STUDIES IN

abnormal behavior

— STUDIES IN

abnormal behavior —

edited by
GLENN D. SHEAN
College of William and Mary

RAND McNALLY & COMPANY / Chicago

616.84
S 539

RAND MℂNALLY PSYCHOLOGY SERIES
Lloyd Humphreys, *Advisory Editor*

PREFACE

Selection of an anthology which is truly representative of the breadth of literature on abnormal behavior is clearly an impossible task. Nevertheless, the author has attempted to select a balanced presentation of various theoretical perspectives and their empirical bases. Given this orientation, there are certain assumptions which have guided the selection of articles: first, that an understanding of the principles derived from the study of normal behavior is most relevant to an understanding of abnormal behavior and, second, that a medical or disease model is more often than not obstructive to the understanding of much of what is labeled abnormal behavior.

This book is organized into three parts: (I) General Issues in the Study of Abnormal Behavior, (II) Patterns of Abnormal Behavior, and (III) Behavior Modification and Psychotherapy. Each of the ten sections is preceded by commentary intended to raise questions and provide a context for evaluation of the articles which follow. Finally a brief discussion and attempt at synthesization follows each section. It may be noted that the heading of Part II rather closely follows standard diagnostic categories. This method has been followed, despite its many inadequacies, because it remains by far the most widely utilized system of classification of abnormal behavior. This organizational framework in no way implies that the current classificatory system is not in need of considerable refinement and revision.

There are several articles in this anthology which represent innovative applications of the basic principles of behavioral science and yet have not, to the author's knowledge, received adequate coverage in recent textbooks of abnormal psychology. Included in this group are Schwitzgebel's experimenter-subject therapy with delinquents, Yablonsky's description of the Synanon House for drug addicts, Sanders' description of a task-group and community-living project with chronic mental patients, Atthowe and Krasner's report of a "token economy" ward, and Sternbach's experimental approach to psychophysiologic disorders.

The contents of this book are appropriate for any group concerned with the study of abnormal behavior and psychotherapy. Courses in counseling, psychiatric nursing, social work, special education, psychiatry, and both undergraduate and advanced courses in abnormal psychology would seem most directly related to the articles included.

Acknowledgements are due the authors and publishers who were kind enough to permit the reprinting of their work. Special thanks are due Karen Van Riper and Suzanne Townsend for their highly competent assistance and organizational skills. Finally, thanks are due Jeanne and Erin Shean for their presence.

Glenn D. Shean

Williamsburg, Virginia
January, 1971

CONTENTS

PART

I

General Issues

Section 1:   MODELS FOR THE STUDY OF
ABNORMAL BEHAVIOR

The scientific study of a set of phenomena requires that one first identify and define its characteristics in a manner which will facilitate reliable identification and classification. Abnormal behavior has presented a special problem in this regard; there is often little or no apparent communality between behaviors classified as forms of "mental illness," e.g., runaway reaction of adolescence, senile dementia, chronic schizophrenia, enuresis, anxiety reactions, and ulcerative colitis.

In addition to the problem of the classification of abnormal behavior, science attempts to conceptualize and understand its causes. As is often the case, man has attempted to understand and explain abnormal behavior through the application of terminology and principles of pre-existing conceptual models. This tendency to superimpose a model derived from the study of other phenomena upon abnormal behavior is advantageous in that it simplifies and seems to explain the phenomena. However, the analogy may also distort our perception, and stifle further study because of the complacency generated by a ready explanation. For centuries abnormal behavior was explained by a supernatural model, whereby such behavior was assumed to be the result of either divine or evil spiritual forces. Today most of us rely upon the model of physical illness to conceptualize abnormal behavior. One need reflect for only a moment to realize how heavily we lean upon the analogy of physical disease to explain abnormal behavior: we speak of mental illness, diagnosis, symptoms, mental hospitals, and therapy.

3

The articles included in this section question the appropriateness of the medical model as an explanation of abnormal behavior and signal the beginning of some dramatic changes in our approach to the study of abnormal behavior.

1

RESEARCH DEFINITIONS OF MENTAL HEALTH AND MENTAL ILLNESS

William A. Scott

A serious obstacle to research in the area of mental illness lies in the lack of a clear definition of the phenomenon to be studied. The term "mental ill health" has been used by different researchers to refer to such diverse manifestations as schizophrenia, suicide, unhappiness, juvenile delinquency, and passive acceptance of an intolerable environment. Whether some or all of these various reactions should be included in a single category of "mental illness" is not clear from a survey of the current literature. Theories describing the nature and antecedents of one sort of disturbance rarely relate it to another, and there is a paucity of research evidence indicating the extent to which such manifestations are empirically intercorrelated.

In the face of such ambiguity it would appear useful to attempt an organized review of the various definitions of mental illness which are explicit or implicit in recent research, with a view toward highlighting their commonalities and discrepancies on both a theoretical and an empirical level. Such a presentation might help students concerned with causative factors to assess the comparability of previous research findings on correlates of "mental illness,"

Reprinted from the *Psychological Bulletin,* 55, 1958, 29–45, with the permission of the American Psychological Association and Dr. Scott.

This review was prepared for the Survey Research Center, University of Michigan, as background material for that organization's national survey of mental health, sponsored by the Joint Commission on Mental Illness and Health. The writer is indebted to Dr. Gerald Gurin of the Survey Research Center, and to Dr. Fillmore Sanford, formerly of the Joint Commission, for their contributions to the ideas presented here. Also appreciation is due the following researchers for their suggestions and for data from current studies which they provided: Harry Beilin, John Clausen, Benjamin Darsky, John Glidewell, Marie Jahoda, Morton Kramer, Thomas Langner, Charles Metzner, M. Brewster Smith, and Shirley Star.

and also point toward some next steps in research to discover the degree to which these diverse phenomena represent either unitary, or multifold, psychological processes.

The research criteria for mental illness to be reviewed here are subsumed under the following categories: (*a*) exposure to psychiatric treatment; (*b*) social maladjustment; (*c*) psychiatric diagnosis; (*d*) subjective unhappiness; (*e*) objective psychological symptoms; and (*f*) failure of positive adaptation. For each category we shall review studies which appear to have employed the definition, either explicitly or implicitly. This will be accompanied by a critical discussion of the adequacy of each definition, together with an assessment, based on empirical data where possible, of the relation between this and other definitions. Finally, we shall attempt to summarize the differences among the definitions, by indicating their divergent approaches to certain basic problems in the conceptualization of mental illness and health.

MENTAL ILLNESS AS EXPOSURE TO PSYCHIATRIC TREATMENT

The most frequently used operational definition of mental illness, at least in terms of the number of studies employing it, is simply the fact of a person's being under psychiatric treatment. And this definition is usually restricted to hospital treatment, rather than outpatient service. Nearly all the ecological studies (e.g., 3, 16, 22, 30, 35, 50) and most of the studies correlating mental illness with demographic characteristics (e.g., 5, 19, 29, 41, 47) use this as a criterion. They obtain their information from hospital records or, in unusual instances (e.g., 28), from psychiatrists in the area who furnish information about persons treated on an outpatient basis.

Such a definition of mental illness is operational rather than conceptual, but its implicit meaning for the interpretation of research results is that anyone who is regarded by someone (hospital authorities, relatives, neighbors, or himself) as disturbed enough to require hospitalization or outpatient treatment is mentally ill, and people who do not fit into such diagnoses are mentally healthy. Use of hospital records, moreover, requires that the criterion of the nature of the mental illness be the diagnosis which appears on the record.

Shortcomings of such an operational definition are recognized by no one better than its users. The reliability of psychiatric diagnosis is of course open to question, and any attempt to determine correlates of particular kinds of mental disturbance must take into account the large error inherent in the measuring process. (One study of the association between diagnosis at Boston Psychopathic Hospital and previous diagnoses of the patients at other hospitals showed only 51 per cent above-chance agreement between the two [cf. 15, pp. 42–43].)

If "under the care of a psychiatrist" is to be regarded as the criterion of mental illness, one must realize the automatic limitation on the size of the mentally ill population that such a definition imposes. Kramer (34, p. 124) has estimated that the maximum possible number of mentally ill, under such a definition, would be less than 7,000,000, given the present number of available psychiatrists.

It has been suggested by both sociologists (7, 10) and physicians (17) that different rates of hospital admissions for different geographical areas may indicate more than anything else about the areas the relative degree to which the communities tolerate or reject persons with deviant behavior (11). Or as the Chief of the National Institute of Mental Health puts it: researchers using hospital records are dependent on the public's rather uneven willingness to give up its mentally ill members and to support them in institutions (17); this in addition to the admittedly unstandardized and often substandard methods of record-keeping used by the various hospitals is likely to render incomparable prevalence and incidence data from various geographical areas.

The effects of such differential thresholds for admission in various communities are difficult to estimate, since they cannot be uniform from study to study. In 1938 a house-to-house survey in Williamson County, Tennessee, yielded nearly one person diagnosed as psychotic, but never having been in a mental hospital, for every hospitalized psychotic from the county (48). By contrast, Eaton found in his study of the Hutterites (14) that more intensive canvassing by psychiatrists did not yield a larger number of persons deemed psychotic than did a more superficial count based on community reports.

Eaton's study *did* yield higher proportions of neurotic diagnoses the more intensive the case findings procedure became, and this observation relates to the finding in New Haven that neurotics under outpatient treatment came disproportionately from the upper socioeconomic strata (28). At first consideration, such differential rates seem readily attributable to the cost of psychiatric treatment, but Hollingshead and Redlich prefer to seek an explanation in the greater social distance between lower-class neurotics and the psychiatrists than in the case of middle- and upper-class neurotics. Whatever the sources of rate differences, it is clear that such correlations as have been reported make one wary of the hospital admissions or outpatient figures as indicative of the "true" incidence of psychiatric disorders. Thus the criterion of exposure to psychiatric treatment is at best a rough indicator of any underlying conceptual definition of mental illness.

MALADJUSTMENT AS MENTAL ILLNESS

Adjustment is necessarily determined with reference to norms of the total society or of some more restricted community within the society. Accordingly, one may conceptually define adjustment as adherence to social norms. Such a definition of mental health has an advantage over the preceding in encompassing a range of more-or-less healthy, more-or-less ill behavior, rather than posing a forced dichotomy. The operation for assessing mental health by this criterion might ideally be a community (or other relevant group) consensus concerning a given subject's degree of adjustment. This has been approximated by at least one set of studies (1, 2).

Rather than assess consensus by pooling many divergent individual opinions, it is possible to assume that a law or other visible sign of social norms constitutes the criterion against which adjustment is determined. Such reference is employed in studies of suicide (12, 26) or juvenile delinquency (25) or divorce (39, 53) as indicants of maladjustment. While the operational criterion may become dichotomous in such cases (whether or not the person comes in contact with the law), this is not necessarily so. Gordon (21) has suggested considering the "biologic gradient" of suicide, extending from contemplation of the act to its actual accomplishment.

Finally, it would be possible to assess degree of adjustment with reference to some externally defined set of requirements for a given social system. Thus a work situation might be seen as demanding a high level of productivity from all its members, and the degree of adherence to this standard becomes the criterion of adjustment, without reference to the individual opinions of the group members or to the manifest norms of the group. This criterion of conformity to the requirements of a given social structure has not been explicitly employed by any of the researchers covered in the present review, but it has been hinted at (37) and remains a possibility, provided that the structural requirements of a social system can be determined independently of the members' behaviors.

Theory of social structure suggests that these three criteria of adjustment would tend toward congruence: The demands of a particular social system lead to the development of social norms, which are expressed in laws or customs and also in the individual participants' notions of what is acceptable behavior. Lack of congruence may be taken as evidence of cultural lag, of poor correspondence between manifest and latent function within the social structure, or of defensive psychological processes within the participating individuals. Since all of these factors supporting discrepancy do occur within most social systems, the criteria may be expected to yield somewhat different results.

When maladjustment is assessed by community consensus, one finds considerable divergence of opinion among various segments of the public regarding what constitutes good and poor adjustment. The Minnesota Child Welfare studies (1) showed differences in criteria for assessing adjustment among different occupational groups in the community. Teachers tended to emphasize standards different from those emphasized by ministers, who in turn displayed some differences from a more heterogeneous group of community adults. Beilin concludes that it is meaningless to discuss "adjustment" in the abstract or to contemplate the prediction of "adjustment" in general. One must specify *adjustment to what, adjustment to whose standards* (2). Lindemann reflects this relativistic conception of mental health when he states: "We find it preferable not to talk about a 'case' in psychiatry—rather we try to assess functional impairment in specific situations as viewed by different professional groups in the community. So a 'case' is really a relationship of possibly pathogenic situation and appropriate or inappropriate behavior to that situation. It is often a matter of arbitrary choice whether such a person becomes an object of psychiatric care" (38, p. 130).

Thus, though adjustment appears a more conceptually adequate criterion of mental health than does exposure to treatment, the necessity for considering different personal frames of reference and the demands of different social structures poses seemingly insurmountable obstacles to the establishment of mutually consistent operational definitions. All such difficulties which lie "hidden," as it were, under the psychiatric treatment criterion, come to the fore to plague the researcher trying to establish a criterion for adjustment which applies to the treated and nontreated alike.

PSYCHIATRIC DIAGNOSIS AS CRITERION FOR MENTAL ILLNESS

There have been a few studies in which entire communities or samples of them have been systematically screened, either by direct examination (44, 48) or by evidence from community records or hearsay (13, 14, 54). Here the criterion for mental illness or health need not be dichotomous, but can be divided into several gradations. Such intensive case-finding can be expected to increase the yield of persons classified as neurotic (34, p. 124) over that provided by the criterion of exposure to treatment, but whether the psychotic group is thereby increased will depend on the community (34, p. 124; 48) and, of course, on the standards for diagnosis employed by the particular investigator.

The lack of standardization of diagnostic procedures and criteria contributes to the incomparability of mental illness rates derived from such studies (34, p. 139; 55). As long as the criterion of assessment is largely dependent on the psychiatrist's subjective integration of a different set of facts for each subject, nonuniform results can be anticipated. Expensive and unreliable though the method may be, it at least places the judgment regarding mental illness or health in the hands of professionals, which is not the case when adjustment is the criterion. And though hospitalization is in part determined by the judgment of professionals, *who* is sent to the hospitals for psychiatric diagnosis is, for the most part, out of the hands of the psychiatrists. As Felix and Bowers (17) have observed, it is the community rather than the clinician that operates the case-finding process today, and this will continue to be so until diagnostic examinations are given regularly to all people.

MENTAL ILLNESS DEFINED SUBJECTIVELY

It has been maintained by some that a major indication of need for psychotherapy is the person's own feeling of unhappiness or inadequacy. Conversely, the degree of mental health may be assessed by manifestations of subjective happiness, self-confidence, and morale. Lewis (36) quotes Ernest Jones to the effect that the main criterion for effect of therapy is the patient's subjective sense of strength, confidence, and well-being. Terman (52, 53) has used a "marriage happiness" test, composed largely of subjective items, and Pollak (43) has suggested that old-age adjustment be assessed in terms of the person's degree of happiness or well-being in various areas of his life.

That such criteria of mental health correlate somewhat with independent diagnoses by physicians has been indicated in two sorts of studies. In the Baltimore Eastern Health District (9), cases diagnosed psychoneurotic were found to express complaints about their own physical health; it is suggested that persons who report chronic nervousness can be classified as suffering from a psychiatric condition. Rogers has maintained that a marked discrepancy between one's "perceived self" and "ideal self" constitutes evidence of psychiatric disturbance (45), and some empirical studies lend support to this position. When Q sorts of subjects' self concepts are compared with Q sorts of their ideal selves, it is possible to distinguish psychiatric groups from nonpsychiatric groups on the basis of the degree of discrepancy between these two measures (4). Furthermore, progress in therapy (as judged by the therapist) tends to be associated with increasing similarity between the patient's self concept and ideal self (46).

Though subjective well-being is an appealing criterion for mental health in ordinary daily living, it might be presumed that under some circumstances psychological defense mechanisms could operate to prevent the person's reporting, or becoming aware of, his own underlying unhappiness and disturbance. Jahoda (33) has rejected happiness as a criterion for mental health on somewhat different grounds: Happiness, she says, is a function not only of the person's behavior patterns, but of the environment in which he moves. If one wants to relate mental health to characteristics of the environment, then one must not take as a criterion of mental health something that already presupposes a benign environment. "There are certain circumstances in which to be happy would make it necessary first to be completely sick" (33, p. 105).

Such objections to this criterion imply that it is possible to find persons

who are mentally ill by some other criterion, yet who nevertheless report themselves as happy or self-satisfied. Empirical demonstration of this implication is
not available at present. In fact, while one study predicted defensively high Q
sorts for the self concept of paranoid psychotics, they were found to have a
greater discrepancy between self- and ideal-sorts than normals, and no less discrepancy between these measures than psychoneurotics (4).

MENTAL ILLNESS DEFINED BY OBJECTIVE
PSYCHOLOGICAL SYMPTOMS

It is generally accepted almost by definition that mental illness entails
both a disordering of psychological processes and a deviation of behavior from
social norms (6). The latter aspect of disturbance may be assessed as maladjustment to one's social environment (discussed above); the former aspect
can presumably be assessed by psychological inventories aimed at the assumedly
critical processes. The distinction between the psychological inventory approach
and the subjective assessment procedure discussed above is not really a clear
one. Subjective well-being may be regarded as one of the psychological processes
which becomes disordered. Yet more "objective" measures of psychological
process, which do not require the subject's verbal report of his degree of happiness, are frequently preferred, both to guard against purposeful distortion and to
tap areas of disorder which may not be accompanied by subjective counterparts.

Such "objective" psychological inventories may represent various degrees
of manifest purpose. For some, the objective of assessment is transparent, and
the only reason they are not classed as devices for subjective report is that they
stop just short of requiring the subject to report his over-all level of well-being.
Such a manifest-level inventory is Halmos' questionnaire concerning the respondent's difficulties in social relations (24).

At a somewhat less obvious level are such inventories as the MMPI, the
War Department Neuropsychiatric Screening Battery, and the Cornell Medical
Index, which require subjects to check the presence of various subjective and
objective symptoms (e.g., "I smoke too much"). Once validated against an
accepted criterion, such as psychiatric diagnosis, these are frequently used as
criteria themselves. Rennie constructed a composite instrument of this type to
assess his respondents' levels of mental health in the Yorkville study (44); at the
same time, a validity analysis of the index was undertaken, by correlating each item
with independent psychiatric diagnosis on a subsample of the respondents. On the
basis of their experience with such a composite instrument, one of Rennie's colleagues (Langner, personal communication, August 1956) suggests caution in
abstracting parts of previously validated batteries, since the item validities are sometimes not maintained when they are used out of context of the total instrument.

An adaptation of the psychiatric screening battery approach for use with children is suggested in the work of the St. Louis County Public Health Department (20). It involves obtaining information about symptoms from the children's mothers rather than from the children themselves. Naturally, the symptoms covered must be of the "objective" type ("Does Johnny wet the bed?") rather than of the "subjective" type ("Does Johnny worry a lot?"). As validated by an outside criterion (teachers' and psychiatric social workers' ratings of the child's level of adjustment), the number of symptoms reported by the mothers appears to be a promising index of the child's mental health.

A general characteristic of the types of psychological inventories reviewed so far is that each item in the battery is assumed, a priori, to involve a "directional" quality, such that one type of answer (e.g., "yes" to "Are you troubled with nightmares?") may be taken as indicative of psychological disorder, and the opposite answer as indicative of normal functioning. Thus the index of disturbance is computed by adding all the positive indicators, weighted equally. That alternative methods of test construction may yield equally, or more, valid indices of mental illness is indicated by the extensive investigations of McQuitty (40).

McQuitty proposes several different methods of diagnostic test scoring, each based on explicit assumptions about the diagnostic procedure which the test is supposed to represent. One of the simplest assumptions, for example, is that an individual is mentally ill to the extent that his psychological processes deviate from the culturally modal processes. Thus, any type of multiple-alternative test may be administered to a group of subjects representing a "normal" population. Each alternative of each item is then scored for its "popularity." The score for a subject is then computed by adding the popularity scores of the items he checks (McQuitty calls this the T method of scoring); a high popularity score is taken as evidence of mental health (by this "typicality" criterion).

An alternative assumption proposed by McQuitty as underlying the diagnostic procedure might be that mental health is manifest to the degree that the subject's responses conform to *any* pattern of answers represented by a significant number of community people, regardless of whether that pattern is the most popular one. Such an assumption leads to a scoring procedure (H method) whereby a subject's index of "cultural harmony" is based on the degree to which his responses to different questions "go together" in the same manner as do the responses of all people in the sample who check the same alternatives he does.

Elaborations on these basic procedures provide for differential weighting of responses depending on their degree of deviance (WH method), and correction for "linkage" between successive pairs of items (WHc method).

The Bernreuter Personality Test and the Strong Vocational Interest Inventory were administered by McQuitty to a group of mental patients and to a group of university students; they were scored by different methods, the scores for the two tests were correlated, and the mean scores of the two groups compared. Results of the comparisons indicate: (*a*) when appropriately scored, the Strong can discriminate mental patients from normals, though not as well as the Bernreuter; (*b*) better resuts are obtained if, instead of treating each answer as a separate, independent measure, it is evaluated in terms of the pattern of other answers with which it occurs (WHc scoring method); (*c*) within the Bernreuter, those items which correlated best with the test score (McQuitty's WHc method of scoring) and provided the best discrimination between patients and normals tended to be of the "subjective" type (i.e., they depended on the subject's introspection, as in "Do you often have disturbing thoughts?") rather than the "objective" (items which an observer could report, such as "Do you talk very much?") ; (*d*) different scoring procedures appeared differentially appropriate for the "subjective" and "objective" items; (*e*) when the "subjective" items were scored by the method most appropriate to them (i.e., the method which best discriminated patients from normals), and the "objective" items by their most appropriate method, the correlation between the two scores on the same group of subjects was about zero, indicating that two independent dimensions of mental health were being tapped by these two sets of items.

A separate study reported by McQuitty (40) indicated that the simple T method of scoring (based on the popularity of the subject's responses) both subjective and objective items significantly discriminated groups of school children classified on the basis of independent criteria of mental health. There is considerable evidence from these studies that, especially with respect to those traits measured by the "objective" items, the person may be regarded as mentally ill to the extent that he deviates from the dominant community pattern.

The foregoing studies provide a certain amount of evidence that measures of mental illness according to psychometric criteria relate to two of the criteria discussed earlier—maladjustment and psychiatric diagnosis. That such concurrent validation may yield somewhat different results from studies of predictive validity is indicated in Beilin's report of the Nobles County study (2). Two indices of student adjustment predictors were constructed, one (the "pupil index") based on students' responses to five different instruments, and the other (the "teacher index") based on teacher ratings. Both were concurrently validated against juvenile court judges' nominations of delinquent youngsters and against teachers' descriptions of the youngsters. Four years later the mental health of the youth was assessed by a number of different criteria—community reputation, interviewers' ratings, self-assessment, and an adaptation of the Rundquist-Sletto morale scale. The predictors correlated significantly with only some of the subsequent criteria, and all of the correlations were at best moderate. The "pupil index" correlated better with the interviewer's rating than with the community reputation criterion; while the "teacher index" correlated better with the subject's subsequent community reputation than with the interviewer's rating. Or, stated more generally, the psychologist's predictor predicted better to a psychologist's criterion, and a community predictor predicted better to a community criterion. Though the time span (four years) between the predictor and criterion measures may have been such as to allow for considerable change in the subjects, one is nevertheless reminded by these results that various criteria for mental health are not necessarily highly correlated.

In summarizing the various studies of mental health and illness defined by psychological testing batteries, we may note that many of them lack an underlying conception of the nature of mental illness from which to derive items and scoring procedures (a notable exception being McQuitty's measures), that some of them challenge the notion of the unidimensional nature of mental health, and that their degree of correlation with other criteria, such as adjustment or psychiatric diagnosis, depends on the nature of the criterion.

MENTAL HEALTH AS POSITIVE STRIVING

A radically different approach to the assessment of mental health is indicated in the definitions proposed by some writers with a mental hygiene orientation. Gruenberg suggests that, though failure to live up to the expectations of those around him may constitute mental illness, one should also consider the person's failure to live up to his own potentialities (23, p. 131). Frank speaks of the "positive" aspect of mental health—healthy personalities are those who "continue to grow, develop, and mature through life, accepting responsibilities, finding fulfillments, without paying too high a cost personally or socially, as they participate in maintaining the social order and carrying on our culture" (18). In a less exhortative tone, Henry (27) discusses successful adaptation of the person in the "normal stressful situation." He sees many normal situations as situations of inherent stress. Some individuals in them develop mental disease, while others may develop out of them a more complex, but more successful, personality. It is this successful coping with the "normal stressful situation" that Henry regards as indicative of mental health.

Jahoda has translated this kind of emphasis on the positive, striving aspects of behavior into a set of criteria amenable to empirical research. She proposes three basic features of mental health (31): (a) The person displays active adjustment, or attempts at mastery of his environment, in contrast to lack of adjustment or indiscriminate adjustment through passive acceptance of social conditions. (b) The person manifests unity of personality—the maintenance of a stable integration which remains intact in spite of the flexibility of behavior which derives from active adjustment. (c) The person perceives the world and himself correctly, independent of his personal needs.

Active mastery of the environment, according to Jahoda, presupposes a deliberate choice of what one does and does not conform to, and consists of the deliberate modification of environmental conditions. "In a society in which regimentation prevails, active adjustment will hardly be possible; in a society where overt regimentation is replaced by the invisible compulsiveness of conformity pressures, active adjustment will be equally rare. Only where there exists social recognition of alternative forms of behavior is there a chance for the individual to master his surroundings and attain mental health." (31, p. 563).

Such an approach is quite at odds with the subjective criterion of personal happiness, and with the conformity criterion referred to above as "adjustment." Attempted adjustment does not necessarily result in success, for success is dependent on the environment. The best mode of adjustment only maximizes the chances of success. It is mentally healthy behavior even if the environment does not permit a solution of the problem (33). Jahoda proposes that the criterion of happiness be replaced with some more "objective" definition of mental health, based on an explicit set of values.

In an unpublished community study, Jahoda apparently attempted to assess only two of the aspects of mental health incorporated in her definition. Veridicality of perception (actually, of judgment) was determined by asking respondents to estimate certain characteristics of their communities concerning which objective data were available (e.g., proportion of people with only gradeschool education), and at the same time inferring needs to distort reality from the respondent's evaluative statements about the problem (e.g., how important R believed education to be). This method of assessing need-free perception was regarded as something less than satisfactory (Jahoda, personal communication, August 1956), since the need was so difficult to determine, and it was difficult to establish unambiguously that distortion of judgment was due to the operation of a need rather than simply to lack of valid information.

The degree of attempted active adjustment was assessed by first asking a respondent to mention a particular problem in the community, then determining what he had done, or tried to do, about it, and how he felt about the problem at the time of interview (33). Three aspects of respondents' reactions were coded from their replies (32): (a) the stage of problem solution—mere consideration of the problem, consideration of solutions, or actual implementation; (b) the feeling tone associated with the problem—continued worry or improvement in feeling (either through partial solution or through passive acceptance); (c) the directness or indirectness of the approach—i.e., whether R went to the heart of the problem in his attempted solution or merely dealt temporarily with recurrent nuisances.

In her analysis Jahoda relates her measures of problem-solving and need-free perception to various characteristics of the respondents and of the communities in which they live. The relationships are interesting (e.g., in one of the communities the level of problem-solving was related to the degree of community participation of the respondent), but they appear to leave unanswered a basic question about the appropriateness of the criteria. If one accepts Jahoda's definition of mental health as involving the two components assessed in the study, then the results can be interpreted as showing what patterns of social interaction are associated with mental health. But if one is skeptical about the meaningfulness of the definition, then he is impelled to search for correlations between her two measures and other, more commonly accepted, criteria of mental health. These are not reported, although it would appear to be a fair question to ask about the relation of her concepts to those employed by other researchers.

If one is wedded to the happiness criterion of mental health, for example, one may speculate about the possibility of a negative relation between it and those provided by Jahoda. Unhappiness could conceivably lead to excessive coping behavior (attempted adjustment), or excessive coping behavior might elicit negative reactions from others which, in turn, would increase one's unhappiness. In like fashion, it could be that need-free perception would lead to increased unhappiness, since psychological defenses are not available to bolster one's self image. Though Jahoda might reject the suggestion that happiness is even relevant to her criteria, it would appear useful to explore, both conceptually and empirically, the interrelations between other measures of mental health and the novel one proposed by her.

Clausen (6) has maintained that researchers must ultimately face the task of relating mental health defined in positive terms to the individual's ability to resist mental illness under stress. At present it is not known whether they represent a common factor or are independent characteristics. Jahoda (personal communication, August 1956) suspects that positive mental health, as she defines it, may indeed represent a dimension orthogonal to that represented by the conventional psychological symptoms of mental illness. Thus, from a different approach from that employed by McQuitty comes the suggestion that mental health and illness may be a multidimensional phenomenon.

In employing these particular criteria, especially that of active adaptation, Jahoda seems willing to defend the evaluative standards implicit in it. And it may well be that values relating to attempted mastery of problems are every bit as defensible as the values of conformity implied in the adjustment criteria discussed above. Nevertheless, the former appear to exemplify the application of the Protestant ethic to the mental health movement in a manner which might introduce culture and class biases into one's conclusions. Miller and Swanson (42) have hypothesized that lower-class children will show more defeatism than middle-class children, as a result of different interpersonal and environmental experiences. Would they thereby be less mentally healthy by any standards besides those of the middle class? Truly, the problems posed in setting up absolute values from which to judge mental health and illness are perplexing.

BASIC PROBLEMS IN THE DEFINITION OF MENTAL HEALTH AND ILLNESS

Underlying the diversities in definition of mental illness one can discern certain basic differences of viewpoint concerning how the phenomena should be conceptualized. We may abstract certain foci of disagreement by posing the following four points of contention: (*a*) Does mental illness refer to a unitary concept or to an artificial grouping of basically different specific disorders? (*b*) Is mental illness an acute or chronic state of the organism? (*c*) Is maladjustment (or deviance from social norms) an essential concomitant of mental illness? (*d*) Should mental illness be explicitly defined according to values other than social conformity?

Each of the proposed definitions takes a stand, either explicitly or implicitly, on one or more of these issues. It is likely that resolution of disagreements will depend in part on the outcome of future empirical research. But at least some of the divergence inheres in the theoretical formulation of the problem, and is more a matter of conceptual predilection than of empirical fact. In either case, if one is to arrive at consistent theoretical and operational definitions of mental illness, it would be well to make explicit one's bias concerning each of these issues, and attempt to rationalize it in terms of his conception of the causes of disturbance.

The Unitary or Specific Nature of Mental Illness

The position that mental illness is manifest in some rather general form, regardless of the specific diagnostic category in which the patient is placed, would appear to be implicit in the subjective definition of the phenomenon. If the person's feeling of happiness or adequacy is regarded as the crucial indicator of his mental state, this would appear to imply that over-all health or illness can be assessed for a particular person, regardless of the area of functioning referred to. Likewise, the definition of mental health in terms of purposeful striving or active adjustment tends to ignore differences in the underlying bases for such striving or lack thereof. Such a position has been stated explicitly by Stieglitz: "The mensuration of health . . . closely parallels the measurement of biological age as contrasted to chronological age. . . .

We are no longer seeking to discover specific disease entities, or even clinical syndromes, but attempting to measure biological effectiveness in adaptation" (51, p. 79). And such a unitary view of the phenomenon is implied in Schneider's comment: "The major 'cause' of mental disease is seen as some form of disorientation between the personality and society" (49, p. 31).

By contrast, the specific view of mental illness is taken by Gordon: "What we choose to call mental disease is an artificial grouping of many morbid processes. The first essential, in my opinion, is to separate the various entities, and in the approach to an epidemiology of mental diseases, to center attention on some one condition, or a few selected conditions, which have functions in common with other mass diseases well understood in their group relationships" (15, p. 107). McQuitty offers empirical evidence in favor of a specific view, in his isolation of two quite independent measures of mental illness (by psychological testing), both of which correlate with external diagnostic criteria. And he further speculates that the number of areas in which the degree of personality integration varies rather independently is probably greater than the two which he has isolated. "One might expect that mental illness might develop within any one or more patterns. In order to understand the mental illness of a particular subject, we must isolate the pattern, or patterns, of characteristics to which his mental illness pertains" (40, p. 22).

While the weight of opinion and evidence appears to favor the multidimensional view, this may simply be a function of the operational definitions employed (e.g., mental health defined by responses to a battery of tests is bound to turn out multidimensional to the extent that intercorrelations between the test items are low). But there are yet insufficient empirical data collected from the unitary point of view to test whether its assumption is correct. Indeed, it seems quite plausible that both happiness and active adaptation may be partially a function of the situation, hence the concept of mental health implied by them must become multidimensional to the extent that they allow for intersituational variability.

The Acute or Chronic Nature of Mental Illness

The psychologist's testing approach to assessing mental illness inclines him toward a view of the condition as chronic. That is, the predisposing conditions within the organism are generally presumed to be relatively enduring, though perhaps triggered off into an actual psychotic break by excessively stressful situations. The epidemiological approach, on the other hand, is usually concerned with the counting of actual hospitalized cases, and this may incline one toward a view of mental illness as predominantly acute. Felix has espoused this position explicitly: "Unless the kinds of mental illness are specified, I can't conceive that mental illness is a chronic disease. More mental illnesses by far are acute and even short term than there are mental illnesses which are chronic and long term." (15, p. 163). Of course, the epidemiological approach traditionally considers characteristics of the host, as well as characteristics of the agent and the environment. But the predisposing factors within the organism seem to be regarded, like "low resistance," not as a subliminal state of the disease, but rather as a general susceptibility to any acute attack precipitated by external factors.

It is easier to regard a psychosis as acute than it is similarly to regard a neurosis, since in the former disorder the break with normal behavior appears more precipitate. However, such a judgment, based on easily observed external behaviors, may be unduly superficial. Even in the case of such a discrete disturbance as suicide, at least cne writer (21) recommends considering the biologic gradient of the disorder. He distinguishes varying degrees of suicide, with successful accomplishment as merely a possible end product. Where such continuity between morbid and non-morbid states can be discerned, the possibility of chronic disturbance might well be considered.

The Problem of Mental Health as Conformity to Social Norms

The criterion of mental health based on adjustment clearly implies that conformity to the social situation in which the individual is permanently imbedded is a healthy response. And such an assumption would appear to be lurking, in various shapes, behind nearly all of the other definitions considered (with the possible exception of some of the "positive striving" criteria, which stress conformity to a set of standards independent of the person's immediate social group). In fact, McQuitty's methods of scoring psychological inventories are all explicitly based on the assumption that conformity (either to the total community or to a significant subgroup) is healthy.

If the stability of the larger social system be regarded as the final good, or if human development be seen as demanding harmony in relation to that social system, then such an assumption would appear basic and defensible. But one is still impelled to consider the possibility that the social system, or even an entire society, may be sick, and conformity to its norms would constitute mental illness, in some more absolute sense. If any particular behavior pattern is considered both from the standpoint of its adaptability within the social structure to which the individual maintains primary allegiance and from the standpoint of its relation to certain external ideal standards imposed by the observer, perhaps a comparison of the two discrepancy measures would yield information about the degree to which the social system approaches the ideal. On the other hand, such a comparison might be interpreted as merely indicating the degree to which the researcher who sets the external standards is himself adapted to the social system which he is studying. The dilemma appears insoluble.

The Problem of Values in Criteria for Mental Health

The mental hygiene movement has traditionally been identified with one or another set of values—ideal standards from which behavior could be assessed as appropriate or inappropriate. The particular set of values adopted probably depends to a considerable degree on who is doing the judging. Such a diversity of evaluative judgments leads to chaos in the popular literature and to consider-able confusion in the usage of the term "mental health" in scientific research. Kingsley Davis (8) presented a rather strong case for the proposition that mental hygiene, being a social movement and source of advice concerning personal conduct, has inevitably been influenced by the Protestant ethic inherent in our culture. The main features of this Protestant ethic, as seen by him, are its democratic, worldly, ascetic, individualistic, rationalistic, and utilitarian orientations.

To the extent that research on mental health is based on criteria [evolved] from such an ideology, it is middle-class-Protestant biased. To the extent that it is based on some other set of "absolute" norms for behavior, it is probably biased toward some other cultural configuration. At least one researcher, Jahoda (33), has clearly taken the position that mental health criteria must be based on an explicit set of values. There is some advantage in allowing the assumptions to come into full view, but in this case the resulting criteria appear to be rather specialized and not comparable with those used by other researchers. Perhaps the difficulty lies not so much in the existence of explicit assumptions as in their level of generality. If a more basic set of assumptions could be found, from which the diverse criteria for mental health and illness can be derived, then comparability among researches might better be achieved. One would be in a better position to state when mental illness, as defined by psycho-logical tests or by absence of active adjustment, is likely to be displayed in mental illness defined by psychiatric diagnosis or deviance from community standards.

SUMMARY

The various categories of definitions of mental illness discussed here have been distinguished primarily on the basis of their differing operational defini-tions: the dependent variables employed in empirical research on the phenomena are clearly different. Moreover the conceptualizations of mental illness explicit or implicit in the empirical criteria are often quite divergent—viz., the radically different viewpoints underlying the "maladjustment," "subjective unhappiness," and "lack of positive striving" definitions.

Certain conceptual and methodological difficulties in each of these types of definition have been noted: "Exposure to treatment" is deficient in that only a limited proportion of those diagnosable as mentally ill ever reach psychiatric treatment. "Social maladjustment" is open to question because of the varying requirements of different social systems and the diversity of criteria for adjustment employed by community members. "Psychiatric diagnosis" provides an expensive, and often unreliable, method of assessing the state of mental health. "Subjective unhappiness" can be criticized as a criterion since it may be a functional of intolerable environmental conditions as well as the psychological state of the person, and is subject to distortion by defense mechanisms. The validity of "objective testing procedures" appears to depend considerably on the method by which they are scored, and there is strong evidence that a major component of their score may simply be the degree of conformity of the person to the community average. Finally, criteria included under the heading of "positive striving" are subject to question in that they are inevitably based on disputable value systems of their proponents.

While many of these difficulties would not be considered damaging from the point of view of certain of the definitions of mental illness, they run into conflict with others. Also they suggest certain basic incompatibilities among the various approaches to conceptualization of mental illness. Whether these incompatibilities should be reconciled by further theoretical and empirical exploration, or whether they should be regarded as valid indicators that mental health and illness constitute multidimensional phenomena is still a moot question. We can only note that various studies employing two or more of these different categories of criteria have tended to yield moderate, but not impressive, interrelations.

The criterion of "exposure to psychiatric treatment" has been related to "maladjustment," "psychiatric diagnosis," "subjective unhappiness," and "objective psychometrics." Also "maladjustment" has been related to "psychiatric diagnosis" and to certain "objective" measures; and "psychiatric diagnosis" has been related to both "subjective" and "objective" measures of mental illness. The areas of interrelationship for which no empirical studies have been found are between "subjective" measures and both "maladjustment" and "objective" assessment; also between the "positive striving" criteria and all of the other types of measures.

Two directions for future theory and research are indicated by these results. First, more investigations are needed of the extent of relationship among the various criteria, and of the conditions under which the magnitudes of the intercorrelations vary. Second, assuming absence of high intercorrelations under many conditions, it would be worthwhile to explore the implications of poor congruence between one measure and another—implications both for the person and for the social system in which he lives.

REFERENCES

1. Beilin, H. The effects of social (occupational) role and age upon the criteria of mental health. *J. soc. Psychol.*, in press.
2. Beilin, H. The prediction of adjustment over a four year interval. *J. clin. Psychol.*, 1957, 13, 270–274.
3. Belknap, I. V., & Jaco, E. G. The epidemiology of mental disorders in a political-type city, 1946–1952. In *Interrelations between the social environment and psychiatric disorders:* N. Y.: Milbank Memorial Fund, 1953.
4. Chase, P. Concepts of self and concepts of others in adjusted and maladjusted hospital patients. Unpublished doctor's dissertation, Univer. of Colorado, 1956.
5. Clark, R. E. Psychoses, income and occupational prestige. *Amer. J. Social.*, 1949, 54, 433–440.
6. Clausen, J. A. *Sociology and the field of mental health.* N. Y.: Russell Sage Foundation, 1956.
7. Clausen, J. A., & Kohn, M. L. The ecological approach in social psychiatry. *Amer. J. Sociol.*, 1954, 60, 140–151.
8. Davis, K. Mental hygiene and the class structure. *Psychiatry*, 1938, 1, 55–65.
9. Downes, Jean, & Simon, Katherine. Characteristics of psychoneurotic patients and their families as revealed in a general morbidity study. *Milbank Memorial Fund Quarterly*, 1954, 32, 42–64.
10. Dunham, H. W. Current status of ecological research in mental disorder. *Social Forces*, 1947, 25, 321–326.
11. Dunham, H. W. Some persistent problems in the epidemiology of mental disorders. *Amer. J. Psychiat.*, 1953, 109, 567–575.
12. Durkheim, E. *Le suicide.* Paris: F. Alcan, 1897. (English translation, Glencoe, Ill.: Free Press, 1951.)
13. Eaton, J. W. *Culture and mental disorders.* Glencoe, Ill.: Free Press, 1955.
14. Eaton, J. W., & Weil, R. J. The mental health of the Hutterites. In A. M. Rose (Ed.), *Mental health and mental disorder.* N. Y.: Norton, 1955.
15. *Epidemiology of mental disorder.* N. Y.: Milbank Memorial Fund, 1950.
16. Faris, R. E. L., & Dunham, H. W. *Mental disorders in urban areas.* Chicago: Chicago Univer. Press, 1939.
17. Felix, R. H., & Bowers, R. V. Mental hygiene and socio-environmental factors. *Milbank Memorial Fund Quarterly*, 1948, 26, 125–147.

18. Frank, L. K. The promotion of mental health. *Ann. Amer. Acad. of Pol. Soc. Sic.,* 1953, 286, 167–174.

19. Frumkin, R. M. Occupation and major mental disorders. In A. M. Rose (Ed.), *Mental health and mental disorder.* N. Y.: Norton, 1955.

20. Glidewell, J. C., et al. Behavior symptoms in children and degree of sickness. *Amer. J. Psychiat,* 1957, 114, 47–53.

21. Gordon, J. E., et al. An epidemiologic analysis of suicide. In *Epidemiology of mental disorder.* N. Y.: Milbank Memorial Fund, 1950.

22. Gruenberg, E. M. Community conditions and psychoses of the elderly. *Amer. J. Psychiat.,* 1954, 110, 888–896.

23. Gruenberg, E. M. Comment in *Interrelations between the social environment and psychiatric disorders.* N. Y.: Milbank Memorial Fund, 1953.

24. Halmos, P. *Solitude and privacy.* London: Routledge and Kegan Paul, 1952.

25. Hathaway, S. R., & Monachesi, E. D. The Minnesota Multiphasic Personality Inventory in the study of juvenile delinquents. In A. M. Rose (Ed.), *Mental health and mental disorder.* N. Y.: Norton, 1955.

26. Henry, A. F., & Short, J. *Suicide and homicide.* Glencoe, Ill.: Free Press, 1954.

27. Henry, W. E. Psychology. In *Interrelations between the social environment and psychiatric disorders.* N. Y.: Milbank Memorial Fund, 1953.

28. Hollingshead, A. B. & Redlich, F. C. Social stratification and psychiatric disorders. *Amer. sociol. Rev.,* 1953, 18, 163–169.

29. Hyde, P. W., & Kingsley, L. V. Studies in medical sociology. I: The relation of mental disorders to the community socio-economic level. *New England J. Med.,* 1944, 231, 543–548.

30. Jaco, E. G. The social isolation hypothesis and schizophrenia. *Amer. sociol. Rev.,* 1954, 19, 567–577.

31. Jahoda, Marie. Toward a social psychology of mental health. In A. M. Rose (Ed.), *Mental health and mental disorder.* N. Y.: Norton, 1955.

32. Jahoda, Marie. The meaning of psychological health. *Soc. Casewk,* 1953, 34, 349–354.

33. Jahoda, Marie. Social psychology. In *Interrelations between the social environment and psychiatric disorders.* N. Y.: Milbank Memorial Fund, 1953.

34. Kramer, M. Comment in *Interrelations between the social environment and psychiatric disorders.* N.Y.: Milbank Memorial Fund, 1953.

35. Lemert, E. M. An exploratory study of mental disorders in a rural problem area. *Rural Sociol.,* 1948, 13, 48–64.

36. Lewis, A. Social aspects of psychiatry. *Edinburgh med. J.,* 1951, 58, 241–247.

37. Lindemann, E., et al. Minor disorders. In *Epidemiology of mental disorders.* N. Y.: Milbank Memorial Fund, 1950.

38. Lindemann, E. Comment in *Interrelations between the social environment and psychiatric disorders.* N. Y.: Milbank Memorial Fund, 1953.

39. Locke, H. *Predicting adjustment in marriage: a comparison of a divorced and a happily married group.* N. Y.: Holt, 1951.
40. McQuitty, L. L. Theories and methods in some objective assessments of psychological well-being. *Psychol. Monogr.,* 1954, 68, No. 14.
41. Malzberg, B. *Social and biological aspects of mental disease.* Utica: State Hosp. Press, 1940.
42. Miller, D. R., & Swanson, G. E. A proposed study of the learning of techniques for resolving conflicts of impulses. In *Interrelations between the social environment and psychiatric disorders.* N. Y.: Milbank Memorial Fund, 1953.
43. Pollak, O. Social adjustment in old age. *Soc. Sci. Res. Council Bull.* No. 59, 1948.
44. Rennie, T. A. C. The Yorkville community mental health research study. In *Interrelations between the social environment and psychiatric disorders.* N. Y.: Milbank Memorial Fund, 1953.
45. Rogers, C. *Client-centered therapy.* Boston: Houghton Mifflin, 1951.
46. Rogers, C., & Dymond, Rosalind. *Psychotherapy and personality change.* Chicago: Univer. of Chicago Press, 1954.
47. Rose, A. M., & Stub, H. R. Summary of studies on the incidence of mental disorders. In A. M. Rose (Ed.), *Mental health and mental disorder.* N. Y.: Norton, 1955.
48. Roth, W. F., & Luton, F. H. The mental health program in Tennessee. *Amer. J. Psychiat.,* 1943, 99, 662–675.
49. Schneider, E. V. Sociological concepts and psychiatric research. *In Interrelations between the social environment and psychiatric disorders.* N. Y.: Milbank Memorial Fund, 1953.
50. Schroeder, C. W. Mental Disorders in cities. *Amer. J. Sociol.,* 1942, 48, 40–47.
51. Stieglitz, E. J. The integration of clinical and social medicine. In I. Galdston (Ed.), *Social medicine—its derivations and objectives.* N. Y. Acad. of Med., 1947. N. Y.: Commonwealth Fund, 1949.
52. Terman, L. M., et al. *Psychological factors in marital happiness.* N. Y.: McGraw-Hill, 1938.
53. Terman, L. M., & Wallin, P. The validity of marriage prediction and marital adjustment tests. *Amer. sociol. Rev.,* 1949, 14, 497–505.
54. Tietze, C., et al. Personal disorder and spatial mobility. *Amer. J. Sociol.,* 1942, 48, 29–39.
55. Tietze, C., et al. A survey of statistical studies on the prevalence and incidence of mental disorders in sample populations. *Publ. Hlth Rep.,* 1943, 58, 1909–1927.

2

THE MYTH OF MENTAL ILLNESS

Thomas S. Szasz

My aim in this essay is to raise the question "Is there such a thing as mental illness?" and to argue that there is not. Since the notion of mental illness is extremely widely used nowdays, inquiry into the ways in which this term is employed would seem to be especially indicated. Mental illness, of course, is not literally a "thing"—or physical object—and hence it can "exist" only in the same sort of way in which other theoretical concepts exist. Yet, familiar theories are in the habit of posing, sooner or later—at least to those who come to believe in them—as "objective truths" (or "facts"). During certain historical periods, explanatory conceptions such as deities, witches, and microorganisms appeared not only as theories but as self-evident *causes* of a vast number of events. I submit that today mental illness is widely regarded in a somewhat similar fashion, that is, as the cause of innumerable diverse happenings. As an antidote to the complacent use of the notion of mental illness—whether as a self-evident phenomenon, theory, or cause—let us ask this question: What is meant when it is asserted that someone is mentally ill?

In what follows I shall describe briefly the main uses to which the concept of mental illness has been put. I shall argue that this notion has outlived whatever usefulness it might have had and that it now functions merely as a convenient myth.

MENTAL ILLNESS AS A SIGN OF BRAIN DISEASE

The notion of mental illness derives its main support from such phenomena as syphilis of the brain or delirious conditions—intoxications, for in-

Reprinted from the *American Psychologist,* 15, 1960, 113–118, with the permission of the American Psychological Association and Dr. Szasz.

stance—in which persons are known to manifest various peculiarities or disorders of thinking and behavior. Correctly speaking, however, these are diseases of the brain, not of the mind. According to one school of thought, *all* so-called mental illness is of this type. The assumption is made that some neurological defect, perhaps a very subtle one, will ultimately be found for all the disorders of thinking and behavior. Many contemporary psychiatrists, physicians, and other scientists hold this view. This position implies that people *cannot* have troubles—expressed in what are *now called* "mental illnesses"—because of differences in personal needs, opinions, social aspirations, values, and so on. *All problems in living* are attributed to physicochemical processes which in due time will be discovered by medical research.

"Mental illnesses" are thus regarded as basically no different from all other diseases (that is, of the body). The only difference, in this view, between mental and bodily diseases is that the former, affecting the brain, manifest themselves by means of mental symptoms; whereas the latter, affecting other organ systems (for example, the skin, liver, etc.), manifest themselves by means of symptoms referable to those parts of the body. This view rests on and expresses what are, in my opinion, two fundamental errors.

In the first place, what central nervous system symptoms would correspond to a skin eruption or a fracture? It would *not* be some emotion or complex bit of behavior. Rather, it would be blindness or a paralysis of some part of the body. The crux of the matter is that a disease of the brain, analogous to a disease of the skin or bone, is a neurological defect, and not a problem in living. For example, a *defect* in a person's visual field may be satisfactorily explained by correlating it with certain definite lesions in the nervous system. On the other hand, a person's *belief*—whether this be a belief in Christianity, in Communism, or in the idea that his internal organs are "rotting" and that his body is, in fact, already "dead"—cannot be explained by a defect or disease of the nervous system. Explanations of this sort of occurrence—assuming that one is interested in the belief itself and does not regard it simply as a "symptom" or expression of something else that is *more interesting*—must be sought along different lines.

The second error in regarding complex psychosocial behavior, consisting of communications about ourselves and the world about us, as mere symptoms of neurological functioning is *epistemological*. In other words, it is an error pertaining not to any mistakes in observation or reasoning, as such, but rather to the way in which we organize and express our knowledge. In the present case, the error lies in making a symmetrical dualism between mental and physical (or bodily) symptoms, a dualism which is merely a habit of speech and to which no known observations can be found to correspond. Let us see if this is so. In medical practice, when we speak of physical disturbances, we mean either signs (for example, a fever) or symptoms (for example, pain). We speak of mental symptoms, on the other hand, when we refer to a patient's *communications about himself, others, and the world about him.* He might state that he is Napoleon or that he is being persecuted by the Communists. These would be considered mental symptoms *only* if the observer believed that the patient was *not* Napoleon or that he was *not* being persecuted by the Communists. This makes it apparent that the statement that "X is a mental symptom" involves rendering a judgment. The judgment entails, moreover, a covert comparison or matching of the patient's ideas, concepts, or beliefs with those of the observer and the society in which they live. The notion of mental symptom is therefore inextricably tied to the *social* (including *ethical*) *context* in which it is made in much the same way as the notion of bodily symptom is tied to an *anatomical* and *genetic context* (Szasz, 1957a, 1957b).

To sum up what has been said thus far: I have tried to show that for those who regard mental symptoms as signs of brain disease, the concept of mental illness is unnecessary and misleading. For what they mean is that people so labeled suffer from diseases of the brain; and, if that is what they mean, it would seem better for the sake of clarity to say that and not something else.

MENTAL ILLNESS AS A NAME FOR PROBLEMS IN LIVING

The term "mental illness" is widely used to describe something which is very different from a disease of the brain. Many people today take it for granted that living is an arduous process. Its hardship for modern man, moreover, derives not so much from a struggle for biological survival as from the stress and strains inherent in the social intercourse of complex human personalities. In this context, the notion of mental illness is used to identify or describe some feature of an individual's so-called personality. Mental illness—as a deformity of the personality, so to speak—is then regarded as the *cause* of the human disharmony. It is implicit in this view that social intercourse between people is regarded as something *inherently harmonious,* its disturbance being due solely to the presence of "mental illness" in many people. This is obviously fallacious reasoning, for it makes the abstraction "mental illness" into a *cause,* even though this abstraction was created in the first place to serve only as a shorthand expression for certain types of human behavior. It now becomes necessary to ask: "What kinds of behavior are regarded as indicative of mental illness, and by whom?"

The concept of illness, whether bodily or mental, implies *deviation from some clearly defined norm.* In the case of physical illness, the norm is the structural and functional integrity of the human body. Thus, although the desirability of physical health, as such, is an ethical value, what health *is* can be stated in anatomical and physiological terms. What is the norm deviation from which is regarded as mental illness? This question cannot be easily answered. But whatever this norm might be, we can be certain of only one thing: namely, that it is a norm that must be stated in terms of *psychosocial, ethical,* and *legal* concepts. For example, notions such as "excessive repression" or "acting out an unconscious impulse" illustrate the use of psychological concepts for judging (so-called) mental health and illness. The idea that chronic hostility, vengefulness, or divorce are indicative of mental illness would be illustrations of the use of ethical norms (that is, the desirability of love, kindness, and a stable marriage relationship). Finally, the widespread psychiatric opinion that only a mentally ill person would commit homicide illustrates the use of a legal concept as a norm of mental health. The norm from which deviation is measured whenever one speaks of a mental illness is a *psychosocial and ethical one.* Yet, the remedy is sought in terms of *medical* measures which —it is hoped and assumed—are free from wide differences of ethical value. The definition of the disorder and the terms in which its remedy are sought are therefore at serious odds with one another. The practical significance of this covert conflict between the alleged nature of the defect and the remedy can hardly be exaggerated.

Having identified the norms used to measure deviations in cases of mental illness, we will now turn to the question: "Who defines the norms and hence the deviation?" Two basic answers may be offered: (*a*) It may be the person himself (that is, the patient) who decides that he deviates from a norm. For example, an artist may believe that he suffers from a work inhibition; and he may implement this conclusion by seeking help *for* himself from a psychotherapist. (*b*) It may be someone other than the patient who decides that the latter is deviant (for example, relatives, physicians, legal authorities, society generally, etc.). In such a case a psychiatrist may be hired by others to do something *to* the patient in order to correct the deviation.

These considerations underscore the importance of asking the question "Whose agent is the psychiatrist?" and of giving a candid answer to it (Szasz, 1956, 1958). The psychiatrist (psychologist or nonmedical psychotherapist), it now develops, may be the agent of the patient, of the relatives, of the school, of the military services, of a business organization, of a court of law, and so forth. In speaking of the psychiatrist as the agent of these persons or organizations, it is not implied that his values concerning norms, or his ideas and aims concerning the proper nature of remedial action, need to coincide exactly with those of his employer. For example, a patient in individual psychotherapy may believe that his salvation lies in a new marriage; his psychotherapist need not share this hypothesis. As the patient's agent, however, he must abstain from bringing social or legal force to bear on the patient which would prevent him from putting his beliefs into action. If his *contract* is with the patient, the psychiatrist (psychotherapist) may disagree with him or stop his treatment; but he cannot engage others to obstruct the patient's aspirations. Similarly, if a psychiatrist is engaged by a court to determine the sanity of a criminal, he need not fully share the legal authorities' values and intentions in regard to the criminal and the means available for dealing with him. But the psychiatrist is expressly barred from stating, for example, that it is not the criminal who is "insane" but the men who wrote the law on the basis of which the very actions that are being judged are regarded as "criminal." Such an opinion could be voiced, of course, but not in a courtroom, and not by a psychiatrist who makes it his practice to assist the court in performing its daily work.

To recapitulate: In actual contemporary social usage, the finding of a mental illness is made by establishing a deviance in behavior from certain psychosocial, ethical, or legal norms. The judgment may be made, as in medicine, by the patient, the physician (psychiatrist), or others. Remedial action, finally, tends to be sought in a therapeutic—or covertly medical—framework, thus creating a situation in which *psychosocial, ethical,* and/or *legal deviations* are claimed to be correctible by (so-called) *medical action.* Since medical action is designed to correct only medical deviations, it seems logically absurd to expect that it will help solve problems whose very existence had been defined and established on nonmedical grounds. I think that these considerations may be fruitfully applied to the present use of tranquilizers and, more generally, to what might be expected of drugs of whatever type in regard to the amelioration or solution of problems in human living.

THE ROLE OF ETHICS IN PSYCHIATRY

Anything that people *do*—in contrast to things that *happen* to them (Peters, 1958)—takes place in a context of value. In this broad sense, no human activity is devoid of ethical implications. When the values underlying certain activities are widely shared, those who participate in their pursuit may lose sight of them altogether. The discipline of medicine, both as a pure science (for example, research) and as a technology (for example, therapy), contains many ethical considerations and judgments. Unfortunately, these are often denied, minimized, or merely kept out of focus; for the ideal of the medical profession as well as of the people whom it serves seems to be having a system of medicine (allegedly) free of ethical value. This sentimental notion is expressed by such things as the doctor's willingness to treat and help patients irrespective of their religious or political beliefs, whether they are rich or poor, etc. While there may be some grounds for this belief—albeit it is a view that is not impressively true even in these regards—the fact remains that ethical considerations encompass a vast range of human affairs. By making the practice of medicine neutral in regard to some specific issues of value need not, and cannot, mean that it can be kept free from all such values. The practice of medicine is intimately tied to ethics; and the first thing that we must do, it seems to me, is to try to make this clear and explicit. I shall let this matter rest here, for it does not concern us specifically in this essay. Lest there be any vagueness, however, about how or where ethics and medicine meet, let me remind the reader of such issues as birth control, abortion, suicide, and euthanasia as only a few of the major areas of current ethicomedical controversy.

Psychiatry, I submit, is very much more intimately tied to problems of ethics than is medicine. I use the word "psychiatry" here to refer to that contemporary discipline which is concerned with *problems in living* (and not with diseases of the brain, which are problems for neurology). Problems in human relations can be analyzed, interpreted, and given meaning only within given social and ethical contexts. Accordingly, it *does* make a difference—arguments to the contrary notwithstanding—what the psychiatrist's socioethical orientations happen to be; for these will influence his ideas on what is wrong with the patient, what deserves comment or interpretation, in what possible directions change might be desirable, and so forth. Even in medicine proper, these factors play a role, as for instance, in the divergent orientations which physicians, depending on their religious affiliations, have toward such things as birth control and therapeutic abortion. Can anyone really believe that a psychotherapist's ideas concerning religious belief, slavery, or other similar issues play no role in his practical work? If they do make a difference, what are we to infer from it? Does it not seem reasonable that we ought to have different psychiatric therapies—each expressly recognized for the ethical positions which they embody—for, say, Catholics and Jews, religious persons and agnostics, democrats and communists, white supremacists and Negroes, and so on? Indeed, if we look at how psychiatry is actually practiced today (especially in the United States), we find that people do seek psychiatric help in accordance with their social status and ethical beliefs (Hollingshead & Redlich, 1958). This should really not surprise us more than being told that practicing Catholics rarely frequent birth control clinics.

The foregoing position which holds that contemporary psychotherapists deal with problems in living, rather than with mental illnesses and their cures, stands in opposition to a currently prevalent claim, according to which mental illness is just as "real" and "objective" as bodily illness. This is a confusing claim since it is never known exactly what is meant by such words as "real" and "objective." I suspect, however, that what is intended by the proponents of this view is to create the idea in the popular mind that mental illness is some sort of disease entity, like an infection or a malignancy. If this were true, one could *catch* or *get* a "mental illness," one might *have* or *harbor* it, one might *transmit* it to others, and finally one could get *rid* of it. In my opinion, there is not a shred of evidence to support this idea. To the contrary, all the evidence is the other way and supports the view that what people now call mental ill-nesses are for the most part *communications* expressing unacceptable ideas, often framed, moreover, in an unusual idiom. The scope of this essay allows me to do no more than mention this alternative theoretical approach to this problem (Szasz, 1957c).

This is not the place to consider in detail the similarities and differences between bodily and mental illnesses. It shall suffice for us here to emphasize only one important difference between them: namely, that whereas bodily disease refers to public, physicochemical occurrences, the notion of mental illness is used to codify relatively more private, sociopsychological happenings of which the observer (diagnostician) forms a part. In other words, the psy-chiatrist does not stand *apart* from what he observes, but is, in Harry Stack Sullivan's apt words, a "participant observer." This means that he is *committed* to some picture of what he considers reality—and to what he thinks society considers reality—and he observes and judges the patient's behavior in the light of these considerations. This touches on our earlier observation that the notion of mental symptom itself implies a comparison between observer and observed, psychiatrist and patient. This is so obvious that I may be charged with belabor-ing trivialities. Let me therefore say once more that my aim in presenting this argument was expressly to criticize and counter a prevailing contemporary tendency to deny the moral aspects of psychiatry (and psychotherapy) and to substitute for them allegedly value-free medical considerations. Psychotherapy, for example, is being widely practiced as though it entailed nothing other than restoring the patient from a state of mental sickness to one of mental health. While it is generally accepted that mental illness has something to do with man's social (or interpersonal) relations, it is paradoxically maintained that problems of values (that is, of ethics) do not arise in this process.[1] Yet, in one sense, much of psychotherapy may revolve around nothing other than the elucidation and weighing of goals and values—many of which may be mutually contra-dictory—and the means whereby they might best be harmonized, realized, or relinquished.

The diversity of human values and the methods by means of which they may be realized is so vast, and many of them remain so unacknowledged, that they cannot fail but lead to conflicts in human relations. Indeed, to say that human relations at all levels—from mother to child, through husband and wife, to nation and nation—are fraught with stress, strain, and disharmony is, once

[1]Freud went so far as to say: "I consider ethics to be taken for granted. Actually I have never done a mean thing" (Jones, 1957, p. 247). This surely is a strange thing to say for someone who has studied man as a social being as closely as did Freud. I mention it here to show how the notion of "illness" (in the case of psychoanalysis, "psychopathology," or "mental illness") was used by Freud—and by most of his followers—as a means for classifying certain forms of human behavior as falling within the scope of medicine, and hence (by *fiat*) outside that of ethics!

again, making the obvious explicit. Yet, what may be obvious may be also poorly understood. This I think is the case here. For it seems to me that—at least in our scientific theories of behavior—we have failed to *accept* the simple fact that human relations are inherently fraught with difficulties and that to make them even relatively harmonious requires much patience and hard work. I submit that the idea of mental illness is now being put to work to obscure certain difficulties which at present may be inherent—not that they need be un-modifiable—in the social intercourse of persons. If this is true, the concept functions as a disguise; for instead of calling attention to conflicting human needs, aspirations, and values, the notion of mental illness provides an amoral and impersonal "thing" (an "illness") as an explanation for *problems in living* (Szasz, 1959). We may recall in this connection that not so long ago it was devils and witches who were held responsible for men's problems in social living. The belief in mental illness, as something other than man's trouble in getting along with his fellow man, is the proper heir to the belief in demon-ology and witchcraft. Mental illness exists or is "real" in exactly the same sense in which witches existed or were "real."

CHOICE, RESPONSIBILITY, AND PSYCHIATRY

While I have argued that mental illnesses do not exist, I obviously did not imply that the social and psychological occurrences to which this label is currently being attached also do not exist. Like the personal and social troubles which people had in the Middle Ages, they are real enough. It is the labels we give them that concerns us and, having labelled them, what we do about them. While I cannot go into the ramified implications of this problem here, it is worth noting that a demonologic conception of problems in living give rise to therapy along theological lines. Today, a belief in mental illness implies—nay, requires—therapy along medical or psychotherapeutic lines.

What is implied in the line of thought set forth here is something quite different. I do not intend to offer a new conception of "psychiatric illness" nor a new form of "therapy." My aim is more modest and yet also more ambitious. It is to suggest that the phenomena now called mental illnesses be looked at afresh and more simply, that they be removed from the category of illnesses, and that they be regarded as the expressions of man's struggle with the problem of *how* he should live. The last mentioned problem is obviously a vast one, its enormity reflecting not only man's inability to cope with his environment, but even more his increasing self-reflectiveness.

By problems in living, then, I refer to that truly explosive chain reaction which began with man's fall from divine grace by partaking of the fruit of the tree of knowledge. Man's awareness of himself and of the world about him seems to be a steadily expanding one, bringing in its wake an ever larger *burden of understanding* (an expression borrowed from Susanne Langer, 1953). *This burden, then, is to be expected and must not be misinterpreted.* Our only *rational* means for lightening it is *more understanding,* and appropriate *action* based on such understanding. The main alternative lies in acting as though the burden were not what in fact we perceive it to be and taking refuge in an outmoded theological view of man. In the latter view, man does not fashion his life and much of his world about him, but merely lives out his fate in a world created by superior beings. This may logically lead to pleading nonresponsibility in the face of seemingly unfathomable problems and difficulties. Yet, if man fails to take increasing responsibility for his actions, individually as well as collectively, it seems unlikely that some higher power or being would assume this task and carry this burden for him. Moreover, this seems hardly the proper time in human history for obscuring the issue of man's responsibility for his actions by hiding it behind the skirt of an all-explaining conception of mental illness.

CONCLUSIONS

I have tried to show that the notion of mental illness has outlived whatever usefulness it might have had and that it now functions merely as a convenient myth. As such, it is a true heir to religious myths in general, and to the belief in witchcraft in particular; the role of all these belief-systems was to act as *social tranquilizers,* thus encouraging the hope that mastery of certain specific problems may be achieved by means of substitutive (symbolic-magical) operations. The notion of mental illness thus serves mainly to obscure the everyday fact that life for most people is a continuous struggle, not for biological survival, but for a "place in the sun," "peace of mind," or some other human value. For man aware of himself and of the world about him, once the needs for preserving the body (and perhaps the race) are more or less satisfied, the problem arises as to what he should do with himself. Sustained adherence to the myth of mental illness allows people to avoid facing this problem, believing that mental health, conceived as the absence of mental illness, automatically insures the making of right and safe choices in one's conduct of life. But the facts are all the other way. It is the making of good choices in life that others regard, retrospectively, as good mental health!

The myth of mental illness encourages us, moreover, to believe in its logical corollary: that social intercourse would be harmonious, satisfying, and the secure basis of a "good life" were it not for the disrupting influences of mental illness or "psychopathology." The potentiality for universal human happiness, in this form at least, seems to me but another example of the I-wish-it-were-true type of fantasy. I do believe that human happiness or well-being on a hitherto unimaginably large scale, and not just for a select few, is possible. This goal could be achieved, however, only at the cost of many men, and not just a few being willing and able to tackle their personal, social, and ethical conflicts. This means having the courage and integrity to forego waging battles on false fronts, finding solutions for substitute problems—for instance, fighting the battle of stomach acid and chronic fatigue instead of facing up to a marital conflict.

Our adversaries are not demons, witches, fate, or mental illness. We have no enemy whom we can fight, exorcise, or dispel by "cure." What we do have are *problems in living*—whether these be biologic, economic, political, or sociopsychological. In this essay I was concerned only with problems belonging in the last mentioned category, and within this group mainly with those pertaining to moral values. The field to which modern psychiatry addresses itself is vast, and I made no effort to encompass it all. My argument was limited to the proposition that mental illness is a myth, whose function is to disguise and thus render more palatable the bitter pill of moral conflicts in human relations.

REFERENCES

Hollingshead, A. B., & Redlich, F. C. *Social class and mental illness.* New York: Wiley, 1958.

Jones, E. *The life and work of Sigmund Freud.* Vol. III. New York: Basic Books, 1957.

Langer, S. K. *Philosophy in a new key.* New York: Mentor Books, 1953.

Peters, R. S. *The concept of motivation.* London: Routledge & Kegan Paul, 1958.

Szasz, T. S. Malingering: "Diagnosis" or social condemnation? *AMA Arch Neurol. Psychiat.,* 1956, 76, 432–443.

Szasz, T. S. *Pain and pleasure: A study of bodily feelings.* New York: Basic Books, 1957. (a)

Szasz, T. S. The problem of psychiatric nosology: A contribution to a situational analysis of psychiatric operations. *Amer. J. Psychiat.,* 1957, 114, 405–413. (b)

Szasz, T. S. On the theory of psychoanalytic treatment. *Int. J. Psycho-Anal.,* 1957, 38, 166–182. (c)

Szasz, T. S. Psychiatry, ethics and the criminal law. *Columbia law Rev.,* 1958, 58, 183–198.

Szasz, T. S. Moral conflict and psychiatry. *Yale Rev.,* 1959, in press.

3

ON THE FUTILITY OF THE PROPOSITION THAT SOME PEOPLE BE LABELED "MENTALLY ILL"

Theodore R. Sarbin

The writing of a dispassionate account of the current utility of the mental-illness concept reflects a noble purpose. Ellis (1967), by juxtaposing pro et contra arguments, tries to implement this purpose. On the one hand, he recognizes the massive negative utilities that result from the use of the mental-illness label; on the other hand, he points to occasions where the employment of the label appears to have positive utility. His studied conclusion is that the label, when used by professional diagnosticians in an operational way, identifies a limited number of people who are "really mentally ill." He adds the caution that the person who uses the label must subtract from it the pejorative components that have become part and parcel of the concept. Of several definitions, the following is representative of Ellis's viewpoint:

> This is what we really mean when we say that an individual is "mentally ill"—that he has *symptoms of mental malfunctioning or illness.* More operationally stated, he thinks, emotes, and acts *irrationally* and he can usually uncondemningly acknowledge and change his acts. If this, *without any moralistic overtones,* is the definition of "mental illness," then it can distinctly help the *afflicted* individual to accept himself while he is *ill* . . . [p. 440; italics added].

The general conclusions drawn by Ellis must be rejected on logical grounds. They represent not so much a lack of attention to the rules of evidence (to be mentioned later) as the acceptance of an entrenched and unwarranted belief that operates as a major premise. When operative, the premise may be stated:

Reprinted from the *Journal of Counsulting Psychology,* 31, 1967, 447–453, with the permission of the American Psychological Association and Dr. Sarbin.

The label "mental illness" reliably denotes certain forms of conduct that are discriminable from forms of conduct that may be reliably denoted as "not mentally ill."

Since Ellis does not establish the ontological argument for "mental illness," his conclusions are illicit. That is to say, he assumes the truth of the proposition he sets out to demonstrate. (Note the italicized phrases in the quotation above.) The fundamental question is by-passed; to wit, is there a set of observations for which the dual metaphor "mental illness" is appropriate?

Most of Ellis's (and others', for example Ausubel, 1961) arguments aimed at retaining the mental-illness label flow from concealed, tacit, and disguised implications now contained within the label itself. Further, such arguments do not take into account the fact that the choice of label not only constrains further descriptive elaborations of the conduct under observation, but also indirectly restricts alternatives to action. The sentence "A child . . . is known to have tendencies toward severe (mental) illness . . ." contains implications different from "A child has tendencies to hit other children."

To anticipate a criticism of the semiotic approach as a legitimate entrée into the argument, let me assert that the choice of a metaphor to designate an object or event is not inconsequential. Every metaphor contains a wealth of connotations, each connotation has the potential for manifold implications, and each implication is a directive to action. While metaphors are ordinarily used by people to facilitate communication, the peril is always at hand that people may be used by metaphors (Turbayne, 1960). Such a peril is activated when the user of a metaphor ignores, forgets, or purposely drops syntactical modifiers (e.g., *as if*) that denote the metaphor and, instead, employs the word in a literal fashion. To say "Jones is a saint" carries one set of implications if we supply the tacit modifier ("It is *as if* Jones is a saint"); the sentence carries a radically different set of implications if the predicate is treated as literal. The effects of permanently ignoring the metaphoric properties of a word, that is, of dropping the expressed or tacit modifiers, is to hypostatize an entity. Such hypostatization sets the stage for myth making.

Most of Ellis's arguments topple off their own structural defects, defects related to the uncritical acceptance of "illness of the mind" as the proper concept for describing the conduct of people who violate propriety norms (the mores of Sumner, 1906). Much of the undiagnosed confusion currently noted in the helping professions and in relevant juridical decisions is reflected in Ellis's paper. Such confusion might be reduced if we looked at the metaphorical background of our constraining vocabularies. First, let us look at "illness."

The basic referent for illness and for synonyms such as sickness and disease is a stable one, extending over centuries. The referent is discomfort of some kind, such as aches, pains, cramps, chills, paralyses, and so on. The discomfort is a self-appraisal through attention to unusual proximal stimuli, that is, stimuli located "inside" the oganism. These proximal stimuli, when they occur simultaneously with dysfunction of bodily organs, are the so-called symptoms of illness. A diagnosis of illness or disease meant not only that a person reported discomforts, but that the associated somatic dysfunction interfered with the performance of some of his customary roles. This general paradigm of sickness or illness is widespread and may be found in ancient writings and in ethnographic reports.

A compelling question arises: How did the concept "illness" come to include gross behavior, that is, misconduct, rather than complaints and somatic symptoms which were the defining criteria of pre-Renaissance diagnosis? What additional criteria were employed to increase the breadth of the concept "illness"?

The inclusion of behavior disorders in the concept "illness" did not come about suddenly or accidentally. Rather, the label "illness" was at first used as a metaphor and later transformed into a myth.

The beginning of this metaphor-to-myth transformation may be located in the 16th century. The demoniacal model of conduct disorders, codified in the 15th century *Malleus Mallificarum,* had embraced all conduct that departed from the existing norms and was policed by zealous church and secular authorities. The most outstanding result of this thought model was the Inquisition, a social movement that among other things influenced the diagnosis and treatment of unusual imaginings, esoteric beliefs, and extraordinary conduct. The diagnosis of witchcraft and the prescription of treatment (burning) was the province of ecclesiastical specialists. The 16th century witnessed the beginnings of a reaction against the excesses of the Inquisition. The beginnings of humanistic philosophy, the discovery and serious study of Galen and other classical writers, the renunciation of scholasticism—the whole thrust of the Renaissance was opposite that of the Inquisition. In this atmosphere, Teresa of Avila, an outstanding figure of the Counter-Reformation, contributed to the shift from demons to "illness" as the cause of conduct disturbances. A group of nuns was exhibiting conduct which at a later date would have been called hysteria. By declaring these women to be infirm or ill, Teresa was able to fend off the Inquisition. However, the appeal that a diagnosis should be changed from witchcraft to illness required some cognitive elaboration. She invoked the notion of natural causes. Among the natural causes were (a) melancholy (Galenic humoral pathology), (b) weak imagination, and (c) drowsiness. If a person's conduct could be accounted for by such natural causes, it was to be regarded not as evil, but comas enfermas, *as if sick.* By employing the metaphor "as if sick," she implied that practitioners of physic rather than clergymen should be the responsible social specialists (Sarbin & Juhasz, 1967).

When employing metaphorical expressions there is a common human tendency to drop the qualifying "as if" (Turbyane, 1960). That is to say, the metaphor is used without a qualifier to designate it as figurative rather than literal. In the case of illness as a metaphor for conditions not meeting the usual criteria of illness, the dropping of the "as if" was facilitated by the practitioners of physic. It was awkward for them to talk about two kinds of illness, "real" illness and "as if" illness. When Galenic classifications were reintroduced, the "as if" was dropped. Thus, post-Renaissance physicians could concern themselves with illness as traditionally understood and also with norm violations as illness. A review of the 16th and 17th century treatises on "physic" reveals clearly that Galen's humoral theory was the standard for diagnosis and treatment. The diagnostic problem was how to construct inferences about the balance of humors inside the organism.

The decline of the power of church authorities in diagnosing extraordinary imaginings and perplexing conduct was parallel to the rise of science. The prestige of the scientist helped in establishing the model of Galen for both kinds of "illness"—those with somatic complaints and observable somatic symptoms and those without somatic complaints but with unusual behavior standing for somatic symptoms.

Whereas the concept illness had been satisfied by the exclusive use of conjunctive criteria (complaints and observable somatic symptoms), it was now satisfied by the use of disjunctive criteria (complaints and somatic symptoms or complaints by others of perplexing, embarrassing, mystifying conduct). As a result of the uncritical acceptance of the humoral pathology of Galen as the overriding explanation for both somatic and behavior disorders, the latter became assimilated to the former. That is to say, to meet the requirements of the basic Galenic model, symptoms of disease had to be observed, so the observed behavior sequences were regarded as if they were symptoms. Thus, the verbal report of strange imaginings on the one hand and fever on the other, were treated as belonging to the same class, that is, symptoms. As a result of shifting from a metaphoric to a literal interpretation of gross behavior as symptom, Galenic medicine embraced not only everything somatic but also all conduct. Now, any bit of behavior—laughing, crying, threatening, spitting, silence, imagining, lying, and believing—could be called symptoms of underlying internal pathology.

The basic Galenic model was not rejected by psychiatry or clinical psychology. Microbes, toxins, and growths, which were material and operated according to mechanical principles, were appropriate "causes" of disease of the body. They were inside. The appropriate causes for abnormal behavior had to be sought on different dimensions. Since the mind-body conception was taken as truth, the hypothesis could be entertained that the causes of abnormal conduct were in the mind. If this were so, then the most appropriate label for such nonsomatic diseases would be "mental illness."

Before considering the meaning of "mental" in the phrase "mental illness," let me recapitulate. "Illness," as in mental illness, is an illicit transformation of a metaphorical concept to a literal one. To save unfortunate people from being labeled witches, it was humane to treat persons who exhibited misconduct of certain kinds as if they were ill. The Galenic model facilitated the eliding of the hypothetical phrase, the "as if," and the concept of illness was thus deformed to include events that did not meet the original conjunctive criteria for illness. A second transformation assured the validity of the Galenic model. The mystifying behaviors could be treated as if they were symptoms equivalent to somatic symptoms. By dropping the "as if" modifier, observed behavior could be interpreted as symptomatic of underlying internal pathology.

How did the notion of "illness of the mind" become so widely accepted that it served as the groundwork for several professions? A searching historical analysis makes clear that mind was originally employed as a metaphor to denote such events as remembering and thinking. (Colloquial English has retained this formulation, as in "mind your manners.") The shift of meaning to that of a substantive or agency can best be understood as another instance of metaphor-to-myth transformation (Ryle, 1948).

The modern practitioner of Galenic psychiatry and psychology operates from the principle that the "illness" about which he is concerned is in the mind (or psyche, or psychic apparatus). But the mind, even for Galenic practitioners, was to abstract and undifferentiated a concept.

Since the mind was invisible and immaterial, it could not have the same properties as the body—properties that could be denoted by physicalistic terms. Visual palpable organs being the components of the material body, what differentiating components of the invisible impalpable mental entity could one discover or invent? A new metaphor was required—the metaphor of states of mind. States of love, fear, anxiety, apathy, etc., were invented to account for differences in observed conduct. The practitioner now had the job of discovering through chains of inferences which mental states were responsible for normal and abnormal conduct.

MIND AS AN ORGAN OF ILLNESS

Three developments contributed to the construction of mind as the repository of special states and as an organ that was subject to "illness": (1) the ready availability of dispositional terms, (2) the introduction of new terms of faith and religion that located religious experience "inside" the person, and (3) the development of a scientific lexicon.

1. Dispositional terms are shorthand expressions for combinations or orderings of distal and/or proximal events—in principle, a dispositional term can be reduced to a series of observable occurrences. For example, "bravery"

implies a set of concrete behaviors under certain conditions. No implication is carried that the referent is an internal mental state. The development of dispositional terms, however, appears to be a necessary (though not sufficient) prerequisite for the postulation of mental states. In time, dispositional terms become elided and remote from the original metaphorical beginnings.

2. Dispositional terms were conveniently borrowed to denote religious conceptions which followed the shift from an emphasis on ritual and ceremony to inward, personal aspects of faith. Theologians and preachers gave a new set of referents to these dispositional terms, referents that changed dispositional terms from brief notations of observable conduct to states of the soul. The context in which mental states are employed is best expressed by the polarity inside-outside. The problem for the medieval thinker was to find a paradigm for locating events on the inside. Such a model could have been constructed from the following observations: Two classes of proximal inputs may be identified. The first occurs in a context of distal events: for example, pain in the ankle occurs in a context of tripping over a curb; a burning irritation in the fingers occurs in the context of leaning on a hot radiator. The second class of proximal inputs occurs in the absence of associated distal events, such as toothache, headache, gastritis, neuritis, etc. Since the antecedents of the latter inputs could not be located in the outside world, the locus of the somatic perception inside the body was taken as the causal locus. Medieval man had little reliable knowledge of anatomy save that there were bones, sinews, tubes, and fluids and there were also empty spaces. Under the authority of the priests, he acquired the belief that an immaterial and invisible soul resided in these otherwise empty spaces. On this belief system, events for which there were no observed distal contexts could be attributed to the workings of this inner entity or soul. Such an analysis probably prepared the way for locating dispositions inside the person and calling them states of mind. If the cause of an event had no obvious external locus, then it must have an internal locus. Dispositions, when they are codified as substantives, tend to be treated in the same way as other nouns, as possessing "thingness." Thus bravery, lust, conscience, purity, devotion—all dispositional terms originally tied to orderings of behavior—are framed as nouns. If nouns are names of things, and things have location, the problem emerged: where to locate the referents for these nouns? The answer is similar to the process of locating inside the person the cause of pain and discomfort in the absence of external occurrences. Thus, anger, joy, courage, happiness, etc., came to be located in the soul.

3. The replacement of theologians by scientists in the 16th and 17th centuries in matters pertaining to strange and mysterious conduct made necessary a shift from such theological terms as "soul" to scientific metaphors. However, the scientists could not break completely with the entrenched dualistic philosophy. They took as their point of departure the facts of thinking and knowing

and, as a substitute for the soul, employed *mind* as the organ for such activities. With the development of classical scholarship, Greek terms were substituted for the vernacular, the most popular being "psyche" (Boring, 1966). The efforts of the post-Renaissance Galenic practitioners, then, were directed toward analyzing states of mind or psychic events. Those sequences of perplexing conduct that could not be related to external occurrences were declared to be outcomes of internal mental or psychic processes.

Thus mental states—the objects of interest and study for the diagnostician of "mental illness'—were postulated to fill gaps in early knowledge. Through historical and linguistic processes, the construct was reified. Contemporary users of the mental-illness concept are guilty of illicitly shifting from metaphor to myth. Instead of maintaining the metaphorical rhetoric "it is as if there were states of mind," and "it is as if some 'states of mind' could be characterized as sickness," the contemporary mentalist conducts much of his work as if he believes that minds are "real" entities and that, like bodies, they can be sick or healthy.

The most potent implication of the metaphor is that persons labeled mentally ill are categorized as significantly discontinuous from persons labeled with the unmodified term "ill." Of course, referring to persons simply as ill or sick suggests that they belong to a class different from the mutually exclusive class "not ill" or "healthy." Assigning persons to the class "ill" carries the meaning of objective symptoms of a recognized or named disease, in addition to subjectively experienced discomfort. In most societies, persons so classified are temporarily excused from the performance of selected role obligations. The label carries no hint of negative valuation. Sickness, in general, is something for which one is not responsible.

However, when the adjective "mental" is prefixed, a whole new set of implications follows. Contrary to the humane intent of those who resisted the Inquisitors by employing the nonpejorative diagnostic label of illness, present usage is transparently pejorative.

In adding the word "mental" to "illness," the whole meaning structure changes. In the first place, the necessity for adding a prefix to "illness" imposes a special constraint on the interpreter: He asks, "What about this person or his behavior calls for such a special designation?" Since it is a special kind of illness, does the same expectation hold that he (the patient) is to be temporarily excused from the enactment of his roles?

The answers to these questions may be found in a number of studies (Cumming & Cumming, 1962; Goffman, 1961; Nunnally, 1961; Phillips, 1963). Persons who are labeled mentally ill are not regarded as merely sick; they are regarded as a special class of beings, to be feared or scorned, sometimes to be pitied, but nearly always to be degraded. Coincident with such negative valuations are the beliefs that such "mentally ill" persons discharge obligations only of the most simple kinds. The author has elsewhere argued that the process whereby a person is converted into a mental patient carries with it the potential for self-devaluation. The stigmatization, then, may work in the nature of a self-fulfilling prophecy (Sarbin, 1967c).

Further, because of the inherent vagueness in the concept of mind, its assumed independence from the body, and its purported timelessness (derived from the immortal soul), there is a readiness to regard this special kind of sickness as permanent. Thus, a person with a fractured wrist or a patient suffering from influenza, that is, a sick person, may take up his customary roles upon being restored to health. A person diagnosed as mentally ill, however, is stigmatized. Although "cured" of the behavior that initiated the sequence of social and political acts that resulted in his being classified as mentally ill, his public will not usually accept such "cures" as permanent. It is as if the mental states were capable of disguising the person as healthy, although the underlying mental illness remains in a dormant or latent state.

The pejorative connotation is an integral part of the concept. Ellis's advice to subtract the "moralistic overtones" is gratuitous. One can no more delete by fiat the valuational component from "mental illness" than eliminate the "pleasantness" from the act of eating a preferred food.

Another implication of the mental-illness concept stemming from the demonstrated utility of germ theory for nonmental illness is the internal causal locus of mental illness. But the shadowy interior of the mind is not easily entered. The experts must depend on chains of inference forged out of the verbal and nonverbal communications of patients and informants. From such communications, today's experts draw conclusions about the mental structures, their dynamic properties, and their relation to observed behavior in the same manner as Galenic practitioners drew conclusions about the distribution of the humors. One outcome of the exclusive verbal preoccupation with psychic states is the neglect and avoidance of events in the social systems that might be antecedent to instances of misconduct illicitly and arbitrarily called symptoms.

The heuristic implications of the mental-illness metaphor are no less important than the practical implications. Scientists of many kinds have discovered the causes for many (nonmental) illnesses by looking inside the body. By adding a postulate that all mental states are caused by organic conditions (the somatopsychic hypothesis) and also accepting disordered conduct as symptomatic of underlying disease entities, the corollary follows that the ultimate causal agents will be discovered through searching for biochemical, toxicological, and bacteriological substrates. Again, such search methods deploy attention and effort away from the social ecology as a possible source of antecedent conditions of misconduct.

REJECTION OF THE MENTAL-ILLNESS CONCEPT

The analysis offered so far supports the argument that the label "mental illness" should be eliminated from our vocabulary. Following from the implications contained in the label, the logical arguments by themselves would predict the social discrimination and self-denigration consequent to the establishment of social institutions to segregate, house, treat, manage, and reform norm violators. The tacit semantic relation between sin (or evil) and mental illness (Crumpton, Weinstein, Acker, & Annis, 1967), as well as the juridically endorsed relation of mental illness to danger (Platt & Diamond, 1966; Sarbin, 1967a), also grows out of the label's implications.

It is one thing to demonstrate that "mental illness" has achieved mythic status and that its continued employment stands in the way of developing policies and practices for meeting some important social problems; it is another thing to recognize that some people, sometimes, somewhere, engage in conduct that violates propriety norms, including norms controlling in-group aggression. Ellis is justifiably concerned with the problem of what disposition to make of these norm violators. His solution to the problem is to label them mentally ill (sans "moral overtones"). Such labeling provides a warrant for segregating norm violators in mental hospitals or referring them to psychotherapists. The warrant contains (sometimes explicitly) the notion "for the patient's own good." The history of the mental hospital system and the mental health movement in America witnesses that "the patient's good" is little more than a cliché uttered to offset the degradation and desocialization outcomes.

If my previous arguments are not footless, then Ellis's recommendation that we continue the practice of labeling people mentally ill should be forcefully rejected. If his advice is rejected on the grounds of logic and of humanitarian values, then we are left with a gap in the social fabric. What should citizens and officials of an open society do about the problem of norm violation? What, if anything, should we do about people who are sometimes described as silly, unpredictably eccentric, perturbed, deviant, mute, shameless, rude, impertinent, immodest, dishonest, childish, dangerous, hostile, aggressive, and so on? Current practice is, under some conditions, to regard the behavior described by such terms as symptoms of, or caused by, mental illness. Ellis (1967) illustrates this point nicely. With impressive documentation, he says:

"In the last analysis, almost all neurosis and psychosis consists of some self-dishonesty. . . . When, therefore, one fully faces the fact that one is "mentally ill," that this is not a pleasant way to be, and that one is partially responsible for being so, one becomes at that very point, more honest with oneself and begins to get a little better [p. 440]."

What function is served other than the imputation of a discredited mental-state causality? More continuous with observation would be the substitution of the word "dishonest" for "mentally ill."

In exposing mental illness as a myth that has outlived its usefulness, the label becomes improper and futile. Thus we are left with a far-reaching problem in jurisprudence, law enforcement, social engineering, and community psychology. The problem may be formulated as a question: What criteria should be employed to deprive a man of his liberty, his civil rights, his capacity for self-determinism, and so on? It would be foolhardy for me to try even to suggest answers in this brief paper. However, I can point to some partially charted areas that require further exploration.

All of us must put our heads together and decide how free and open a society we want. This decision is prerequisite for establishing criteria to identify those persons who should not be free. It is my belief that with increasing application of democratic principles the use of "mental illness" will be dropped as an intervening category between overt conduct and juridically established status as free or restrained. The arguments of Szasz (1963); the observations of Goffman (1961); the historico-legal studies of Platt and Diamond (1966); the persisting dissatisfaction with such legal precedents as McNaughten, Durham, and others (Diamond, 1964; Dreher, 1967); the disillusionment of psychiatric and psychological practitioners with mentalistic and scholastic theories (Sarbin, 1964); and the development of community psychology (The Conference Committee, 1966)—these and other forces are converging toward finding a fair and more efficient process for arresting, detaining, and incarcerating individuals whose public conduct violates current propriety norms.

In this connection, we must confront the implications of a currently common practice of regarding deviant conduct (e.g., homosexuality) as equivalent to sickness. The refusal of an individual to accept the pejorative classification of mental illness and, correlatively, his refusal to enter psychotherapy, are taken as signs that he, according to Ellis, does not want "to improve his lot." The careful work of Hooker (1957, 1958) suggests that in the culture of male homosexuals the distributions of conventionally used indicators of psychopathology (e.g., Rorschach variables) are not substantially different from the distributions of heterosexuals. Deviance from cultural norms is a societal problem. It is doubtful whether the use of the mental-illness label or any other epithet of degradation will contribute to the solution of the problem. I know of no evidence that supports the contrary notion that societal problems associated with cultural deviance are ameliorated by diagnosing deviant individuals as "ill."

We turn our attention briefly to the problems in jurisprudence generated by the facts of norm violation and by the continued use of the mental-illness doctrine. A cursory review of legal treatises makes clear that the law, its writers, and interpreters, although deeply involved in the problems of equity and justice, have not been concerned with questioning the ontological status of mental illness. Such verdicts as "not guilty by reason of insanity" reflect the dualism upon which much of our jurisprudence rests, not to mention our theology and metaphysics. This verdict is not unlike many constructions to be found in legal treatises. The hidden metaphor is this: It is as if there is a body and a mind normally functioning in harmony. The body performs actions under the governance of the immaterial invisible mind. Where the acts of the body and the intent of the mind are not in harmony in meeting normative standards of conduct, explanations in terms of rule-following models are inadequate. Under these conditions a causal explanation is required: The mind is not properly controlling the body. Therefore the body is declared "not guilty" and the mind becomes the object of punishment or retribution. The aim of such actions is to exorcise the evil influences or mental states that guided the body to perform improper or sinful acts.

While I may be charged with unrestrained hyperbole, the historical facts are undeniable. The same cultural thought model that generated the medieval demoniacal model also produced the modern mental-illness model to explain conduct that does not meet rule-following prescriptions.

The rejection of such an entrenched thought model by the relevant professionals is in the nature of a scientific revolution. As in all scientific revolutions, a new metaphor is needed to replace an exploded myth. The most likely candidate for such replacement is a metaphor that denotes recent and current observations not convincingly assimilated into the older labels. Elsewhere, I have presented arguments in support of a new metaphor—the transformation of social identity—a metaphor that captures the antecedent and concurrent process of becoming a norm violator (Sarbin, 1967a, 1967b, 1967c; Sarbin, Scheibe, & Kroger, 1965). Because of space limitations, I can say only that the metaphor arises from a comprehensive social theory—a theory that rejects mentalistic metaphors as being feebly inappropriate in the enormity of the theoretical and societal problems that confront us.

In these few pages I have tried to make the case that it is futile to try to support the proposition that some people be labeled "mentally ill." The case stands or falls on the coherence of the ontological argument. My argument declares that the label is vacuous, save as an epithet of pejoration. Further, its scientific utility is suspect because of its reliance on an outworn mentalistic concept—the ghost in the machine, to use Ryle's (1948) apt metaphor.

SUMMARY

By recognizing the metaphorical nature of "symptoms" and "illness" and the hypothetical nature of "mind," the mythical character of the mental concept is exposed. Conclusions lead the author to take a position contrary to Ellis's: Logical canons as well as humanistic value orientations direct us to delete "mental illness" from our vocabulary. Such a deletion does not deny that persons who engage in certain kinds of norm violations, which Ellis would call symptoms of mental illness, present problems to society. How to contain, manage, and reform persons judged to be actual or potential violators of social norms has been and continues to be one of the fundamental problems of social organizations. Creative solutions to such fundamental problems require a new set of metaphors and the sustained effort of experts in jurisprudence, social engineering, law enforcement, and community psychology.

REFERENCES

Ausubel, D. Personality disorder *is* disease. *American Psychologist,* 1961, 16, 69–74.

The Conference Committee. C. C. Bennett (Chm.), *Community psychology, a report of the Boston Conference on the education of psychologists for community mental health.* Boston: Boston University Press, 1966.

Boring, E. G. A note on the origin of the word psychology. *Journal of the History of the Behavioral Sciences,* 1966, 2, 167.

Crumpton, E., Weinstein, A. D., Acker, C. W., & Annis, A. P. How patients and normals see the mental patient. *Journal of Clinical Psychology,* 1967, 23, 46–49.

Cumming, J., & Cumming, E. *Ego and milieu.* New York: Atherton Press, 1962.

Diamond, B. L. Review of T. S. Szasz, *Law, liberty and psychiatry; an inquiry into the social uses of mental health practices. California Law Review,* 1964, 52, 899–907.

Dreher, R. H., Origin, development and present status of insanity as a defense to criminal responsibility in the common law. *Journal of the History of the Behavioral Sciences,* 1967, 3, 47–57.

Ellis, A. Should some people be labeled mentally ill? *Journal of Consulting Psychology,* 1967, 31, 435–446.

Goffman, E. *Asylums.* Chicago: Aldine, 1961.

Hooker, E. The adjustment of the male overt homosexual. *Journal of Projective Techniques and Personality Assessment,* 1957, 21, 18–31.

Hooker, E. Male homosexuality in the Rorschach. *Journal of Protective Techniques and Personality Assessment,* 1958, 22, 31–54.

Nunnally, J. C. *Popular conceptions of mental health.* New York: Holt, Rinehart & Winston, 1961.

Phillips, D. L. Rejection as a consequence of seeking help for mental disorders. *American Sociology Review*, 1963, 28, 963–972.

Platt, A. M., & Diamond, B. L. The origins and development of the "wild beast" concept of mental illness and its relation to theories of criminal responsibility. *Journal of the History of the Behavioral Sciences*, 1965, 1, 355–367.

Ryle, G. *The concept of mind*. Oxford: Hutchinson's University Press, 1948.

Sarbin, T. R. Anxiety: The reification of a metaphor. *Archives of General Psychiatry*, 1964, 10, 630–638.

Sarbin, T. R. The dangerous individual: An outcome of social identity transformations. *British Journal of Criminology*, 1967, in press. (a)

Sarbin, T. R. Notes on the transformation of social identity. In N. S. Greenfield, M. L. Miller, & L. M. Roberts (Eds.), *Comprehensive mental health: The challenge of evaluation*. Madison: University of Wisconsin Press, 1968. (b)

Sarbin, T. R. Role theoretical analysis of schizophrenia. In J. H. Mann (Ed.), *Reader in general psychology*. New York: Rand McNally, 1967, in press. (c)

Sarbin, T. R. The scientific status of the mental illness concept. In S. Plog (Ed.), *Determinants of mental illness—A handbook*. New York: Holt, Rinehart & Winston, 1967, in press. (d)

Sarbin, T. R., & Juhasz, J. B. The historical background of the concept of hallucination. *Journal of the History of the Behavioral Sciences*, 1967, in press.

Sarbin, T. R., Scheibe, K. E., & Kroger, R. O. *The transformation of social identity*. Unpublished manuscript, University of California, Berkeley, 1965.

Sumner, W. G. *Folkways*. Boston: Ginn, 1906.

Szasz, T. S. *Law, liberty and psychiatry; an inquiry into the social uses of mental health practices*. New York: Macmillan, 1963.

Turbayne, C. *Myth of metaphor*. New Haven: Yale University Press, 1960.

DISCUSSION

Attempts to define normality and abnormality often appear to be confusing and of limited application. Perhaps, as Scott suggests, much of the difficulty in defining abnormality results from basic incompatibilities in the manner in which we define and conceptualize the causes of abnormal behavior. Indeed, the fact that such diverse phenomena as mental retardation (determined primarily by performance on an intelligence test), diseases of the nervous system (classified on the basis of observed neurological change), and functional disorders (classified on the basis of patterns of behavior) are listed as psychiatric illnesses indicates such incompatibilities. The original assumption underlying psychiatric nosology was that such diverse behavioral phenomena resulted from underlying disease processes and that application of the procedures, terminology and rationale of physical medicine would most effectively enable us to understand and modify such phenomena. The articles by Sarbin and Szasz clearly challenge this assumption, since, as these authors indicate, indiscriminately extending the assumptions of the disease analogy to account for all abnormal behavior can serve only to obscure and obstruct progress in the delineation of the variables which result in abnormal behavior. Many of the articles which follow indicate the promising results obtained when the principles of behavioral science are consistently applied to the modification and study of abnormal behavior.

Section 2:   THE CLASSIFICATION OF ABNORMAL BEHAVIOR

All systems for the classification of abnormal behavior are derived from an associated conceptual model. Thus, the supernatural model classifies abnormal behavior on the basis of indices of witchcraft, the medical model diagnoses behaviors assumed to be indicative of mental illness, and the behavioral model attempts to delineate consistent patterns of maladaptive behavior. Whether we label this process witchcraft, diagnosis, or the classification of behavior, does not alter the fact that some taxonomic system is necessary to all scientific studies. The articles included in this section are concerned with the rationale and utility of our current classificatory system, psychiatric diagnosis.

4

THE PROBLEM OF PSYCHIATRIC NOSOLOGY: A CONTRIBUTION TO A SITUATIONAL ANALYSIS OF PSYCHIATRIC OPERATIONS

Thomas S. Szasz

The problem of psychiatric nosology has posed a persistent difficulty during the past half-century because, it seems to me, it is one of those problems that is insoluble in the form in which it is usually tackled. Certain fundamental concepts and technical aims must be clarified first. Only after this has been accomplished will we be in a position to return to the problem of psychiatric nosology and re-examine it in a new light.

WHAT DOES PSYCHIATRIC NOSOLOGY CLASSIFY?

I want to emphasize the need to scrutinize the very notion of "psychiatric nosology" and to divide it into workable fragments. The reason for this suggestion is that this problem encompasses, as far as I can see, the following, often mutually exclusive, methods and tasks. First, in relation to the word "psychiatric," there is ambiguity about the domain of this field. Is psychiatry a branch of medicine? And if so, do we mean by this that it is a therapeutic discipline based (as far as possible) on the methods of physics and chemistry? Or do we mean that it is the study of human behavior and human relationships? And if so, do we conceive of it as a branch of, or allied to, psychology and sociology? If this is what we mean, then we are committed to the psychological

This is an abbreviated version of a paper read with the title "Psychiatric Nosology: Clinical and Sociological Implications" in the theoretical symposium on "Psychiatric Nosology," at 113th annual meeting of The American Psychiatric Association, Chicago, Ill., May 13-17, 1957. The full length text will appear elsewhere.

50

method and frame of reference. We cannot have both, or a combination of the two, either by simply wishing or by coining a word like "psychosomatic" (39). To illustrate this, let us consider the diagnosis of general paresis. Does this diagnosis refer to a physico-chemical or a psychological phenomenon? Clearly it refers to the former. It is not characteristic, or even descriptive, of any particular behavioral event. How then can we hope to bring it into a meaningful relationship with other "psychiatric diagnoses" such as hysteria, reactive depression or situational maladjustment? These, and many others, refer to behavioral events and are meaningless in a physico-chemical frame of reference. (They are, however, modelled after, and are not meaningless in, a medical framework of concepts.) Yet, such dissimilar concepts are now all subsumed under the heading of "psychiatric diagnosis." This is as though in the periodic table of elements, we would find coal, steel, and petroleum interspersed among items such as helium, sulfur and carbon. In my opinion, this is one of the reasons why the taxonomic system known as "psychiatric nosology" does not work and why attempts to improve it—which have not taken this factor into account—have failed to satisfy anyone but their authors.

A second source of difficulties arises as a result of the several implications of the word "nosology." Nosology means the classification of "diseases." This immediately casts psychiatry into the medical (and physico-chemical) mold into which it fits only according to the first definition of this discipline (36). In this view, psychiatry is the study of diseases of the brain, and psychiatric nosology is the classification of these diseases. Others, however, regard psychiatry as the study of diseases of the "mind"; "psychopathology" is the nosology based on this scheme (15). The trouble here stems from the concept "mind." Still others have attempted to overcome this difficulty by recourse to a system of "disorders of behavior" (8). Thus far we have enumerated three categories of concepts (brain, mind and behavior). To the taxonomy of each of these, the expression "psychiatric nosology" is applied. Not only do psychiatrists use different categories, usually without specifying their scheme, but often concepts from two or all three of these categories are combined within a single taxonomic scheme (e.g., general paresis, latent schizophrenia and homosexuality).

Although the expression "psychiatric nosology" means principally the classification of psychiatric disorders (whatever these may be), modern developments in psychiatry have led to further taxonomic possibilities. This state of affairs has resulted from the fact that psychiatry consists of both a "basic science" and of a "clinical technique" (or several such techniques). It is only the latter that is oriented toward "diseases," "diagnosis" and "treatment." The former is oriented, like all sciences, toward an essentially non-judgmental (non-evaluative) understanding of the phenomena which it studies. "Nosology" in this context becomes akin to the taxonomic systems of the physical sciences in that it aims at a system of *ordering* phenomena that is useful not for "treatment" but for "scientific mastery" (whatever that may mean, depending upon the developmental stage in which the science finds itself and upon social factors). Some of the classificatory concepts of psychoanalysis (*e.g.,* repression as a characteristic feature of "hysteria") resemble most closely such nonevaluative concepts of classification. Unfortunately, however, most of these concepts have been re-introduced into a medically modeled system of psychopathology (20).

AN OPERATIONAL APPROACH TO PSYCHIATRIC NOSOLOGY

Classification is but a special case of the more general psychological phenomenon of category-formation. This process depends, as we know, upon the psychological characteristics of the person engaged in forming categories and upon the social situation in which he participates. The dependence of the psychological variable upon brain function, for example, has been studied and demonstrated in an impressive fashion by Kurt Goldstein (16-18). The role of the latter factor, that is, the effect of the social situation on category-formation, is a matter of common knowledge and may escape attention precisely because it is so obvious. In other words, it would be banal to stress that from the point of view of the economist or of the jeweler there are no "similarities" between coal and diamond. In an economic situation, one may distinguish diamond, gold, platinum and money as members of the (same) category that pertains to *economic value.* The chemist, on the other hand, may classify diamond and coal as "chemically similar" members of the category called *carbon.* Surely, there is no need to belabor this point. The example cited illustrates what I mean by an operational approach to nosology; the word "operational" is used in this context to denote not only the characteristic methods of observation but also the social situation in which the observation is made and its purposes. This extension is inherent in the philosophy of operationalism (14). Let us look at psychiatric nosology in this light.

It is apparent at once that the social situations in which so-called psychiatric observations are made are diverse, and yet it is generally assumed that one and the same system of classification should be useful for all of them. We may name but a few of the major "psychiatric situations," without implying that our list is exhaustive: the mental hospital, private psychiatric practice (including the psychoanalytic situation), the child guidance clinic, the psychoanalytic training system, military service, the court of law and jail. Psychiatric diagnoses are made and used in each of these settings (10, 13, 30, 34). *Yet the methods employed and the purposes for which diagnoses are made differ.* I submit, therefore, that we can not expect to be able to take a system of psychiatric nosology developed in one situation and expect it to be meaningful and serviceable in another.

Unfortunately space does not permit a detailed consideration of the characteristics of the various psychiatric situations that have been listed. To do so would require, at the very least, a separate treatise for each. I have offered fragments of such operational descriptions of specific psychiatric situations elsewhere (*e.g.,* for the psychoanalytic situation [37, 38], for the psychotherapeutic situation with the schizophrenic [32], and for the legal situation [40]).

Someone might ask, what is it that corresponds in these situations to the differences in the classificatory schemes of the jeweler and the chemist, in the example cited. My comments shall be restricted to answering this question. I hope that this will illustrate and clarify the general problem under discussion. For this purpose, we may consider three situations: that of the psychiatrist in a state mental hospital, the psychoanalytic situation and the situation in the court of law (psychiatric expert testimony). In the first of these, the relevant category into which the patient must be fitted is principally that of psychosis versus non-psychosis (4, 9). The former tends to justify forcible retention in the hospital; the latter does not. Also, the diagnosis of psychosis, in this context, legitimizes the use of various, sometimes drastic, therapies. In the psychoanalytic situation, the same term, that is "psychosis" (or "psychotic"), refers *only* to certain mental mechanisms or patterns of human relationships; it does not refer to overt behavior or social judgment. This method of classification is somewhat analogous to that of the chemist, and consequently the concept "psychosis," as used here, will *not* point to any significant phenomenological similarities between the patient under study and others who may be either inside or outside of mental hospitals (32, 33). Finally, in the legal situation, psychiatric diagnostic terms must be categorized in terms of two mutually exclusive classes, those who are punishable and those who are not (35). This is inherent in the legal situation just as it is inherent in our present economic situation that diamond is more valuable than coal. A non-judgmental, purely descriptive system of classification—while it may be as accurate as it would be to state that both diamond and coal are forms of carbon—is no more appropriate to the legal situation, than would be its analogue for purposes of banking.

Let us now take a brief glimpse at the recent history of psychiatry, viewed in this light. We may restate our problem by recalling that the questions that we have asked were: *Whom do we study, where, and with what methods?* We have called attention to how various "psychiatric situations" on the current scene differ from one another. Let us ask the same questions now about the principal psychiatric figures since Kraepelin.

Kraepelin's chief objects of observation were inmates of mental hospitals (21). He studied them by direct common-sense observation. The underlying assumption was first that they suffered from diseases much the same as other diseases with which physicians were familiar, and second that society and the physicians who studied them were "normal" and constituted the standards with which their behavior was compared. Accordingly, patients were subsumed under categories ("diagnoses") based on the behavioral phenomena ("symptoms") that were judged to be dominant. The spirit of the inquiry precluded emphasis on specifically individualistic features and determinants. Kraepelin's approach, as Zilboorg (43) noted, was therefore at once humane and inhuman. He was interested in man, but was not interested in the patient as an individual.

The psychiatric situation that characterized Bleuler's work (2) was essentially similar to Kraepelin's. The main difference lay, I think, in the fact that Bleuler had a much greater interest in the patient as an individual. He, therefore, noted more personally unique phenomena and saw, for example, that patients with dementia praecox were not really "demented."

Now we come to Freud, who, most of us will agree, saw much more than his predecessors. I would like to suggest that he saw more partly because he was not fettered in making his observations in a single situation with limited techniques. Indeed, he enlarged the psychiatric situation to include almost anything that came across his horizon. Thus, he rapidly shifted from pure clinical observation with or without hypnosis, to observations of himself, of other socially normal individuals, so-called neurotics, as well as to observations of the biographies and autobiographies of artists, "psychotics" and others. On the whole, he too tended to use society and the observer as norms against which the patient and his conduct were measured. In contrast to his predecessors, however, he made this standard explicit. Prior to this time, it was not fully realized that such a standard was implicit in the then current schemes of psychiatric nosology. The nosological scheme that Freud used, as might be expected from what has just been said, was chaotic. He retained the Kraepelinian scheme as far as the diagnostic words were concerned but used them as he pleased. This has resulted, among other things, in repeated forays of re-labeling his cases by later authors (28). Once again, Zilboorg (42) clarified this matter by emphasizing that Freud cared little about the diagnostic labels he used. He concentrated, as we know, on accurate description, reconstruction and on the formulation of new abstractions to account for what he observed (*e.g.,* transference, repression, reaction-formation, etc.).

There have been attempts to use psychoanalytic abstractions in the formation of new psychiatric nosologies. These have failed because they have mimicked the Kraepelinian and Bleulerian systems (*e.g.,* by suggesting that hysteria be diagnosed by the presence of repression as the chief mechanism of defense). Such attempts could succeed, if at all, only by limiting their range of applicability and by adhering to operational criteria (*e.g.,* the patient's reaction to the analytic situation [11]).

Adolf Meyer's approach was a great departure from the basic concepts of Kraepelin and Bleuler in that he did not subscribe to the notion that mental disorder is a phenomenon akin to physical disease (24, 25). Yet he remained more closely allied in his work to these men than to psychoanalysis, probably chiefly because he continued to focus attention principally on so-called "clinical material" that is, on those who are mentally ill by social criteria. His method was, by his own statement, that of "common sense" (22), but in his thinking he combined biological, historical, psychological and social considerations. He developed a system of classification not of "diseases" but of "reaction types," meaning thereby that disorders of behavior may be classified according to their predominant symptoms. It is important to note that the technical terms—the "ergasias"—which Meyer suggested for these categories were never widely accepted in spite of his great influence on American psychiatry. Within a few decades his system of nosology became an historical relic.

Kurt Goldstein has become well-known for his observations in still another psychiatric situation: he studied the brain injured, combining in his approach the methods of neurology, clinical psychiatry and psychological testing (16). In addition, he introduced certain philosophical and linguistic considerations (17) in his studies which have also proved significant. While his name is not customarily associated with any nosological innovations, it should be noted that he did create two new categories—the concrete and the abstract attitudes (18)— and that these grew out of the particular situation in which his observations were made.

We may also note, at this point, that Bleuler's, Freud's and Goldstein's nosological categories continue to be used. All make good sense in the situations in which they originated. They have, however, since been removed, transplanted and combined with one another, and used in all manner of situations. Is it then surprising that our current psychiatric nosology is a modern Tower of Babel?

Considerations of some recent work in psychoanalysis would throw further light on the interrelations of the social structure, the methods of, and the classificatory schemes appropriate to, various psychiatric situations. Suffice it to note that most of these developments have increasingly abandoned the traditional nosological concepts and have developed new concepts and terms of their own. Harry Stack Sullivan's contributions (31), for example, cannot be fitted into our current official nosology without doing the utmost violence both to him and to our nosology. The same is true of other current contributions to the psychology of "schizophrenia" and of the entire trend toward an object-relationship type of approach (12). These considerations underscore the need to develop adequate systems of classification, rather than to continue paying lip-service to an outmoded nosology, as we progress in our psychiatric knowledge.

PANCHRESTONS IN PSYCHIATRY

In connection with the word "protoplasm," Hardin has recently called attention to the danger of words that "explain everything." He wrote:

> Such enemies of thought, like all enemies, may be easier to spot if we label them. Such "explain-alls" need a name. As we borrow from the Greek to call a "cure-all" a *panacea,* so let us christen an "explain-all" a *panchreston.* The history of science is littered with the carcasses of discarded panchrestons: the Galenic *humours,* the Bergsonian *élan vital,* and the Drieschian *entelechy* are a few biological cases in point. A panchreston, which "explains-all," *explains* nothing (19, p. 113).

Clearly, panchrestons have played, and continue to play, an enormous role in psychiatry and psychoanalysis. Percival Bailey's address (1) last year to this Association may indeed be regarded as a discourse on the existence of panchrestons in psychiatry and on the uses to which they are put. He overlooked, however, all that we *do know,* and all that has been discovered during the past half century. By concentrating attention on panchrestons, one naturally limits himself to that which remains to be elucidated. I would like to emphasize this point, in order to make it clear that my subsequent comments are not intended as a wholesale criticism of psychiatry, or any of its branches, but are offered simply as additional considerations to be taken into account in connection with the problem of how to improve our nosology.

It is clear that many terms—some diagnostic, like schizophrenia, others non-diagnostic, like libido—function as panchrestons. In other words, "schizophrenia" is supposed to "explain" so-called insane behavior in much the same way as "protoplasm" explained the nature of life, and "ether" the manner in which energy travels through space. Not only do these words *not* explain the phenomena in question, but, as Hardin (19) rightly emphasized, they hinder understanding or explanation. If this is so, it means that just as "ether" and "protoplasm" obscured important problems in physics and biology, so "schizophrenia" (and many other psychiatric words) may obscure fundamental problems in psychiatry.

We touch here on an exceedingly important problem, but one that is in no way peculiar to psychiatry. Accordingly, we need not dwell on it and may assume that analogous developments in other sciences constitute a lesson that we must learn. From a point of view of psychiatric nosology this means that categories such as "schizophrenia" may be doubly harmful: first, such categories are unsatisfactory as readily validable concepts for purposes of classification, and secondly, they give rise to the misleading impression that there "exists" a more-

or-less homogoneous group of phenomena which are designated by the word in question (*e.g.,* "schizophrenia," "hysteria," "malingering"). If this line of thought is correct—as I believe it is—it leads to the realization that the "problem of schizophrenia," which many consider to be the core-problem of psychiatry today, may be truly akin to the "problem of the ether." To put it simply: there is no such problem. The task is, rather, to redefine our questions so that they become manageable with the technical tools at our command. In the case of "schizophrenia" this will mean, first a conceptual clarification of the manifold meanings of the word, and then work along clearly defined methodological lines—whether biochemical or psychoanalytic—aimed at elucidating specific "facts" rather than "explaining" global concepts. Thus biochemical studies may throw light on disorders of brain function, much as the discovery of the histological lesions of general paresis threw light on the presence of a physically damaged brain in these patients. There is no reason to believe that this may not prove to be the case for *some* patients who by curent criteria might be labeled "schizophrenic." Similarly, studies along psychological and social lines should prove enlightening about processes of object relationships, the use of language and symbol-formation and other features characteristic of the behavior, in certain situations, of so-called "schizophrenic" patients. It would be a mistake to believe—or so I submit—that such researches will "explain schizophrenia."[1] Instead what may happen is that various behavioral processes will be better understood and the need for the word "schizophrenia" will disappear.

A RECAPITULATION AND SOME FURTHER CONCLUSIONS

In the preceding pages, psychiatric situations and nosologies (more-or-less) appropriate to each were discussed in the light of the philosophy of operationalism. This word is used to designate that principle of scientific philosophy which emphasizes the over-riding importance of an explicit awareness of the particular methods of observation used in each study. I have extended its use, somewhat, to include in the concept of "method" the nature of the social setting in which the observation took place. This extension is implicit in the

[1]In last year's theoretical symposium Pauling stated: "I am sure that most mental disease is chemical in origin, and that the chemical abnormalities involved are usually the result of abnormalities in the genetic constitution of the individual" (27, p. 492). This is a sweeping claim that is buttressed, at present, by little more than the scientific prestige (derived from another field) of its distinguished author. It seems to me entirely plausible that investigations into what Pauling calls "molecular diseases" may prove exceedingly fruitful for our understanding of the physical basis of some aspects of human behavior. It is not in keeping with the spirit of the "scientific attitude," however, to hold out this (or for that matter any other) specific investigative technique as one that promises wholesale solution to a problem as poorly defined as that of "mental disease" (an expression that no doubt will also soon qualify for the title of panchreston).

principles of operational philosophy and it has been explicitly developed by students of what is often referred to as the "sociology of science." The relevance of this extension to the study of psychiatry need not be belabored, since we are fully aware today of the immense significance of the interpersonal and social matrix in this area of knowledge.

The brief sketches of the various psychiatric situations that have been presented were offered to clearly identify these situations and to show that they differ in one or several parameters. Thus, there may be differences in the person and position of the observer and the observed, and there may be variations in the aims for which the classification ("diagnosis") is made, or in the principal action patterns inherent in the situation. It must be concluded that to hope that one and the same system of psychiatric nosology should be serviceable in all of these situations is to expect too much. Contrariwise, it is reasonable to assume that multiple nosological systems, each serviceable for one situation but not for others, may be developed without undue difficulties. Indeed, there are some in everyday use today, as for example, the categories of "sane-insane" as used in jurisprudence of "transference-reality" as used in the psychoanalytic situation. The notions of sane and insane pertain to the legal situation and can be correlated with the action-patterns of punishment and acquittal (40). The notion of transference pertains to the psychoanalytic situation and expresses the analyst's inference concerning some aspects of the patient's behavior: to the extent to which it is patterned upon past object relationships that are now re-experienced in relation to the analyst, it is "transference"; in so far as the behavior reflects the patient's current orientation to (external) objects, it is not "transference" but is considered to be "reality-oriented." None of these concepts can be readily applied in other situations, although our so-called common sense, and the needs of society, often press us, as psychiatrists, to use all available psychiatric notions in every conceivable situation. This sort of tendency has led the psychiatrist to be viewed—both by himself and by others—as a "universal social expert" who can offer "scientific" advice on all manner of problems ranging from how to raise children to how to pick men who will be "safe" political leaders. This "global" (not to say "megalomanic") view of psychiatry not only cannot lay claim to being "scientific," but—and this may be even more damaging in the long run—it distracts attention from the truly worth-while advances that have been made, and that are being made, in this field.

All of this, as I have said, runs counter to "common sense," and much of it runs counter to a currently prevalent tendency toward unbridled eclecticism (almost as if this were a "good" thing in itself) as well as to a widespread predilection of a "global" type of psychiatric research (*e.g.,* attacks on the problem of "mental health" or "schizophrenia"). The need for science to deny (or more precisely, to transcend) "common sense" has been repeatedly emphasized, particularly by Bridgman (6). It was cogently re-emphasized recently by Hardin, when he stated,

In the necessity of discarding 'protoplasm,' biology is now confronted with a painful decision of the sort that faced its older sister science, physics, more than half a century ago—the necessity of denying 'common sense' (19, p. 120).

Psychiatry, too, is confronted with the need to abandon "common sense." Thus "common sense" has assumed that insights gained from the psychoanalytic situation should be *directly* applicable to other situations, for instance to problems of child rearing or to the disposition of criminals in courts of law. Our experience shows that this is *not* possible. So we criticize, in turn, psychoanalysis, parents or lawyers, and refuse to draw the obvious conclusion which is that most psychoanalytic concepts make good sense in the psychoanalytic situation, but their relevance in other situations is a matter for careful and critical judgment. Psychoanalysis is here used for purposes of illustration only. Similar considerations hold true for concepts developed and used in other settings, such as in the state hospital ("manic-depressive psychosis"), in jail ("the Ganser syndrome") or in the military situation ("malingering").

Attention is also called to the role that words that purport to "explain"—when, in fact they merely "name"—play in psychiatry and in psychiatric nosology. The word "schizophrenia" is singled out as probably the most important of these words. Its secure place in the taxonomy of our discipline, it is suggested, interferes with a better comprehension of the data for which this word allegedly accounts. The notion of "schizophrenia" further lends itself to the creation of a reified picture of this disorder, so that we imagine it to constitute a problem similar to others with which we are familiar in medicine, such as poliomyelitis or arteriosclerotic heart disease. It seems more likely that instead of "schizophrenia" being akin to such serviceable models of "disease," its common bonds are with such panchrestons as "protoplasm" in biology and "ether" in physics. If so, it is useless to search for the "cause" and "treatment" of the "entity" that will account for the observed phenomena now labeled "schizophrenia." Rather, a better comprehension of the "real facts"—if I may be excused for this expression—will probably lead to the gradual disappearance of this word, whose function, like that of all panchrestons, is to fill a scientific void.

In closing, I would like to mention a thought that has occurred to me in reflecting on this subject. It struck me as odd—however obvious it may seem—that our officially accepted nosological system is such that everyone pays lip-service to it, but almost no one considers it satisfactory. Often one hears such statements as "Nosology is a necessary evil," or "Nosology is the expression of the immaturity of psychiatry as a science." Such utterances are misleading. There is no science without classification. What matters is whether the taxonomic system used is appropriate for the endeavor at hand or not. The present situation with respect to psychiatric nosology may be compared to posting a blind policeman on a new superhighway and then expecting him to enforce the speed-laws. The rules of psychiatric nosology are not only being constantly violated, but they are violated gleefully. Nowadays, a contemptuous disregard for the rules of nosology has even become a part of the cloak of psychiatric authority.

An interpretation of this mode of social behavior would prompt one to assume that psychiatrists behave as if their system of nosology was created by "alien others" for no purpose other than to hinder them. Few feel sufficiently identified with this cause to do work along this line or to inspire their colleagues to change their ways. Yet, if one wants to work, all will agree that social order is better than anarchy. Similarly, nosological order would be better than the nosological anarchy which is our present state. Perhaps this symposium will prove to be the soil from which new nosological orders in psychiatry will grow.

SUMMARY

The thesis of this essay is that most problems of psychiatric nosology, as currently formulated, are refractory to solution because of certain basic ambiguities in psychiatric concepts and operations. Scientific clarity and progress in this area depend upon clear agreement on the following issues: 1. the scope and subject matter that is to be designated as "psychiatry" (*e.g.,* brain, mind, or behavior); 2. the scientific and technical methods that characterize this branch of knowledge (*e.g.,* physics or psychology, physico-chemical techniques or psychotherapy); 3. the precise nature of the phenomena that we seek to classify (*e.g.,* physical or chemical changes in the brain, social behavior, or behavior toward specific individuals). These are not three separate categories, but represent rather interlocking aspects of what must be, in the last analysis, operational descriptions of specific "psychiatric situations."

It is suggested that we distinguish sharply between the following principal psychiatric situations on the current American scene: the mental hospital, private psychiatric practice (including the psychoanalytic situation), the child guidance clinic, the psychoanalytic training system, military service, the court of law and jail. Illustrative samples of an operational analysis of a few of these situations are presented. A similar scrutiny of the psychiatric situations that characterized the work of each of the principal figures in the history of psychiatry since Kraepelin is suggested and briefly sketched. This mode of approach prompts one to take a more "relativistic" view of psychiatry, by which is meant the appreciation that different observational methods imply differences in the very nature of the observed "material." Thus, global approaches to psychiatry may have to be abandoned in favor of more limited, and socially and methodologically better defined, plans of attack on specific problems. It is further inherent in this line of thought that a nosological system developed in, and appropriate to, one type of psychiatric situation cannot be validly transferred to another, radically different psychiatric situation. This is a principle familiar to us from other branches of science and technology and the various systems of classification that they employ.

Considerations of nosology also prompt a scrutiny of the specific items that are classified. At present, probably the single most important diagnostic label in psychiatry is "schizophrenia." Some epistemological aspects of the problem of schizophrenia are briefly discussed, and it is suggested that this word may now function as a "panchreston" (or "explain-all") which, instead of illuminating, obscures the essential problems that face psychiatry today. . . .

REFERENCES

1. Bailey, P. *Am. J. Psychiat.*, 113:387, 1956.

2. Bleuler, E. *Dementia Praecox or the Group of Schizophrenia.* New York: International Universities Press, 1950.

3. Blitzsten, N. L. *Am. J. Psychiat.*, 94:1431, 1938.

4. Bowman, K. M., and Rose, M. *Am. J. Psychiat,* 108:161, 1951.

5. Breuer, J., and Freud, S. *Studies in Hysteria* (1895). New York: *Nervous and Mental Disease Monographs,* 1947.

6. Bridgman, P. W. *Scient. Monthly,* 79:32, 1954.

7. Cameron, D. E. A theory of diagnosis. *In* Hoch, P. H., and Zubin, J. (Editors): *Current Problems in Psychiatric Diagnosis,* pp. 33–45. New York: Grune & Stratton, 1953.

8. Cameron, N., and Magaret, A. *Behavior Pathology.* New York: Houghton Mifflin Co., 1951.

9. Diethelm, O. The fallacy of the concept: psychosis. *In* Hoch, P. H., and Zubin, J. (Editors): *Current Problems in Psychiatric Diagnosis,* pp. 24–32. New York: Grune & Stratton, 1953.

10. Ebaugh, F. G., Solomon, H. C., and Bamford, T. E. (Editors). *Military Neuro-Psychiatry. Res. Publ. Ass. Nerv. Ment. Dis.,* Vol. XXV. Baltimore: The Williams and Wilkins Co., 1946.

11. Eissler, K. R. *J. Amer. Psychoanal. Assoc.,* 1:104, 1953.

12. Fairbairn, W. R. D. *Psychoanalytic Studies of the Personality.* London: Tavistock Publications, Ltd., 1952.

13. Foxe, A. N. *Psychiat. Quart.,* 12:617, 1938.

14. Frank, P. *Modern Science and Its Philosophy.* New York: George Braziller, 1955.

15. Glover, E. *J. Ment. Sc.,* 78:819, 1932.

16. Goldstein, K. *Aftereffects of Brain Injuries in War.* New York: Grune & Stratton, 1948.
17. Goldstein, K. *Human Nature in the Light of Psychopathology.* Cambridge, Mass.: Harvard University Press, 1951.
18. Goldstein, K., and Scheerer, M. Abstract and concrete behavior: an experimental study with special tests. *Psychol. Monographs,* 53:No. 2 (Whole No. 239), 1941.
19. Hardin, G. *Scient. Monthly,* 82:112, 1956.
20. Hoch, P. H., and Zubin, J. (Editors). *Current Problems in Psychiatric Diagnosis.* New York: Grune & Stratton, 1953.
21. Kraepelin, E. *Manic-Depressive Insanity and Paranoia.* Edinburg: E. and S. Livingstone, 1921.
22. Lief, A. *The Commonsense Psychiatry of Adolf Meyer.* New York: McGraw-Hill Book Co., 1948.
23. Macalpine, I. *Psychoanalyt. Quart.,* 19:501, 1950.
24. Meyer, A. Genetic-dynamic psychology versus nosology (1926). *In,* E. F. Winters (General Editor): *The Collected Papers of Adolph Meyer,* Vol. III, Baltimore: The Johns Hopkins Press, 1951.
25. Meyer, A. Preparation for psychiatry (1933). *In E. F. Winters* (General Editor): *The Collected Papers of Adolph Meyer,* Vol. III, Baltimore: The Johns Hopkins Press, 1951.
26. Noyes, A. P. *Modern Clinical Psychiatry* (4th ed.). Philadelphia: W. B. Saunders Co., 1953.
27. Pauling, L. *Am. J. Psychiat.,* 113:492, 1956.
28. Reichard, S. *Psychoanalyt. Quart.,* 25:155, 1956.
29. Solomon, H. C., and Yakovlev, P. I. *Manual of Military Neuropsychiatry.* Philadelphia: W. B. Saunders Co., 1945.
30. Stanton, A. H., and Schwartz, M. S. *The Mental Hospital.* New York: Basic Books, 1954.
31. Sullivan, H. S. *Conceptions of Modern Psychiatry* (2nd ed.). New York: W. W. Norton & Co., 1954.
32. Szasz, T. S. *Arch. Neurol. & Psychiat.,* 77:420, 1957.
33. Szasz, T. S. *J. Nerv. & Ment. Dis.,* in press.
34. Szasz, T. S. Malingering. *Arch. Neurol. & Psychiat.,* 76:432, 1956.
35. Szasz, T. S. *Arch. Neurol. & Psychiat.,* 75:297, 1956.
36. Szasz, T. S. *Arch. Neurol. & Psychiat.,* 77:86, 1957.
37. Szasz, T. S. *J. Amer. Psychoanal. Assoc.,* 4:197, 1956.
38. Szasz, T. S. *Internat. J. Psychoanal.,* 38:166, 1957.
39. Szasz, T. S. *Pain and Pleasure: A Study of Bodily Feelings.* New York: Basic Books, 1957.
40. Szasz, T. S. *Psychiatry,* in press.
41. Szasz, T. S. *Internat. J. Psychoanal.,* to be published.
42. Zilboorg, G. *Internat. J. Psychoanal.,* 35:90, 1954.
43. Zilboorg, G., and Henry, G. W. *A History of Medical Psychology.* New York: W. W. Norton & Co., 1941.

5

PSYCHIATRIC DIAGNOSIS: A CRITIQUE

Edward Zigler and Leslie Phillips

The inadequacies of conventional psychiatric diagnosis have frequently been noted (Ash, 1949; Cattell, 1957; Eysenck, 1952; Foulds, 1955; Harrower, 1950; Hoch & Zubin, 1953; Jellinek, 1939; King, 1954; Leary & Coffey, 1955; Mehlman, 1952; Menninger, 1955; Noyes, 1953; Phillips & Rabinovitch, 1958; Roe, 1949; Rogers, 1951; Rotter, 1954; Scott, 1958; Thorne, 1953; Wittenborn & Weiss, 1952; Wittman & Sheldon, 1948). The responses to this rather imposing body of criticism have ranged from the position that the present classificatory system is in need of further refinement (Caveny, Wittson, Hunt, & Herman, 1955; Foulds, 1955), through steps towards major revisions (Cattell, 1957; Eysenck, 1952; Leary & Coffey, 1955; Phillips & Rabinovitch, 1958; Thorne, 1953; Wittman & Sheldon, 1948), to a plea for the abolishment of all "labeling" (Menninger, 1955; Noyes, 1953; Rogers, 1951). As other investigators have noted (Caveny et al., 1955; Jellinek, 1939), this last position suggests that the classificatory enterprise is valueless. This reaction against classification has gained considerable popularity in clinical circles. The alacrity with which many clinicians have accepted this view seems to represent more than a disillusionment with the specific current form of psychiatric diagnosis. These negative attitudes appear to reflect a belief that diagnostic classification is inherently antithetical to such clinically favored concepts as "dynamic," "idiographic," etc. Thus, a question is raised as to whether any diagnostic schema can be of value. Let us initially direct our attention to this question.

Reprinted from the *Journal of Abnormal and Social Psychology,* 3, 1961, 607–618, with the permission of the American Psychological Association and the authors.

This investigation was supported by the Dementia Praecox Research Project, Worcester State Hospital, and a research grant (M-896) from the National Institute of Mental Health, United States Public Health Service.

ON CLASSIFICATION

The growth among clinicians of sentiment against categorization has coincided with a period of critical reappraisal within the behavioral sciences generally (Beach, 1950; Brower, 1949; Cronbach, 1957; Guthrie, 1950; Harlow, 1953; Koch, 1951; MacKinnon, 1953; Marquis, 1948; Rapaport, 1947; Roby, 1959; Scott, 1955; Tolman, 1953; Tyler, 1959). This parallel development is more than coincidental. The reaction against "labeling" can be viewed as an extreme outgrowth of this self-evaluation, i.e., that psychology's conceptual schemata are artificial in their construction, sterile in terms of their practical predictions, and lead only to greater and greater precision about matters which are more and more irrelevant. It it little wonder that in this atmosphere, conceptualization has itself become suspect or that Maslow's (1948) exposition of the possible dangers of labeling or naming has been extended (Rotter, 1954) as a blanket indictment of the categorizing process.

The error in this extension is the failure to realize that what has been criticized is not the conceptual process but only certain of its products. The criticisms mentioned above have not been in favor of the abolishment of conceptualization, but have rather been directed at the prematurity and rarifications of many of our conceptual schemata and our slavish adherence to them. Indeed, many of these criticisms have been accompanied by pleas for lower-order conceptualization based more firmly on observational data (Koch, 1951; MacKinnon, 1953; Tolman, 1953).

In the clinical area, the sentiment against classification has become sufficiently serious that several investigators (Cattell, 1957; Caveny et al, 1955; Eysenck, 1952; Jellinek, 1939) have felt the need to champion the merits of psychiatric categorization. They have pointed out that diagnosis is a basic scientific classificatory enterprise to be viewed as essentially the practice of taxonomy, which is characteristic of all science. Eysenck (1952) puts the matter quite succinctly in his statement, "Measurement is essential to science, but before we can measure, we must know what it is we want to measure. Qualitative or taxonomic discovery must precede quantitative measurement" (p. 34).

Reduced to its essentials, diagnostic classification involves the establishment of categories to which phenomena can be ordered. The number of class systems that potentially may be constructed is limited only by man's ability to abstract from his experience. The principles employed to construct such classes may be inductive, deductive, or a combination of both, and may vary on a continuum from the closely descriptive to the highly abstract.

Related to the nature of the classificatory principle are the implications to be derived from class membership. Class membership may involve nothing more than descriptive compartmentalization, its only utility being greater ease in the handling of data. Obversely, the attributes or correlates of class membership may be widespread and far-reaching in their consequences. The originators of a classificatory schema may assert that specified behavioral correlates accompany class membership. This assertion is open to test. If the hypothesized correlates represent the full heuristic value of the diagnostic schema and class membership is found not to be related to these correlates, then revision or discard is in order. A somewhat different type of problem may also arise. With the passage of time, correlates not originally related to the schema may erroneously be attributed to class membership. Nevertheless, the original taxonomy may still possess a degree of relevance to current objectives in a discipline. In these circumstances, its maintenance may be the rational choice, although a clarification and purification of categories is called for. The relationship of the two problems outlined here to the criticism of contemporary psychiatric diagnosis will be discussed later. What should be noted at this point is that the solution to neither problem implies the abolishment of the attempt at classification.

Another aspect of taxonomy is in need of clarification. When a phenomenon is assigned to a class, certain individual characteristics of that phenomenon are forever lost. No two class members are completely identical. Indeed, a single class member may be viewed as continuously differing from itself over time. It is this loss of uniqueness and an implied unconcern with process that have led many clinicians to reject classification in principle. While classificatory schemata inevitably involve losses of this type, it must be noted that they potentially offer a more than compensatory gain. This gain is represented in the significance of the class attributes and correlates. Class membership conveys information ranging from the descriptive similarity of two phenomena to a knowledge of the common operative processes underlying the phenomena.

A conceptual system minimizes the aforementioned loss to the extent that only irrelevant aspects of a phenomenon are deleted in the classificatory process. The implicit assumption is made that what is not class relevant is inconsequential. The dilemma, of course, lies in our lacking divine revelation as to what constitutes inconsequentiality. It is this issue which lies at the heart of the idiographic versus nomothetic controversy (Allport, 1937, 1946; Beck, 1953; Eysenck, 1954; Falk, 1956; Hunt, 1951a, 1951b; Skaggs, 1945, 1947). The supporters of the idiographic position (Allport, 1937; Beck, 1953) have criticized certain conceptual schemata for treating idiosyncratic aspects of behavior as inconsequential when they are in fact pertinent data which must be utilized if a comprehensive and adequate view of human behavior is to emerge. However, the idiographic position is not a movement toward the abolishment of classification, a fact emphasized by Allport (1937) and Falk (1956). Rather, it represents a plea for broader and more meaningful classificatory schemata.

A conceptually different type of argument against the use of any diagnostic classification has been made by the adherents of nondirective psychotherapy

(Patterson, 1948; Rogers, 1946, 1951). This position has advanced the specific contention that differential diagnosis is unnecessary for, and perhaps detrimental to, successful psychotherapy. This attitude of the nondirectivists has been interpreted (Thorne, 1953) as an attack on the entire classificatory enterprise. To argue against diagnosis on the grounds that it affects therapeutic outcome is to confuse diagnosis as an act of scientific classification with the present clinical practice of diagnosis with its use of interviewing, psychological testing, etc. The error here lies in turning one's attention away from diagnosis as an act of classification, a basic scientific enterprise, and attending instead to the immediate and prognostic consequences of some specific diagnostic technique in a specific therapeutic situation, i.e., an applied aspect. To reject the former on the basis of the latter would appear to be an unsound decision.

Although the nondirectivists' opposition to diagnosis seems to be based on a confusion between the basic and applied aspects of classification, implicitly contained within their position is a more fundamental argument against the classificatory effort. Undoubtedly, the diagnosis both articulates and restricts the range of assumptions which may be entertained about a client. However, the philosophy of the nondirectivist forces him to reject any theoretical position which violates a belief in the unlimited psychological growth of the client. It would appear that this position represents the rejection, in principle, of the view that any individual can be like another in his essential characteristics, or that any predictable relationship can be established between a client's current level of functioning and the ends which may be achieved. In the setting of this assumption, a transindividual classificatory schema is inappropriate. There is no appeal from such a judgment, but one should be cognizant that it rejects the essence of a scientific discipline. If one insists on operating within the context of a predictive psychology, one argues for the necessity of a classificatory system, even though particular diagnostic schemata may be rejected as irrelevant, futile, or obscure.

Let us now direct our discussion toward some of the specific criticisms of conventional psychiatric diagnosis—that the categories employed lack homogeneity, reliability, and validity.

HOMOGENEITY

A criticism often leveled against the contemporary diagnostic system is that its categories encompass heterogeneous groups of individuals, i.e., individuals varying in respect to symptomatology, test scores, prognosis, etc. (King, 1954; Rotter, 1954; Wittenborn, 1952; Wittenborn & Bailey, 1952; Wittenborn & Weiss, 1952). Contrary to the view of one investigator (Rotter, 1954), a lack of homogeneity does not necessarily imply a lack of reliability. King (1954) has clearly noted the distinction between these two concepts. Reliability refers to the agreement in assigning individuals to different diagnostic categories, whereas homogeneity refers to the diversity of behavior subsumed within categories. While the two concepts may be related, it is not difficult to conceptualize categories which, though quite reliable, subsume diverse phenomena.

King (1954) has argued in favor of constructing a new diagnostic classification having more restrictive and homogeneous categories. He supports his argument by noting his own findings and those of Kantor, Wallner, and Winder (1953), which have indicated that within the schizophrenic group subcategories may be formed which differ in test performance. King found further support for the construction of new and more homogeneous diagnostic categories in a study by Windle and Hamwi (1953). This study indicated that two subgroups could be constructed within a psychotic population which was composed of patients with diverse psychiatric diagnoses. Though matched on the distribution of these diagnostic types, the subgroups differed in the relationship obtained between test performance and prognosis. On the basis of these studies, King suggests that the type of homogeneous categories he would favor involves such classificatory dichotomies as reactive versus process schizophrenics and chronic versus nonchronic psychotics.

An analysis of King's (1954) criticism of the present diagnostic system discloses certain difficulties. The first is that King's heterogeneity criticism does not fully take into consideration certain basic aspects of classification. A common feature of classificatory systems is that they utilize classes which contain subclasses. An example drawn from biology would be a genus embracing a number of species. If schizophrenia is conceptualized as a genus, it cannot be criticized on the grounds that all its members do not share a particular attribute. Such a criticism would involve a confusion between the more specific attributes of the species and the more general attributes of the genus. This is not to assert that schizophrenia does in fact possess the characteristics of a genus. It is, of course, possible that a careful analysis will reveal that it does not, and the class schizophrenia will have to be replaced by an aggregate of entities which does constitute a legitimate genus. However, when a genus is formulated, it cannot be attacked because of its heterogeneous nature since genera are characterized by such heterogeneity.

A more serious difficulty with King's (1954) heterogeneity criticism lies in the inherent ambiguity of a homogeneity-heterogeneity parameter. To criticize a classificatory system because its categories subsume heterogeneous phenomena is to make the error of assuming that homogeneity is a quality which inheres in phenomena when in actuality it is a construction of the observer or classifier. In order to make this point clear, let us return to King's argument. What does it mean to assert that chronic psychosis is an example of an homogeneous class, while schizophrenia is an example of an heterogeneous one? In terms of the descriptively diverse phenomena encompassed, the latter would appear to have the greater homogeneity. The statement only has meaning insofar as a particular correlate—for instance, the relationship of test score to prognosis—is shared by all members of one class but not so shared by the members of the other class. Thus, the meaningfulness of the homogeneity concept is ultimately dependent on the correlates or attributes of class membership or on the classificatory principle related to these correlates or attributes. The intimacy of the relationship between the attributes of classes and the classificatory principle can best be exemplified by the extreme case in which a class has but a single attribute, and that attribute is defined by the classificatory principle, e.g., the classification of plants on the basis of the number of stamens they possess. Therefore, the heterogeneity criticism of a classificatory system is nothing more than a plea for the utilization of a new classificatory principle so that attention may be focused on particular class correlates or attributes not considered in the original schema. While this plea may be a justifiable one, depending on the significance of the new attributes, it has little to do with the homogeneity, in an absolute sense, of phenomena. Indeed, following the formulation of a new classificatory schema, the heterogeneity criticism could well be leveled against it by the adherents of the old system, since the phenomena encompassed by the new categories would probably not be considered homogeneous when evaluated by the older classificatory principle.

Although differing in its formulation, the heterogeneity criticism of present psychiatric classification made by Wittenborn and his colleagues (Wittenborn, 1952; Wittenborn & Bailey, 1952; Wittenborn & Weiss, 1952) suffers from the same difficulties as does King's (1954) criticism. Wittenborn's findings indicated that individuals given a common diagnosis showed differences in their symptom cluster score profiles based on nine symptom clusters isolated earlier by means of factor analytic techniques (Wittenborn, 1951; Wittenborn & Holzberg, 1951). It is upon the existence of these different profiles within a diagnostic category that Wittenborn bases his heterogeneity criticism. Here again the homogeneity-heterogeneity distinction is only meaningful in terms of an independent criterion, a particular symptom cluster score profile. Had it been discovered that all individuals placed into a particular diagnostic category shared a common symptom cluster score profile, then this category would be described as subsuming homogeneous phenomena. But the phenomena—the symptoms mirrored by the symptom profile—are not homogeneous in any absolute sense because the pattern of symptoms may involve the symptoms in descriptively diverse symptom clusters. Thus, the homogeneity ascribed to the category would refer only to the fact that individuals within the category homogeneously exhibited a particular pattern of descriptively diverse behaviors. However, the organization of symptoms mirrored by the symptom cluster profiles is not in any fundamental sense different from that observed in conventional

diagnostic syndromes. Both methods of categorization systematize diverse behaviors because of an observed regularity in their concurrent appearance.

The difference between these two approaches, then, lies only in the pattern
of deviant behaviors that define the categories. Indeed, Eysenck (1953) has
noted that both the clinician and the factor analyst derive syndromes in essentially the same manner, i.e., in terms of the observed intercorrelations of various
symptoms. It is the difference in method, purely observational versus statistical,
that explains why the final symptom structure may differ. The assumption must
not be made that the advantage lies entirely with the factor analytic method.
The merit accruing through the greater rigor of factor analysis may be out-
weighed by the limitations imposed in employing a restricted group of symptoms
and a particular sample of patients. Thus, the factor analyst cannot claim that
the class-defining symptom pattern he has derived is a standard of homogeneity
against which classes within another schema can be evaluated. The plea that
symptom cluster scores, derived from factor analytic techniques, substitute for
the present method of psychiatric classification has little relevance to the heterogeneity issue.

In the light of this discussion we may conclude that the concept of homogeneity has little utility in evaluating classificatory schemata. Since the heterogeneity criticism invariably involves an implicit preference for one classificatory
principle over another, it would perhaps be more fruitful to dispense entirely
with the homogeneity-heterogeneity distinction, thus, allowing us to direct our
attention to the underlying problem of the relative merits of different classificatory principles.

RELIABILITY AND VALIDITY

A matter of continuing concern has been the degree of reliability of the
present diagnostic system. Considerable energy has been expended by both those
who criticize the present system for its lack of reliability (Ash, 1949; Boisen,
1938; Eysenck, 1952; Mehlman, 1952; Roe, 1949; Rotter, 1954; Scott, 1958)
and those who defend it against this criticism (Foulds, 1955; Hunt, Wittson,
& Hunt, 1953; Schmidt & Fonda, 1956; Seeman, 1953). Certain investigators
(Foulds, 1955; Schmidt & Fonda, 1956) who have offered evidence that the
present system is reliable have also pointed out that the earlier studies emphasizing the unreliability of psychiatric diagnosis have suffered from serious conceptual and methodological difficulties.

In evaluating the body of studies concerned with the reliability of psychiatric diagnosis, one must conclude that so long as diagnosis is confined to
broad diagnostic categories, it is reasonably reliable, but the reliability diminishes
as one proceeds from broad, inclusive class categories to narrower, more specific

ones. As finer discriminations are called for, accuracy in diagnosis becomes increasingly difficult. Since this latter characteristic appears to be common to the classificatory efforts in many areas of knowledge, it would appear to be inappropriate to criticize psychiatric diagnosis on the grounds that it is less than perfectly reliable. This should not lead to an underestimation of the importance of reliability. While certain extraclassificatory factors, e.g., proficiency of the clinicians, biases of the particular clinical settings, etc., may influence it, reliability is primarily related to the precision with which classes of a schema are defined. Since the defining characteristic of most classes in psychiatric diagnosis is the occurrence of symptoms in particular combinations, the reliability of the system mirrors the specificity with which the various combinations of symptoms (syndromes) have been spelled out. It is manadatory for a classificatory schema to be reliable since reliability refers to the definiteness with which phenomena can be ordered to classes. If a system does not allow for such a division of phenomena, it can make no pretense of being a classificatory schema.

While reliability is a prerequisite if the diagnostic system is to have any value, it must not be assumed that if human effort were to make the present system perfectly reliable, it could escape all the difficulties attributed to it. This perfect reliability would only mean that individuals within each class shared a particular commonality in relation to the classificatory principle of symptom manifestation. If one were interested in attributes unrelated or minimally related to the classificatory principle employed, the perfect reliability of the system would offer little cause for rejoicing. Perfect reliability of the present system can only be the goal of those who are interested in nothing more than the present classificatory principle and the particular attributes of the classes constructed on the basis of this principle.

When attention is shifted from characteristics which define a class to the correlates of class membership, this implies a shift in concern from the reliability of a system to its validity. The distinction between the reliability and validity of a classificatory system would appear to involve certain conceptual difficulties. It is perhaps this conceptual difficulty which explains why the rather imposing body of literature concerned with diagnosis has been virtually silent on the question of the validity of the present system of psychiatric diagnosis. Only one group of investigators (Hunt, 1951; Hunt, Wittson, & Barton, 1950a, 1950b; Hunt, Wittson, & Hunt, 1953; Wittson & Hunt, 1951) has specifically been concerned with the predictive efficacy of diagnosis and, thus, to the validity of psychiatric classifications; and even in this work, the distinction between validity and reliability is not clearly drawn.

In order to grasp the distinction between the reliability and the validity of a classificatory schema, one must differentiate the defining characteristics of the classes from the correlates of the classes. In the former case, we are interested in the principles upon which classes are formed; in the latter, in the predictions or valid statements that can be made about phenomena once they are classified. The difficulty lies in the overlap between the classifying principles and the class correlates. If a classificatory system is reliable, it is also valid to the extent that we can predict that the individuals within a class will exhibit certain characteristics, namely, those behaviors or attributes which serve to define the class.

It is the rare class, however, that does not connote correlates beyond its defining characteristics. The predictions associated with class membership may vary from simple extensions of the classificatory principles to correlates which would appear to have little connection with these principles. Let us examine a simple illustration and see what follows from categorizing an individual. Once an individual has been classified as manifesting a manic-depressive reaction, depressed type, on the basis of the symptoms of depression of mood, motor retardation, and stupor (American Psychiatric Association, 1952), the prediction may be made that the individual will spend a great deal of time in bed, which represents an obvious extension of the symptom pattern. One may also hypothesize that the patient will show improvement if electroshock therapy is employed. This is a correlate which has little direct connection with the symptoms themselves. These predictions are open to test, and evidence may or may not be found to support them. Thus, measures of validity may be obtained which are independent of the reliability of the system of classification.

The problem of validity lies at the heart of the confusion which surrounds psychiatric diagnosis. When the present diagnostic schema is assailed, the common complaint is that class membership conveys little information beyond the gross symptomatology of the patient and contributes little to the solution of the pressing problems of etiology, treatment procedures, prognosis, etc. The criticism that class membership does not predict these important aspects of a disorder appears to be a legitimate one. This does not mean the present system has no validity. It simply indicates that the system may be valid in respect to certain correlates but invalid in respect to others. Much confusion would be dispelled if as much care were taken in noting the existing correlates of classes as is taken in noting the classificatory principles. A great deal of effort has gone into the formalization of the defining characteristics of classes (American Psychiatric Association, 1952), but one looks in vain for a formal delineation of the extraclassificatory attributes and correlates of class membership. As a result, the various diagnostic categories have been burdened with correlates not systematically derived from a classificatory principle but which were attributed to the classes because they were the focal points of clinical interest. A major question is just what correlates can justifiably be attributed to the class categories. To answer this question we must turn our attention to the purposes and philosophy underlying contemporary psychiatric diagnosis.

PHILOSOPHY AND PURPOSE OF CONVENTIONAL DIAGNOSIS

The validity of the conventional diagnostic system is least ambiguous and most free from potential criticism as a descriptive schema, a taxonomy of mental disorders analogous to the work of Ray and Linnaeus in biology. In this sense, class membership confirms that the inclusion of an individual within a class guarantees only that he exhibit the defining characteristics of that class. Only a modest extension of this system, in terms of a very limited number of well established correlates, makes for a system of impressive heuristic value, even though it falls considerably short of what would now be considered an optimal classificatory schema. As has been noted (Caveny et al., 1955; Hunt et al., 1953), the present diagnostic system is quite useful when evaluated in terms of its administrative and, to a lesser extent, its preventive implications. Caveny et al. (1955), and Wittenborn, Holzberg, and Simon (1953) should be consulted for a comprehensive list of such uses, but examples would include legal determination of insanity, declaration of incompetence, type of ward required for custodial care, census figures and statistical data upon which considerable planning is based, screening devices for the military services or other agencies, etc. In view of the extensive criticism of contemporary diagnosis, the surprising fact is not that so few valid predictions can be derived from class membership, but that so many can.

The value of the present psychiatric classification system would be further enhanced by its explicit divorcement from its Kraepelinian heritage by an emphasis on its descriptive aspect and, through careful empirical investigation, the cataloging of the reliable correlates of its categories. That this catalog of correlates would be an impressive one is expressed in Hoch's (1953) view that the present system is superior to any system which has been evolved to replace it. It is an open question whether the system merits this amount of praise. In general, however, the defense of the present system—or, for that matter, diagnosis in general (Caveny et al., 1955; Eysenck, 1952; Hunt et al., 1953; Jellinek, 1939)—tends to rest on the merits of its descriptive, empirical, and nondynamic aspects.

The present classificatory system, even as a purely descriptive device, is still open to a certain degree of criticism. Its classificatory principle is organized primarily about symptom manifestation. This would be adequate for a descriptive system if this principle were consistently applied to all classes of the schema and if the symptoms associated with each diagnostic category were clearly specified. There is some question, however, whether the system meets these requirements (Phillips & Rabinovitch, 1958; Rotter, 1954). The criticism has been advanced that the present system is based on a number of diverse principles of classification. Most classes are indeed defined by symptom manifestation, but the organic disorders, for example, tend to be identified by etiology, while such other factors as prognosis, social conformity, etc., are also employed as classificatory principles. This does not appear, however, to be an insurmountable problem, for the system could be made a completely consistent one by explicitly defining each category by the symptoms encompassed. The system would appear to be eminently amenable to the unitary application of this descriptive classificatory principle, for there are actually few cases where classes are not so defined. Where reliable relations between the present categories and etiology and prognosis have been established, these also could be incorporated explicitly within the system. Etiology and prognosis would be treated not as inherent attributes of the various classifications, but rather as correlates of the particular classes to which their relationship is known. They would, thus, not be confounded with the classificatory principle of the system.

This course of action would satisfy the requirement of consistency in the application of the classificatory principle. A remaining area of ambiguity would be the lack of agreement in what constitutes a symptom. In physical medicine, a clear distinction has been made between a symptom, which is defined as a subjectively experienced abnormality, and a sign, which is considered an objective indication of abnormality (Holmes, 1946). This differentiation has not, however, been extended to the sphere of mental disorders. A source of difficulty may lie in the definition of what is psychologically abnormal. In psychiatric terminology, symptoms include a wide range of phenomena from the grossest type of behavior deviation, through the complaints of the patient, to events almost completely inferential in nature. One suggestion (Yates, 1958) has been to eliminate the term "symptom" and direct attention to the manifest responses of the individual. This suggestion appears to be embodied in the work of Wittenborn and his colleagues (Wittenborn, 1951, 1952; Wittenborn & Bailey, 1952; Wittenborn & Holzberg, 1951; Wittenborn et al., 1953; Wittenborn & Weiss, 1952). Wittenborn's diagnostic system, in which symptoms are defined as currently discernible behaviors, represents a standard of clarity for purely descriptive systems of psychiatric classification. This clarity was achieved by clearly noting and limiting the group of behaviors which would be employed in the system. But even here a certain amount of ambiguity remains. The number of responses or discernible behaviors which may be considered for inclusion within a diagnostic schema borders on the infinite. The question arises, then, as to how one goes about the selection of those behaviors to be incorporated in the classificatory system. Parsimony demands that only "meaningful" items of behavior be chosen for inclusion, and this selective principle has certainly been at work in the construction of all systems of diagnosis. In this sense, the present method of psychiatric classification is not a purely descriptive one, nor can any classification schema truly meet this criterion of purity. Meaning and utility inevitably appear among the determinants of classificatory systems.

Several investigators (Cameron, 1956; Jellinek, 1939; Magaret, 1952) have stressed the inappropriateness of discussing diagnosis in the abstract, pointing out that such a discussion should center around the question of "diagnosis for what?" Indeed, a diagnostic system cannot be described as "true" or "false," but only as being useful or not useful in attaining prescribed goals. Therefore, when a system is devised, its purposes should be explicitly stated so that the system can be evaluated in terms of its success or failure in attaining these objectives. Furthermore, these goals should be kept explicit throughout the period during which the system is being employed. The present diagnostic schema has not met this requirement. Instead, its goals have been carried along in an implicit manner and have been allowed to become vague. The result has been that some see the purpose of the schema as being an adequate description of mental disorders (Hunt et al., 1953), others view it as being concerned with prognosis (Hoch, 1953), and still others view the schemata goal as the discovery of etiology (Cameron, 1953).

Typically, the present schema has been conceptualized as descriptive in nature, but a brief glance at its history indicates that the original purposes and goals in the construction of this schema went far beyond the desire for a descriptive taxonomy. As Zilboorg and Henry (1941) clearly note, Kraepelin not only studied the individual while hospitalized, but also the patient's premorbid history and posthospital course. His hope was to make our understanding of all mental disorders as precise as our knowledge of the course of general paresis. He insisted on the classification of mental disorders according to regularities in symptoms and course of illness, believing this would lead to a clearer discrimination among the different disease entities. He hoped for the subsequent discovery of a specific somatic malfunction responsible for each disease. For Kraepelin, then, classification was related to etiology, treatment, and prognosis. Had the system worked as envisaged, these variables would have become the extraclassificatory attributes of the schema. When matched against this aspiration, the present system must be considered a failure since the common complaint against it is that a diagnostic label tells us very little about etiology, treatment, or prognosis (Miles, 1953). However, it would be erroneous to conclude that the present system is valueless because its classes are only minimally related to etiology and prognosis.

What should be noted is that etiology and prognosis, though important, are but two of a multitude of variables of interest. The importance of these variables should not obscure the fact that their relationship to a classificatory system is exactly the same as that of any other variables. This relationship may take one of two forms. Etiology and prognosis may be the correlates of the classes of a diagnostic system which employs an independent classificatory principle like symptom manifestation. Optimally, we should prefer a classificatory schema in which the indices of etiology and preferred modes of treatment would be incorporated's (Hunt et al., 1953; Pepinsky, 1948). In essence, this was Kraepelin's approach, and it continues to underlie some promising work in the area of psychopathology. Although Kraepelin's disease concept is in disrepute (Hoch & Zubin, 1953; Marzoff, 1947; Rotter, 1954), it is the opinion of several investigators (Eysenck, 1953; Phillips & Rabinovitch, 1958; Wittenborn, et al., 1953) that further work employing the descriptive symptomatic approach could well lead to a greater understanding of the etiology underlying abnormal "processes."

Another manner in which etiology, treatment, or prognosis could be related to a classificatory schema is by utilizing each of these variables as the classificatory principle for a new diagnostic system. For instance, we might organize patients into groups which respond differentially to particular forms of treatment like electroshock, drugs, psychotherapy, etc. The new schemata which might be proposed could be of considerable value in respect to certain goals but useless in regard to others. Since we do not possess a diagnostic system based on all the variables of clinical interest, we might have to be satisfied with the construction of a variety of diagnostic systems, each based on a different principle of classification. These classificatory techniques would exist side by side, their use being determined by the specific objectives of the diagnostician.

ETIOLOGY VERSUS DESCRIPTION IN DIAGNOSIS

The classical Kraepelinian classification schema shows two major characteristics: a commitment to a detailed description of the manifest symptomatic behaviors of the individual and an underlying assumption that such a descriptive classification would be transitory, eventually leading to and being replaced by a system whose classificatory principle was the etiology of the various mental disorders. Major criticism of this classificatory effort has been directed at the first of these. The reservations are that, in practice, such a descriptive effort allows no place for a process interpretation of psychopathology and that it has not encouraged the development of prevention and treatment programs in the mental disorders.

The authors do not feel that the failure of the Kraepelinian system has demonstrated the futility of employing symptoms as the basis for classification. It does suggest that if one approaches the problem of description with an assumption as to the necessary correlates of such descriptions, then the diagnostic system may well be in error. Kraepelin's empiricism is contaminated in just this way. For example, he refused to accept as cases of dementia praecox those individuals who recovered from the disorder, since as assumed irreversibility as a necessary concomitant of its hypothesized neurophysiological base. Bleuler, on the other hand, who was much less commited to any particular form of causality in this illness, readily recognized the possibility of its favorable outcome. It is not, then, the descriptive approach itself which is open to criticism, but description contaminated by preconception. An unfettered description of those schizophrenics with good prognosis in contrast to those with poor prognosis reveals clear differences in the symptom configuration between these kinds of patients (Farina & Webb, 1956; Phillips, 1953).

Kraepelin's basic concern with the problem of etiology has remained a focus of efforts in the clinical area. Although his postulate of central nervous system disease as the basis of mental disorder is in disrepute, and his systematic classificatory efforts are assailed, one nevertheless finds a striking congruence between Kraepelin's preconceptions and certain current attempts at the solution of the problem of psychopathology. There is an unwavering belief that some simple categorical system will quickly solve the mysteries of etiology. The exponents of these newer classificatory schemata have merely replaced symptoms by other phenomena like test scores (King, 1954), particular patterns of interpersonal relations (Leary & Coffey, 1955), etc. It is the author's conviction that these new efforts to find short-cut solutions to the question of etiology will similarly remain unsuccessful. The amount of descriptive effort required before etiological factors are likely to be discovered has been underestimated (Kety, 1959a, 1959b), and the pursuit of etiology should represent an end point rather than a beginning for classificatory systems. The process of moving from an empirical orientation to an etiological one is of necessity, inferential and therefore susceptible to the myriad dangers of premature inference. We propose that the greatest safeguard against such prematurity is not to be found in the scrapping of an empirical descriptive approach, but in an accelerated program of empirical research. What is needed at this time is a systematic, empirical attack on the problem of mental disorders. Inherent in this program is the employment of symptoms, broadly defined as meaningful and discernible behaviors, as the basis of a classificatory system. Rather than an abstract search for etiologies, it would appear more currently fruitful to investigate such empirical correlates of symptomatology as reactions to specific forms of treatment, outcome in the disorders, case history phenomena, etc.

The pervasive concern with etiology may derive from a belief that if this were known, prevention would shortly be forthcoming, thus making the present complex problems of treatment and prognosis inconsequential. Unfortunately, efforts to short-circuit the drudgery involved in establishing an empirically founded psychiatry has not resulted in any major breakthroughs. Etiology is typically the last characteristic of a disorder to be discovered. Consequently, we would suggest the search for etiology be put aside and attempted only when a greater number of the correlates of symptomatic behaviors have been established.

The authors are impressed by the amount of energy that has been expended in both attacking and defending various contemporary systems of classification. We believe that a classificatory system should include any behavior or phenomenon that appears promising in terms of its significant correlates. At this stage of our investigations, the system employed should be an open and expanding one, not one which is closed and defended on conceptual grounds. Systems of classification must be treated as tools for further discovery, not as bases for polemic disputation.

As stated above, it is possible that a number of systems of classification may be needed to encompass the behaviors presently of clinical interest. It may appear that the espousal of this position, in conjunction with a plea for empirical exploration of the correlates of these behaviors, runs headlong into a desire for conceptual neatness and parsimony. It may be feared that the use of a number of classificatory systems concurrently, each with its own correlates, may lead to the creation of a gigantic actuarial table of unrelated elements. However, the authors do not feel that such a fear is well founded because it assumes that the correlates of these systems have no eventual relation one to the other.

We believe that this latter view is unnecessarily pessimistic. While in principle a multiplicity of classificatory systems might be called for, results from the authors' own research program suggests that a single, relatively restricted and coherent classification system can be derived from an empirical study of the correlates of symptomatic behaviors (Phillips & Rabinovitch, 1958; Zigler & Phillips, 1960). Such a system might serve a number of psychiatrically significant functions, including the optimum selection of patients for specific treatment programs and the prediction of treatment outcomes. In conclusion, a descriptive classificatory system appears far from dead, and if properly employed, it can lead to a fuller as well as a more conceptually based understanding of the psychopathologies.

REFERENCES

Allport, G. *Personality: A psychological interpretation.* New York: Holt, 1937.

Allport, G. Personalistic psychology as science: A reply. *Psychol. Rev.,* 1946, 53, 132–135.

American Psychiatric Association, Mental Hospital Service, Committee on Nomenclature and Statistics of the American Psychiatric Association. *Diagnostic and statistical manual: Mental disorders.* Washington, D.C.: APA, 1952.

Ash, P. The reliability of psychiatric diagnosis. *J. abnorm. soc. Psychol.,* 1949, 44, 272–277.

Beach, F. The snark was a boojum. *Amer. Psychologist,* 1950, 5, 115–124.

Beck, S. The science of personality: Nomothetic or idiographic? *Psychol. Rev.* 1953, 60, 353–359.

Boisen, A. Types of dementia praecox: A study in psychiatric classification. *Psychiatry,* 1938, 1, 233–236.

Brower, D. The problem of quantification in psychological science. *Psychol. Rev.*, 1949, 56, 325–333.

Cameron, D. A theory of diagnosis. In P. Hoch & J. Zubin (Eds.), *Current problems in psychiatric diagnosis*. New York: Grune & Stratton, 1953. Pp. 33–45.

Cattell, R. *Personality and motivation structure and measurement*. New York: World Book, 1957.

Caveny, E., Wittson, C., Hunt, W., & Herman, R. Psychiatric diagnosis, its nature and function. *J. nerv. ment. Dis.*, 1955, 121, 367–380.

Cronbach, L. The two disciplines of scientific psychology. *Amer. Psychologist*, 1957, 12, 671–684.

Eysenck, H. *The scientific study of personality*. London: Routledge & Kegan Paul, 1952.

Eysenck, H. The logical basis of factor analysis. *Amer. Psychologist*, 1953, 8, 105–113.

Eysenck, H. The science of personality: Nomothetic. *Psychol. Rev.*, 1954, 61, 339–341.

Falk, J. Issues distinguishing idiographic from nomothetic approaches to personality theory. *Psychol. Rev.*, 1956, 63, 53–62.

Farina, A., & Webb, W. Premorbid adjustment and subsequent discharge. *J. nerv. ment. Dis.*, 1956, 124, 612–613.

Foulds, G. The reliability of psychiatric and the validity of psychological diagnosis. *J. ment. Sci.*, 1955, 101, 851–862.

Guthrie, E. The status of systematic psychology. *Amer. Psychologist*, 1950, 5, 97–101.

Harlow, H. Mice, monkeys, men, and motives. *Psychol. Rev.*, 1953, 60, 23–32.

Harrower, Molly. (Ed.) *Diagnostic psychological testing*. Springfield, Ill.: Charles C. Thomas, 1950.

Hoch, P. Discussion. In P. Hoch & J. Zubin (Eds.), *Current problems in psychiatric diagnosis*. New York: Grune & Stratton, 1953, Pp. 46–50.

Hoch, P., & Zubin, J. (Eds.) *Current problems in psychiatric diagnosis*. New York: Grune & Stratton, 1953.

Holmes, G. *Introduction to clinical neurology*. Edinburgh: Livingstone, 1946.

Hunt, W. Clinical psychology—science or superstition. *Amer. Psychologist*, 1951, 6, 683–687. (a)

Hunt, W. An investigation of naval neuropsychiatric screening procedures. In H. Gruetskaw (Ed.), *Groups, leadership, and men*. Pittsburgh, Pa.: Carnegie Press, 1951. Pp. 245–256. (b)

Hunt, W., Wittson, C., & Barton, H. A further validation of naval neuropsychiatric screening. *J. consult. Psychol.*, 1950, 14, 485–488. (a)

Hunt, W., Wittson, C., & Barton, H. A validation study of naval neuropsychiatric screening. *J. consult. Psychol.*, 1950, 14, 35–39. (b)

Hunt, W., Wittson, C., & Hunt, E. A theoretical and practical analysis of the diagnostic process. In P. Hoch & J. Zubin (Eds.), *Current problems in psychiatric diagnosis.* New York: Grune & Stratton, 1953. Pp. 53–65.

Jellinek, E. Some principles of psychiatric classification. *Psychiatry,* 1939, 2, 161–165.

Kantor, R., Wallner, J., & Winder, C. Process and reactive schizophrenia. *J. consult. Psychol.,* 1953, 17, 157–162.

Kety, S. Biochemical theories of schizophrenia. Part I. *Science,* 1959, 129, 1528–1532. (a)

Kety, S. Biochemical theories of schizophrenia. Part II. *Science,* 1959, 129, 1590–1599. (b)

King, G. Research with neuropsychiatric samples. *J. Psychol.,* 1954, 38, 383–387.

Koch, S. The current status of motivational psychology. *Psychol. Rev.,* 1951, 58, 147–154.

Leary, T., & Coffey, H. Interpersonal diagnosis: Some problems of methodology and validation. *J. abnorm. soc. Psychol.,* 1955, 50, 110–126.

MacKinnon, D. Fact and fancy in personality research. *Amer. Psychologist,* 1953, 8, 138–146.

Magaret, Ann. Clinical methods: Psychodiagnostics. *Annu. Rev. Psychol.,* 1952, 3, 283–320.

Marquis, D. Research planning at the frontiers of science. *Amer. Psychologist,* 1948, 3, 430–438.

Marzoff, S. S. The disease concept in psychology. *Psychol. Rev.,* 1947, 54, 211–221.

Maslow, A. Cognition of the particular and of the generic. *Psychol. Rev.,* 1948, 55, 22–40.

Mehlman, B. The reliability of psychiatric diagnosis. *J. abnorm. soc. Psychol.,* 1952, 47, 577–578.

Menninger, K. The practice of psychiatry. *Dig. Neurol. Psychiat.,* 1955, 23, 101.

Miles, H. Discussion. In P. Hoch & J. Zubin (Eds.), *Current problems in psychiatric diagnosis.* New York: Grune & Stratton, 1953. Pp. 107–111.

Noyes, A. *Modern clinical psychiatry.* Philadelphia: Saunders, 1953.

Patterson, C. Is psychotherapy dependent on diagnosis? *Amer. Psychologist,* 1948, 3, 155–159.

Pepinsky, H. B. Diagnostic categories in clinical counseling. *Appl. psychol. Monogr.,* 1948, No. 15.

Phillips, L. Case history data and prognosis in schizophrenia. *J. nerv. ment. Dis.,* 1953, 117, 515–525.

Phillips, L., & Rabinovitch, M. Social role and patterns of symptomatic behaviors. *J. abnorm. soc. Psychol.,* 1958, 57, 181–186.

Rapaport, D. The future of research in clinical psychology and psychiatry. *Amer. Psychologist,* 1947, 2, 167–172.

Roby, T. An opinion on the construction of behavior theory. *Amer. Psychologist,* 1959, 14, 129–134.

Roe, Anne. Integration of personality theory and clinical practice. *J. abnorm. soc. Psychol.,* 1949, 44, 36–41.

Rogers, C. Significant aspects of client-centered therapy. *Amer. Psychologist,* 1946, 1, 415–422.

Rogers, C. *Client-centered therapy.* Boston: Houghton Mifflin, 1951.

Rotter, J. *Social learning and clinical psychology.* New York: Prentice-Hall, 1954.

Schmidt, H., & Fonda, C. The reliability of psychiatric diagnosis: A new look. *J. abnorm. soc. Psychol.,* 1956, 52, 262–267.

Scott, J. The place of observation in biological and psychological science. *Amer. Psychologist,* 1955, 10, 61–63.

Scott, W. Research definitions of mental health and mental illness. *Psychol. Bull.,* 1958, 55, 1–45.

Seeman, W. Psychiatric diagnosis: An investigation of interperson-reliability after didactic instruction. *J. nerv. ment. Dis.,* 1953, 118, 541–544.

Skaggs, E. Personalistic psychology as science. *Psychol. Rev.,* 1945, 52, 234–238.

Skaggs, E. Ten basic postulates of personalistic psychology. *Psychol. Rev.,* 1947, 54, 255–262.

Thorne, F. Back to fundamentals. *J. clin. Psychol.,* 1953, 9, 89–91.

Tolman, R. Virtue rewarded and vice punished. *Amer. Psychologist,* 1953, 8, 721–733.

Tyler, Leona. Toward a workable psychology of individuality. *Amer. Psychologist,* 1959, 14, 75–81.

Windle, C., & Hamwi, V. An exploratory study of the prognostic value of the complex reaction time tests in early and chronic psychotics. *J. clin. Psychol.,* 1953, 9, 156–161.

Wittenborn, J. Symptom patterns in a group of mental hospital patients. *J. consult. Psychol.,* 1951, 15, 290–302.

Wittenborn, J. The behavioral symptoms for certain organic psychoses. *J. consult. Psychol.,* 1952, 16, 104–106.

Wittenborn, J., & Bailey, C. The symptoms of involutional psychosis. *J. consult. Psychol.,* 1952, 16, 13–17.

Wittenborn, J., & Holzberg, J. The generality of psychiatric syndromes. *J. consult. Psychol.,* 1951, 15, 372–380.

Wittenborn, J., Holzberg, J., & Simon, B. Symptom correlates for descriptive diagnosis. *Genet. psychol. Monogr.,* 1953, 47, 237–301.

Wittenborn, J., & Weiss, W. Patients diagnosed manic-depressive psychosis-manic state. *J. consult. Psychol.,* 1952, 16, 193–198.

Wittman, P., & Sheldon, W. A proposed classification of psychotic behavior reactions. *Amer. J. Psychiat.*, 1948, 105, 124–128.

Wittson, C., & Hunt, W. The predictive value of the brief psychiatric interview. *Amer. J. Psychiat.*, 1951, 107, 582–585.

Yates, A. Symptoms and symptom substitution. *Psychol. Rev.*, 1958, 65, 371–374.

Zigler, E., & Phillips, L. Social effectiveness and symptomatic behaviors. *J. abnorm. soc. Psychol.*, 1960, 61, 231–238.

Zilboorg, G., & Henry, G. W. *History of medical psychology.* New York: Norton, 1941.

DISCUSSION

The current system of psychiatric diagnosis has undergone little funda-mental modification since Kraepelin. Nevertheless, there seems to be no agreement as to what the goals of psychiatric classification should be. As indicated in the preceding articles by Szasz, and Zigler and Phillips, much of the current confusion and dissatisfaction with nosology results from the inconsistencies implicit in the orientation of modern psychiatry, contradic-tory situational demands placed upon diagnosis, and the varied observa-tional bases utilized.

This confusion is reflected in the referents of current psychiatric nosology: organic disease processes, inferred mediational processes, and patterns of abnormal behavior. To further complicate matters, this heter-ogenous system is utilized for such diverse purposes as the determination of criminal responsibility, prediction of response to psychotherapy, military screening, and placement in a mental hospital.

Given the above inconsistencies it seems inevitable that several sys-tems of classification which are consistent with a given model, observa-tional base, and function must eventually evolve to replace our current system.

PART

II

Patterns of
Abnormal Behavior

Section 3: CHARACTER DISORDERS

The patterns of abnormal behavior to be considered in this section have variously been labelled Conduct Disorders, Character Disorders, Impulse Neuroses, and/or Personality Disorders. Whatever the label, critics have argued that there seems to be little value in grouping such diverse phenomena as alcoholism, drug addiction, sexual deviancy, juvenile delinquency, and psychopathy together. Nevertheless, several characteristics common to individuals so categorized have been cited as justification for the continued acceptance of the general heading Character Disorders: 1) Such abnormalities typically constitute a violation of the codes and conventions of society. 2) The problem behaviors most often result in immediate positive reinforcing consequences, although the delayed or long term effects are usually negative. 3) Such individuals do not seem to experience guilt over repeated violation of societal conventions and are rarely genuinely motivated to change their behavior. The articles which follow represent several attempts to refine our system of classifying and understanding the origin of such behavior, as well as descriptions of innovative approaches to the modification of the patterns of behavior classed as character disorders which represent dramatic changes from traditional therapeutic practice.

6

PHASES OF ALCOHOL ADDICTION

E. M. Jellinek

In 1946 E. M. Jellinek, on the basis of a questionnaire study of members of Alcoholics Anonymous, first formulated his concept of phases in the drinking history of alcoholics. With the original publication[1] of this concept Jellinek outlined a more detailed questionnaire, which in the intervening years has been administered to some 2,000 alcoholics. The elaboration of the phases concept resulting from analysis of these additional materials has been presented by Jellinek in lectures at the Yale Summer School of Alcohol Studies (July 1951 and July 1952) and at the European Seminar on Alcoholism (Cophenhagen, October 1951). The summary of these lectures, as published under the auspices of the Alcoholism Subcommittee of the World Health Organization,[2] is reproduced here in full.

Reprinted from the *Quarterly Journal of Studies on Alcohol,* 13, 1952, 673–684, with the permission of the Publications Division of Rutgers Center of Alcohol Studies, copyright by Journal of Studies on Alcohol, Inc., New Brunswick, N.J. 08903. (Footnotes have been renumbered.)

[1]Jellinek, E. M. Phases in the drinking history of alcoholics. Analysis of a survey conducted by the official organ of Alcoholics Anonymous. (Memoirs of the Section of Studies on Alcohol, Yale University, No. 5.) *Quart. J. Stud. Alc.,* 7 (1946), 1–88. Published also as a monograph (Hillhouse Press, New Haven, 1946) under the same title; the monograph is now out of print.

[2]Expert Committee on Mental Health, Alcoholism Subcommittee, Second Report. Annex 2, The Phases of Alcohol Addiction. World Hlth. Org. Techn. Rep. Ser., No. 48, Aug. 1952.

INTRODUCTION

Only certain forms of excessive drinking—those which in the present report are designated as alcoholism—are accessible to medical-psychiatric treatment. The other forms of excessive drinking, too, present more or less serious problems, but they can be managed only on the level of applied sociology, including law enforcement. Nevertheless, the medical profession may have an advisory role in the handling of these latter problems and must take an interest in them from the viewpoint of preventive medicine.

The conditions which have been briefly defined by the Subcommittee as alcoholism are described in the following pages in greater detail, in order to delimit more definitely those excessive drinkers whose rehabilitation primarily requires medical-psychiatric treatment.

Furthermore, such detailed description may serve to forestall a certain potential danger which attaches to the disease conception of alcoholism, or more precisely of addictive drinking.

With the exception of specialists in alcoholism, the broader medical profession and representatives of the biological and social sciences and the lay public use the term "alcoholism" as a designation for any form of excessive drinking instead of as a label for a limited and well-defined area of excessive drinking behaviors. Automatically, the disease conception of alcoholism becomes extended to all excessive drinking irrespective of whether or not there is any physical or psychological pathology involved in the drinking behavior.

Such an unwarranted extension of the disease conception can only be harmful, because sooner or later the misapplication will reflect on the legitimate use too and, more importantly, will tend to weaken the ethical basis of social sanctions against drunkenness.

THE DISEASE CONCEPTION OF ALCOHOL ADDICTION

The Subcommittee has distinguished two categories of alcoholics, namely "alcohol addicts" and "habitual symptomatic excessive drinkers." For brevity's sake the latter will be referred to as nonaddictive alcoholics. Strictly speaking, the disease conception attaches to the alcohol addicts only, not to the habitual symptomatic excessive drinkers.

In both groups the excessive drinking is symptomatic of underlying psychological or social pathology, but in one group after several years of excessive drinking "loss of control" over the alcohol intake occurs, while in the other group this phenomenon never develops. The group with the "loss of control" is designated as "alcohol addicts." (There are other differences between these two groups and these will be seen in the course of the description of the "phases.")

The disease conception of alcohol addiction does not apply to the excessive drinking, but solely to the "loss of control" which occurs in only one group of alcoholics and then only after many years of excessive drinking. There is no intention to deny that the nonaddictive alcoholic is a sick person; but his ailment is not the excessive drinking, but rather the psychological or social difficulties from which alcohol intoxication gives temporary surcease.

The "loss of control" is a disease condition per se which results from a process that superimposes itself upon those abnormal psychological conditions of which excessive drinking is a symptom. The fact that many excessive drinkers drink as much as or more than the addict for 30 or 40 years without developing loss of control indicates that in the group of "alcohol addicts" a superimposed process must occur.

Whether this superimposed process is of a psychopathological nature or whether some physical pathology is involved cannot be stated as yet with any degree of assurance, the claims of various investigators notwithstanding. Nor is it possible to go beyond conjecture concerning the question whether the "loss of control" originates in a predisposing factor (psychological or physical), or whether it is a factor acquired in the course of prolonged excessive drinking.

The fact that this "loss of control" does not occur in a large group of excessive drinkers would point towards a predisposing X factor in the addictive alcoholics. On the other hand this explanation is not indispensable as the difference between addictive and nonaddictive alcoholics could be a matter of acquired modes of living—for instance, a difference in acquired nutritional habits.

THE MEANING OF SYMPTOMATIC DRINKING

The use of alcoholic beverages by society has primarily a symbolic meaning, and secondarily it achieves "function." Cultures which accept this custom differ in the nature and degree of the "functions" which they regard as legitimate. The differences in these "functions" are determined by the general pattern of the culture, e.g., the need for the release and for the special control of aggression, the need and the ways and means of achieving identification, the nature and intensity of anxieties and the modus for their relief, and so forth. The more the original symbolic character of the custom is preserved, the less room will be granted by the culture to the "functions" of drinking.

Any drinking within the accepted ways is symptomatic of the culture of which the drinker is a member. Within that frame of cultural symptomatology there may be in addition individual symptoms expressed in the act of drinking. The fact that a given individual drinks a glass of beer with his meal may be the symptom of the culture which accepts such a use as a refreshment, or as a "nutritional supplement." That this individual drinks at this given moment may be a symptom of his fatigue, or his elation or some other mood, and thus an individual symptom, but if his culture accepts the use for these purposes it is at the same time a cultural symptom.

In this sense even the small or moderate use of alcoholic beverages is symptomatic, and it may be said that all drinkers are culturally symptomatic drinkers or, at least, started as such.

The vast majority of the users of alcoholic beverages stay within the limits of the culturally accepted drinking behaviors and drink predominantly as an expression of their culture, and while an individual expression may be present in these behaviors its role remains insignificant.

For the purpose of the present discussion the expression "symptomatic drinking" will be limited to the predominant use of alcoholic beverages for the relief of major individual stresses.

A certain unknown proportion of these users of alcoholic beverages, perhaps 20 per cent, are occasionally inclined to take advantage of the "functions" of alcohol which they have experienced in the course of its "cultural use." At least at times, the individual motivation becomes predominant and on those occasions alcohol loses its character as an ingredient of a beverage and is used as a drug.

The "occasional symptomatic excessive drinker" tends to take care of the stresses and strains of living in socially accepted—i.e., "normal"—ways, and his drinking is most of the time within the cultural pattern. After a long accumulation of stresses, however, or because of some particularly heavy stress, his tolerances for tension is lowered and he takes recourse to heroic relief of his symptoms through alcoholic intoxication.[3] Under these circumstances the "relief" may take on an explosive character, and thus the occasional symptomatic excessive drinker may create serious problems. No psychological abnormality can be claimed for this type of drinker, although he does not represent a well-integrated personality.

Nevertheless, within the group of apparent "occasional symptomatic excessive drinkers" there is a certain proportion of definitely deviating personalities who after a shorter or longer period of occasional symptomatic relief take recourse to a constant alcoholic relief, and drinking becomes with them a "mode of living." These are the "alcoholics" of whom again a certain proportion suffer "loss of control," i.e., become "addictive alcoholics."

The proportion of alcoholics (addictive and nonaddictive) varies from country to country, but does not seem to exceed in any country 5 per cent or 6 per cent of all users of alcoholic beverages. The ratio of addictive to nonaddictive alcoholics is unknown.

---

[3]This group does not include the regular "periodic alcoholics."

THE CHART OF ALCOHOL ADDICTION

The course of alcohol addiction is represented graphically in Figure 1. The diagram is based on an analysis of more than two thousand drinking histories of male alcohol addicts. Not all symptoms shown in the diagram occur

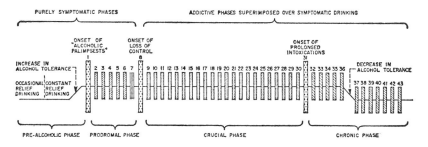

Figure 1

THE PHASES OF ALCOHOL ADDICTION

The large bars denote the onset of major symptoms which initiate phases. The short bars denote the onset of symptoms within a phase. Reference to the numbering of the symptoms is made in the text.

necessarily in all alcohol addicts, nor do they occure in every addict in the same sequence. The "phases" and the sequences of symptoms within the phases are characteristic, however, of the great majority of alcohol addicts and represent what may be called the average trend.

For alcoholic women the "phases" are not as clear-cut as in men and the development is frequently more rapid.

The "phases" vary in their duration according to individual characteristics and environmental factors. The "lengths" of the different phases on the diagram do not indicate differences in duration, but are determined by the number of symptoms which have to be shown in any given phase.

The chart of the phases of alcohol addiction serves as the basis of description, and the differences between addictive and nonaddictive alcoholics are indicated in the text.

THE PREALCOHOLIC SYMPTOMATIC PHASE

The very beginning of the use of alcoholic beverages is always socially motivated in the prospective addictive and nonaddictive alcoholic. In contrast to the average social drinker, however, the prospective alcoholic (together with the occasional symptomatic excessive drinker) soon experiences a rewarding relief in the drinking situation. The relief is strongly marked in his case because either his tensions are much greater than in other members of his social circle, or he has not learned to handle those tensions as others do.

Initially this drinker ascribes his relief to the situation rather than to the drinking and he seeks therefore those situations in which identical drinking will occur. Sooner or later, of course, he becomes aware of the contingency between relief and drinking.

In the beginning he seeks this relief occasionally only, but in the course of 6 months to 2 years his tolerance for tension decreases to such a degree that he takes recourse to alcoholic relief practically daily.

Nevertheless his drinking does not result in overt intoxication, but he reaches toward the evening a stage of surcease from emotional stress. Even in the absence of intoxication this involves fairly heavy drinking, particularly in comparison to the use of alcoholic beverages by other members of his circle. The drinking is, nevertheless, not conspicuous either to his associates or to himself.

After a certain time an increase in alcohol tolerance may be noticed, i.e., the drinker requires a somewhat larger amount of alcohol than formerly in order to reach the desired stage of sedation.

This type of drinking behavior may last from several months to two years according to circumstances and may be designated as the prealcoholic phase, which is divided into stages of occasional relief-drinking and constant relief-drinking.

THE PRODROMAL PHASE

The sudden onset of a behavior resembling the "blackouts" in anoxemia marks the beginning of the prodromal phase of alcohol addiction. The drinker who may have had not more than 50 to 60 g. of absolute alcohol and who is not showing any signs of intoxication may carry on a reasonable conversation or may go through quite elaborate activities without a trace of memory the next day, although sometimes one or two minor details may be hazily remembered. This amnesia, which is not connected with loss of consciousness, has been called by Bonhoeffer the "alcoholic palimpsests," with reference to old Roman manuscripts superimposed over an incompletely erased manuscript.

"Alcoholic palimpsests" (1)[4] may occur on rare occasions in an average drinker when he drinks intoxicating amounts in a state of physical or emotional exhaustion. Nonaddictive alcoholics, of course, also may experience "pal-

[4]The italicized figures in parentheses following the designations of the individual symptoms represent their order as given in Figure 1.

impsests," but infrequently and only following rather marked intoxication. Thus, the frequency of "palimpsests" and their occurrence after medium alcohol intake are characteristic of the prospective alcohol addict.

This would suggest heightened susceptibility to alcohol in the prospective addict. Such a susceptibility may be psychologically or psysiologically determined. The analogy with the "blackouts" of anoxemia is tempting. Of course, an insufficient oxygen supply cannot be assumed, but a malutilization of oxygen may be involved. The present status of the knowledge of alcoholism does not permit of more than vague conjectures which, nevertheless, may constitute bases for experimental hypotheses.

The onset of "alcoholic palimpsests" is followed (in some instances preceded) by the onset of drinking behaviors which indicate that, for this drinker, beer, wine, and spirits have practically ceased to be beverages and have become sources of a drug which he "needs." Some of these behaviors imply that this drinker has some vague realization that he drinks differently from others.

Surreptitious drinking (2) is one of these behaviors. At social gatherings the drinker seeks occasions for having a few drinks unknown to others, as he fears that if it were known that he drinks more than the others he would be misjudged: those to whom drinking is only a custom or a small pleasure would not understand that because he is different from them alcohol is for him a necessity, although he is not a drunkard.

Preoccupation with alcohol (3) is further evidence of this "need." When he prepares to go to a social gathering his first thought is whether there will be sufficient alcohol for his requirements, and he has several drinks in anticipation of a possible shortage.

Because of this increasing dependence upon alcohol, the onset of *avid drinking* (4) (gulping of the first or first two drinks) occurs at this time.

As the drinker realizes, at least vaguely, that his drinking is outside of the ordinary, he develops *guilt feelings about his drinking behavior* (5) and because of this he begins to *avoid reference to alcohol* (6) in conversation.

These behaviors, together with an *incrasing frequency of "alcoholic palimpsests"* (7), foreshadow the development of alcohol addiction; they are premonitory signs, and this period may be called the prodromal phase of alcohol addiction.

The consumption of alcoholic beverages in the prodromal phase is "heavy," but not conspicuous, as it does not lead to marked, overt intoxications. The effect is that the prospective addict reaches towards evening a state which may be designated as emotional anesthesia. Nevertheless, this condition requires drinking well beyond the ordinary usage. The drinking is on a level which may begin to interfere with metabolic and nervous processes as evidenced by the frequent "alcoholic palimpsests."

The "covering-up" which is shown by the drinker in this stage is the first sign that his drinking might separate him from society, although initially the drinking may have served as a technique to overcome some lack of social integration.

As in the prodromal phase rationalizations of the drinking behavior are not strong and there is some insight as well as fear of possible consequences, it is feasible to intercept incipient alcohol addiction at this stage. In the United States of America, the publicity given to the prodromal symptoms begins to bring prospective alcoholics to clinics as well as to groups of Alcoholics Anonymous.

It goes without saying that even at this stage the only possible modus for this type of drinker is total abstinence.

The prodromal period may last anywhere from 6 months to 4 or 5 years according to the physical and psychological make-up of the drinker, his family ties, vocational relations, general interests, and so forth. The prodromal phase ends and the crucial or acute phase begins with the onset of loss of control, which is the critical symptom of alcohol addiction.

THE CRUCIAL PHASE

Loss of control (8) means that any drinking of alcohol starts a chain reaction which is felt by the drinker as a physical demand for alcohol. This state, possibly a conversion phenomenon, may take hours or weeks for its full development; it lasts until the drinker is too intoxicated or too sick to ingest more alcohol. The physical discomfort following this drinking behavior is contrary to the object of the drinker, which is merely to feel "different." As a matter of fact, the bout may not even be started by any individual need of the moment, but by a "social drink."

After recovery from the intoxication, it is not the "loss of control"—i.e., the physical demand, apparent or real—which leads to a new bout after several days or several weeks; the renewal of drinking is set off by the original psychological conflicts or by a simple social situation which involves drinking.

The "loss of control" is effective after the individual has started drinking, but it does not give rise to the beginning of a new drinking bout. The drinker has lost the ability to control the quantity once he has started, but he still can control whether he will drink on any given occasion or not. This is evidenced in the fact that after the onset of "loss of control" the drinker can go through a period of voluntary abstinence ("going on the water wagon").

The question of why the drinker returns to drinking after repeated disastrous experiences is often raised. Although he will not admit it, the alcohol addict believes that he has lost his will power and that he can and must regain it. He is not aware that he has undergone a process which makes it impossible for him to control his alcohol intake. To "master his will" becomes a matter of the greatest importance to him. When tensions rise, "a drink" is the natural remedy for him and he is convinced that this time it will be one or two drinks only.

Practically simultaneously with the onset of "loss of control" the alcohol addict begins to *rationalize his drinking behavior* (9): he produces the well-known alcoholic "alibis." He finds explanations which convince him that he did not lose control, but that he had a good reason to get intoxicated and that in the absence of such reasons he is able to handle alcohol as well as anybody else. These rationalizations are needed primarily for himself and only secondarily for his family and associates. The rationalizations make it possible for him to continue with his drinking, and this is of the greatest importance to him as he knows no alternative for handling his problems.

This is the beginning of an entire "system of rationalizations" which progressively spreads to every aspect of his life. While this system largely originates in inner needs, it also serves to counter *social pressures* (10) which arise at the time of the "loss of control." At this time, of course, the drinking behavior becomes conspicuous, and the parents, wife, friends, and employer may begin to reprove and warn the drinker.

In spite of all the rationalizations there is a marked loss of self-esteem, and this of course demands compensations which in a certain sense are also rationalizations. One way of compensation is the *grandiose behavior* (11) which the addict begins to display at this time. Extravagant expenditures and grandiloquence convince him that he is not as bad as he had thought at times.

The rationalization system gives rise to another system, namely, the "system of isolation." The rationalizations quite naturally lead to the idea that the fault lies not within himself but in others, and this results in a progressive withdrawal from the social environment. The first sign of this attitude is a *marked aggressive behavior* (12).

Inevitably, this latter behavior generates guilt. While even in the prodromal period remorse about the drinking arose from time to time, now *persistent remorse* (13) arises, and this added tension is a further source of drinking.

In compliance with social pressures the addict now goes on *periods of total abstinence* (14). There is, however, another modus of control of drinking which arises out of the rationalizations of the addict. He believes that his trouble arises from his not drinking the right kind of beverages or not in the right way. He now attempts to control his troubles by *changing the pattern of his drinking* (15), by setting up rules about not drinking before a certain hour of the day, in certain places only, and so forth.

The strain of the struggle increases his hostility towards his environment and he begins to *drop friends* (16) and *quit jobs* (17). It goes without saying that some associates drop him and that he loses some jobs, but more frequently he takes the initiative as an anticipatory defense.

The isolation becomes more pronounced as his entire *behavior becomes alcohol-centered* (*18*), i.e., he begins to be concerned about how activities might interfere with his drinking instead of how his drinking may affect his activities. This, of course, involves a more marked egocentric outlook which leads to more rationalizations and more isolation. There ensue a *loss of outside interests* (*19*) and a *reinterpretation of interpersonal relations* (*20*) coupled with *marked self-pity* (*21*). The isolation and rationalizations have increased by this time in intensity and find their expression either in contemplated or actual *geographic escape* (*22*).

Under the impact of these events, a *change in family habits* (*23*) occurs. The wife and children, who may have had good social activities, may withdraw for fear of embarrassment or, quite contrarily, they may suddenly begin intensive outside activities in order to escape from the home environment. This and other events lead to the onset of *unreasonable resentments* (*24*) in the alcohol addict.

The predominance of concern with alcohol induces the addict to *protect his supply* (*25*), i.e., to lay in a large stock of alcoholic beverages, hidden in the most unthought-of places. A fear of being deprived of the most necessary substance for his living is expressed in this behavior.

Neglect of proper nutrition (*26*) aggravates the beginnings of the effects of heavy drinking on the organism, and frequently the *first hospitalization* (*27*) for some alcoholic complaint occurs at this time.

One of the frequent organic effects is a *decrease of the sexual drive* (*28*) which increases hostility toward the wife and is rationalized into her extramarital sex activities, which gives rise to the well-known *alcoholic jealousy* (*29*).

By this time remorse, resentment, struggle between alcoholic needs and duties, loss of self-esteem, and doubts and false reassurance have so disorganized the addict that he cannot start the day without steadying himself with alcohol immediately after arising or even before getting out of bed. This is the beginning of *regular matutinal drinking* (*30*), which previously had occurred on rare occasions only.

This behavior terminates the crucial phase and foreshadows the beginnings of the chronic phase.

During the crucial phase intoxication is the rule, but it is limited to the evening hours. For the most part of this phase drinking begins sometime in the afternoon and by the evening intoxication is reached. It should be noted that the "physical demand" involved in the "loss of control" results in continual rather than continuous drinking. Particularly the "matutinal drink" which occurs toward the end of the crucial phase shows the continual pattern. The first drink at rising, let us say at 7 A.M., is followed by another drink at 10 or 11 A.M., and another drink around 1 P.M., while the more intensive drinking hardly starts before 5 P.M.

Throughout, the crucial phase presents a great struggle of the addict against the complete loss of social footing. Occasionally the aftereffects of the evening's intoxication cause some loss of time, but generally the addict succeeds in looking after his job, although he neglects his family. He makes a particularly strong effort to avoid intoxication during the day. Progressively, however, his social motivations weaken more and more, and the "morning drink" jeopardizes his effort to comply with his vocational duties as this effort involves a conscious resistance against the apparent or real "physical demand" for alcohol.

The onset of the "loss of control" is the beginning of the "disease process" of alcohol addiction which is superimposed over the excessive symptomatic drinking. Progressively, this disease process undermines the morale and the physical resistance of the addict.

THE CHRONIC PHASE

The increasingly dominating role of alcohol, and the struggle against the "demand" set up by matutinal drinking, at last break down the resistance of the addict and he finds himself for the first time intoxicated in the daytime and on a weekday and continues in that state for several days until he is entirely incapacitated. This is the onset of *prolonged intoxications* (*31*), referred to in the vernacular as "benders."

This latter drinking behavior meets with such unanimous social rejection that it involves a grave social risk. Only an originally psychopathic personality or a person who has later in life undergone a psychopathological process would expose himself to that risk.

These long-drawn-out bouts commonly bring about *marked ethical deterioration* (*32*) and *impairment of thinking* (*33*) which, however, are not irreversible. True *alcoholic psychoses* (*34*) may occur at this time, but in not more than 10 per cent of all alcoholics.

The loss of morale is so heightened that the addict *drinks with persons far below his social level* (*35*) in preference to his usual associates—perhaps as an opportunity to appear superior—and, if nothing else is available, he will *take recourse to "technical products"* (*36*) such as bay rum or rubbing alcohol.

A *loss of alcohol tolerance* (*37*) is commonly noted at this time. Half of the previously required amount of alcohol may be sufficient to bring about a stuporous state.

Indefinable fears (*38*) and *tremors* (*39*) become persistent. Sporadically these symptoms occur also during the crucial phase, but in the chronic phase they are present as soon as alcohol disappears from the organism. In consequence the addict "controls" the symptoms through alcohol. The same is true of *psychomotor inhibition* (*40*), the inability to initiate a simple mechanical act—

as winding a watch—in the absence of alcohol.

The need to control these symptoms of drinking exceeds the need of relieving the original underlying symptoms of the personality conflict, and the *drinking takes on an obsessive character* (41).

In many addicts, approximately 60 per cent, some *vague religious desires develop* (42) as the rationalizations become weaker. Finally, in the course of the frequently prolonged intoxications, the rationalizations become so frequently and so mercilessly tested against reality that the entire *rationalization system fails* (43) and the addict admits defeat. He now becomes spontaneously accessible to treatment. Nevertheless, his obsessive drinking continues as he does not see a way out.

Formerly it was thought that the addict must reach this stage of utter defeat in order to be treated successfully. Clinical experience has shown, however, that this "defeat" can be induced long before it would occur of itself and that even incipient alcoholism can be intercepted. As the latter can be easily recognized it is possible to tackle the problem from the preventive angle.

THE "ALCOHOLIC PERSONALITY"

The aggressions, feelings of guilt, remorse, resentments, withdrawal, etc., which develop in the phases of alcohol addiction, are largely consequences of the excessive drinking, but at the same time they constitute sources of more excessive drinking.

In addition to relieving, through alcohol, symptoms of an underlying personality conflict, the addict now tends to relieve, through further drinking, the stresses created by his drinking behavior.

By and large, these reactions to excessive drinking—which have quite a neurotic appearance—give the impression of an "alcoholic personality", although they are secondary behaviors superimposed over a large variety of personality types which have a few traits in common, in particular a low capacity for coping with tensions. There does not emerge, however, any specific personality trait or physical characteristic which inevitably would lead to excessive symptomatic drinking. Apart from psychological and possibly physical liabilities, there must be a constellation of social and economic factors which facilitate the development of addictive and nonaddictive alcoholism in a susceptible terrain.

THE NONADDICTIVE ALCOHOLIC

Some differences between the nonaddictive alcoholic and the alcohol addict have been stated passim. These differences may be recapitulated and elaborated, and additional differential features may be considered.

The main difference may be readily visualized by erasing the large bars of the diagram (see Figure 1). This results in a diagram which suggests a progressive exacerbation of the use of alcohol for symptom relief and of the social and health consequences incumbent upon such use, but without any clear-cut phases.

The prealcoholic phase is the same for the nonaddictive alcoholic as for the alcohol addict, i.e., he progresses from occasional to constant relief of individual symptoms through alcohol.

The behaviors which denote that alcohol has become a drug rather than an ingredient of a beverage (symptoms 2 to 6) occur also in the nonaddictive drinker, but, as mentioned before, the "alcoholic palimpsests" occur rarely and only after overt intoxication.

"Loss of control" is not experienced by the nonaddictive alcoholic, and this is the main differentiating criterion between the two categories of alcoholics. Initially, of course, it could not be said whether the drinker had yet reached the crucial phase, but after 10 or 12 years of heavy drinking without "loss of control," while symptoms 2 to 6 were persistent and "palimpsests" were rare and did not occur after medium alcohol intake, the differential diagnosis is rather safe.

The absence of "loss of control" has many involvements. First of all, as there is no inability to stop drinking within a given situation there is no need to rationalize the inability. Nevertheless, rationalizations are developed for justifying the excessive use of alcohol and some neglect of the family attendant upon such use. Likewise, there is no need to change the pattern of drinking, which in the addict is an attempt to overcome the "loss of control." Periods of total abstinence, however, occur as a response to social pressure.

On the other hand, there is the same tendency toward isolation as in the addict, but the social repercussions are much less marked as the nonaddictive alcoholic can avoid drunken behavior whenever the social situation requires it.

The effects of prolonged heavy drinking on the organism may occur in the nonaddictive alcoholic too; even delirium tremens may develop. The libido may be diminished and "alcoholic jealousy" may result.

Generally, there is a tendency toward a progressive dominance of alcohol resulting in greater psychological and bodily effects. In the absence of any grave initial psychopathy, however, the symptoms of the chronic phase as seen in addicts do not develop in the nonaddictive alcoholic. In the presence of grave underlying psychopathies a deteriorative process is speeded up by habitual alcoholic excess, and such a nonaddictive drinker may slide to the bottom of society.

7

THE ANTICRIMINAL SOCIETY: SYNANON

Lewis Yablonsky

A reader of the *Terminal Island News* of April 12, 1962, would be somewhat surprised to note an unusual statement called "Breaking the Invisible Wall" authored by a former criminal and inmate of the Federal Correctional Institution at Terminal Island, California, the U.S. Public Health Service Hospital at Fort Worth, Texas, the State Prison of Southern Michigan, and various juvenile reformatories. James Middleton, the writer of the statement, had served a total of 15 years in these institutions. He has currently been clean of his past lengthy addiction and criminal history for almost 3 years. Middleton is one of a group of seven ex-offenders and former prisoners who go to the Terminal Island institution once a week to run group counseling sessions with about 25 addict inmates. This is the way Middleton described this project in the Terminal Island News:

> As a former using addict and inmate of Terminal Island and other prisons, having been free from the use of drugs for the past 2½ years by being a resident of Synanon House, I have been aware of the lack of communication between inmates and all those in positions of authority. Perhaps the most difficult problem to overcome for penologists, prison officials, and others dealing with the socially rejected group, the criminal, is the problem of establishing an area of communication, some feeling of rapport. The convict, criminal, or any rebellious delinquent has a defiance of all authority. This he carried to such an extent that he will refuse to even talk to a person

Reprinted from *Federal Probation*, 26, 1962, 50–57 with the permission of the publisher and Dr. Yablonsky.

in any position of authority whom he considers his enemy. He takes the attitude that "If you are not on my side, you are against me."

On November 26, 1961, six members of the Synanon Foundation were invited to the Terminal Island correctional institution by Chief Parole Officer Frank E. Saunders who believed that the Synanon approach might have something to offer the prisoners who had an addiction history.

Of paramount significance perhaps is the effect synanon has had in bridging this gap in communication between prisoner and official. This has been accomplished by the prisoners being encouraged to verbalize their problem, frustration, attitudes, opinions, etc., in the synanon.

Synanon is a form of intense group interaction. In these meetings synanites and inmate addicts are encouraged to break down this wall and see their problems in a more realistic light. Part of the success of these meetings can be attributed to the fact that an inmate can often lie to the officials and get away with it, however with his fellow inmates, those who know him intimately, and can identify with his problems and his unsatisfactory reaction to them, he can't get away with as much. They see him as he is. Once a person has admitted his failures and inadequacies to others, and as an eventual consequence, to himself, he finds that he can discuss these things with almost anyone.

They are no longer deep, dark secrets which he must hide from others and himself. As Dr. Yablonsky, U.C.L.A. criminologist said, "This is the most significant break-through in the field of criminology in the past 50 years."

It is conceivable to me as an ex-inmate myself that someday Synanon could become an established part of the prison program throughout the United States.

THE BACKGROUND OF SYNANON

The Synanon organization,[1] of which Middleton is a significant member, has been in operation about 4 years. As a result of exposure to this unique social system approximately 100 persons, most with long criminal and addiction records, no longer find it necessary to use drugs or commit crimes. Some Synanon residents have been clean of these deviant patterns for periods of up to 4 years.

[1]The name Synanon was derived from the slip-of-the-tongue of a confused addict attempting to say seminar. It was adopted because it is a new word for describing a new phenomenon.

This antiaddiction society originated with Charles E. Dederich, a former business executive, who had worked through an alcoholic problem and was motivated to transmit the forces which had led to his own recovery. A strong personality with characteristics of a charismatic leader, Dederich attracted to his residence by the beach in Ocean Park a coterie of alcoholics and drug addicts who found stimulating and interesting the lengthy philosophical discussions which he led. Many of these persons had no roots and moved into Dederich's "pad." Within a short time a small colony of about 15 addicts moved into the various apartments in the immediate area and emerged as the early core of the Synanon movement. At this point, about 6 months after its inception, there emerged an idealized assumption that no one was using drugs; although this fact was only true for about half the residents at the time.

Two incidents sharply changed the nature of this unusual collectivity and projected the evolution of a clean Synanon community. One was what later became known as the "big cop-out." This involved the open admission of occasional use by several key residents. Shortly after this episode the balance of power shifted over to a community with a majority of *clean addicts*. This new situation gave strength and credence to an antiaddiction, anticriminal ethos. To my knowledge, it was the first time anywhere that a group of nonprisoner ex-addicts could be found in one location.

By the summer of 1959 about 40 to 50 men and women, not using drugs, were living in a Synanon colony in one large building. The Synanon movement has become more established and aroused the interest of many significant professionals. *Time* magazine in its April 7, 1961 issue published an extensive description of the Synanon organization at that time.

S.S. HANG TOUGH

Early in August 1959, homeowners along the stylish Pacific Ocean beaches in Santa Monica, Calif., were dismayed to get a new set of neighbors: a bedraggled platoon of half a hundred men and women, who moved into a run-down, three story, red brick building that once was a National Guard armory. White and black, young and middle-aged, criminals and innocents, artists and loafers, the unlikely assortment shared one trait: they were narcotics addicts determined to kick their habit for good.

Scrounging lumber, paint and old furniture, the group converted the top floor of the armory into a barracks-style men's dormitory. They turned the second floor into offices, kitchen, dining hall and living room, and the main floor into women's sleeping quarters. Over the doors in the living room they hung their emblem: a life preserver with the words *"S.S. Hang Tough,"* slang for "don't give up." . . .

Such was the formal dedication of Synanon House, a self-run, haphazardly financed experiment in human reclamation whose success has been hailed by Dr. Ronald Cressey, University of California at Los Angeles sociologist, as "the most significant attempt to keep addicts off drugs that has ever been made." . . . The technique was patterned roughly after the group-therapy methods of Alcoholics Anonymous. . . . Dr. Cressey describes the psychology: "A group in which Criminal A joins with some noncriminals to change Criminal B is probably most effective in changing Criminal A."

In the often brutally frank personal exchanges, the addicts slowly reveal themselves . . . and through daily contact with similarly beset persons are reinforced in their determination to quit narcotics permanently. Says the founder of Synanon House, 48-year-old Charles E. Dederich . . . . once an alcoholic but never a drug addict: "It is something that works."

The Synanon curriculum is divided into three stages. During the first phase, the emotionally shaken, physically weak addict gradually adjusts to his new surroundings. . . . During the second stage, the ex-addict works at a regular job on the outside, contributes part of his wages to the group, continues to live at the house. . . . In its final stage, Synanon sends its member out into society.

Interestingly, the potential of this type of an anticriminal society for modifying difficult offenders had been forecast by Professor Cressey in an article published in 1955 in *The American Journal of Sociology*.[2] His projection of the need for this treatment approach was based upon Sutherland's causal theory of criminal "differential association." Cressey logically speculated that, "if the behavior of an individual is an intrinsic part of the groups to which he belongs, attempts to change the behavior must be directed at groups." [3]

Cressey, utilizing "differential association" theory as a diagnostic base, projected the necessity for an anticriminal society to modify deviant behavior.

The differential association theory of criminal behavior presents implications for diagnosis and treatment consistent with the group-relations principle for changing behavior and could be advantageously utilized in correctional work. According to it, persons become criminals principally because they have been relatively isolated from groups whose behavior patterns (including attitudes, motives, and rationalizations) are anticriminal, or because their residence, employment, social position, native capacities, or something else has brought them

[2]Donald R. Cressey, "Changing Criminals: The Application of the Theory of Differential Association," *American Journal of Sociology*, September 1955, pp. 116–120.
[3]*Ibid.* p. 117.

into relatively frequent association with the behavior patterns of criminal groups. A diagnosis of criminality based on this theory would be
directed at analysis of the criminal's attitudes, motives, and rationalizations regarding criminality and would recognize that those characteristics depend upon the groups to which the criminal belongs. Then if
criminals are to be changed, either they must become members of anticriminal groups, or their present procriminal group relations must be
changed.[4]

Life in the Synanon anticriminal society revolves around a set of educational and apparently group therapeutic procedures developed by Dederich and
the group of ex-addict leaders he had personally trained. Synanon by this time
had many characteristics of an extended father-dominated family. As Dederich
himself described it in an address before The Southern California Parole Officers
Association:

> We have here a climate consisting of a family structure similar
> in some areas to a primitive tribal structure, which seems to affect
> individuals on a sub-conscious level. The structure also contains over-
> tones of a 19th century family set-up of the type which produced
> inner-directed personalities. It is the feeling of the Synanon Founda-
> tion that an undetermined percentage of narcotic addicts are potentially
> inner-directed people as differentiated from tradition-directed people.
> A more or less autocratic family structure appears to be necessary as a
> pre-conditioning environment to buy time for the recovering addict.
>   . . . The autocratic overtone of the family structure demands that
> the patients or members of the family perform tasks as part of the
> group. As a member is able to take direction in small tasks such as
> helping in the preparation of meals, housecleaning and so forth,
> regardless of his rebellion of being "told what to do," his activity
> seems to provide exercise of emotions of giving or creating which
> have lain dormant. As these muscles strengthen, it seems that the
> resistance to cooperating with the group tends to dissipate.

SYNANON GROUP THERAPY

The daily program for the Synanon resident includes some type of work,
a noon educational seminar, the synanon (a form of leaderless group therapy
in which all residents participate three times a week), and daily interaction

[4]*Ibid.* p. 118.

and communication with hundreds of "squares" (nonaddicts) from all walks of life who visit the building regularly.

The synanon, a form of group interaction vital to the overall approach, tends to be a unique form of aggressive leaderless nonprofessional group psychotherapy, directed by what Dederich has referred to as a Synanist. According to Dederich:

> The Synanist leans heavily on his own insight into his own problems of personality in trying to help others find themselves, and will use the weapons of ridicule, cross-examination, and hostile attack as it becomes necessary. Synanon sessions seem to provide an emotional catharsis and trigger an atmosphere of truth-seeking which is reflected in the social life of the family structure. The Synanist does not try to convey to another that he himself is a stable personality. In fact, it may very well be the destructive drives of the recovered or recovering addictive personality embodied in a Synanist which makes him a good therapeutic tool—fighting fire with fire.

This form of group therapy is ideally suited for the overall Synanon community. The group sessions do not have any official leader. They are autonomous; however, leaders emerge in each session in a natural fashion. The emergent leader tells much about himself in his questioning of another. Because he is intensely involved with the subject or the problem in the particular session he begins to direct, he is in a natural fashion the "most qualified" session leader for that time and place. In short, the expert of the moment may be emotionally crippled in many personal areas, but in the session where he is permitted by the group to take therapeutic command, he may be the most qualified therapeutic agent.

Synanon, as a side effect, trains people to become a new brand of therapeutic agent in the correctional field. The system provides the opportunity for offenders to modify their own deviant behavior and then work with other offenders. In this context I view the phenomenon of Synanon at Terminal Island as a major break-through in the field of correction.

Although ex-offenders have been randomly used over the years in the processes of correction, Synanon provides a unique contribution. One can view the seven 2-year-clean Synanon participants in the Terminal Island project as a new type of "therapeutic agent" for dealing with the crime problem. Unlike most professional or ex-offender workers in the field the trained Synanist has three levels of experience which uniquely qualify him for work with other offenders.

1. He has a lengthy history of criminal experience. He himself has made the "scene." He knows the crime problem in its many dimensions—at first hand.

2. At Synanon, this individual has deeply experienced the emotional up-heaval of rejecting one way of life for another. He has "in his gut" gone through a resocialization process and knows something about the set of experiences and the pain involved in the transition.

3. He knows the Synanon social system. He has a subconscious conception of the processes at work for helping others and he is himself a functional part of this organization. He has been trained at "the Synanon College" for working with recalcitrant offenders.

This triad of experiences qualified the Synanist uniquely for the task at hand. Terminal Island inmates in the Synanon project know they are encountering in the Synanist a new breed of "treatment man." The Synanist is difficult to con or juggle out of position. The Synanist cannot easily be out-maneuvered from his zeal to point up a new direction in life to replace the roles of crime and addiction which he now views as wasteful and stupid behavior. This point of view of the Synanist seems to get across to the inmate seeking a noncriminal mode of existence.

Although the synanon form of group therapy is an important aspect of the method, the basic therapeutic force is the overall synanon social system. The best way to reveal this overall dynamic is to examine its impact on one successful resident.

FRANKIE: A CASE STUDY OF THE SYNANON SYSTEM[5]

Frankie, 2-year-clean Synanon resident, first came to the author's attention in an unusual fashion. While listening to some tapes being played on the Egyptian King gang killing (an incident studied intensively by the author), Dederich detected a familiar voice. Hearing one King comment, "I kicked him in the head, it was the least I could do," Dederich remarked, "That sounds like Frankie." It was later confirmed that Frankie was this Egyptian King gang member's older brother. It was also determined that Frankie's early case history and violent gang life pattern paralleled his young brother's. Frankie later turned to using and pushing drugs, a criminal career, which carried him to the Federal Correctional Institution at Danbury, Conn., New York City's Riker's Island Penitentiary, and finally Bellevue Hospital in New York City. As a result of his experience at Synanon, Frankie was at the time free and clear of drugs and violence for over 2 years.

"Frankie would never use a knife; unless he had to. Mostly with his fists he would beat a guy down and try to kill him right there. They pulled him off this big guy one time—he wouldn't stop punching him in the face." This was

<hr/>

[5]This section is partially derived from a recent volume by the author, *The Violent Gang* (New York: The Macmillan Company, 1962).

a casual observation made by Frankie's ex-"crime partner," the girl with whom he had lived for 5 years in New York. (She is also currently a successful resident at Synanon.)

Frankie's first reaction to Synanon was confusion. "The first thing they hit me with flipped me. This tough looking cat says to me—'there are two things you can't do here, shoot drugs and fight.' " Frankie said, scratching his head, "I was all mixed up—these were the only two things I knew how to do."

Frankie first came West at the insistence of his parents "to try a new way of life." "The family chipped in, gave me a plane ticket, and told me to straighten out or drop dead." He accepted the plane ticket they gave him and came West under the assumption of continuing his old way of life. In the Los Angeles situation he had trouble getting a good drug connection and stealing enough money to supply his habit. He heard about Synanon, and decided to try it. His initial motives were not pure. His thought was "to get cleaned up a little" and either get organized for a new onslaught on Los Angeles or steal enough to return to New York and his old criminal pattern. Something happened at Synanon to make Frankie stay "clean" for 2 years and later assume the administrative role of "coordinator" at Synanon.[6]

The Synanon environment was interesting and exciting for Frankie. There were, in the addicts' jargon, "lots of hip people." Jimmy the Greek, who at 48 had been an addict for 20 years and a criminal and conman for over 30 years[7] and Jimmy Middleton who now ran the kitchen at Synanon. In the kitchen Frankie received his first job scouring pots and pans and mopping floors. According to Frankie, Jimmy M. could not be conned or manipulated out of position like the therapist Frankie had encountered at Riker's Island Prison. Jimmy M., of course, knew the score and to him Frankie with all his exploits

---

[6]A coordinator works a 4-hour shift, answering phones, catering to visitors and generally handling the House's business as it emerges. It requires some ingenuity and administrative ability.

[7]Jimmy's personal statement in the *Synanon Issue* of the *Terminal Island News* further reveals his criminal background and current view of life: "My addiction history goes back to when I was 12 years old (I am close to 50) but up until the time I came to Synanon, 31 months ago, I never knew what it was to be "clean" on the streets. I have done just about everything illegal to obtain money; work was not a part of this life, for I could not support a habit working. I have spent almost 10 years in county jails, the Lewisburg federal penitentiary, and chain-gangs. I can go so far as to say that I had never met a 'clean' dope-fiend until I came to Synanon. . . .

"I have been a resident of Synanon for 31 months. I plan on staying for some time to come. For the first time in my life I like what I am doing—Synanon is growing and I am part of it. There is a group from Synanon attending meetings at Terminal Island every week, for the past 4½ months; I am project director of this group. There are plans in the making to start Synanon meetings on the women's side at Terminal Island— and eventually, men and women together. I am sure with the cooperation we have been getting this plan will come about in the near future."—JAMES (GREEK) GEORGELAS.

was a "young punk," who could give him no trouble. "I've met kids like this all my life—in and out of the joint."

According to Frankie, "I hated this '. . .' for no good reason. I used to sometimes sit and plan ways to kill him." When Frankie wanted to fight Jimmy over a disagreement about work (no fighting allowed at Synanon) Jimmy laughed and told him if he wanted to fight he would be thrown out of Synanon.

The usual prison situation was reversed and confusing to Frankie. In the "joint" (prison) if Frankie got in trouble confinement became increasingly severe with the "hole" (solitary confinement) as an end point. At the Bellevue Hospital psychiatric ward where Frankie had also "done time" it was a straight-jacket. What made Frankie remain, even behave in order to stay at Synanon with its open door?

The fact that Frankie was exported from New York to Los Angeles was a significant force initially in keeping him at Synanon, as he stated it: "At times I felt like splitting [leaving], then I thought it will be hard to make it back to New York. I didn't know Los Angeles and I was afraid to make it out there —cause I didn't know the people. Synanon was better than anything else I could do—at the time."

Also, Synanon House was on the beach. The meals were good. In the evening many ex-addict top musicians would play cool jazz.[8] Also there were, according to Frankie, "broads to dance with and get to know." But highly important in this antiaddiction, antidelinquency society there were others who understood him, had made the same "scenes" and intuitively knew his problems and how to handle him. He respected people he could not con. He belonged and was now part of a "family" he could accept.

At Synanon Frankie could also make a "rep" without getting punished or locked up. In prison, the highest he could achieve in terms of the values of "his people" was to become "King" of the sociopathic inmate system, acquire a "stash" of cigarettes, obtain some unsatisfactory homosexual favors, and land in the "hole." In the "inmate system" of Synanon he could achieve any role he was "big enough of a man" to acquire and this carried the highest approval of his fellows. He could actually become a *director* in this organization—which was now in the national spotlight.[9] Articles on Synanon had been published in national magazines like *Time, Life,* and *Nation,* and were coming out daily in the press. For the first time in his life, Frankie was receiving status for being clean and nondelinquent.

Of course, when he first arrived at Synanon, Frankie attempted to gain a

---

[8]The Synanon Band recently produced a widely acclaimed professional record album, appropriately called: *Sounds of Synanon.*

[9]There are currently 8 directors of the Synanon Foundation. This is the highest and most respected status level of achievement in the organization.

"rep" by conniving and making deals in accord with his old mode of relating. He was laughed at, ridiculed and given a "hair-cut" (a verbal dressing down) by other "old-time con men" members of the organization. He was accused of "shucking and sliding" (simply not performing adequately). The oldtime Synanists were ferocious about keeping the organization, which had literally saved their lives and given them a new life status, operating smoothly.

Frankie found that "rep" was acquired in this social system (unlike ones he had known) by truth, honesty, and industry. The values of his other life required reversal if he was to gain a "rep" at Synanon. These values were not goals *per se* which someone moralized about in a meaningless vacuum; they were means to the end of acquiring prestige in this tough social system with which he now intensely identified.

In the small *s* synanons, three nights a week Frankie participated in a form of leaderless group psychotherapy. In these synanons the truth was viciously demanded. Any system of rationalizations about past or current experience were brutally demolished by the group. There was an intensive search for self-identity.

In the process the individual attempted to learn what goes on beneath the surface of his thoughts. For Frankie this was the first time in his life he discovered others had some idea about what he was thinking underneath. He had individual group therapy in prison—but there he could "con" the therapist and most important, "I said what I thought they wanted to hear so I could hit the street sooner."

Most important Frankie began to get some comprehension of what others thought in a social situation. The fact of empathy or identifying with the thoughts and feelings of others became a significant reality.

Frankie was at first empathic in his usual pattern of sociopathic self-centered manipulation. However, a new force was introduced into the situation —he began to care about what happened to others at Synanon. This was at first selfish. Synanon was for him a good interesting way of life. He had identified with the system and learned "gut level" that if any Synanon member failed, he too was diminished and failed. In Cressey's words which Frankie learned to quote (since after all Professor Cressey was a friend of his) "When I help another guy, it helps me personally."

In the status system, Frankie's rise to the role of coordinator was not quick nor easy. He moved from the "dishpan" to serving food at the kitchen counter.

After several months he was allowed to work outside on a pickup truck which acquired food and other donations. With two other individuals who worked with him on the truck a group decision was made one day "that one shot wouldn't hurt." One individual knew a "connection" on the route. They went to his home. All they could get were some pills.

When they arrived back at Synanon their slightly "loaded" appearance immediately became apparent to the group ("they spotted us right away") and they were hauled into the main office and viciously (verbally) attacked to tell all ("copout") or get out of the building. A general meeting was called and they were forced to reveal "all" before the entire group.[10] Frankie was back at work on the dishpan that evening.

Such "slips" often come out in the synanon. In a sense, in addition to other forces of growth from the synanon it serves as a form of "first-aid" therapy. If anyone reveals a minor "slip," the personal wound is examined and cleaned up by the group before a serious act of misbehavior occurs. (The synanon situation has some of the characteristics of an underground organization operating during wartime. If any member "falls," it may entail the destruction of the entire organization.)

The norms of synanon society are the reverse of the criminal code. On one occasion Frankie, with two other members of Synanon, went for a walk into town. One individual suggested buying a bottle of wine. (No drinking is permitted.) The other two (including Frankie) smashed the idea. However, no one revealed the incident until 2 days later it came up in a synanon. The group jumped hardest on Frankie and the other individual who did not reveal the potential "slip," rather than on the transgressor who had suggested the wine. Frankie and the other "witness" were expected to report such "slips" immediately, since the group's life depended on keeping each other "straight." For the first time in his life Frankie was censured for *"not squealing."* The maxim "thou shalt not squeal" basic to the existence of the usual underworld criminal culture was reversed at Synanon and just as ferociously sanctioned. An individual could get "kicked out" of Synanon for *not* being a "stoolie."

The rule of no physical violence was at first extremely difficult for Frankie to grasp and believe. Since his usual response to a difficult situation would be to leap fists-first past verbal means of communication into assault. As a result of the synanons and other new patterns of interaction, Frankie's social ability for communication increasingly minimized his assaultive impulse. Although at first he was controlled from commiting violence by the fear of ostracism, he later no longer had a need to use violence since he now had some ability to interact effectively. He could express himself with a new form of communication on a nonviolent, verbal level.

On occasion Frankie would regress and have the motivation for assault— but the system had taken hold. In one synanon session I heard him say, "I was

[10]This process known as a "fireplace" may be called at anytime, day or night. The "transgressor" is placed at the fireplace in the main living room in front of all other residents. They are ridiculed into an open-honest revelation of their "offense." The group may then decide to evict or give the individual another chance.

so . . . . mad yesterday, I wished I was back at Rikers [prison]. I really wanted to hit that bastard Jimmy in the mouth."

Frankie had a sketchy work record prior to Synanon. Other than gang fights, "pimping," armed robbery, pushing heroin, and some forced work in prison, he seldom acted in any role resembling formal work. His theme had been "work was for squares." He learned how to work at Synanon automatically as a side effect of his desire to rise in the status system. He also learned as a side effect of the work process, the startling fact "that talking to someone in the right way made them do more things than belting them."

Frankie's most recent position involves the overall supervision of Synanon's number two building. Here 12 mothers (ex-addicts) in residence at Synanon live with their children. Frankie supervises a budget, the care and feeding of the establishment and the inevitable daily counseling of his "wards." Although it is not apparent on the surface of his efficient administration, Frankie beneath maintains a state of personal amazement about his new social role in society.

As a consequence of living in the Synanon social system, Frankie developed an increasing residual of social learning and ability. His destructive pattern of relating to others withered away because it was no longer functional for him within this new way of life. Synanon developed his empathic ability, produced an attachment to different, more socially acceptable values, and reconnected him adequately to the larger society within which Synanon functioned as a valid organization.

PRINCIPAL FORCES AT WORK IN THE SYNANON SOCIETY

Involvement

Initially, Synanon society is able to involve and control the offender. This is accomplished through providing an interesting social setting comprised of associates who understand him and will not be out-maneuvered by his manipulative behavior.

An Achievable Status System

Within the context of this system he can (perhaps, for the first time) see a realistic possibility for legitimate achievement and prestige. Synanon provides a rational and attainable opportunity structure for the success-oriented individual. He is no longer restricted to inmate status since there is no inmate-staff division. All residents are staff.

New Social Role

Synanon creates a new social role which can be temporarily or indefinitely occupied in the process of social growth and development. (Some residents have made the decision to make Synanon their life's work.) This new role is a legitimate one supported by the ex-offender's own community as well as the inclusive society. Within the opening of new Synanons and increasing development of projects like the one at Terminal Island, Synanon-trained persons are increasingly in demand. Since the Synanon organization is not a hospital or an institution, there is no compulsion to move out of this satisfying community.

Social Growth

In the process of acquiring legitimate social status in Synanon the offender necessarily, as a side effect, develops the ability to relate, communicate and work with others. The values of truth, honesty, and industry become necessary means to this goal of status achievement. After a sufficient amount of practice and time, the individual socialized in this way in a natural fashion develops the capability of behaving adequately with reference to these values.

Social Control

The control of deviance is a by-product of the individual's status-seeking. Conformity to the norms is necessary in order to achieve. Anomie, the dislocation of goals and means, becomes a minimal condition. The norms are valid and adhered to within this social system since means are available for legitimate goal attainment.

Another form of control is embodied in the threat of ostracism which becomes a binding force. After being initially involved in Synanon, the individual does not at the time feel adequate for participation in the larger society. After a sufficient residue of Synanon social living has been acquired the individual no longer fears banishment; however, at the same time he is then better prepared for life on the outside (if this is his choice). He no longer fears ostracism and may remain voluntarily because he feels Synanon is a valid way of life for him. In Synanon he has learned and acquired a gratifying social role which enables him as a "coordinator" or a "director" to help others who can benefit from Synanon treatment.

Other forms of immediate social control include ridicule ("hair-cuts," the "fireplace") and the synanon sessions. The individual is required to tell the truth in the synanon. This also regulates his behavior. Real life transgressions are often prevented by the knowledge that the individual's deviance will auto-matically, rapidly, and necessarily be brought to the attention of his community within the synanon session. He is living within a community where others know about and, most important, are concerned with his behavior.

Empathy and Self-Identity

The constant self-assessment required in his daily life and in the synanon sessions fosters the consolidation of self-identity and empathy. His self-estimation is under constant assessment and attack by relevant others, who become sensitive to and concerned about him. The process provides the oppor-tunity for the individual almost literally "to see himself as others do." He is also compelled as part of this process to develop the ability to identify with and understand others. A side consequence is the development of self-growth, social awareness, the ability to communicate and empathic effectiveness. When these socialization processes are at work and take hold the youth becomes reconnected with the legitimate society and no longer finds it necessary to use drugs or assume a deviant role.

SYNANON'S FUTURE

From its unusual beginnings the Synanon Foundation has emerged as a highly efficient organization. The Foundation has federal tax exempt status and is a corporate entity in the State of California. The State Legislature passed and the Governor signed into law The Petris Bill on June 15, 1961, officially sanctioning Synanon as a "Place" for rehabilitating drug addicts.[11]

[11]The Petris Bill especially passed for Synanon is here presented in full:
Assembly Bill No. 2626 (State of California). An act to amend Section 11391 of the Health and Safety Code, relating to narcotic addiction.
The people of the State of California do enact as follows:
Section 1. Section 11391 of the Health and Safety Code is amended to read:
11391. No person shall treat an addict for addiction except in one of the following:
(a) An institution approved by the Board of Medical Examiners, and where the patient is at all times kept under restraint and control.
(b) A city or county jail.
(c) A state prison.
(d) A state narcotic hospital.
(e) A state hospital.
(f) A county hospital.
This section does not apply during emergency treatment or where the patient's addic-tion is complicated by the presence of incurable disease, serious accident, or injury, or the infirmities of old age.
Neither this section nor any other provision of this division shall be construed to

Synanon, over the past year, as a partial consequence of donations and the earning power of its residents, has rented four buildings with a total rental of over $1500 a month. Although its budgeting is tight, comparable to other nonprofit organizations, it has met all of its financial obligations as a result of community support. The organization over the past year has sustained approximately 85 residents in food and clothing, and has entertained approximately 19,000 guests (mostly professional visitors). In addition to the Terminal Island project a Synanon educational and addiction-prevention program has involved most of the 100 Synanon members in over 400 speaking engagements delivered to business, professional, religious, youth, and college and university groups. One evening a week about 40 nonaddicts from all segments of society participate in the so-called "Square Synanons." Here the variety of human problems are examined through utilization of the Synanon method involving Synanon residents mixed with "squares." This interaction and cross-fertilization of ideas and insights appear to be of benefit to all.

As a social science research center Synanon is unique. In this open-door environment run by ex-offenders themselves, persons with long addiction and criminal background freely provide important data unavailable in the usual custodial setting. Synanon thus enables the systematic gathering of much useful information about crime, addiction, and the solution of these problems.

The Synanon approach which has emerged under the creative and capable leadership of Dederich and his uniquely trained staff of directors as an effective anticriminal and antiaddiction society, also involves an organization of distinguished citizens from all walks of life called "S.O.S." or Sponsors of Synanon. This supportive organization has a national membership of over 600 persons who donate money, goods, and services. They are currently launching a building program for an ideal Synanon community.

The organization is naturally committed to expansion. Synanon-trained personnel of the type carrying out the program at Terminal Island will no doubt shortly be utilized as the core staff for Synanon Houses planned for other

prohibit the maintenance of a place [Synanon] in which persons seeking to recover from narcotic addiction reside and endeavor to aid one another and receive aid from others in recovering from such addiction, nor does this section or such division prohibit such aid, provided that no person is treated for addiction in such place [Synanon] by means of administering, furnishing, or prescribing of narcotics. The preceding sentence is declaratory of pre-existing law. Every such place [Synanon] shall register with and be approved by the Board of Medical Examiners. The board may inspect such places [Synanons] at reasonable times and, if it concludes that the conditions necessary for approval no longer exist, it may withdraw approval. Every person admitted to such a place [Synanon] shall register with the police department of the city in which it is located or, if it is outside of the city limits, with the sheriff's office. The place [Synanon] shall maintain its own register of all residents. It shall require all its residents to register with said police department or sheriff's office and, upon termination of the residence of any person in said place [Synanon], it shall report the name of the person terminating residence to said police department or sheriff's office.

communities. Each new establishment has the potential for "cleaning-up" another hundred offenders.

As viewed by its founder, Charles Dederich, Synanon is still in its infancy. The fact of 100 individuals with long addiction and criminal histories currently clean attests to its effectiveness. However, Synanon, as a social movement or community way of life, appears to have possibilities beyond exclusive application to the addiction problem. As Middleton commented at the outset: "It is conceivable to me as an ex-inmate myself that someday Synanon could become an established part of the prison program throughout the United States."

8

HOMOSEXUALITY AND FAMILY DYNAMICS

Daniel G. Brown

In considering the subject of sexual development and behavior, it is necessary to differentiate three different, independently varying components. These are: (1) the *biological-constitutional* component, which refers to hereditary, congenital, and maturational factors; (2) the *sex role* component, which pertains to the individual's identification with one sex or the other, and (3) the *genital* component which refers to the source, aim, and direction of sexual stimulation, desire, activity, and satisfaction.

Disturbances in any one of these areas have occasioned confusion in the mind of the public, at least. Physical disturbances, such as hermaphroditism, are not evidence of abnormality in other components. Disturbance in the sex role is particularly variable in degree, ranging from very mild forms to such practices as transvestitism. It does not necessarily involve inverted sex relations. On the other hand, individuals who seek sexual activity with persons of the same sex as themselves may or may not display evidence of abnormality in the other two realms. The situation is further confused by the fact that these individuals are sometimes active sexually with both sexes.

The term homosexuality is properly applied only to the specific deviation from the norm in the third component, in which sexual desire and activity is directed toward the same sex.

There is a need for clarification in the area of disturbances in sexual development, but this study is concerned only with the relationship of male homosexuality (as defined above) to certain parent-child experiences and particular family dynamics.

Research studies (7, 8) indicate there are several million individuals in the

Reprinted with the permission of the *Bulletin of the Menninger Clinic, Vol. 27,* 227–232, copyright 1963 by The Menninger Foundation, and Dr. Brown.

Paper presented at the Annual Air Force Clinical Psychology Meeting, USAF School of Aerospace Medicine, Brooks AFB, Texas, January 10, 1963.

United States who are predominately or exclusively homosexual and that among these millions, there are two or three times more males than females. The widespread occurrence of homosexuality has prompted the reference to homosexuals as those individuals within our society who do not biologically reproduce themselves, yet whose number seems to be steadily increasing. Why is this so? And, parenthetically, the question might be raised, why has so little been done by society (and the social, psychological, and medical sciences) to understand, to correct, to prevent, to cope with this behavioral abnormality? While millions have been spent on research for the control and prevention of various ailments of mankind, very little has been spent on psychological disturbances such as homosexuality, although certainly the unhappiness and misery that are often found in such individuals and their families may be as real and painful as other human afflictions.

There are a number of factors that occur in childhood which appear to be related to the development of homosexuality in adults. Such conditions as prolonged segregation of the sexes; specific, intensely exciting, and gratifying homosexual experiences in childhood; seduction by adult homosexuals; threatening and painful experiences in connection with sex play or relationships with the opposite sex; these and related factors in childhood and adolescence are correlated with the occurrence of homosexuality in adulthood. The focus of the present discussion, however, is on the child's early experiences and relationships with parental figures, specifically with the opposite-sex parent compared to the same-sex parent in the etiology of male homosexuality.

There is now sufficient evidence to warrant the following general conclusion: male children who become predominantly or exclusively homosexual in adulthood often have childhoods in which there was an excessively close and abnormally strong mother-son relationship. Typically, this relationship involved exaggerated amounts of fondling, caressing, and petting by the mother who, at the same time, was dominating and overcontrolling her son. Such activities as dressing and undressing, bathing, and sleeping with the boy along with frequent and overintense "love" attachments long after infancy appear to provide the kind of psychological climate that results in a developmental predisposition for the boy later becoming homosexually rather than heterosexually adjusted. In simple learning terms, such a relationship early becomes and remains a source of fear arousal and avoidance conditioning. With the incest barrier in human society, the boy is conditioned against the female figure as a sexual love object because of the prolonged attachment and *excessive* emotional-physical contacts with the mother.* This psychologically unhealthy attachment

---

*This underlying dynamic factor probably explains in part why the typical adult male homosexual finds the heterosexual relationship revolting and even frightening. To him there is nothing sexually attractive or exciting about the female figure; he is impotent as far as women are concerned.

seems to be instigated by the mother who, consciously or unconsciously, handles the boy in an erotic and often seductive manner. In addition, the family constellation usually involves a father who is, in one way or another, a predominantly negative figure as far as the son is concerned. Such a father either is passive, weak, and ineffective as a member of the family and in relation to the son, or else is abusive, hostile, rejecting, or indifferent to the son. There is consequently an absence of emotional closeness and attachment between the male child and the father. It is this family pattern that sets the stage for the development of homosexuality in males.

How valid and well substantiated is the above formulation? What evidence is there for it? Before briefly reviewing the major clinical and research investigations, mention might be made of observations of the author during the past eight years of active duty in the Air Force. During this period there was the opportunity to interview and test approximately 40 male airmen in whom predominant or exclusive homosexuality was the major problem. In more than 30 of these cases, the mother-son and father-son relationships conformed to the family pattern described above. Not one of these airmen had a close, warm, affectionate attachment to his father or a father-substitute in childhood. There may be such cases but they were not among his group.

Some 30 years ago, Terman and Miles (11), on the basis of a careful study of 77 male homosexuals, 17 to 44 years of age, concluded as follows: "If the case history data supplied by these individuals can be accepted as anywhere near the truth, the psychosocial formula for developing homosexuality in boys would seem to run somewhat as follows: 'Too demonstrative affection from an excessively emotional mother—a father who is unsympathetic, autocratic, brutal, much away from home, or deceased; treatment of the child as a girl, coupled with lack of encouragement to associate with boys—overemphasis of neatness, niceness, and spirituality; lack of vigilance against the danger of seduction by older homosexual males.' "

Psychoanalytic theory also has emphasized the mother-son factor in the development of male homosexuality. Freud (5), Schilder (9), Fenichel (4) and other psychoanalytic writers refer to a *very intense* mother fixation in childhood in practically all cases of adult, male homosexuality. In Hamilton's report (6) of his study and evaluation of a number of male homosexuals, invariably one factor stood out in childhood: the presence of an intense mother-son relationship that made it difficult for the boy to accept his own sexual feelings as natural and acceptable. Hamilton refers to the "unmistakable eroticism" and "incestuous aggressiveness" that mothers expressed toward their sons who became homosexual adults; he considers the fear of incest to be the most important factor involved. Bender and Paster (1), in a study of 19 actively homosexual children, found either a grossly deficient or very negative relationship with the same-sex parent, coupled with an overly intimate attachment to the opposite-sex parent. And, in a recent publication by West (12), a number of contemporary investigators are cited who independently have reached the same conclusion concerning the mother-son factor in male homosexuality. In this same publication, West presents his own study in England of 50 homosexual males and 50 matched control (nonhomosexual) males. His findings clearly show that male homosexuals are much more likely to come from a family constellation involving an overintense mother *and* unsatisfactory father relationship. West emphasizes that it is this *combination* of parental relationship that characterized the homosexual group. This suggests clearly that it is not simply the psychologically "smothering mother" but also the psychologically "starving father" that provides the basis for predisposing the male child to homosexuality. Thus, even with a smothering mother, homosexuality probably will not develop provided the father maintains a close, positive relationship with the son.

Finally, the most recent research study of family dynamics and homosexuality is the book by Bieber and collaborators (2). This reference reports in detail the findings of a study of 106 homosexual males and a comparison group of 100 heterosexual males, all of whom had received psychoanalytic therapy. This study represents a comprehensive analysis of the problem and is one of the most significant contributions that has yet appeared. The basic over-all finding is summarized as follows: "The 'classical' homosexual triangular pattern is one where the mother is close-binding-intimate with the son and is dominant and minimizing toward a husband who is a detached father, particularly a hostile-detached one. From our statistical analysis, the chances appear to be high that any son exposed to this parental combination will become homosexual or develop severe homosexual problems." In the clear majority of these cases *the mother* was described as "close-binding-intimate" and seductive; she suppressed normal heterosexual interests and discouraged masculine patterns; she interfered with the father-son relationship by preferring the son to the father, fostering father-son rivalry, and using the son as a romantic substitute for the father; she interfered with the peer relations of the son and discouraged friendships with "regular" boys; and she interfered with the development of the son's independence by overprotection, "babying," etc. Concerning the role of the father, the authors write: "The father played an essential and determining role in the homosexual outcome of his son." "Profound interpersonal disturbance is unremitting in the homosexual father-son relationships. Not one of the fathers (of homosexual sons) . . . could be regarded as reasonably 'normal' parents. . . ." These fathers typically were emotionally detached and hostile, spent little time with their sons, failed to serve as a masculine model, and failed to protect the son from destructive maternal influences.

It is recognized that individuals with this family constellation do not necessarily or invariably become homosexual, *i.e.,* this pattern may be found in the childhood of individuals who do not become adult homosexuals. It might be predicted that many such nonhomosexuals would show other kinds of psychiatric disturbance, immaturity reactions, or character problems. The question then arises: given the psychopathological family dynamics described in this paper, what psychosocial factors differentiate those males who become or do not become adult homosexuals?

More research is necessary, of course, before this question can be answered. One important over-all variable would be the *timing* and *continuity or discontinuity* of the family pattern, *i.e.,* did this pattern exist from the birth of the son, continue through childhood, and into adolescence? For example, it would make a difference if the child were exposed to this configuration before rather than after the second or third or fourth year of life. What would be the effect on a child's psychosexual development of a change in the family structure by the death of a parent or the prolonged or permanent separation of the parents? Also, what would be the effect of the subsequent replacement of one parent by a step-parent? It would seem safe to assume that the particular effect would depend to a significant degree on the *age* of the child at the time he experiences the loss, and the availability of a parental substitute. In other words, the concept of a "critical period" in the child's development and learning is relevant here (10). It is quite conceivable that there is a crucial period in the early years of a child for establishing the basic capacity for heterosexual adjustment. In this connection, evidence indicates that sex role differentiation and identity occur in most children between the ages of one and one-half and three, and that heterosexual stimulation and responsiveness develop between the third and sixth year of life (2, 3).

In summary, then, it would seem that the family pattern involving a combination of a dominating, overly intimate mother *plus* a detached, hostile or weak father is beyond doubt related to the development of male homosexuality. Beginning with the penetrating clinical insights of Freud 50 years ago, the systematic investigation by Terman and Miles some 30 years ago, the independent findings of a number of clinical and research workers, and the recent noteworthy contributions of West and Bieber, there is now strong evidence and considerable agreement as to family dynamics in the development of male homosexuality. It is surprising there has not been greater recognition of this relationship among the various disciplines that are concerned with children. A problem that arises in this connection is how to inform and educate teachers and parents relative to the decisive influence of the family in determining the course and outcome of the child's psychosexual development. There would seem to be no justification for waiting another 25 or 50 years to bring this information to the attention of those who deal with children. And there is no excuse for professional workers in the behavioral sciences to continue avoiding their responsibility to disseminate this knowledge and understanding as widely as possible.

REFERENCES

1. Bender, Lauretta and Paster, Samuel: Homosexual Trends in Children. *Amer. J. Orthopsychiat.* 11:730–743, 1941.

2. Bieber, Irving and others: *Homosexuality.* New York, Basic Books, 1962.

3. Brown, D. G.: Sex-Role Development in a Changing Culture. *Psychol. Bull.* 54:232–242, 1958.

4. Fenichel, Otto: *The Psychoanalytic Theory of Neurosis.* New York, Norton, 1945.

5. Freud, Sigmund: Three Contributions to the Theory of Sex. In *The Basic Writings of Sigmund Freud,* A. A. Brill, ed. New York, Modern Library, 1938.

6. Hamilton, G. V.: Incest and Homosexuality. In *Encyclopaedia Sexualis,* Victor Robinson, ed. New York, Crown, 1936.

7. Kinsey, A. C. and others: *Sexual Behavior in the Human Male.* Philadelphia, Saunders, 1948.

8. ———: *Sexual Behavior in the Human Female.* Philadelphia, Saunders, 1953.

9. Schilder, Paul: On Homosexuality. *Psa. Rev.* 16:377–389, 1929.

10. Scott, J. P.: Critical Periods in Behavioral Development. *Science* 138:949–958, Nov. 30, 1962.

11. Terman, L. M. and Miles, C. C.: *Sex and Personality.* New York, McGraw-Hill, 1936.

12. West, D. J.: Parental Figures in the Genesis of Male Homosexuality. *Int. J. Soc. Psychiat.* 5:85–97, 1959.

PRELIMINARY SOCIALIZATION FOR PSYCHOTHERAPY OF BEHAVIOR-DISORDERED ADOLESCENTS

Robert L. Schwitzgebel

A common problem in treating adolescent delinquents is their failure to participate in traditional psychotherapeutic procedures. Small cash bonuses given contingent on participation in tape-recorded nondirective interviews were shown to be effective in shaping dependable and prompt attendance. Using a variable schedule of reinforcement, extrinsic rewards could be gradually reduced without corresponding decrement in attendance behavior. The rationale for using such a procedure is emphasized.

A patient cannot be treated in absentia. A minimum expectation in traditional psychotherapy is that the patient will come to a specified location at a predetermined time on a fairly regular basis for a person-to-person verbal exchange. And generally it is assumed that voluntary participation is highly desirable, if not essential, for success of the treatment (cf. Hollingshead & Redlich, 1958).

Unfortunately, a substantial number of persons whose behavior often represents some social threat (e.g., psychotics, psychopaths, adolescent delinquents) may be among the least likely to volunteer for therapy. In a follow-up study of 54 adolescents with behavior disorders referred to a psychiatric clinic, Hammar and Holterman (1965) found that 21 would-be patients failed to appear, and 11 more discontinued after the initial contact. Rosen, Bahn, Shellow, and Bower (1965) reported that of an estimated 194,000 adolescents treated in outpatient clinics in the United States in 1962, approximately one-third withdrew from treatment. Similar lack of adequate voluntary attendance is

Reprinted from the *Journal of Consulting and Clinical Psychology,* 33, 1969, 71–77, with the permission of the American Psychological Association and Dr. Schwitzgebel. (Footnotes have been renumbered.)

reflected in employment data cited by Gordon (1965). Of 234,000 under-privileged youths invited by letter to visit an employment counselor, only 42,000 appeared for interviews. Of these, fewer than 13,000 were referred to jobs, and less than 7,000 were hired—some for only a few days. Similar to orthodox psychotherapists, the typical employer expects or demands a high rate of goal behavior (e.g., "After all, I'm running a business"). Failure of the youth to meet this criterion usually results in threats and punishment which may antagonize the youth and cause him to devaluate himself further as a potential employee.

The statistics which have been cited simply confirm a persistent and widely acknowledged difficulty confronting virtually every practitioner who deals with this population. Anna Freud (1958), for example, wrote that adolescents are very difficult to get into treatment because they do not cooperate, they miss appointments, they are unpunctual, they cannot or will not introspect, and their rapidly changing emotional patterns leave little energy available to invest in the analyst. Stieper and Wiener (1965) have claimed that developing motivation in behavior-disordered patients "is probably the single most crucial problem with which therapy must grapple [p. 123]." The purpose of this paper is to summarize briefly a strategy for dealing with adolescent delinquents and certain other groups of prospective patients who are often minimally motivated to participate in psychotherapy.

RATIONALE

The reasons usually given for poor participation involve the adolescent's desire for independence, revolt against authority, a narcissistic belief in his ability to solve his own problems, reluctance to talk about hostile or sexual thoughts, etc. (e.g., Pelpz, 1957). In Aichhorn's classic work, *Wayward Youth* (1955), he argued that one of the chief difficulties in treatment was the fact that a delinquent "does not suffer discomfort from his symptoms [p. 27]" in the way which a neurotic does. Alternately, one might hypothesize that traditional psychotherapeutic procedures simply appear more threatening to some potential patients than others. In this respect, it should be noted that many of the characteristics attributed here to delinquents which tend to make them unsuitable for traditional psychotherapy may be class-linked rather than related to age or pathology. That is, these predispositions characterize a large number of persons, especially in the lower socioeconomic class, who are neither adolescent nor delinquent (cf. Riessman, Cohen, & Pearl, 1964).

Therapy procedures which seemingly require adolescent delinquents (particularly males) to acknowledge feelings of weakness, ignorance, helplessness, or passivity may be extremely aversive. From the adolescent's point of view, accepting help may imply that he is weak or sick or "queer." He is likely to believe that psychotherapists are [strange doctors] who do mysterious things to crazy people. The delinquent knows that he is not like the crazy people he has seen in television movies. To the contrary, he may pride himself on being active, strong, and clever. This image is especially valued in his peer group subculture. In exchange for an adult's promise of something better in the future, it seems to the delinquent that he must sacrifice, in advance, his social identity and his place on the street corner. These may not be much, but they are all he has.

Should the delinquent happen to volunteer or be forced into an initial interview, the experience may be embarrassing and punitive because traditional mental health procedures are not designed to treat patients with his characteristic reactions. For example, he may, having had no other experience, relate to the psychotherapist as he has to (other) medical doctors. He waits for questions, gives brief answers (not always accurate), and waits for the next question or for some specific advice. The therapist, on the other hand, who is often a trainee or resident in the clinic, may rigidly wait for the patient to verbally elaborate on feelings. The ensuing silences and awkward exchanges are likely to confirm the patient's doubts regarding the possibility of getting "real help," and the therapist may become more convinced that psychotherapy is appropriately restricted to individuals who exhibit what Schofield (1964, p. 133) has referred to as the "Yavis" syndrome—persons who are youthful, attractive, verbal, intelligent, and successful.

Unfortunately, the patient's willingness to become involved has often been attributed to factors (e.g., "motivation" or "intelligence") which seem to lie outside the province of treatment. Attendance at psychotherapeutic interviews is not, however, an intrinsic attribute of prospective patients. It is the result of innumerable variables such as physical setting and the nature of verbal and nonverbal communications as well as the patient's predispositions. Cooperation is more practicably viewed not as "something" which the patient *brings to* therapy but as a *product* of therapy.

Since cooperative behavior among delinquents is likely to be minimal and of short duration, the therapist may have only one or two opportunities to strengthen the desired responses. Therefore some relatively simple, direct, but flexible strategies are mandatory. Again, Aichhorn (1955) appropriately noted:

I consider this first moment of our coming together of the utmost importance. It is more than a "feeling out" of the situation; it must have the appearance of certainty and sureness and must be put through as quickly as possible because in most cases it forms the foundation for our later relationship. The adolescent does the same thing when he comes in contact with me. He wants to know right away what kind of person he is dealing with [p. 99].

Passivity on the part of the therapist may be misinterpreted as weakness, lack of concern, or hostile withholding of information. On the other hand, gestures of friendship and attention such as a sincere compliment about clothes or appearance may actually prove threatening. This is particularly true in the case of adolescent delinquents whose personal histories confirm that attention from elders is usually paired with punishment. The occasions on which parents, teachers, or public officials have given attention to our prospective patient *without* some form of punishment may be indeed rare. We can assume that fear and counter-hostility will generalize to the therapy situation unless the therapist's actions are sufficiently unique to force the delinquent to make new discriminations. Thus, one of the primary tasks of the initial interview is to break up stereotyped response patterns with minimal aversiveness to the patient.

STRATEGIES

Despite theoretical differences, a survey of the techniques actually employed during the initial phases of treatment of behavior-disordered adolescents by a number of well-known therapists shows remarkable conformity. Slavson (1956) noted, for example, that in group work, "elements of surprise and novelty were constantly being introduced into the group therapy situation in the form of variations in activity and unexpected refreshments [p. 20]." Aichhorn (1955) reported:

I usually begin with a friendly look or attitude, sometimes I say, 'How do you do?' or I may only shake hands in silence. I say that there is nothing here to be afraid of, that this is neither a police station nor a court. Sometimes I tell a joke by way of introduction [p. 99].

Shmideberg (1949), who will "make a point of shaking hands with some of these patients as often as possible" and accept an invitation to tea, has claimed that her "spontaneous and unprofessional manner helps to break down their depersonalization which is an important defense mechanism of the 'callous' criminal [p. 186]."

Neill (1962) has provided an example of what might be considered positive reinforcement of attendance behavior at his psychoanalytically oriented interviews known as "private lessons":

> With young children, the technique was more spontaneous. I followed the child's lead. Here is a typical first P.L. with a six-year-old girl named Margaret. She comes into my room and says, 'I want a P.L.' 'Righto,' I say.
> She sits down in an easy chair.
> 'What is a P.L.?' she asks.
> 'It isn't anything to eat,' I say, 'but somewhere in this pocket I have a caramel. Ah, here it is.' And I give her the sweet.
> 'Why do you want a P.L.?' I ask.
> 'Evelyn has one, and I want one too.'
> 'Good. You begin it. What do you want to talk about?' [p. 42]

Eissler (1949) wrote, "It is a general rule of therapy of the delinquent never to act the way he expects, but unceasingly to introduce new and unforeseen elements in order to keep alive his interest in the therapeutic situation [p. 19]." Specifically, he recommends the use of money, although he cautions that the situation "is wrought with danger and therefore requires special skill and tact."

Gradually, as certain commonalities emerge, successful treatment should become less a matter of "special skill" and more a matter of definable technique. As a rather simple demonstration of a way in which dependable attendance at psychotherapeutic sessions could be obtained, a program of instrumental conditioning was instituted among adolescent delinquents by the present writer. No referral procedure was involved. Prospective Ss were contacted randomly in poolhalls, amusement centers, etc. Inasmuch as details of the experimental results have been reported elsewhere (Schwitzgebel, 1967), this report will emphasize initial socialization procedures which have, over a period of years, become sufficiently systematized and successful to eliminate the problem of obtaining an adequate number of nonincarcerated delinquents for research and clinical training purposes.

METHOD AND RESULTS

Specification or Goal Behavior

The terminal or goal behavior in the present demonstration was dependent upon prompt arrival at a clinic office for tape-recorded interviews.

Estimation of Goal Behavior Base Rate

The Ss were selected from a population with a low probability of dependable attendance at a clinic. Twenty-one male adolescent offenders, ranging in age from 12 to 21 years and averaging 15 months of probation, were contacted directly on street corners or in amusement centers by Es and ask to participate in tape-recorded interviews. It was explained that S's task would be to express his opinion and feelings about parents, teachers, policemen, schools, reformatories, etc.; they would be paid $1.00 an hour, but one of the "qualifications" for the job was a court record. (Records were verified later.)

Eight members of the experimental group had histories of active refusal to participate in psychiatric treatment, and seven Ss had been incarcerated an average of 18 months. The base rate for attendance among Ss for the first four interviews showed a group mean of 38 minutes late. (Failure to arrive for the scheduled appointment was scored as 60 minutes; nine out of 21 Ss failed to appear for the first interview, and approximately 50% of those who did arrive were late.) Most Ss who missed an interview were able to be contacted a few days later at the original meeting place.

Selection of Reinforcing Conseqences

Eissler (1949) has claimed that "usually no successful therapy of a delinquent is possible without his obtaining money from his analyst during that introductory phase of treatment when all possibilities must be mobilized to make the analyst a valuable person in the delinquent's eyes [p. 20]." Money is not only a readily exchanged generalized reinforcer for most delinquents, but it frequently serves to "protect" the prospective patient from criticism by the peer group. Almost any activity is approved in the delinquent subculture if the participant can "make a fast buck"—this includes visits to a psychotherapist. Other tangible "face-saving" consequences or valued activities will sometimes suffice. If money is used in the initial phase, it can be gradually replaced by more personalized and idiosyncratic reinforcers. These usually prove to be more effective and are well-received by the patient.

Premack (1963, 1965) has suggested that any activity which has a higher probability of occurring can be used as a reinforcer for a response of lesser probability. Thus, if at a given time the independent response rates in a "free choice" situation for an adolescent would show the following rank order: watching a movie (M) > playing pool (P) > eating candy (C) > reading a comic book (B), then P could reinforce C and B but not M. If true, this principle suggests that literally hundreds of potential reinforcers are available for use by the therapist. An obvious difficulty arises, however, in estimating the respective probabilities of various activities unless one has knowledge of previous deprivations. In work with retarded children, Addison and Homme (1966) have used what they term a "behavior menu." The "menu" consists of a booklet of pictures and descriptions of brief activities (e.g., a child being pushed down the hallway on a chair by E) which the child may choose when he becomes eligible for reinforcement. Another simple way of determining what tangible consequences might serve as reinforcers is to take a leisurely walk through a department store with the patient and to note various items which receive favorable comment.

In addition to administrative, ethical, and financial considerations in selecting reinforcers, it is generally held that the reinforcing activity should not be directly incompatible with the goal behavior. For example, dismissing a child from school as a reinforcing consequence for regular attendance at school, even though such might have a relatively high probability at a given moment, is not considered advisable. Dismissal from school may be reinforcing (not punishing) for truants; detention is also likely to be ineffective since it is a direct pairing of a noxious event with presence at school. Counter-conditioning is probably the procedure of choice.[1]

Arranging Contingencies

In our demonstration project, the basic wage of $1.00 an hour was supplemented by positive consequences contingent on dependable and prompt attendance. The first problem, of course, is just to get the delinquent into the office under what he views as favorable conditions. The following conversation is a sample street-corner contact. In this particular instance, two Es saw five prospective Ss standing in a row in front of a dime store. It was mid-winter. The boys were huddled in their jackets; there was no conversation.

$E:$ (approaching Ss) We're looking for some real people.
$S1:$ That's us!

[1]An unpublished study by Schwitzgebel, Faltico, and Feeney (1967) selected 10 junior high school students from an underprivileged urban area who had never attended all 5 days of school in a given week for a period of 2 years. Home visits and small gifts contingent on gradual improvement of attendance showed significant results over a 6-week period. Due to the ending of the school year, no data were obtained regarding the maintenance of such behavior following termination of reinforcement. It might be noted, however, that in contrast to school attendance officers, who typically apply aversive sanctions following undesired behavior, the experimental procedure produced at least temporary gain. (One parent of Spanish-American descent commented to a graduate assistant that he was the first white person who had come to their house not to collect the rent or "tell us we done something wrong.")

S2: See, look we move! (Waves arms; all laugh.)

E: Hey, you really are! (Exaggeratedly imitates arm waving, more laughing.)

We're from college and trying to find out what kids think about cops and teachers and school and stuff like that. Instead of reading a bunch of books, we decided just to go out and ask the kids themselves. We usually pay $1 an hour or a little more for kids to talk into a tape recorder. . . . We'll pay you a dollar if you want to come with us to some restaurant around here; you can get some good food too. You don't have to say anything you don't want to—no names or places or stuff likè that. We're straight, and we're not cops.

S3: There's a pizza place down there (pointing).

S2: You mean we get a buck and mooch some free food?

E: Ya.

S2: (Offering E some peanuts from a small crumpled bag) Want some of these?

E: No thanks.

S4: I can tell you that the cops in (names a town) are a lot worse than those in (names another nearby town).

E: We want kids who know what they're talking about—not just a bunch of bull. You've got to have a record or know what you're talking about.

S2: Ha! I'm eligible all right! (Laughs) Here's my probation card. (Pulls out a partly torn probation card from his pocket and hands it to the E. E reads some of the rules aloud, such as "not keeping bad company"; group laughs.)

E: Anybody else got a record to qualify for the restaurant? (Several boys point to a member of the group who reluctantly admits he does. Soon the Es and two boys go off to the pizza parlor. The E apologizes to the remaining three boys without records for not being able to take them along. Once the group gets to the restaurant, the boys ask if it would be all right just to order a coke and receive cash in place of food. The E agrees. Approximately 20 minutes is spent in the restaurant talking in a general way about police. The boys are then taken to the project office, play briefly with the tape recorder, are given a small cash bonus, and an appointment for another meeting is scheduled for the same time the following day.)

Obviously the delinquents are suspicious. They typically speculate that E is a gangster, policeman, homosexual, escaped mental patient, or—as one of them put it later—"just some new kind of nut." The task of E is not to make guesses regarding the cognitions of the prospective patients, but to establish environmental conditions in which desired behavior will be prompted and reinforced. This is not excessively difficult. Delinquents often stand in collective boredom waiting for something to happen. The offer of a little free food, adventure, and money under a situation in which *S*s outnumber *E*s in a safe public place has resulted in acceptance by an estimated 70% of eligible adolescents. It might be noted that food is used in this situation not only as a generalized reinforcer contingent on cooperative behavior but also as an unconditioned stimulus incompatible with anxiety (cf. desensitization procedures of Wolpe & Lazarus, 1966).

One group of nine *S*s was then selected to receive reinforcers contingent on attendance, while a matched group of *S*s served as controls by receiving bonuses contingent on an unrelated behavior. The *S*s did not know when they would become eligible for a reinforcement or the nature of the reinforcement (i.e., a variable interval-variable ratio schedule).

In difficult cases when the patient does not have the necessary repertoire of social skills, it may be necessary to use a shaping procedure. In another study (Schwitzgebel, 1964), two boys were met at successively closer geographical locations to the office. The *E* arranged to meet the boys on the first two occasions at a downtown amusement center, the next meeting outside a subway station near the amusement center, then inside the subway station *after* the toll gate, eventually outside the subway station near the office, and finally at the office. Arrival at the designated location was casually rewarded with a cigarette or candy bar or perhaps money (in the form of a token put into the toll gate for *S*). The shaping required approximately six to eight meetings over a period of 2 weeks.

Recording Dependent Variable(s)

Both demonstration project groups improved in promptness and dependability of attendance over the first 20 sessions; however, the contingent-reinforcement group had a discrepancy of 11.2 minutes between appointment time and arrival time, while the noncontingent-reinforcement group showed a 15.6 minute discrepancy (Fisher test, $p < .025$). Since the noncontingent-reinforcement group received bonuses for other socially desirable behavior (e.g., putting coke bottles away at the end of the interview), generalization effects possibly obscured differences which might have occurred if more orthodox procedures had been used. Most *S*s came to look upon the interviews as an interesting and challenging game; anticipatory approach behaviors became stabilized at a fairly high rate. Skinner (1953) and others have pointed out that gambling establishments use variable schedules of reinforcement. On one occasion, we noticed an *S* standing outside the office door, waiting for the chimes of a nearby church to ring, so that he could enter just at the appointed moment. Using the VI-VR schedule, nonverbal consequences could be faded out between the fifteenth and twenty-fifth session without noticeable decrement in promptness of attendance.

DISCUSSION

The strategy outlined here for introducing delinquents to psychotherapy is by no means entirely novel. Indeed, the implicit use of reinforcement techniques by therapists of widely divergent orientations has important implications since it suggests that an empirically based technology may begin to be established. In this way, the potential replicability of clinical procedures should be improved, and, at the same time, alternative methods should become more obvious. For example, Redl and Wineman (1952), in a chapter entitled "Techniques for the antiseptic manipulation of surface behavior," note the ineffectiveness of making promises to behavior-disordered children and recommend that a group leader give "gratification grants without strings attached [p. 229]." They asert further that to tie these gratification grants to a condition would be "like promising a child cough medicine provided he goes without coughing for a day." That is, they recommend the use of noncontingent consequences since they believe, apparently, that it is impossible to set appropriate criteria for future performance. What is not explicitly considered by Redl and Wineman, however, is making such grants contingent on modest *past* improvements of behavior (i.e., shaping).

Occasionally, clinicians will agree that "paying delinquents" is a form of bribery or a dishonest maneuver. Again, some ambiguity appears to be involved regarding very basic details of the reinforcement procedure. "Bribery" is usually defined as a promise of payment for a future performance. In instrumental conditioning, consequences follow desired behavior. On the variable schedule used in the study reported here, Ss were explicitly told that while they could depend on the base wage, bonuses were entirely the decision of E. Furthermore, the amount and frequency of reinforcers decreased over time in contrast to bribery situations where the victim usually demands increased payoffs as he becomes aware of the exploitation. Technically speaking, a promise to deliver a specified payoff following a specified performance is considered a "prompt." These may be useful in initiating behavior which is then subsequently reinforced by an operant procedure. Kubie (1958), apparently referring to the technique of prompting, has argued that a therapist may be required occasionally to use a "symbolic bribe."

We might also consider the frequently voiced objection to reinforcement procedures on the grounds that patients will become excessively dependent. This possibility exists, but its actual occurrence would likely be a result of poor therapeutic management. As previously mentioned, in our study, nonverbal consequences for attendance behavior were faded out between their fifteenth and twenty-fifth session. Extinction can be minimized, of course, by using variable schedules and gradually increasing the interval and ratio components.

In addition, other aspects of the therapy situation may take on secondary reinforcing properties, including the therapist himself. Therefore extrinsic consequences are not required. This situation may be particularly common in the case of therapists whom adolescents find "exciting" or "stimulating." Physiologically, one might attempt to measure such attributes by the occurrence in the patient of the "orienting reflex" (peripheral vasoconstriction, cephalic dilation, galvanic skin response, alpha desynchronization; see Sokolov, 1963) which seems to be both a prerequisite for learning and an intrinsically reinforcing event. The charismatic and colorful personalities of well-known therapists who work with behavior-disordered patients (cf. Federn, 1962; Josselyn, 1957; Levenson, 1961) might be analyzed in terms of their ability to elicit orienting responses from patients who typically have a high threshold for arousal. One might even speculate further that the percentage of orienting and defensive reflexes during an initial interview with a given therapist could serve as a prognostic index.

This writer believes that a minimal technology now exists for introducing adolescent delinquents to psychotherapy or other "work" situations. Except for youths who persistently use narcotics, shaping dependable and prompt attendance of prospective patients has become for our experienced staff almost a routine matter. But just as any continuing social relationship tends to move from initial stereotyped patterns to those which are more subtle and unique, the preliminary socialization technique suggested here neither encompasses nor excludes the complexities and excitement of therapeutic interaction. It, at best, increases the probability that a continuing dialogue will occur.

REFERENCES

Addison, R. M., & Homme, L. E. The reinforcing event (RE) menu. *National Society for Programmed Instruction Journal,* 1966, 5, 8–9.

Aichhorn, A. *Wayward youth.* New York: Viking Press, 1935. (Reprinted New York: Meridian Books, 1955.)

Eissler, K. R. *Searchlights on delinquency.* New York: International Universities Press, 1949.

Federn, E. The therapeutic personality as illustrated by Paul Federn and August

Aichhorn. *The Psychiatric Quarterly* (New York State Department of Mental Hygiene, Utica), 1962, 1–15.

Freud, A. Adolescence. *The Psychoanalytic Study of the child,* 1958, 13, 255–277.

Gordon, J. E. Project Cause, the federal anti-poverty program, and some implications of subprofessional training. *American Psychologist,* 1965, 20, 334–342.

Hammar, S. L., & Holterman, V. L. Referring adolescents for psychotherapy. *Clinical Pediatrics,* 1965, 4, 462–467.

Hollingshead, A. B., & Redlich, F. C. *Social class and mental illness.* New York: Wiley, 1958.

Josselyn, I. M. Psychotherapy of adolescents at the level of private practice. In B. B. Balser (Ed.), *Psychotherapy of the adolescent.* New York: International Universities Press, 1957.

Kubie, L. S. *Neurotic distortion of the creative process.* Lawrence, Kansas: University of Kansas Press, 1958.

Levenson, E. A. Jam tomorrow—jam yesterday. *Etc.,* 1961, 18, 167–178.

Neill, A. S. *Summerhill: A radical approach to child rearing.* London: Victor Gollancz, 1962.

Pelpz, W. L. Psychotherapy of adolescents in private practice. In B. H. Balser (Ed.), *Psychotherapy of the adolescent.* New York: International Universities Press, 1957.

Premack, D. Rate differential reinforcement in monkey manipulation. *Journal of the Experimental Analysis of Behavior,* 1963, 6, 81–89.

Premack, D. Reinforcement theory. *Nebraska Symposium on Motivation,* 1965, 13, 123–180.

Redl, S., & Wineman, D. *Controls from within.* Glencoe, Ill.: The Free Press, 1952.

Riessman, F., Cohen, J., & Pearl, A. (Eds.) *Mental health of the poor.* New York: The Free Press of Glencoe, 1964.

Rosen, B., Bahn, A. K., Shellow, R., & Bower, E. M. Adolescent patients served in outpatient psychiatric clinics. *American Journal of Public Health,* 1965, 55, 1563–1577.

Schmideberg, M. The analytic treatment of major criminals: Therapeutic results and technical problems. In K. R. Eissler (Ed.), *Searchlights on delinquency.* New York: International Universities Press, 1949.

Schofield, W. *Psychotherapy: The purchase of friendship.* Englewood Cliffs, New Jersey: Prentice-Hall, 1964.

Schwitzgebel, R. K. *Street corner research: An experimental approach to the juvenile delinquent.* Cambridge, Mass.: Harvard University Press, 1964.

Schwitzgebel, R. L. Short-term operant conditioning of adolescent offenders on socially relevant variables. *Journal of Abnormal Psychology,* 1967, 72, 134–142.

Schwitzgebel, R. L., Faltico, G., & Feeney, S. Instrumental conditioning of school attendance. Unpublished manuscript, Department of Psychology, University of California, Los Angeles, 1967.

Skinner, B. F. *Science and human behavior.* New York: Macmillan, 1953.

Slavson, S. R. *The fields of group psychotherapy.* New York: International Universities Press, 1956.

Sokolov, E. N. *Perception and the conditioned reflex.* New York: Macmillan, 1963.

Stieper, D. R., & Wiener, D. N. *Dimensions of psychotherapy: An experimental and clinical approach.* Chicago: Adline, 1965.

Wolpe, J., & Lazarus, A. A. *Behavior therapy techniques.* New York: Pergamon Press, 1966.

DISCUSSION

The diversity of problems subsumed under the heading Character Disorders is reflected in the articles included in this section. Jellinek's paper represents a major contribution to the refinement of our classification of the subtypes and antecedents of alcoholism. Such empirical research into the correlates and patterns of alcoholic behavior serves both to enhance our understanding of the process of alcohol addiction and generate additional research hypotheses. Brown's review of clinical and research literature on the family background of male homosexuals both illustrates the value of clinical observation in generating research hypotheses and enhances our understanding of the environmental factors which result in homosexuality. Perhaps the derivation of a more precise and refined system for the classification of the various patterns of homosexual behavior, such as Jellinek has derived for alcoholics, will enable us to further specify the relative importance of precipitating conditions within the family.

Despite the progress made in our ability to classify and delineate the conditions which result in the character disorders, these behaviors by and large remain refractory to traditional forms of therapeutic intervention. Thus, the articles by Schwitzgebel and Yablonsky assume considerable importance, in that they describe highly innovative and successful approaches to the modification of previously "unreachable" patterns of abnormal behavior. Schwitzgebel's use of the principles of instrumental conditioning to shape the behaviors and attitudes necessary to introduce delinquents to counseling represents a refreshing pragmatism. Yablonsky's description of the highly effective total environmental approach in the Synanon group represents one of the few methods which has been successful in modifying the complex behavioral problem of drug addiction. Clearly, Synanon represents only the beginning of a great number of nontraditional applications of psychological principles to chronic behavioral problems, which have proven refractory to traditional medically oriented therapies.

PSYCHOSOMATIC DISORDERS

The disorders to be considered in this section are differentiated from other patterns of abnormal behavior in that they are classified on the basis of changes in the structure and function of internal organ systems, rather than overt motor behavior. Thus, psychosomatic disorders are thought to result from prolonged inappropriate firing of the automatic nervous system which regulates the activity of the internal visceral organs, rather than activity of skeletal nervous system which controls motor behavior. During the early 1930s several psychoanalytic theorists reported observing consistent underlying emotional patterns which characterized individuals suffering from various organic conditions. This clinical finding eventually resulted in the classification of psychosomatic disorders as patterns of abnormal behavior. The general formula arrived at by the psychoanalysts is that whenever the expression of certain impulses and tensions is inhibited, a chronic state of emotional arousal develops, which in turn exerts a continued influence upon selected visceral functions and ultimately results in permanent physical symptoms. This is not to say that every individual suffering from psychosomatic disorders is emotionally disturbed, but rather that at least some proportion of these individuals may have developed the symptom as a result of inhibiting the discharge of emotional tensions, rather than some constitutional weakness or disease process. As can be seen in the article which follows, this formulation has generated a great deal of research activity, the results of which have necessitated considerable refinement and revision of the original psychoanalytic hypotheses.

10

PSYCHOSOMATIC DISEASES

Richard A. Sternbach

. . . To make an analogy, psychophysiology is to the psychosomatic diseases what physiology is to pathology. That is, both psychophysiology and psychosomatic disorders are special ways of thinking about general physiology and general pathology. What is special is that the roles of ideas and feelings are placed in some relationship to physiological function and dysfunction.

Now we must hasten to point out that there are several kinds of models for thinking about the psychosomatic diseases, and in addition there are a great many definitions of the term. There has also been a good deal of argument about which diseases are psychosomatic, and the extent to which any particular disease is psychosomatic. Without presenting all the arguments or evidence concerning these issues, let us at least clarify what we mean by the term and how we conceptualize the problems involved.

The terms "psychosomatic disease" and "psychosomatic medicine" were originally coined to impress on the users that mind (psyche) and body (soma) are interacting processes, not separate entities. This was necessary because, as philosophers continually point out, ever since Descartes we have tended to be dualistic in our thinking about human functions—they are *either* mental *or* physical. The word "psychosomatic" should remind us that all functioning and all diseases are both mental and physical, because both mental and physiological processes are going on continuously. Unfortunately, many persons persist in making the dualistic dichotomy even while acknowledging mental-physical interactions. "Sure, emotions are involved in ulcers, but do they *cause* the ulcers?" Although most workers in this field no longer ask such questions (partly because they are not answerable, and partly because they beg the question), the dualistic approach is so built into our way of thinking and into our

Reprinted from *Principles of Psychophysiology,* 1966, pp. 139–157, with the permission of Academic Press, Inc., and Dr. Sternbach. (Figures have been renumbered.)

language that it is difficult to avoid. Even the most ardent monist is likely at times to lapse into speculating about how certain fantasies *result* in allergic reactions, or what role is played by the emotions in *causing* tuberculosis. It is very difficult to maintain a holistic-organismic approach. But, it is also very difficult to take seriously those who maintain that all feelings are only by-products (epiphenomena) of physiological events, or that the opposite is true—all physiological responses are only the results of our feelings. Both extremes seem hard to justify.

Although there are emotions involved in all diseases, the attempt to show a cause-and-effect relationship between an emotion and the pathology is very difficult. This is because, when determining cause, it is necessary to show that A is always followed by B before being able to say that A is a cause or part of the cause of B. If B occurs once in a while without A, then A becomes only a sufficient or partly sufficient cause of B, but not a necessary one. Since it is difficult to determine how much emotion preceded the onset of a given disease, let alone to determine which emotion, with what frequency, etc., the extent of emotions as causative factors in pathology is not clear.

However, over the years it has appeared that, in certain illnesses, emotional antecedents were more frequent or striking than in other diseases. These illnesses have come to comprise a list which is identified as psychosomatic. The list is different from writer to writer, and is continually expanding. What makes these "traditionally" psychosomatic diseases different from others is that specific emotions have been noted frequently to occur at some time prior to the onset of symptoms, whereas this is not so clear in the other diseases. In some illnesses, specific emotions have been found to accompany or to follow symptoms (diabetes, tuberculosis), but many are reluctant to call any illness psychosomatic until there is good evidence for emotional participation that is antecedent, and therefore possibly causative.

This is too bad, in a way, because it tends to foster the impression many people (both professional and non-professional) seem to have, that if an illness is psychosomatic, it is therefore "all in the head," and so either imaginary, or a sign of malingering, or due to a defect in character. But it is easy to show that even the most traditional psychosomatic illnesses (such as ulcers) are not like that. An ulcer is not imaginary, it is a real hole in the stomach. And the person who has one is usually quite the opposite of a malingerer. In fact, it is thought by some that ulcer patients are those who (among other things) work too hard without letup, and have, if anything, too much "character."

The point of view we are proposing here is that all illness and all normal functioning is psychosomatic. Walking down the street is psychosomatic and so is falling down and breaking a leg. This is because all responses have both physiological and mental or emotional aspects. If, however, we want to consider certain diseases as having more clear emotional or "psychological" aspects than others, that is all right, provided we remember that at no point can we say with any certainty that an emotion "caused" this psychosomatic disease, or that other diseases do not have their emotional components. The problem lies in the tendency to confuse emotional correlates with causes; not every concomitant of a response can be its cause.

Now with this lengthy and cautionary introduction, let us turn to the main problem. Granted that certain diseases are usually considered psychosomatic, and that they are so considered because of frequently identified emotional antecedents, how can emotions cause or contribute to the cause of tissue pathology? Several explanations have been offered. One class of explanations concerns itself with the adaptive or maladaptive nature of emotions. The reasoning goes something like this.

In the course of evolution, emotions served to mobilize energy in such a way as to insure man's survival. Strong arousal led to fight-or-flight responses which would enable an individual to overcome or flee a threatening situation, and thus he would be more likely to survive and produce offspring than one who could not be so mobilized. Therefore a selection would have taken place in primitive times to create a population of emotional responders, simply because these strong emotions were adaptive. Now, however, such violent physical responses are no longer adaptive in our complex cilivilzation. The individual who is angered by his boss, or frightened by a crowd, cannot strike or flee. Such responses are incompatible with survival in the sense that our society imposes physical restraints on the person who acts that way. Consequently, although the individual may experience the emotions and have the accompanying intense physiological changes, he is unable to discharge the increased energy which has been mobilized by taking appropriate action. Therefore the organic changes persist and result in pathology.

This interpretation obviously combines the views of Darwin and Cannon, and in a sense lays the "blame" for psychosomatic diseases on the mores of a society which does not allow the appropriate expression of once adaptive emotional responses. A similar approach which has a different emphasis is one which considers emotions as maladaptive. Emotions are thought of as vestigial responses which may once have had survival value, but which no longer do so, and the individual who has such fight-or-flight reactions frequently is responding to inadequate stimuli, and thus is responding inappropriately.

Another psychosomatic model emphasizes failures of adaptation, rather than adaptiveness. In this view, a psychosomatic disorder results whenever any physiological response in an emotion is too much or too little. That is, mechanisms of homeostatic control fail to keep the functioning within optimal limits, resulting in excessive responses (as in too much gastric acid) or inadequate ones (as in too little blood supply). This sort of model can apply to all diseases, of course, including those whose major components may be infection or injury.

What is different about the psychosomatic diseases is that infections or injuries are not readily discernible antecedent events; the failure in feedback control seems to occur as an extreme at one or another end of a continuum of normal functioning, and frequently does so in conjunction with strong emotions. This model may be used to stress either innate (constitutional) defects, or failures of control which are acquired. Familial dysautonomia is an example of the former (the Riley-Day syndrome: inherited defects in several autonomic functions, often associated with mental retardation); and conditioned autonomic responses are examples of the latter. . . .

The general framework of the adaptation model is the one which fits our approach, in that it is compatible with the principles we have described. But before we go into these in any detail, let us just mention briefly one other class of explanations which has been offered, the psychoanalytic ones. Despite some variations, these approaches in general have stressed the subjective aspects of psychosomatic diseases. The patient is often seen as having regressed to an earlier developmental stage, and primitive emotions or fantasies associated with unfulfilled and unconscious childhood wishes are thought to be causative antecedents of symptoms. Consequently, pathology results from the continued presence of provoking situations, or because the individual is of a personality type which responds to any situation with archaic emotions. Except for the stress on the psychic phenomena *causing* the tissue damage, this model is quite similar to one which would propose a stimulus-response specificity or individual response-stereotype as an explanation. Indeed, the latter principles can be thought of as up-to-date refinements of the psychoanalytic theories, although they were arrived at by different procedures.

Now let us examine the psychosomatic diseases. There are many, and as we said the lists vary, but here are those about which there seems to be frequent agreement: metabolic edema; hypertension; regional enteritis; Raynaud's disease; hives; anorexia nervosa; acne; hyperthyroidism; psoriasis; asthma; eczema; constipation; colitis; backache; migraine; duodenal ulcer; rheumatoid arthritis. We cannot discuss all of these, but let us use three as examples in the following discussions: duodenal ulcers, hypertension, and hives. Ulcers, as you know, are erosions in the gastric lining; hypertension is high blood pressure, usually defined as a diastolic pressure of at least 90; and hives are a reddening, swelling, and itching of the skin.

From what we have said of the psychophysiological principles, how can we understand the formation of these pathologies? Let us begin with individual response-stereotype. We can safely assume that a patient who has ulcers, hypertension, or hives is a gastric, blood pressure, or skin "reactor," respectively, and not only by definition. [Earlier chapters reported] real evidence to support the view that, regardless of the nature of the stimuli, psychosomatic patients show their greatest physiological responses in the system in which they have their symptoms;

as compared with normals, they display a far greater degree of "physiological rigidity," in the sense that there is a greater invariance in the hierarchies of response magnitudes of the systems measured. (It complicates the picture somewhat, but is not inconsistent with the schemes we are presenting, to point out that there are individuals who display two or more kinds of psychosomatic disorders.)

Thus the first postulate which can be made is that the appearance of psychosomatic symptoms requires an organ system which is maximally responsive to most situational stimuli, as compared with the other physiological systems. For gastric symptoms to appear, it is necessary that the individual's stomach be the viscus which shows the greatest responses to various inputs; similarly for the blood pressure and skin disorders—they must consistently be the most reactive systems. Now when we say that it is "necessary," or that this kind of response hierarchy "must occur," it should be clear that we are referring to the statistical correlations which we discussed earlier. An individual is more likely to develop an ulcer, for example, if he shows response-stereotypy with gastric activity as the maximally reactive system. It may be that it is also necessary, in a causative sense, that an ulcer patient always respond maximally with gastric hypersecretions or hypermotility and that other responses (blood pressure, skin temperature) follow in order of magnitude, but we do not know this for certain. We are really only describing a statistical association. This response-stereotypy, then, constitutes a predisposing condition, and as such it is a necessary but not a sufficient cause.

We must admit that it is not clear what causes the stereotypy in the first place. Certainly in some instances this is a genetic matter. In many patients with hypertension, for example, it is possible to show that the disease runs in the family and is associated with a defect in the control of a substance called renin. Yet autonomic responses are easily conditioned, as we have noted, and so it seems to us unreasonable to assume that in any given instance of stereotypy the patterning of responses (or the predisposition) is *either* inherited *or* acquired. Probably both factors are always involved, but we would have difficulty in knowing to what extent. The problems of separating genetic transmission from early conditioning in a family are considerable. For the present time we must simply begin with the fact of response stereotypy as a given.

Now let us turn to the principle of stimulus-response specificity. We have seen that there is a good idea of evidence that certain response systems tend to be activated more in certain emotions (stimuli-situations) than in others. In anger, for example, there is greater gastric activity than in fear, which tends to inhibit gastric functions. The same is true for hypertensive symptoms—anger regularly is associated with a greater diastolic blood pressure increase than is fear. On the other hand, we are all aware that certain emotions are easily observed in vascular responses of the skin: flushing with anger or blushing in embarrassment are two of the most common. It is interesting that anger is the emotion that most frequently is associated with psychosomatic types of responses. Actually this may be partly an artifact of the limited number of emotions that have been examined successfully in the laboratory. Partly, too, it may be because we have directed our attention to the emotions whose immediate effects are similar to those observed in the psychosomatic diseases. But . . . there are other possibilities in the production of symptoms. For example, the inhibition of gastric activity in fear or anxiety may be followed by a hyper-activity which is indistinguishable from that directly associated with anger or resentment.

Accordingly we may postulate as a second "necessary" (but not necessarily sufficient) condition for psychosomatic symptoms, the exposure of the individual to certain emotion-arousing situations. From the limited experimental information we have, we may assume that anger and fear are the two kinds of emotions most likely to be associated with the appearance of symptoms. Anger perhaps is most frequently involved, but fear may be also, both in its own right and as a prelude to rebound. All of us experience these emotion-provoking situations, of course, yet we do not all experience symptoms. Therefore we would have to assume that the emotions must be of sufficient intensity and duration to produce changes. That is, the physiological responses must be great enough, and occur with sufficient frequency, to produce the tissue damage which is given a disease label. This would require, therefore, that the individual continually receive exposure to such activating situations.

Now you can see that, if an individual with marked response-stereotypy were involved in situations which regularly provoked emotional responses, this may be sufficient to result in the production of symptoms. But another principle is involved here, that concerning homeostasis. If a person with marked response-stereotypy is continually exposed to stressful situations, he may nevertheless avoid having psychosomatic symptoms if his autonomic feedback and control mechanisms operate efficiently. The individual's own autonomic balance (homeostasis) may be kept within the limits of normal functioning by the reflex mechanisms we have discussed, which prevent either responses or rebounds from being of such magnitude that tissue damage occurs. Thus even though he may have "physiological rigidity" in the sense that one organ system always shows greater responses than the others, and even though these responses are continually and frequently activated by intensely provoking situations, reflexive control of the response systems may make it possible to avoid the appearance of symptoms.

Therefore we must add a third condition as necessary for psychosomatic disorders—the inadequacy of homeostatic restraints on the response systems. These three conditions may be put in the form of a logical If-Then proposition:

$$\text{If } \left\{ \begin{array}{l} \text{Individual} \\ \text{Response} \\ \text{Stereotypy} \end{array} \right\} \text{ and } \left\{ \begin{array}{l} \text{Inadequate} \\ \text{Homeostatic} \\ \text{Restraints} \end{array} \right\} \text{ and } \left\{ \begin{array}{l} \text{Exposure to} \\ \text{Activating} \\ \text{Situations} \end{array} \right\} \text{ Then } \left\{ \begin{array}{l} \text{Psychosomatic} \\ \text{Episodes} \end{array} \right\}$$

In this scheme of conditions leading to psychosomatic episodes what we are attempting to do is to account for individual differences. We are essentially asking, Why does this person and not that one show symptoms? and, Why does he have this symptom and not those others? and, Why now and not another time? The outline suggests some possible answers. In the first place, an individual at any given time must have a "constitutional predisposition," as evidenced by the response hierarchy who have called stereotypy. This stereotypy may be present at birth or may be due to exposure to situations in the past in which responses were differentially reinforced, or some combination of these. But together with homeostatic failure, the stereotypy can account for the reason why this person his this symptom. On the other hand, the exposure to the activating situations is necessary for the responses to occur and can account for the time of symptom formation. In addition, if the stimulus-situation is one which will maximally activate a certain organ system (stimulus-response specificity), and this coincides with the individual's response specificity and homeostatic weakness, then the likelihood of a psychosomatic episode is greatly increased.

At this point psychotherapists may point out that psychosomatic patients show other attributes that seem to make them unique. Inasmuch as our knowledge of these disorders is very far from complete, we should consider such data suggested by clinical experience, and see how they fit with the other information we have. Many clinical descriptions concern the unconscious fantasies of the patients which are associated with the specific diseases. Without going into each of them, we can say that in general these fantasies seem to be related to the psychoanalytic concepts of the various stages of psychosexual development. Clinicans working with patients are frequently able to predict the appearance of symptoms on the basis of certain fantasy material (and the emotions associated with them). More commonly, it is possible retrospectively to draw parallels between productions offered by a patient in therapy and the appearance and disappearance of symptoms.

It is for this reason that the psychoanalytically oriented have assumed, as we mentioned earlier, that the fantasies stand in a causative relationship to the symptoms, using as a model the somatization of psychic energy. Assuming the validity of these clinical observations (and there seems every reason to do so), we may be able to use an explanatory model that is more parsimonious than the concepts of "somatization" and "psychic energy," one which is perhaps better related to the psychophysiological approach we have been following. ("Parsimony" in this sense refers to theoretical or explanatory economy. It is not necessarily a more accurate or valid representation of the true—but not yet known—state of affairs.)

It is possible to conceive of unconscious fantasies, to the extent that we know what they are or can obtain evidence of them, as particular instances of sets. [Sets] are defined as predispositions to perceive or respond in certain ways. In the sense in which we have used the term, fantasies may parallel in subjective experience the physiological responses (stereotypy!) which constitute an important condition of psychosomatic symptoms.

Although this may seem like psychophysical parallelism, we are not suggesting this philosophical view. We do not know, nor can we, whether fantasy material is merely an epiphenomenon of physiological events, or the reverse, or whether the two are independent but "parallel." What we are saying is that the same kinds of lawfulness of behavior may apply to both psychic and physiological processes, and that the concept of sets may be useful in describing some of these events that seem to occur in both. We want to avoid, where possible, lapsing into a dualistic discussion such as we have just been doing, and we may avoid this by translating the clinical concepts into the psychophysiological terminology.

Accordingly we may think of fantasy productions as evidence of predispositions to perceive and think in certain ways. And if perceptual and thought processes are thought of as responses, then the fantasies are signs of predispositions to make certain responses, just as autonomic response hierarchies are evidence of such predispositions. This is what we have called sets—those tendencies to respond in certain ways which may be inferred as intervening variables from examining the relationships between inputs and outputs. When psychosomatic patients show a relationship between the appearance of certain (perhaps unconscious) ideas or feelings and the appearance of their symptoms, we may consider this as evidence of a common set to perceive and respond to the world in a certain way. In this sense the concept of sets cuts across the other necessary conditions we postulated for psychosomatic episodes . . . . Given stereotypy and homeostatic inadequacy, the existence of an appropriate set can trigger the appearance of a symptom even when there is no real life stimulating situation to do so. This is because the set is such (due to previous exposures) that the patient perceives otherwise innocuous stimuli in a distorted way. It is this set which results in physiological responses to situations *as if* they were appropriate stressors; it is this set which results in emotions which are inappropriate to the situation in which they occur; and it is this set which leads therapists to the conviction that unconscious fantasies *cause* the symptoms. Actually, as we have noted, the unconscious fantasies and the physiological responses may be different aspects of the same sets.

Is there any advantage, other than conceptual, in making this sort of translation? There is, if it results in data which supply new information about the psychosomatic disorders. This approach leads to different kinds of questions, which can be examined experimentally. For example, what are the sets associated with the various psychosomatic symptoms? Fortunately, there have been studies of this problem, and data are available which support the point of view which we have been presenting. Up to now our discussion has been theoretical. Let us turn to some of the evidence concerning the psychosomatic disorders.

The Grahams and their colleagues have conducted a series of studies on the specific relationships between attitudes and physiological responses. The attitudes were obtained in interviews with psychosomatic patients. The hypothesis they investigated was that there exists a specific relation between the attitude toward a stressful stimulus and the disease which occurs in response to the stimulus. Three different kinds of studies were employed: judgments and ratings of interviews with the patients; selections by patients of cartoon illustrations representing attitudes; and suggestions of these attitudes to normal subjects. This is a step-by-step zeroing-in on the role of those intervening variables we have called sets. Therefore let us examine their findings in some detail.

The attitudes arose first in a clinical study of 128 patients with 12 different psychosomatic diseases or symptoms (Grace & Graham, 1952). It was found that patients with the same disease used similar words to describe their attitudes toward events which occurred just before the appearance or exacerbation of symptoms. Attitudes were defined as the way the patient felt about what happened to him in the situation, and what he wanted to do about it. Further studies of patients using similar interviewing techniques resulted in a list of 18 diseases and attitudes. It was from these interviews that the investigators proposed the hypothesis that there is a relationship between the attitude of a person toward a stressful event, and the physiological changes which occur in response to the event.

The first step in testing the hypothesis was to make sure that the attitudes which had been obtained were not due to either observer or sampling bias. Therefore two interview studies were carried out (Graham *et al.*, 1962), the first using 16 patients with eight different diseases and the second using 20 patients with ten different diseases. Patients were not specially selected for emotional problems, but taken from a hospital medical ward in a prearranged order. The possibility of bias in conducting the interviews was controlled by using, for half the patients in each of the two studies, a psychologist interviewer, who was unfamiliar with the predictions about the relationships between the attitudes and the diseases; his interviews are referred to below as "blind," in the sense that he was "blind" to the details of the hypothesis, while the other interviews, conducted by Graham, are called "nonblind." All interviews were recorded, and then edited to remove references to symptoms before being evaluated by judges. Control of biases by judges was obtained by using four judges, of whom two were not medically trained, and who had no extensive experience with either the attitude hypothesis or with other psychodynamic approaches. The task of the judges was to select from the list of 18 attitude descriptions the three which were most similar to those expressed by the patient in the interview; and also to rank all 18 attitudes in the order in which they applied to the patient.

The percentage of correctly predicted choices was significantly greater than that expected by chance in both studies, and in both the blind and the nonblind interviews. The average of correctly predicted choices in the two studies were 28% and 45% for the blind interviews, and 38% and 62% for the nonblind interviews. Three judges chose the predicted attitudes significantly often from the interviews conducted blind, and all four judges did so from the nonblind interviews. The judges showed significant agreement with each other, and the nonmedical judges did as well as the medical ones. It was also found that a particular attitude was judged more applicable to a patient when he had the disease predicted to be associated with it than when he had another disease. The ranks for predicted attitude-disease associations were significantly more applicable in the blind interviews of the second study and in the nonblind interviews of both studies.

From these results the investigators concluded that different psychosomatic diseases were indeed associated with different attitudes, and that the association could be demonstrated even when a naive interviewer and naive judges were used. Now let us look at the 18 diseases and the attitudes which had been correctly predicted to be associated with them.

1. *Hives*. Feels he is taking a beating and is helpless to do anything about it.
2. *Ulcers*. Feels deprived of what is due him and wants to get even.
3. *Hypertension*. Feels threatened with harm and has to be ready for anything.
4. *Asthma*. Feels left out in the cold and wants to shut the person or situation out.
5. *Colitis*. Feels he is being injured or degraded and wishes he could get rid of the responsible agent.
6. *Eczema*. Feels he is being frustrated and can do nothing about it except take it out on himself.
7. *Acne*. Feels he is being picked on or at and wants to be let alone.
8. *Psoriasis*. Feels there is a constant gnawing at him and that he has to put up with it.
9. *Hyperthyroidism*. Feels he might lose somebody or something he loves and takes care of, and tries to prevent the loss.
10. *Vomiting*. Feels something wrong has happened, usually for which he feels responsible, and he wishes it hadn't happened.
11. *Constipation*. Feels in a situation from which nothing good could come but keep on with it grimly.
12. *Migraine*. Feels something has to be achieved and then relaxes after the effort.
13. *Multiple Sclerosis*. Feels forced to undertake some kind of physical activity, usually hard work, and wants not to.

14. *Metabolic Edema.* Feels he is carrying a heavy load and wants somebody else to carry all or part of it.
15. *Rheumatoid Arthritis.* Feels tied down and wants to get free.
16. *Raynaud's Disease.* Wants to take hostile physical action.
17. *Regional Enteritis.* Feels he has received something harmful and wants to get rid of it.
18. *Low Backache.* Wants to run away.

There is an important point to note about these attitudes. Those [attitudes] which were predicted (from earlier interviews) to be associated with the diseases were significantly more applicable to patients having the disease in question than to patients who did not have the disease. Also, these findings obtained for the naive interviewer and the naive judges.

In a second type of study (Graham, 1962) cartoons were prepared to illustrate the attitudes, and these were presented to hospitalized patients having one or another of the relevant diseases. Figure 1 shows some sample cartoons. The hypothesis was that a patient with a disease related to a cartoon would respond to that cartoon differently from patients with other diseases. The psychophysical method of paired comparisons was used in which cartoons were presented two at a time and the patients had to compare every cartoon with every other one. Their instructions were to choose, in every pair, the one which reminded them the most of a situation they had been in and their feelings at the time. The choices made by each patient were scored by ranking the 18 cartoons according to the frequency with which they had been chosen. For each patient there was only one relevant cartoon, the one corresponding to his disease, and so the cartoon's rank by all the other patients served as a control. Then it was determined whether the rank given the cartoon by the patient with the related disease fell into the top, middle, or bottom quartiles of its control distribution. However, it was noticed that some patients seemed to treat their relevant cartoon differently by choosing it much less often than would be expected. When the patients were divided into groups above and below the median score on the WAIS Vocabulary Scale, it turned out that the more intelligent half chose their relevant cartoon significantly more often. These results support a phenomenon long known to clinicians, that is, that denial as a defense mechanism appears more frequently among the less intelligent. The results also support the original hypothesis, when this grouping by intelligence is used, that whether selection or rejection is the response, patients respond to the cartoon relevant to their disease in a way which is different from patients with different diseases which are not relevant to that cartoon.

Thus far, the results of the two kinds of studies support the hypothesis that specific attitudes are related to specific symptoms, but the studies have used only patients as controls for other patients. A more compelling study would be one in which normal subjects were used, and the nature of the relationship

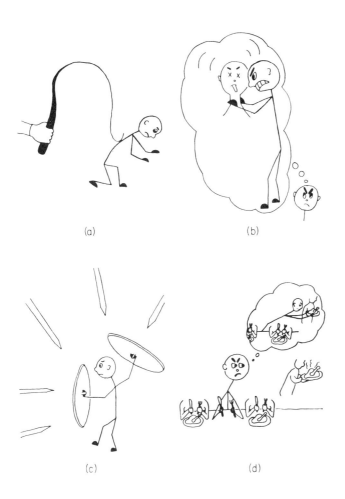

Figure 1

Sample cartoons, illustrating attitudes expressed by patients having certain psychosomatic diseases. (a) Hives: This person feels he is taking a beating (being unfairly treated or mistreated), and is helpless to do anything about it. (b) Raynaud's disease: This person wishes to take hostile action, such as hitting or strangling. (c) Essential hypertension: This person feels that he is threatened with harm and has to be on guard. (d) Duodenal ulcer: This person feels deprived of what is due him and wants to get even. These attitudes were those expressed by the patients about a situation or incident which occurred prior to the onset or exacerbation of their symptoms. (From Graham, 1962. Courtesy of the author and Univ. of Wisconsin Press and the Regents of the Univ. of Wisconsin.)

between attitudes and physiological responses could be specified. From the above studies, it is really not clear that the attitudes are responses to pre-symptomatic stressful situations; they could well be, wholly or in part, responses to the symptoms themselves. Consequently a third type of study has been performed, in which the attitudes of selected diseases are suggested to normal subjects, while physiological responses are being measured.

In the first of these studies (Graham *et al.*, 1958) normal subjects were hypnotized and told to assume the attitudes associated with hives and Raynaud's disease. Since a rise in skin temperature is related to the development of hives and a fall of skin temperature is part of Raynaud's disease (severe peripheral vasoconstriction, usually of the fingers), it was predicted that skin temperature would rise with the hives suggestion and fall with Raynaud's suggestion. Evaluating 22 experimental sessions with 8 subjects and 41 separate attitude suggestions, these predictions were confirmed. Furthermore, the difference between the temperature responses to the two suggestions was statistically significant and for each suggestion, temperature changes reached a point significantly different from the last previous control temperature. These results clearly support the hypothesis. Figure 2 illustrates the findings.

In a second study (Stern *et al.*, 1961), 28 hypnotic sessions were analyzed, in which 18 normal subjects were given the attitude suggestions of hives, Raynaud's disease, and hypertension. The specific predictions made were that diastolic blood pressure should rise under the hypertension attitude, and as before, skin temperature should rise with the hives suggestion and fall with the Raynaud's suggestion. Although systolic blood pressure, heart rate and respiration rate were also recorded, no predictions were made concerning them. Results were generally confirmatory. With the hypertension attitude, there was a rise

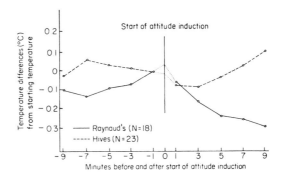

Figure 2

Mean differences in hand temperatures during the induction of attitudes specific for hives and Raynaud's disease. . . . (From Graham, Stern & Winokur, 1958. Courtesy of the authors and Hoeber Medical Division, Harper & Row.)

in diastolic blood pressure greater than the one in Raynaud's and significantly greater than with the hives attitude. Although there was a drop in skin temperature during the first four minutes of the attitude period for all attitudes, during the last six minutes of the attitude period the skin temperature rose for hives and remained low for Raynaud's and were significantly different. There were no significant differences among attitudes in systolic blood pressure, heart rate or respiration. Consequently, these findings replicate and extend the previous one, and further support the hypothesis.

In a third experiment (Graham, Kabler, & Graham, 1962) similar procedures were followed, using an improved experimental design, to compare hives and hypertension responses. Once again predictions were confirmed. Mean change, maximal rise, and rate of change of skin temperature during the hives suggestion were significantly greater than the corresponding changes during the hypertension suggestion. All three measures of change in diastolic blood pressure were significantly greater during the hypertension than during the hives suggestion. And there were no differential effects of the two attitude suggestions on systolic blood pressure, heart rate, or respiratory rate. . . .

The reason why just these three diseases have received experimental test so far is, of course, the ease of measuring the physiological responses related to the symptoms. It is much more difficult, technically speaking, to measure in a laboratory the responses relevant to the other diseases, or to find relevant response systems that change rapidly enough for experimental manipulation. Nevertheless, it is clear from the work of these investigators that certain attitudes are specifically related to certain psychosomatic symptoms; and that when these attitudes are adopted by normals, a set is induced such that physiological responses occur which are analogous to the symptom formation.

Now let us relate the formula. We begin with a person who has response-stereotypy to the extent that whatever the nature of the activating stimulus, one response system always or usually shows the greatest magnitudes of change as compared to his other response systems. This person also has a deficiency in feedback control so that either in initial responsiveness, or in rebound, some limit is expected by this maximally reactive system which results in some tissue damage or symptom appearance. This event will occur either when a stressful situation arises which is specifically stimulating to the response system in which the individual is also maximally reactive, or when any stressful situation occurs which is of sufficient intensity and/or frequency to result in maximum and/or frequent reactivity. In the absence of objective real-life stressors, this condition may be met by the individual whose set is such that he perceives ordinary events as if they were those stressors, and who will reveal the existence of that set both by the appearance of symptoms and by verbal expressions of attitudes (or fantasies).

This explanatory scheme for the psychosomatic disorders has the advantage of using only the psychophysiological principles we have described earlier. As additional research is performed the principles will be modified, and so too will this scheme. It is now in such a form that hypotheses may be derived for testing, either in respect to the psychosomatic disorders themselves, or directly concerning the underlying principles. The author will be pleased if this book helps to stimulate research in any area of psychophysiology.

REFERENCES

Alexander, F. *Psychosomatic Medicine, Its Principles and Applications.* New York: W. W. Norton & Co., 1950.

Ax, A. F. The physiological differentiation between fear and anger in humans. *Psychosom. Med.,* 1953, 15, 433–442.

Barber, T. X., and Hahn, K. W., Jr. Physiological and subjective responses to pain-producing stimulation under hypnotically-suggested and waking-imagined "analgesia." *J. abn. soc. Psychol.,* 1962, 65, 411–418.

Beecher, H. K. Increased stress and effectiveness of placebos and "active" drugs. *Science,* 1960, 132, 91–92.

Benjamin, L. S. Statistical treatment of the law of initial values (LIV) in autonomic research: A review and recommendation. *Psychosom. Med.,* 1963, 25, 556–566.

Bonvallet, M., Dell, P., and Hiebel, G. Tonus sympathique et activite' electrique corticale. *EEG clin. Neurophysiol.,* 1954, 6, 119–144.

Bruner, J. S., and Goodman, C. C. Value and need as organizing factors in perception. *J. abn. soc. Psychol.,* 1947, 42, 33–44.

Cameron, D. E. *Objective and Experimental Psychiatry.* (2nd ed.) New York: Macmillan, 1941.

Cannon, W. B. The mechanism of emotional disturbance of bodily functions. *New Eng. J. Med.,* 1928, 198, 877–884.

Cannon, W. B. *Bodily changes in pain, hunger, fear and rage.* (2nd ed.) New York: Appelton-Century, 1936.

Damaser, E. C., Shor, R. E., and Orne, M. T. Physiological effects during hypnotically requested emotions. *Psychosom. Med.,* 1963, 25, 334–343.

Davis, R. C., Buchwald, A. M. and Frankmann, R. W. Autonomic and muscular responses, and their relation to simple stimuli. *Psychol. Monogr.,* 1955 (No. 20), 69, 1–71 (whole No. 405).

Duffy, E. *Activation and Behavior.* New York: John Wiley & Sons, 1962.

Dunbar, H. F. *Emotions and Bodily Changes.* New York: Columbia Univ. Press, 1935.

Dunbar, H. F. *Mind and Body: Psychosomatic Medicine.* New York: Random House, 1947.

Engel, B. T. Some physiological correlates of hunger and pain. *J. exp. Psychol.,* 1959, 57, 389–396.

Engel, B. T. Stimulus-response and individual-response specificity. *Arch. gen. Psychiat.,* 1960, 2, 305–313.

Engel, B. T., and Bickford, A. F. Response-specificity: Stimulus-response and individual-response specificity in essential hypertensives. *Arch. gen. Psychiat.,* 1961, 5, 478–489.

Eppinger H., and Hess, L. *Vagotonia.* Ment. nerv. Dis. Monogr. No. 20. New York: Nerv. & Ment. Dis. Publ. Co., 1915.

Eysenck, H. J. *The Structure of Human Personality.* New York: John Wiley, 1953.

Funkenstein, D. H. Nor-epinephrine-like and epinephrine-like substances in relation to human behavior. *J. nerv. ment. Dis.,* 1956, 124, 58–67.

Gellhorn, E., Cortell, L., and Feldman, J. The effect of emotion, sham rage and hypothalamic stimulation on the vago-insulin system. *Am. J. Physiol.,* 1941, 133, 532–541.

Gellhorn, E., and Loofbourrow, G. N. *Emotions and Emotional Disorders.* New York: Hoeber Medical Division, Harper & Row, 1963.

Grace, W. J., and Graham, D. T. Relationship of specific attitudes and emotions to certain bodily diseases. *Psychosom. Med.,* 1952, 14, 243–251.

Graham, D. T. Some research on psychophysiologic specificity and its relation to psychosomatic disease. In R. Roessler & N. S. Greenfield (eds.), *Physiological Correlates of Psychological Disorder.* Madison: Univ. of Wisconsin Press, 1962.

Graham, D. T., Kabler, J. D., and Graham, F. K. Physiological response to the suggestion of attitudes specific for hives and hypertension. *Psychosom. Med.,* 1962, 24, 159–169.

Graham, D. T., Lundy, R. M., Benjamin, L. S., Kabler, J. D., Lewis, W. C., Kunish, N. O., and Graham, F. K. Specific attitudes in initial interviews with patients having different "psychosomatic" diseases. *Psychosom. Med.,* 1962, 24, 257–266.

Graham, D. T., Stern, J. A., and Winokur, G. Experimental investigation of the specificity of attitude hypothesis in psychosomatic disease. *Psychosom. Med.,* 1958, 20, 446–457.

Graham, F. K., and Kunish, N. O. Physiological responses of unhypnotized subjects to attitude suggestions. *Psychosom. Med.,* 1965, 27, 317–329.

Gunderson, E. Autonomic balance in schizophrenia. Unpublished doctoral dissertation, University of California, Los Angeles, 1953.

Herrnstein, R. J. Placebo effect in the rat. *Science,* 1962, 138, 677–678.

Hord, D. J., Johnson, L. C., and Lubin, A. Differential effect of the law of initial value (LIV) on autonomic variables. *Psychophysiol.,* 1964, 1, 79–87.

Jasper, H. H. Electroencephalography. In W. Penfield and T. C. Erickson, *Epilepsy and Cerebral Localization.* Springfield: Charles C. Thomas, 1941.

Johnson, L. C., Hord, D. J., and Lubin, A. Response specificity for difference scores and autonomic lability scores. *USN Med. NP Res. Unit Rep. 63-12,* Aug., 1963.

Kuntz, A. *The Autonomic Nervous System.* Philadelphia: Lea & Febiger, 1953.

Lacey, J. I. The evaluation of autonomic responses: Toward a general solution. *Ann. N.Y. Acad. Sci.,* 1956, 67, 123–164.

Lacey, J. I. Psychophysiological approaches to the evaluation of psychotherapeutic process and outcome. In E. A. Rubinstein and M. B. Parloff (eds.), *Research in Psychotherapy.* Washington, D.C.: Am. Psychol. Assn., 1959.

Lacey, J. I., Bateman, D. E., and VanLehn, R. Autonomic response specificity and Rorschach color responses. *Psychosom. Med.,* 1952, 14, 256–260.

Lacey, J. I., Bateman, D. E., and VanLehn, R. Autonomic response specificity: An experimental study. *Psychosom. Med.,* 1953, 15, 8–21.

Lacey, J. I., and Lacey, B. C. Verification and extension of the principle of autonomic response-stereotypy. *Am. J. Psychol.,* 1958, 71, 50–73.

Lacey, J. I., and Lacey, B. C. The law of initial value in the longitudinal study of autonomic constitution: Reproducibility of autonomic responses and response patterns over a four-year interval. *Ann. N.Y. Acad. Sci.,* 1962, 98, 1257–1290; 1322–1326.

Lacey, J. I., Kagan, J., Lacey, B. C., and Moss, H. A. The visceral level: Situational determinants and behavioral correlates of autonomic response patterns. In P. H. Knapp (ed.), *Expression of the Emotions in Man.* New York: International Univ. Press, 1963.

Lindsley, D. B. Emotion. In S. S. Stevens (ed.), *Handbook of Experimental Psychology.* New York: John Wiley & Sons, 1951, 473–516.

Lindsley, D. B. Psychological phenomena and the electroencephalogram. *EEG clin. Neurophysiol.,* 1952, 4, 443–456.

Lindsley, D. B. Psychophysiology and motivation. In M. R. Jones (ed.), *Nebraska Symposium on Motivation.* Lincoln: Univ. Nebraska Press, 1957, 44–105.

Malmo, R. B. Activation: A neuropsychological dimension. *Psychol. Rev.,* 1959, 66, 367–386.

Malmo, R. B., and Shagass, C. Physiologic study of symptom mechanisms in psychiatric patients under stress. *Psychosom. Med.,* 1949, 11, 25–29.

Malmo, R. B., Shagass, C., and Davis, F. H. Symptom specificity and bodily reactions during psychiatric interview. *Psychosom. Med.,* 1950, 12, 362–376. (a)

Malmo, R. B., Shagass, C., and Davis, F. H. Specificity of bodily reactions under stress: A physiological study of somatic mechanisms in psychiatric patients. *Res. Publ. Ass. Res. nerv. ment. Dis.,* 1950, 29, 231–261. (b)

Markwell, E. D., Jr. An investigation of autonomic balance in tuberculous patients. *Psychosom. Med.,* 1961, 23, 392–399.

Markwell, E. D., Jr. Autonomic nervous system measures and factor correlates with personality indices in a tuberculous population. *J. consult. Psychol.,* 1962, 26, 194.

McNemar, Q. *Psychological Statistics.* New York: John Wiley & Sons, 1955.

Obrist, P. A. Cardiovascular differentiation of sensory stimuli. *Psychosom. Med.,* 1963, 25, 450–459.

Oken, D., Grinker, R. R., Heath, H. A., Hertz, M., Korchin, S. J., Sabshin, M., and Schwartz, N. B. Relation of physiological response to affect expression. *Arch. gen. Psychiat.,* 1962, 6, 336–351.

Orne, M. T. The nature of hypnosis: Artifact and essence. *J. abn. soc. Psychol.,* 1959, 58, 277–299.

Orne, M. T. On the social psychology of the psychological experiment: With particular reference to demand characteristics and their implications. *Amer. Psychologist,* 1962, 17, 776–783.

Porter, R. W., Brady, J. V., Conrad, D., Mason, J. W., Galambos, R., and Rioch, D. McK. Some experimental observations on gastrointestinal lesions in behaviorally conditioned monkeys. *Psychosom. Med.,* 1958, 20, 379–394.

Rosenthal, R. Experimenter outcome-orientation and the results of the psychological experiment. *Psychol. Bull.,* 1964, 61, 405–412.

Schachter, J. Pain, fear and anger in hypertensives and normotensives. *Psychosom. Med.* 1957, 19, 17–29.

Selye, H. The general adaptation syndrome and diseases of adaptation. *J. clin. Endocrin.,* 1946, 6, 217–230.

Sokolov, E. N. Higher nervous functions: The orienting reflex. *Ann. Rev. Physiol.,* 1963, 25, 545–580.

Stern, J. A. Toward a definition of psychophysiology. *Psychophysiol.,* 1964, 1, 90–91.

Stern, J. A., Winokur, G., Graham, D. T., and Graham, F. K. Alterations in physiological measures during experimentally induced attitudes. *J. psychosom. Res.,* 1961, 5, 73–82.

Sternbach, R. A. Correlates of differences in time to recover from startle. *Psychosom. Med.,* 1960, 22, 143–148. (a)

Sternbach, R. A. A comparative analysis of autonomic responses in startle. *Psychosom. Med.,* 1960, 22, 204–210. (b)

Sternbach, R. A. Two independent indices of activation. *EEG clin. Neurophysiol.,* 1960, 12, 609–611. (c)

Sternbach, R. A. Some relationships among various "dimensions" of autonomic activity. *Psychosom. Med.,* 1960, 22, 430–434. (d)

Sternbach, R. A. Assessing differential autonomic patterns in emotions. *J. psychosom. Res.,* 1962, 6, 87–91.

Sternbach, R. A. The effects of instructional sets on autonomic responsivity. *Psychophysiology,* 1964, 1, 67–72.

Sternbach, R. A. Autonomic responsivity and the concept of sets. In N. S. Greenfield & W. C. Lewis (eds.), *Psychoanalysis and Current Biological Thought.* Madison: Univ. of Wisconsin Press, 1965.

Sternbach, R. A., and Tursky, B. Ethnic differences among housewives in psychophysical and skin potential responses to electric shock. *Psychophysiology,* 1965, 1, 241–246.

Troffer, S. A., and Tart, C. T. Experimenter bias in hypnotist performance. *Science,* 1964, 145, 1330–1331.

Wenger, M. A. The measurement of individual differences in autonomic balance. *Psychosom. Med.,* 1941, 3, 427–434.

Wenger, M. A. The stability of measurement of autonomic balance. *Psychosom. Med.,* 1942, 4, 94–95.

Wenger, M. A. Preliminary study of the significance of measures of autonomic balance. *Psychosom. Med.,* 1947, 9, 301–309.

Wenger, M. A. Studies of autonomic balance in Army Air Forces personnel. *Comp. Psychol. Monogr.,* Vol. 19, No. 4, Berkeley: Univ. of Calif. Press, 1948.

Wenger, M. A. Clemens, T. L., Coleman, D. R., Cullen, T. D., and Engel, B. T. Autonomic response specificity. *Psychosom. Med.,* 1961, 23, 185–193.

Wenger, M. A., Clemens, T. L., and Cullen, T. D. Autonomic functions in patients with gastrointestinal and dermatological disorders. *Psychosom. Med.,* 1962, 24, 267–273.

Wenger, M. A., Clemens, T. L., Darsie, M. L., Engel, B. T., Estess, F. M. and Sonnenschein, R. R. Autonomic response patterns during intravenous infusion of epinephrine and nor-epinephrine. *Psychosom. Med.,* 1960, 22, 294–307.

Wenger, M. A., and Cullen, T. D. ANS response patterns to fourteen stimuli. *Amer. Psychol.,* 1958, 13, 423 (abstract).

Wenger, M. A., and Ellington, M. The measurement of autonomic balance in children: Method and normative data. *Psychosom. Med.,* 1943, 5, 241–253.

Wenger, M. A., Jones, F. N., and Jones, M. H. *Physiological Psychology.* New York: Henry Holt & Co., 1956.

Wilder, J. The law of initial values in neurology and psychiatry: Facts and problems. *J. nerv. ment. Dis.,* 1957, 125, 73–86.

Wolf, S., and Wolff, H. G. *Human Gastric Function.* (2nd ed.). New York: Oxford Univ. Press, 1947.

Woodworth, R. S., and Schlosberg, H. *Experimental Psychology.* (Rev. ed.). New York: Henry Holt & Co., 1954.

Zborowski, M. Cultural components in responses to pain. *J. soc. Issues,* 1952, 8, 16–30.

DISCUSSION

The article by Sternback attempts to integrate current research evidence into a general theory on the origins of psychosomatic disorders. Like all good theory this one is solidly based upon empirical evidence and is formulated in such a fashion as to generate further research hypotheses. Sternbach's incorporation of the research on autonomic stimulus and response specificity as well as the incorporation of research on personality variables associated with these response characteristics represents a much needed integration of diverse research findings. Whatever the outcome of the studies which attempt to test Sternbach's theory it is apparent that complete understanding of the origin of psychosomatic disorders must await further research and theoretical revision.

Section 5:   PSYCHONEUROTIC DISORDERS

The psychoneuroses are generally defined as patterns of abnormal behavior which interefere with the optimal functioning of the individual and frequently result in feelings of depression, tension and anxiety, but are usually not so severe as to require hospitalization. The American Psychiatric Association has classed neurotic symptom types as follows: Anxiety Reaction, Phobic Reaction, Depressive Reaction, Dissociative Reaction, Obsessive-Compulsive Reaction, Conversion Reaction, and Psychoneurotic Reaction. This system, basically a continuation of Kraepelinian nomenclature, has been widely criticized because of its relatively low reliability.

Classificatory systems in abnormal psychology are convenient methods of grouping and communicating about patterns of maladaptive behavior; nevertheless such behaviors are dependent variables and the value of a classificatory system must ultimately be judged on the basis of its effectiveness in facilitating our understanding of the variables which result in and maintain such behaviors. The articles which follow represent two quite divergent theoretical attempts to specify the variables which result in neurotic patterns of behavior.

11

CULTURE AND NEUROSIS

Karen Horney

In the psychoanalytic concept of neuroses a shift of emphasis has taken place: whereas originally interest was focussed on the dramatic symptomatic picture, it is now being realized more and more that the real source of these psychic disorders lies in character disturbances, that the symptoms are a manifest result of conflicting character traits, and that without uncovering and straightening out the neurotic character structure we cannot cure a neurosis. When analyzing these character traits, in a great many cases one is struck by the observation that, in marked contrast to the divergency of the symptomatic pictures, character difficulties invariably center around the same basic conflicts.

These similarities in the content of conflicts present a problem. They suggest, to minds open to the importance of cultural implications, the question of whether and to what extent neuroses are moulded by cultural processes in essentially the same way as "normal" character formation is determined by these influences; and, if so, how far such a concept would necessitate certain modifications in Freud's views of the relation between culture and neurosis.

In the following remarks I shall try to outline roughly some characteristics typically recurring in all our neuroses. The limitations of time will allow us to present neither data—good case histories—nor method, but only results. I shall try to select from the extremely complex and diversified observational material the essential points.

There is another difficulty in the presentation. I wish to show how these neurotic persons are trapped in a vicious circle. Unable to present in detail the factors leading up to the vicious circle, I must start rather arbitrarily with one of the outstanding features, although this in itself is already a complex product

Reprinted from the *American Sociological Review,* 1, 1936, 221–230, with the permission of the American Sociological Association.

of several interrelated, developed mental factors. I start, therefore, with the problem of competition.

The problem of competition, or rivalry, appears to be a never-failing center of neurotic conflicts. How to deal with competition presents a problem for everyone in our culture; for the neurotic, however, it assumes dimensions which generally surpass actual vicissitudes. It does so in three respects:

(1) There is a constant measuring-up with others, even in situations which do not call for it. While striving to surpass others is essential for all competitive situations, the neurotic measures up even with persons who are in no way potential competitors and have no goal in common with him. The question as to who is the more intelligent, more attractive, more popular, is indiscriminately applied towards everyone.

(2) The content of neurotic ambitions is not only to accomplish something worthwhile, or to be successful, but to be absolutely best of all. These ambitions, however, exist in fantasy mainly—fantasies which may or may not be conscious. The degree of awareness differs widely in different persons. The ambitions may appear in occasional flashes of fantasy only. There is never a clear realization of the powerful dramatic role these ambitions play in the neurotic's life, or of the great part they have in accounting for his behavior and mental reactions. The challenge of these ambitions is not met by adequate efforts which might lead to realization of the aims. They are in queer contrast to existing inhibitions towards work, towards assuming leadership, towards all means which would effectually secure success. There are many ways in which these fantastic ambitions influence the emotional lives of the persons concerned: by hyper-sensitivity to criticism, by depressions or inhibitions following failures, etc. These failures need not necessarily be real. Everything which falls short of the realization of the grandiose ambitions is felt as failure. The success of another person is felt as one's own failure.

This competitive attitude not only exists in reference to the external world, but is also internalized, and appears as a constant measuring-up to an ego-ideal. The fantastic ambitions appear on this score as excessive and rigid demands towards the self, and failure in living up to these demands produces depressions and irritations similar to those produced in competition with others.

(3) The third characteristic is the amount of hostility involved in neurotic ambition. While intense competition implicitly contains elements of hostility—the defeat of a competitor meaning victory for oneself—the reactions of neurotic persons are determined by an insatiable and irrational expectation that no one in the universe other than themselves should be intelligent, influential, attractive, or popular. They become infuriated, or feel their own endeavors condemned to futility, if someone else writes a good play or a scientific paper or plays a prominent role in society. If this attitude is strongly accentuated, one may observe in the analytical situation, for example, that these patients regard

any progress made as a victory on the part of the analyst, completely disregarding the fact that progress is of vital concern to their own interests. In such situations they will disparage the analyst, betraying, by the intense hostility displayed, that they feel endangered in a position of paramount importance to themselves. They are as a rule completely unaware of the existence and intensity of this "no one but me" attitude, but one may safely assume and eventually always uncover this attitude from reactions observable in the analytical situation, as indicated above.

This attitude easily leads to a fear of retaliation. It results in a fear of success and also in a fear of failure: "If I want to crush everyone who is successful, then I will automatically assume identical reactions in others, so that the way to success implies exposing me to the hostility of others. Furthermore, if I make any move towards this goal and fail, then I shall be crushed." Success thus becomes a peril and any possible failure becomes a danger which must at all costs be avoided. From the point of view of all these dangers it appears much safer to stay in the corner, be modest and inconspicuous. In other and more positive terms, this fear leads to a definite recoiling from any aim which implies competition. This safety device is assured by a constant, accurately working process of automatic self-checking.

This self-checking process results in inhibitions, particularly inhibitions towards work, but also towards all steps necessary to the pursuit of one's aims, such as seizing opportunities, or revealing to others that one has certain goals or capacities. This eventually results in an incapacity to stand up for one's own wishes. The peculiar nature of these inhibitions is best demonstrated by the fact that these persons may be quite capable of fighting for the needs of others or for an impersonal cause. They will, for instance, act like this:

When playing an instrument with a poor partner, they will instinctively play worse than he, although otherwise they may be very competent. When discussing a subject with someone less intelligent than themselves, they will compulsively descend below his level. They will prefer to be in the rank and file, not to be identified with the superiors, not even to get an increase in salary, rationalizing this attitude in some way. Even their dreams will be dictated by this need for reassurance. Instead of utilizing the liberty of a dream to imagine themselves in glorious situations, they will actually see themselves, in their dreams, in humble or even humiliating situations.

This self-checking process does not restrict itself to activities in the pursuit of some aim, but going beyond that, tends to undermine the self-confidence, which is a prerequisite for any accomplishment, by means of self-belittling. The function of self-belittling in this context is to eliminate oneself from any competition. In most cases these persons are not aware of actually disparaging themselves, but are aware of the results only as they feel themselves inferior to others and take for granted their own inadequacy.

The presence of these feelings of inferiority is one of the most common psychic disorders of our time and culture. Let me say a few more words about them. The genesis of inferiority feelings is not always in neurotic competition. They present complex phenomena and may be determined by various conditions. But that they do result from, and stand in the service of, a recoiling from competition, is a basic and ever-present implication. They result from a re-coiling inasmuch as they are the expression of discrepancy between high-pitched ideals and real accomplishment. The fact, however, that these painful feelings at the same time fulfill the important function of making secure the recoiling attitude itself, becomes evident through the vigor with which this position is defended when attacked. Not only will no evidence of competence or attractive-ness ever convince these persons, but they may actually become scared or angered by any attempt to convince them of their positive qualities.

The surface pictures resulting from this situation may be widely divergent. Some persons appear thoroughly convinced of their unique importance and may be anxious to demonstrate their superiority on every occasion, but betray their insecurity in an excessive sensitivity to every criticism, to every dissenting opinion, or every lack of responsive admiration. Others are just as thoroughly convinced of their incompetence or unworthiness, or of being unwanted or unappreciated; yet they betray their actually great demands in that they react with open or concealed hostility to every frustration of their unacknowledged demands. Still others will waver constantly in their self-estimation between feeling themselves all-important and feeling, for instance, honestly amazed that anyone pays any attention to them.

If you have followed me thus far, I can now proceed to outline the par-ticular vicious circle in which these persons are moving. It is important here, as in every complex neurotic picture, to recognize the vicious circle, because, if we overlook it and simplify the complexity of the processes going on by assuming a simple cause-effect relation, we either fail to get an understanding of the emotions involved, or attribute an undue importance to some one cause. As an example of this error, I might mention regarding a highly emotion-charged rivalry attitude as derived directly from rivalry with the father. Roughly, the vicious circle looks like this:

The failures, in conjunction with a feeling of weakness and defeat, lead to a feeling of envy towards all persons who are more successful, or merely more secure or better contented with life. This envy may be manifest or it may be repressed under the pressure of the same anxiety which led to a repression of, and a recoiling from, rivalry. It may be entirely wiped out of consciousness and represented by the substitution of a blind admiration; it may be kept from awareness by a disparaging attitude towards the person concerned. Its effect, however, is apparent in the incapacity to grant to others what one has been forced to deny oneself. At any rate, no matter to what degree the envy is repressed or expressed, it implies an increase in the existing hostility against people and consequently an increase in the anxiety, which now takes the particular form of an irrational fear of the envy of others.

The irrational nature of this fear is shown in two ways: (1) it exists regardless of the presence or absence of envy in the given situation; and (2) its intensity is out of proportion to the dangers menacing from the side of the envious competitors. This irrational side of the fear of envy always remains unconscious, at least in nonpsychotic persons, therefore it is never corrected by a reality-testing process, and is all the more effective in the direction of reinforcing the existing tendencies to recoil.

Consequently the feeling of own insignificance grows, the hostility against people grows, and the anxiety grows. We thus return to the beginning, because now the fantasies come up, with about this content: "I wish I were more powerful, more attractive, more intelligent than all the others, then I should be safe, and besides, I could defeat them and step on them." Thus we see an ever-increasing deviation of the ambitions towards the stringent, fantastic, and hostile.

This pyramiding process may come to a standstill under various conditions, usually at an inordinate expense in loss of expansiveness and vitality. There is often some sort of resignation as to personal ambitions, in turn permitting the diminution of anxieties as to competition, with the inferiority feelings and inhibitions continuing.

It is now time, however, to make a reservation. It is in no way self-evident that ambition of the "no-one-but-me" type must necessarily evoke anxieties. There are persons quite capable of brushing aside or crushing everyone in the way of their ruthless pursuit of personal power. The question then is: Under what special condition is anxiety invoked in neurotically competitive people?

The answer is that they at the same time want to be loved. While most persons who pursue an asocial ambition in life care little for the affection or the opinion of others, the neurotics, although possessed by the same kind of competitiveness, simultaneously have a boundless craving for affection and appreciation. Therefore, as soon as they make any move towards self-assertion, competition, or success, they begin to dread losing the affection of others, and must automatically check their aggressive impulses. This conflict between ambition and affection is one of the gravest and most typical dilemmas of the neurotics of our time.

Why are these two incompatible strivings so frequently present in the same individual? They are related to each other in more than one way. The briefest formulation of this relationship would perhaps be that they both grow out of the same sources, namely, anxieties, and they both serve as a means of reassurance against the anxieties. Power and affection may both be safeguards. They generate each other, check each other, and reinforce each other. These interrelations can be observed most accurately within the analytic situation, but sometimes are obvious from only a casual knowledge of the life history.

In the life history may be found for instance, an atmosphere in childhood lacking in warmth and reliability, but rife with frightening elements—battles between the parents, injustice, cruelty, over-solicitousness—generation of an increased need for affection—disappointments—development of an outspoken competitiveness—inhibition—attempts to get affection on the basis of weakness, helplessness, or suffering. We sometimes hear that a youngster has suddenly turned to ambition after an acute disappointment in his need for affection, and then given up the ambition on falling in love.

Particularly when the expansive and aggressive desires have been severely curbed in early life by a forbidding atmosphere, the excessive need for reassuring affection will play a major role. As a guiding principle for behavior this implies a yielding to the wishes or opinions of others rather than asserting one's own wishes or opinions; an overvaluation of the significance for one's own life of expressions of fondness from others, and a dependence on such expressions. And similarly, it implies an overvaluation of signs of rejection and a reacting to such signs with apprehension and defensive hostility. Here again a vicious circle begins easily and reinforces the single elements: In diagram it looks somewhat like this:

> Anxiety plus repressed hostility
> Need for reassuring affection
> Anticipation of, sensi-
> tivity to, rejection
> Hostile reactions
> to feeling
> rejected

These reactions explain why emotional contact with others that is attained on the basis of anxiety can be at best only a very shaky and easily shattered bridge between individuals, and why it always fails to bring them out of their emotional isolation. It may, however, serve to cope with anxieties and even get one through life rather smoothly, but only at the expense of growth and personality develpment, and only if circumstances are quite favorable.

Let us ask now, which special features in our culture may be responsible for the frequent occurrence of the neurotic structures just described?

We live in a competitive, individualistic culture. Whether the enormous economic and technical achievements of our culture were and are possible only on the basis of the competitive principle is a question for the economist or sociologist to decide. The psychologist, however, can evaluate the personal price we have paid for it.

It must be kept in mind that competition not only is a driving force in economics activities, but that it also pervades our personal life in every respect.

The character of all our human relationships is moulded by a more or less out-spoken competition. It is effective in the family between siblings, at school, in social relations (keeping up with the Joneses), and in love life.

In love, it may show itself in two ways: the genuine erotic wish is often overshadowed or replaced by the merely competitive goal of being the most popular, having the most dates, love letters, lovers, being seen with the most desirable man or woman. Again, it may pervade the love relationship itself. Marriage partners, for example, may be living in an endless struggle for supremacy, with or without being aware of the nature or even of the existence of this combat.

The influence on human relations of this competitiveness lies in the fact that it creates easily aroused envy towards the stronger ones, contempt for the weaker, distrust towards everyone. In consequence of all these potentially hostile tensions, the satisfaction and reassurance which one can get out of human relations are limited and the individual becomes more or less emotionally isolated. It seems that here, too, mutually reinforcing interactions take place, so far as insecurity and dissatisfaction in human relations in turn compel people to seek gratification and security in ambitious strivings, and vice versa.

Another cultural factor relevant to the structure of our neurosis lies in our attitude towards failure and success. We are inclined to attribute success to good personal qualities and capacities, such as competence, courage, enterprise. In religious terms this attitude was expressed by saying that success was due to God's grace. While these qualities may be effective—and in certain periods, such as the pioneer days, may have represented the only conditions necessary —this ideology omits two essential facts: (1) that the possibility for success is strictly limited; even external conditions and personal qualities being equal, only a comparative few can possibly attain success; and (2) that other factors than those mentioned may play the decisive role, such as, for example, un-scrupulousness or fortuitous circumstances. Inasmuch as these factors are over-looked in the general evaluation of success, failures, besides putting the person concerned in a factually disadvantageous position, are bound to reflect on his self-esteem.

The confusion involved in this situation is enhanced by a sort of double moral. Although, in fact, success meets with adoration almost without regard to the means employed in securing it, we are at the same time taught to regard modesty and an undemanding, unselfish attitude as social or religious virtues, and are rewarded for them by praise and affection. The particular difficulties which confront the individual in our culture may be summarized as follows: for the competitive struggle he needs a certain amount of available aggressive-ness; at the same time, he is required to be modest, unselfish, even self-sacrificing. While the competitive life situation with the hostile tensions involved in it creates an enhanced need of security, the chances of attaining a feeling of safety in human relations—love, friendship, social contacts—are at the same time diminished. The estimation of one's personal value is all too dependent on the degree of success attained, while at the same time the possibilities for success are limited and the success itself is dependent, to a great extent, on fortuitous circumstances or on personal qualities of an asocial character.

Perhaps these sketchy comments have suggested to you the direction in which to explore the actual relationship of our culture to our personality and its neurotic deviations. Let us now consider the relation of this conception to the views of Freud on culture and neurosis.

The essence of Freud's views on this subject can be summarized, briefly, as follows: Culture is the result of a sublimation of biologically given sexual and aggressive drives—"sexual" in the extended connotation Freud has given the term. Sublimation presupposes unwitting suppression of these instinctual drives. The more complete the suppression of these drives, the higher the cultural development. As the capacity for sublimating is limited, and as the intensive suppression of primitive drives without sublimation may lead to neurosis, the growth of civilization must inevitably imply a growth of neurosis. Neuroses are the price humanity has to pay for cultural development.

The implicit theoretical presupposition underlying this train of thought is the belief in the existence of biologically determined human nature, or, more precisely, the belief that oral, anal, genital, and aggressive drives exist in all human beings in approximately equal quantities.[1] Variations in character formation from individual to individual, as from culture, are due, then, to the varying intensity of the suppression required, with the addition that this suppression can affect the different kinds of drives in varying degrees.

This viewpoint of Freud's seems actually to encounter difficulties with two groups of data. (1) Historical and anthropological findings[2] do not support the assumption that the growth of civilization is in a direct ratio to the growth of instinct suppression. (2) Clinical experience of the kind indicated in this paper suggests that neurosis is due not simply to the quantity of suppression of one or the other instinctual drives, but rather to difficulties caused by the conflicting character of the demands which a culture imposes on its individuals. The differences in neuroses typical of different cultures may be understood to be conditioned by the amount and quality of conflicting demands within the particular culture.

In a given culture, those persons are likely to become neurotic who have met these culturally determined difficulties in accentuated form, mostly through the medium of childhood experiences, and who have not been able to solve their difficulties, or have solved them only at great expense to personality.

[1] I pass over Freud's recognition of individual constitutional difference.

[2] Ruth Benedict, *Patterns of Culture;* Margaret Mead, *Sex and Temperament in Three Savage Societies.*

12

ETIOLOGY OF HUMAN NEUROSIS

Joseph Wolpe

THE CAUSAL RELATIONS OF PERVASIVE ("FREE-FLOATING") ANXIETY

Under certain circumstances it is not only to well-defined stimulus configurations that anxiety responses are conditioned, but also to more or less omnipresent properties of the environment, of which extreme examples would be light, light and shade contrasts, amorphous noise, spatiality, and the passage of time. Since each of these enters into most, if not all, possible experience, it is to be expected that if any of them becomes connected to anxiety responses the patient will be persistently, and apparently causelessly anxious. He will be suffering from what is erroneously called "free-floating" anxiety, and for which a more suitable label would be *pervasive anxiety*.

It must be unequivocally stated, in case it is not quite self-evident, that there is no sharp dividing line between specific anxiety-evoking stimuli and stimuli to pervasive anxiety. The pervasiveness of the latter is a function of the pervasiveness of the stimulus element conditioned; and there are degrees of pervasiveness ranging from the absolute omnipresence of time itself through very common elements like room walls to rarely encountered configurations like hunchbacks.

What reason is there for believing that pervasive anxiety has definable stimulus sources?

Questioning of patients with pervasive anxiety usually reveals that definable aspects of the environment are especially related to this anxiety. For example, one patient reported increased anxiety in the presence of any very large object;

Reprinted from *Psychotherapy by Reciprocal Inhibition,* 1958, pp. 83–94, with the permission of the Stanford University Press (©1958 by the Board of Trustees of the Leland Stanford Junior University) and Dr. Wolpe.

another an uncomfortable intrusiveness of all sharp contrasts in his visual field —even the printed words on a page, and particularly contrasts in the periphery of the field. A third felt overwhelmed by physical space. Frequently, patients with pervasive anxiety observe that noise causes a rise in the level of their anxiety. In some cases the noise need not be loud, and in some even music is disturbing.

Although pervasive anxiety is usually felt less when the patient lies down and closes his eyes, it does not disappear. To some extent this may be explained on the basis of perseveration due to prolonged reverberation of the effects of the stimulus in the nervous system. But this does not accout for the fact that usually *some* anxiety is already felt at the moment of waking. An obvious explanation is that anxiety evocable by stimuli that enter into the very structure of experience is likely to be produced by the first contents of the awakening subject's imagination. Anxiety increases when the outside world makes its impact; and it is consonant with this that, very commonly, the level of pervasive anxiety gradually rises as the day goes on.

This diurnal rise in level is less likely to occur when the general level of pervasive anxiety is low; for then there is a greater likelihood of the arousal, during a normal day's experience, of other emotions which may be physiologically antagonistic to anxiety, so that the anxiety will be inhibited and its habit strength each time slightly diminished. On the other hand, invariably (in my experience) the patient with pervasive anxiety also has unadaptive anxiety reaction to specific stimuli, and if he should encounter and react to any one of the latter during that day, the level of pervasive anxiety will promptly rise. In the normal course of events it is to be expected that the level of pervasive anxiety will fluctuate because of "chance" occurrences which strengthen or weaken its habit strength.

Sometimes when a patient is fortunate enough not to meet with any specific disturbing stimuli over an extended period, his pervasive anxiety may practically cease, but subsequent response to a relevant specific anxiety-evoking stimulus will condition it lastingly again. This reconditioning was beautifully demonstrated in one of my patients, who, in addition to pervasive anxiety, had a number of severe phobias on the general theme of illness. The pervasive anxiety responded extremely well to La Verne's carbon dioxide–oxygen inhalation therapy. The patient stopped coming for treatment until several months later when the pervasive anxiety was reinduced after he had witnessed an epileptic fit in the street. The pervasive anxiety was again speedily removed by carbon dioxide–oxygen and the patient again stopped treatment after a few more interviews. The essence of this sequence was repeated about ten times before the patient finally allowed desensitization to the phobic stimuli to be completed.

The question naturally arises: What factors determine whether or not pervasive anxiety will be part of a patient's neurosis? At the moment two possible factors may be suggested on the basis of clinical impressions. One seems to be the intensity of anxiety evocation at the time of the induction of the neurosis. It is hypothesized that the more intense the anxiety the more stimulus aspects are likely to acquire *some* measure of anxiety conditioning. Indirect support for this hypothesis comes from the observation that, on the whole, it is the patient who reacts more severely to specific stimuli who is also likely to suffer from pervasive anxiety.

The second possible factor is a lack of clearly defined environmental stimuli at the time of neurosis induction. For example, one patient's pervasive anxiety began after a night in a hotel during which he had attempted intercourse with a woman to whom he felt both sexual attraction and strong revulsion. He had felt a powerful and strange, predominantly nonsexual excitation, and ejaculation had occurred very prematurely without pleasure. The light had been switched off, and *only the dark outlines of objects could be seen.* After this, so great was his feeling of revulsion to the woman that he spent the remainder of the night on the carpet. This experience left him, as he subsequently found, with an anxiety toward a wide range of sexual objects, along with much pervasive anxiety, characterized by a special intrusiveness of all heavy dark objects.

THE CAUSAL PROCESS IN HYSTERIA

Hysterical reactions are clearly distinguishable from the rather diffuse discharges of the autonomic nervous system that characterize anxiety reactions. In most instances hysterical reactions do not find expression in the autonomic nervous system at all, but in the sensory system, the motor system, or groups of functional units involved in the production of imagery or of consciousness in general. Thus, they may take the form of anesthesias, paresthesias, hyperesthesias, or disturbances of vision or hearing; of paralyses, pareses, tics, tremors, disturbances of balance, contractures or fits; of amnesias, fugues, or "multiple personality" phenomena. Occasionally, hysterical reactions do appear to involve functions within the domain of the autonomic nervous system—in the form of vomiting (or nausea) or enuresis, but it is noteworthy that each of the two functions involved is to some extent within voluntary control.

Anxiety frequently accompanies hysterical reactions and then they occur side by side as two distinct forms of *primary* neurotic response. This state of affairs must be sharply distinguished from that in which sensory or motor phenomena are secondary effects of the normal components of anxiety, and as such do not qualify as hysterical. For example, a headache due to tension of the temporal muscles, backache due to tension of the longitudinal spinal muscles, or paresthesia due to hyperventilation are not to be regarded as hysterical.

It is necessary also to differentiate hysterical from obsessional reactions.

Hysterical reactions are at a relatively low level of organization, affecting well-defined sensory areas and specific motor units, and causing changes in the general character of consciousness of "blocks" of experience limited in terms of a time span or some other broad category. The details of the reactions tend to be fixed and unchanging. Obsessional reactions consist by contrast of highly organized movements or of elaborate and complex thinking, in either of which there is a great variety in the individual instances of expression of a specific constant theme.

Like other neurotic reactions, hysterical reactions are acquired by learning. It is intriguing to note that Freud's very early observations on hysterical subjects could easily have led him to this conclusion had he not been sidetracked by a spurious deduction from observations on therapeutic effects. In a paper published in 1893, speaking of the relation of the symptoms of hysteria to the patients' reactions at the time of the precipitating stress, he states:

> The connection is often so clear that it is quite evident how the exciting event has happened to produce just this and no other manifestation; the phenomenon is determined in a perfectly clear manner by the cause; to take the most ordinary example, a painful effect, which was originally excited while eating, but was suppressed, produces nausea and vomiting, and this continues for months, as hysterical vomiting. A child who is very ill at last falls asleep, and its mother tries her utmost to keep quiet and not to wake it; but just in consequence of this resolution (hysterical counterwill) she makes a clucking noise with her tongue. On another occasion when she wishes to keep absolutely quiet this happens again, and so a tic in the form of tongue-clicking develops which for a number of years accompanies every excitement. . . . A highly intelligent man assists while his brother's ankylosed hip is straightened under an anesthetic. At the instant when the joint gives way with a crack, he feels a violent pain in his own hip joint which lasts almost a year. . . . [pp. 25–26]
>
> The attack then arises spontaneously as memories commonly do; but they may also be provoked, just as any memory may be aroused according to the laws of association. Provocation of an attack occurs either by stimulation of a hysterogenic zone or by a new experience resembling the pathogenic experience. We hope to be able to show that no essential difference exists between the two conditions, apparently so distinct; and in both cases a hyperaesthetic memory has been stirred. [p 40]

Apart from the reference to the possibility of attacks arising "spontaneously" (which Freud later explicitly repudiated) we have here an account of the formation by learning of stimulus-response connections. That Freud did not *see* this was mainly because, having observed patients cured when they recalled and narrated the story of the precipitating experience, he concluded that the symptoms were due to the imprisonment of emotionally disturbing memories. He states ". . . we are of opinion that the psychical trauma, or the memory of it acts as a kind of foreign body constituting an effective agent in the present, even long after it has penetrated. . . ." There can be little doubt that this statement would not have been made, and the mind-structure theory that is psychoanalytic theory would not have been born, if Freud could have known that memories do not exist in the form of thoughts or images in some kind of repository within us, but depend on the establishment, through the learning process, of specific neural interconnections that give *a potentiality* of evocation of particular thoughts and images when and only when certain stimulus conditions, external or internal, are present.

When a clear history of the onset of hysterical symptoms is obtained, it is usually found, as illustrated in Freud's cases quoted above, that the hysterical reaction displays a repetition of features that were present in response to the initiating disturbing experience. The stimulus to the reaction varies. Sometimes it is a fairly specific sensory stimulation. For example, a 33-year-old woman had as a hysterical reaction an intolerable sensation of "gooseflesh" in her calves in response to any rectal sensation such as a desire to defecate, ever since, three years previously, a surgeon had unceremoniously performed a rectal examination upon her, while, drowsy from premedication with morphia, she was awaiting the administration of an anesthetic for an abdominal operation.

In other cases it appears that the hysterical reaction is aroused by ubiquitous stimuli, being then the hysterical equivalent of pervasive ("free-floating") anxiety. An example of this is wryneck that is present throughout the working day and relaxes the moment the patient falls asleep. In yet others anxiety appears to *mediate* the hysterical reaction. The hysteria of one of my patients had both a pervasive component and an anxiety-mediated component. This was a 58-year-old woman who 18 months earlier had encountered a deadly snake in a copse. She had been terrified and momentarily paralyzed; her ears were filled with the sound of waves and she had been unable to speak for two hours. The sound of waves had never left her, and any considerable anxiety such as might arise from tension in her home would intensify this sound and then lead to vertigo, loss of balance, and a feeling of great weakness in her limbs, so that she sometimes fell.

The central feature of hysterical reactions is the conditioning, in situations of stress, of neurotic reactions other than anxiety, although anxiety is often also conditioned as well. It is necessary to ask what determines this. There are two possible answers. One is that these reactions are conditioned when they happen to be evoked in addition to anxiety. The other is that although such reactions may be evoked by stress in all subjects, they become the neurotic responses conditioned only in those in whom some special factor is present that gives preference to nonanxiety conditioning. Since, in fact, the immediate response to neurotigenic stimulation always seems to implicate all response systems, the latter possibility is the more likely to be relevant. And there is evidence that it is people with distinct personality features who usually develop hysterical reactions.

Jung (1923) long ago observed that hysterics tend to exhibit extravert character traits while other neurotic subjects tend to be introverted. In this partition of personalities he was followed by other writers who, while differing in many ways, agreed, as Eysenck (1947, p. 58) concluded from a survey, in the following particulars: (a) the introvert has a more subjective, the extravert a more objective outlook; (b) the introvert shows a higher degree of cerebral activity, the extravert a higher degree of behavioral activity; (c) the introvert shows a tendency to self-control (inhibition), the extravert a tendency to lack of such control. Eysenck (1955b) has pointed out on the basis of experiments performed by Franks (1956) and himself (1955a) that extraverted subjects besides learning more poorly also generate reactive inhibition more readily than introverts do. He postulates (1955b, p. 35) that subjects in whom reactive inhibition is generated quickly and dissipated slowly "are predisposed thereby to develop extraverted patterns of behavior and to develop hysterico-psychopathic disorders in cases of neurotic breakdown." Clearly what his facts actually demonstrate is that the hysterical type of breakdown is particularly likely in subjects in whom reactive inhibition has the feature stated. The *causal* role of reactive inhibition is not shown, nor is a possible mechanism suggested.

A possibility is this: that in addition to their easily generated and persistent reactive inhibition (and perhaps in some indirect way bound up with it) extraverted people have one or both of the following characteristics: (a) when exposed to anxiety-arousing stimuli they respond with relatively low degrees of anxiety so that other responses are unusually prominent; (b) when anxiety and other responses are simultaneously evoked in them, contiguous stimuli become conditioned to the other responses rather than to the anxiety—by contrast with introverts.

This hypothesis lends itself readily to direct experimentation. In the meantime a survey from my records of the 22 patients with hysterical symptoms has yielded some suggestive evidence. Nine of them (41 per cent) had initial Willoughby scores below 30. This is in striking contrast to 273 nonhysterical neurotic patients, in only 50 (18 per cent) of whom were the initial scores below this level. The Kolmogorov-Smirnov test shows the difference to be significant at the .05 level. It is interesting to note that insofar as this supports our hypothesis it accords with the time-worn conception of the hysterical patient with little or no anxiety—*la belle indifference.* It is relevant to the same point that the hysterical patients with low Willoughby scores all benefited by procedures that varied greatly but did not obviously affect anxious sensitivity. By contrast, in the 13 patients whose hysterical reactions were accompanied by much anxiety there was a direct correlation between diminution of anxious sensitivity and decreased strength of hysterical reactions except in two cases where this consisted purely of amnesia, which was unaffected. (In one of these the events of the forgotten period were later retrieved under hypnosis, in the other they remained forgotten. It seemed to make no difference either way to the patient's recovery.)

Summarizing the above facts, it may be said that hysterical reactions may either accompany anxiety or occur on their own. In the former case their treatment of anxiety, in the latter it is different in a way that will be discussed in the chapter [later in his book] on treatment. It is supposed that anxiety is a feature when hysteria occurs in subjects relatively far from the extraverted extreme of Eysenck's introversion-extraversion dimension, just because the hypothetical preferential conditioning of responses other than anxiety to neurotigenic stimuli is less marked in these people. This supposition needs to be tested.

Meanwhile it may be noted that there is experimental evidence of a competitive relationship in certain contexts between autonomic and motor responses. Mowrer and Viek (1948), using two groups of rats, placed each animal after a period of starvation on the electrifiable floor of a rectangular cage and offered him food on a stick for ten seconds. Whether the animal ate or not, shock was applied ten seconds later. In the case of one group of ten rats, jumping into the air resulted in the experimenter switching off the shock (shock-controllable group). Each animal in this group had an experimental "twin" to which the shock was applied for the same length of time as it had taken its counterpart to jump into the air (shock-uncontrollable group). One trial a day was given to each animal. The animals in each group whose eating responses during the ten seconds were inhibited (by conditioned anxiety responses resulting from the shocks) were charted each day, and it was found that in the shock-controllable group the number of eating inhibitions was never high and declined to zero, whereas in the shock-uncontrollable group the number rose to a high level and remained there. Apparently, the constant evocation of jumping in the former group resulted in gradual development of conditioned inhibition of anxiety. By contrast with this, in the typical Cornell technique for producing experimental neuroses (p. 43) a very localized musculoskeletal conditioned response comes to be increasingly dominated by autonomic anxiety responses. This whole matter has been discussed in more detail elsewhere (Wolpe, 1953a).

OBSESSIONAL BEHAVIOR

Sometimes, besides the autonomic discharges characteristic of anxiety, ideational, motor, and sensory responses are prominent in a neurosis. If simple and invariate in character, they are labeled *hysterical*. The term *obsessional* is applied to behavior that is more complex and variable in detail, consisting of well-defined and often elaborate thought sequences or relatively intricate acts which, though they may differ in outward form from one occasion to the next, lead or tend to lead to the same kind of result. The term is applicable even to those cases characterized by an obstinate impulse to behavior that rarely or never becomes manifest. Examples of obsessions predominantly of thought are a woman's insistent idea that she might throw her child from the balcony of her apartment, or a man's need to have one of a restricted class of "pleasant" thoughts in his mind before he can make any well-defined movement such as entering a doorway or sitting down. Exhibitionism and compulsive handwashing are characteristic examples of predominantly motor obsessional behavior.

Sometimes the word *compulsive* has been preferred to obsessional for those cases in which motor activity predominates. However, as most cases display both elements, there is little practical value in the distinction. Furthermore, the term compulsive is open to the objection that *all* behavior is compulsive in a sense, for causal determinism implies that the response that occurs is always the only one that could have occurred in the circumstances. The feature of any example of obsessional behavior is not its inevitability but its *intrusiveness*. Its elicitation or the impulse toward it is an encumbrance and an embarrassment to the patient.

If hysterical and obsessional reactions involve similar elements, we may expect that borderline cases will be found. An example of this is a 47-year-old male nurse employed in an industrial first-aid room who for 17 years had an uncontrollable impulse to mimic any rhythmic movements performed before him, e.g., waving of arms or dancing, and to obey any command no matter from whom. In this was combined the basic simplicity of hysteria and the situationally determined variability of obsessional behavior.

It may be stated almost as dogma that the strength and frequency of evocation of obsessional behavior is directly related to the amount of anxiety being evoked in the patient. Pollitt (1957) in a study of 150 obsessional cases noted that obsessional symptoms became more severe and prominent "when anxiety and tension increased for whatever causes." However, it is not always that the source of the anxiety is irrelevant. Sometimes the obsessional behavior is evident only when anxiety arises from specific, usually neurotic sources. For example, an exhibitionist experienced impulses to expose himself when he felt inadequate and inferior among his friends but not when he was anxious about the results of a law examination.

Anxiety-Elevating Obsessions

Two types of obsessional behavior are clearly distinguishable in clinical practice. One type appears to be part and parcel of the immediate response to anxiety-evoking stimulation and has secondary effects entirely in the direction of increasing anxiety. When a motor mechanic of 45 had neurotic anxiety exceeding a certain fairly low level, he would have a terrifying though always controllable impulse to strike people. From the first moment of awareness of the impulse he would feel increased anxiety, and if at the time he was with an associate or even among strangers—for example, in a bus—he would thrust his hands firmly into his pockets "to keep them out of trouble." In the history of such patients one finds that behavior similar to that constituting the obsession was present during an earlier situation in which conditioning of anxiety took place. In 1942 this motor mechanic, on military service, had been sentenced to 30 days' imprisonment in circumstances which he had with some justice felt to be grossly unfair. Then, as he had resisted the military police rather violently in protest, he was taken to a psychiatrist who said there was nothing wrong with him and that the sentence should be carried out. At this his feeling of helpless rage had further increased and he was taken out by force. Then for the first time he had had "this queer feeling" in his abdomen and had struck a military policeman who tried to compel him to work. Horror at the implications of this act intensified his disturbed state. The obsession to strike people made its first appearance in 1953, eleven years later. He had been imprisoned over-night (for the first time since 1942) because, arriving home one night to find his house crowded with his wife's relatives, he had shouted and been violent until his wife had called the police. After emerging from jail, burning with a sense of injustice much like that experienced during his imprisonment in the army, he had felt the impulse to strike a stranger who was giving him a lift in an automobile, and then again, much more strongly, a few days later toward his wife at their first meeting since his night in jail. This time he had gone into a state of panic, and since then, for a period of five months, the obsession had recurred very frequently and in an increasing range of conditions, e.g., at work he would often have a fear-laden desire to hit fellow workmen with any tool he happened to be holding. (There was subsequently a secondary conditioning of anxiety to the *sight* of tools, including knives and forks.)

Anxiety-Reducing Obsessions

The second type of obsessional behavior occurs as a *reaction* to anxiety, and its performance *diminishes* anxiety to some extent, for at least a short time. It occurs in many forms—tidying, handwashing, eating, buying—activities which are of course "normal" when prompted by usual motivation and not by anxiety; rituals like touching poles, perversions like exhibitionism, and various thinking activities. In some of these cases secondary heightening of anxiety occurs as a response to some aspect of the obsessional behavior. For example, in a case of obsessional eating, the anxiety was at first reduced by the eating and then its level would rise in response to the idea of getting fat.

Obsessional behavior of this kind owes its existence to previous conditioning of anxiety-relieving responses. This has been strikingly demonstrated in a recent experiment by Fonberg (1956). This writer conditioned each of several dogs to perform a definite movement in response to several auditory and visual stimuli using food reinforcement. When these instrumental conditioned responses had been firmly established, she proceeded to elaborate defensive instrumental conditioned responses, employing stimuli and responses distinct from those of the alimentary training. The noxious stimulus used was either an electric shock to the right foreleg or a strong air puff to the ear. As a result of this conditioning, upon presentation of the conditioned stimulus an animal would be able to avert the noxious stimulus—for example, by lifting a particular foreleg. The dogs were then made neurotic by conditioning an excitatory alimentary response to a strong tone of 50 cycles and an inhibitory response to a very weak tone of the same frequency, and then bringing the two differentiated tones nearer and nearer to each other from session to session either by progressive strengthening of the inhibitory tone or by both strengthening the inhibitory and weakening the excitatory. In all animals, as soon as neurotic behavior appeared it was accompanied by the previously elaborated defensive motor reaction. Besides this deliberately conditioned reaction, "shaking off" movements were observed in those dogs in whom the noxious stimulation had originally been air puffed into the ear. The more intense the general disturbance the more intense and frequent were the defensive movements. The alimentary conditioned reflexes disappeared completely. With the disappearance of general disturbed symptoms, the defensive movements subsided, reappearing with any new outburst of behavioral disturbance.

It appears clear from these observations that in elaborating the conditioned defensive reaction to the auditory stimulus, anxiety-response-produced stimuli were also conditioned to evoke the defensive reaction, and this reaction was consequently evocable *whenever* the animal had anxiety responses, no matter what the origin of these may have been.

Similarly, in the history of patients displaying this kind of obsessional behavior, it is found that at an earlier period, some important real threat was consistently removed by a single well-defined type of behavior, and this behavior later appears as a response to *any* similar anxiety. The behavior must owe its strength to its association with exceptionally strong reinforcement-favoring conditions—either very massive or very numerous anxiety-drive reductions or both. Its development is also, no doubt, greatly favored when from the outset no other significant anxiety-relieving activity has occurred to compete with it. Its maintenance depends upon the reduction of anxiety it is able to effect at each performance.

One patient was the youngest daughter of a man who despised females and would not forgive his wife for failing to bear him a son. She was very clever at school, and found that intellectual achievement, and that alone, could for brief periods abate her father's blatant hostility and therefore her own anxiety. Consequently, "thinking things out" became her automatic response to *any* anxiety. Since there are many objective fears for which careful thought is useful, there were no serious consequences for years. But when a series of experiences in early adult life led to a severe anxiety state in her, she automatically resorted to her characteristic "problem-solving" behavior. Because the anxiety responses now arose from such sources as imaginary social disapproval, and could not be removed by the solution of a well-defined problem, she began to set herself complex problems in which she usually had to decide whether given behavior was morally "good" or "bad". Partial and brief alleviation of anxiety followed both the formulation of a "suitable" problem and the solution thereof, while prolonged failure to solve a problem increased anxiety sometimes to terror. Although the anxiety soon returned in full force, its temporary decrements at the most appropriate times for reinforcement maintained the problem-finding and problem-solving obsessions, and could well have continued to do so indefinitely.

In other cases obsessional behavior is less episodically determined because everyday circumstances contain aspects of the special situation in which the obsessional mode of behavior alone brought relief from severe anxiety. A history of more than 100 undetected thefts of money by a 17-year-old university student began at the age of 5 when his mother joined the army and left him in the care of an elder sister who beat him severely or tied him to a tree for a few hours if he was slightly dirty or did anything "wrong." He feared and hated her and retaliated by stealing money from her. He was never caught and the possession of the stolen gains gave him a feeling of "munificence and security." The kleptomania continued all through the early home life and school life and was clearly connected with the chronic presence of punishment-empowered authority in the shape of parents or teachers.

It is not surprising, if obsessional behavior is so consistently followed by reduction of anxiety drive, that it is apt to become conditioned to other stimuli too, especially any that happen to be present on repeated occasions. Thus, after therapy had rendered the young woman with the problem-solving obsession mentioned above practically free from neurotic anxieties, mild problem-solving activity was still occasionally aroused by a trifling question, such as "Is it cloudy enough to rain?" The conditioned stimulus was apparently the mere awareness of doubt. Similarly an exhibitionist whose exhibiting had almost entirely disappeared with the overcoming of his anxious sensitivities, still had some measure of the impulse when he saw a girl dressed in a school ("gym") uniform, because he had in the past exhibited to schoolgirls particularly frequently and with special relish. Of course, in this instance sex-drive reduction may have played as important a role in the reinforcement as anxiety-drive reduction.

AMNESIA AND "REPRESSION"

The amnesias that are usually encountered in the course of neurotic states can be conveniently divided into two classes, according to the emotional importance of the incidents forgotten. Patients who are in a chronic state of emotional disturbance frequently fail to register many trifling events that go on around them. For example, a patient may go into a room and conduct a brief conversation with his wife and an hour later have no recollection whatever that he went into that room at all. Here we seem to have a simple case of deficient registration of impressions (retrograde amnesia). Apparently, the patient's attention is so much taken up by his unpleasant anxious feelings that very little is left to be devoted to what goes on around him.

The forgetting of the content of highly emotionally charged experiences has been given foremost importance by Freud and his followers as the cause of neurosis. It seems, however, that forgetting of this character is rather unusual, and when it does occur it appears to be merely one more of the conditionable occurrences in the neurotigenic situation. It does not appear that the repression as such plays any part in the maintenance of neurosis. It is quite possible for the patient to recover emotionally although the forgotten incidents remain entirely forgotten.

REFERENCES

Eysenck, H. J. (1947) *Dimensions of Personality*. London, Routledge.

Eysenck, H. J. (1955a) A dynamic theory of anxiety and hysteria. *J. Ment. Sci.* 101: 28.

Eysenck, H. J. (1955b) Cortical inhibition, figural after-effect and theory of personality. *J. Abnorm. Soc. Psychol.* 51: 94.

Fonberg, E. (1956) On the manifestation of conditioned defensive reactions in stress. *Bull. Soc. Sci. Lettr. Lodz. Class III. Sci. Math. Natur.* 7: 1.

Franks, C. M. (1956) Conditioning and personality: A study of normal and neurotic subjects. *J. Abnorm. Soc. Psychol.* 52: 143.

Freud, S. (1893) On the psychical mechanism of hysterical phenomena. In *Collected Works of Freud,* Vol. I. London, Hogarth Press, 1949.

Jung, C. G. (1923) *Psychological Types.* New York, Harcourt, Brace.

Mowrer, O. H., and Viek, P. (1948) Experimental analogue of fear from a sense of helplessness. *J. Abnorm. Soc. Psychol.* 43: 193.

Pollitt, J. (1957) Natural history of obsessional states: A study of 150 cases. *Brit. Med. J.* 1: 194.
Wolpe, J. (1953*a*) Learning theory and "abnormal fixations." *Psychol. Rev.* 60: 111.

DISCUSSION

The articles included in this section succinctly present the conflicting theoretical interpretations of neurotic patterns of behavior set forth by Intrapsychic and Behavior theorists. The progenitor of all intrapsychic formulations is the psychoanalytic theory of Sigmund Freud, whereas behavioral theorists have derived their basic explanatory principles from theories of learning and conditioning. Horney, consistent with her intrapsychic orientation, views neurotic behavior as simply the surface phenomena of the underlying "neurosis";—the outcome of the trauma, conflict, anxiety, and defense mechanisms characteristic of deep-seated psychic character disturbances. Thus, this underlying disturbance must be modified if the life circumstance of the neurotic individual is to be meaningfully improved. Wolpe, representative of the behavioristic approach, argues that the "neurosis" is the maladaptive neurotic behavior; that once these maladaptive responses are modified or extinguished the individual is no longer neurotic. As will be seen in Part III these conflicting orientations have profound implications for the manner in which the clinician goes about attempting to modify such behavior.

It is interesting that despite their theoretical differences, both Horney and Wolpe have not attempted to significantly revise our current classificatory system, but rather have attempted to explain the patterns of behavior listed in diagnostic manuals. Perhaps this indirectly indicates some validity of observational bases for current diagnostic practice.

Section 6:   AFFECTIVE DISORDERS—SUICIDE

Most individuals who either attempt or commit suicide evidence prior signs of emotional depression; thus suicidal phenomena are frequently considered to be a manifestation of an underlying affective disorder. However, this association is only partly valid, for a significant number of suicidal individuals do not manifest the clinical features of depression, and many depressed individuals are not suicidal. Thus it appears that suicide merits separate consideration from that given the affective disorders and that research efforts must be directed toward the delineation of a classificatory system which will enhance our ability to better understand and predict the causes of this phenomena. The article which follows represents a significant contribution to this end.

13

CAMPUS TRAGEDY: A STORY OF STUDENT SUICIDE

Richard H. Seiden

The act of self-destruction rudely challenges our supposed love of life and fear of death. It is always a puzzlement, but in no case is suicide more shocking or bewildering than it is in the college student. For here is a relatively privileged group of persons enjoying valued advantages of youth, intelligence and educational opportunity. Why should persons, seemingly so rewarded, seek to kill themselves, and, indeed, to commit suicide at a rate significantly in excess of their noncollege peers (Bruyn & Seiden, 1965, p. 76)?

This perplexing question—"Why do students suicide?"—has motivated a great deal of concern among college health authorities leading to several studies and evaluations of the problem in American universities (Braaten & Darling, 1962; Jensen, 1955; Parish, 1957; Raphael, Power, & Berridge, 1937; Temby, 1961). Unfortunately, these studies have all had an exclusively descriptive approach. They have drawn conclusions about certain characteristics of suicidal students but, seemingly, without appreciation for the degree to which these same characteristics are shared by the entire student body population. What has been conspicuously omitted is a baseline—a standard of comparison against which the diagnostic value of their findings might be judged. One is reminded of the gentleman who, when asked, "How is your wife?" astutely responded, "Compared to what?" This very question of relative comparison must also be asked in the study of student suicides.

The present study attempted to remedy this situation by applying a reasonable standard of comparison, namely, the great majority of fellow college

Reprinted from the *Journal of Abnormal and Social Psychology,* 71, 1966, 389–399, with the permission of the American Psychological Association and Dr. Seiden.

This study was supported in part by a grant from the National Institute of Mental Health.

students who do not commit suicide. By investigating what characteristics significantly differentiate suicidal students from their classmates plus examining those situational-temporal conditions associated with campus suicides, it was hoped to achieve a clearer diagnostic picture. Once the high-risk, suicide-prone student can be identified, a large and necessary step will have been taken toward the ultimate objective of effective prophylaxis.

METHOD

The approach used in the present study was one of analytic epidemiology, that is, comparing for particular characteristics the subset of student suicides with the total student body population from which they were drawn. This particular procedure meets the methodological criteria for selection of comparison groups, as stated by MacMahon, Pugh, and Ipsen (1960):

> A comparison group is a group of unaffected individuals believed to reflect the characteristics of the population from which the affected group was drawn. Ideally the comparison group should not differ from the affected group in any respect (other than not being affected) which might be likely to influence the frequency of the variable or variables suspected of being casually connected. This means either that both the patient and comparison groups must be representative of the same population or that if selective factors enter into the choice of the patterns, the same factors ought to enter into the selection of the comparison group [p. 235].

The method of the present study involved a comparison of the sample of 23 University of California at Berkeley (UCB) students who committed suicide during the 10-year period 1952 through 1961, with the entire UCB student body population during this same decade. The objective of this comparison was to determine what special characteristics differentiated the suicide-prone student from his classmates. Within this framework the following working definitions were employed: (*a*) *Student*—the definition of a student was established by registration on the Berkeley campus of the University of California, in either graduate or undergraduate status, during the regular college semester periods. Summer sessions were not included because of the unreliability of data for these periods and changes in the usual composition of the student body population during summer sessions. (*b*) *Suicide*—refers to a completed suicide, established by a death certificate stating suicide as the legal cause of death. In one instance, involving a jump from the Golden Gate bridge, this was not possible. Since the body was never recovered, a certificate was not issued; however, the case was well-documented in police and newspaper files. By keeping to this legalistic definition of suicide, one runs the very likely probability that the true number of suicides will be underenumerated. For example, cases of equivocal student deaths, such as by falls or drowning, were regarded as accidental, in keeping with the coroner's findings, even though these deaths, listed as accidents, could have been suicides which were covered up to avoid the social stigma related to suicide. Indeed, it has been estimated that only about 70% of successful suicides are ever recorded as such (Dublin, 1963, p. 3). The advantage in using this definition is that one can be quite certain that deaths recorded as suicide are bona fide cases since the error is, almost always, in the direction of underreporting. (*c*) *Exposure to risk*—the period of exposure to risk comprised the 10-year span 1952–1961 inclusive, a total of 10 academic or 7½ calendar years. This important variable, the length of exposure, was to some degree controlled since both the suicidal and nonsuicidal students were exposed to the same period of risk. (*d*) *Population at risk*—population at risk was the total student body of UCB during the 10-year period cited. Case finding procedures were extremely painstaking, requiring several months of effort to detect and verify 23 bona fide study cases. Numerous sources of information were used, but for the suicidal students the primary source was the standard death certificate, obtained from the state health department. Secondary sources consisted of newspaper clippings, police files, and University records. The source of materials for the baseline data for the total student body population was the UCB Office of the Registrar. Their publication, *A Ten-Year Survey of Certain Demographic Characteristics of the Student Population* (Suslow, 1963), was indispensable.

In terms of research design, the procedures consisted of collecting and analyzing data regarding selected attributes of the total student population. These data were then used as a baseline to which the sample of suicidal UCB students could be compared. Since suicide may also involve a strong volitional component, further analyses were made with respect to certain situational-temporal features of the academic environment.

RESULTS AND DISCUSSION

Results are presented in tabular and graphic form and discussed in the text by order of their appearance. The various comparisons were statistically analyzed by testing the significance of the difference between two proportions (Hill, 1961, pp. 122–123), specifically, the significance of proportional differences between the suicidal sample and expected population values as based upon knowledge of the student universe. All probability statements are two-tailed probabilities.

Incidence and Prevalence

Previous research on the UCB population (Bruyn & Seiden, 1965) investigated the general question of student suicide risk. By comparing the student suicide experience with the suicide incidence among a comparable group of non-college-age cohorts, it was established that the incidence of suicide among students was significantly greater than for non-student-age peers ($p = .004$). Conversely, the general mortality experience from all causes was significantly more favorable for students when compared to their non-academic-age peers ($p < .001$). In terms of total mortality, suicides accounted for 23 of the 68 student deaths which occurred during the 10-year study period. Proportionally, it ranked as the second leading cause of death (34%), exceeded only by accidents (37%).

Age

For the United States as a whole, there is a well-documented positive correlation between age and suicide (Dublin, 1963, p. 22). This same relationship holds for the student population. If the student body is divided on the basis of those who are above and below age 25, one finds that the percentage of suicides in the older age group is approximately twice their proportional percentage in the population (see Table 1). This distinction is graphically portrayed in Figure 1 which presents the relative frequency of suicidal and nonsuicidal students by 5-year age groups. It is notable that only about 6% of all students fall in the 30- to 34-year age category while more than 26% of the suicidal students are found in this interval. In fact, the median age for the student body population is 22 years, 6 months, while the median age for the suicidal students, 26 years, 5 months, is greater by almost 4 years.

Class Standing

Directly correlated with, and, indeed, almost identical to, chronological age, is the class standing of individual students. Median class standing for the entire student population was the junior year, for the suicidal subset it was the senior year. When the groups are divided on the basis of graduate or undergraduate standing, one finds that graduate students committed suicide in numbers significantly greater than could be expected from their proportions in the student body at large (see Table 1).

Table 1

SELECTED DEMOGRAPHIC CHARACTERISTICS OF SUICIDAL AND NONSUICIDAL
STUDENTS, UCB, 1952–61

Demographic characteristics	Suicidal students		Total student body population	
	Frequency distribution ($n = 23$)	% distribution	% distribution	p
Age				
Under 25	9	39	70	.001
25 and above	14	61	30	
Class standing				
Undergraduate	12	52	72	.033
Graduate	11	48	28	
Sex				
Male	17	74	67	ns
Female	6	26	33	
Marital status[a]				
Married	3	14	23	ns
Never married	19	86	77	
Race				
White	20	87	89	ns
Nonwhite	3	13	11	
Religion				
Protestant	15	65	60	
Jewish	5	22	18	ns
Catholic	3	13	22	
Nationality				
U.S.A.	19	83	96	.002
Foreign	4	17	04	
Major subject[b]				
Mechanical-mathematic	10	50	64	ns
Aesthetic-social	10	50	36	
Grade-point average[c]				
Above average	14	67	50	ns
Below average	7	33	50	
Mental-health service				
Psychiatric patient	8	34	10	$<.001$
Nonpatient	15	66	90	

a Excludes one divorced student.

b Excludes three students who had not declared majors.

c Excludes two students who did not complete a semester.

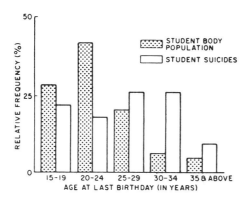

Figure 1

AGE DISTRIBUTIONS OF STUDENT SUICIDES AND TOTAL STUDENT
BODY POPULATION, UCB, 1952–61.

Sex

Of the 23 student suicides, 17 were male, 6 female, a sex ratio approximating 3:1 (see Table 1). This finding accords with those sex ratios reported in previous studies of completed suicide (Dublin, 1963, p. 23). However, an adjustment is necessary to correctly relate this information to the college population. Whereas the sexes are about equally distributed in the general United States population, they are not equally distributed on campus. For the years under study, males outnumbered females in the student body population by approximately 2:1. Accordingly, the obtained sex ratio of 3:1 must be halved to yield an adjusted student ratio of about 1.5 male suicides for each female suicide. This student sex ratio is considerably narrower than the sex ratio for the country at large. It seems to indicate a heightened risk of suicide among female students as compared to the general female population. However, this indication must remain somewhat speculative since the female suicides were considerably older (median age 30 years, 1 month) than were male suicides (median age 26 years, 1 month). As a consequence one cannot be entirely sure that the constricted ratio is not an effect of confounding between age and sex. Should further research confirm that there is, in fact, a greater risk of suicide among female students as opposed to female nonstudents, it would follow the predictions of Gibbs and Martin (1964). They proposed a rise in female suicides due to increasing social pressures. According to their status-integration theory,

as more women enter the labor force they encounter cross-pressures from conflicting social roles. They postulate that these stresses will lead to increasing
numbers of female suicides.

Marital Status

Of the 23 student suicides, it was possible to classify 22 persons into the
categories of "married" or "never married," which corresponded to the available student population data. One divorced student was thereby excluded from
the analysis. There was no remarkable disparity between the suicidal and nonsuicidal students on the basis of marital status (see Table 1). For the entire
United States population, suicide is less common among married persons
(Dublin, 1963, p. 26), but this was not the case for campus suicides. Only
three of the student suicides were married, and only one of those married had
children. The remaining two cases, both females, committed suicide shortly
after their marriages.

Race

Of the 23 known suicides, only three were nonwhite and all three of
these nonwhite students were Chinese. There were no suicides among Negro,
East Indian, or American Indian students who, at any event comprised only
about 3% of the student body population. The distribution of suicides by race
corresponded closely to the racial proportions found in the student population
(see Table 1). It should be mentioned, however, that there is a good reason to
question the adequacy of these racial data. Since University records do not ask
for nor indicate students' race, these breakdowns, furnished by the University
Dean of Students Office, were presumably obtained from simple headcounts
with all the imprecision that this method implies.

Religion

Religion was not a significant factor in differentiating suicidal students
from the general campus population (see Table 1). As was the case with racial
statistics, the religious data, likewise, must be regarded with great skepticism.
The University does not conduct a religious census of its students. Consequently,
the religious population figures were estimated from student residence information cards on which "religious affiliation" is an optional item. Very frequently
it is left unanswered.

Nationality

Only 4 of the 23 student suicides were foreign students. Nonetheless, their representation in the student body was so negligible (only 4%) that they appear among the suicides in approximately four times the magnitude one would expect from their proportions in the student population (see Table 1). As a group, these four "international student" suicides were characterized by some striking similarities. As youngsters, all of the four had known and suffered from the ravages of war, and three of them were forced to flee from their childhood homes. Two of the students, natives of mainland China, had been dispossessed by the Communist revolution; another student, born in Austria, lost his family in the horrors of the Nazi concentration camps and subsequently migrated to Israel. The fourth student, a native Israeli, had grown up amidst the Arab-Jewish war over the Palestine partition.

Moreover, they shared a similar pattern of conflicts, centering to a large degree around strong feelings of shame. These feelings were reflected in a deep dread that they would not meet expectations that others had set for them. There was some reality to these fears, in that other persons had sent them abroad, were paying their expenses, and probably did expect from them some measure of academic achievement. Still, their excessive concern about "what others would

Table 2

SUICIDES AMONG LANGUAGE AND
LITERATURE MAJORS VS. ALL OTHER
SUBJECT MAJORS

Major subject group	Suicidal students		Total student body population %	p
	n	%		
Language and literature	5	25	9	
All other majors	15	75	91	.012

Note.—Excludes three students who had not declared major subjects.

think" was unduly frenetic. All four of them were known to the Student Mental Health Service where they had been seen for psychiatric treatment. These findings, however, must be interpreted with some caution since the median age of foreign students (26 years, 1 month), exceeded the median age of American students (24 years), raising the possibility that the differences were due in some degree to age rather than nationality.

Major Subject

For this comparison, the suicidal subjects were divided into two categories, corresponding somewhat to William James' distinction between the "tough" and "tender minded." Of the 20 suicidal students who had declared majors, the breakdown was 10 students in the "tough-minded" or mechanical-mathematics group (Engineering, Professional, Physical Sciences, Biological Sciences, Agricultural majors) and 10 students in the "tender-minded" or aesthetic-social group (Arts, Social Sciences, Language and Literature majors). Relative to their population proportions, there was a greater incidence of suicides in the tender-minded group, but not a large enough imbalance to achieve statistical significance. Further analysis, by individual subject groups, revealed that suicides were significantly more frequent among students majoring in languages and literature (five cases), especially English majors, who comprised three of the five cases (see Table 2).

Grade-Point Average

Grade-point analysis required some basic adjustments since graduate and undergraduate grading systems are not directly comparable. In practice, an undergraduate "C" is approximately equivalent to a graduate "B". For the student population, the grade-point average (GPA) for undergraduates was 2.50, while for graduates it was 3.35 (calculated to the scale: $A = 4$, $B = 3$, $C = 2$, $D = 1$, $F = 0$). Given this discrepancy, it is obviously necessary to separately compare undergraduate and graduate students with reference to their respective grade-point distributions. When the suicidal students (excluding two who did not complete a full semester at UCB) are ranked by means of achievement above or below their population GPA, we find that two-thirds of them were above average while, by definition, only half of the general student body achieved this mark. Although suggestive of a tendency toward higher grades among suicidal students, the difference, in fact, did not achieve statistical significance. However, further analysis, distributing GPA by class standing, revealed a marked discrepancy between graduate and undergraduate students. This breakdown is detailed in Table 3 and reveals that of the 11 undergraduate students who committed suicide (after one complete semester at the University), 10 of them had surpassed the undergraduate GPA. For graduate student suicides, only 4 of the 10 who had completed a semester exceeded the graduate

GPA. Despite the differential grading system that rewards the graduate student with more grade points for a similar level of work, the suicidal undergraduate students received a higher overall GPA than the graduate student suicides (see Table 4).

Table 3

GRADE-POINT AVERAGES FOR GRADUATE
AND UNDERGRADUATE STUDENT SUICIDES

GPA	Suicidal students		Student population %	p
	n	%		
Class standing				
Undergraduate				
Above mean	10	91	50	
Below mean	1	09	50	.006
Graduate				
Above mean	4	40	50	
Below mean	6	60	50	ns

Note.—Excludes two students; one graduate, one undergraduate, who suicided during their first semester.

This finding seems to indicate that undergraduate and graduate suicides differ markedly from one another in terms of academic achievement. The undergraduate suicides performed on a level well above their fellow classmates and performed considerably better than did graduate suicides. Looking at the

Table 4

OBSERVED AND EXPECTED GPA OF
STUDENT SUICIDES BY CLASS STANDING

Class standing	GPA	
	Observed	Expected
Undergraduate	3.18	2.50
Graduate	2.90	3.35

personal histories of these undergraduate students one discovers an interesting paradox. To an external observer, say someone viewing their transcripts, these students achieved splendidly in their academic pursuits. They had all been A or B students in high school since a B or better average is required for under-graduate admission, a policy which is estimated to limit entrance to the top 10–12% of graduating high school seniors. Reports from family and friends, however, reveal that self-satisfaction was not the case with these students. Rather, they seemed filled with doubts of their adequacy, dissatisfied with their grades, and despondent over their general academic aptitude. This exacerbated fear of failure was tempered somewhat by the fact that in every case of under-graduate suicide the final semester's GPA was lower (mean = 2.53) than the previous cumulative GPA (mean = 3.34). Another consideration is whether these students aspired to graduate school which requires a higher than average GPA (2.5–3.0 at UCB). Unfortunately, these exact data are not available; how-ever, a check of those students in major subjects which definitely indicated future graduate work, for example, pre-medicine, revealed academic achievement in excess of grade requirements. Nevertheless, on balance, they were still achieving loftily above the average of their classmates. How can one explain their deep self-dissatisfaction despite contrary and objective indications of their competence? Two possible explanations suggest themselves: (a) The in-ternal standards these students applied to themselves were so Olympian, the demands they imposed upon themselves so exacting, that they were destined to suffer frustration and disappointment no matter how well they fared; and/or (b) Whereas they had previously been crackerjack students in high school or junior college, excelling without much difficulty, the precipitous drop in grade points over the final semester threatened their feelings of self-esteem. Thus, faced by a sudden loss of status, they may have suicided as a response to this egoistic conflict. In any case, the discrepancy between perceived self-concept and objective reality indicates that a purely objective approach often obscures more than it reveals. What one needs to try and understand is the phenomenological response of the individual student. What is necessary to know is what inner standards, what idealized fantasy he uses to judge himself and his own personal worth. For the graduate student suicides as a group, there was no discrepancy between their academic achievements and what might be expected on the basis of the general population of graduate students. While they produced slightly below their population mean, the variation in this instance was primarily due to two students who were in considerable scholastic straits. Contrary to the under-graduates, graduate suicides showed no pattern of decline in their terminal semester GPA. Confirmation of the scholastic disparity between graduate and undergraduate suicides is further revealed by the irregular distribution of aca-demic awards. Inspection of Table 5 indicates that undergraduate students garnered scholarship honors at a rate well beyond the general undergraduate population, while the graduate student suicides did not differ significantly from their classmates in earning academic awards. Even though graduate student awards were far more plentiful, the great majority of awards (10 of 11) were held by undergraduate student suicides.

Table 5

SCHOLASTIC AWARDS BY CLASS STANDING

Class standing	Suicidal students		Student population	
	n	%	%	p
Undergraduate				
Scholarship	7	58	05	<.001
Nonscholarship	5	42	95	
Graduate				
Scholarship	1	10	23	ns
Nonscholarship	10	90	77	

Mental Health

Of the 23 student suicides, 8 had been referred to the student mental health service for psychiatric treatment (of the 8 students, apparently only 2 were diagnosed as psychotic reactions). These 8 cases comprised better than one-third of the student suicides, significantly exceeding the approximately 10% of the total student body population seen at the mental health facilities (see Table 1). Besides the 8 students known to the student psychiatric service, an additional 3 students were in private psychiatric treatment, making a total of almost 50% of the suicidal group who gave this particular indication of prior mental disturbance.

Temporal-Situational Relationships

Among all causes of death, suicide allows for the greatest degree of volition. The suicidal person is in a position to choose the date, place, and method of his death, and it has long been speculated that there may be a special psychological significance to these choices. Through tracing the time, place, and method of student suicides; the following particular patterns were observed:

Time. When student suicides were charted by calendar months they formed a bimodal curve with peaks occurring during February and October. A more meaningful comparison obtained when the academic semester was used as the time interval. This distribution, as illustrated in Figure 2, challenges a frequently held belief about campus suicides. Academic folklore often explains student suicides as a response to the anxieties and stresses of final examinations. Yet, surprisingly, the data showed that almost the reverse relationship held.

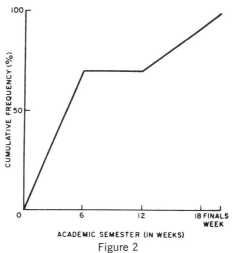

Figure 2

TIME DISTRIBUTION OF STUDENT SUICIDES,
UCB, 1952–61.

Only 1 of the 23 student suicides was committed during finals. (Even that single instance may be dubiously related to final exams since this student was doing well in school and had expressed satisfaction with his "finals" performance.) Most of the suicides occurred at the beginning of the semester. When the semester is divided into three equivalent parts, the vast majority of cases, 16 out of 23, are found to occur during the first 6-week segment. (Actually, the period is only 5 weeks from when instruction begins; the first week is confined to registration procedures.) No cases were found during the second 6-week period which includes the mid-term examinations. Over the remaining third of the semester there were seven cases, just one of which occurred during finals week itself (always the last week of the semester). This irregular time distribution of student suicides departed significantly from uniform expectations ($x^2_2 = 16.8$, $p < .001$). Clearly, the old saw about suicides and finals was not supported. Instead, the danger period for student suicide was found to be the start, not the finish, of the school semester. Incidentally, the day of the week departed significantly from the null hypothesis of uniformity ($x^2_1 = 4.18$, $p < .05$) with almost one-half the cases occurring on Monday or Friday, terminals of the school week. Unfortunately, the data were none too precise since some cases were based on coroner's estimates as to the data of death.

The unexpectedly low correspondence between final examinations and the commission of student suicide bears some resemblance to a parallel phenomenon involving student mental health during the recent free speech activities on the UCB campus. In the course of these supposedly stressful times, there was a striking drop in admissions to the student mental health service (20% below average) and no recorded student suicides during the 1965 academic year. (Such behavior corresponds to the drop in suicides, psychosomatic illness, and neurotic conditions observed during both World Wars.) Why, in the midst of all the controversy, turmoil, and tempest was student mental health apparently enhanced? One possibility is that some students who had previously been grappling with internal problems now had the opportunity to act out, to ventilate their inner conflicts, and to displace their intrapunitive anger and hostility by redirecting it toward an external symbol, namely, the University. Perhaps it was the galvanized and heightened sense of community that facilitated mental well-being. Certainly many students felt involved in a common cause; probably, for some it imparted meaning to their lives where previously they had felt alienated and purposeless. If so, it was also a perfect antidote to the kinds of feelings that often drive people to self-destruction.

Place.   Most of the students, 12 of 23, committed suicide at their residences. The next most frequent location was the University itself, upon whose grounds 4 students ended their lives. Three students were found dead in parked autos on isolated suburban roads. Another 3 suicided in out-of-town hotel rooms, and 1 student leaped from the San Francisco Golden Gate Bridge. It is difficult to determine any significance to the site of these suicides, except for the 4 cases who killed themselves on the university grounds. Of these, the most symbolic suicide was the 1 student who jumped from the Campanile, an architectural landmark of the Berkeley campus.

Method.   The most frequent agent of choice was firearms, followed by ingestions and asphyxiations. A comparison with the methods used by Yale student suicides (see Table 6) revealed considerable similarity in the methods employed by the two groups of students. The relatively larger number of poisonings among UCB students is most likely due to the more recent availability of tranquilizers and barbiturates.

For only two of the Berkeley cases was there the least equivocation about assigning suicide as the cause of death. These two cases, both involving ingestions of poisonous substances, were qualified as "probably suicide" but routinely coded as "deaths due to suicide." In at least 10 instances, suicide notes were left by the decedents. These notes ranged from simple instructions concerning the disposal of personal belongings to lengthy, literary dissertations, one of which finished by tersely quoting Camus: "Life as a human being is absurd."

Table 6

METHODS OF SUICIDE USED BY UCB AND
YALE STUDENTS

Method	UCB (1952–1961)		Yale (1920–1955)[a]	
	n	%	n	%
Firearms	8	35	10	40
Poisonings	6	26	3	12
Asphyxiation	4	17	5	20
Hanging	2	09	6	24
Jumping from high place	2	09	1	04
Cutting instruments	1	04	—	—
Total	23	100	25	100

[a] Source: Parrish, 1957, p. 589.

Psychological Factors

A statistical approach, per se, can go just so far in describing the suicide-prone student. The additional use of case history materials provides a fuller, more clinically oriented dimension to the portrayal. As such, the following inferences were derived from anecdotal reports of friends and acquaintances of the students, along with those members of the University community whose lives they touched. From a preventive standpoint, the most pertinent questions which might be asked are, "What prodromal signs, what clues to suicide could be discerned from the personal lives of these students? Specifically, were there any indications or harbingers of their ultimate destinies?" Lastly, "Was there a characteristic conflict which precipitated their self-destructive actions?" The question of prodromal indications can be flatly answered "yes." There were numerous warnings in almost every case. At least five of the students had made past suicide attempts. Warnings of a more subtle nature could be discovered in the histories of the remaining students. For example, the pupil who went out of his way to modify an item on the medical history form. Where it had requested, "Whom shall we notify in case of emergency?" he crossed out the word "emergency" and substituted "death." Or the student who confided that he sometimes takes 10 or so nembutals because "I am an adventurer." Other students evidenced a long-standing infatuation with death, often initiating "bull sessions" about the futility of life, or making wry jokes about killing themselves. Prior to their suicides a disproportionately large number of these students were involved in psychiatric treatment. As a group, they presented similar symptomatic patterns featuring symptoms of insomnia, anorexia, and extreme moodiness, especially moods of despondency; in all, it was a psychological picture compatible with the general diagnosis of agitated depression.

Although their prodromal response to stress was very similar, the particular crises that precipitated their suicides were not. Bearing in mind that each individual case was unique, for purposes of description, the main prodromal conflicts could be classified into the following three categories:

1. *Concern over studies*—In many cases acquaintances of the students made such judgments as "he pushed himself too hard," "worried over grades," "felt his grades were not good as he thought they should be," or similar scholastic anxieties which, they felt, triggered the suicidal crisis. It is difficult to evaluate these inferences since "worry over grades" is often seen by informants as a most likely explanation. At any event, if true, their exaggerated concern over studies contrasted vividly with generally excellent academic grades.

2. *Unusual physical complaints*—A number of the students complained of inability to eat or sleep, one student warranting a diagnosis of "avitaminosis." Others worried about possible deterioration such as the student who feared that his "failing sight" might ruin a prospective medical career. A few pupils, however, presented physical complaints of a bizarre semidelusional quality, for instance, the young man whose stomach literally persecuted him. From childhood on he had suffered from anorexia and "stomach ache." Although an exploratory laparotomy did not disclose anything, by the time he entered the University he was at least 50 pounds underweight, still wracked by chronic stomach pains. He then moved from his fraternity house, in the hope of gaining weight by selecting his own food. This plan proved to no avail, nor did extensive medical testing at the student health service, all of which proved negative. He finally ended his torment, perhaps symbolically, by ingesting cyanide.

3. *Difficulties with interpersonal relationships*—Combined under this heading were two different types of conflicts, both reflecting problems in personal relationships. First were the students involved in stormy love affairs. Here the critical stresses were feelings of rejection which had been engendered by broken romances. In the one recorded instance of double suicide, the precipitating event was parental opposition to the youngsters' marriage. Much more

typical, however, was the essentially asocial, withdrawn student. These particular students were uniformly described as terribly shy, virtually friendless individuals, alienated from all but the most minimal social interactions. Frequently they had compensated for their personal solitude by increased study and almost total absorption in schoolwork. The most calamitous example of such human isolation was the student, dead for 18 days before he was found in his lonely room. It is a tragic commentary to his existence, and perhaps a cause for his suicide, that there were no friends, no people involved enough in his life to know, or to care, that he had been missing for well over 2 weeks.

Interpretation

Reviewing the results of the present study, one can reasonably conclude that significant associations between student suicide and numerous variables, both personal and environmental, have been demonstrated. Nonetheless, one cannot, with certitude, infer that these relationships are causal ones. This type of inference would require procedures more exacting than the limited epidemiological methods herein employed. For instance, the total student body population, used as a matched control or comparison group, included a number of students who had unsuccessfully attempted suicide. Quite possibly their inclusion diluted the significance of the obtained differences between suicidal and presumably nonsuicidal students. This is a relatively minor concern, compared to other more cautionary limitations. A primary concern is to what degree the observed relationships were spuriously increased by a common variable. For example, the correlation between student suicide and declining terminal GPA may very well be due to a third factor—emotional disturbance—which both depressed scholastic grades and led to self-destruction. As a corollary, it should be recognized that not all of the selected variables were independent of one another. It is known for one that age and class standing are highly dependent, and it was observed, also, that the variable of age probably confounded to some degree the comparisons by sex and by nationality. Another area of uncertainty concerns the time-order sequence of student suicide. One is unable to state, with certainty, which comes first, the disturbed student or the stresses of student life. Are the suicides due to selection into colleges of mentally unstable individuals or are they due to competitive pressures of the academic environment? The fullest answer to these questions will only come from further research. Toward this goal some salient lines of inquiry could include: the investigation of student suicide attempters and student accident cases, postcollegiate follow-up studies, and the use of "psychological autopsy" procedures, as described by Shneidman and Farberow (1961).

Within the expressed limits of the study design, what predictions about the future suicide problem are warranted? Extrapolating from results of the present study, it appears that a future increase of student suicides may be expected. This increase should occur as a function of two variables, that is, age and academic competition, both of which are directly correlated to student suicides, and both of which are slated to increase in future student body populations. Average student age is already rising as a result of ever increasing proportions of graduate students in the American university system. For example, architects of the UCB educational master plan are considering an ultimate 50:50 graduate-undergraduate ratio. The second variable, academic competition, will likely increase as a result of mounting public demands for quasi-universal college education. As a case in point, the enrollment demands at UCB have already exceeded the available academic supply. Consequently, it has been necessary to restrict enrollment to the uppermost fraction of high school graduating classes. If accepted, the pressure on the student to achieve and maintain very high GPAs gives no indication of abatement. In fact, the situation ominously resembles a suicidal problem which prevails among the youth of Japan. In the Japanese case there are tremendous pressures to attend college, and those students who fail to gain entrance frequently turn to suicide as a solution to their dilemmas. Such conflicts, in addition to a more accepting cultural attitude, have probably helped to make Japan "a country of youthful suicides where suicide has become the number one cause of death in individuals under 30 [DeVos, 1964, p. 6]."

SUMMARY

The purpose of this study was to identify distinctive attributes of the suicidal student, and to determine those environmental conditions which heighten his susceptibility to suicide.

Using an epidemiological approach, demographic comparisons were made between the sample of 23 UCB students who committed suicide during the years 1952–1961 inclusive, and the total student body population for those years. As an additional procedure, the temporal-situational characteristics of student suicides were described and analyzed.

The main findings of the research were:

1. Suicidal students could be significantly differentiated from their classmates on the variables of age, class standing, major subject, nationality, emotional condition, and academic achievement. Compared to the student population at large, the suicidal group was older, contained greater proportions of graduates, language majors, and foreign students, and gave more indications of emotional disturbance. In addition, the undergraduate suicides fared much better than their fellow students in matters of academic achievement.

2. Contrary to the popular belief that suicides frequently occur during final examinations week, time relationships indicated that the peak danger period for student suicides was the beginning (first 6 weeks), not the midterm, nor end of the semester.

3. Most of the students gave recurrent warnings of their suicidal intent. Many of them presented a similar prodromal pattern marked by anorexia, insomnia, and periods of despondency.

4. Major precipitating factors were: Worry over schoolwork, chronic concerns about physical health (sometimes of a decidedly bizarre nature), and difficulties with interpersonal relationships. This last category contained some students who had reacted to romantic rejections but, for the most part, comprised the emotionally withdrawn and socially isolated student.

5. A future increase of student suicides was predicted on the basis of changes taking place in the age structure of college populations and in the competitive pressures of student life.

REFERENCES

Braaten, J., & Darling, C. Suicidal tendencies among college students. *Psychiatric Quarterly,* 1962, 36, 665–692.

Bruyn, H. B., & Seiden, R. H. Student suicide: Fact or fancy? *Journal of the American College Health Association,* 1965, 14, 69–77.

DeVos, G. Role narcissism and the etiology of Japanese suicide. Berkeley Calif.: Institute of International Studies, University of California, 1964. (Mimeo)

Dublin, L. I. *Suicide: A sociological and statistical study.* New York: Ronald, 1963.

Gibbs, J. P., & Martin, W. T. *Status integration and suicide.* Eugene: Oregon University Press, 1964.

Hill, A. B. *Principles of medical statistics.* New York: Oxford University Press, 1961.

Jensen, V. W. Evaluating the suicidal impulse in the university setting. *Journal Lancet,* 1955, 75, 441–444.

MacMahon, B., Pugh, T. F., & Ipsen, J. *Epidemiological methods.* Boston: Little, Brown, 1960.

Parrish, H. M. Epidemiology of suicide among college students. *Yale Journal of Biology and Medicine,* 1957, 29, 585–595.

Raphael, T., Power, S. H., & Berridge, W. L. The question of suicide as a problem in college mental hygiene. *American Journal of Orthopsychiatry,* 1937, 7, 1–14.

Shneidman, E. S., & Farberow, N. L. Sample investigations of equivocal deaths.

In N. L. Farberow & E. S. Shneidman (Eds.), *The cry for help*. New York: McGraw-Hill, 1961. Pp. 118–128.

Suslow, S. A *ten-year survey of certain demographic characteristics of the student population*. Berkeley: Office of the Registrar, University of California, 1963. (Mimeo)

Temby, W. D. Suicide. In G. B. Blaine & C. G. McArthur (Eds.), *Emotional problems of the student*. New York: Appleton-Century-Crofts, 1961. Pp. 133–152.

DISCUSSION

Seiden's article represents a significant contribution to the scientific understanding of a phenomenon which has been investigated too often in the past solely through the method of the descriptive clinical case report. His results differentiate between suicidal and nonsuicidal students as well as determine some of the situational variables associated with student suicide. Clearly, these findings represent only one small but necessary step toward the formulation of a classificatory system which will eventually enable us to better predict and prevent suicidal behavior.

The functional psychoses are divided into three subclasses: manic-depressive disorders, the paranoid reactions, and schizophrenia. Schizophrenia is the most common form of psychosis by far, accounting for approximately fifty percent of all hospitalized mental patients. This fact is probably not as indicative of the great prevalence of schizophrenia as it is the result of indiscriminate grouping of individuals characterized by severely disturbed behavior resulting from a variety of causes. The articles included in this section present quite diverse attempts to explain the origins of schizophrenic behavior. Perhaps some of the apparent lack of overlap in these articles is due to the fact that the authors appear to be discussing quite unique subpopulations of individuals labelled schizophrenic.

14

SCHIZOTAXIA, SCHIZOTYPY, SCHIZOPHRENIA

Paul E. Meehl

In the course of the last decade, while spending several thousand hours in the practice of intensive psychotherapy, I have treated—sometimes unknowingly except in retrospect—a considerable number of schizoid and schizophrenic patients. Like all clinicians, I have formed some theoretical opinions as a result of these experiences. While I have not until recently begun any systematic research efforts on this baffling disorder, I felt that to share with you some of my thoughts, based though they are upon clinical impressions in the context of selected research by others, might be an acceptable use of this occasion.

Let me begin by putting a question which I find is almost never answered correctly by our clinical students on PhD orals, and the answer to which they seem to dislike when it is offered. Suppose that you were required to write down a procedure for selecting an individual from the population who would be diagnosed as schizophrenic by a psychiatric staff; you have to wager $1,000 on being right; you may not include in your selection procedure any behavioral fact, such as a symptom or trait, manifested by the individual. What would you write down? So far as I have been able to ascertain, there is only one thing you could write down that would give you a better than even chance of winning such a bet—namely, "Find an individual X who has a schizophrenic identical twin." Admittedly, there are many other facts which would raise your odds somewhat above the low base rate of schizophrenia. You might, for example, identify X by first finding mothers who have certain unhealthy child-rearing attitudes; you might enter a subpopulation defined jointly by such demographic

Reprinted in part from the *American Psychologist,* 17, 1962, 827–831, with the permission of the American Psychological Association and Dr. Meehl.

Address of the President of the seventieth Annual Convention of the American Psychological Association, St. Louis, September 2, 1962.

variables as age, size of community, religion, ethnic background, or social class. But these would leave you with a pretty unfair wager, as would the rule, "Find an X who has a fraternal twin, of the same sex, diagnosed as schizophrenic" (Fuller & Thompson, 1960, pp. 272–283; Stern, 1960, pp. 581–584).

Now the twin studies leave a good deal to be desired methodologically (Rosenthal, in press); but there seems to be a kind of "double standard of methodological morals" in our profession, in that we place a good deal of faith in our knowledge of schizophrenic dynamics, and we make theoretical inferences about social learning factors from the establishment of group trends which may be statistically significant and replicable although of small or moderate size; but when we come to the genetic studies, our standards of rigor suddenly increase. I would argue that the concordance rates in the twin studies need not be accepted uncritically as highly precise parameter estimates in order for us to say that their magnitudes represent the most important piece of etiological information we possess about schizophrenia.

It is worthwhile, I think, to pause here over a question in the sociology of knowledge, namely, why do psychologists exhibit an aversive response to the twin data? I have no wish to argue *ad hominem* here—I raise this question in a constructive and irenic spirit, because I think that a substantive confusion often lies at the bottom of this resistance, and one which can be easily dispelled. Everybody readily assents to such vague dicta as "heredity and environment interact," "there need be no conflict between organic and functional concepts," "we always deal with the total organism," etc. But it almost seems that clinicians do not fully believe these principles in any concrete sense, because they show signs of thinking that *if* a genetic basis were found for schizophrenia, the psychodynamics of the disorder (especially in relation to intrafamilial social learnings) would be somehow negated or, at least, greatly demoted in importance. To what extent, if at all, is this true?

Here we run into some widespread misconceptions as to what is meant by *specific etiology* in nonpsychiatric medicine. By postulating a "specific etiology" one does *not* imply any of the following:

1. The etiological factor always, or even usually, produces clinical illness.

2. If illness occurs, the particular form and content of symptoms is derivable by reference to the specific etiology alone.

3. The course of the illness can be materially influenced only by procedures directed against the specific etiology.

4. All persons who share the specific etiology will have closely similar histories, symptoms, and course.

5. The largest single contributor to symptom variance is the specific etiology.

In medicine, not one of these is part of the concept of specific etiology, yet they are repeatedly invoked as arguments against a genetic interpretation of schizophrenia. I am not trying to impose the causal model of medicine by analogy; I merely which to emphasize that *if* one postulates a genetic mutation as the specific etiology of schizophrenia, he is not thereby committed to any of the above as implications. Consequently such familiar objections as "Schizophrenics differ widely from one another" or "Many schizophrenics can be helped by purely psychological methods" should not disturb one who opts for a genetic hypothesis. In medicine, the concept of specific etiology means the *sine qua non*—the causal condition which is necessary, but not sufficient, for the disorder to occur. A genetic theory of schizophrenia would, in this sense, be stronger than that of "one contributor to variance"; but weaker than that of "largest contributor to variance." In analysis of variance terms, it means an interaction effect such that no other variables can exert a main effect when the specific etiology is lacking.

Now it goes without saying that "clinical schizophrenia" as such cannot be inherited, because it has behavioral and phenomenal contents which are learned. As Bleuler says, in order to have a delusion involving Jesuits one must first have learned about Jesuits. It seems inappropriate to apply the geneticist's concept of "penetrance" to the crude statistics of formal diagnosis— if a specific genetic etiology exists, its phenotypic expression in *psychological* categories would be a quantitative aberration in some parameter of a behavioral acquisition function. What could possibly be a genetically determined functional parameter capable of generating such diverse behavioral outcomes, including the preservation of normal function in certain domains?

The theoretical puzzle is exaggerated when we fail to conceptualize at different levels of molarity. For instance, there is a tendency among organically minded theorists to analogize between catatonic phenomena and various neurological or chemically induced states in animals. But Bleuler's masterly *Theory of Schizophrenic Negativism* (1912) shows how the whole range of catatonic behavior, including diametrically opposite modes of relating to the interpersonal environment, can be satisfactorily explained as instrumental acts; thus even a convinced organicist, postulating a biochemical defect as specific etiology, should recognize that the causal linkage between this etiology and catatonia is indirect, requiring for the latter's derivation a lengthy chain of statements which are not even formulable except in molar psychological language.

What kind of behavioral fact about the patient leads us to diagnose schizophrenia? There are a number of traits and symptoms which get a high weight, and the weights differ among clinicians. But thought disorder continues to hold its own in spite of today's greater clinical interest in motivational (especially interpersonal) variables. If you are inclined to doubt this for yourself, consider the following indicators: Patient experiences intense ambivalence, readily reports conscious hatred of family figures, is pananxious, subjects therapist to a long series of testing operations, is withdrawn, and says, "Naturally, I am growing my father's hair."

While all of these are schizophrenic indicators, the last one is the diagnostic bell ringer. In this respect we are still Bleulerians, although we know a lot more about the schizophrenic's psychodynamics than Bleuler did. The significance of thought disorder, associative dyscontrol (or, as I prefer to call it so as to include the very mildest forms it may take, "cognitive slippage"), in schizophrenia has been somewhat de-emphasized in recent years. Partly this is due to the greater interest in interpersonal dynamics, but partly also to the realization that much of our earlier psychometric assessment of the thought disorder was mainly reflecting the schizophrenic's tendency to underperform because uninterested, preoccupied, resentful, or frightened. I suggest that this realization has been overgeneralized and led us to swing too far the other way, as if we had shown that there really *is* no cognitive slippage factor present. One rather common assumption seems to be that if one can demonstrate the potentiating effect of a motivational state upon cognitive slippage, light has thereby been shed upon the etiology of schizophrenia. Why are we entitled to think this? Clinically, we see a degree of cognitive slippage not found to a comparable degree among nonschizophrenic persons. Some patients (e.g., pseudoneurotics) are highly anxious and exhibit minimal slippage; others (e.g., burnt-out cases) are minimally anxious with marked slippage. The demonstration that we can intensify a particular patient's cognitive dysfunction by manipulating his affects is not really very illuminating. After all, even ordinary neurological diseases can often be tremendously influenced symptomatically via emotional stimuli; but if a psychologist demonstrates that the spasticity or tremor of a multiple sclerotic is affected by rage or fear, we would not thereby have learned anything about the etiology of multiple sclerosis.

Consequent upon our general assimilation of the insights given us by psychoanalysis, there is today a widespread and largely unquestioned assumption that when we can trace out the motivational forces linked to the content of aberrant behavior, then we understand why the person has fallen ill. There is no compelling reason to assume this, when the evidence is mainly our dynamic understanding of the patient, however valid that may be. The phrase "why the person has fallen ill" may, of course, be legitimately taken to include these things; an account of how and when he falls ill will certainly include them. But they may be quite inadequate to answer the question, "Why does X fall ill and not Y, granted that we can understand both of them?" I like the analogy of a color psychosis, which might be developed by certain individuals in a society entirely oriented around the making of fine color discriminations. Social, sexual, economic signals are color mediated; to misuse a color word is strictly taboo; compulsive mothers are horribly ashamed of a child who is retarded in color development, and so forth. Some color-blind individuals (not all, perhaps not most) develop a color psychosis in this culture; as adults, they are found on the couches of color therapists, where a great deal of *valid* understanding is achieved about color dynamics. Some of them make a social recovery. Nonetheless, if we ask, "What was basically the matter with these patients?" meaning, "What is the specific etiology of the color psychosis?" the answer is that mutated gene on the X chromosome. This is why my own therapeutic experience with schizophrenic patients has not yet convinced me of the schizophrenogenic mother as a specific etiology, even though the picture I get of my patients' mothers is pretty much in accord with the familiar one. There is no question here of accepting the patient's account; my point is that *given* the account, and taking it quite at face value, does not tell me why the patient is a patient and not just a fellow who had a bad mother.

Another theoretical lead is the one given greatest current emphasis, namely, *interpersonal aversiveness.* The schizophrene suffers a degree of social fear, distrust, expectation of rejection, and conviction of his own unlovability which cannot be matched in its depth, pervasity, and resistance to corrective experience by any other diagnostic group.

Then there is a quasi-pathognomonic sign, emphasized by Rado (1956; Rado & Daniels, 1956) but largely ignored in psychologists' diagnostic usage, namely, *anhedonia*—a marked, widespread, and refractory defect in pleasure capacity which, once you learn how to examine for it, is one of the most consistent and dramatic behavioral signs of the disease.

Finally, I include *ambivalence* from Bleuler's cardinal four (1950). His other two, "autism" and "dereism," I consider derivative from the combination of slippage, anhedonia, and aversiveness. Crudely put, if a person cannot think straight, gets little pleasure, and is afraid of everyone, he will of course learn to be autistic and dereistic.

If these clinical characterizations are correct, and we combine them with the hypothesis of a genetic specific etiology, do they give us any lead on theoretical possibilities?

Granting its initial vagueness as a construct, requiring to be filled in by neurophysiological research, I believe we should take seriously the old European notion of an "integrative neural defect" as the only direct phenotypic consequence produced by the genic mutation. This is an aberration in some parameter of single cell function, which may or may not be manifested in the functioning of more molar CNS systems, depending upon the organization of the mutual feedback controls and upon the stochastic parameters of the reinforcement regime. This neural integrative defect, which I shall christen *schizotaxia,* is all that can properly be spoken of as inherited. The imposition of a social learning history upon schizotaxic individuals results in a personality organization which I shall call, following Rado, the *schizotype.* The four core behavior traits are obviously not innate; but I postulate that they are universally learned by schizotaxic individuals, given any of the actually existing social reinforcement regimes, from the best to the worst. If the interpersonal regime is favorable, and the schizotaxic person also has the good fortune to inherit a low anxiety readiness, physical vigor, general resistance to stress and the like, he will remain a well-compensated "normal" schizotype, never manifesting symptoms of mental disease. He will be like the gout-prone male whose genes determine him to have an elevated blood uric acid titer, but who never develops clinical gout.

Only a subset of schizotypic personalities decompensate into clinical schizophrenia. It seems likely that the most important causal influence pushing the schizotype toward schizophrenic decompensation is the schizophrenogenic mother.

I hope it is clear that this view does not conflict with what has been established about the mother-child interaction. If this interaction were totally free of maternal ambivalence and aversive inputs to the schizotaxic child, even compensated schizotypy might be avoided; at most, we might expect to find only the faintest signs of cognitive slippage and other minimal neurological aberrations, possibly including body image and other proprioceptive deviations, but not the interpersonal aversiveness which is central to the clinical picture.

Nevertheless, while assuming the etiological importance of mother in determining the course of aversive social learnings, it is worthwhile to speculate about the modification our genetic equations might take on this hypothesis. Many schizophrenogenic mothers are themselves schizotypes in varying degrees of compensation. Their etiological contribution then consists jointly in their passing on the gene, *and* in the fact that being schizotypic, they provide the kind of ambivalent regime which potentiates the schizotypy of the child and raises the odds of his decompensating. Hence the incidence of the several parental genotypes among parent pairs of diagnosed proband cases is not calculable from the usual genetic formulas. For example, given a schizophrenic proband, the odds that mother is homozygous (or, if the gene were dominant, that it is mother who carries it) are different from those for father; since we have begun by selecting a decompensated case, and formal diagnosis as the phenotype involves a potentiating factor for mother which is psychodynamically greater than that for a schizotypic father. Another important influence would be the likelihood that the lower fertility of schizophrenics is also present, but to an unknown degree, among compensated schizotypes. Clinical experience suggests that in the semicompensated range, this lowering of fertility is greater among males, since many schizotypic women relate to men in an exploited or exploitive sexual way, where as the male schizotype usually displays a marked deficit in heterosexual aggressiveness. Such a sex difference in fertility among decompensated cases has been reported by Meyers and Goldfarb (1962).

Since the extent of aversive learnings is a critical factor in decompensation, the inherited anxiety readiness is presumably greater among diagnosed cases. Since the more fertile mothers are likely to be compensated, hence themselves to be relatively low anxiety if schizotaxic, a frequent parent pattern should be a compensated schizotypic mother married to a neurotic father, the latter being the source of the proband's high-anxiety genes (plus providing a poor paternal model for identification in male patients, and a weak defender of the child against mother's schizotypic hostility).

These considerations make ordinary family concordance studies, based upon formal diagnoses, impossible to interpret. The most important research need here is development of high-validity indicators for compensated schizotypy. I see some evidence for these conceptions in the report of Lidz and co-workers, who in studying intensively the parents of 15 schizophrenic patients were surprised to find that "minimally, 9 of the 15 patients had at least one parent who could be called schizophrenic, or ambulatory schizophrenic, or clearly paranoid in behavior and attitudes" (Lidz, Cornelison, Terry, & Fleck, 1958, p. 308). As I read the brief personality sketches presented, I would judge that all but two of the probands had a clearly schizotypic parent. These authors, while favoring a "learned irrationality" interpretation of their data, also recognize the alternative genetic interpretation. Such facts do not permit a decision, obviously; my main point is the striking difference between the high incidence of parental schizotypes, mostly quite decompensated (some to the point of diagnosable psychosis), and the zero incidence which a conventional family concordance study would have yielded for this group.

Another line of evidence, based upon a very small sample but exciting because of its uniformity, is McConaghy's report (1959) that among non-diagnosed parent pairs of 10 schizophrenics, subclinical thought disorder was psychometrically detectable in at least one parent of every pair. Rosenthal (in press) reports that he can add five tallies to this parent-pair count, and suggests that such results might indicate that the specific heredity is dominant, and completely penetrant, rather than recessive. The attempt to replicate these findings, and other psychometric efforts to tap subclinical cognitive slippage in the "normal" relatives of schizophrenics, should receive top priority in our research efforts.

Summarizing, I hypothesize that the statistical relation between schizotaxia, schizotypy, and schizophrenia is class inclusion: All schizotaxics become, *on all actually existing social learning regimes,* schizotypic in personality organization; but most of these remain compensated. A minority, disadvantaged by other (largely polygenically determined) constitutional weaknesses, and put on a bad regime by schizophrenogenic mothers (most of whom are themselves schizotypes) are thereby potentiated into clinical schizophrenia. What makes schizotaxia etiologically specific is its role as a *necessary* condition. I postulate that a nonschizotaxic individual, whatever his other genetic makeup and whatever his learning history, would at most develop a character disorder or a psychoneurosis; but he would not become a schizotype and therefore could never manifest its decompensated form, schizophrenia.

What sort of quantitative aberration in the structural or functional parameters of the nervous system can we conceive to be directly determined by a mutated gene, and to so alter initial dispositions that affected individuals will, in the course of their childhood learning history, develop the four schizotypal source traits: cognitive slippage, anhedonia, ambivalence, and interpersonal aversiveness? To me, the most baffling thing about the disorder is the phenotypic heterogeneity of this tetrad. If one sets himself to the task of doing a theoretical Vigotsky job on this list of psychological dispositions, he may manage part of it by invoking a sufficiently vague kind of descriptive unity between ambivalence and interpersonal aversiveness; and perhaps even anhedonia could be somehow subsumed. But the cognitive slippage presents a real roadblock. Since I consider cognitive slippage to be a core element in schizophrenia, any characterization of schizophrenic or schizotypic behavior which purports to abstract its essence but does not include the cognitive slippage must be deemed unsatisfactory. I believe that an adequate theoretical account will necessitate moving downward in the pyramid of the sciences to invoke explanatory constructs not found in social, psychodynamic, or even learning theory language, but instead at the neurophysiological level.

Perhaps we don't know enough about "how the brain works" to theorize profitably at that level; and I daresay that the more a psychologist knows about the latest research on brain function, the more reluctant he would be to engage in etiological speculation. Let me entreat my physiologically expert listeners to be charitable toward this clinician's premature speculations about how the schizotaxic brain might work. I feel partially justified in such speculating because there are some well-attested general truths about mammalian learned behavior which could almost have been set down from the armchair, in the way engineers draw block diagrams indicating what kinds of parts or subsystems a physical system *must* have, and what their interconnections *must* be, in order to function "appropriately." Brain research of the last decade provides a direct neurophysiological substrate for such cardinal behavior requirements as avoidance, escape, reward, drive differentiation, general and specific arousal or activation, and the like (see Delafresnaye, 1961; Ramey & O'Doherty, 1960). The discovery in the limbic system of specific positive reinforcement centers by Olds and Milner in 1954, and of aversive centers in the same year by Delgado, Roberts, and Miller (1954), seems to me to have an importance that can scarcely be exaggerated; and while the ensuing lines of research on the laws of intracranial stimulation as a mode of behavior control present some puzzles and paradoxes, what *has* been shown up to now may already suffice to provide a theoretical framework. As a general kind of brain model let us take a broadly

Hebbian conception in combination with the findings on intracranial stimulation.

To avoid repetition I shall list some basic assumptions first but introduce others in context and only implicitly when the implication is obvious. I shall assume that:

When a presynaptic cell participates in firing a postsynaptic cell, the former gains an increment in firing control over the latter. Coactivation of anatomically connected cell assemblies or assembly systems therefore increases their stochastic control linkage, and the frequency of discharges by neurons of a system may be taken as an intensity variable influencing the growth rate of intersystem control linkage as well as the momentary activity level induced in the other systems. (I shall dichotomize acquired cortical systems into "perceptual-cognitive," including central representations of goal objects; and "instrumental," including overarching monitor systems which select and guide specific effector patterns.)

Most learning in mature organisms involves altering control linkages between systems which themselves have been consolidated by previous learnings, sometimes requiring thousands of activations and not necessarily related to the reinforcement operation to the extent that perceptual-to-instrumental linkage growth functions are.

Control linkage increments from coactivation depend heavily, if not entirely, upon a period of reverberatory activity facilitating consolidation.

Feedback from positive limbic centers is facilitative to concurrent perceptual-cognitive or instrumental sequences, whereas negative center feedback exerts an inhibitory influence. (These statements refer to initial features of the direct wiring diagram, not to all long-term results of learning.) Aversive input also has excitatory effects via the arousal system, which maintain activity permitting escape learning to occur because the organism is alerted and keeps doing things. But I postulate that this overall influence is working along with an opposite effect, quite clear from both molar and intracranial experiments, that a major biological function of aversive-center activation is to produce "stoppage" of whatever the organism is currently doing.

Perceptual-cognitive systems and limbic motivational control centers develop two-way mutual controls (e.g., discriminative stimuli acquire the reinforcing property; "thoughts" become pleasantly toned; drive-relevant perceptual components are "souped-up.")

What kind of heritable parametric aberration could underlie the schizotaxic's readiness to acquire the schizotypic tetrad? It would seem, first of all, that the defect is much more likely to reside in neurone's synaptic control function than in its storage function. It is hard to conceive of a general defect in storage which would on the one hand permit so many perceptual-cognitive functions, such as tapped by intelligence tests, school learning, or the high order cognitive powers displayed by some schizotypes, and yet have the diffuse motivational and emotional effects found in these same individuals. I am not saying that a storage deficit is clearly excludable, but it hardly seems the best place to look. So we direct our attention to parameters of control.

One possibility is to take the anhedonia as fundamental. What is *phenomenologically* a radical pleasure deficiency may be roughly identified *behaviorally* with a quantitative deficit in the positive reinforcement growth constant, and each of these—the "inner" and "outer" aspects of the organism's appetitive control system—reflect a quantitative deficit in the limbic "positive" centers. The anhedonia would then be a direct consequence of the genetic defect in wiring. Ambivalence and interpersonal aversiveness would be quantitative deviations in the balance of appetitive-aversive controls. Most perceptual-cognitive and instrumental learnings occur under mixed positive and negative schedules, so the normal consequence is a collection of habits and expectancies varying widely in the intensity of their positive and negative components, but mostly "mixed" in character. Crudely put, everybody has *some* ambivalence about almost everything, and everybody has *some* capacity for "social fear." Now if the brain centers which mediate phenomenal pleasure and behavioral reward are numerically sparse or functionally feeble, the aversive centers meanwhile functioning normally, the long-term result would be a general shift toward the aversive end, appearing clinically as ambivalence and exaggerated interpersonal fear. If, as Brady believes, there is a wired-in reciprocal inhibiting relation between positive and negative centers, the long-term aversive drift would be further potentiated (i.e., what we see at the molar level as a sort of "softening" or "soothing" effect of feeding or petting upon anxiety elicitors would be reduced).

Cognitive slippage is not as easy to fit in, but if we assume that normal ego function is acquired by a combination of social reinforcements and the self-reinforcements which become available to the child via identification, then we might say roughly that "everybody has to learn *how* to think straight." Rationality is socially acquired; the secondary process and the reality principle are slowly and imperfectly learned, by even the most clear headed. Insofar as slippage is manifested in the social sphere, such an explanation has some plausibility. An overall aversive drift would account for the paradoxical schizotypic combination of interpersonal distortions and acute perceptiveness of others' unconscious, since the latter is really a hypersensitivity to aversive signals rather than an overall superiority in realistically discriminating social cues. On the output side, we might view the cognitive slippage of mildly schizoid speech as originating from poorly consolidated second-order "monitor" assembly systems which function in an editing role, their momentary regnancy constituting the "set to communicate." At this level, selection among competing verbal operants involves slight differences in appropriateness for which a washed-out social reinforcement history provides an insufficiently refined monitor system. However, if one is impressed with the presence of a pervasive and primary slippage, showing up in a diversity of tests (cf. Payne, 1961) and also on occasions when the patient is desperately trying to communicate, an explanation on the basis of deficient positive center activity is not too convincing.

This hypothesis has some other troubles which I shall merely indicate. Schizoid anhedonia is mainly interpersonal, i.e., schizotypes seem to derive adequate pleasure from esthetic and cognitive rewards. Secondly, some successful psychotherapeutic results include what appears to be a genuine normality of hedonic capacity. Thirdly, regressive electroshock sometimes has the same effect, and the animal evidence suggests that shock works by knocking out the aversive control system rather than by souping up appetitive centers. Finally, if the anhedonia is really general in extent, it is hard to conceive of any simple genetic basis for weakening the different positive centers, whose reactivity has been shown by Olds and others to be chemically drive specific.

A second neurological hypothesis takes the slippage factory as primary. Suppose that the immediate consequence of whatever biochemical aberration the gene directly controls were a specific alteration in the neurone's membrane stability, such that the distribution of optional transmission probabilities is more widely dispersed over the synaptic signal space than in normals. That is, presynaptic input signals whose spatio-temporal configuration locates them peripherally in the neurone's signal space yield transmission probabilities which are relatively closer to those at the maximum point, thereby producing a kind of dedifferentiation or flattening of the cell's selectivity. Under suitable parametric assumptions, this synaptic slippage would lead to a corresponding dedifferentiation of competing interassembly controls, because the elements in the less frequently or intensely coactivated control assembly would be accumulating control increments more rapidly than normal. Consider a perceptual-cognitive system whose regnancy is preponderantly associated with positive-center coactivation but sometimes with aversive. The cumulation of control increments will draw these apart; but if synaptic slippage exists, their difference, at least during intermediate stages of control development, will be attenuated. The intensity of aversive-center activation by a given level of perceptual-cognitive system activity will be exaggerated relative to that induced in the positive centers. For a preponderantly aversive control this will be reversed. But now the different algebraic sign of the feedbacks introduces an important asymmetry. Exaggerated negative feedback will tend to lower activity level in the predominantly appetitive case, retarding the growth of the control linkage; whereas exaggerated positive feedback in the predominantly aversive case will tend to heighten activity levels, accelerating the linkage growth. The long-term tendency will be that movement in the negative direction which I call *aversive drift*. In addition to the asymmetry generated by the difference in feedback signs, certain other features in the mixed-regime setup contribute to aversive drift. One factor is the characteristic difference between positive and negative reinforcers in their role as strengtheners. It seems a fairly safe generalization to say that positive centers function only weakly as strengtheners when "on" continuously, and mainly when they are turned on as terminators of a cognitive or instrumental sequence; by contrast, negative centers work mainly as "off" signals, tending to inhibit elements while steadily "on." We may suppose that the former strengthen mainly by facilitating post-activity reverberation (and hence consolidation) in successful systems, the latter mainly by holding down such reverberation in unsuccessful ones. Now a slippage-heightened aversive steady state during predominantly appetitive control sequences reduces their activity level, leaves fewer recently active elements available for a subsequent Olds-plus "on" signal to consolidate. Whereas a slippage-heightened Olds-plus steady state during predominantly aversive control sequences (*a*) increases their negative control *during* the "on" period and (*b*) leaves relatively more of their elements recently active and hence further consolidated by the negative "off" signal when it occurs. Another factor is exaggerated competition by aversively controlled sequences, whereby the appetitive chains do not continue to the stage of receiving socially mediated positive reinforcement, because avoidant chains (e.g., phobic behavior, withdrawal, intellectualization) are getting in the way. It is worth mentioning that the schizophrenogenic mother's regime is presumably "mixed" not only in the sense of the frequent and unpredictable aversive inputs she provides in response to the child's need signals, but also in her greater tendency to present such aversive inputs *concurrently* with drive reducers—thereby facilitating the "scrambling" of appetitive-and-aversive controls so typical of schizophrenia.

The schizotype's dependency guilt and aversive overreaction to offers of help are here seen as residues of the early knitting together of his cortical representations of appetitive goals with punishment-expectancy assembly systems. Roughly speaking, he has learned that to want anything interpersonally provided is to be endangered.

The cognitive slippage is here conceived as a direct molar consequence of synaptic slippage, potentiated by the disruptive effects of aversive control and inadequate development of interpersonal communication sets. Cognitive and instrumental linkages based upon sufficiently massive and consistent regimes, such as reaching for a seen pencil, will converge to asymptotes hardly distinguishable from the normal. But systems involving closely competing strengths and automatized selection among alternatives, especially when the main basis of acquisition and control is social reward, will exhibit evidences of malfunction.

My third speculative model revives a notion with a long history, namely, that the primary schizotaxic defect is a quantitative deficiency of inhibition. (In the light of Milner's revision of Hebb, in which the inhibitory action of Golgi Type II cells is crucial even for the formation of functionally differentiated cell assemblies, a defective inhibitory parameter could be an alternative basis for a kind of slippage similar in its consequences to the one we have just finished discussing.) There are two things about this somewhat moth-eaten "defective inhibition" idea which I find appealing. First, it is the most direct and un-complicated neurologizing of the schizoid cognitive slippage. Schizoid cognitive slippage is neither an incapacity to link, nor is it an unhealthy overcapacity to link; rather it seems to be a defective *control* over associations which are also accessible to the healthy (as in dreams, wit, psychoanalytic free association, and certain types of creative work) but are normally "edited out" or "automatically suppressed" by those superordinate monitoring assembly systems we lump to-gether under the term "set." Secondly, in working with pseudoneurotic cases one sees a phenomenon to which insufficient theoretical attention has been paid: Namely, these patients cannot turn off painful thoughts. They suffer con-stantly and intensely from painful thoughts about themselves, about possible adverse outcomes, about the past, about the attitudes and intentions of others. The "weak ego" of schizophrenia means a number of things, one of which is failure of defense; the schizophrenic has too ready access to his own id, and is too perceptive of the unconscious of others. It is tempting to read "failure of defense" a "quantitatively deficient inhibitory feedback." As mentioned earlier, aversive signals (whether exteroceptive or internally originated) must exert both an exciting effect via the arousal system and a quick-stoppage effect upon cortical sequences which fail to terminate the on-going aversive signal, leading the organism to shift to another. Suppose the gene resulted in an insufficient pro-duction (or too rapid inactivation) of the specific inhibitory transmitter sub-stance, rendering all inhibitory neurones quantitatively weaker than normal. When aversively linked cognitive sequences activate negative limbic centers, these in turn soup up the arousal system normally but provide a subnormal in-hibitory feedback, thereby permitting their elicitor to persist for a longer time and at higher intensity than normal. This further activates the negative control center, and so on, until an equilibrium level is reached which is above normal in intensity all around, and which meanwhile permits an excessive linkage growth in the aversive chain. (In this respect the semicompensated case would differ from the late-stage deteriorated schizophrenic, whose aversive drift has gradually proliferated so widely that almost any cognitive or instrumental chain elicits an overlearned defensive "stoppage," whereby even the inner life undergoes a pro-found and diffuse impoverishment.)

The mammalian brain is so wired that aversive signals tend to produce stoppage of regnant cognitive or instrumental sequences without the aversive signal having been specifically connected to their controlling cues or motiva-tional systems. E.g., lever pressing under thirst or hunger can be inhibited by shock-associated buzzer, even though the latter has not been previously con-nected with hunger, paired with the discriminative stimulus, nor presented as punishment for the operant. A deficient capacity to inhibit concurrent activity of fringe elements (aversively connected to ambiguous social inputs from ambivalent mother) would accelerate the growth of linkages between them and appetitive systems not hitherto punished. Sequential effects are here especially important, and combine with the schizophrenogenic mother's tendency not to provide differential cues of high consistency as predictors of whether aversive or appetitive consequences will follow upon the child's indications of demand.

Consider two cortical systems having shared "fringe" subsystems (e.g., part percepts of mother's face). When exteroceptive inputs are the elicitors, negative feedback from aversive centers cannot usually produce stoppage; in the absence of such overdetermining external controls, the relative activity levels are determined by the balance of facilitative and inhibitory feedbacks. "Fringe" assemblies which have already acquired more aversive control, if they begin to be activated by regnant perceptual-cognitive sequences, will increase inhibitory feedback; and being "fringe" they can thereby be held down. The schizotaxic, whose aversive-feedback stoppage of fringe-element activity is weakened, accumulates excessive intertrial Hebbian increments toward the aversive side, the predominantly aversive fringe elements being more active and becoming more knit into the system than normally. One subsequent exteroceptively controlled trials, whenever the overdetermining stimulus input activates predominantly aversive perceptual-cognitive assemblies, their driving of the negative centers will be heightened. The resulting negative feedback may now be strong enough that, when imposed upon "fringe" assemblies weakly activated and toward the appetitive side, it can produce stoppage. On such occasions the more appetitive fringe elements will be retarded in their linkage growth, receiving fewer Hebbian increments. And those which do get over threshold will become further linked during such trials to the concurrent negative center activity. The result is two-fold: a retarded growth of appetitive perceptual-cognitive linkages; and a progressive drawing of fringe elements into the aversive ambit.

"Ambiguous regimes," where the pairing of S^+ and S^- inputs occurs very unpredictably, will have a larger number of fringe elements. Also, if the external schedule is dependent upon regnant appetitive drive states as manifested in the child's instrumental social acts, so that these are often met with mixed S^+ (drive-relevant) and S^- (anxiety-eliciting) inputs, the appetitive and aversive assemblies will tend to become linked, and to activate positive and negative centers concurrently. The anhedonia and ambivalence would be consequences of this plus-minus "scrambling," especially if the positive and negative limbic centers are mutually inhibitory but here deficiently so. We would then expect schizotypic anhedonia to be basically interpersonal, and only derivatively present, if at all, in other contexts. This would in part explain the schizotype's preservation of relatively normal function in a large body of instrumental domains. For example, the acquisition of basic motor and cognitive skills would be relatively less geared to a mixed input, since "successful" mastery is both mechanically rewarded (e.g., how to open a door) and also interpersonally rewarded as "school success," etc. The hypercathexis of intellect, often found even among nonbright schizotypes, might arise from the fact that these performances are rewarded rather "impersonally" and make minimal demands on the reinforcing others. Also, the same cognitive and mechanical instrumental acts can often be employed both to turn on positive center feedback and to turn off negative, an equivalence much less true of purely social signals linked to interpersonal needs.

Having briefly sketched three neurological possibilities for the postulated schizotaxic aberration, let me emphasize that while each has sufficient merit to be worth pursuing, they are mainly meant to be illustrative of the vague concept "integrative neural defect." I shall myself not be surprised if all three are refuted, whereas I shall be astounded if future research shows no fundamental aberration in nerve-cell function in the schizotype. Postulating schizotaxia as an open concept seems at first to pose a search problem of needle-in-haystack proportions, but I suggest that the plausible alternatives are really somewhat limited. After all, what does a neuron do to another neuron? It excites, or it inhibits! The schizotypic preservation of relatively normal function in selected domains directs our search toward some minimal deviation in a synaptic control parameter, as opposed to, say, a gross defect in cell distribution or structure, or the kind of biochemical anomaly that yields mental deficiency. Anything which would give rise to defective storage, grossly impaired transmission, or sizable limitations on functional complexity can be pretty well excluded on present evidence. What we are looking for is a quantitative aberration in synaptic control—a deviation in amount or patterning of excitatory or inhibitory action—capable of yielding cumulative departures from normal control linkages under mixed appetitive-aversive regimes; but slight enough to permit convergence to quasi-normal asymptotes under more consistent schedules (or when massive repetition with motive-incentive factors unimportant is the chief basis for consolidation). The defect must generate aversive drift on mixed social reinforcement regimes, and must yield a primary cognitive slippage which, however, may be extremely small in magnitude except as potentiated by the cumulative effects of aversive drift. Taken together these molar constraints limit our degrees of freedom considerably when it comes to filling in the neurophysiology of schizotaxia.

Leaving aside the specific nature of schizotaxia, we must now raise the familiar question whether such a basic neurological defect, however subtle and nonstructural it might be, should not have been demonstrated hitherto? In reply to this objection I shall content myself with pointing out that there are several lines of evidence which, while not strongly arguing *for* a neurological theory, are rebuttals of an argument presupposing clear and consistent *negative* findings. For example: Ignoring several early European reports with inadequate controls, the literature contains a half-dozen quantitative studies showing marked vestibular system dysfunction in schizophrenics (Angyal & Blackman, 1940, 1941; Angyal & Sherman, 1942; Colbert & Koegler, 1959; Freeman & Rodnick, 1942; Leach, 1960; Payne & Hewlett, 1960; Pollock & Krieger, 1958). Hoskins (1946) concluded that a neurological defect in the vestibular system was one of the few clear-cut biological findings in the Worcester studies. It is of prime importance to replicate these findings among compensated and pseudoneurotic cases, where the diffuse withdrawal and deactivation factor would not provide the explanation it does in the chronic, burnt-out case (cf. Collins, Crampton, & Posner, 1961). Another line of evidence is in the work of King (1954) on psychomotor deficit, noteworthy for its careful use of task simplicity, asymptote performance, concern for patient cooperation, and inclusion of an outpatient pseudoneurotic sample. King himself regards his data as indicative of a rather basic behavior defect, although he does not hold it to be schizophrenia-specific. Then we have such research as that of Barbara Fish (1961) indicating the occurrence of varying signs of perceptual-motor maldevelopment among infants and children who subsequently manifest clinical schizophrenia. The earlier work of Schilder and Bender along these lines is of course well known, and there has always been a strong minority report in clinical psychiatry that many schizophrenics provide subtle and fluctuating neurological signs of the "soft" variety, if one keeps alert to notice or elicit them. I have myself been struck by the frequent occurrence, even among pseudoneurotic patients, of transitory neurologic-like complaints (e.g., diplopia, localized weakness, one-sided tremor, temperature dyscontrol, dizziness, disorientation) which seem to lack dynamic meaning or secondary gain and whose main effect upon the patient is to produce bafflement and anxiety. I have seen preliminary findings by J. McVicker Hunt and his students in which a rather dramatic quantitative deficiency in spatial cognizing is detectable in schizophrenics of above-normal verbal intelligence. Research by Cleveland (1960; Cleveland, Fisher, Reitman, & Rothaus, 1962) and by Arnhoff and Damianopoulos (in press) on the clinically well-known body-image anomalies in schizophrenia suggests that this domain yields quantitative departures from the norm of such magnitude that with further instrumental and statistical refinement it might be used as a quasi-pathognomonic sign of the disease. It is interesting to note a certain thread of unity running through this evidence, which perhaps lends support to Rado's hypothesis that a kinesthetic integrative defect is even more characteristic of schizotypy than is the radical anhedonia.

All these kinds of data are capable of a psychodynamic interpretation. "Soft" neurological signs are admittedly ambiguous, especially when found in the severely decompensated case. The only point I wish to make here is that *since* they exist and are at present unclear in etiology, an otherwise plausible neurological view cannot be refuted on the ground that there is a *lack* of any sign of neurological dysfunction in schizophrenia; there is no such lack.

Time forces me to leave detailed research strategy for another place, but the main directions are obvious and may be stated briefly: The clinician's Mental Status ratings on anhedonia, ambivalence, and interpersonal aversiveness should be objectified and preferably replaced by psychometric measures. The research findings on cognitive slippage, psychomotor dyscontrol, vestibular malfunction, body image, and other spatial aberrations should be thoroughly replicated and extended into the pseudoneurotic and semicompensated ranges. If these efforts succeed, it will be possible to set up a multiple sign pattern, using optimal cuts on phenotypically diverse indicators, for identifying compensated schizotypes in the nonclinical population. Statistics used must be appropriate to the theoretical model of a dichotomous latent taxonomy reflecting itself in otherwise independent quantitative indicators. Family concordance studies should then be run relating proband schizophrenia to schizotypy as identified by this multiple indicator pattern. Meanwhile we should carry on an active and varied search for more direct neurological signs of schizotaxia, concentrating our hunches on novel stimulus inputs (e.g., the stabilized retinal image situation) which may provide a better context for basic neural dysfunction to show up instead of being masked by learned compensations or imitated by psychopathology.

In closing, I should like to take this unusual propaganda opportunity to play the prophet. It is my strong personal conviction that such a research strategy will enable psychologists to make a unique contribution in the near future, using psychological techniques to establish that schizophrenia, while its content is learned, is fundamentally a neurological disease of genetic origin.

REFERENCES

Angyal, A., & Blackman, N. Vestibular reactivity in schizophrenia. *Arch. Neurol. Psychiat.*, 1940, 44, 611–620.

Angyal, A., & Blackman, N. Paradoxical reactions in schizophrenia under the influence of alcohol, hyperpnea, and CO_2 inhalation. *Amer. J. Psychiat.*, 1941, 97, 893–903.

Angyal, A., & Sherman, N. Postural reactions to vestibular stimulation in schizophrenic and normal subjects. *Amer. J. Psychiat.*, 1942, 98, 857–862.

Arnhoff, F., & Damianopoulos, E. Self-body recognition and schizophrenia: An exploratory study. *J. abnorm. soc. Psychol.*, in press.

Bleuler, E. *Theory of schizophrenic negativism.* New York: Nervous and Mental Disease Publishing, 1912.

Bleuler, E. *Dementia praecox.* New York: International Universities Press, 1950.

Cleveland, S. E. Judgment of body size in a schizophrenic and a control group. *Psychol. Rep.,* 1960, 7, 304.

Cleveland, S. E., Fisher, S., Reitman, E. E., & Rothaus, P. Perception of body size in schizophrenia. *Arch, gen. Psychiat.,* 1962, 7, 277–285.

Colbert, G., & Koegler, R. Vestibular dysfunction in childhood schizophrenia. *AMA Arch. gen. Psychiat.,* 1959, 1, 600–617.

Collins, W. E., Crampton, G. H., & Posner, J. B. The effect of mental set upon vestibular nystagmus and the EEG. *USA Med. Res. Lab. Rep.,* 1961, No. 439.

Delafresnaye, J. F. (Ed.) *Brain mechanisms and learning.* Springfield, Ill.: Charles C Thomas, 1961.

Delgado, J. M. R., Roberts, W. W., & Miller, N. E. Learning motivated by electrical stimulation of the brain. *Amer. J. Physiol.,* 1954, 179, 587–593.

Fish, Barbara. The study of motor development in infancy and its relationship to psychological functioning. *Amer. J. Psychiat.,* 1961, (117) 17, 1113–1118.

Freeman, H., & Rodnick, E. H. Effect of rotation on postural steadiness in normal and schizophrenic subjects. *Arch. Neurol. Psychiat.,* 1942, 48, 47–53.

Fuller, J. L., & Thompson, W. R. *Behavior genetics.* New York: Wiley, 1960. Pp. 272–283.

Hoskins, R. G. *The biology of schizophrenia.* New York: Norton, 1946.

King, H. E. *Psychomotor aspects of mental disease.* Cambridge: Harvard Univer. Press, 1954.

Leach, W. W. Nystagmus: An integrative neural deficit in schizophrenia. *J. abnorm. soc. Psychol.,* 1960, 60, 305–309.

Lidz, T., Cornelison, A., Terry, D., & Fleck, S. Intrafamilial environment of the schizophrenic patient: VI. The transmission of irrationality. *AMA Arch. Neurol. Psychiat.,* 1958, 79, 305–316.

McConaghy, N. The use of an object sorting test in elucidating the hereditary factor in schizophrenia. *J. Neurol. Neurosurg. Psychiat.,* 1959, 22, 243–246.

Meyers, D., & Goldfarb, W. Psychiatric appraisals of parents and siblings of schizophrenic children. *Amer. J. Psychiat.,* 1962, 118, 902–908.

Olds, J., & Milner, P. Positive reinforcement produced by electrical stimulation of septal area and other regions of rat brain. *J. comp. physiol. Psychol.,* 1954, 47, 419–427.

Payne, R. W. Cognitive abnormalities. In H. J. Eysenck (Ed.), *Handbook of abnormal psychology.* New York: Basic Books, 1961. Pp. 248–250.

Payne, R. S., & Hewlett, J. H. G. Thought disorder in psychotic patients. In H. J. Eysenck (Ed.), *Experiments in personality.* Vol. 2. London: Routledge, Kegan, Paul, 1960. Pp. 3–106.

Pollack, M., & Krieger, H. P. Oculomotor and postural patterns in schizophrenic children. *AMA Arch. Neurol. Psychiat.,* 1958, 79, 720–726.

Rado, S. *Psychoanalysis of behavior.* New York: Grune & Stratton, 1956.

Rado, S., & Daniels, G. *Changing concepts of psychoanalytic medicine.* New York: Grune & Stratton, 1956.

Ramey, E. R., & O'Doherty, D. S. (Ed.) *Electrical studies on the unanesthetized brain.* New York: Hoeber, 1960.

Rosenthal, D. Problems of sampling and diagnosis in the major twin studies of schizophrenia. *J. psychiat. Res.,* in press.

Stern, K. *Principles of human genetics.* San Francisco: Freeman, 1960. Pp. 581–584.

15

BIOCHEMICAL HYPOTHESES AND STUDIES

Seymour S. Kety

Biochemistry, which has had notable success in elucidating etiologic factors in many areas of medicine, has also been brought to bear on the problem of schizophrenia. Although these efforts have not to date been successful in demonstrating a biochemical "lesion," a number of arguments can be made to support the viewpoint that chemical factors operate significantly and specifically in schizophrenia.

Perhaps the strongest of these arguments is the good evidence for the operation of genetic factors in the transmission of schizophrenia (92), consisting of a higher concordance rate for the disorder in the monozygotic twins of afflicted individuals (43, 57, 59, 67, 99), and in the biologic families of schizophrenics where early adoption or removal from their natural parents has served to disentangle the operation of genetic and environmental factors in its transmission (50, 64, 93).

Another argument which has been used is the ability of a number of exogenous chemical substances (iodides, mescaline, LSD, amphetamine, iproniazid, psilocybin) or some endogenous biochemical disturbances (porphyria, thyroid disorders) to produce psychoses resembling schizophrenia is some or many of its features.

Biochemical hypotheses and findings related to schizophrenia have been the subject of several exhaustive and critical reviews of which only a few are cited for further reference (22, 61, 63, 109). In spite of the large number of abnormal chemical findings which have been reported in schizophrenia, few have been independently confirmed and on none is there general agreement with regard to its significance. This may be attributed to the operation of an inordinate number of variables, difficult to control, which are associated with the clinical studies of schizophrenia.

Reprinted from the *Schizophrenic Syndrome,* L Bellak and L. Loeb (Eds.) 1969, pp. 155–171 with the permission of Grune & Stratton, Inc. and Dr. Kety.

Despite the phenomenologic similarities which permitted the concept of schizophrenia to emerge, there is little evidence that all of its forms have a common etiology or pathogenesis. Errors involved in the study of relatively small samples from heterogeneous populations may help to explain the frequency with which findings of one group fail to be confirmed by another.

Most biochemical research in schizophrenia has been carried out in patients with a long history of hospitalization in institutions where overcrowding is difficult to avoid and hygienic standards cannot always be maintained. It is easy to imagine the spread of chronic infections such as infectious hepatitis among such patients, and one wonders how often this may account for findings attributable to disturbed hepatic function or elevated plasma titres of antibody globulins. Even in the absence of previous or current infection, the development of a characteristic pattern of intenstinal flora in a group of patients living together for long periods of time may occasionally contribute to the finding of what appear to be deviant metabolic pathways.

The variety and quality of the diet of the institutionalized schizophrenic is rarely comparable to that of the nonhospitalized normal control. In the case of the acute schizophrenic, the weeks of continual turmoil which precede recognition of the disorder are hardly conducive to a normal dietary intake. It is not surprising that a dietary vitamin deficiency has been found to account for at least one biochemical abnormality which had been attributed to schizophrenia (77). Horwitt (55) found signs of liver dysfunction during long periods of borderline protein ingestion.

Emotional stress is known to cause profound changes in men, in adrenocortical and thyroid function, in excretion of water, electrolytes, creatinine, epinephrine and norepinephrine, to mention only a few recently reported findings. On the other hand, physical inactivity would be expected to produce changes in a number of body functions. Schizophrenic illness is often characterized by indolence and lack of exercise or by marked emotional disturbance in the basal state and frequently exaggerated anxiety in response to routine and research procedures. The disturbances in behavior and activity which mark the schizophrenic process would also be expected to cause deviations from the normal in many biochemical and metabolic measures: in urinary volume and concentration, in energy and nitrogen metabolism, in the state and activity of numerous organ systems and metabolic pathways. The biochemical changes which are secondary to the psychologic and behavioral state of the patient are often of interest in themselves; it is important, however, not to attribute to them etiologic roles.

Another incidental feature of the schizophrenic patient which differentiates him from the normal control and from many other types of patient is the long list of therapies to which he may have been exposed. The ataractic drugs which are often used over extended periods of time are particularly prone to produce metabolites which appear in the urine and interfere with a number of chemical determinations long after the drug has been withdrawn.

With this combination of many variables and the subjective judgments necessary for diagnosis and the evaluation of clinical course, it is not unexpected that subjective bias would from time to time affect the results of research in schizophrenia and make even more necessary in that field than in many others the employment of rigorous research design.

ENERGY METABOLISM

A decrease in basal metabolism was found in schizophrenia by earlier workers, although more recent work has not confirmed this (89), and hypotheses attributing the disease to disturbances in the fundamental mechanisms of energy supply or conversion in the brain have been formulated but on the basis of rather inadequate evidence. Kelsey and co-workers (60) found a decreased B.M.R. in their series of schizophrenics to be associated with an increased uptake of ^{131}I by the thyroid, correctible by the addition of iodine to the diet, and attributed it to a lack of that element in the institutional diet. Periodic catatonia and some other schizophreniform psychoses seem to be associated with disturbances in thyroxine or thyrotropic hormone regulation (21, 40), but little evidence exists to suggest that such disturbances are characteristic of schizophrenia generally.

The oxygen consumption and blood flow of the brain as a whole have been found to lie within the normal range in a variety of forms of schizophrenia (65), and although localized changes in these functions have sometimes been postulated, there is no evidence to support this supposition. The clear consciousness usually present in schizophrenia does not suggest the manifestation of cerebral anoxia.

Richter (89) has pointed out the uncontrolled factors in earlier work which implicated a defect in carbohydrate metabolism as a characteristic of the schizophrenic process. The finding in schizophrenia of an abnormal glucose tolerance in conjunction with other evidence of hepatic dysfunction, or evidence of a retarded metabolism of lactate by the schizophrenic (2), does not completely exclude incidental hepatic disease, nutritional deficiencies or the psychophysiologic influences on carbohydrate metabolism as possible sources of error. Horwitt and associates (56) were able to demonstrate and correct similar abnormalities by altering the dietary intake of the B group of vitamins.

A deficiency of glucose-6-phosphate dehydrogenase, known to occur in 10–20 per cent of American Negroes, has been found to show an incidence significantly different from normal in Negro catatonic and paranoid schizophrenics (19), an observation which has received partial confirmation by an independent group (29). Findings that schizophrenia is associated with cellular changes in oxidative phosphorylation or in the uptake (44) or metabolism of glucose (35) require further confirmation (17).

It is difficult to believe that a generalized defect in energy metabolism, a process fundamental to every cell in the body, could be responsible for the highly specialized features of schizophrenia. For this reason, perhaps, interest has developed in other aspects of metabolism, the substrates or products of which appear to have some special role in the brain.

PROTEIN

Although Gjessing (40) found definite alterations in bodily nitrogen balance correlated with and sometimes preceding the changes in mental state of periodic catatonics, there has been no evidence to indicate a major change in protein metabolism for schizophrenia generally. On the other hand, some interest has been focused recently on more specific protein constituents or the metabolism of particular amino acids or their amines.

Interest in the possible presence of an abnormal protein constituent of blood of schizophrenics were stimulated by a report, in 1958, that a serum fraction obtained from schizophrenic patients was capable of causing some of the symptoms of that disorder when injected into nonschizophrenic volunteers (49). This material, which was given the name "taraxein," appeared to have some relationship to ceruloplasmin, the copper-containing globulin of normal plasma which the same group had found to be elevated in schizophrenia (71) and, upon its intravenous injection, to produce rapid clinical improvement (48). Very recently, Martens, in a thorough examination of the relationships between ceruloplasmin and schizophrenia (76), has reported an equivalent elevation of serum copper in that disorder and in delirium tremens. In a controlled, double blind series he was unable to confirm the earlier report of clinical improvement following intravenous injections of ceruloplasmin. One attempt to replicate the production of psychotic symptoms in volunteers by means of taraxein was not successful (91), and to date the original findings have not been confirmed in a significant and well controlled series.

A number of groups, however, have reported evidence compatible with the thesis that an abnormal protein is present to a greater extent in the blood of some schizophrenics than in normals and that this substance is capable of producing certain behavioral, metabolic, or cellular changes in lower animals. Haddad and Rabe (45), replicating and extending an earlier report by Malis (73), found some evidence for an antigenic abnormality in the pooled serum of chronically ill schizophrenic patients. More recent studies by this group using different immunologic methods have yielded negative results which they do not regard as conclusive. Faurbye, Lundberg and Jensen (23) were unable to confirm Malis' results. Using another approach, Vartanyan (108) has found evidence for an immunologic abnormality in schizophrenia. Heath and co-workers (47) have advanced an auto-immune concept as the biologic basis of schizophrenia. The studies with fluorescent antibodies, electrophysiologic, immunologic and behavioral observations, on which the concept is based, await independent confirmation. Precipitin reactions have yielded positive (79) and negative (58, 84, 90) results with respect to the occurrence of specific proteins in the serum of schizophrenics.

Fessel and co-workers (26, 28) have reported increases in 4S and 19S macroglobulins in a considerable proportion of schizophrenic patients and the ability to differentiate schizophrenic from manic depressive patients on this basis. Mental stress in nonpsychotic individuals was found to elevate the same macroglobulins (27). Certain of these findings have been confirmed by two independent groups (66, 97). Gammack and Hector (37), while failing to confirm Fessel's findings, observed a highly significant increase in the α-globulin fraction and the haptoglobin component in the serum of schizophrenics. They also questioned the specificity of such findings which occur frequently in many types of chronic disease. Others have not confirmed this increase in haptoglobins (72). It seems fair to conclude that to the present time no abnormal protein characteristic of schizophrenia has been characterized by physico-chemical technics.

Some special properties of the plasma of schizophrenics have been reported by workers using various biologic assays. Bishop (11) has reported evidence for the effect of plasma from schizophrenic patients upon learning and retention of learning in the rat. Other investigators (8, 112) found a slowing of rope climbing activity in rats injected with whole serum or certain fractions from schizophrenic patients as compared with normal fractions. The specificity of this response for schizophrenia has not been demonstrated and later findings were not confirmatory (96). German (38) reported an effect of serum of schizophrenics on cortical evoked responses in rates which in later, more rigorously controlled studies he and his associates were unable to confirm (39). In well controlled studies of the effects of plasma from psychotic patients on behavior, Ferguson and Fisher (25) have reported observations using a precision timing task in cebus monkeys in which a highly significant delay in responsiveness was produced by the injection of plasma from some newly admitted catatonic patients. It is of interest that in their studies plasma from normal individuals under preoperative stress produced a similar but not as marked slowing of response.

Frohman and his associates (34) have reported increases in the ratio of lactate-to-pyruvate in the medium after chicken erythrocytes are incubated with plasma or plasma fractions of some schizophrenic patients as compared to normal controls. Mangoni and associates (74) have been unable to confirm this. In a subsequent paper, Frohman and associates (36) were able to demonstrate this difference in the lactate: pyruvate ratio only when the subjects had engaged in moderate exercise before the blood samples were drawn; no appreciable difference was found when the subjects were at complete rest, in normal activity, or exercising vigorously. This, plus the fact that exercise affected the lactate: pyruvate ratio in the incubation mixture, more than did the presence or absence of schizophrenia, suggests the need for better definition of what may be a large number of variables involved in this reaction.

Recently, Ryan, Brown and Durell (94) have succeeded in clarifying some of the fundamental processes involved in the ability of human plasma to affect the lactate production of chicken erythrocytes, which appears to be the determining variable of the lactate:pyruvate ratio. In their test system, lactate production by aerobic glycolysis did not occur in completely intact erythrocytes but was contingent upon and correlated with hemolysis. This, in turn, was caused by a complement-requiring antibody present in variable titre in all human plasma tested. The plasma of schizophrenics could not be reliably distinguished from that of nonschizophrenic patients from the same hospital (95). Turner and Chipps (107) found a higher heterophile hemolysin titre in the blood of schizophrenics than of nonschizophrenics. Chronic alcoholics, however, also showed a higher titre of the hemolysin. Although Frohman and his associates have consistently found this phenomenon with higher frequency among schizophrenics, a possibility which remains to be ruled out is that the titre of this antibody is more closely related to a history of chronic hospitalization and greater exposure to a variety of antigens than to the presence of schizophrenia. An interesting further possibility is the significantly greater antibody responsiveness of schizophrenic patients than normal or depressed individuals to a standard antigen challenge (33a).

The evidence with regard to the biologic or behavioral effects of the plasma of schizophrenics is far from conclusive at the present time. Most of the effects reported have failed of confirmation and none have been shown to be properties of plasma which are characteristic of schizophrenia.

Further work is necessary to determine to what extent the abnormalities in plasma found by physico-chemical analysis, when they are confirmed, are characteristic of schizophrenia or a reflection of the stress, exposure to chronic endemic infections, dietary or other adventitious factors which accompany the disorder and are associated with chronic institutionalization (61).

AMINO ACIDS AND AMINES

Although an earlier report indicated abnormalities in amino acid excretion in schizophrenia (114), this has not been further confirmed. Much interest, on the other hand, has been attached to the possibility that abnormal metabolism of one or another amine could be of etiologic importance in schizophrenia (51).

The great sensitivity and relative nonspecificity of chromatographic methods and the ease with which findings may be affected by exogenous factors such as diet or drugs increase the likelihood of false positives in this area, and great caution must be exercised in identifying the particular metabolite which appears to be involved or interpreting the significance which should be attached to it (42, 75).

The significance of an unidentified Ehrlich positive substance ("the mauve spot") attributed to a new form of schizophrenia by Hoffer and Osmond (52) has been brought into question by O'Reilly and his associates (80, 81) who found it with high frequency in the urines of patients with affective psychosis, alcoholism, psychoneurosis, personality disorders and cancer.

TRANSMETHYLATION

In 1952, Osmond and Smythies (82) pointed out some similarities between mescaline psychosis and schizophrenia and between that drug and epinephrine. They included a biochemical note by Harley-Mason which stated, in part:

"It is extremely probable that the final stage in the biogenesis of adrenaline is a transmethylation of noradrenaline, the methyl group arising from methionine or choline. It is just possible that a pathological disordering of its transmethylation mechanism might lead to methylation of one or both of its phenolic hydroxyl groups instead of its amino group. . . . Methylation of phenolic hydroxyl groups in the animal body is of rare occurrence but a significant case has been reported recently. . . . It is particularly interesting to note that out of a series of phenylethylamine derivations tested by Noteboom, 3,4-dimethoxyphenylethylamine was the most potent in producing catatonia in animals."

Since that time the transmethylation of norepinephrine to epinephrine has been established (12), while Axelrod, Senoh and Witkop (5) have demonstrated the O-methylation of both catecholamines as an important step in their normal metabolism.

The suggestion that pathologic transmethylation may occur in schizophrenia was further strengthened by the recognition that a number of psychotomimetic agents, in addition to mescaline, were methylated congeners of normal body metabolites. On this basis, Hoffer and associates (53) used niacin and niacinamide, methyl accepters, in an effort to inhibit competitively the possible abnormal process. They reported beneficial results which have not been independently confirmed. In 1961, Pollin, Cardon and Kety (86) tested this hypothesis by administering large doses of L-methionine to chronic schizophrenic patients in conjunction with a monoamine oxidase inhibitor to permit the accumulation of any monoamines formed. This substance is an essential precursor of S-adenosylmethionine, the active substance which was shown by Cantoni (18) to transfer its methyl group to accepter compounds in the process of transmethylation. In some of the patients during the administration of the L-methionine there was a brief intensification of psychosis which involved an exacerbation of some of the schizophrenic symptoms. No other amino acids tested (glycine, tyrosine, phenylalanine, tryptophan, histidine, glutamine) were associated with this phenomenon. The intensification of psychosis in schizophrenics with methionine has since, in essence, been confirmed by four other groups (1, 15, 46, 83) and, in addition, Brune and Himwich (16) found that betaine, another methyl donor, was equally effective in accentuating psychotic symptoms in schizophrenics. Baldessarini and Kopin (6) found that feeding L-methionine to rats produced a significant increase in S-adenosylmethionine concentration in the liver and brain. Axelrod (4) demonstrated the presence in normal mammalian tissue of an enzyme capable of methylating normal metabolities, i.e., tryptamine and serotonin to their dimethyl derivatives for which psychotomimetic properties have been reported.

DIMETHOXYPHENYLETHYLAMINE

In 1962, Friedhoff and Van Winkle (32) examined the urine of patients with early schizophrenia and reported the occurrence of 3,4-dimethoxyphenylethylamine (DMPEA), to which Harley-Mason had alluded as a possible abnormally methylated metabolite. This compound is a dimethylated derivative of dopamine and closely related to mescaline, which represents a trimethylated cogener of this biogenic amine.

Since 1962 a number of groups have attempted to confirm the excretion of DMPEA in schizophrenia and further to define the variables which affect it. Friedhoff and Van Winkle (32) had found it in the urine of 15 of 19 schizophrenics and in none of 14 normal urines. Kuehl and associates (68) confirmed its presence in 7 of 22 schizophrenics and in none of 10 normals. Takesada and associates (105) found it in 70 of 78 (90 per cent) schizophrenics but also in 35 of 67, or 52 per cent, of normals. Faurbye and Pind (24), who modified the method to increase its sensitivity and to avoid interference by phenothiazine metabolites, were unable to detect DMPEA in the urine of 15 schizophrenics and 10 normals. Perry, Hansen and Macintyre (85) were unable to find the compound in 10 schizophrenics on a diet free of fruits and vegetables. After finding DMPEA in the urine of 4 out of 6 schizophrenics and 2 of 3 controls, Studnitz and Nyman (104) demonstrated its disappearance when the same individuals were placed on a pure carbohydrate regimen.

In an extensive series in which biochemical determinations and psychiatric diagnoses were made independently, Bourdillon and his associates (14) reported the presence of a "pink spot" having some of the characteristics of DMPEA in the urines of 46 of 85 (55 per cent) schizophrenics, while it was absent in all of 17 nonschizophrenic patients and 149 normal controls. A second experiment with less striking results showed a low incidence (3 per cent) of the spot in the urine of paranoid patients and a 29 per cent incidence in nonparanoid schizophrenics. Drug administration which was not controlled could have been different in type of drug or dosage for different diagnostic categories. Drugs or their metabolites are known to interfere with DMPEA determinations, and at least one group (24) has observed a phenothiazine metabolite with Rf value and color reactions similar to DMPEA which persisted in the urine for as long as 25 days after withdrawal of the drug. Williams (110) has examined the technique used by Bourdillon and found it relatively insensitive to DMPEA. Further studies by this group (111) and by others using more specific technics (7, 13) have indicated that Bourdillon's "pink spot" was not, in fact, DMPEA and that DMPEA is not excreted in abnormal amounts by schizophrenics. Friedhoff (33), on the other hand, on the basis of its behavior in six solvent systems, a number of color reactions, thin layer and gas chromatography and melting point determinations, has concluded that the material he has found in the urine of schizophrenics is identical to DMPEA. Although this substance, when administered to schizophrenics, is rapidly converted to 3,4-dimethoxyphenyl-acetic acid (31), Kuehl and associates (69) could not detect a significant difference in the excretion of that acid between normal subjects and schizophrenics.

These findings—the intensification of psychosis in schizophrenics by methionine or betaine, the increase in S-adenosylmethionine in the brain and liver of rats by methionine feeding, the existence of at least one enzyme capable of transmethylating normal metabolites to psychoto-mimetic compounds, the evidence obtained by some workers for the excretion of DMPEA in a substantial number of schizophrenics—are compatible with the hypothesis that the process of biologic transmethylation is somehow disturbed in schizophrenia with the production of persistence of excessive amounts of methylated derivatives of normal metabolites capable of inducing some of the symptoms of schizophrenia. That hypothesis, however, is far from having been validated. Although methionine and betaine are the only ones of a large number of amino acids which have been shown capable of briefly exacerbating psychosis in some schizophrenics, it has not been established that the clinical changes resulted from any specific methylated derivatives, and the possibility that this was a nonspecific toxic psychosis or a peculiarly schizophrenic response to nonspecific toxic changes has not been ruled out. Haydu, et al. (46), who confirm the ability of methionine to exacerbate schizophrenic symptomatology, found an ameliorating effect from hydroxychloroquine and suggest that the clinical effects of these agents result from their activation or suppression of thiol groups. A special sensitivity of schizophrenics to methionine has not been established although a similar regimen of methionine without iproniazid in a small number of normal volunteers produced no hint of a psychotic reaction (62). The accumulated evidence for the excretion of dimethoxyphenylethylamine in association with some forms of schizophrenia is as yet inconclusive. Several groups have been unable to confirm it and the possibility that it is an artifact of drug therapy has not been completely ruled out. There is evidence that some dietary factors are necessary for its appearance although the same is true for phenylketonuria and does not argue against its significance or relevance to schizophrenia. On parenteral administration to man, DMPEA has not been shown to produce perceptible mental effects (31), but this does not preclude an effect from higher concentrations locally within the brain. The transmethylation hypothesis appears to require and merit further examination and development.

INDOLEAMINES

Although Woolley (113) was impressed with indirect evidence for the possibility of a disorder in serotonin metabolism in schizophrenia, significant differences between schizophrenic and normal populations with respect to this amine or its metabolites have not been established (61). Earlier findings of indolic compounds (indole acetamide and 6-hydroxyskatole) with abnormal frequency in the urine of schizophrenics (78, 101) have more recently been found to a similar extent in the urine of other types of mental patients and are probably to be attributed to exogenous or nondisease-related factors (20, 100, 115).

Tryptamine excretion may have some significance in schizophrenia since an increase has been found to occur in such patients before a period of exacerbation (9). An increase in urinary tryptophan metabolites has also been observed following the administration of methionine (10, 102, 103), and it has been suggested that the conversion of tryptamine to its hallucinogenic methylated derivative may occur. Aside from one positive report (30), the search for dimethyltryptamine or dimethylserotonin in the urine of schizophrenics has yielded negative results (98, 102, 106).

EPINEPHRINE

The hypothesis that adrenochrome or other abnormal metabolites of circulating epinephrine were formed in schizophrenia and accounted for many of the symptoms (54) has received careful scrutiny made possible by the recently acquired knowledge of the normal metabolism of this hormone (3). No evidence was found for the abnormal metabolism of labeled epinephrine infused into schizophrenic patients (88), and in one study which accounted almost entirely for the excreted label in terms of unchanged epinephrine and four metabolites (3-methoxy-4-hydroxymandelic acid, metanephrine, 3,4-dihydroxymandelic acid, and 3-methoxy-4-hydroxyphenylglycol), no qualitative or quantitative differences were found in this pattern between chronic schizophrenics and normal volunteers (70). The infusion of epinephrine into schizophrenics was not found to intensify the psychosis (87) which would have been expected if the psychosis were associated with abnormal metabolites of circulating epinephrine.

SUMMARY AND CONCLUSIONS

Although it would be difficult to demonstrate that a definitive increase in our knowledge of biochemical mechanisms in the schizophrenic psychoses has occurred in the past decade, substantial progress has nonetheless been made. There is an increasing awareness of the complexity of the problem and of the sophistication of research design necessary to cope with it. Most important, there has been a burgeoning of fundamental knowledge in biochemistry and neurochemistry and their interaction with behavior on which depend meaningful hypotheses relating to schizophrenia and from which may eventually come an understanding of whatever biochemical mechanisms operate significantly in its etiology, pathogenesis, or therapy.

Before the etiology of any syndrome has been established, it is idle to regard it as a single disease, and, in the case of schizophrenia, the striking resemblance which certain temporal lobe epilepsies or chronic intoxications (bromidism, iodism, amphetamine psychosis, porphyria) bear to it makes tenable the possibility that the syndrome may emerge from different etiologic pathways. Recognition of such a possibility aids in the interpretation of genetic and biologic findings and would facilitate the characterization of more specific subgroups.

Those interested in exploring the biologic aspects of schizophrenic disorders cannot with impunity ignore the psychologic, social, and other environmental factors which operate significantly at various stages of their development. Leaving aside etiology considerations, it is clear that exogenous factors may precipitate, intensify, or ameliorate the symptoms and confound the biologic picture. To what extent the classical psychologic features of chronic schizophrenia are created by prolonged isolation and hospitalization will become apparent with the increasing adoption of community-oriented treatment. Examples are readily found in which uncontrolled nutritional, infectious, or pharmacologic variables may have accounted for specific biochemical abnormalities in populations of chronic schizophrenics. These secondary variables are so manifold that it is hard to imagine a design which could anticipate and control them all, and successive studies concentrating on particularly relevant controls will probably continue to be called for. There is, in addition, much to be said for broadening the scope of the typical sample from chronic hospitalized schizophrenia to the early, more acute, remitting, episodic, or periodic forms (21, 41) in which it may not only be possible to obviate some of the difficulties imposed by chronic hospitalization and drug administration but, by study of the same patient in psychotic and nonpsychotic states, to avoid the effects of interindividual variance.

An unavoidable difficulty at the present time is the fact that the crucial processes of diagnosis and evaluation of change are based almost entirely on subjective estimates. It is not insensitivity which diminishes the reliability of such measures as much as their vulnerability to bias; failure to recognize and guard against this source of error probably accounts for much of the inconsistency in the study of schizophrenia not only from biologic but also from sociologic and psychologic points of view.

The single-gene-single-enzyme concept of the biologic disorder in schizophrenia was encouraged by the very high concordance rate found in monozygotic twins in earlier studies. More recent twin studies in which selective bias in sampling has been more effectively controlled have yielded a concordance rate of 40 per cent or less. Studies with adopted schizophrenics (64, 93) where environmental factors can be more successfully controlled have still reinforced the importance of genetic factors but have emphasized the genetic transmission of a vulnerability to schizophrenia or to a variety of personality or character disorders. This suggests that personality or intelligence may be more appropriate models for schizophrenia than phenylketonuria. A polygenic inadequacy interacting with particular life situations seems more compatible with all of the evidence (92). The biologic component of the schizophreniform illnesses may lie in the mechanisms which underlie arousal, inhibition, perception, cognition, affect, or the complex relationships among them, all of which appear to be involved at one time or another. Although a single chemical substance such as mescaline or lysergic acid diethylamide may produce disturbances in all of these areas, it would be well to keep in mind the possibility that more complex neurochemical, neurophysiologic and psychologic interactions may form the biologic substrate of schizophrenia.

REFERENCES

1. Alexander, F., Curtis, G. C., Sprince, H., and Crosley, A. P.: L-Methionine and L-tryptophan feedings in nonpsychotic and schizophrenic patients with and without tranylcypromine. *J. Nerv. Ment. Dis.* 137:135–142, 1963.

2. Altschule, M. D., Henneman, D. H., Holliday, P., and Goncz, R.-M.: Carbohydrate metabolism in brain disease. VI. Lactate metabolism after infusion of sodium d-lactate in manic-depressive and schizophrenic psychoses. *AMA Arch. Intern. Med.* 98:35–38, 1956.

3. Axelrod, J.: Metabolism of epinephrine and other sympathomimetic amines. *Physiol. Rev.* 39:751–776, 1959.

4. Axelrod, J.: Enzymatic formation of psychotomimetic metabolites from normally occurring compounds. *Science* 134:343, 1961.

5. Axelrod, J., Senoh, S., and Witkop, B.: O-Methylation of catecholamines *in vivo. J. Biol. Chem.* 233:697–701, 1958.

6. Baldessarini, R. J., and Kopin, I. J.: Assay of tissue levels of S-adenosylmethionine. *Anal. Biochem.* 6:289–292, 1963.

7. Bell, C. E., and Somerville, A. R.: Identity of the "pink spot." *Nature* 211:1405–1406, 1966.

8. Bergen, J. F., Pennell, R. B., Saravis, C. A., and Hoagland, H.: Further experiments with plasma proteins from schizophrenics. *In* Heath, R. G. (Ed.) *Serological Fractions in Schizophrenia.* New York, Harper & Row, 1963, pp. 67–76.

9. Berlet, H. H., Bull, C., Himwich, H. E., Kohl, H., Matsumoto, K., Pscheidt, G. R., Spaide, J., Tourlentes, T. T., and Valverde, J. M.: Endogenous metabolic factor in schizophrenic behavior. *Science* 114: 311–313, 1964.

10. Berlet, H. H., Matsumoto, K., Pscheidt, G. R., Spaide, J., Bull, C., and Himwich, H. E.: Biochemical correlates of behavior in schizophrenic patients. *Arch. Gen. Psychiat.* 13:521–531, 1965.

11. Bishop, M. P.: Effects of plasma from schizophrenia subjects upon learning and retention in the rat. *In* Heath, R. G. (Ed.) *Serological Fractions in Schizophrenia.* New York, Harper & Row, 1963, pp. 77–91.

12. Blaschko, H.: The development of current concepts of catecholamine formation. *Pharmacol. Rev.* 11:307–316, 1959.

13. Boulton, A. A., and Felton, C. A.: The "pink spot" and schizophrenia. *Nature* 211:1404–1405, 1966.

14. Bourdillon, R. E., Clarke, C. A., Ridges, A. P., Sheppard, P. M., Harper, P., and Leslie, S. A.: "Pink spot" in the urine of schizophrenics. *Nature* 208:453–455, 1965.

15. Brune, G. G., and Himwich, H. E.: Effects of methionine loading on the behavior of schizophrenic patients. *J. Nerv. Ment. Dis.* 134:447–450, 1962.

16. Brune, G. G., and Himwich, H. E.: Biogenic amines and behavior in schizophrenic patients. *In Recent Advances in Biological Psychiatry,* Vol. 5. New York, Plenum Press, 1963, pp. 144–160.

17. Buhler, D. R., and Ihler, G. S.: Effect of plasma from normal and schizophrenic subjects on the oxidation of labeled glucose by chicken erythrocytes. *J. Lab. Clin. Med.* 62:306–318, 1963.

18. Cantoni, G. L.: S-Adenosylmethinine: a new intermediate formed enzymatically from L-methionine and adenosine-triphosphate. *J. Biol. Chem.* 204: 403–416, 1953.

19. Dern, R. J., Glynn, M. F., and Brewer, G. J.: Studies on the influence of hereditary G-6-PD deficiency in the expression of schizophrenic patterns. *Clin. Res.* 10:80, 1962.

20. Dohan, F. C., Ewing, J., Graff, H., and Sprince, H.: Schizophrenia: 6-hydroxyskatole and environment. *Arch. Gen. Psychiat.* 10:420–422, 1964.

21. Durell, J., Lidow, L. S., Kellam, S. F., and Shader, R. I.: Interrelationships between regulation of thyroid gland function and psychosis. *Res. Publ. Ass. Res. Nerv. Ment. Dis.* 43:387–399, 1966.

22. Durell, J., and Schildkraut, J. J.: Biochemical studies of the schizophrenic and affective disorders. *In* Arieti, S. (Ed.) *American Handbook of Psychiatry,* Vol. III. New York, Basic Books, 1966, pp. 423–457.

23. Faurbye, A., Lundberg, L., and Jensen, K. A.: Studies on the antigen demonstrated by Malis in serum from schizophrenic patients. *Acta Path. Micro-biol. Scand.* 61:633–651, 1964.

24. Faurbye, A., and Pind, K.: Investigation on the occurrence of the dopamine metabolite 3,4-dimethoxyphenylethylamine in the urine of schizophrenics. *Acta Psychiat. Scand.* 40:240–243, 1964.

25. Ferguson, D. C., and Fisher, A. E.: Behavior disruption in cebus monkeys as a function of injected substances. *Science* 139:1281–1282, 1963.

26. Fessel, W. J.: Macroglobulin elevations in functional mental illness. *Nature* 193:1005, 1962.

27. Fessel, W. J.: Mental stress, blood proteins and the hypothalamus: experimental results showing effect of mental stress upon 4S and 19S proteins. *Arch. Gen. Psychiat.* 7:427–435, 1962.

28. Fessel, W. J., and Grunbaum, B. W.: Electrophoretic and analytical ultracentrifuge studies in sera of psychotic patients: elevation of gamma globulins and macro-globulins, and splitting of alpha$_2$ globulins. *Ann. Intern. Med.* 54:1134–1145, 1961.

29. Fieve, R. R., Brauninger, G., Fleiss, J., and Cohen, G.: Glucose-6-phosphate dehydrogenase deficiency and schizophrenic behavior. *J. Psychiat. Res.* 3:255–262, 1965.

30. Fischer, E., Fernández Lagravere, T. A., Vázquez, A. J., and Di Stefano, A. O.: A bufotenin-like substance in the urine of schizophrenics. *J. Nerv. Ment. Dis.* 133:441–444, 1961.

31. Friedhoff, A. J., and Hollister, L. E.: Comparison of the metabolism of 3,4-dimethoxyphenylethylamine and mescaline in humans. *Biochem. Pharmacol.* 15:269–273, 1966.

32. Friedhoff, A. J., and Van Winkle, E.: The characteristics of an amine found in the urine of schizophrenic patients. *J. Nerv. Ment. Dis.* 135: 550–555, 1962.

33. Friedhoff, A. J., and Van Winkle, E.: New developments in the investigation of the relationship of 3,4-dimethoxyphenylethylamine to schizophrenia. *In* Himwich, H. E.: Kety, S. S., and Smythies, J. R. (Eds.) *Amines and Schizophrenia.* Oxford, Pergamon Press, 1967, pp. 19–21.

33a. Friedman, S. B., Cohen, J., and Iker, H.: Antibody response to cholera vaccine. Differences between depressed, schizophrenic, and normal subjects. *Arch. Gen. Psychiat.* 16:312–315, 1967.

34. Frohman, C. E., Czajkowski, N. P., Luby, E. D., Gottlieb, J. S., and Senf, R.: Further evidence of a plasma factor in schizophrenia. *Arch. Gen. Psychiat.* 2:263–267, 1960.

35. Frohman, C. E., Latham, L. K., Beckett, P. G. S., and Gottlieb, J. S.: Evidence of a plasma factor in schizophrenia. *Arch. Gen. Psychiat.* 2: 255–262, 1960.

36. Frohman, C. E., Latham, L. K., Warner, K. A., Brosius, C. O., Beckett, P. G. S., and Gottlieb, J. S.: Motor activity in schizophrenia; effect on plasma factor. *Arch. Gen. Psychiat.* 9: 83–88, 1963.

37. Gammack, D. B., and Hector, R. I.: A study of serum proteins in acute schizophrenia. *Clin. Sci.* 28:469–475, 1965.

38. German, G. A.: Effects of serum from schizophrenics on evoked cortical potentials in the rat. *Brit. J. Psychiat.* 109:616–623, 1963.

39. German, G. A., Antebi, R. N., Dear, E. M. A., and McCance, C.: A further study of the effects of serum from schizophrenics on evoked cortical potentials in the rat. *Brit. J. Psychiat.* 111:345–347, 1965.

40. Gjessing, R.: Disturbances of somatic functions in catatonia with a periodic course, and their compensation. *J. Ment. Sci.* 84:608–621, 1938.

41. Gjessing, L. R.: Studies of periodic catatonia. II. The urinary excretion of phenolic amines and acids with and without loads of different drugs. *J. Psychiat. Res.* 2:149–162, 1964.

42. Goldenberg, H., Fishman, V., Whittier, J., and Brinitzer, W.: Urinary aromatic excretion patterns in schizophrenia. *Arch. Gen. Psychiat.* 2:221–230, 1960.

43. Gottesman, I. I., and Shields, J.: Schizophrenia in twins: sixteen years' consecutive admissions to a psychiatric clinic. *Dis. Nerv. Syst.* 27 (Suppl.): 11–19, 1966.

44. Haavaldsen, R., Lingjaerde, O., and Walaas, O.: Disturbances of carbohydrate metabolism in schizophrenics: effect of serum fractions from schizophrenics on glucose uptake of rat diaphragm *in vitro. Confin. Neurol.* 18:270, 1958.

45. Haddad, R. K., and Rabe, A.: An antigenic abnormality in the serum of chronically ill schizophrenic patients. *In* Heath, R. G. (Ed.) *Serological Fractions in Schizophrenia.* New York, Harper & Row, 1963, pp. 151–157.

46. Haydu, G. G., Dhrymiotis, A., Korenyi, C., and Goldschmidt, L.: Effects of methionine and hydroxychloroquine in schizophrenia. *Amer. J. Psychiat.* 122:560–564, 1965.

47. Heath, R. G., and Krupp, I. M.: The biologic basis of schizophrenia: an autoimmune concept. *In* Walaas, O. (Ed.) *Molecular Basis of Some Aspects of Mental Activity,* Vol. 2. London, Academic Press, 1967, pp. 313–344.

48. Heath, R. G., Leach, B. E., Byers, L. W., Martens, S., and Feigley, C. A.: Pharmacological and biological psychotherapy. *Amer. J. Psychiat.* 114: 683–689, 1958.

49. Heath, R. G., Martens, S., Leach, B. E., Cohen, M., and Feigley, C. A.: Behavioral changes in nonpsychotic volunteers following the administration of taraxein, the substance obtained from serum of schizophrenic patients. *Amer. J. Psychiat.* 114:917–920, 1958.

50. Heston, L. L.: Psychiatric disorders in foster home reared children of schizophrenic mothers. *Brit. J. Psychiat.* 112:819–825, 1966.

51. Himwich, H. E., Kety, S. S., and Smythies, J. R. (Eds.): *Amines and Schizophrenia.* Oxford, Pergamon Press, 1967.

52. Hoffer, A., and Osmond, H.: Malvaria: A new psychiatric disease. *Acta Psychiat. Scand.* 39:335–366, 1963.

53. Hoffer, A., Osmond, H., Callbeck, M. J., and Kahan, I.: *Treatment of* schizophrenia with nicotinic acid and nicotinamide. *J. Clin. Exp. Psychopathol.* 18:131–158, 1957.

54. Hoffer, A., Osmond, H., and Smythies, J.: Schizophrenia: A new approach. II. Result of a year's research. *J. Ment. Sci.* 100:29–45, 1954.

55. Horwitt, M. K.: Report of Elgin Project No. 3 with emphasis on liver dysfunction. *In Nutrition Symposium Series No. 7.* New York, National Vitamin Foundation, 1953, pp. 67–83.

56. Horwitt, M. K., Liebert, E., Kreisler, O., and Wittman, P.: Investigations of human requirements for B-complex vitamins. *In National Research Council Bulletin No. 116.* Washington, D.C., National Academy of Sciences, 1948.

57. Inouye, E.: Similarity and dissimilarity of schizophrenia in twins. *In Proceedings of the Third World Congress of Psychiatry,* Vol. I, Montreal, 1961, pp. 524–530.

58. Jensen, K., Clausen, J., and Osterman, E.: Serum and cerebrospinal fluid proteins in schizophrenia. *Acta Psychiat. Scand.* 40:280–286, 1964.

59. Kallmann, F. J.: The genetic theory of schizophrenia. An analysis of 691 schizophrenic twin index families. *Amer. J. Psychiat.* 103:309–322, 1946.

60. Kelsey, F. O., Gullock, A. H., and Kelsey, F. E.: Thyroid activity in

hospitalized psychiatric patients. *AMA Arch. Neurol. Psychiat.* 77:543–548, 1957.

61. Kety, S. S.: Biochemical theories of schizophrenia. *Science* 129:1528–1532, 1590–1596, 1959.

62. Kety, S. S.: Possible relation of central amines to behavior in schizophrenic patients. *Fed. Proc.* 20:894–896, 1961.

63. Kety, S. S.: Current biochemical approaches to schizophrenia. *New Eng. J. Med.* 276:325–331, 1967.

64. Kety, S. S., Rosenthal, D., Wender, P. H., and Schulsinger, F.: The types and prevalence of mental illness in the biological and adoptive families of adopted schizophrenics. *J. Psychiat. Res.* 6: Suppl., 1968 (in press).

65. Kety, S. S., Woodford, R. B., Harmel, M. H., Freyhan, F. A., Appel, K. E., and Schmidt, C. F.: Cerebral blood flow and metabolism in schizophrenia. The effects of barbiturate semi-narcosis, insulin coma and electroshock. *Amer. J. Psychiat.* 104:765–770, 1948.

66. Kopeloff, L. M., and Fischel, E.: Serum levels of bactericidin and globulin in schizophrenia. *Arch. Gen. Psychiat.* 9:524–528, 1963.

67. Kringlen, E.: Schizophrenia in twins: An epidemiological-clinical study. *Psychiatry* 29:172–184, 1966.

68. Kuehl, F. A., Jr., Hichens, M., Ormond, R. E., Meisinger, M. A. P., Gale, P. H., Cirillo, V. J., and Brink, N. G.: Para-O-methylation of dopamine in schizophrenic and normal individuals. *Nature* 203:154–155, 1964.

69. Kuehl, F. A., Jr., Ormond, R. E., and Vandenheuvel, W. J. A.: Occurrence of 3,4-dimethoxyphenylacetic acid in urines of normal and schizophrenic individuals. *Nature* 211:606–608, 1966.

70. LaBrosse, E. H., Mann, J. D., and Kety, S. S.: The physiological and psychological effects of intravenously administered epinephrine and its metabolism in normal and schizophrenic men. III. Metabolism of 7-H³-epinephrine as determined in studies on blood and urine. *J. Psychiat. Res.* 1:68–75, 1961.

71. Leach, B. E., Cohen, M., Heath, R. G., and Martens, S.: Studies of the role of ceruloplasmin and albumin in adrenaline metabolism. *AMA Arch. Neurol. Psychiat.* 76:635–642, 1956.

72. Lovegrove, T. D., and Nicholls, D. M.: Haptoglobin subtypes in a schizophrenic and control population. *J. Nerv. Ment. Dis.* 141:195–196, 1965.

73. Malis, C. Y.: *K Etiologii Schizofrenii.* Medgiz, Moscow, 1959.

74. Mangoni, A., Balazs, R., and Coppen, A. J.: The effect of plasma from schizophrenic patients on the chicken erythrocyte system. *Brit. J. Psychiat.* 109:231–234, 1963.

75. Mann, J. D., and LaBrosse, E. H.: Urinary excretion of phenolic acids by normal and schizophrenic male patients. *Arch. Gen. Psychiat.* 1:547–551, 1959.

76. Martens, S.: *Effects of exogenous human ceruloplasmin in the schizophrenia syndrome.* Stockholm, Tryckeri Balder AB, 1966.

77. McDonald, R. K., Weise, V. K., Evans, F. T., and Patrick, R. W.: Studies on plasma ascorbic acid and ceruloplasmin levels in schizophrenia. *In* Folch-Pi, J. (Ed.) *Chemical Pathology of the Nervous System*. Oxford, Pergamon Press, 1961, pp. 404–412.

78. Nakao, A., and Ball, M.: The appearance of a skatole derivative in the urine of schizophrenics. *J. Nerv. Ment. Dis*. 130:417–419, 1960.

79. Noval, J. J., and Mao, T. S. S.: Abnormal immunological reaction of schizophrenic serum. *Fed. Proc*. 25:560, 1966.

80. O'Reilly, P. O., Ernest, M., and Hughes, G.: The incidence of malvaria. *Brit. J. Psychiat*. 111:741–744, 1965.

81. O'Reilly, P. O., Hughes, G., Russell, S., and Ernest, M.: The mauve factor: An evaluation. *Dis. Nerv. Syst*. 26:562–568, 1965.

82. Osmond H., and Smythies, J.: Schizophrenia: A new approach. *J. Ment. Sci*. 98:309–315, 1952.

83. Park, L., Baldessarini, R. J., and Kety, S. S.: Methionine effects on chronic schizophrenics. *Arch. Gen. Psychiat*. 12:346–351, 1965.

84. Pennell, R. B., Pawlus, C., Saravis, C. A., and Scrimshaw, G.: Further characterization of a human plasma component which influences animal behavior. *Trans. NY Acad. Sci*. 28:47–58, 1965.

85. Perry, T. L., Hansen, S., and Macintyre, L.: Failure to detect 3,4-dimethoxyphenylethylamine in the urine of schizophrenics. *Nature* 202:519–520, 1964.

86. Pollin, F., Cardon, P. V., and Kety, S. S.: Effects of amino acid feedings in schizophrenic patients treated with iproniazid. *Science* 113:104–105, 1961.

87. Pollin, W., and Goldin, S.: The physiological and psychological effects of intravenously administered epinephrine and its metabolism in normal and schizophrenic men. II. Psychiatric observations. *J. Psychiat. Res*. 1:50–67, 1961.

88. Resnick, O., and Elmadjian, F.: Excertion and metabolism of dl-epinephrine-7-C^{14}-d-bitartrate infused into schizophrenic patients. *Amer. J. Physiol*. 187:626, 1956.

89. Richter, D.: Biochemical aspects of schizophrenia. *In* Richter, D. (Ed.) *Schizophrenia: Somatic Aspects*. London, Pergamon Press, 1957, pp. 53–75.

90. Rieder, H. P., Ritzel, G., Spiegelberg, H., and Gnirss, F.: Serologische Versuche zum Nachweis von "Taraxein." *Experientia* 16:561–562, 1960.

91. Robins, E., Smith, K., and Lowe, I. P.: Discussion of clinical studies with taraxein. *In* Abramson, H. A. (Ed.) *Neuropharmacology: Transactions of the Fourth Conference*. New York, Josiah Macy Jr. Foundation, 1957, pp. 123–135.

92. Rosenthal, D., and Kety, S. S. (Eds.): The Transmission of Schizophrenia. *J. Psychiat. Res*. 6: Suppl., 1968 (in press).

93. Rosenthal, D., Wender, P. H., Kety, S. S., Schulsinger, F., Welner, J., and Ostergaard, L.: Schizophrenics' offspring reared in adoptive homes. *J. Psychiat. Res.* 6: Suppl., 1968 (in press).

94. Ryan, J. W., Brown, J. D., and Durrell, J.: Antibodies affecting metabolism of chicken erythrocytes: examination of schizophrenic and other subjects. *Science* 151:1408–1410, 1966.

95. Ryan, J. W., Steinberg, H. R., Green, R., Brown, J. D., and Durell, J.: Controlled study of effects of plasma of schizophrenic and non-schizophrenic psychiatric patients on chicken erythrocytes. *J. Psychiat. Res.* 6: 33–34, 1968.

96. Sanders, B. E., Small, S. M., Ayers, W. J., Oh, Y. H., and Axelrod, S.: Additional studies on plasma proteins obtained from schizophrenics and controls. *Trans. NY Acad. Sci.* 28:22–39, 1965.

97. Sapira, J. D.: Immunoelectrophoresis of the serum of psychotic patients. *Arch. Gen. Psychiat.* 10:196–198, 1964.

98. Siegel, M.: A sensitive method for the detection of N,N-dimethylserotonin (bufotenin) in urine; failure to demonstrate its presence in the urine of schizophrenic and normal subjects. *J. Psychiat. Res.* 3:205–211, 1965.

99. Slater, E.: *Psychotic and Neurotic Illnesses in Twins.* London, H. M. Stationery Office, 1953.

100. Sohler, A., Noval, J. J., and Renz, R. H.: 6-Hydroxyskatole sulfate excretion in schizophrenia. *J. Nerv. Ment. Dis.* 137:591–596, 1963.

101. Sprince, H., Houser, E., Jameson, D., and Dohan, F. C.: Differential extraction of indoles from the urine of schizophrenic and normal subjects. *Arch. Gen. Psychiat.* 2:268–270, 1960.

102. Sprince, H., Parker, C. M., Jameson, D., and Alexander, F.: Urinary indoles in schizophrenic and psychoneurotic patients after administration of tranylcypromine (parnate) and methionine or tryptophan. *J. Nerv. Ment. Dis.* 137:246–251, 1963.

103. Sprince, H., Parker, C. M., Jameson, D., and Josephs, J. A.: Effect of methionine on nicotinic acid and indoleacetic acid pathways of tryptophan metabolism *in vivo. Proc. Soc. Exp. Biol. Med.* 119:942–946, 1965.

104. Studnitz, W. v., and Nyman, G. E.: Excretion of 3,4-dimethoxyphenylethylamine in schizophrenia. *Acta Psychiat. Scand.* 41:117–121, 1965.

105. Takesada, M., Kakimoto, Y., Sano, I., and Kaneko, Z.: 3,4-Dimethoxyphenylethylamine and other amines in the urine of schizophrenic patients. *Nature* 199:203–204, 1963.

106. Takesada, M., Miyamoto, E., Kakimoto, Y., Sano, I., and Kaneko, Z.: Phenolic and indole amines in the urine of schizophrenics. *Nature* 207: 1199–1200, 1965.

107. Turner, W. J., and Chipps, H. I.: A heterophil hemolysin in human blood. I. Distribution in schizophrenics and nonschizophrenics. *Arch. Gen. Psychiat.* 15:373–377, 1966.

108. Vartanyan, M. E.: Immunological investigation of schizophrenia. *Zh. Neuropat. Psikhiat. Korsakov* 63:3–12, 1963.

109. Weil-Malherbe, H.: The biochemistry of the functional psychoses. *In Advances in Enzymology,* Vol. XXIX. New York, Interscience Publishers, 1967, pp. 479–553.

110. Williams, C. H.: The pink spot. *Lancet* 1:599–600, 1966.

111. Williams, C. H., Gibson, J. G., and McCormick, W. O.: 3,4-Dimethoxyphenylethylamine in schizophrenia. *Nature* 211:1195, 1966.

112. Winter, C. A., Flataker, L., Boger, W. P., Smith, E. V. C., and Sanders, B. E.: The effects of blood serum and of serum fractions from schizophrenic donors upon the performance of trained rats. *In* Folch-Pi, J. (Ed.) *Chemical Pathology of the Nervous System.* Oxford, Pergamon Press, 1961, pp. 641–646.

113. Woolley, D. W.: *The Biochemical Bases of Psychoses.* New York, John Wiley & Sons, 1962.

114. Young, H. K., Berry, H. K., Beerstecher, E., and Berry, J. S.: Metabolic patterns of schizophrenic and control groups. *In Biochemical Institute Studies* IV, University of Texas Publication No. 5109. Austin, University of Texas, 1951, pp. 189–197

115. Yuwiler, A., and Good, M. H.: Chromatographic study of "Reigelhaupt" chromogens in urine. *J. Psychiat. Res.* 1:215–227, 1962.

16

THE PARANOID PSEUDO-COMMUNITY REVISITED

Norman Cameron

A decade of experience with intensive clinical studies of paranoid thinking, in the course of psychoanalyzing psychoneurotics and in the long-term therapy of ambulatory psychotics, has led me to a reworking of the concept of the pseudo-community as formulated in this *Journal*[1] and further developed elsewhere.[2] The social aspects of the concept require little change. It is in its individual aspects—in a greater concern with the evidence of internal changes and with the signs that forces are operative which are not open to direct observation—that the pseudo-community acquires deeper roots and greater usefulness.

ORIGINAL PRESENTATION

In the normal evolution and preservation of socially organized behavior the most important factor is the developing and maintaining of genuine communication. In each individual, language behavior grows out of preverbal interchange between infant and older person. It evolves in accordance with whatever traditional patterns prevail in the immediate environment, since communication is always, at first, between a child who operates at preverbal levels and older

Reprinted from the *American Journal of Sociology*, 65, 1959, 52–62, with the permission of The University of Chicago Press and Dr. Cameron.

[1]Norman Cameron, "The Paranoid Pseudo-Community," *American Journal of Sociology*, XLIX (1943), 32–38. Reprinted in A. M. Rose (ed.), *Mental Health and Mental Disorder: A Sociological Approach* (New York: W. W. Norton & Co., 1955).

[2]Norman Cameron, *The Psychology of Behavior Disorders: A Biosocial Interpretation* (Boston: Houghton Mifflin Co., 1947), and "Perceptual Organization and Behavior Pathology," in R. Blake and G. Ramsey (eds.), *Perception: An Approach to Personality* (New York: Ronald Press Co., 1951); and Norman Cameron and A. Magaret, *Behavior Pathology* (Boston: Houghton Mifflin Co., 1951), chap. xiii, "Pseudo-Community and Delusion."

individuals whose language is already a highly organized interactive system. Through sharing continuously in such language and prelanguage interchange, each child develops shared social perspectives and skill in shifting from one perspective to another in time of need.

A highly significant result of this gradual process is that, as time goes on, the child normally acquires an increasingly realistic grasp of how other people feel, what their attitudes, plans, hopes, fears, and intentions are, and in what ways these all relate to his own. Eventually, he is able to take the roles of other people around him in imagination and to view things more or less realistically from their perspectives as well as from his own. In this way he also develops a workable degree of objectivity toward himself, learning to respond to his body, his personality, and his behavior more or less as others do. In the final product, there is considerable difference between the socialization achieved in behavior publicly shared and genuinely communicated and behavior that has remained private and little formulated or expressed in language.

The adult who is especially vulnerable to paranoid developments is one in whom this process of socialization has been seriously defective. His deficient social learning and poorly developed social skills leave him unable to understand adequately the motivations, attitudes, and intention of others. When he becomes disturbed or confused under stress, he must operate under several grave handicaps imposed by a lifelong inability to communicate freely and effectively, to suspend judgment long enough to share his tentative interpretations with someone else, to imagine realistically the attitudes that others might have toward his situation and himself, and to imagine their roles and thus share their perspectives.

Left to his own unaided devices in a crisis, the paranoid person is able only to seek and find "evidence" that carries him farther in the direction he is already going—toward a more and more delusional interpretation of what seems to be going on around him[3]. This process may culminate in a conviction that he himself is the focus of a community of persons who are united in a conspiracy of some kind against him. It is this supposed functional community of real persons whom the patient can see and hear, and of other persons whom he imagines, that we call the *paranoid pseudo-community*. It has no existence as a social organization and as soon as he attempts to combat it, or to flee, he is likely to come into conflict with his actual social community.

INCOMPLETENESS OF THE DESCRIPTIVE PSEUDO-COMMUNITY

This, in brief, is the background and structure of the paranoid pseudo-community, as originally described. As it stands, it still seems valid; but it is

[3]For a detailed discussion of this process of *desocialization* see "Desocialization and Disorganization," in Cameron and Magaret, *op. cit.*, pp. 448–517.

unnecessarily restricted. In the first place, the account of the delusional development pays scant attention to internal dynamics because of the limits imposed by a behavioristic orientation. Patients, of course, recognize no such limitations. In the course of long-term intensive therapy they can sometimes furnish important information about what is going on within them to a therapist who is ready to receive it. Some of this they describe as it happens, in their own terms, and often in their own idiom. Some of it one can infer from what is said and done, with the help of material communicated in parallel cases. Some of it one must postulate in an effort to make one's observations and direct inferences more intelligible, just as is done in other empirical sciences.

In the original account not enough emphasis was given to the positive achievements of delusion formation. As we shall see, the pseudo-community is the best means a paranoid patient has at the time for bridging the chasm between his inner reality and social reality. Its use for this purpose may lead to a progressive reduction in desocialization and the reappearance of more normal communicative channels.

And, finally, the concept of the pseudo-community needs a background of structural postulates. In order to make sense out of the experiences which people actually have in fantasies, daydreams, dreams, and psychoses, one is obliged to go beyond such impermanent concepts as perception, response, and behavior—upon which the writer earlier relied—and to assume probable forces and mechanisms operating within personality systems and interacting subsystems. Here, again, the patient often comes to the rescue with empirical data. And, every now and then, one comes across a patient who describes with naive simplicity and directness—but consistently over a long period of time—phenomena which seem purely theoretical and highly abstruse, as reported in the literature. Exposed to such material the therapist may still be left with a sense of strangeness; but his previous feeling of their abstruseness and incredulity sooner or later vanishes.[4]

PARANOID LOSS OF SOCIAL REALITY

Paranoid delusional development begins with an impairment of social communication. It is preceded by experiences of frustration to which, like many normal persons, the paranoid individual reacts by turning away from his surroundings, and taking refuge in fantasy and daydream. This is the phase of withdrawal and preoccupation which is sometimes obvious even to an untrained observer.

[4]See, e.g., the clinical material in Norman Cameron's "Reprojection and Introjection in the Interaction between Schizophrenic Patients and Therapists" (submitted for publication).

When a paranoid person withdraws like this, he is far more likely than a normal person to lose effective contact with his social environment (i.e., with social reality) and to undergo regression. If this happens, he may abandon social reality for a time completely and become absorbed in primitive regressive thinking and feeling. Occasionally, a patient openly expresses some of his regressive experiences at the time; more often they can be inferred only from what emerges later on.

PRECURSORS OF THE PSEUDO-COMMUNITY

I. Beginning Restitution

It is a fact, of both clinical observation and subjective report, that paranoid patients, while still wihdrawn, preoccupied, and regressed, begin to make attempts to regain their lost relationships with social reality. We may conceptualize these as marking the tapering-off of regression and the beginning of the reintegration of personality. The attempts fail to recover the lost social reality, however, because the patient's internal situation is not what it was before his regression. It is no longer possible for him to regain social reality as, for example, a normal person does when he wakes up in the morning. Instead, as we shall see, paranoid reintegration involves a restitutive process, the construction of a pseudo-reality which culminates in the paranoid pseudo-community.

Paranoid personalities suffer all their lives from defective repressive defenses and a heavy reliance upon the more primitive defenses of denial and projection. If thy undergo a psychotic regression, which involves partial ego disintegration, their repressive defenses become still more defective. Primitive fantasies and conflicts now begin to emerge and to threaten ego disruption. The patient is forced to deal with them somehow, if he is to preserve what personality integration he still has and avoid further regression. Since he cannot successfully regress them, he vigorously denies them and projects them. An immediate result of the intense projective defense is that the products of the patient's emerging fantasies and conflicts now appear to him to be coming from outside him. Thus he seems to escape disintegration from within only to be threatened with destruction from without.

II. Estrangement and Diffuse Vigilance

In the process of denying and projecting, the paranoid patient makes a start toward regaining contact with his surroundings. But this process neither simplifies nor clarifies the situation for him; and it does not bring about a return to social reality. On the contrary, the surroundings now seem somehow strange and different. Something has unquestionably happened. The patient misidentifies this "something" as basically a change in the makeup of his environment instead of what it actually is, a fundamental change within himself. If he expresses his feelings at this point, he is likely to say that things are going on which he does not understand; and this, of course, is literally true.

It is hardly surprising that the patient, finding himself in a world grown suddenly strange, should become diffusely vigilant. He watches everything uneasily; he listens alertly for clues; he lookes everywhere for hidden meanings. Here his lifelong social incompetence makes matters still worse. He lacks even ordinary skill in the common techniques for testing social reality. He is unable to view his threatening situation even temporarily from the perspective of a neutral person. The more anxious and vigilant he grows, the less he can trust anybody, the less he dares to share with anyone his uneasiness and suspicion. He is condemned to pursue a solitary path, beset by primal fears, hates, and temptations which he cannot cope with nor escape.

III. Increased Self-reference

Strong tendencies toward self-reference are characteristic of paranoid personalities. When a paranoid adult becomes deeply and regressively preoccupied, his habitually egocentric orientation is greatly increased. And when he next resorts to wholesale projection, he in effect converts his environment into an arena for his projected fantasies and conflicts. This destroys whatever neutrality and objectivity the environment may have previously possessed for him. He is now engrossed in scrutinizing his surroundings for signs of the return of what he is denying and projecting. To these he has become selectively sensitive. He is watching out for something that will explain away the strangeness and enable him to escape his frightening sense of isolation.

It is an unfortunate fact that a badly frightened person—even a normal one—is likely to notice things and make interpretations that increase rather than diminish his fear. And this is especially the case if he feels alone, in strange surroundings, and threatened by an unknown danger. Many nonparanoid adults, for example, walking alone through a large cemetery at night, or lost at night in a forest, become extremely alert and feel personally threatened by harmless things wholly unrelated to them. The paranoid adult, who is peopling his surroundings with projected phantoms from his own past, likewise creates a situation in which everything seems somehow dangerously related to him. Since he cannot escape, he tries to understand the situation he has unconsciously created, in the vain hope that he may then be able to cope with it.

IV. Preliminary Hypotheses

Being human, the paranoid patient is driven irresistibly to make hypotheses; but, having partially regressed, and being paranoid as well, he cannot test them. He tends, therefore, to pass from one guess or one suspicion to another like it. Using the materials provided by his environment and by his projected fantasies and conflicts, he constructs a succession of provisional hypotheses, discarding each as it fails to meet the contradictory demands of his internal needs and the environment. This is characteristic also of complex normal problem-solving. It is an expression of what is called the synthetic function of the ego.

Everyone who works with paranoid patients discovers that some kind of delusional reconstruction of reality is essential to their continued existence as persons. Even a temporary and unsatisfactory delusional hypothesis may be at the time a patient's sole means of bridging the gap between himself and his social environment. It gives a distorted picture of the world; but a distorted world is better than no world at all. And this is often a regressed person's only choice. To abandon his projected fears, hates, and temptations might mean to abandon all that he has gained in the reconstruction of reality, to have his world fall apart and fall apart himself. Patients sense this danger, even expressing it in these words, and they rightly refuse to give up their delusional reality. Their fear is not unrealistic, for clinically such catastrophes actually occur, ending in personality disintegration.

A great many paranoid persons never go beyond the phase of making and giving up a succession of preliminary delusional hypotheses. Some of them regain a good working relationship with social reality, something approaching or equaling their premorbid status. Some are less successful and remain chronically suspicious, averse, and partially withdrawn but manage even so to go on living otherwise much as they had lived before. They may appear morose, irascible, and bitter; but they do not fix upon definite enemies or take definite hostile action. At most they suffer brief outbursts of protest and complaint without losing their ability to retreat from an angry delusional position. In this paper, however, we are concerned primarily with paranoid patients—by no means incurable—who go on to crystallize a more stable delusional organization.

FINAL CRYSTALLIZATION: THE PSEUDO-COMMUNITY

A great many paranoid persons succeed in crystallizing a stable conceptual organization, the pseudo-community, which gives them a satisfactory cognitive explanation of their strange altered world and a basis for doing something about the situation as they now see it. Their problem is exceedingly complex. It is impossible for them to get rid of the unconscious elements which they have denied and projected, but which now return apparently from the outside. They cannot abandon or even ignore their environment without facing a frightening regression into an objectless world. Their task is somehow to integrate these internal and external phenomena which appear before them on a single plane into a unified world picture.

The human environment which others share (*social reality*) provides the patient with real persons having social roles and characteristics which he can utilize in making his delusional reconstruction. It also provides real interaction among them, including interaction with the patient himself. Many things actually happen in it, some of them in direct relation to the patient, most of them actually not.

Internal reality provides two sets of functions. One is made up of the previously unconscious impulses, conflicts, and fantasies—now erupted, denied and projected. This, as noted, introduces imagined motivation, interaction, and intentions into the observed activities of other persons. It gives apparent meaning to happenings which do not have such meaning for the consensus. The other set of functions is included in the concept of ego adaptation. It is the ego synthesis mentioned above, by means of which the demands of internal reality and the structure of social reality are integrated into a meaningful, though delusional, unity.

What the paranoid patient does is as follows: Into the organization of social reality, as he perceives it, he unconsciously projects his own previously unconscious motivation, which he has denied but cannot escape. This process now requires a perceptual and conceptual reorganization of object relations in his surroundings into an apparent community, which he represents to himself as organized wholly with respect to him (delusion of self-reference). And since the patient's erupted, denied, and projected elements are overwhelmingly hostile and destructive, the motivation he ascribes to the real persons he has now organized into his conceptual pseudo-community is bound to be extremely hostile and destructive.

To complete his conceptual organization of a paranoid conspiracy, the patient also introduces imaginary persons. He ascribes to them, as to real persons, imagined functions, roles, and motivations in keeping with his need to unify his restitutional conception and make it stable. He pictures helpers, dupes, stooges, go-betweens, and master-minds, of whose actual existence he becomes certain.

It is characteristic of the pseudo-community that it is made up of both real and imaginary persons, all of whom may have both real and imaginary functions and interrelations.[5] In form it usually corresponds to one or another of the

[5]This is in contrast to the autistic community, which is composed of wholly imaginary persons (see "Autistic Community and Hallucination," in Cameron and Magaret, *op. cit.*, pp. 414–447).

common dangerous, hostile groups in contemporary society, real or fictional—gangs, dope and spy rings, secret police, and groups of political, radical, and religious fanatics. Many paranoid patients succeed in creating a restitutional organization which has well-formulated plans. The chief persecutor is sometimes a relative or acquaintance, or a well-known public figure, while the rest of the imaginary personnel forms a vague, sinister background. Sometimes one finds the reverse—the chief persecutor is unknown, a malevolent "brain" behind everything, while the known dangerous persons play supporting roles in the delusional cast.

The final delusional reconstruction of reality may fall into an integrated conceptual pattern that brings an experience of closure: "I suddenly realized what it was all about!" the patient may exclaim with obvious relief at sudden clarification. The intolerable suspense has ended: the strangeness of what has been "going on" seems to disappear, and confusion is replaced by "understanding," and wavering doubt by certainty. A known danger may be frightening; but at least it is tangible, and one can do something about it. In short, the pseudo-community reduces the hopeless complexity and confusion to a clear formula. This formula—"the plot"—the patient can now apply to future events as he experiences them and fit them into the general framework of his reconstruction.

The organization of a conceptual pseudo-community is a final cognitive step in paranoid problem-solving. It re-establishes stable object relations, though on a delusional basis, and thus makes integrated action possible. To summarize what this reconstruction of reality has achieved for its creator:

Reduction in estrangement. As a direct result of paranoid problem-solving, experienced external reality is distorted so as to bring it into line with the inescapable projected elements. This lessens confusion and detachment and allows the patient to recover some of his lost sense of ego integrity. The world seems dangerous but familiar.

Internal absorption of aggression. Construction and maintenance of a conceptual pseudo-community absorb aggression internally, in the same sense that organizing a baseball team, a political ward, or a scientific society absorbs aggression. This reduces the threat of ego disintegration which the id eruptions pose.

Basis for action. Any new cognitive construct can serve as a basis for new action; in this respect the paranoid pseudo-community is no exception. It organizes the drive-directed cognitive processes, leads to meaningful interpretations in a well-defined pseudo-reality structure, and paves the way for overt action with a definite focus. The patient is enabled to go ahead as anyone else might who had powerful urges and felt sure that he was right.

Justification of aggressive action. Finally, a persecutory pseudo-community justifies attack or flight, either of which involves a direct aggressive discharge in overt action. Fighting or running away is less disintegrative psychologically than prolonged frightened inaction. And under the circumstances, as the patient now conceptualizes them, he need feel neither guilt for attacking nor shame for fleeing.

PARANOID COGNITION AND PARANOID ACTION

When a patient succeeds in conceptualizing a pseudo-community, he has taken the final cognitive step in paranoid problem-solving. He now "knows" what his situation is. But he is still faced with his need to do something about it. As a matter of fact, the crystallization of a hostile delusional structure usually increases the urge to take action. A circular process may quickly develop. The imagined threats of the now structured imaginary conspiracy seem to the patient concrete and imminent. They stimulate more and more his anxiety and defensive hostility—and the latter, being as usual projected, further increases the apparent external threat. Often this kind of self-stimulation spirals upward, while more and more "incidents" and people may be drawn into the gathering psychotic storm.

Paranoid action, however inappropriate it may be, still represents the completion of restitutional relationships and the fullest contact with his human environment of which the patient is capable at the time. He switches from his previous passive role of observer and interpreter, with all its indecision and anxiety, to that of an aggressive participant in what he conceives as social reality. For him this is genuine interaction, and he experiences the gratification that comes with certainty and with a massive discharge of pent-up aggressiveness. He may give a preliminary warning to the supposed culprits or make an appeal for intervention to someone in authority before taking direct action himself, which, when it comes, may be in the form of an attack or sudden flight, either of which may be planned and executed with considerable skill.

MAKING SOCIAL REALITY CONFORM TO THE
PSEUDO-COMMUNITY

Paranoid patients who take aggressive action often achieve a pyrrhic victory. They succeed finally in making social reality act in conformity with the delusional reality which they have created. As long as a patient confines himself to watching, listening, and interpreting, he need not come into open conflict with the social community. But, when he takes overt action appropriate only in his private pseudo-community, a serious social conflict will arise.

Social reality is the living product of genuine sharing, communication, and interaction. Valid social attitudes, interpretations, and action derive continuously from these operations. The restitutional reality in which the patient believes himself to be participating has no counterpart outside of himself: it is illusory. Other persons cannot possibly share his attitudes and interpretations because they do not share his paranoid projections and distortions. Therefore they do not understand action taken in terms of his delusional reconstruction. The patient, for his part, cannot share their attitudes and interpretations because he is driven by regressive needs which find no place in adult social reality.

When an intelligent adult expresses beliefs and makes accusations which seem unintelligible to others, as well as threatening, he may make the people around him exceedingly anxious. This is particularly the case when his words tend to activate their unconscious fantasies and conflicts. And when such a person begins to take aggressive action, which seems unprovoked as well as unintelligible, he inevitably arouses defensive and retaliatory hostility in others. The moment the social community takes action against him, it provides him with the confirmation he has been expecting—that there is a plot against him.

Thus, in the end, the patient manages to provoke action in the social community that conforms to the expectation expressed in his pseudo-community organization. His own internal need to experience hostility from without—as a defense against being overwhelmed by internal aggression—is satisfied when actual persons behave in accordance with his projections. His need for a target against which to discharge hostility is also met. This is his victory and his defeat.

The defeat need not be final. Much will depend, of course, upon the patient's basic personality organization, particularly his emotional flexibility, his potentiality for internal change, and his residual capacity for establishing new ego and superego identifications. The depth and extent of his regression are also important, as are the fixity and inclusiveness of his delusional structure. Much will also depend upon his potential freedom to communicate, to develop reciprocal role-taking skills with another person, and to include another's alternative perspectives in his own therapeutic orientation.

THERAPY

The primary therapeutic consideration, of course, is not the character of the delusional structure but what makes it necessary. A reduction in anxiety is among the first objectives. The source of anxiety lies in the regressive changes and in the threat these have brought of an unconscious breakthrough. But it is also aggravated by anything in the environment which tends to increase the patient's hostility and fear. Once the setting has been made less anxiety-provoking, the most pressing need is for someone in whom the patient can ultimately put his trust—someone not made anxious by the patient's fear and hostility or driven to give reassurances and make demands.

For the paranoid patient who is ready to attempt social communication, an interested but neutral therapist can function as a living bridge between psychotic reality and social reality. Through interacting with such a person, who neither attacks the delusional structure nor beats the drums of logic, a patient may succeed in gaining new points of reference from which to build a new orientation. The therapeutic process now involves another reconstruction of reality, one which undoes the restitutional pseudo-community without destroying the patient's defenses and forcing him to regress further.

As anxiety and the threat of disintegration subside, paranoid certainty becomes less necessary to personality survival. The patient can begin to entertain doubts and consider alternative interpretations. Such changes, of course, must come from within if they are to come at all. If he is able to work through some of the origins and derivatives of his basic problems, the patient may succeed eventually in representing to himself more realistically than ever before how other people feel and think. In this way the conceptual structure of his pseudo-community may be gradually replaced by something approaching the conceptual structure of social reality.

17

TOWARD A THEORY OF SCHIZOPHRENIA

Gregory Bateson, Don D. Jackson, Jay Haley and
John Weakland

This is a report on a research project which has been formulating and testing a broad, systematic view of the nature, etiology, and therapy of schizophrenia. Our research in this field has proceeded by discussion of a varied body of data and ideas, with all of us contributing according to our varied experience in anthropology, communications analysis, psychotherapy, psychiatry, and psychoanalysis. We have now reached common agreement on the broad outlines of a communicational theory of the origin and nature of schizophrenia; this paper is a preliminary report on our continuing research.

THE BASE IN COMMUNICATIONS THEORY

Our approach is based on that part of communications theory which Russell has called the Theory of Logical Types (17). The central thesis of this theory

Reprinted from *Behavioral Science,* 1 (4), 1956, 251–264, with the permission of the publishers and the authors. (Footnotes have been renumbered.)

This paper derives from hypotheses first developed in a research project financed by the Rockefeller Foundation from 1952-54, administered by the Department of Sociology and Anthropology at Stanford University and directed by Gregory Bateson. Since 1954 the project has continued, financed by the Josiah Macy, Jr. Foundation. To Jay Haley is due credit for recognizing that the symptoms of schizophrenia are suggestive of an inability to discriminate the Logical Types, and this was amplified by Bateson who added the notion that the symptoms and etiology could be formally described in terms of a double bind hypothesis. The hypothesis was communicated to D. D. Jackson and found to fit closely with his ideas of family homeostasis. Since then Dr. Jackson has worked closely with the project. The study of the formal analogies between hypnosis and schizophrenia has been the work of John H. Weakland and Jay Haley.

is that there is a discontinuity between a class and its members. The class cannot be a member of itself nor can one of the members *be* the class, since the term used for the class is of a *different level of abstraction*—a different Logical Type —from terms used for members. Although in formal logic there is an attempt to maintain this discontinuity between a class and its members, we argue that in the psychology of real communications this discontinuity is continually and inevitably breached (2), and that a priori we must expect a pathology to occur in the human organism when certain formal patterns of the breaching occur in the communication between mother and child. We shall argue that this pathology at its extreme will have symptoms whose formal characteristics would lead the pathology to be classified as a schizophrenia.

Illustrations of how human beings handle communication involving multiple Logical Types can be derived from the following fields:

1. *The use of various communicational modes in human communication.* Examples are play, nonplay, fantasy, sacrament, metaphor, etc. Even among the lower mammals there appears to be an exchange of signals which identify certain meaningful behavior as "play," etc.[1] These signals are evidently of higher Logical Type than the messages they classify. Among human beings this framing and labeling of messages and meaningful actions reachs considerable complexity, with the peculiarity that our vocabulary for such discrimination is still very poorly developed, and we rely preponderantly upon nonverbal media of posture, gesture, facial expression, intonation, and the context for the communication of these highly abstract, but vitally important, labels.

2. *Humor.* This seems to be a method of exploring the implicit themes in thought or in a relationship. The method of exploration involves the use of messages which are characterized by a condensation of Logical Types or communicational modes. A discovery, for example, occurs when it suddenly becomes plain that a message was not only metaphoric but also more literal, or vice versa. That is to say, the explosive moment in humor is the moment when the labeling of the mode undergoes a dissolution and resynthesis. Commonly, the punch line compels a re-evaluation of earlier signals which ascribed to certain messages a particular mode (e.g., literalness or fantasy). This has the peculiar effect of attributing *mode* to those signals which had previously the status of that higher Logical Type which classifies the modes.

3. *The falsification of mode-identifying signals.* Among human beings mode identifiers can be falsified, and we have the artificial laugh, the manipulative simulation of friendliness, the confidence trick, kidding, and the like. Similar falsifications have been recorded among mammals (3, 13). Among human beings we meet with a strange phenomenon—the unconscious falsification of

[1]A film prepared by this project, "The Nature of Play; Part I, River Otters," is available.

these signals. This may occur within the self—the subject may conceal from himself his own real hostility under the guise of metaphoric play—or it may occur as an unconscious falsification of the subject's understanding of the other person's mode-identifying signals. He may mistake shyness for contempt, etc. Indeed most of the errors of self-reference fall under this head.

4. *Learning.* The simplest level of this phenomenon is exemplied by a situation in which a subject receives a message and acts appropriately on it: "I heard the clock strike and knew it was time for lunch. So I went to the table." In learning experiments the analogue of this sequence of events is observed by the experimenter and commonly treated as a single message of a higher type. When the dog salivates between buzzer and meat powder, this sequence is accepted by the experimenter as a message indicating that "the dog has *learned* that buzzer means meat powder." But this is not the end of the hierarchy of types involved. The experimental subject may become more skilled in learning. He may *learn to learn* (1, 7, 9,), and it is not inconceivable that still higher orders of learning may occur in human beings.

5. *Multiple levels of learning and the Logical Typing of signals.* These are two inseparable sets of phenomena—inseparable because the ability to handle the multiple types of signals is itself a *learned* skill and therefore a function of the multiple levels of learning.

According to our hypothesis, the term "ego function" (as this term is used when a schizophrenic is described as having "weak ego function") is precisely *the process of discriminating communicational modes either within the self or between the self and others.* The schizophrenic exhibits weakness in three areas of such functions: (*a*) He has difficulty in assigning the correct communicational mode to the messages he receives from other persons. (*b*) He has difficulty in assigning the correct communicational mode to those messages which he himself utters or emits nonverbally. (*c*) He has difficulty in assigning the correct communicational mode to his own thoughts, sensations and percepts.

At this point it is appropriate to compare what was said in the previous paragraph with von Domarus' (16) approach to the systematic description of schizophrenic utterance. He suggests that the messages (and thought) of the schizophrenic are deviant in syllogistic structure. In place of structures which derive from the syllogism, Barbara, the schizophrenic, according to this theory, uses structures which identify predicates. An example of such a distorted syllogism is:

Men die.
Grass dies.
Men are grass.

But as we see it, von Domarus' formulation is only a more precise—and therefore valuable—way of saying that schizophrenic utterance is rich in metaphor. With that generalization we agree. But metaphor is an indispensable tool of thought and expression—a characteristic of all human communication, even of that of the scientist. The conceptual models of cybernetics and the energy theories of psychoanalysis are, after all, only labeled metaphors. The peculiarity of the schizophrenic is not that he uses metaphors, but that he uses *unlabeled* metaphors. He has special difficulty in handling signals of that class whose members assign Logical Types to other signals.

If our formal summary of the symptomatology is correct and if the schizophrenia of our hypothesis is essentially a result of family interaction, it should be possible to arrive a priori at a formal description of these sequences of experience which would induce such a symptomatology. What is known of learning theory combines with the evident fact that human beings use *context* as a guide for mode discrimination. Therefore, we must look not for some specific traumatic experience in the infantile etiology but rather for characteristic sequential patterns. The specificity for which we search is to be at an abstract or formal level. The sequences must have this characteristic: that from them the patient will acquire the mental habits which are exemplified in schizophrenic communication. That is to say, *he must live in a universe where the sequences of events are such that his unconventional communicational habits will be in some sense appropriate.* The hypothesis which we offer is that sequences of this kind in the external experience of the patient are responsible for the inner conflicts of Logical Typing. For such unresolvable sequences of experiences, we use the term "double bind."

The Double Bind

The necessary ingredients for a double bind situation, as we see it, are:

1. *Two or more persons.* Of these, we designate one, for purposes of our definition, as the "victim." We do not assume that the double bind is inflicted by the mother alone, but that it may be done either by mother alone or by some combination of mother, father, and/or siblings.

2. *Repeated experience.* We assume that the double bind is a recurrent theme in the experience of the victim. Our hypothesis does not invoke a single traumatic experience, but such repeated experience that the double bind structure comes to be an habitual expectation.

3. *A primary negative injunction.* This may have either of two forms: (*a*) "Do not do so and so, or I will punish you," or (*b*) "If you do not do so and so, I will punish you." Here we select a context of learning based on avoidance

of punishment rather than a context of reward seeking. There is perhaps no formal reason for this selection. We assume that the punishment may be either the withdrawal of love or the expression of hate or anger—or most devastating—the kind of abandonment that results from the parent's expression of extreme helplessness.[2]

4. *A secondary injunction conflicting with the first at a more abstract level, and like the first enforced by punishments or signals which threaten survival.* This secondary injunction is more difficult to describe than the primary for two reasons. First, the secondary injunction is commonly communicated to the child by nonverbal means. Posture, gesture, tone of voice, meaningful action, and the implications concealed in verbal comment may all be used to convey this more abstract message. Second, the secondary injunction may impinge upon any element of the primary prohibition. Verbalization of the secondary injunction, may, therefore, include a wide variety of forms; for example, "Do not see this as punishment"; "Do not see me as the punishing agent"; "Do not submit to my prohibitions"; "Do not think of what you must not do"; "Do not question my love of which the primary prohibition is (or is not) an example"; and so on. Other examples become possible when the double bind in inflicted not by one individual but by two. For example, one parent may negate at a more abstract level the injunctions of the other.

5. *A tertiary negative injunction prohibiting the victim from escaping from the field.* In a formal sense it is perhaps unnecessary to list this injunction as a separate item since the reinforcement at the other two levels involves a threat to survival, and if the double binds are imposed during infancy, escape is naturally impossible. However, it seems that in some cases the escape from the field is made impossible by certain devices which are not purely negative, e.g., capricious promises of love, and the like.

6. Finally, the complete set of ingredients is no longer necessary when the victim has learned to perceive his universe in double bind patterns. Almost any part of a double bind sequence may then be sufficient to precipitate panic or rage. The pattern of conflicting injunctions may even be taken over by hallucinatory voices (14).

The Effect of the Double Bind

In the Eastern religion, Zen Buddhism, the goal is to achieve Enlightenment. The Zen Master attempts to bring about enlightenment in his pupil in various ways. One of the things he does is to hold a stick over a pupil's head and say fiercely, "If you say this stick is real, I will strike you with it. If you say this

---

[2] Our concept of punishment is being refined at present. It appears to us to involve perceptual experience in a way that cannot be encompassed by the notion of "trauma."

stick is not real, I will strike you with it. If you don't say anything, I will strike you with it." We feel that the schizophrenic finds himself continually in the same situation as the pupil, but he achieves something like disorientation rather than enlightenment. The Zen pupil might reach up and take the stick away from the Master—who might accept this response, but the schizophrenic has no such choice since with him there is no not caring about the relationship, and his mother's aims and awareness are not like the Master's.

We hypothesize that there will be a breakdown in any individual's ability to discriminate between Logical Types whenever a double bind situation occurs. The general characteristics of this situation are the following:

1. When the individual is involved in an intense relationship; that is, a relationship in which he feels it is vitally important that he discriminate accurately what sort of message is being communicated so that he may respond appropriately.

2. And, the individual is caught in a situation in which the other person in the relationship is expressing two orders of message and one of these denies the other.

3. And, the individual is unable to comment on the messages being expressed to correct his discrimination of what order of message to respond to, i.e., he cannot make a metacommunicative statement.

We have suggested that this is the sort of situation which occurs between the pre-schizophrenic and his mother, but it also occurs in normal relationships. When a person is caught in a double bind situation, he will respond defensively in a manner similar to the schizophrenic. An individual will take a metaphorical statement literally when he is in a situation where he must respond, where he is faced with contradictory messages, and when he is unable to comment on the contradictions. For example, one day an employee went home during office hours. A fellow employee called him at his home, and said lightly, "Well, how did you get *there*?" The employee replied, "By automobile." He responded literally because he was faced with a message which asked him what he was doing at home when he should have been at the office, but which denied that this question was being asked by the way it was phrased. (Since the speaker felt it wasn't really his business, he spoke metaphorically.) The relationship was intense enough so that the victim was in doubt how the information would be used, and he therefore responded literally. This is characteristic of anyone who feels "on the spot," as demonstrated by the careful literal replies of a witness on the stand in a court trial. The schizophrenic feels so terribly on the spot at all times that he habitually responds with a defensive insistence on the literal level when it is quite inappropriate, e.g., when someone is joking.

Schizophrenics also confuse the literal and metaphoric in their own utterance when they feel themselves caught in a double bind. For example, a patient may wish to criticize his therapist for being late for an appointment, but he may be unsure what sort of a message that act of being late was—particularly if the therapist has anticipated the patient's reaction and apologized for the event. The patient cannot say, "Why were you late? Is it because you don't want to see me today?" This would be an accusation, and so he shifts to a metaphorical statement. He may then say, "I knew a fellow once who missed a boat, his name was Sam and the boat almost sunk . . . etc.," Thus he develops a metaphorical story and the therapist may or may not discover in it a comment on his being late. The convenient thing about a metaphor is that it leaves it up to the therapist (or mother) to see an accusation in the statement if he chooses, or to ignore it if he chooses. Should the therapist accept the accusation in the metaphor, then the patient can accept the statement he has made about Sam as metaphorical. If the therapist points out that this doesn't sound like a true statement about Sam, as a way of avoiding the accusation in the story, the patient can argue that there really was a man named Sam. As an answer to the double bind situation, a shift to a metaphorical statement brings safety. However, it also prevents the patient from making the accusation he wants to make. But instead of getting over his accusation by indicating that this is a metaphor, the schizophrenic patient seems to try to get over the fact that it is a metaphor by making it more fantastic. If the therapist should ignore the accusation in the story about Sam, the schizophrenic may then tell a story about going to Mars in a rocket ship as a way of putting over his accusation. The indication that it is a metaphorical statement lies in the fantastic aspect of the metaphor, not in the signals which usually accompany metaphors to tell the listener that a metaphor is being used.

It is not only safer for the victim of a double bind to shift to a metaphorical order of message, but in an impossible situation it is better to shift and become somebody else, or shift and insist that he is somewhere else. Then the double bind cannot work on the victim, because it isn't he and besides he is in a different place. In other words, the statements which show that a patient is disoriented can be interpreted as ways of defending himself against the situation he is in. The pathology enters when the victim himself either does not know that his responses are metaphorical or cannot say so. To recognize that he was speaking metaphorically he would need to be aware that he was defending himself and therefore was afraid of the other person. To him such an awareness would be an indictment of the other person and therefore provoke disaster.

If an individual has spent his life in the kind of double bind relationship described here, his way of relating to people after a psychotic break would have a systematic pattern. First, he would not share with normal people those signals which accompany messages to indicate what a person means. His metacommunicative system—the communications about communication—would have broken down, and he would not know what kind of message a message was. If a person said to him, "What would you like to do today?" he would be unable to judge accurately by the context or by the tone of voice or gesture whether he was being condemned for what he did yesterday, or being offered a sexual invitation, or just what was meant. Given this inability to judge accurately what a person really means and an excessive concern with what is really meant, an individual might defend himself by choosing one or more of several alternatives. He might, for example, assume that behind every statement there is a concealed meaning which is detrimental to his welfare. He would then be excessively concerned with hidden meanings and determined to demonstrate that he could not be deceived—as he had been all his life. If he chooses this alternative, he will be continually searching for meanings behind what people say and behind chance occurrences in the environment, and he will be characteristically suspicious and defiant.

He might choose another alternative, and tend to accept literally everything people say to him; when their tone or gesture or context contradicted what they said, he might establish a pattern of laughing off these metacommunicative signals. He would give up trying to discriminate between level of message and treat all messages as unimportant or to be laughed at.

If he didn't become suspicious of metacommunicative messages or attempt to laugh them off, he might choose to try to ignore them. Then he would find it necessary to see and hear less and less of what went on around him, and do his utmost to avoid provoking a response in his environment. He would try to detach his interest from the external world and concentrate on his own internal processes and, therefore, give the appearance of being a withdrawn, perhaps mute, individual.

This is another way of saying that if an individual doesn't know what sort of message a message is, he may defend himself in ways which have been described as paranoid, hebephrenic, or catatonic. These three alternatives are not the only ones. The point is that he cannot choose the one alternative which would help him to discover what people mean; he cannot, without considerable help, discuss the messages of others. Without being able to do that, the human being is like any self-correcting system which has lost its governor; it spirals into never-ending, but always systematic, distortions.

A DESCRIPTION OF THE FAMILY SITUATION

The theoretical possibility of double bind situations stimulated us to look for such communication sequences in the schizophrenic patient and in his family situation. Toward this end we have studied the written and verbal reports of psychotherapists who have treated such patients intensively; we have studied tape recordings of psychotherapeutic interviews, both of our own patients and others; we have interviewed and taped parents of schizophrenics; we have had two mothers and one father participate in intensive psychotherapy; and we have interviewed and taped parents and patients seen conjointly.

On the basis of these data we have developed a hypothesis about the family situation which ultimately leads to an individual suffering from schizophrenia. This hypothesis has not been statistically tested; it selects and emphasizes a rather simple set of interactional phenomena and does not attempt to describe comprehensively the extraordinary complexity of a family relationship.

We hypothesize that the family situation of the schizophrenic has the following general characteristics.

1. A child whose mother becomes anxious and withdraws if the child responds to her as a loving mother. That is, the child's very existence has a special meaning to the mother which arouses her anxiety and hostility when she is in danger of intimate contact with the child.

2. A mother to whom feelings of anxiety and hostility toward the child are not acceptable, and whose way of denying them is to express overt loving behavior to persuade the child to respond to her as a loving mother and to withdraw from him if he does not. "Loving behavior" does not necessarily imply "affection"; it can, for example, be set in a framework of doing the proper thing, instilling "goodness," and the like.

3. The absence of anyone in the family, such as a strong and insightful father, who can intervene in the relationship between the mother and child and support the child in the face of the contradictions involved.

Since this is a formal description we are not specifically concerned with why the mother feels this way about the child, but we suggest that she could feel this way for various reasons. It may be that merely having a child arouses anxiety about herself and her relationships to her own family; or it may be important to her that the child is a boy or a girl, or that the child was born on the anniversary of one of her own siblings (8), or the child may be in the same sibling position in the family that she was, or the child may be special to her for other reasons related to her own emotional problems.

Given a situation with these characteristics, we hypothesize that the mother of a schizophrenic will be simultaneously expressing at least two orders of message. (For simplicity in this presentation we shall confine ourselves to two orders.) These orders of message can be roughly characterized as (a) hostile or withdrawing behavior which is aroused whenever the child approaches her, and (b) simulated loving or approaching behavior which is aroused when the child responds to her hostile and withdrawing behavior, as a way of denying that she is withdrawing. Her problem is to control her anxiety by controlling the closeness and distance between herself and her child. To put this another way, if the mother begins to feel affectionate and close to her child, she begins to feel endangered and must withdraw from him; but she cannot accept this hostile act and to deny it must simulate affection and closeness with her child. The important point is that her loving behavior is then a comment on (since it is compensatory for) her hostile behavior and consequently it is of a different *order* of message than the hostile behavior—it is a message about a sequence of messages. Yet by its nature it denies the existence of these messages which it is about, i.e., the hostile withdrawal.

The mother uses the child's responses to affirm that her behavior is loving, and since the loving behavior is simulated, the child is placed in a position where he must not accurately interpret her communication if he is to maintain his relationship with her. In other words, he must not discriminate accurately between orders of message, in this case the difference between the expression of simulated feelings (one Logical Type) and real feelings (another Logical Type). As a result the child must systematically distort his perception of meta-communicative signals. For example, if mother begins to feel hostile (or affectionate) toward her child and also feels compelled to withdraw from him, she might say, "Go to bed, you're very tired and I want you to get your sleep." This overtly loving statement is intended to deny a feeling which could be verbalized as "Get out of my sight because I'm sick of you." If the child correctly discriminates her metacommunicative signals, he would have to face the fact that she both doesn't want him and is deceiving him by her loving behavior. He would be "punished" for learning to discriminate orders of messages accurately. He therefore would tend to accept the idea that he is tired rather than recognize his mother's deception. This means that he must deceive himself about his own internal state in order to support mother in her deception. To survive with her he must falsely discriminate his own internal messages as well as falsely discriminate the messages of others.

The problem is compounded for the child because the mother is "benevolently" defining for him how he feels; she is expressing overt maternal concern over the fact that he is tired. To put it another way, the mother is controlling the child's definitions of his own message, as well as the definition of his responses to her (e.g., by saying, "You don't really mean to say that," if he should criticize her) by insisting that she is not concerned about herself but only about him. Consequently, the easiest path for the child is to accept mother's simulated loving behavior as real, and his desires to interpret what is going on are undermined. Yet the result is that the mother is withdrawing from him and defining this withdrawal as the way a loving relationship should be.

However, accepting mother's simulated loving behavior as real also is no solution for the child. Should he make this false discrimination, he would approach her, this move toward closeness would provoke in her feelings of fear and helplessness, and she would be compelled to withdraw. But if he then withdrew from her, she would take his withdrawal as a statement that she was not a loving mother and would either punish him for withdrawing or approach him to bring him closer. If he then approached, she would respond by putting him at a distance. *The child is punished for discriminating accurately what she is expressing, and he is punished for discriminating inaccurately—he is caught in a double bind.*

The child might try various means of escaping from this situation. He might, for example, try to lean on his father or some other member of the family. However, from our preliminary observations we think it is likely that the fathers of schizophrenics are not substantial enough to lean on. They are also in the awkward position where if they agreed with the child about the nature of mother's deceptions, they would need to recognize the nature of their own relationships to the mother, which they could not do and remain attached to her in the *modus operandi* they have worked out.

The need of the mother to be wanted and loved also prevents the child from gaining support from some other person in the environment, a teacher, for example. A mother with these characteristics would feel threatened by any other attachment of the child and would break it up and bring the child back closer to her with consequent anxiety when the child became dependent on her.

The only way the child can really escape from the situation is to comment on the contradictory position his mother has put him in. However, if he did so, the mother would take this as an accusation that she is unloving and both punish him and insist that his perception of the situation is distorted. By preventing the child from talking about the situation, the mother forbids him to use the metacommunicative level—the level we use to correct our perception of communicative behavior. The ability to communicate about communication, to comment upon the meaningful actions of oneself and others, is essential for successful social intercourse. In any normal relationship there is a constant interchange of metacommunicative messages such as "What do you mean?" or "Why did you do that?" or "Are you kidding me?" and so on. To discriminate accurately what people are really expressing we must be able to comment directly or indirectly on that expression. The metacommunicative level the schizophrenic seems unable to use successfully (2). Given these characteristics of the mother, it is apparent why. If she is denying one order of message, then any statement about her statements endangers her and she must forbid it. Therefore, the child grows up unskilled in his ability to communicate about communication and, as a result, unskilled in determining what people really mean and unskilled in expressing what he really means, which is essential for normal relationships.

In summary, then, we suggest that the double bind nature of the family situation of a schizophrenic results in placing the child in a position where if he responds to his mother's simulated affection her anxiety will be aroused and she will punish him (or insist, to protect herself, that *his* overtures are simulated, thus confusing him about the nature of his own messages) to defend herself from closeness with him. Thus the child is blocked off from intimate and secure associations with his mother. However, if he does not make overtures of affection, she will feel that this means she is not a loving mother and her anxiety will be aroused. Therefore, she will either punish him for withdrawing or make overtures toward the child to insist that he demonstrate that he loves her. If he then responds and shows her affection, she will not only feel endangered again, but she may resent the fact that she had to force him to respond. In either case in a relationship, the most important in his life and the model for all others, he is punished if he indicates love and affection and punished if he does not; and his escape routes from the situation, such as gaining support from others, are cut off. This is the basic nature of the double bind relationship between mother and child. This description has not depicted, of course, the more complicated interlocking gestalt that is the "family" of which the "mother" is one important part (11, 12).

ILLUSTRATIONS FROM CLINICAL DATA

An analysis of an incident occurring between a schizophrenic patient and his mother illustrates the "double bind" situation. A young man who had fairly well recovered from an acute schizophrenic episode was visited in the hospital by his mother. He was glad to see her and impulsively put his arm around her shoulders, whereupon she stiffened. He withdrew his arm and she asked, "Don't you love me any more?" He then blushed, and she said, "Dear, you must not be so easily embarrassed and afraid of your feelings." The patient was able to stay with her only a few minutes more and following her departure he assaulted an aide and was put in the tubs.

Obviously, this result could have been avoided if the young man had been able to say, "Mother, it is obvious that you become uncomfortable when I put my arm around you, and that you have difficulty accepting a gesture of affection from me." However, the schizophrenic patient doesn't have this possibility open to him. His intense dependency and training prevents him from commenting upon his mother's communicative behavior, though she comments on his and forces him to accept and to attempt to deal with the complicated sequence. The complications for the patient include the following:

1. The mother's reaction of not accepting her son's affectionate gesture is masterfully covered up by her condemnation of him for withdrawing, and the patient denies his perception of the situation by accepting her condemnation.

2. The statement "Don't you love me any more" in this context seems to imply:

(*a*) "I am lovable."

(*b*) "You should love me and if you don't you are bad or at fault."

(*c*) "Whereas you did love me previously you don't any longer," and thus focus is shifted from his expressing affection to his inability to be affectionate. Since the patient has also hated her, she is on good ground here, and he responds appropriately with guilt, which she then attacks.

(*d*) "What you just expressed *was not* affection," and in order to accept this statement the patient must deny what she and the culture have taught him about how one expresses affection. He must also question the times with her, and with others, when he thought he was experiencing affection and when they *seemed* to treat the situation as if he had. He experiences here loss-of-support phenomena and is put in doubt about the reliability of past experience.

3. The statement, "You must not be so easily embarrassed and afraid of your feelings," seems to imply;

(*a*) "You are not like me and are different from other nice or normal people because we express our feelings."

(*b*) "The feelings you express are all right, it's only that *you* can't accept them." However, if the stiffening on her part had indicated "These are unacceptable feelings," then the boy is told that he should not be embarrassed by unacceptable feelings. Since he has had a long training in what is and is not acceptable to both her and society, he again comes into conflict with the past. If he is unafraid of his own feelings (which mother implies is good), he should be unafraid of his affection and would then notice it was she who was afraid, but he must not notice that because her whole approach is aimed at covering up this shortcoming in herself.

The impossible dilemma thus becomes: "If I am to keep my tie to mother I must not show her that I love her, but if I do not show her that I love her, then I will lose her."

The importance to the mother of her special method of control is strikingly illustrated by the interfamily situation of a young woman schizophrenic who greeted the therapist on their first meeting with the remark, "Mother had to get married and now I'm here." This statement meant to the therapist that:

1. The patient was the result of an illegitimate pregnancy.

2. This fact was related to her present psychosis (in her opinion).

3. "Here" referred to the psychiatrist's office and to the patient's presence on earth for which she had to be eternally indebted to her mother, especially since her mother had sinned and suffered in order to bring her into the world.

4. "Had to get married" referred to the shot-gun nature of mother's wedding and to the mother's response to pressure that she must marry, and the reciprocal, that she resented the forced nature of the situation and blamed the patient for it.

Actually, all these suppositions subsequently proved to be factually correct and were corroborated by the mother during an abortive attempt at psychotherapy. The flavor of the mother's communications to the patient seemed essentially this: "I am lovable, loving, and satisfied with myself. You are lovable when you are like me and when you do what I say." At the same time the mother indicated to the daughter both by words and behavior: "You are physically delicate, unintelligent, and different from me ('not normal'). You need me and me alone because of these handicaps, and I will take care of you and love you." Thus the patient's life was a series of beginnings, of attempts at experience, which would result in failure and withdrawal back to the maternal hearth and bosom because of the collusion between her and her mother.

It was noted in collaborative therapy that certain areas important to the mother's self-esteem were especially conflictual situations for the patient. For example, the mother needed the fiction that she was close to her family and that a deep love existed between her and her own mother. By analogy the relationship to the grandmother served as the prototype for the mother's relationship to her own daughter. On one occasion when the daughter was seven or eight years old the grandmother in a rage threw a knife which barely missed the little girl. The mother said nothing to the grandmother but hurried the little girl from the room with the words, "Grandmommy really loves you." It is significant that the grandmother took the attitude toward the patient that she was not well enough controlled, and she used to chide her daughter for being too easy on the child. The grandmother was living in the house during one of the patient's psychotic episodes, and the girl took great delight in throwing various objects at the mother and grandmother while they cowered in fear.

Mother felt herself very attractive as a girl, and she felt that her daughter resembled her father closely, although by damning with faint praise it was obvious that she felt the daughter definitely ran second. One of the daughter's first acts during a psychotic period was to announce to her mother that she was going to cut off all her hair. She proceeded to do this while the mother pleaded with her to stop. Subsequently the mother would show a picture of *herself* as a girl and explain to people how the patient would look if she only had her beautiful hair.

The mother, apparently without awareness of the significance of what she was doing, would equate the daughter's illness with not being very bright and with some sort of organic brain difficulty. She would invariably contrast this with her own intelligence as demonstrated by her *own* scholastic record. She treated her daughter with a completely patronizing and placating manner which was insincere. For example, in the psychiatrist's presence she promised her daughter that she would not allow her to have further shock treatments, and as soon as the girl was out of the room she asked the doctor if he didn't feel she should be hospitalized and given electric shock treatments. One clue to this deceptive behavior arose during the mother's therapy. Although the daughter had had three previous hospitalizations the mother had never mentioned to the doctors that she herself had had a psychotic episode when she discovered that she was pregnant. The family whisked her away to a small sanitarium in a nearby town, and she was, according to her own statement, strapped to a bed for six weeks. Her family did not visit her during this time, and no one except her parents and her sister knew that she was hospitalized.

There were two times during therapy when the mother showed intense emotion. One was in relating her own psychotic experience; the other was on the occasion of her last visit when she accused the therapist of trying to drive her crazy by forcing her to choose between her daughter and her husband. Against medical advice, she took her daughter out of therapy.

The father was as involved in the homeostatic aspects of the intrafamily situation as the mother. For example, he stated that he had to quit his position as an important attorney in order to bring his daughter to an area where competent psychiatric help was available. Subsequently, acting on cues from the patient (e.g., she frequently referred to a character named "Nervous Ned") the therapist was able to elicit from him that he had hated his job and for years had been trying to "get out from under." However, the daughter was made to feel that the move was initiated for her.

On the basis of our examination of the clinical data, we have been impressed by a number of observations including:

1. The helplessness, fear, exasperation and rage which a double bind situation provokes in the patient, but which the mother may serenely and ununderstandingly pass over. We have noted reactions in the father that both create double bind situations, or extend and amplify those created by the mother, and we have seen the father passive and outraged, but helpless, become ensnared in a similar manner to the patient.

2. The psychosis seems, in part, a way of dealing with double bind situations to overcome their inhibiting and controlling effect. The psychotic patient may make astute, pithy, often metaphorical remarks that reveal an insight into the forces binding him. Contrariwise, he may become rather expert in setting double bind situations himself.

3. According to our theory, the communication situation described is essential to the mother's security, and by inference to the family homeostasis. If this be so, then when psychotherapy of the patient helps him become less vulnerable to mother's attempts at control, anxiety will be produced in the mother. Similarly, if the therapist interprets to the mother the dynamics of the situation she is setting up with the patient, this should produce an anxiety response in her. Our impression is that when there is a perduring contact between patient and family (especially when the patient lives at home during psychotherapy), this

leads to a disturbance (often severe) in the mother and sometimes in both mother and father and other siblings (10, 11).

CURRENT POSITION AND FUTURE PROSPECTS

Many writers have treated schizophrenia in terms of the most extreme contrast with any other form of human thinking and behavior. While it is an isolable phenomenon, so much emphasis on the differences from the normal—rather like the fearful physical segregation of psychotics—does not help in understanding the problems. In our approach we assume that schizophrenia involves general principles which are important in all communication and therefore many informative similarities can be found in "normal" communication situations.

We have been particularly interested in various sorts of communication which involve both emotional significance and the necessity of discriminating between orders of message. Such situations include play, humor, ritual, poetry, and fiction. Play, especially among animals, we have studied at some length (3). It is a situation which strikingly illustrates the occurrence of metamessages whose correct discrimination is vital to the cooperation of the individuals involved; for example, false discrimination could easily lead to combat. Rather closely related to play is humor, a continuing subject of our research. It involves sudden shifts in Logical Types as well as discrimination of those shifts. Ritual is a field in which unusually real or literal ascriptions of Logical Type are made and defended as vigorously as the schizophrenic defends the "reality" of his delusions. Poetry exemplifies the communicative power of metaphor—even very unusual metaphor—when labeled as such by various signs, as contrasted to the obscurity of unlabeled schizophrenic metaphor. The entire field of fictional communication, defined as the narration or depiction of a series of events with more or less of a label of actuality, is most relevant to the investigation of schizophrenia. We are not so much concerned with the content interpretation of fiction—although anlysis of oral and destructive themes is illuminating to the student of schizophrenia—as with the formal problems involved in simultaneous existence of multiple levels of message in the fictional presentation of "reality." The drama is especially interesting in this respect, with both performers and spectators responding to messages about both the actual and the theatrical reality.

We are giving extensive attention to hypnosis. A great array of phenomena that occur as schizophrenic symptoms—hallucinations, delusions, alterations of personality, amnesias, and so on—can be produced temporarily in normal subjects with hypnosis. These need not be directly suggested as specific phenomena, but can be the "spontaneous" result of an arranged communication sequence.

For example, Erickson (4) will produce a hallucination by first inducing catalepsy in a subject's hand and then saying, "There is no conceivable way in which your hand can move, yet when I give the signal, it must move." That is, he tells the subject his hand will remain in place, yet it will move, and in no way the subject can consciously conceive. When Erickson gives the signal, the subject hallucinates the hand moved, or hallucinates himself in a different place and therefore the hand was moved. This use of hallucination to resolve a problem posed by contradictory commands which cannot be discussed seems to us to illustrate the solution of a double bind situation via a shift in Logical Types. Hypnotice responses to direct suggestions or statements also commonly involve shifts in type, as in accepting the words "Here's a glass of water" or "You feel tired" as external or internal reality, or in literal response to metaphorical statements, much like schizophrenics. We hope that further study of hypnotic induction, phenomena and waking will, in this controllable situation, help sharpen our view of the essential communicational sequences which produce phenomena like those of schizophrenia.

Another Erickson experiment (12) seems to isolate a double bind communication sequence without the specific use of hypnosis. Erickson arranged a seminar so as to have a young chain smoker sit next to him and to be without cigarettes; other participants were briefed on what to do. All was ordered so that Erickson repeatedly turned to offer the young man a cigarette, but was always interrupted by a question from someone so that he turned away, "inadvertently" withdrawing the cigarettes from the young man's reach. Later another participant asked this young man if he had received the cigarette from Dr. Erickson. His reply, "What cigarette?", showed clearly that he had forgotten the whole sequence. He even refused a cigarette offered by another member, saying that he was too interested in the seminar discussion to smoke. This young man seems to us to be in an experimental situation paralleling the schizophrenic's double bind situation with mother: An important relationship, contradictory messages (here of giving and taking away), and comment blocked —because there was a seminar going on, and anyway it was all "inadvertent." And note the similar outcome: Amnesia for the double bind sequence and reversal from "He doesn't give" to "I don't want."

Although we have been led into these collateral areas, our main field of observation has been schizophrenia itself. All of us have worked directly with schizophrenic patients and much of this case material has been recorded on tape for detailed study. In addition, we are recording interviews held jointly with patients and their families, and we are taking sound motion pictures of mothers and disturbed, presumably preschizophrenic, children. Our hope is that these operations will provide a clearly evident record of the continuing repetitive double binding which we hypothesize goes on steadily from infantile beginnings in the family situation of individuals who become schizophrenic. This basic family situation, and the overtly communicational characteristics of schizo-phrenia, have been the major focus of this paper. However, we expect our concepts and some of these data will also be useful in future work on other problems of schizophrenia, such as the variety of other symptoms, the character of the "adjusted state" before schizophrenia becomes manifest, and the nature and circumstances of the psychotic break.

THERAPEUTIC IMPLICATIONS OF THIS HYPOTHESIS

Psychotherapy itself is a context of multilevel communication, with explora-tion of the ambiguous lines between the literal and metaphoric, or reality and fantasy, and indeed, various forms of play, drama, and hypnosis have been used extensively in therapy. We have been interested in therapy, and in addition to our own data we have been collecting and examining recordings, verbatim transcripts, and personal accounts of therapy from other therapists. In this we prefer exact records since we believe that how a schizophrenic talks depends greatly, though often subtly, on how another person talks to him; it is most difficult to estimate what was really occurring in a therapeutic interview if one has only a description of it, especially if the description is already in theo-retical terms.

Except for a few general remarks and some speculation, however, we are not yet prepared to comment on the relation of the double bind to psycho-therapy. At present we can only note:

1. Double bind situations are created by and within the psychotherapeutic setting and the hospital milieu. From the point of view of this hypothesis we wonder about the effect of medical "benevolence" on the schizophrenic patient. Since hospitals exist for the benefit of personal as well as—as much as—more than—for the patient's benefit, there will be contradictions at times in sequences where actions are taken "benevolently" for the patient when actually they are intended to keep the staff more comfortable. We would assume that whenever the system is organized for hospital purposes and it is announced to the patient that the actions are for *his* benefit, then the schizophrenogenic situation is being perpetuated. This kind of deception will provoke the patient to respond to it as a double bind situation, and his response will be "schizophrenic" in the sense that it will be indirect and the patient will be unable to comment on the fact that he feels that he is being deceived. One vignette, fortunately amusing, illustrates such a response. On a ward with a dedicated and "benevolent" physician in charge there was a sign on the physician's door which said "Doctor's Office. Please Knock." The doctor was driven to distraction and finally capitulation by the obedient patient who carefully knocked every time he passed the door.

2. The understanding of the double bind and its communicative aspects may lead to innovations in therapeutic technique. Just what these innovations may be is difficult to say, but on the basis of our investigation we are assuming that double bind situations occur consistently in psychotherapy. At times these are inadvertent in the sense that the therapist is imposing a double bind situation similar to that in the patient's history, or the patient is imposing a double bind situation on the therapist. At other times therapists seem to impose double binds, either deliberately or intuitively, which force the patient to respond differently than he has in the past.

An incident from the experience of a gifted psychotherapist illustrates the intuitive understanding of a double bind communicational sequence. Dr. Frieda Fromm-Reichmann (5) was treating a young woman who from the age of seven had built a highly complex religion of her own replete with powerful gods. She was very schizophrenic and quite hesitant about entering into a therapeutic situation. At the beginning of the treatment she said, "God R says I shouldn't talk with you." Dr. Fromm-Reichmann replied, "Look, let's get something into the record. To me God R doesn't exist, and that whole world of yours doesn't exist. To you it does, and far be it from me to think that I can take that away from you, I have no idea what it means. So I'm willing to talk with you in terms of that world, if only you know I do it so that we have an understanding that it doesn't exist for me. Now go to God R and tell him that we have to talk and he should give you permission. Also you must tell him that I am a doctor and that you have lived with him in his kingdom now from seven to sixteen—that's nine years—and he hasn't helped you. So now he must permit me to try to see whether you and I can do that job. Tell him that I am a doctor and this is what I want to try."

The therapist has her patient in a "therapeutic double bind." If the patient is rendered doubtful about her belief in her god then she is agreeing with Dr. Fromm-Reichmann, and is admitting her attachment to therapy. If she insists that God R is real, then she must tell him that Dr. Fromm-Reichmann is "more powerful" than he—again admitting her involvement with the therapist.

The difference between the therapeutic bind and the original double bind situation is in part the fact that the therapist is not involved in a life and death struggle himself. He can therefore set up relatively benevolent binds and gradually aid the patient in his emancipation from them. Many of the uniquely appropriate therapeutic gambits arranged by therapists seem to be intuitive. We share the goal of most psychotherapists who strive toward the day when such strokes of genuis will be well enough understood to be systematic and commonplace.

REFERENCES

1. Bateson, G. Social planning and the concept of "deutero-learning." *Conference on Science, Philosophy, and Religion, Second Symposium*. New York: Harper, 1942.

2. Bateson, G. A. A theory of play and fantasy. *Psychiatric Research Reports,* 1955, 2, 39–51.

3. Carpenter, C. R. A field study of the behavior and social relations of howling monkeys. *Comp. Psychol. Monogr.,* 1934, 10, 1–168.

4. Erickson, M. H. Personal communication, 1955.

5. Fromm-Reichmann, F. Personal communication, 1956.

6. Haley, J. Paradoxes in play, fantasy, and psychotherapy. *Psychiatric Research Reports,* 1955, 2, 52–58.

7. Harlow, H. F. The formation of learning sets. *Psychol. Rev.,* 1949, 56, 51–65.

8. Hilgard, J. R. Anniversary reactions in parents precipitated by children. *Psychiatry,* 1953, 16, 73–80.

9. Hull, C. L., *et al. Mathematico-deductive theory of rote learning.* New Haven: Yale Univ. Press, 1940.

10. Jackson, D. D. An episode of sleepwalking. *J. Amer. Psychoanal. Assn.,* 1954, 2, 503–508.

11. Jackson, D. D. Some factors influencing the Oedipus complex. *Psychoanal. Quart.,* 1954, 23, 566–581.

12. Jackson, D. D. The question of family homeostasis. Presented at the Amer. Psychiatric Assn. Meeting, St. Louis, May 7, 1954.

13. Lorenz, K. Z. *King Solomon's ring.* New York: Crowell, 1952.

14. Perceval, J. A narrative of the treatment experienced by a gentleman during a state of mental derangement, designed to explain the causes and nature of insanity, etc. London: Effingham Wilson, 1836 and 1840.

15. Ruesch, J., & Bateson, G. *Communication: the social matrix of psychiatry.* New York: Norton, 1951.

16. von Domarus, E. The specific laws of logic in schizophrenia. In J. S. Kasanin (Ed.), *Language and thought in schizophrenia.* Berkeley: Univ. of California Press, 1944.

17. Whitehead, A. N., & Russell, B. *Principia mathematica.* Cambridge: Cambridge Univ. Press, 1910.

18

AN APPROACH TO FAMILY PATHOLOGY

Stephen Fleck

Historically all behavioral sciences and the helping professions have concerned themselves with the family. In antiquity, writers and philosophers were preoccupied and fascinated with the subject, and humanity's universal concern with family life and structure is reflected in most religious systems. As the primary transmitter of human experience and institutions across the generations, the family, whatever its structure or composition, has therefore often been the historians' or politicians' scapegoat, being held accountable for cultural, social, or political decline of a group or nation. However, it must be appreciated that the family, although the primary environment for each person, is but one institution in society, and modifications in family styles and characteristics are as likely to arise from within that institution as through forces outside it. Changing cultural mores, political, economic, or climactic factors, or technologic innovations are among the factors that affect family life, and vice versa.

Family pathology therefore cannot be considered as something absolute, a "Ding in sich" apart either from external influences which affect it or from internal forces, including the individual personality patterns and the emotionally charged interrelationships, none of which is static or unidirectional. The individuals who compose the family undergo evolutionary and nonevolutionary changes, and the adults in it (the parents in the nuclear family) bring to it personalities and behavioral techniques which derive largely from their respective family experiences, which in turn shaped their developing personalities.

Even if we knew such a thing as a "normal" or "average" family, it would

Reprinted from *Comprehensive Psychiatry,* 7 (5), 1966, 307–320, with the permission of Grune & Stratton, Inc. and Dr. Fleck.

The author is indebted to Theodore Lidz and Alice Cornelison with whom many of the concepts advanced here have been evolved collaboratively, but only the author is responsible for the formulations and views expressed here.

still have to be defined on different levels of organization ranging from the cellular to the social, from different perspectives and vantage points, and also for different cultures if not for every socioeconomic class. For instance, Mrs. Marguerite Oswald, twice married and unable to take care of her children much of the time, claimed that hers was just "an average American family" (30), and an infertile couple, both Ph.D.'s, in the pursuit of adopting a child described themselves in the same terms. We cannot deal with family pathology as we can with liver slices, for example, which we establish as normal or abnormal through various chemical and optical measurements. Defining family abnormalities is complex, and the examination and evaluation of family functions or tasks seems the most appropriate approach to determining the outlining family pathology. It is therefore necessary to present first a brief resume of our current concepts of basic and essential family functions before discussing family pathology as deviations from or deficiencies in family functioning. These functions are "normal" in the sense of being indispensable to the establishment of a family and to the fulfillment of its mission in a given culture.

This paper deals with the nuclear family unless stated otherwise, because it is increasingly the typical family unit in modern Western society and because our clinical experience as well as most of our relevant concepts pertain to the nuclear family. It should be noted briefly that, compared with the extended family, the nuclear unit imposes on family life certain disadvantages and special burdens. In the isolated nuclear family the personalities of the parents are more crucial than in the extended family, because each parent must function as a model for the child of the same sex. In extended family systems alternate models and sometimes more wholesome ones than those of the progenitors are readily and continuously available to offspring. The sharing of tangible and intangible tasks within the family, especially when a parent becomes sick, is more difficult in the isolated nuclear family, and a child may have to substitute for a parent. Furthermore, industrialization, together with child labor laws, have rendered offspring and grandparents economic liabilities, in contrast to earlier generations when both were more likely assets especially on the farm (4, 21, 26).

Before outlining family functions as a preliminary to considering pathology, two important and basic divisions that govern family structure and dynamics must be understood. These can be viewed as the two axes of family life. One is the generation boundary which divides the group into parents who nurture, lead, direct, and teach, and offspring who are dependent and who follow and learn. This line also divides those members who are sexually active with each other, the parents, from those to whom sexual activity within the family is interdicted. The other division is that of the two sexes, the family being the environment in which sons first learn to be boys and men, and daughters learn to become girls and women. While much identity consolidation, especially with regard to gender security and gender-linked behavior characteristics, is influenced from outside the family, especially by peers in adolescence, the identity anlagen are preoedipal, and basic gender awareness and security derive from constructive resolution of oedipal issues. Effecting and maintaining these two boundaries is the most important task of family life, a task accomplished more by example and nonverbal cues than explicitly. This paradigm can also be stated as the effective establishment of the incest taboo within the family (21, 25).

I

Family functions will be outlined briefly under the following headings: (1) parental coalition, (2) nurturant tasks, (3) enculturation of the younger generation, (4) emancipation of offspring from the family, and (5) family crises. These functions are presented as if separate for the purpose of discussion, but in actuality they are interrelated and overlap. They parallel in many ways the development, especially the personality development, of the child, and much of what is stated here has also been outlined by Erickson in his eight stages of development (11, 12), and also by Parsons (26, 27).

1. The marital coalition may be defined as those interactional patterns which the spouses evolve at first for their mutual needs and satisfaction. Later, in the evolving structure and dynamics of the family, this coalition must serve the age-appropriate needs of the children and still maintain an area of exclusive relationship and mutuality between parents. One of these parental sectors is sexual activity, interdicted to children in most societies. Mutuality denotes the spouses' interactive patterns on implicit and explicit levels, the sharing of feelings and conveying of respect and appreciation of the spouse one to the other as well as to other people.

An important function of this coalition in family life is the mutual reinforcement of the spouses' complementary sex-linked roles, so that as parents they represent, respectively, culture-determined masculinity and femininity, not only as individuals but also through the other spouse's support and approval. Another facet of the coalition is the conjugal role divisions and reciprocities the spouses establish for themselves, but it should be noted that role allocations in a marriage as well as the decision-making methods vary with different socioeconomic classes (6, 29).

The coalition must serve the establishment of triangular relationships when children are born, and these triangles must be flexible as each additional child at first must be very close to the mother and absorbs a great deal of her attention and energy to which the older family members must adapt. The older child must give up his primary closeness with his mother and learn to tolerate his replacement by a younger sibling. Parental role complementarity is essential to this task.

In the psychodynamic and sociodynamic sense, this role complementarity evolved by the parents is an important facet of the group which the family must become. Role allocations affect and involve all family members, and they must change with the age of the family group. In contrast to synthetic or therapy groups the family group has built in it bio-psycho-social givens and a predeterminant evolutionary history with rather distinct age-related tasks and functions. Role flexibility within the family is therefore a necessity and also demonstrates that the needs or welfare of the group sometimes precedes individual needs, and vice versa at other times (4). Yet basically, according to Parsons, fathers are predominantly the instrumentalists in our culture; their activities usually determine the family's social position, whereas mothers are more responsible for the affective and emotional climate in the family (21, 26).

Parental role allocations are therefore important demonstrations of how the two sexes divide tasks and attitudes in a particular society. If the parents' behavior in this respect is markedly and consistently deviant from the social norms, we must entertain the likelihood of abnormal family dynamics and a pathogenic impact on the personality developments of the children.

2. The nurturant tasks are primarily assigned to the mother, but she can perform these adequately only if supported tangibly and emotionally by a spouse. Even if the spouse is absent or dead, the knowledge of his approval of the mother and her mothering behavior is important. Nurturant functions encompass more than food and the psychological aspects of feeding, especially the establishment of basic trust. The early nurturance of the child includes helping him learn how to manage and control his body, and how to observe, distinguish, and communicate about inner and external experiences; it also includes providing him with appropriate experiences and learning opportunities. The importance of these "nurturant" functions very early in the child's life has been appreciated clearly only in recent times. The potential damage to personality development, social adjustment, and educational capacities, if these nurturant tasks are not fulfilled adequately, is now a source of much concern and investigation (5, 7, 21, 24).

Weaning is part of nurturance but more is involved with withdrawing bottle or breast. The intricate physical closeness with the mother must be weaned and an essentially nonphysical intimacy established with all family members. Weaning involves still more, in that both the process of weaning and its accomplishment are foundation stones in the acquisition of ego boundaries and a sense of separateness (12).

Mastery of separation can be defined as the child's experiencing the pain of acute loss of supportive closeness to another person and good feeling toward, or of dissatisfaction with, such a significant person (the parent) without losing faith and trust in the continuity of the relationship and in the ultimate restoration of good feeling and a sense of security. Through separation experiences the child learns and grows; he becomes more able to avoid the same impasse and he is less vulnerable to and threatened by subsequent separations or emotional distance from others. This mastery must be facilitated by the opportunity to observe, imitate, and eventually internalize how other family members cope with frustration and this kind of "separation anxiety."

3. Obviously any clear line between nurturant and enculturating tasks is arbitrary because these family functions are continuous and overlap, but the passage of the oedipal phase may be considered the turning from predominantly nurturant issues to enculturating ones. At this point the child should not only have mastered body control together with gender awareness, but also he should have acquired communicative competence and accepted the incest taboo in the sense of feeling comfortable in his de-eroticized relationship to each parent. Latency can then begin in the sense of an abeyance of sexual and erotic problems, freeing the child for instrumental learning and increasing his investment into peer relationships. Family tasks become at this time those of facilitating peer relationships—that is, allowing the child greater distance from the family circle, as well as teaching him within the family many of the instrumental modes of the culture in shared work and games.

Together with instrumental teaching, the family helps to inculcate the communicative and social skills and modes of the culture, and defines the sociocultural norms of relationships by example rather than explicitly (22, 27).

Communicative styles and competence in the family are crucial because significant deviance from the culturally valid patterns will usually create disturbance within the family and certainly handicap its members in interacting with the surrounding community. Faulty, inadequate or idiosyncratic intrafamilial communication is, of course, related to other conditions or defects, such as parental psychopathology, or to cultural differences between the family and the community in which they live. Furthermore, language is the basis for conceptual and abstract thinking; therefore, the younger generation's formal education and emotional development depend on instrumentally and relationally valid verbal and nonverbal communication (22, 32).

4. Emancipation of offspring from the parental family is an evolutionary task in a nuclear family system and culture. Emancipation must occur physically and geographically as well as psychologically and socially. To be accomplished successfully this final separation cannot be sudden; it must be the culmination of many forms of increasing psychosocial separatenesses between parents and child. The first step in this evolution was weaning followed by many partial steps of emancipation and vectorial independence which the family must abet and effect as the child moves through his developmental stages. Among such steps are the first school entrance, camp or other living-away-from-home experiences, dating, job or college, and the final achievement of a solid identity and inner self-direction, culminating ideally in marriage and parenthood.

The family tasks in this connection demand mutual tolerance and resilience, for adolescents especially experiment with independent behavior and often teeter between their still-important needs for dependence and guidance, and their strivings for independence. The parental coalition is on trial during the emancipation phases, because the parents must be prepared and able to live again as a dyad. Emancipation is therefore also the evolutionary dissolution of the family as a group, because grandparental functions are limited and not continuous in a nuclear family system (4, 6).

5. Many of the functions and tasks outlined can also be viewed as normal or evolutionary family "crises." Here lies one key to our approach to family pathology. Coping with crises is an important standard of family and of individual mental health, even though this standard is not measurable in any easy or simple manner at this time (8).

Moving from the parental dyad to a triad is one of these important crisis issues. For instance, do the parents at this time clearly establish a generation boundary or does one parent remain overly dependent on the other, thereby competing with the child for his spouse's parental nurturance? Equivalent questions arise around the oedipal phase. For example, does one parent fail to de-eroticize his or her relationships to and behavior with the child? During the offspring's puberty and adolescence, does the parental coalition present a consistent front against which emancipation experiments can proceed, or does the front give and waver, engulfing the offspring in inconsistency and indecision? Do parents show a capacity to return to dyadic living and face the issues of aging and infirmity together and independently for as long as possible? These are some of the crises in which deficiencies in parental personalities and in family functioning can be discerned most readily.

One form of family crisis should be mentioned because its usual absence in present-day family life unavoidably creates an experience deficiency which affects adults often adversely, because they may live as adults and parents for many years before a death in the immediate family occurs. The absence of shared tragedy and mourning early in life has wrought certain difficulties for families and individuals in facing death and gaining reassurance in the continuity of individual and family life after the loss of a loved one. Stated another way, the work of mourning is best learned as a shared family experience. Paul (28) considers unresolved and unshared mourning on the part of a parent a common source of pathological family interaction.

II

This brief compendium of family tasks and functions may permit us now to consider family pathology as deficiencies in family task performance. Such an approach to family pathology is anchored in present knowledge and data from family studies, but it will not lend itself to establishing very specific correlations between types of family disfunctions and psychiatric entities.

Like family functions, family disturbances must be considered on many levels, and one must be constantly mindful that any one pathogenic "focus" affects all the members and the family dynamics on more than one level, and that these interactive and reactive forces in turn influence the "focus." If so considered, a concept such as "schizophrenogenic" mother, for instance, becomes untenable. Symbiotic mother-child relationships or incestuous patterns do not exist in vacuo, but are part of a family's structure and dynamics. Distinct levels of disturbance or deficiency can be separated therefore only at the expense of ignoring other levels of the reactive and interactive forces in the life of the family. However, for the purpose of discussion we shall treat these levels as if they were rather discrete. Besides, a particular defect can be overwhelming and pervasive in the life of a particular family and should alert the physician much in the way a high fever would direct his thinking about possible causes into the realm of infections.

We shall follow as far as possible our outline for family functions, but the discussion must begin with intrapersonal problems.

1. Inborn defects in a child, whether inherited or not, have serious implications for the entire family and may distort structure and dynamics to a pathological degree. If the condition is familial and therefore presumably hereditary, family life may become centered around the parents' guilt or shame and other maladaptive mechanisms. A shared defect can dominate family life, as in so-called nests of severely feeble-minded individuals. While almost every clinician has encountered such family-wide psychological and psychosocial pathology, no systematic study of such problems seems to have been made.

A pathological phenomenon similar to that created by the presence of a defective child has been pointed out by Solnit, who found that families with a child who recovered, despite a fatal prognosis, can suffer from an inability to accept the fact that a mistake in diagnosis had been made, or that despite the acute danger from which recovery was not expected the child's health and expected lifespan did return to normal. Overprotection, infantilization of that child, and even of his siblings may ensue, and secondary rejection and scapegoating of the child may occur because of his resentment and adverse reactions to this situation (16). Rather similar findings have been reported in detail by Caplan with regard to prematurity; in particular, the search for whom or what to blame was evidence of familial pathology and inadequate crisis coping (8).

The most common familial pathology which clinicians encounter incident to handicapped offspring concerns denial of realistic implications and consequences of the condition. We cannot here consider or even list the many possibilities and underlying reasons for such a development—among them denial, guilt, whether realistic or unrealistic, and immaturity, evidenced often by confusing the wish for a magic solution with its realizability. A complete discussion of these reactions would require a treatise of all known defense mechanisms on intrapsychic and interactional levels (10).

All too often, iatrogenic contributions to familial pathology occur in the form of confusing or evasive statements, meant to be soothing when they should educate and help the family toward realistic appraisal and action, even though such a step may be upsetting and painful to all concerned (15).

Parallel considerations of familial pathology are relevant to any chronic illness in the family, especially the problem of dying. The infrequency of acute death and the lack of opportunity for shared mourning have already been stressed, but another element of modern family life concerns the adjustment or maladjustment to dying rather than to death. Most often, death now is not sudden or unexpected but "occurs" over a long period of time. This imposes on the family the task of adjusting to an inevitable loss through anticipatory mourning which healthily would result in a gradual emotional disengagement and disinvestment at a pace commensurate with the patient's declining capacity for involvement. There are many important facets to this process which are not altogether relevant here, but without detailed discussion of them we can state that unrealistic and pathological family processes are commonly observed in the situation of a dying family member similar to those briefly indicated in connection with chronic illness or the presence of defective offspring.

In general, whether a condition is transitory or permanent, congenital, hereditary, or acquired postnatally, and regardless of whether it is located in parent or offspring, the potential for family pathology is increased, but the opportunity for such a family to develop special forms of strength also exists (8, 29). The decision to turn over the care of nurturant and enculturating tasks to an extrafamilial agent can be realistic and constructive for the family or it can constitute abdication of responsibilities, in which case it indicates a serious limitation of the parents' nurturant capacities which probably would affect all their offspring adversely.

2. Consideration of deviant parental personalities is especially germane to our approach to family pathology; this, of course, does not exclude organic defects or illness in a parent, but they comprise also the entire range of neurotic, psychotic, or psychopathic abnormalities. However, their impact on family life and family task performance is not determined by the intrapersonal abnormality itself. Schizophrenic mothers can have children whose personality and adjustment may fall within normal range, and psychopathic or alcoholic fathers need not produce offspring with like abnormalities, although these intrapersonal abnormalities leave their mark on the family (2, 22). Moreover, symptoms and behavior are copied and incorporated by offspring, although we do not know how frequently. It is an impression that neurotic and psychopathic traits, espe-

cially conversion mechanisms, are transmitted more frequently than psychotic processes (15), but investigations of trait-specific and mechanism-specific intrafamilial transmission are very much needed. Psychopathy is probably the best documented form of intrafamilial learning of abnormal behavior (18). Young psychopaths often act out overt and covert wishes of parents who themselves may not misbehave grossly. We also noted a high incidence of occupation of public relations type among the fathers of a small series of young upper-class delinquents (22).

Parental personality patterns largely determine the character of the parental coalition or lack thereof. Chronic parental disharmony has been found by us to be a common occurrence among parents of young schizophrenics, especially female patients (22). We have termed the marriages of such parents "schismatic," resulting in a "schismatic family" with the children forced to join one or the other camp of two warring spouses. In a sense the "coalition" is a negative one. One of the major problems for offspring in such a family is that the spouses devalue each other, making it difficult for the child to want to be like either of them or to appreciate the parent of the opposite sex as the prototype of a desirable love object. This interferes with the development of a clear sexual identity and maturation toward heterosexual orientation. Besides homosexual proclivities being potentially fostered in this manner, incestuous problems also persist, because one or both parents engender intimate closeness with one or the other offspring in their war with the devalued spouse. In such a family the child may perceive correctly that one parent values him above his or her spouse. Stated another way, in such situations both axes of family life are violated (13, 22).

Overt incest is evidence in itself of gross parental psychopathology as well as of defective family structure. Father-daughter incest is commonest (at least as far as is known, because intersibling incest is much more likely to remain undisclosed, if temporary), but both parents are involved in any form of incest pattern, because it is very difficult for one spouse "not to know" of such a relationship within the family. Incest may represent a pattern that serves to maintain a tenuous equilibrium. For instance in daughter-father incest, the daughter often fulfills many of the mother's functions, the latter having withdrawn from parental tasks, often to work outside the home. But the parents maintain in this manner a facade of role competence, and after the "discovery" of incest behavior such families often break up (31).

Another form of defective coalition occurs when one or both spouses remain primarily attached to and involved with their families of origin so that parental roles are not really assumed with the nuclear group, and the weight of the decision-making lies outside the primary family. This situation can compound a schismatic marriage but it also occurs apart from it—for instance, when incompletely emancipated spouses live geographically as a nuclear family, but psychologically and emotionally as an extended family. The spouses then abrogate essential parental tasks (20, 22).

Another distortion of the parental coalition has been described as skewed (22). This condition is also rooted in severe psychopathology of at least one spouse, but the other, although usually aware of the severe abnormalities of his or her partner, gives in, appeases, and generally assumes a submissive role to preserve the marriage. Only a very passive person could tolerate such a mode of adjustment, which demands abrogating realistic views in the home while being effectively responsive to reality ouside, so that the marital pair can be said to consist of two partners with complementary personality patterns, but the coalition balance is very lopsided and unsuited to many basic family tasks. In its severe form it has been observed in families with schizophrenic offspring (22). In less severe forms such a coupling of psychopathology in two people has been described as a "neurotic marriage", that is, the spouses' neurotic difficulties are interlocking (1, 10).

All these coalition deviations and other difficulties can, of course, result in divorce or desertion, which occur significantly more often in the backgrounds of psychopaths and of schizophrenics than in other groups (22).

One-parent childhood, at least in the lower socioeconomic classes, is significantly related to school underachievement (2, 4, 23). Another risk for the one-parent child, especially for an only child, is overattachment to and overdependence on the parent and parental overcloseness to the child.

3. Nurturance can be defective because the husband either fails to support or actively interferes with the mother's tending to the infant. In other instances, the mother may be ill and cannot nurture adequately or procure an adequate substitute. Some mothers of schizophrenics were found (retrospectively) to have been too anxious and obsessively indecisive to accomplish what they wanted—namely, to function as "normal" mothers (2, 22).

Pathology on the level of parental personality can, of course, have serious consequences in itself, and because parents with deviant personalities are apt to effect very faulty family patterns, the nurturant disfunction rarely stands out as a single pathologic or pathogenic item. A mother too anxious and obsessive to work out a realistic feeding pattern for her baby or too afraid to bathe him lest he drown is likely to find decisions about the child's play activities and range of distance no easier. The so-called symbiotic mother must be included as another example of deficient nurturance, because she cannot wean the child effectively. Most probably her personality difficulties, unless relieved, will adversely affect her children's development at many stages, and she is not likely to change her overprotective role in the family as its biosocial evolution demands. Similarly, a father jealous of the firstborn child is not likely to change with subsequent offspring, although the sex of the child can make a difference.

Deficient nurturance can occur because parents may quickly acquire more children than they would have opted for, had they been able to foresee and predict their limitations to function as parents with decreasing time, energy, and material resources available to provide for their own needs and ambitions. Nurturant functions then become deficient because the requirements for nurturance exceed parental resources (23). This phenomenon has been observed in psychosomatic illnesses of parents, but it can also be a factor in a child's illness, since the sick child may receive preferential attention in a large family, rendering the sick role an "adaptive" one in the sense that it procures important emotional satisfaction. However, limitations in fulfilling nurturant tasks as defined here are found in smaller families too for the reasons already described in connection with defective coalitions or because of chronic illness of one parent. The battered child is a manifestation of severe parental and family pathology and disfunction, which has recently been the cause of much concern and legislative action (14). It indicates malfunction of nurturance but could be listed under any of the deficiency sections.

4. Parental expectations of offspring with respect to enculturation may be overly severe, stringent, and even unrealistic. Cohen et al. found this in the family background of depressed patients, the central issue being family prestige (9). However, depression also plays a causative role in family malfunction, especially in the form of unresolved mourning. Paul (28), on the basis of family studies, and Lindeman and Caplan (8), on the basis of both clinical and epidemiological observations, stress the preventive value of accomplishing the "work of mourning" and the possible ill effects of "bypassing" the mourning experience after a significant emotional loss or trauma. They consider that the stoic family member, who may gain applause for not being upset in the face of having lost a loved one, is headed for emotional troubles. We have stressed already that learning how to mourn is a family task, although it is more common today that a family may have no death to mourn before the children reach the ages of their emancipation from their family of origin; yet the evolutionary crises such as separations or sicknesses or accidents do occur, and the family's modes of dealing with these may help to strengthen or to weaken family functioning or promote or hinder emotional growth in the individual members. The continuum of successive separations and their mastery by the family as well as by each individual in it can be extended to the issues of loss or death, but if no death occurs, separation experiences can serve to some extent as prototypes for shared grief and pain.

Culturally deprived parents, especially single parents, are apt to raise culturally undernourished children, leading to mental ill health in the form of undereducation, communicative disabilities, and culturally deviant behavior. It is true that definitions of health, especially of mental health, are impossible in absolute terms, but it is possible to distinguish between "healthier" and "less healthy" in a particular culture. Rather than seeking definitions that have absolute cross-cultural validity, it must be appreciated that the differences have more to do with values, including health as a cultural value than with health standards per se. In a society where dentistry is unknown defective teeth are the "norm"; or one might say that whatever the reasons, the culture gives a low priority to dental health. Similarly, a society without formal educational institutions puts a low value on abstract thought or scientific inquiry, so that relationships are accepted through fixed role ascriptions and expectations instead of through individual aspirations and subtle interpersonal processes. Value discrepancies also exist within a society in the different socioeconomic classes in Western culture, but here the argument is specious that middle class standards of health, family health in particular, are not relevant to other classes, especially lower socioeconomic groups. Such a formulation may serve to avoid considering effective remedial action with regard to family pathology because of the complexities of assessment and because of the well-documented treatment difficulties, if there is a marked class differential between therapist and patient or family. Although it is true that studies with lower class families have tended to be extensive rather than intensive and that modifications of concepts, especially with regard to sources of strength in a family, must be considered, it is also true that the paradigms of family functions as outlined here and the effects of deficiencies and malfunctioning family dynamics are relevant in a major degree to all classes. If we accept health, optimal education, and individuation within a particular society as valid goals, the family's enculturating effectiveness can be examined and evaluated in these respects. That is, do the family structure and interaction serve these goals, or not, or do they do so more or less (5)?

Normal or abnormal familial interaction depends on the parental personalities and the parental coalition, if any, and children learn through this interaction or fail to learn how to interact with their environment at crucial stages of their development (21). Manifestations of parental mental ill health are learned by children, if not copied, and there is ample evidence that if the parental interaction is starkly atypical of the culture or subculture surrounding them, the entire family suffers estrangement, and children will be handicapped in their interactions outside the family and can develop serious intrapersonal conflicts or neurotic or psychotic proportions (4, 6, 19, 22).

Alanen, who earlier described characteristics of the mothers of schizophrenics (2), has more recently focused on family process and interaction. Comparison of families with neurotic and schizophrenic offspring respectively disclosed some significant differences. In the schizophrenic group he found two types of background: (1) "chaotic" families which lacked suitable identification figures, contained no consistent relationship patterns, and tended to teach paralogical ideation; and (2) rigid families which permitted only very stereotyped and limited interactions, and where the patient's personality was usually an extension of that of one of the parents. Neither type occurred among the families of neurotics. Symptomatic behavior was similar in the patient and one parent in 17 per cent of schizophrenic and 22 per cent of neurotic patients (3).

The single most important learning instrument is communication, and the family is the major and primary teacher. Verbal communication must fit the nonverbal interaction, and language competence is a sine qua non for conceptual and abstract thinking, for reading and for the cultural ways and styles of perceiving. Bateson and Jackson observed and analyzed the frequent contradictory messages in families with a schizophrenic member, a situation which they named "double bind" (17). Wynne and Singer (23) have discovered that analysis of thought and communication styles is more relevant to family pathology than the communicative contents transmitted or educational levels as such. Styles of intrafamilial communication called "amorphous" and "fragmented," respectively, by Wynne and Singer have been found specifically related to different types of schizophrenic patients, and Lidz et al. have documented how irrationality is transmitted in families with schizophrenic offspring (22). Abnormal intrafamilial communication is not only important as a manifestation of family pathology, but also holds the best promise to yield to further analysis and classification of family pathology either in itself or as an indication of thought disorders in individual family members (22, 32, 33).

It has already been stated that the evolution of the nuclear family demands its eventual contraction to the parental dyad after the emancipation of the young from it. Deficient emancipation is usually rooted in earlier defects in family task accomplishments. Cultural deviations between the generations may also be an important impediment to children's separation from parents and the parental home (4, 20). The pathology of incomplete emancipation is probably best known to college mental health services (19), but in less educated groups is more likely to appear as individual psychopathology after the incompletely emancipated person has undertaken marriage and parenthood (24, 29). Obviously a cycle of successive generations with psychopathology and family pathology can occur in this way, and we and others have documentary data for this phenomenon up to four generations (5, 15, 22).

COMMENT

It would have been tempting and rewarding, were it possible, to relate specific family problems and constellations to specific psychiatric diagnostic entities. It is not possible at this stage of our understanding of family dynamics, and our conceptual frameworks of family functions may not be sufficiently succinct to permit this. Equally weighty, however, is the imprecision of psychiatric diagnosis and the lack of specific quantifiable indicators for most diagnostic entities. Further revision and greater precision may result from more acute understanding of familial and other psychosocial deficiencies and abnormalities. It is clear now that issues and concepts of health are interwined with sociocultural and educational issues. The family is the original sociocultural milieu as well as the original teacher for every human being. Crucial to both these functions are communication and thinking and conceptual styles and values. Attention to and analysis of these processes as family functions, as exemplified by the works of Wynne and Singer (33), Kluckhohn and Spiegel (19), and Lidz et al. (21, 22), seem more promising and fruitful in elucidating psychopathology than attempts to deal with total family constellations or with specific personality features of a parent or child or the particular mode of their pathological relationships. The difficulty of correlating individual and family abnormalities is compounded, because some abnormalities, such as communication style, pervade the entire family and if severe will affect all members, but not necessarily in the same way. While each child lives in the same family, he also lives in a family unique for him. No parent-child triad is identical, not even those of twins, as has been demonstrated (3, 22). It is necessary to understand both the family-wide deviations and the specific distortions of family paradigms in each child's dynamic position and role in the family vis-a-vis his parents and vis-a-vis his siblings.

Research must begin with present knowledge and plausibly derived theories. This points presently toward functional analysis of family health and strengths and of family pathology. Grasping the entire bio-psycho-social complex is difficult and no one method will suffice, but a concerted and multidisciplinary approach should prove fruitful and rewarding at this time when total health is becoming an integral part and goal of total human welfare.

Most important, such an approach has therapeutic relevance, because the approach of analyzing family functioning and coping can be accomplished in its entirety only through a therapeutically oriented group process. Certain tests, especially those devised by Wynne, Singer (33), and Wild (23), are important, but intrafamilial communication and interaction can be studied best through participant observation incident to a therapeutic effort or at least—and next best—in a task-oriented session (1, 7, 20).

SUMMARY

An approach to family pathology has been proposed which focuses on deficiencies in and deviations from salient family functions and tasks. It is not possible at present to establish specific correlation between such defects and clinical psychiatric entities. It may, however, be suggested that from such an approach to family pathology, revisions and reclassification of psychiatric diagnoses could follow. Although for discussion purposes some distinction has been made among intrapersonal, interparental, and family-wide pathological phenomena, it can be concluded that all these are relevant, but each alone is insufficient to understand family process. The most promising approaches to family functioning are the examinations of familial communication styles and interaction modes through relevant tests and therapeutically oriented participant observation. These observations, together with the family's history, must be evaluated in terms of the validity and effectiveness of the family behavior with regard to basic family tasks, which were briefly outlined in the first part of this paper.

REFERENCES

1. Ackerman, N. W.: *The Psychodynamics of Family Life*. New York, Basic Books, 1958.
2. Alanen, Y. O.: The mothers of schizophrenic patients. *Acta Psychiat. Neurol. Scand.* Suppl. 124, 1958.
3. Alanen, Y. O.: The family in the pathogenesis of schizophrenia and neurotic disorders. *Acta Psychiat. Neurol. Scand.* Suppl. 189 (Vol. 24), 1966.
4. Bell, N. W., and Vogel E.: Toward a framework for functional analysis of family behavior. *In: A Modern Introduction to the Family* (N. W. Bell and E. Vogel, Eds.) Glencoe, Ill., Free Press, 1960.
5. Bloom, B. S.: *Stability and Change in Human Characteristics*. New York. John Wiley and Sons, 1964.
6. Bott, E.: *Family and Social Network*. London, Tavistock Publications, 1957.
7. Bowlby, J.: *Maternal Care and Mental Health*. Geneva, World Health Organization, 1952.
8. Caplan, G.: *Principles of Preventive Psychiatry*. New York. Basic Books, 1964.
9. Cohen, M. B., et al.: An intensive study of twelve cases of manic-depressive psychosis. *Psychiatry* 17:103–137, 1954.
10. Ehrenwald, J.: Family diagnosis and mechanisms of psychosocial defense. *Family Process* 2:121–131, 1963.
11. Erikson, E.: *Childhood and Society*. New York, Norton, 1950.
12. Erikson, E.: *Insight and Responsibility*. New York, Norton, 1964.
13. Fleck, S., Lidz, T., Cornelison, A., Schafer, S., and Terry D.: The intrafamilial environment of the schizophrenic patient: Incestuous and homosexual problems. *In: Individual and Familial Dynamics* (J. Masserman, Ed.) New York, Grune & Stratton, 1959.
14. Fleck, S.: *Family welfare, mental health and birth control*. Journal Family Law 3:241–247, 1964.
15. Fleck, S.: Unpublished data.

16. Green, M., and Solnit, A. J.: Reactions to the threatened loss of a child: a vulnerable child syndrome. *Pediatrics* 34:58–66, 1964.

17. Jackson, D. D., and Satir, V.: A review of psychiatric developments in family diagnosis and therapy. *In: Exploring the Case for Family Therapy* (N. W. Ackerman, F. Beatman, and S. Sherman, Eds.) New York, Family Assoc. of America, 1961.

18. Johnson, A. M., and Szurek, S. A.: The genesis of antisocial acting out in children and adults. *Psychoanal. Quart.* 21:323–343, 1952.

19. Keniston, K.: *The Uncommitted.* New York, Harcourt. Brace and World, Inc., 1965.

20. Kluckhohn, F.: Variants in Value Orientations. Evanston, Ill., Row Peterson, 1957.

21. Lidz, T.: *The Family and Human Adaptation.* New York, International Universities Press, 1963.

22. Lidz, T., Fleck, S., and Cornelison, A.: *Schizophrenia and the Family.* New York, International Universities Press, 1966.

23. Lieberman, E. J.: Preventive psychiatry and family planning. *J. Marriage Family* 26:471, 1964.

24. Moynihan, D. P.: *The Negro Family: A Case for National Action.* Washington, D. C., U. S. Gov. Printing Bureau, 1965.

25. Parsons, T.: The incest taboo in relation to social structure and the socialization of the child. *Brit. J. Sociol.* 5:101, 1954.

26. Parsons, T., and Bales, R. F. Family, Socialization and Interaction Process. Glencoe, Ill., Free Press, 1955.

27. Parsons, T.: Social Structure and Personality. Glencoe, Ill., Free Press, 1964.

28. Paul, N., and Grosser, G.: The role of loss and mourning in conjoint family therapy. Presented Aug. 18, 1964, at 1st Int. Congress of Social Psychiatry, London.

29. Rainwater, L.: Family Design. Chicago, Aldino Publ. Co., 1965.

30. Stafford, J.: *An American Mother in History.* New York, Farar, Strauss and Group, 1965.

31. Weinberg, S. K.: *Incest Behavior.* New York, Citadel Press, 1955.

32. Whorf, B.: *Language, Thought, and Reality: Selected Writings of Benjamin Lee Whorf* (J. Carroll, Ed.). New York, J. Wiley & Sons and M.I.T. Press, 1956.

33. Wynne, L. C., and Singer, M. T.: Thought disorder and family relations of schizophrenics. II. A classification of forms of thinking. *Arch. Gen. Psychiat,* 9:199–206, 1963.

19

THE PROCESS-REACTIVE CLASSIFICATION OF SCHIZOPHRENIA

William G. Herron

The heterogeneity of schizophrenic patients and the lack of success in relating variable schizophrenic functioning to diagnostic subtypes (King, 1954) have indicated the serious limitations of the current neuropsychiatric classification of schizophrenia. In response to these limitations interest has arisen in a two-dimensional frame of reference for schizophrenia. Such a conception is based on the patient's life history and/or prognosis. A number of terms—malignant-benign, dementia praecox-schizophrenia, chronic-episodic, chronic-acute, typical-atypical, evolutionary-reactive, true-schizophreniform, process-reactive—have appeared in the literature describing these two syndromes. Process schizophrenia involves a long-term progressive deterioration of the adjustment pattern with little chance of recovery, while reactive schizophrenia indicates a good prognosis based on a history of generally adequate social development with notable stress precipitating the psychosis.

In view of the current favorable interest in this approach to the understanding of schizophrenia (Rabin & King, 1958) the present investigation is designed as an evaluative review of the literature on the process-reactive classification.

EARLY PROGNOSTIC STUDIES

The process-reactive distinction had its implicit origin in the work of Bleuler (1911). Prior to this the Kraepelinian influence had prevailed, with dementia praecox considered an incurable deteriorative disorder. Bleuler, while adhering to an organic etiology for schizophrenia, nonetheless observed that

Reprinted from the *Psychological Bulletin*, 59, 1962, 329–343, with the permission of the American Psychological Association and Dr. Herron.

some cases recovered. This conclusion opened the field to a series of subsequent prognostic studies (Benjamin, 1946; Chase & Silverman, 1943; Hunt & Appel, 1936; Kant, 1940, 1941, 1944; Kretschmer, 1925; Langfeldt, 1951; Lewis, 1936, 1944; Malamud & Render, 1939; Mauz, 1930; Milici, 1939; Paskind & Brown, 1940; Wittman, 1941, 1944; Wittman & Steinberg, 1944a, 1944b) eventuating in formalized descriptions of the process and reactive syndromes in terms of specific criteria.

These early studies can be classified in three general categories: studies correlating the outcome of a specific type of therapy with certain prognostic variables, studies descriptively evaluating prognostic criteria, and studies validating a prognostic scale.

The first category is illustrated by the attempt of Chase and Silverman (1943) to correlate the results of Metrazol and insulin shock therapy with prognosis, using 100 schizophrenic patients treated with Metrazol and 40 schizophrenic patients treated with insulin shock.

In the first part of this study the probable outcome of each of the 150 patients was estimated on the basis of prognostic criteria. The criteria considered of primary importance for a favorable prognosis were: short duration of illness, acute onset, obvious exogenic precipitating factors, early prominence of confusion, and atypical symptoms (marked by strong mixtures of manic-depressive, psychogenic, and symptomatic trends), and minimal process symptoms (absence of depersonalization, derealization, massive primary persecutory ideas, and sensations of influence, conscious realization of personality disintegration, bizarre delusions and hallucinations, marked apathy, and dissociation of affect). When these conditions were reversed the prognosis was least favorable. The following factors were considered less important for a favorable prognosis: history of previous illness, pyknic body type, extrovert temperament and adequate prepsychotic life adjustment, catatonic and atypical subtypes. Asthenic body type, introversion, inadequacy of prepsychotic reactions to life situations, onset of illness after the age of 40, and hebephrenic and paranoid subtypes were considered indicative of unfavorable prognosis. Age of onset under 40, sex, education, and abilities, and hereditary background were not considered of prognostic importance. An analysis of the prognostically significant factors resulted in the evaluation of the prognosis for each case as good, fair, or poor.

Following termination of shock treatment all patients were followed up for an average of 10 months and divided into three groups; much improved, improved, and unimproved. A comparison of the prognostic assessments with the results of shock indicated that of 43 cases in which the prognosis was considered good, 33 showed remissions, while of 74 cases with a poor prognosis, 63 did not improve. It was concluded that shock therapies were effective in cases of schizophrenia in which the prognosis was favorable, but were of little value when the prognosis was poor.

The second part of the research involved a reanalysis of the prognostic criteria in the light of the results of shock treatment. Short duration of illness and the absence of process symptoms were the most significant factors for favorable outcome, while long duration of illness (more than 2 years) and the presence of process symptoms were primary in determining poor prognosis.

A descriptive review of prognostic factors is seen in Kant's (1944) description of the benign (reactive) syndrome as cases in which clouding and confusion prevail, or in which the schizophrenic symptoms centered around manic-depressive features or cases with alternating states of excitement and stupor with fragmentation of mental activity. Malignant (process) cases are characterized by direct process symptoms. These include changes in the behavior leading to disorganization, dulling and autism, preceding the outbreak of overt psychosis. The most subtle manifestation of this is the typical schizophrenic thought disturbance. The patient experiences the process as a loss of normal feeling of personality activity and the start of experiencing a foreign influence applied to mind or body.

The third category includes the Elgin Prognostic Scale, constructed by Wittman (1941) to predict recovery in schizophrenia. It is comprised of 20 rating scales weighted according to prognostic importance: favorable factors are weighted negatively, and unfavorable factors are assigned positive weights. Initial validation involved 343 schizophrenic cases placed on shock treatment. Wittman and Steinberg (1944a) performed a follow-up study on 804 schizophrenics and 156 manic-depressive patients. The Elgin scale proved effective in predicting the outcome of therapy in 80–85% of the cases in both studies, and has been utilized in the work of Becker (1956, 1959), King (1958), and McDonough (1960) to distinguish the process-reactive syndrome. Included in the subscales of the Elgin scale are evaluations of prepsychotic personality, nature of onset, and typicality of the psychosis relative to Kraepelin's definition.

STUDIES WITH DETAILED PROCESS-REACTIVE CRITERIA

The synthesis of early studies is found in the research of Kantor, Wallner, and Winder (1953) establishing detailed criteria for distinguishing the two syndromes on the basis of case history material. A process patient would exhibit the following characteristics: early psychological trauma, severe or long physical illness, odd member of the family, school difficulties, family troubles paralleled by sudden changes in the patient's behavior, introverted behavior trends and interests, history of a breakdown of social, physical, and/or mental functioning, pathological siblings, overprotective or rejecting mother, rejecting father, lack of heterosexuality, insidious gradual onset of psychosis without pertinent stress, physical aggression, poor response to treatment, lengthy stay in the hospital, massive paranoia, little capacity for alcohol, no manic-depressive component, failure under adversity, discrepancy between ability and achievement, awareness of a change in the self, somatic delusions, a clash between the culture and the environment, and a loss of decency. In contrast, the reactive patient has these characteristics: good psychological history, good physical health, normal family member, well adjusted at school, domestic troubles unaccompanied by behavioral disruptions in the patient, extroverted behavior trends and interests, history of adequate social, physical, and/or mental functioning, normal siblings, normally protective accepting mother, accepting father, heterosexual behavior, sudden onset of psychosis with pertinent stress present, verbal aggression, good response to treatment, short stay in the hospital, minor paranoid trends, good capacity for alcohol, manic-depressive component present, success despite adversity, harmony between ability and achievement, no sensation of self-change, absence of somatic delusions, harmony between the culture and the environment, and retention of decency.

The first three criteria apply to the patient's behavior between birth and the fifth year; the next seven, between the fifth year and adolescence; the next five, from adolescence to adulthood; the last nine, during adulthood. Using these 24 points to distinguish the two syndromes they tried to answer three questions:

1. Do diagnoses based upon the Rorschach alone label as nonpsychotic a portion of the population of mental patients who are clinically diagnosed as schizophrenic?

2. Can case histories of clinically diagnosed schizophrenics be differentiated into two categories: process and reactive?

3. Are those cases rated psychotic from the Rorschach classed as process on the basis of case histories, and are those cases judged nonpsychotic from the Rorschach classified as reactive from the case histories?

Two samples of 108 and 95 patients clinically diagnosed as schizophrenic were given the Rorschach and rated according to the process-reactive criteria. In the first sample of 108 patients, 57 were classified as psychotic and 51 nonpsychotic on the basis of the Rorschach alone, while in the second sample, of 74 patients who could be rated as process or reactive, 36 were classified as psychotic, and 38 as nonpsychotic from their Rorschach protocols. Those patients who were rated as reactive from their history were most often judged nonpsychotic from the Rorschach, and those rated process from the case histories were most often judged as psychotic from the Rorschach.

Only one judge was used in the second sample to rate the patients as process or reactive, but two judges were used in the first sample. Of the 108 patients in this sample, both judges rated 86 cases, and were in agreement on 64 of these, which is greater than would be expected by chance.

However, the accuracy of the schizophrenic diagnosis is questionable in this study. If the Rorschach diagnosis is followed, then it appears that reactive schizophrenics are not psychotic. Furthermore, the psychiatric diagnosis appears to be somewhat contaminated because it was established on the basis of data collected by all appropriate services of the hospital, including psychological examinations. A similar type of contamination may have been present in classifying patients as process or reactive because one judge had reviewed each case previously and had seen psychological examination and history materials together prior to making his ratings. Three difficulties can be found with the criteria for process-reactive ratings. First, case histories are often incomplete and the patient is unable or unwilling to supply the necessary information. Second, it is difficult to precisely apply some of the criteria. For example, what is the precise dividing line between oddity and normality within the family? Third, in order to classify a patient it is necessary to set an arbitrary cut off point based on the number of process or reactive characteristics a patient has. Such a procedure needs validation.

Nonetheless, the results of this study support the view that schizophrenics can be classified as process or reactive, and that these syndromes differ in psychological functioning.

Another rating scale which has been used extensively to distinguish prognostically favorable and prognostically unfavorable schizophrenics was developed by Phillips (1953). The scale was developed from the case histories of schizophrenic patients who were eventually given shock treatment. The scale evaluates each patient in three areas; premorbid history, possible precipitating factors, and signs of the disorder. Premorbid history includes seven items on the social aspects of sexual life during adolescence and immediately beyond, seven items on the social aspects of recent sexual life, six items on personal relations, and six items on recent premorbid adjustment in personal relations. The sections of the scale which reflect the recent sexual life and its social history are the most successful in predicting the outcome of treatment. The items in the scales are arranged in order of increasing significance for improvement and nonimprovement away from the score of three, which is the dividing point between improved and unimproved groups. The premorbid history subscale has been utilized as the ranking instrument in the studies described by Rodnick and Garmezy (1957; Garmezy & Rodnick, 1959).

Another approach to the separation of schizophrenics into prognostic groups uses the activity of the autonomic nervous system as the basis for division (Meadow & Funkenstein, 1952; Meadow, Greenblatt, Funkenstein, & Solomon, 1953; Meadow, Greenblatt, & Solomon, 1953). Meadow and Funkenstein (1952) worked with 58 schizophrenic patients tested for autonomic reactivity and for abstract thinking. Following therapy the patients were divided into two groups, good or poor, depending on the outcome of the treatment. The battery of psychological tests included the similarities and block design subtests of the Wechsler-Bellevue scale, the Benjamin Proverbs test, and the object sorting tests. The physiological test involved the systolic blood pressure reaction to adrenergic stimulation (intravenous Epinephrine) and cholinergic stimulation (intramuscular Mecholyl). On the basis of the physiological and psychological testing, schizophrenic cases were divided into three types: Type I, characterized by marked response to Epinephrine, low blood pressure, and failure of the blood pressure to rise under most stresses, loss of ability for abstract thinking, inappropriate affect, and a poor prognosis; Type II, characterized by an entirely different autonomic pattern, relatively intact abstract ability, anxiety or depression, and a good prognosis; Type III, showing no autonomic disturbance, relatively little loss of abstract ability, little anxiety, well organized paranoid delusions, and a fair prognosis.

However, as Meadow and Funkenstein (1952) point out, there is considerable overlap of the measures defining these types so that the classification must be tentative. Also, of the psychological tests used, only Proverbs distinguished significantly between the patients when they were classified according to autonomic reactivity, while Block Design failed to distinguish significantly among any of the types. Further research using this method of division (Meadow, Greenblatt, Funkenstein, & Solomon, 1953; Meadow, Greenblatt, & Solomon, 1953) served as a basis for investigations of the process-reactive syndromes by King (1958) and Zuckerman and Grosz (1959).

King (1958) hypothesized that predominantly reactive schizophrenics would exhibit a higher level of autonomic responsiveness after the injection of Mecholyl than predominantly process schizophrenics. The subjects were 60 schizophrenics who were classified as their process or reactive by the present investigator and an independent judge using the criteria of Kantor et al. (1953). Only those subjects were used on which there was classificatory agreement. This resulted in 22 process and 24 reactive patients. In order to consider the process-reactive syndrome as a continuum, 16 subjects were randomly selected from these two groups and were ranked by two independent rates.

While the patient was lying in bed shortly after awakening in the morning the resting systolic blood pressure was determined. The patient then received 10 milligrams of Mecholyl intramuscularly, and the systolic blood pressure was recorded at intervals up to 20 minutes. Then the maximum fall in systolic blood pressure (MFBP) below the resting blood pressure following the injection of Mecholyl was computed for the different time intervals. There was a significant difference in the MFBP score for the reactives as compared with the normals. For the 16 subjects, the correlation between the sets of ranks on the process-reactive dimension and MFBP was −.58.

In a second part of the study 90 schizophrenics, none of whom had participated in the first part, were classified as either process, process-reactive, or reactive, using the criteria of Kantor et al. (1953). On this basis the subjects were divided into three groups of 24. Also, scores for 22 subjects were obtained on the Elgin Prognostic Scale, and 12 of these were rated independently by two raters. The MFBP scores were 17.04 for the process group, 22.79 for the process-reactive group, and 26.62 for the reactive. Using an analysis of variance a significant F score occurs at the .01 level. The correlation between the Elgin Prognostic Scale and the MFBP scores for 22 patients were −.49.

Results of both parts of the study revealed that the patients classified as reactive exhibited a significantly greater fall in blood pressure after the administration of Mecholyl than the process patients. This evidence points to diminished physiological responsiveness in process, but not in reactive schizophrenia. However, Zuckerman and Grosz (1959) found that process schizophrenics showed a significantly greater fall in blood pressure following the administration of Mecholyl than reactives. Since these results contradict King's findings the question of the direction of responsiveness to Mecholyl in these two groups requires further investigation before a conclusion can be reached.

PROCESS-ORGANIC VERSUS REACTIVE-PSYCHOGENIC

Brackbill and Fine (1956) suggested that process schizophrenics suffer from an organic impairment not present in the reactive case. They hypothesized that there would be no significant differences in the incidence of "organic signs" on the Rorschach between a group of process schizophrenics and a group of known cases of central nervous system pathology, and that both organic and process groups would show significantly more signs of organic involvement than the reactive group.

The subjects consisted of 36 patients diagnosed as process schizophrenics and 24 reactive schizophrenics. The criteria of Kantor et al. (1953) were used to describe the patients as process or reactive. Patients were included only when there was complete agreement between judges as the category of schizophrenia. Also included in the sample were 28 cases of known organic involvement. All patients were given the Rorschach, and the protocols were scored using Piotrowski's (1940) 10 signs of organicity.

Using the criterion of five or more signs as a definite indication of organic involvement there was no significant difference between the organic and process groups, but both groups were significantly different from the reactives. Considering individual signs, four distinguished between the reactive and organic group, while two distinguished between process and reactive groups. The authors concluded that the results supported the hypothesis that process schizophrenics react to a perceptual task in a similar manner to that of patients with central nervous system pathology. No specific hypothesis was made about individual Rorschach signs, but color naming, completely absent in the reactives, was indicated as an example of concrete thinking and inability to abstract, suggesting that one of the critical differences between process and reactive groups is in terms of a type of thought disturbance.

This study does not provide detailed information about the manner of establishing the diagnosis of schizophrenia or about the judges deciding the process and reactive syndromes. Also, a further difficulty is the admitted inadequacy of the organic signs, since 66% of cases with organic pathology in this study were false negatives according to the Rorschach criteria. Thus while the existence of the process and reactive syndromes is supported by the results of this investigation, there is less evidence of an organic deficit in process schizophrenics.

Becker (1956) pointed out that the consistency of the prognostic findings in schizophrenia has led to postulating two kinds of schizophrenia: process, with an organic basis, and reactive, with a psychological basis. He rejects this conclusion because research data in this area shows considerable group overlap, making it clinically difficult and arbitrary to force all schizophrenics into one group or the other. Also, if schizophrenia is a deficit reaction which may be brought about by any combination of 40 or more etiological factors, then the conception of two dichotomous types of schizophrenia is not useful. Finally, he maintains that 20 years of research have failed to find clear etiological differences between any subgroupings.

Instead, Becker stated that process and reactive syndromes should be conceived as end points on a continuum of levels of personality organization. Process reflects a very primitive undifferentiated personality structure, while reactive indicates a more highly organized one. He hypothesized that schizophrenics more nearly approximating the process syndrome would show more regressive and immature thinking processes than schizophrenics who more nearly approximate the reactive syndromes. His sample consisted of 51 schizophrenics, 24 males and 27 females, all under 41 years of age. Their thinking processes were evaluated by the Rorschach and the Benjamin Proverbs test. The 1937 Stanford-Binet vocabulary test was used to estimate verbal intelligence. A Rorschach scoring system was used which presumably reflected the subjects' level of perceptual development, while a scoring system was devised for the Proverbs which reflected levels of abstraction. Since there is a high relationship between intelligence and ability to interpret proverbs, a more sensitive index of a thinking disturbance was considered to be a discrepancy score based on the standard score difference between a vocabulary estimate of verbal intelligence and the proverbs score. Process and reactive ratings were made on the Elgin Prognostic Scale.

The Rorschach mean perceptual level score and the Elgin Prognostic Scale correlated −.599 for men and −.679 for women, indicating a significant relationship between the process-reactive dimension as evaluated from case history data and disturbances of thought processes as measured by the Rorschach scoring system. The Proverbs vocabulary discrepancy score was significantly related to the process-reactive dimension for men, but not for women. No adequate explanation was found for this sex difference, which mitigates the results. A further difficulty occurs because the case history and test evaluations were made by the same person. However, the results in part support the hypothesis, indicating evidence for a measurable dimension of regressive and immature thinking related to the process-reactive dimension.

McDonough (1960), acting on the assumption that process schizophrenia involves central nervous system pathology specifically cortical in nature, hypothesized that brain damaged patients and process schizophrenics would have significantly lower critical flicker frequency (CFF) thresholds and would be unable to perceive the spiral aftereffect significantly more often than reactive schizophrenics and normals. Four groups of 20 subjects each were tested. The organic group consisted of individuals with known brain damage. One hundred and sixty-one schizophrenic case histories were examined, and 76 were chosen from this group to be rated on the Elgin Prognostic Scale. The 20 patients receiving the lowest point totals were selected as being most reactive, while those with the 20 highest scores were considered most process.

Results of the experiment revealed that organic patients were significantly different from all other groups in CFF threshold and ability to perceive the spiral aftereffect. Process and reactive schizophrenics did not differ from each other on either task, but reactive schizophrenics had higher CFF thresholds than normals. These results do not indicate demonstrable cortical defect in either process or reactive schizophrenia.

PROCESS-POOR PREMORBID HISTORY VERSUS
REACTIVE-GOOD PREMORBID HISTORY

Rodnick and Garmezy (1957), discussing the problem of motivation in schizophrenia, reviewed a number of studies in which the Phillips prognostic scale was used to classify schizophrenic patients into two groups, good and poor. For example, Bleke (1955) hypothesized that patients whose prepsychotic life adjustment was markedly inadequate would have greater interferences and so show more reminiscence following censure than patients whose premorbid histories were more adequate.

The subjects were presented with a list of 14 neutrally toned nouns projected successively on a screen. Each subject was required to learn to these words a pattern of pull-push movements of a switch lever. For half the subjects in each group learning took place under a punishment condition, while the remaining subjects were tested under a reward condition. The subjects consisted of 40 normals, 20 poor premorbid schizophrenics, and 20 good premorbid schizophrenics. The results confirmed the hypothesis.

A reanalysis of Dunn's (1954) data indicated that a poor premorbid group showed discrimination deficits when confronted with a scene depicting a mother and a young boy being scolded, but good premorbid and normal subjects did not show this deficit.

Mallet (1956) found that poor premorbid subjects in a memory task for verbal materials showed significantly poorer retention of hostile and nonhostile thematic contents than did good premorbid and normal subjects. Harris (1955) has found that in contrast to goods and normals poor premorbids have more highly deviant maternal attitudes. They attribute more rejective attitudes to their mothers, and are less able to critically evaluate their mothers. Harris (1957) also found differences among the groups in the size estimation of mother-child pictures. The poors significantly overestimated, while the goods underestimated, and the normals made no size error.

Rodnick and Garmezy (1957) reported a study using Osgood's (1952) semantic differential techniques in which six goods and six poors rated 20 concepts on each of nine scales selected on the basis of high loadings on the evaluative, potency, and activity factors. Good and poor groups differed primarily on potency and activity factors. The poors described words with negative value, as more powerful and active. The goods could discriminate among concepts, but the poors tended to see most concepts as powerful and active.

Rodnick and Garmezy (1957) also investigated differences in authority roles in the family during adolescence in good and poor premorbid patients. While results were tentative at that time, they suggested that the mothers of poor premorbid patients were perceived as having been more dominating, restrictive, and powerful, while the fathers appeared ineffectual. The pattern was reversed in the good premorbid patients.

Alvarez (1957) found significantly greater preference decrements to censured stimuli by poor premorbid patients. This result was consistent with the results of Bleke's (1955) and Zahn's (1959) observations of reversal patterns of movement of a switch lever following censure. These experiments suggested an increased sensitivity of the poor premorbid schizophrenic patient to a threatening environment.

These studies reported by Rodnick and Garmezy (1957) indicated that it was possible, using the Phillips scale, to effectively dichotomize schizophrenic patients. However, the Phillips scale had predictive validity only when applied to male patients. Within this form of reference it was also possible to demonstrate differences between goods and poors in response to censure, and in perception of familial figures. Variability in the results of schizophrenic performance was considered reduced by dichotomizing the patients, but it was often impossible to detect significant differences between the performance of good premorbid schizophrenics and normals. Rodnick and Garmezy (1957) suggest

that the results be considered as preliminary findings pending further corrobora-
tion, though providing support for the concept of premorbid groups of schizophrenics differing in certain psychological dimensions.

PROCESS-REACTIVE EMPIRICAL-THEORETICAL
FORMULATIONS

Fine and Zimet (1959; Zimet & Fine, 1959) used the same population
employed by Kantor et al. (1953) and the same criteria for distinguishing the
process and reactive patients. For this study only those cases were included
where there was complete agreement among the judges as to the category of
schizophrenia. They studied the level of perceptual organization of the patients
as shown on their Rorschach records. The process group was found to have
significantly more immature, regressive perceptions, while the reactive group
gave more mature and more highly organized responses. The findings indicated that archaic and impulse-ridden materials break through more freely in
process schizophrenia, and that there is less ego control over the production of
more regressive fantasies. Zimet and Fine (1959) speculated that process schizophrenia mirrors oral deprivation of early ego impoverishment, so that either
regression or fixation to an earlier developmental stage is reflected in his perceptual organization. In contrast, it is possible that the reactive schizophrenic's
ego weakness occurs at a later stage in psychosexual development, and any one
event may reactivate the early conflict.

An amplification of the process-reactive formation has been suggested by
Kantor and Winder (1959). They hypothesized that schizophrenia can be
understood as a series of responses reflecting the stage of development in the
patient's life at which emotional support was severely deficient. Schizophrenia
can be quantitatively depicted in terms of the level in life to which the schizophrenic has regressed, and beyond which development was severely distorted
because of disturbing life circumstances. The earlier in developmental history
that severe stress occurs, the more damaging the effect of subsequent interpersonal relationships. Sullivan (1947) suggested five stages in the development
of social maturity: empathic, prototaxic, parataxic, autistic, and syntaxic. The
most malignant schizophrenics are those who were severely traumatized in the
empathic stage of development when all experience is unconnected, there is no
symbolism, and functioning is at an elementary biological level. The schizophrenic personality originating at this stage may show many signs of organic
dysfunction. Prognosis will be most unfavorable, and delusional formation will
tend to be profound.

In view of the primitive symbolic conduct and the lack of a self-concept
in the prototaxic stage, the schizophrenic personality referable to this stage will

be characterized by magical thinking and disturbed communication. The delusion of adoption often occurs. However, these patients are more coherent than those of the previous level.

The parataxic schizophrenic state involves the inability of the self-system to prevent dissociation. The autonomy of the dissociations result in the patient's fear of uncontrollable inward processes. Schizophrenic symptoms appear as regressive behavior attempting to protect the self and regain security in a threatening world. Delusional content usually involves world disaster coupled with bowel changes. Nihilistic delusions are common. While there is evidence of a self-system in these patients, prognosis remains unfavorable.

The patient who has regressed to the autistic stage, although more reality oriented than in the previous stages, is characterized by paranoid suspiciousness, hostility, and pathological defensiveness against inadequacy feelings. A consistent system of delusions will be articulated and may bring the patient into conflict with society. However, prognosis is more favorable at this stage than previously.

An individual at the syntaxic level has reached concensus with society, so that if schizophrenia occurs it will be a relatively circumscribed reaction. Onset will be sudden with plausible environmental stresses, and prognosis is relatively good.

Becker (1959) also elaborated on the lack of a dichotomy in schizophrenia. Individual cases spread out in such a way that the process syndrome moves into the reactive syndrome, so that the syndromes probably identify the end points of a dimension of severity. At the process end of the continuum the development of personality organization is very primitive, or involves severe regression. There is a narrowing of interests, rigidity of structure, and inability to establish normal heterosexual relationships and independence. In contrast, the reactive end of the continuum represents a higher level of personality differentiation. The prepsychotic personality is more normal, heterosexual relations are better established, and there is greater tolerance of environmental stresses. The remains of a higher developmental level are present in regression and provide strength for recovery.

Becker (1959) factor analyzed some of the data from his previous study (Becker, 1956). The factored matrix included a number of background variables, the 20 Elgin Prognostic Scale subscores, and a Rorschach genetic level score (GL) based on the first response to each card. Seven centroid factors were extracted from the correlation matrix. Factors 4, 6, and 7 represented intelligence, cooperativeness, and marital status of parents, respectively. The highest loadings on Factor 5 were history of mental illness in the family, excellent health history, lack of precipitating factors, and clouded sensorium. The Rorschach GL score and the Elgin scales did not load significantly on Factors 4 through 7.

The remaining three factors parallel the factors Lorr, Wittman, and Schanberger (1951) found with 17 of the 20 Elgin scales using an oblique solution instead of the orthogonal solution used in this study. Factor 1 is called schizophrenic withdrawal, loading on defect of interest, insidious onset, shut-in personality, long duration of psychosis, and lack of precipitating factors. At one end this factor defines the typical process syndrome, while the other end describes the typical reactive syndrome. The Rorschach *GL* score loaded −.46 on Factor 1.

Factor 2, reality distortion, loads on hebephrenic symptoms, bizarre delusions, and inadequate affect. Rorschach *GL* score loaded −.64 on this factor. Factor 3 loaded on indifference and exclusiveness-stubborness. The opposite pole of this factor involves insecurity, inferiority, self-consciousness, and anxiety. Rorschach *GL* score loaded .25 on this factor.

Further analysis indicated that when Factors 1 and 2 were plotted against each other an oblique rotation was required, introducing a correlation of from .60 to .70 between schizophrenic withdrawal and reality distortion factors. Similar obliqueness was found between Factors 2 and 3, suggesting the presence of a second-order factor.

However, the sampling of behavior manifestations in the Elgin scale overweights the withdrawal factor, which gives Factor 1 undue weight and biases the direction of a second-order factor toward the withdrawal factor. Also, it is not possible to accurately locate second-order factors with only seven first-order factors as reference points. In addition, sample size and related sampling errors limited inferences about a second-order factor. There is the suggestion, however, of the existence of a general severity factor, loading primarily schizophrenic withdrawal and reality distortion.

The author suggests utilizing the evidence from this study to form an index of severity of psychosis which could be used to make diagnoses with prognostic significance. This diagnostic procedure would include factor estimates of schizophrenic withdrawal and emotional rigidity, based on Elgin scale ratings, and reality distortion, based on the Rorschach *GL* score.

Garmezy and Rodnick (1959) pointed out that despite failure to find support for a fundamental biological deviation associated with schizophrenia (Kety, 1959), the view of schizophrenia as a dichotomous typology influenced either by somatic or psychic factors has continuously been advanced. They maintain that on the basis of empirical evidence there is little support for a process-organic versus reactive-psychogenic formulation of schizophrenic etiology.

Reviewing a series of studies using the Phillips scale as a dichotomizing instrument (Alvarez, 1957; Bleke, 1955; Dunham, 1959; Dunn, 1954; Englehart, 1959; Farina, 1960; Garmezy, Stockner, & Clarke, 1959; Harris, 1957; Kreinik, 1959; Rodnick & Garmezy, 1957; Zahn, 1959) Garmezy and Rodnick concluded that the results indicate two groups of schizophrenic patients differing both in prognostic potential and sensitivity to experimental cues. There is an interrelationship among the variables of premorbid adequacy, differential sensitivity to censure, prognosis, and types of familial organization. This suggests a relationship between varying patterns of early experience and schizophrenia, though it does not embody the acceptance of a given position regarding psychological or biological antecedents in schizophrenia.

Reisman (1960), in an attempt to explain the heterogeneous results of psychomotor performance in schizophrenics, suggested that there were two groups of schizophrenics, process and reactive, differing in motivation. The process group was seen as more withdrawn and indifferent to their performance, and consequently reflecting a psychomotor deficit not present in reactives. In order to test this hypothesis 36 reactives, 36 process patients, and 36 normals performed a card-sorting task. The groups were distinguished according to the criteria of Kantor, Wallner, and Winder (1953). On Trial 1 all subjects were requested to sort as rapidly as possible. Then the subjects were assigned to one of four experimental conditions, with an attempt made to equate across the experimental conditions for age, estimated IQ, length of hospitalization, and initial sorting time. Condition 1 (FP) involved sorting the cards seven more times and if the sort was fast the subjects were shown stress-arousing photographs. If they sorted slowly no photographs were shown. Condition 2 (SP) was the reverse of this. Condition 3 (FL) and Condition 4 (SL) were similar to the first two conditions except that a nonreinforcing light was used instead of the pictures. After Trial 8 all subjects were informed that there would be no more pictures or light, but were asked to sort rapidly for three more trials. With four conditions on Trials 2 through 8, 10 subjects from each of the three groups participated in each of the two picture conditions, while eight subjects from each group participated in each of the light conditions.

The results indicated that the normals performed about the same under all conditions. The process group under FP sorted as fast as normals, but performed slowly under the other three conditions, while the reactives were slowest under FP but were as fast as normals under the other three conditions. Within all three groups performance under FL did not differ significantly from performance under SL. Under FL and SL, however, reactives and normals sorted more rapidly than the process group. These results supported the hypothesis of a motivational deficit for process schizophrenics. The results also indicated that the pictures were negatively reinforcing for the reactives, while the process patients were motivated to see them. This suggested a withdrawal differential. The withdrawal of the process patients is of such duration that supposedly threatening photographs cause little anxiety. In contrast, reactive withdrawal is motivated by an environment that recently became unbearable. Confronted with pictures representing this environment the reactive patient experiences anxiety and avoidance. However, the results of this experiment are in contrast to the findings of Rodnick and Garmezy (1957) that prolonged exposure to social censure will result in greater sensitivity to that stimulation.

SUMMARY

This review of all research on the process-reactive classification of schizophrenia strongly indicates that it is possible to divide schizophrenic patients into two groups differing in prognostic and life-history variables. Using such a division it is also possible to demonstrate differences between the two groups in physiological measures and psychological dimensions.

The result of such an approach has been to clarify many of the heterogenous reactions found in schizophrenia. It also appears that the dichotomy is somewhat artificial and really represents end points on a continuum of personality organization. The most process patient represents the extreme form of personality disintegration, while the most reactive patient represents the extreme form of schizophrenic integration. The reactions of this type of patient are often difficult to distinguish from behavior patterns of normal subjects. There does not appear to be any significant evidence to support the contention of a process-organic versus a reactive-psychogenic formulation of schizophrenic etiology.

It is difficult to decide on the most appropriate criteria for selecting schizophrenic subjects so as to reduce their response variability. Preferences are generally found for one of three sets of criteria: Kantor, Wallner, and Winder's (1953) items, the Elgin Prognostic Scale (1944), or the Phillips scale (1953). The criteria of Kantor et al. (1953) does not provide a quantitative ordering of the variables, and is descriptively vague in several dimensions as well as depending upon life history material which is not always available. While the Elgin scale does provide a quantitative approach, it also has the disadvantages of descriptive vagueness and excessive dependence upon life history material. The Phillips scale eliminates some of these difficulties, but its validity is limited to the adequacy or inadequacy of social-sexual premorbid adjustment. The need for more feasible criteria may be met by the factor analysis of pertinent variables to obtain a meaningful severity index (Becker, 1959), or by using rating scales in which the patient verbally supplies the necessary information. An example of the latter is the Ego Strength scale (Barron, 1953), recently utilized in distinguishing two polar constellations of schizophrenia; a process type with poor prognosis and grossly impaired abstract ability, and a reactive type characterized by good prognosis and slight abstractive impairment (Herron, in press).

This need for more efficient differentiating criteria mitigates some of the significance of present findings using the process-reactive dimension. Nonetheless, the process-reactive research up to this time has succeeded in explaining schizophrenic heterogeneity in a more meaningful manner than previous interpretations adhering to various symptom pictures and diagnostic subtypes. Consequently, there appears to be definite value in utilizing the process-reactive classification of schizophrenia.

REFERENCES

Alvarez, R. R. A comparison of the preferences of schizophrenic and normal subjects for rewarded and punished stimuli. Unpublished doctoral dissertation, Duke University, 1957.

Barron, F. An ego-strength scale which predicts response to psychotherapy. *J. consult. Psychol.,* 1953, 17, 327–333.

Becker, W. A genetic approach to the interpretation and evaluation of the process-reactive distinction in schizophrenia. *J. abnorm. soc. Psychol.,* 1956, 53, 229–236.

Becker, W. C. The process-reactive distinction: A key to the problem of schizophrenia? *J. nerv. ment. Dis.,* 1959, 129, 442–449.

Benjamin, J. D. A method for distinguishing and evaluating formal thinking disorders in schizophrenia. In J. S. Kasanin (Ed.), *Language and thought in schizophrenia.* Berkeley: Univer. California Press, 1946, Pp. 66–71.

Bleke, R. C. Reward and punishment as determiners of reminiscence effects in schizophrenics and normal subjects. *J. Pers.,* 1955, 23, 479–498.

Bleuler, E. *Dementia-praecox.* New York: International Univer. Press, 1911.

Brackbill, G., & Fine, H. Schizophrenia and central nervous system pathology. *J. abnorm. soc. Psychol.,* 1956, 52, 310–313.

Chase, L. S., & Silverman, S. Prognosis in schizophrenia: An analysis of prognostic criteria in 150 schizophrenics treated with Metrazol or insulin. *J. nerv. ment. Dis.,* 1943, 98, 464–473.

Dunham, R. M. Sensitivity of schizophrenics to parental censure. Unpublished doctoral dissertation, Duke University, 1959.

Dunn, W. L. Visual discrimination of schizophrenic subjects as a function of stimulus meaning. *J. Pers.,* 1954, 23, 48–64.

Englehart, R. S. Semantic correlates of interpersonal concepts and parental attributes in schizophrenia. Unpublished doctoral dissertation, Duke University, 1959.

Farina, A. Patterns of role dominance and conflict in parents of schizophrenic patients. *J. abnorm. soc. Psychol.,* 1960, 61, 31–38.

Fine, H. J., & Zimet, C. N. Process-reactive schizophrenia and genetic levels of perception. *J. abnorm. soc. Psychol.,* 1959, 59, 83–86.

Garmezy, N., & Rodnick, E. H. Premorbid adjustment and performance in schizophrenia: Implications for interpreting heterogeneity in schizophrenia. *J. nerv. ment. Dis.,* 1959, 129, 450–466.

Garmezy, N., Stockner, C., & Clarke, A. R. Child-rearing attitudes of mothers and fathers as reported by schizophrenic and normal control patients. *Amer. Psychologist,* 1959, 14, 333. (Abstract)

Harris, J. G., Jr. A study of the mother-son relationship in schizophrenia. Unpublished doctoral dissertation, Duke University, 1955.

Harris, J. G., Jr. Size estimation of pictures as a function of thematic content for schizophrenic and normal subjects. *J. Pers.,* 1957, 25, 651–672.

Herron, W. G. Abstract ability in the process-reactive classification of schizophrenia. *J. gen. Psychol.,* in press.

Hunt, R. C., & Appel, K. E. Prognosis in psychoses lying midway between schizophrenia and manic-depressive psychoses. *Amer. J. Psychiat.,* 1936, 93, 313–339.

Kant, O. Differential diagnosis of schizophrenia in light of concepts of personality stratification. *Amer. J. Psychiat.,* 1940, 97, 342–357.

Kant, O. A comparative study of recovered and deteriorated schizophrenic patients. *J. nerv. ment. Dis.,* 1941, 93, 616–624.

Kant, O. The evaluation of prognostic criteria in schizophrenia. *J. nerv. ment. Dis.,* 1944, 100, 598–605.

Kantor, R., Wallner, J., & Winder C. Process and reactive schizophrenia. *J. consult. Psychol.,* 1953, 17, 157–162.

Kantor, R. E., & Winder, C. L. The process-reactive continuum: A theoretical proposal. *J. nerv. ment. Dis.,* 1959, 129, 429–434.

Kety, S. S. Biochemical theories of schizophrenia. *Science,* 1959, 129, 1528–1532, 1590–1596, 3362–3363.

King, G. Differential autonomic responsiveness in the process-reactive classification of schizophrenia. *J. abnorm. soc. Psychol.,* 1958, 56, 160–164.

King, G. F. Research with neuropsychiatric samples. *J. Psychol.,* 1954, 38, 383–387.

Kreinik, P. S. Parent-child themas and concept attainment in schizophrenia. Unpublished doctoral dissertation, Duke University, 1959.

Kretschmer, E. *Physique and character.* New York: Harcourt, Brace, 1925.

Langfeldt, G. The diagnosis of schizophrenia. *Amer. J. Psychiat.,* 1951, 108, 123–125.

Lewis, N. D. C. *Research in dementia praecox.* New York: National Committee for Mental Hygiene, 1936.

Lewis, N. D. C. The prognostic significance of certain factors in schizophrenia. *J. nerv. ment. Dis.,* 1944, 100, 414–419.

Lorr, M., Wittman, P., & Schanberger, W. An analysis of the Elgin Prognostic scale. *J. clin. Psychol.,* 1951, 7, 260–263.

McDonough, J. M. Critical flicker frequency and the spiral aftereffect with process and reactive schizophrenics. *J. consult. Psychol.,* 1960, 24, 150–155.

Malamud, W., & Render, N. Course and prognosis in schizophrenia. *Amer. J. Psychiat.,* 1939, 95, 1039–1057.

Mallet, J. J. Verbal recall of hostile and neutral thematic contents by schizophrenic and normal subjects. Unpublished doctoral dissertation, Duke University, 1956.

Mauz, F. *Die Prognostik der endogen Psychosen,* Leipzig: G. Theime, 1930.

Meadow, A., & Funkenstein, D. H. The relationship of abstract thinking to the automatic nervous system in schizophrenia. In P. H. Hoch and J. Zubin (Eds.), *Relation of psychological tests to psychiatry.* New York: Grune & Stratton, 1952. Pp. 131–144.

Meadow, A., Greenblatt, M., Funkenstein, G. H., & Solomon, H. C. The relationship between the capacity for abstraction is schizophrenia and the physiologic response to autonomic drugs. *J. nerv. ment. Dis.,* 1953, 118, 332–338.

Meadow, A., Greenblatt, M., & Solomon, H. C. "Looseness of association" and impairment in abstraction in schizophrenia. *J. nerv. ment. Dis.,* 1953, 118, 27–35.

Milici, P. Postemotive schizophrenia. *Psychiat. Quart.,* 1939, 13, 278–293.

Osgood, C. E. The nature and measurement of meaning. *Psychol. Bull.,* 1952, 49, 197–237.

Paskind, J. A., & Brown, M. Psychosis resembling schizophrenia occurring with emotional stress and ending in recovery. *Amer. J. Psychiat.,* 1940, 96, 1379–1388.

Phillips, L. Case history data and prognosis in schizophrenia. *J. nerv. ment. Dis.,* 1953, 117, 515–525.

Piotrowski, Z. A. Positive and negative Rorschach organic reactions. *Rorschach res. Exch.,* 1940, 4, 143–151.

Rabin, A. J., & King, G. F. Psychological studies. In L. Bellak (Ed.), *Schizophrenia: A review of the syndrome.* New York: Logos, 1958. Pp. 216–278.

Reisman, J. M. Motivational differences between process and reactive schizophrenics. *J. Pers.,* 1960, 28, 12–25.

Rodnick, E. H., & Garmezy, N. An experimental approach to the study of motivation in schizophrenia. In M. R. Jones (Ed.), *Nebraska symposium on motivation: 1957.* Vol. V. Lincoln: Univer. Nebraska Press, 1957. Pp. 109–184.

Sullivan, H. S. *Conceptions of modern psychiatry.* Washington: W. A. White Psychiatric Foundation, 1947.

Wittman, P. A scale for measuring prognosis in schizophrenic patients. *Elgin State Hosp. Pap.,* 1941, 4, 20–33.

Wittman, P. Follow-up on Elgin prognosis scale results. *Ill. psychiat. J.,* 1944, 4, 56–59.

Wittman, P., & Steinberg, L. Follow-up of an objective evaluation of prognosis in dementia praecox and manic-depressive psychoses. *Elgin State Hosp. Pap.,* 1944, 5, 216–227. (a)

Wittman, P., & Steinberg, D. L. Study of prodromal factors in mental illness with special references in schizophrenia. *Amer. J. Psychiat.,* 1944, 100, 811–816. (b)

Zahn, T. P. Acquired and symbolic affective value as determinant of size estimation in schizophrenic and normal subjects. *J. abnorm. soc. Psychol.,* 1959, 58, 39–47.

Zimet, C. N., & Fine, H. J. Perceptual differentiation and two dimensions of schizophrenia. *J. nerv. ment. Dis.,* 1959, 129, 435–441.

Zuckerman, M., & Grosz, H. J. Contradictory results using the mecholyl test to differentiate process and reactive schizophrenia. *J. abnorm. soc. Psychol.,* 1959, 59, 145–146.

DISCUSSION

In many ways the authors included in this section appear to be writing about unique and unrelated phenomena. Meehl is one of the few theorists who has attempted to relate the behavioral characteristics of schizophrenia to current knowledge about possible neurophysiological deficits. He in effect has extended Bleuler's work on schizophrenia to formulate a combined neurological substate—environmental, learning theory of schizophrenia. Nevertheless, this fascinating attempt at theoretical synthesis is of little help with regard to either the prediction or explanation of the many specific behavioral patterns labelled schizophrenia. This is obviously not so much a criticism of the theory as it is indicative of its limited scope. The author would take issue with Meehl's implicit assumption that the term schizophrenia refers to a unitary disorder which is always a result of the interaction of some genetic deficit and environmental stress. For example it seems equally plausible to speculate that many reactive schizophrenics need not be either schizotaxic or polygenetically disadvantaged but rather have developed temporary psychotic behaviors as a result of current stress and having experienced a decidedly schizophrenogenic childhood, perhaps similar to that described by Bateson, et al. In other words it seems equally plausible that genetically sound individuals may become psychotic.

Biochemical researchers for the most part seem also to view schizophrenia as a unitary disorder; essentially biological in nature and caused by some single-gene-single-enzyme deficit. Kety has effectively indicated the many difficulties and complexities of research in this area as well as the limited sample of chronic, institutionalized schizophrenics upon which these studies have been based. Kety's conclusion that schizophrenia results from a polygenic inadequacy interacting with particular life situations closely parallels Meehl's speculation.

Cameron, Bateson et al., and Fleck set forth explanations of the origins and functions of specific subtypes of schizophrenic behavior based on psychological principles. Cameron depicts the functional nature of paranoid delusions as externalizations of previously supressed, unacceptable impulses. The initial susceptibility to anxiety and consequent regression from social reality may be due to some polygenetically determined weakness as postulated by Kety and Meehl; nevertheless such theories in and of themselves do not explain the origin and function of paranoid delusions. Here Cameron's speculations supplement, rather than contradict, and explain delusions as attempts to reconstruct a threatening reality through the mechanism of projecting unacceptable drives. Bateson et al, provide a fascinating account of a family communication pattern that may result in the disturbed communication patterns typical of many schizophrenics.

Fleck's article represents a much more cautious approach to the investigation of the relationship between patterns of family interaction and behavior disorders than the attempts to define the characteristics of the "schizophrenogenic" mother which occurred during the 1950's. His conclusion that no specific interaction pattern of family problems results in a specific disorder is indicative of the fact that many variables must interact in a complex and unspecified fashion in order to result in schizophrenic behavior. Again Fleck's emphasis upon the need to view schizophrenia in the context of the entire bio-psycho-social complex is consistent with the trend away from unifactor theories of schizophrenia. Fleck presents a sophisticated discussion of an approach which focuses upon deficiencies and deviations from family functions and suggests that such an approach may lead to possible refinement revision and reclassification of schizophrenic disorders.

Herron has reviewed research on the process-reactive dimension of schizophrenia. This category represents an attempt to refine our classificatory system by postulating a continuum of schizophrenia which is related to prognosis, life history, and social adjustment variables. Postulation of a process-reactive dimension has generated considerable research which has enabled us to improve our classificatory system. However, the implicit dichotomous nature of this dimension limits its predictive efficacy to those individuals at either extreme and seems not to discriminate between the majority of schizophrenic individuals falling somewhere between. It seems likely that the process-reactive dimension will remain as one of several, along with paranoid-nonparanoid and acute-chronic, which enable us to classify and explain schizophrenic behavior more effectively.

In summary the articles included in this section reflect the great variety of behavior currently labeled schizophrenic. It seems quite likely that this category will eventually be refined into a number of reliable subtypes which will enable us to pinpoint causal factors effectively and to develop rehabilitative techniques tailored to the causes of the specific disorder.

Section 8: PSYCHOPHARMACOLOGY

There are three main categories of drugs which act directly upon psychological processes: the tranquilizers or ataractic drugs, the psychological activators, and the hallucinogens or psychotomimetic drugs. The article which follows summarizes current knowledge as to the effects of the first two categories of drugs. Evidence as to the effectiveness of hallucinogenic drugs as therapeutic agents is as yet inconclusive.

20

THE PSYCHOTROPIC DRUGS: THEIR ACTIONS AND APPLICATIONS

Heinz E. Lehmann

When chlorpromazine and reserpine ushered in the psychopharmacology era in 1952, one of the first effects noticed with these compounds was sedation or tranquilization. The term "tranquilizer" quickly took hold and resisted attempts to substitute such names as ataractic. The World Health Organization is now in the process of establishing uniform and scientifically accurate terminology for the several classes of drugs now used in the treatment of mental illness.

The tranquilizers are now divided into major and minor groupings. The major tranquilizers are more properly called antipsychotics, because of their function, or neuroleptics, because all agents in this class have additional effects on the nervous system. Chlorpromazine and thioridazine are two examples of the major tranquilizers.

The minor tranquilizers, with their antianxiety properties, are used in the treatment of neuroses in general and are the only true tranquilizers. In this classification are meprobamate, chlordiazepoxide, the barbiturates, and alcohol.

Antidepressants are divided into two classes on the basis of physiologic action rather than clinical effect. They are the monamine oxidase (M A O) inhibitors and the non-M A O inhibitors. The latter are usually called tricyclics, because their chemical ring structure resembles that of the phenothiazines. Tranylcypromine is one of the M A O inhibitors; imipramine and amitriptyline are typical of the tricyclic compounds.

The hallucinogens, or "psychedelic" agents, have interesting possibilities in psychiatry, but since their use at present is limited to experimental applications they will not be covered in this article.

Reprinted from *Hospital Practice*, 2 (3), 1967, 74–80, with the permission of the publisher and Dr. Lehmann.

Stimulants, the amphetamines and methylphenidate, have only limited clinical application.

MAJOR TRANQUILIZERS

A discussion of the major tranquilizers is essentially a discussion of the phenothiazines, even though some other compounds are in use and new agents are being tested. To all intents and purposes the phenothiazines are all equally effective. It required large-scale collaborative studies, sponsored by the National Institute of Mental Health and the Veterans Administration and involving large numbers of patients, to turn up any differences among the various phenothiazine compounds. Even then, computers had to tease out the slight variations.

The chlorpromazine type of phenothiazine produces a lower incidence of extrapyramidal symptoms but a higher one of side effects related to the autonomic nervous system. In large doses these compounds produce sedation. Phenothiazines with a piperazine side chain cause fewer autonomic symptoms but more extrapyramidal reactions. These drugs have a slight stimulant effect and are active in much smaller doses than chlorpromazine. On the whole, all phenothiazines have extremely low toxicity. This is demonstrated by the fact that we can give certain patients 50 mg and other patients up to 5,000 mg a day. This provides a tremendously safe margin of therapeutic activity over toxicity.

A combination of effects is selected for each patient, with consideration of side effects the most important factor in making the choice of drug or drugs. These side effects are not necessarily all adverse reactions. Sometimes, as in the case of mild sedation or stimulation, they may well be fringe benefits. With toxicity so low, the fact that one drug is more active at lower dosage than another is of little consequence except in intramuscular administration, where the amount injected should be minimized to avoid irritation.

Reserpine and other rauwolfia compounds are now infrequently used in the treatment of mental illness and are of primarily historical interest in this context. Producing their effects by depleting the biogenic amines serotonin and norepinephrine, they are "hit-and-run" drugs: The biogenic amines remain depleted long after rauwolfia compounds disappear from the body, and the individual who has to cope with stresses such as unanticipated surgery is at a disadvantage.

The effects of phenothiazines are much more easily reversible and their mechanisms of action are quite different. These agents interfere with membrane permeability. By "thickening" the walls of neurons, they seem to block the access of norepinephrine and serotonin—probably excitory transmitting substances— to target neurons.

A new class of compounds, the butyrophenones, has been used for the treatment of mental illness in Europe for some time but has only recently been tested in North America. These compounds, of which haloperidol is one example, are about as effective as the phenothiazines.

Guidelines for therapy

If the drug is effective, the first response in the psychotic patient—within
the first week or two—should be at the arousal level. After two weeks at most,
even the most disturbed patient should be reasonably quiet and sleeping well. If
excitement is unabated, dosage should be increased.

After two to four weeks, the affect level—anxiety, depression, withdrawal,
suspicion—should improve. The patient should be cooperative, less suspicious,
and less withdrawn. As a matter of fact, he may be so improved that his family
and the nursing staff often think he is completely well. The psychiatrist, however, often finds that hallucinations, delusions, and thought disorders are still
present—symptoms referrable to the integration or organization level.

The integration level involves cognitive and perceptual functions. Symptoms at this level often persist for eight to 10 weeks, even under therapy. If
there is no improvement at this time, we increase the dosage again. In addition
to changing dosage, we might substitute a different phenothiazine when the
patient is not responding to the original medication. We generally wait at
least six months before deciding that a patient is treatment-resistant. Drugs are
least effective in the patient who is apathetic and has low drive.

In contrast to the unusual situation in which doctors are sometimes accused
of using medications too freely, the most frequent mistake in the use of phenothiazines is not giving large enough dosages for long enough periods of time.

Many patients will need maintenance therapy after they leave the hospital,
but trial and error is the only way to determine who they are. All patients
should be seen at least once a month after discharge; they are kept on medication for three to six months, when they are tentatively taken off. If the patient
breaks down again, we try to get him over the attack with just medication and
without hospitalization. He is then returned to maintenance therapy for a year
or two, when we again try to take him off. If he then has another attack we
place him on long-term, possibly even permanent, maintenance therapy. The
maintenance doses are much smaller—about a quarter or half that used in treatment of acute attacks.

Side Effects

Extrapyramidal symptoms can be controlled by the use of antiparkinsonism
drugs, but these agents have their own limitations and they cannot always be

used extensively. The extrapyramidal symptoms are usually reversible but can persist, particularly in older patients, in whom persistent choreiform movements are sometimes seen. This is not pleasant, but it is an acceptable price to pay for sanity. It is not hard to choose between having an occasional individual afflicted with uncontrollable chewing movements and a return to the bedlam that prevailed in the violent wards of mental institutions in the pre-psychopharmacologic era.

Chlorpromazine sometimes causes a photosensitivity reaction after long-term use, affecting the eyes and light-exposed areas of the skin. The drug may combine with melanin in the dermis, producing a blue or mauve coloration of the skin. This reaction can be avoided by switching to one of the other phenothiazines, but it is sometimes necessary to stay with chlorpromazine because the patient does not respond to the other drugs. As copper is necessary for the production of melanin, penicillamine, a copper chelating agent, has been used recently to avoid this skin discoloration, which is usually seen only in the patient who has been taking 500 mg of chlorpromazine a day for at least six months.

Probably the same mechanism that affects the skin, chlorpromazine produces opacities in the lens and cornea which are detectable only by slit-lamp examination. This effect has not been seen with any of the other phenothiazines. These opacities look like cataracts, but visual acuity is not affected and they are in no way disabling. For all practical purposes they are not significant and, again, must certainly be regarded as an acceptable price to pay for sanity.

In the early days of chlorpromazine use, the incidence of jaundice was about one to three percent. In the last five or six years this incidence has decreased very markedly. I have not seen a case of phenothiazine-associated jaundice in the past year. (We were among the first to report this complication, and we are alert to the possibility of its presence.) The manufacturers tell us that there have been no changes in the method of making chlorpromazine or in the excipients put in the tablet. We can only hypothesize, therefore, that an unsuspected epidemic of hepatitis coincided with the early administration of the drug.

MINOR TRANQUILIZERS

Although we have to settle for compensatory therapy in schizophrenia, this is not so with the neuroses. A true antianxiety drug—an agent which has only that effect and no other—does not exist, but the minor tranquilizers are useful as adjuncts and for first-aid therapy in the treatment of neuroses.

These drugs—barbiturates, meprobamate, chlordiazepoxide—act as sedatives in small dosages and as hypnotics when larger amounts are given. The three types of agents differ little in effectiveness for short-term therapy. Meprobamate and chlordiazepoxide are more effective for long-term use. For about the first two weeks of administration, barbiturates are comparable to mepro-bamate and chlordiazepoxide. But after three weeks the latter two are more effective than barbiturates, and at about the fourth week of administration chlordiazepoxide probably has some advantages over meprobamate.

The minor tranquilizers have no significant side effects, and this is perhaps their greatest disadvantage. Any drug that reduces stress without producing unpleasant effects—that gives benefit without exacting payment—is apt to cause dependency. Patients taking these drugs are neurotics or under stress, often both, and are thus more prone to dependency to begin with. The longer the patient is on the antianxiety drugs, the more dependency is produced and con-sequently the more the ability to withstand stress is reduced.

Tolerance to the minor tranquilizers develops relatively rapidly, and an increase in dosage becomes necessary to attain the same effects. Such tolerance is, of course, typical of dependency-producing drugs. There is cross-tolerance among the minor tranquilizers, and here alcohol is included, but none between the minor and major tranquilizers.

I have suggested to several manufacturers that unpleasant but minor side effects, such as dry mouth or flushing of the skin, be built into the minor tranquilizers to discourage the development of dependency. Understandably, this suggestion has generated little enthusiasm, and the problem of dependency will still have to be handled by the clinician.

First of all, the first-aid or adjunctive nature of the minor tranquilizers should be kept in mind from the beginning of therapy. If it is necessary to keep the patient on drugs for any length of time, a different minor tranquilizer should be prescribed every few weeks. After about four to eight weeks the patient should be put on a major tranquilizer—not quite as effective as an antianxiety agent, but free of the addiction liability. Making the change is not easy, for the neurotic will often over-react to side effects. The physician will have to see the patient more often to help him over this hurdle. Most patients, how-ever, eventually will develop a tolerance to the side effects that occur with the major tranquilizers.

Drug dependency is always an unhappy alternative, but there is the occa-sional patient who cannot be managed by other means and for whom intensive psychotherapy either has not worked or is not practicable. For this individual, who cannot otherwise function in society, the physician will probably have to prescribe a prolonged course of maintenance therapy with the minor tranquilizers.

ANTIDEPRESSANTS

Terminology and classification for depression are in a state of flux, with the classic descriptions of manic-depressive disorder, involutional melancholia, and reactive depression giving way to endogenous and reactive depressions, or anxious, hostile, or retarded depressions, and to clusters of symptoms designated by simple letters. The important thing to keep in mind is that three major symptom clusters are interwoven in most depressed states—depressive mood, anxiety, and inhibition—and no drug is likely to ameliorate all three simultaneously. The choice of drugs will have to be made on the basis of the physician's evaluation of the presenting symptoms in each patient.

Hospitalization alone may produce a marked improvement in many depressed patients. Whether it is due to removal from the environmental stresses that precipitated the depression, the "shock" of hospitalization, or some other cause, spontaneous recovery or significant and sustained improvement occurs within a month in 20 to 25 percent of unselected depressed patients. Placebos raise the rate of improvement to 50 percent for the hospitalized depressed patient. Antidepressant drugs increase the improvement rate to about 75 percent. Electroconvulsive therapy (E C T) will produce reliable and immediate improvement in approximately 90 percent of these patients.

Where immediate results are the most important consideration, as in the suicidal patient, there is no substitute for E C T, which is both the most effective and rapid treatment for depression. This method of therapy, though, is much more difficult to administer than drugs, causes a particularly unpleasant side effect—impairment of memory—and does not lend itself well to maintenance therapy. Wherever possible, therefore, endeavor to use pharmacotherapy in treating depression.

The tricyclics are probably more effective in the treatment of retarded and severe endogenous depressions and in manic-depressive states; the M A O inhibitors may be preferable in the treatment of hysterical and atypical depressions. The different M A O inhibitors and tricyclics vary in effectiveness, but the tricyclics vary less than the M A O inhibitors.

One problem with antidepressant therapy is the time lag: It takes at least a week for these drugs to show any effect. For this reason, some clinicians prefer tranylcypromine, which has a biphasic action. The drug first produces an immediate amphetamine-like effect and then, in about two or three weeks, the standard antidepressant effect. This dual action, however, may accentuate the difficulties encountered by the patient on M A O inhibitors when he ingests tyramine-containing foods, such as certain cheeses.

Objective improvement in behavior occurs first in the patient taking antidepressants. Subjective improvement takes considerably longer. The patient may still be grumbling about his symptoms long after he has improved to the point where he can function in society and has returned to work. If there is no improvement after two to three weeks, a different type of anti-depressant should be used or the patient given E C T.

The M A O inhibitors increase the supply of biogenic amines in the brain and at the target neurons. The norepinephrine-serotonin ratio is probably related somehow to depression, and this ratio is affected by the M A O inhibitors. The tricyclics do not affect the biogenic amines directly, but by decreasing the membrane permeability of the cell from which the biogenic amines were excreted they prevent the reabsorption of excessive, unused amines and their breakdown by M A O within the cell.

Side Effects

Side effects are much more difficult to handle with the M A O inhibitors; the biogenic amines are affected for at least a week, even with one dose. The "cheese" effect—a tyramine-induced pressor reaction—can persist long after the patient has stopped taking M A O inhibitors. Demerol, epinephrine, thyroid, and many other drugs are incompatible with M A O inhibitors and can produce severe reactions in patients on this type of antidepressant medication. Risky in the irresponsible patient, the M A O inhibitors are best suited for the intelligent patient who checks with his physician before taking so much as an aspirin tablet.

The side effects produced by the tricyclics are more unpleasant than dangerous. They are autonomic in nature and include hypotension. Some caution is needed in older patients with heart disease. The tricyclics dangerously potentiate the anticholinergic effects of antiparkinsonism drugs and should not be used with these agents, but they can be used with the phenothiazines.

Once the tricyclics are out of the system—in two or three days after the last dose—there are no after effects, and a patient could then be switched to M A O inhibitors. But a considerable length of time—at least one, preferably two, weeks—should elapse before a patient who has been taking M A O inhibitors is started on a tricyclic. In certain cases, administering both types of agents together has advantages, but this somewhat risky procedure should be used only if the clinician is absolutely sure he knows what he is doing. Indeed, as a defense against a possible malpractice suit, his records should show that he was aware of and had considered the risk of such combined therapy.

STIMULANTS

There is no such thing as a true "mood lifter." The stimulants are usually tested in normal people, in whom a mild euphoria is produced. In neurotics, however, the effect is often the opposite, and further depression and anxiety are induced. In limited dosages, and under close supervision, amphetamines and methylphenidate have some useful applications. Tolerance to the drugs develops rapidly, however, and the patient needs larger doses, which can be dangerous.

On a short-term basis, the stimulants are useful in the treatment of the kind of depression that often sets in after illnesses such as the flu or mononucleosis and in "housewife's fatigue." In these applications, the amphetamine is best combined with a barbiturate such as amobarbital sodium, which in small dosages has a slight stimulating—or "disinhibiting"—effect of its own. For very limited application, I have observed that amphetamines are practically specific for the treatment of depression following an unhappy love affair. If nothing else, they help the forlorn maiden feel better while nature takes its course.

DISCUSSION

As Lehmann indicates, drugs are frequently a very useful adjunct to psychological approaches in the modification of abnormal behavior. Psychotropic drugs are powerful agents by which we are able to moderate extremes of emotionality and the motor activity level of disturbed individuals. Such effects are of unquestionable therapeutic value, particularly in cases of severe disturbance. Nevertheless, such agents do not alter disturbed patterns of behavior or thought, nor do they compensate for deviant childhood experiences which often lead to such disturbances. Thus, chemotherapy for most individuals must remain an adjunct to psychological intervention.

Behavior Modification and Psychotherapy

Section 9:   **THE MODIFICATION OF THE BEHAVIOR OF INDIVIDUALS**

There are a number of systematic approaches to the modification of abnormal behavior. These approaches can be grouped into two general categories, based on their orientation toward symptoms: behavior therapies and insight or intrapsychic therapies. Behavior therapists emphasize the direct elimination of abnormal behavior and do not concern themselves with underlying causal factors. Abnormal behaviors are viewed as the result of unfortunate conditioning, and are to be modified through the application of learning principles.

Insight therapists on the other hand, are united by the assumption that abnormal behavior is caused by underlying motivational-emotional problems, and that permanent changes in such behaviors must follow reduction of the emotional conflicts producing them. Thus, insight therapy entails facilitating the understanding of underlying motives thereby reducing motivational conflict and resulting in more satisfying patterns of living. To the insight therapists then, abnormal behavior is merely symptomatic of underlying intrapsychic problems, and whatever changes occur in specific behaviors are considered transitory unless such changes result from the alteration of underlying motives. The articles which follow include descriptions and comparisons of the theories and techniques of insight and behavior therapy.

21

FREUDIAN PSYCHOANALYSIS

Lewis R. Wolberg

Reconstructive psychotherapy owes a debt of monumental proportions to Sigmund Freud who introduced the substructure upon which present dynamic psychiatry is based. While many of his original theoretic assumptions have undergone modification, the clinical observations of Freud remain as fundamental foundations for the scientific method in psychiatry.

In 1880, Joseph Breuer discovered that when a hysterical girl under hypnosis was induced to speak freely, she expressed profound emotion and experienced relief from her symptoms. Under the impression that her hysteria originated in certain painful experiences while caring for her sick father, Breuer enjoined her, while she was in an hypnotic state, to remember and to relive the traumatic scenes. This seemed to produce a cure in her hysteria.

Ten years later, in conjunction with Freud, Breuer continued his research, and, in 1895, the two men published their observations in a book, *Studien Uber Hysteria* [1]. Their conclusions were that hysterical symptoms developed as a result of experiences so traumatic to the individual that they were repressed. The mental energy associated with the experiences was blocked off and, not being able to reach consciousness, was converted into bodily innervations. The discharge of strangulated emotions (abreaction), through its normal channels during hypnosis, would relieve the necessity of diverting the energy into symptoms. This method was termed "catharsis."

Freud soon found that equally good therapeutic results could be obtained without hypnosis by permitting the patient to talk freely, expressing whatever ideas came to his mind. Freud invented the term "psychoanalysis" for the process

Reprinted from the *Technique of Psychotherapy,* 1954, pp. 54–63, with the permission of Grune & Stratton, Inc. and Dr. Wolberg. (References have been renumbered.)

of uncovering and permitting the verbal expression of hidden traumatic experiences. Freud found that there were forces that kept memories from invading consciousness, and he discovered that it was necessary to neutralize the repressing forces before recall was possible. An effective way to overcome resistances was to permit the patient to relax and to talk freely about any idea or fantasy that entered his mind no matter how trivial or absurd. Freud could observe in this "free association" a sequential theme that gave clues to the nature of the repressed material.

Mainly through an introspective analysis of his own dreams [2] Freud was able to show how dreams were expressions of unconscious wishes and fears, evading the barriers of repression through the assumption of symbolic disguises. He perfected a technique of arriving at the meaning of the unconscious material through translation of symbols.

Freud also observed that when the patient was encouraged to say whatever came to his mind, he verbalized irrational attitudes toward the therapist, such as deep love, fear, hate, overvaluation, expectancy, disappointment and other strivings that were not justified by the reality situation. He noted too that the patient identified the therapist with significant personages in his past, particularly with his parents, and that this identification motivated the transfer over to the therapist of attitudes similar to those he originally had toward his parents. This phenomenon Freud called "transference." For example, a patient with a phobia of being subject to imminent, but indefinable injury might, at a certain phase in his analysis, begin to develop an aversion and dread of the analyst, expressed in fears of being mutilated. At the same time, incestuous wishes for the mother might appear in dreams. Analysis of the relationship with the analyst (transference) would then possibly reveal an identification of the analyst with the patient's father. It would then become apparent that the patient secretly feared injury by the father for his forbidden wish to possess the mother, and that his phobia was an expression of this fear of mutilation which had been dissociated from awareness by repression. The bringing of the patient's attention to the sources of his fear, and his realization of its irrational nature, would result in an amelioration or cure of his neurosis.

The material uncovered by Freud from his studies of free association, dream interpretation and analysis of the transference, suggested to him that there was a dynamic portion of the psyche, closely associated with the emotional disorder, that did not follow the normal laws of mental functioning. Freud called this aspect of the mind the "unconscious," and he set about to determine the unique laws which dominated the repressed psychic component. In studying the symbols issuing from the unconscious, Freud noted that they were concerned chiefly with sexual material, and he concluded from this that the unconscious was preoccupied for the most part with sexual wishes and fears. Consequently, he assumed that the most important traumatic events which had been repressed were sexual in nature. It was largely on this evidence that he evolved his "theory of instincts" or the "libido theory."

In his theory of instincts, Freud postulated the fact that all energy had its origin in instincts which persistently expressed themselves (repetition compulsion) and were represented mentally as ideas with an emotional charge (cathexis). A fundamental instinct was that of *eros,* the sexual or life instinct, manifesting itself in a force called "libido." Freud hypothesized a permeation of the body by this vital instinctual force, the "libido," which powered the individual's development toward mature sexuality. Libido was, however, subject to many developmental vicissitudes in its destined course to adult genitality. During the first year of life, it concentrated itself around the oral zone, the mouth and lips, the child gaining a kind of erotic pleasure by sucking and later by biting. At the end of the first year, there was a partial shift in libido to the anal zone, and intense pleasures were derived from the retention and expulsion of feces. During this period, the child's interests were more or less concentrated on himself (narcissism), and satisfactions were primarily localized within his own body (autoerotism). Relationships with people were primitive, being circumscribed to only part of the parent (part-object relationships), like the nipple or breast instead of the entire parent.

Around the age of three, libido was centered around the phallic zone—the penis or clitoris. "Object relationships" were less primitive and were extended to a more complete relatedness with the parent. Yet, fundamentally, the child was ambivalent, responding to his parents and other people with a mixture of love and hate.

This stage of psychosexual growth continued into the Oedipal period, during which the little boy developed toward his mother a profound interest, with strong sexual overtones and desires for exclusive ownership. The little girl, envying men for their possession of a penis, created in part by a desire to repudiate her femininity and to become a male (penis envy), and resenting the fact that she had no penis, accused the mother of responsibility for this deprivation and turned to the father with an intensified sexual interest. In the case of the boy, hostility toward the father, due to a desire to eliminate him as a rival, generated a fear of counter-hostility, and particularly a fear of castration, which inspired such anxiety as to induce him to give up his interest in the mother and to make friends with his father. The intensity of fear became so overwhelming and so unendurable that the boy was forced to yield to his more powerful competitor by renouncing, repudiating and repressing sexual feelings toward the maternal love-object. He was obliged also to repress concomitant hostile impulses toward the father. The little girl similarly resolved her enmity toward her mother, as well as her sexual interest in her father. This drama, known as the Oedipus complex, was to Freud the crucial nuclear conflict in the development of the personality contributing to both character formation and neurotic symptoms.

The incorporation of parental injunctions and prohibitions, and the repudiation of sexual and hostile aims as related to the parents, resulted in the crystallization of an aspect of the psyche which took over the judging, prohibiting and punitive functions hitherto vested in the parents. This aspect became the conscience or super-ego. The adequate resolution of the Oedipus complex was associated with channelization of libido into the genital zone, with capacities for complete, mature, unambivalent, "whole-object" relationships.

Following upon the Oedipal period, there was an era characterized by the neutralization of sexual impulses. This Freud called the "latency period." With the advent of puberty, however, increased libido, due to the heightened activity of the genital glands, reactivated the old Oedipal interests. The person then lived through the revived early Oedipal conflict, and his capacity to solve this anew was determined by the extent of previous vicissitudes and the adequacy with which his conflict had formerly been resolved. In "normal" solutions, the child transferred his or her sexual interest to extra-familial persons of the opposite sex. The little girl renounced her boyish interests and accepted a passive female role.

Under certain conditions, normal psychosexual development was impeded by a "fixation" of libido onto oral, anal and phallic zones. The libido, bound down in this way, was unable to participate in the development of full genitality. Freud believed that both constitutional and experiential factors were responsible for this. Most prominent were excessive gratifications or inordinate frustrations experienced at an early stage of growth. Not only did libidinal fixations interfere with the development of mature sexuality, but they constituted stations to which the individual might return when confronted with overwhelming stress or frustration. Under these circumstances, the libidinal stream was said to undergo "regression" to pregenital fixation points. When this happened, there were revived attitudes and interests characteristic of childhood, with immature sexual strivings, interest in "part-objects" and narcissism. Infantile conflicts and patterns were also revivified in this process. Sexual perversions constituted the positive expression of pregenital libidinal fixations, while neurotic symptoms were a negative or converted expression [3].

Freud conceived of the mental apparatus as an organ that prevented the damming up of energy. Pain was related to an increase of energy, and pleasure to a decrease. In order to help understand the operations of the mental apparatus, Freud elaborated a topographic structure of the psyche, as involving a reservoir of instinctual energy, the *id;* a supervisory area serving a censoring and sanctioning function, the *super-ego;* and a structure that mediated internal and external adjustments, the *ego.* These subdivisions, although recognized by Freud as arbitrary, empiric and metapsychologic, were retained by him as a conceptual necessity [4].

Freud classified the id as the original undifferentiated mind, the repository of inherited urges and instinctual energy. It contained the instincts of Eros— the life or sexual instinct, and Thanatos—the death instinct. It provided the individual with dynamic energy (libido), which vitalized every organ and tissue and sought expression in response to a "pleasure principle," along whatever channels were available for it. Through impressions received by the perceptual organs, the id underwent modifications immediately after birth. Differentiation by the child of himself as an entity apart from the world was in keeping with the evolution of the ego, which increasingly assumed the function of an executive organ, harnessing the id to the demands of reality (reality principle). Important impressions, particularly those related to experiences with parents or their surrogates, and frustrations created by prohibitions of pleasure strivings, registered themselves on the child's psyche and stimulated primitive mechanisms of projection and introjection. In projection, aggression was discharged outward and directed toward parents; in introjection, the frustrating parental agencies were "incorporated" within the child's psychic apparatus. Through these mechanisms, rudiments of a super-ego developed which later, with the resolution of the Oedipus complex, crystallized and took over the guiding and prohibitive functions of the parents. One aspect of the super-ego contained constructive ideals toward which the individual felt driven (ego ideal).

Under the lash of the super-ego, the ego created repressions against libidinal strivings and their ideational representatives. Such repressions served to avoid conflict. When, however, for any reason, repression relaxed or proved insufficient, the ego was invaded with some of the content of the repressed. This threat to the individual's security inspired anxiety, a danger signal that indicated a breakthrough of the repressed material.

As Freud continued his work, he laid less and less stress on strangulated emotions due to early traumatic experiences as the primary cause of neurosis. More and more he became cognizant of the purposeful nature of symptoms, and, in 1926, he revised his theory of neurosis drastically, claiming that symptoms were not only manifestations of repressed instinctive strivings, but also represented defenses against these strivings [5].

Freud contended, however, that the essence of a neurosis was a repression of infantile fears and experiences which continually forced the individual to act in the present as if he were living in the past. The neurotic seemed to be dominated by past anxieties that, split off, operated autonomously and served no further function in reality.

Internal dangers were constantly threatened by the efforts of the id to discharge accumulated tension. Such discharge was opposed by the mental force of the super-ego in the form of repression to prevent the release of tension. Repression was a dynamic force which attempted to seal off internal dangers. However, the maintenance of repression required an enormous expenditure of energy. The ego derived this energy from the id in a subversive manner. Thus, an idea or tendency invested with libido (cathexis) would be stripped of libido and this energy used to oppose the idea or tendency (anti-cathexis).

Subtle mechanisms such as symbolization, condensation, distortion and displacement were employed to evade repressive forces and to provide a substitutive discharge of repressed energy, and a consequent relief of tension. Fantasies, dreams and symptoms were expressions of such mechanisms. Where the substitutive expression was in harmony with social values and super-ego ideals, it provided a suitable means of relief (sublimation). Where it was not in harmony, conflict resulted and repressive mechanisms were again invoked. If repression proved ineffective in mediating tension, a regression to earlier modes of adaptation was possible. This happened particularly where the individual was confronted by experiences similar to, or representative of, those which initiated anxiety in childhood. The ego reacted automatically to these experiences, as if the reality conditionings of later years had had no corrective effect on the original danger situation. It responded with essentially the same defenses of childhood, even though these were now inappropriate.

A retention of a relationship to reality, at the expense of an intrapsychic balance, produced a psychoneurotic disturbance. The existing conflict here was between the ego and the id. If an intrapsychic balance developed at the expense of reality relationships, the consequence was psychosis. The latter resulted when the ego was overwhelmed by id forces, the conflict being between the ego and the environment.

In addition to the libido theory described above, Freud elaborated the theory of the death instinct to account for phenomena not explicable in terms of libido. He postulated that an instinct existed in the id which prompted aggressive and destructive drives. This instinct manifested itself in a "repetition compulsion" to undo the forward evolutionary development of the organism, and to return it to its primordial inorganic state. The death instinct, though sometimes libidinized (sadism) was totally different from the sexual instinct.

Freudian psychoanalytic therapy is based on the libido theory described above. It rests on the hypothesis that neurotic illness is nurtured by the repression of vital aspects of the self and its experiences; particularly oral, anal and sexual (including Oedipal) experiences in relation to important parental agencies. This repression is sponsored by fear of the loss of love or of punishment from the parents, which has been internalized in the super-ego. Repressed feelings, attitudes and fears, and the early experiences associated with them, continue to strive for conscious recognition, but are kept from awareness by dread of repetition of parental loss of love or punishment now invested in the super-ego. The removal from the mainstream of consciousness makes it impossible for the individual to come to grips with basic conflicts. These remain in their pristine state, uncorrected by reality and by later experiences. The energy required to maintain repression, as well as to sustain other defenses against anxiety, robs the individual of energy that could be utilized to nurture psychosexual development.

Therapy, of necessity, consists of restoring to consciousness that which was removed by repression, and which has been draining off energies needed to foster personality growth. In therapy, the relationship with the therapist helps strengthen the ego to a point where it can eventually cope with anxiety, mobilized by the return of the repressed to awareness. It is essential that the patient recognize the derivatives of the repressed, since these represent, in an attenuated form, the warded-off material. To minimize the distortion of these derivatives, the obtrusion of current situations and other reality influences must be kept at a minimum. This is fostered by certain technical procedures, such as "free association," the assumption of the couch position, passivity of the therapist, encouragement of transference, the use of dreams, and the focusing of the interview away from reality considerations.

The basis of Freudian psychoanalysis lies in what is perhaps Freud's most vital discovery, that of transference. As has previously been indicated, Freud found that the patient, if not interfered with, inevitably projected into the therapeutic situation feelings and attitudes that were parcels of his past. Sometimes transference manifestations became so intense that the patient actually reproduced and reenacted with the therapist important conflictual situations and traumatic experiences (transference neurosis) which had been subject to infantile amnesia. By recovering and recognizing these repressed experiences and conflictual situations that had never been resolved, and by living them through with a new, less neurotic and non-punitive parental agency, the super-ego was believed to undergo modification. The individual became tolerant of his id, and more capable of altering ego defenses that had crippled his adaptation. There occurred, finally, a mastery of his early conflicts and a liberation of fixated libido which could then enter into the development of a mature personality.

Since the Oedipus complex is considered by Freud to be the nucleus of every neurosis, its analysis and resolution in transference constitutes a primary focus. Where the Oedipus complex is not revealed, where its pathologic manifestations are not thoroughly analyzed and worked through, and where forgotten memories of early childhood experiences are not restored, treatment is considered incomplete.

Because Freudian psychoanalysis *is* transference analysis, all means of facilitating transference are employed. These include the assumption by the therapist of an extremely passive role, the verbalization by the patient of a special kind of communication—"free association"—the analysis of dream material, the maintenance of an intense contact with the patient on the basis of no less than five visits weekly, and the employment of the recumbent couch position.

Passivity on the part of the therapist is judiciously maintained even through long periods of silence. The therapist also refrains from reacting emotionally, or responding positively or negatively to any verbalized or non-verbalized attitude or feeling expressed by the patient. Strict anonymity is observed, no personal information being supplied to the patient irrespective of how importunate he may become. A non-judgmental, non-punitive, non-condoning attitude by the therapist is adhered to, dogmatic utterances of any kind being forbidden.

The only "rule" the patient is asked to obey is the "basic rule" or "fundamental rule" of verbalizing whatever comes to his mind, however fleeting, repulsive or seemingly inconsequential it may seem (free association). This undirected kind of thinking is a most important means of tapping the unconscious, and of reviving unconscious conflicts and the memories that are related to their origin. Most importantly, free association, like passivity, enhances the evolution of transference. So long as the patient continues to associate freely, the therapist keeps silent, even though entire sessions may pass without a comment. The therapist fights off all temptations toward "small talk" or impulses to expound on theory. Only when resistances to free association develop does he interfere, and only until the patient proceeds with his verbalizations.

Dream analysis is utilized constantly as another means of penetrating the unconscious. By activating repressed material and working on defenses as they are revealed in dream structure, the therapist aids the development of transference.

The frequency of visits in Freudian psychoanalysis is important. To encourage transference, no fewer than five visits weekly are required. In some cases four visits may suffice. Fewer visits than this encourage "acting-out" and other resistances to transference.

The use of the recumbent couch position enables the patient to concentrate on the task of free association with as few encumbrances of reality as possible. It helps the therapist, also, to focus on the unconscious content underlying the patient's verbalizations without having to adjust himself to the demands such as would exist in a face-to-face position. Concentrating on his inner life rather than on external reality, helps to bring on the phenomenon of transference.

During the early stages of analysis, the main task is to observe—from his free associations and dreams—unconscious conflicts, and the types of defenses employed by the patient, which form a kind of blueprint of the unconscious problems of the patient. This blueprint is utilized later at the stage of transference. Since repression is threatened by the operation of exploring the unconscious, anxiety is apt to appear, stimulating defensive mechanisms. These function as resistances to productivity, and even to verbalization. Free association may consequently cease, and the patient may exhibit other manifestations that oppose cooperation with the treatment endeavor. Such resistances are dealt with by interpretation. Through interpretation the patient is brought to an awareness of how and why he is resisting, and the conflicts that make resistance necessary.

Sooner or later the patient will "transfer" past attitudes and feelings into the present relationship with the analyst. Observance of the "basic rule," the attack on his resistances through interpretation, and the consideration of unconscious material in dreams and free associations, remove habitual protective devices and façades that permit the patient to maintain a conventional relationship. Toward the therapist he is most apt to express strivings rooted in past experiences, perhaps even reproducing his past in the present. Thus, a revival of pathogenic past conflicts develops. Unlike supportive and reeducative therapy, in which transference may be utilized as a therapeutic vehicle, the transference is interpreted to the patient in order to expose its nature. This is the chief means of resolving resistance, of bringing the individual to an awareness of the warded off content, and of realizing the historical origin of his conflicts.

The development of transference may occur insidiously and manifest itself indirectly, or it may suddenly break out in stark form. It often shows itself in changes in the content of free associations, from inner feelings and past relationships with parents, to more innocuous topics, like current events and situations. This shift is evidence of resistance to deeper material activated by the erupting transference feelings. Sometimes free association may cease entirely, with long stubborn silences prevailing which are engendered by an inability to talk about feelings in relation to the therapist. The purpose of superficial talk or silence is to keep from awareness repressed emotions and forgotten memories associated with early childhood, particularly the Oedipus complex. Until these can be brought out into the open, the emotions relating to them discharged, and the associated memories revived, the conflictual base of neurosis will remain. The transference neurosis offers an opportunity for this revival, since, in the relationship with the therapist, the patient will "act-out" his loves, fears and hates, which were characteristic of his own experiences during the Oedipal period.

Transference, however, acts as a source of powerful resistances that impede therapeutic progress. Once the patient is in the grip of such resistances, he is usually determined to cling to them at the expense of any other motivation, including that of getting well. On the positive side, transference is important diagnostically, since it reveals a most accurate picture of the patient's inner conflicts. Additionally, it induces a coming to grips with and a working-through in a much more favorable setting of those unresolved conflicts that have blocked maturation. The resolution of transference is felt by Freudian psychoanalysts to be the most powerful vehicle known today for producing structural alterations in the personality.

Active interpretations of the transference are essential to its resolution. These include the interpretation of its manifestations, its origin, and its original and present purposes. The working-through of transference is accompanied by a recollection of forgotten infantile and childhood experiences—a recounting of distortions in relationships with parents or parental surrogates. Interpretations will usually be denied at first as part of the resistance manifestation. Acknowledgment of the unreal nature of transference is usually opposed by the patient, because this either constitutes too great a threat for him, or because he does not want to relinquish transference gratifications which are deemed essential to life itself. So long as he continues to accept transference as factual, the analysis will remain interminable, unless forcefully terminated by either participant. With persistence on the part of the therapist, interpretations usually take hold, and the patient is rewarded with greater insight, an increased sense of mastery, liberation from neurotic symptoms, and a genuine growth in maturity.

The therapist must also constantly guard against manifestations of counter-transference, which may be both disguised and varied, and which are mobilized by unresolved problems and pressing needs within the therapist himself. Common forms of counter-transference are subtle sadistic attacks on the patient, impulses to be pompous and omnipotent, or desires to reject the patient or to detach oneself from the relationship. Because of counter-transference, a personal analysis is considered essential for the analyst in order that he can deal with his own unconscious tendencies and resistances precipitated by his contact with his patients.

As the ego of the patient is strengthened by an alliance with the therapist, it becomes more and more capable of tolerating less and less distorted derivatives of unconscious conflict. The continued interpretation by the therapist of the patient's unconscious feelings and attitudes, as well as the defensive devices that he employs against them, enables the patient to work through his problems by seeing how they condition every aspect of his life. In the medium of the therapeutic relationship, the individual is helped to come to grips with early fears and misconceptions, resolving these by living them through in the transference. The patient is finally able to resolve libidinal fixations, and to liberate energy that should originally have gone into the formation of a mature sexual organization [6–27].

Disagreement with certain psychoanalytic concepts is legion. Even those analysts who consider themselves to be "orthodox" Freudians are not in complete accord with Freud in theory and method. For instance, there are many analysts who challenge the death instinct hypothesis. Insofar as technique is concerned, practically every analyst implements psychoanalytic methods in his own specific way. An extensive questionnaire distributed by Glover [28] to a representative group of practicing psychoanalysts demonstrated that deviations from orthodox techniques were extensive. There were differences in the form, timing, amount and depth of interpretation. The degree of adherence to free association varied, as did the assumption of passivity and anonymity, the use of reassurance, and the management of transference. Variation in methods of doing psychoanalysis was indicated by the fact that out of eighty-two questions, there was general agreement on only six, and even here there was not complete conformity.

Criticism of Freudian psychoanalysis is voiced both by those who have had no intimate contact with the psychoanalytic technique, as well as by well-trained psychoanalysts who have been thoroughly schooled in Freudian principles. . . . One commonly voiced criticism of the Freudian method is that some analysts insist upon wedging their patients into a preconceived theoretic structure. When the patient does not produce appropriate material that substantiates accepted notions of dynamics, or when he refuses to accept interpretations, he is credited as being in an obstinate state of resistance. Another criticism expressed by non-Freudians is that, in their eagerness to smuggle "deep" insights into patients, certain "orthodox" analysts make dogmatic interpretations which the patient feels obliged to accept. These may mobilize intense anxiety, which disorganizes patients with weak ego structures. A third criticism is that many Freudian analysts are intolerant toward those who practice any therapies other than Freudian psychoanalysis, considering these to be superficial and of little real value. Accordingly, they are inclined to depreciate the results of treatment by non-analysts, as well as by analysts of non-Freudian orientation.

Freudian psychoanalysis is taught extensively in this country, being sponsored by the American Psychoanalytic Association and by most of the current schools of psychoanalytic training.

REFERENCES

1. Breuer, J., and Freud, S.: *Studies in Hysteria.* Wash., D.C., Nerv. & Ment. Dis. Pub., 1936.
2. Freud, S.: "The Interpretation of Dreams," in *The Basic Writings of Sigmund Freud.* New York, Modern Library, 1938.
3. Freud, S.: "Three Contributions To the Theory of Sex," in *The Basic Writings of Sigmund Freud.* New York, Modern Library, 1938.
4. Freud, S.: *The Ego and the Id.* London, Hogarth, 1930.
5. Freud, S.: *The Problem of Anxiety.* New York, Norton, 1936.
6. Freud, S.: *A General Introduction to Psychoanalysis.* New York, Boni & Liveright, Inc., 1920.
7. Freud, S.: *New Introductory Lectures on Psychoanalysis.* New York, W. W. Norton & Co., 1933.
8. Freud, S.: "Papers on Technique," in *Collected Papers.* London, Hogarth Press, 1924, vol. II.
9. Freud, S.: Analysis terminable and interminable. *Internat. J. Psycho-analysis* 18:373–405, 1937.
10. Glover, E., Fenichel, O., Strachey, J., Bergler, E., Nunberg, H., and Bibring, E.: On the theory of therapeutic results of psychoanalysis. (Symposuim.) *Internat. J. Psycho-analysis* 18:125–189, 1937.
11. Lorand, S.: *Technique of Psychoanalytic Therapy.* New York, International Universities Press, 1946.
12. Sharpe, E. F.: The technique of psychoanalysis. *Internat. J. Psycho-analysis,* vol. II, part 3 and 4, 1930; vol. 12, 1931.

13. Sterba, R.: The dynamics of the dissolution of the transference resistance. *Psychiatric. Quart.*, vol. 9, 1940.

14. Stern, A.: On the counter-transference in psychoanalysis. *Psychoanalyt. Rev.* 9:166–174, 1924.

15. Berg, C.: *Psychotherapy—Practice and Theory.* New York, W. W. Norton & Co., 1948, pp. 349–457.

16. Glover, E.: Lectures on technique in psychoanalysis. *Internat. J. Psychoanalysis,* vols. 8, 9, 1927.

17. Jones, E.: The relation of technique to theory. *Internat. J. Psycho-analysis* 8:1–4, 1924.

18. La Forgue, R.: Exceptions to the fundamental rule of psychoanalysis. *Internat. J. Psycho-analysis,* vol. 18, 1937.

19. Schmideberg, M.: The mode of operation of psychoanalytic therapy. *Internat. J. Psycho-analysis,* vol. 19, 1938.

20. Searl, M. N.: Some queries on principles of technique. *Internat. J. Psycho-analysis,* vol. 17, 1936.

21. Zilboorg, G.: The fundamental conflict with psychoanalysis. *Internat. J. Psycho-analysis* 20:480–492, 1939.

22. Kubie, L.: *Practical and Theoretical Aspects of Psychoanalysis.* New York, International Universities Press, 1950.

23. Fenichel, O.: *Problems of Psychoanalytic Technique.* Albany, The Psychoanalytic Quarterly, Inc., 1941.

24. Strachey, J.: The nature of the therapeutic action of psychoanalysis. *Internat. J. Psycho-analysis* 15:127, 1934.

25. Balint, M.: The final goal of psychoanalytic treatment. *Internat. J. Psycho-analysis,* vol. 17, 1936.

26. Bibring-Lehner, G.: A contribution to the subject of transference resistance. *Internat. J. Psycho-analysis* 17:181–189, 1936.

27. Nunberg, H.: *Practice and Theory of Psychoanalysis.* Nerv. & Ment. Dis. Monog. No. 74, 1948.

28. Glover, E.: *An Investigation of the Technique of Psychoanalysis.* London, Baillière, Tindall and Cox, 1940.

22

IMPLOSIVE THERAPY

Thomas G. Stampfl and Donald J. Levis

A learning-theory-based method of psychotherapy (implosive therapy), which integrates psychodynamic concepts into its theoretical model and leads to a new technique of treatment, is described. The technique has been applied to a wide variety of psychopathology with apparent success. Treatment time ranges from 1 to 30 1-hr. sessions with marked changes in symptomatology usually occurring within 1–15 implosive sessions.

Behavioral or learning-theory approaches to psychotherapy may be divided into several distinct orientations. Differences among the various behavioral methods arrange themselves along both theoretical and applied lines of cleavage. For one group, the emphasis has been placed upon the establishment of empirically derived techniques, which are developed relatively independently of any specific theoretical system (e.g., Ayllon, 1963; Krasner, 1958; Lindsley, 1956; Skinner, 1956). For another group (Dollard & Miller, 1950; Rotter, 1954; Shoben, 1949), the orientation has been predominantly theoretical. For this group, the emphasis has been upon reinterpreting conventional therapeutic strategies and

Reprinted from the *Journal of Abnormal Psychology*, 72, 1967, 496–503, with the permission of the American Psychological Association, and the authors.

This paper is not intended as a complete presentation of the theoretical framework of implosive therapy. Unfortunately, the complexities of features involving both the learning model and certain subtleties associated with the therapeutic technique precluded a completely exhaustive treatment of these issues in the space limitations of this article.

The senior author especially wishes to express his great debt to George Golias, of Hawthornden State Hospital, and Robert Hogan, of Illinois State University, for their help in extending the technique used in the therapy in its early stages of development. The authors also would like to thank Richard Carrera, Cooper Clements, Herbert Caron, Frank Kobler, Perry London, J. McV. Hunt, O. H. Mowrer, Gerald Rosenbaum, John Scanlon, and E. Joseph Shoben, Jr. for their interest and encouragement.

goals from a learning-theory framework. Such fresh looks have generated a number of new hypotheses and concepts which illuminate the basic processes and principles essential for behavioral change. Still a third group is concerned not only with theoretical advances, but also with applying their learning-theory orientation directly to the development of new techniques and approaches (Salter, 1949; Wolpe, 1958; Yates, 1958). Although it is not the purpose of this paper to review the above orientations (for a detailed analysis see Bandura, 1961; Breger & McGaugh, 1965; Grossberg, 1964), such a review points to at least four distinct assets of learning-oriented approaches to the study of psychopathology: (a) It identifies psychotherapy with an objective, experimental discipline that provides a model susceptible to generating testable hypotheses; (b) it establishes a common language between the basic research and applied areas which should in turn enhance communication and the generation of new ideas; (c) it highlights the vast amounts of human and subhuman learning research which have frequently been overlooked by the clinician; (d) it provides a foundation for the development of new treatment techniques.

INTEGRATION OF LEARNING PRINCIPLES WITH PSYCHOPATHOLOGY

The thrust of learning-oriented therapies, for reasons not entirely clear, has been biased heavily toward nonpsychodynamic approaches to the problems of psychopathology. The writings of Salter, Wolpe, and advocates of the Skinnerian methods are almost completely antithetical to conventional psychodynamic approaches. The traditionally oriented practitioners may well be dismayed at the celerity and ease with which the standard dynamic approaches, born of decades of experience, are dispensed. Not fully appreciated and frequently overlooked by both the traditional and behavioral therapists, however, are the numerous analyses proposed by non-applied-learning theorists which are quite consistent with a more dynamic approach to treatment (Brown, 1961; Dollard & Miller, 1950; Holland & Skinner, 1961; Kimble, 1961; Mednick, 1958; Mowrer, 1953; Shoben, 1949). The main disadvantage associated with these analyses is that little effort was made to extend their treatment beyond the area of theory into the realm of practice (Bandura, 1961; Grossberg, 1964).

It is believed (and it is the main purpose of this paper to show) that a better integration between the principles and theory of learning, on the one hand, and traditional dynamic approaches to psychotherapy, on the other, can be effected. Implosive therapy (IT) is an approach which incorporates formulations inherent to dynamic systems of treatment retranslated and reapplied in terms of learning principles; dynamically oriented clinicians need not relinquish their fundamental conceptions of the human situation to use it. The IT technique not only provides a new theoretical orientation, but also alters and in some cases drastically modifies existing treatment procedures and suggests new lines of experimentation with animals. Utilization of principles derived from such research can be used advantageously in the development of new techniques for application to problems of human pathology.

LABORATORY EVIDENCE

Two-factor theory (Mowrer, 1960) states that an organism can be made to respond emotionally to an originally "neutral" stimulus by pairing the "neutral" stimulus with a noxious stimulus. A typical procedure is simply to pair a tone with electric shock. Subsequently, the organism responds to the tone with objectively verifiable changes in his physiological state, such as changes in blood sugar, heart rate, and skin resistance. Descriptively, this state can be labeled as fear or anxiety, and the stimulus which produces the physiological state can be construed to function as a danger signal or warning stimulus. The fear or anxiety state functions as a motivator of behavior, and the reduction or elimination of the fear state serves as a reinforcer of behavior. If the tone is conditioned to produce fear, then any action taken which terminates the tone will be strengthened automatically. A danger signal paired with another neutral stimulus will transfer some of its fear-eliciting properties to the new neutral stimulus (higher-order conditioning). It is important, however, to note that the stimulus preceding noxious stimulation whether applied to subhuman or human fear conditioning ordinarily involves multiple-stimulus patterns sequentially organized in time. Thus, in a sense it is misleading to say that a single discrete stimulus elicits the fear reaction. (For a further discussion and elaboration of the role of contextual and sequential cues, see Levis, 1966; Stampfl, 1960.)

Many studies conducted in the laboratory indicate that Ss can learn a wide variety of responses in order to terminate feared stimuli. In addition, fear states can be developed in the organism leading to behavior which is labeled as neurotic, psychosomatic, or even psychotic (e.g., Brady, Porter, Conrad, & Mason, 1958; Liddell, 1965; Masserman & Pechtel, 1953; Wolpe, 1958). It seems reasonable to assume that many if not all of the anxiety states experienced in the human are a product of numerous conditioning experiences in the life of the individual which can be understood in terms of the conditioning model of the laboratory. Past specific experiences of punishment and pain confer strong anxiety reactions to initially neutral stimuli. These experiences are represented neurally, and the neural engram (memory, image) may be considered as possessing the potential to function as a stimulus. The imagery, thoughts, or other stimuli correlated with the past experience of pain will be avoided, and whatever action or mechanism which prevents them from reoccurring will be learned and maintained on the basis of anxiety reduction. Ideational representation (level of awareness) of the dangerous associations need not be present to function as an elicitation of the anxiety state. Thus, a subliminal area of neural functioning is necessary to account for all of the phenomena associated with the defensive avoidance maneuvers of the individual. Any stimulus object or event in the external environment (e.g., a phobic object) or response-produced stimulation such as the impulse to act sexually or aggressively (or even the impulse to act morally) if associated on a stimulus continuum with the stimulus pattern originally paired with pain will tend to reactivate or redintegrate the anxiety-arousing associations or memories (originally neutral stimuli). The defensive maneuvers of the patient are then seen as a means of avoiding the dangerous associations. Such a viewpoint incorporates many dynamic notions such as placing repression and anxiety as central concepts in the explanation of psychopathology, and points in the direction psychotherapy might proceed.

The question which may then be raised is simply how best the therapist might proceed to divest the anxiety-eliciting stimuli of their potential. Fortunately, both laboratory methods of effective procedures of extinction and evidence which has accrued from the wealth of information available from psychodynamic practice, indicate clearly one way in which therapeutic practice might be developed.

EXPERIMENTAL EXTINCTION

One of the more reliable functions of laboratory research is the original principle of Pavlov that presentation of the conditioned stimulus (CS) without the unconditioned stimulus (UCS) will lead to the extinction of the learned response. An enormous amount of evidence is available which indicates that this principle is a valid one whether overt action or emotional states have been learned.

The knowledge that a CS followed by nonreinforcement leads to extinction of the emotional response has led various writers in the field of learning to describe models for psychotherapy which are based on this principle. Kimble (1961) said:

> The analysis of maladjustment in terms of conflict, anxiety, and repression points the direction in which therapy might proceed. Its method might be to bring traumatic events to consciousness so that the fear they evoke might extinguish [p. 476].

Holland and Skinner (1961) devoted considerable space to the adoption of the same principle to account for traditional methods of psychotherapy—the therapist constitutes a nonpunishing audience so that emotional responses evoked in the patient extinguish by nonreinforcement. Solomon and Wynne (1954, p. 381) pointed out that the transference relationship developed in dynamic therapy duplicates parts of the CS patterns associated with original traumatic experiences to which the emotional responses are attached and thereby leads to extinction. Miller (1951) stated that: "Experimental extinction is more effective when the animal is in the original punished situation that evokes the most intense fear [p. 453]." Since the procedures employed in IT depend very heavily on this principle, it is interesting to observe that Solomon, Kamin, and Wynne (1953) have based their conservation of anxiety hypothesis on exactly the same principle:

> . . . the best way to produce extinction of the emotional response would be to arrange the situation in such a way that an extremely intense emotional reaction takes place in the presence of the CS. This would be tantamount to a reinstatement of the original acquisition situation, and since the US is not presented a big decremental effect should occur [p. 299].

A number of experimental studies have corroborated this interpretation. Studies by Black (1958), Denny, Koons, and Mason (1959), Hunt, Jernberg, and Brady (1952), Knapp (1965), Weinberger (1965), and others indicated that extinction of a learned emotional response proceeds with greatest rapidity when the organism is exposed to stimulus conditions most closely approaching those which were originally associated with painful stimulation. A corollary to this principle is reflected in the experimental studies of Lowenfeld, Rubenfeld, and Guthrie (1956) and Wall and Guthrie (1959) which indicated that the more clearly an S perceives anxiety-eliciting stimuli when followed by non-reinforcement, the more rapid the extinction of the emotional response will be.

THERAPY

The fundamental hypothesis is that a sufficient condition for the extinction of anxiety is to re-present, reinstate, or symbolically reproduce the stimuli (cues) to which the anxiety response has been conditioned, in the absence of primary reinforcement. In a controlled laboratory situation where naive subhuman animals serve as Ss, the above objective presents little challenge to E. In the case of a human patient, however, the contingencies of the conditioning history usually are unknown. The therapist, in his attempt to restructure the conditioning paradigms, is forced to rely mainly upon verbal reports. Considerable time is needed in treatment before sufficient information is available for the reconstruction of the important contingencies. Moreover, the accuracy of the reconstruction is questionable. Thus, at first glance, it would appear that the task of using an extinction procedure is infeasible for a short-term therapeutic approach.

Nevertheless, despite the apparent difficulty of determining the conditioning paradigms, most trained therapists, after only a few diagnostic interviews, usually find themselves speculating upon the etiology of the patient's present pathology; that is, a "good guess" about the significant personal, environmental, and dynamic interactions shaping the patient's behavior often can be made within a relatively short time. In many cases, as therapy progresses, these hypotheses are supported by the verbal report of the patient. Although these initial hypotheses are conceived only as approximations of the original conditioning paradigm, it is quite conceivable that they incorporate a number of the more significant CS components. Unfortunately, these cues are not presented systematically by the therapist using conventional techniques until he believes the patient is ready to accept them in the form of an interpretation.

However, in the implosive procedure, the emphasis is not upon the acceptance of interpretations, but rather upon the extinction of anxiety-evoking conditioned stimuli (cues) which provide both motivational and reinforcing properties for perpetuating the patient's symptoms (avoidance responses). It would also follow from the learning model that it would be irrelevant whether or not the patient "understood" or "accepted" the significance of these cues. All that is necessary for effective treatment is to re-present these conditioned cues in the absence of primary reinforcement. Since the task of accurately establishing the original conditioning cues is difficult, the presentation of hypothesized cues serves as an excellent substitute. Complete accuracy is not essential since some effect, through the principle of generalization of extinction, would be expected when an approximation is presented. The more accurate the hypothesized cues and the more realistically they are presented, the greater the extinction effect would be.

The above analysis is essentially the strategy employed by implosive therapists. Hypotheses are developed about the important cues involved, and these are presented to the patient in the most vivid or realistic manner possible. Because many of the cues presented are believed originally to involve not only auditory but also visual and tactual modalities, an attempt to produce the cues in the patient's imagery, rather than a simple verbal reproduction, seems worthwhile.

The selection of hypotheses can be determined operationally by the therapist. If the cues selected elicit anxiety, the assumption is that the patient has been conditioned to them previously. The greater the degree of anxiety elicited, the greater the reason for continuing the presentations of anxiety-eliciting stimuli. To define the anxiety response, either psychophysiological techniques (e.g., GSR, heart rate) or behavioral observation (e.g., sweating, flushing of the face, increased motor behavior) can be used. In the majority of the cases, for clinical purposes, the latter method is both quite adequate and easily observable. Experience indicates that there is little difficulty in determining whether the patient is anxious. If the hypothesis presented is not confirmed by the patient's reactions, a new hypothesis is selected.

PROCEDURE

Two or three standard clinical diagnostic interviews with the patient usually provide sufficient information to begin IT. A lengthy and detailed dynamic analysis of the patient's difficulties usually is not necessary, as additional information relating to the dynamic motivation of the patient emerges through the implosive process. As treatment progresses, further interviewing may prove beneficial. After a few sessions, patients frequently report recalling various memories which previously had evaded them. Following the initial interviews, the patient is instructed in the implosive procedure. He is asked to playact various scenes which will be presented to him by the therapist. Once the implosive procedure is begun, every effort is made to encourage the patient to "lose himself" in the part that he is playing and "live" the scenes with genuine emotion and affect. He is asked, much like an actor, to portray certain feelings and emotions and to experience them as an important part of the process. The patient is instructed to play the part of himself. Belief or acceptance, in a cognitive sense, of the themes introduced by the therapist is not requested, and little or no attempt is made to secure any admission from the patient that the cues or hypotheses actually apply to him. This factor seems to be especially important in permitting, in a short time, the restatement of cues which are analogous to "depth" interpretations of dynamically oriented therapies.

The scenes which contain the hypothesized cues are described at first by the therapist. The more involved and dramatic the therapist becomes in describing the scenes, the more realistic the presentation, and the easier it is for the patient to participate. At each stage of the process an attempt is made by the therapist to attain a maximal level of anxiety evocation from the patient. When a high level of anxiety is achieved, the patient is held on this level until some sign of spontaneous reduction in the anxiety-inducing value of the cues appears (extinction). The process is repeated, and again, at the first sign of spontaneous reduction of fear, new variations are introduced to elicit an intense anxiety response. This procedure is continued until a significant diminution in anxiety has resulted. After a few repetitions of a particular scene, the patient is given an opportunity to act out the scene by himself. He is encouraged especially to verbalize his own role-playing behavior. Between sessions the patient is instructed to reenact in his imagination the scenes which were presented during the treatment session. This homework provides additional extinction trials. As therapy progresses he is given more instructions on how to handle fearful situations through use of the implosive process. It is hoped that at the termination of treatment the patient will be able to handle new anxiety-provoking situations without the therapist's help.

At no time throughout the procedure is the patient told or encouraged to suppress whatever symptoms he may have. The basic premise is that anxiety is a learned response to sets of cues based on previous trauma in the patient's life. If these cues elicit the anxiety response in the absence of primary reinforcement, the anxiety response will extinguish after repeated evocations. The assumption made here is that these cues essentially consist of avoided (repressed) aspects of the personality, and that by approximating the past dangerous situations and associations without primary reinforcement extinction may be achieved.

Avoidance Serial Cue Hierarchy

The cues selected for reproduction are derived both from an analysis of the patient's present behavior and from dynamic areas thought relevant to the basic problems of the patient. The patient is presumed to be avoiding (repressing) these cues precisely because they have anxiety-evoking value. Since it is maintained that the patient's maladaptive behavior is based on the secondary-drive value of these cues, it follows that reduction or elimination, through extinction, of the drive value of the cues should lead to a proportional reduction or elimination of the maladaptive behavior which was based upon the cues. At the same time, since the anxiety level itself is being reduced, substitute symptom formation (new avoidance responses) should not occur.

The question asked continually by the therapist is, "What are the exteroceptive and interoceptive conditioned stimuli that the patient is avoiding?" The assumption is made that these cues are multiple, involve varied forms of stimulation, and are possibly interdependent. They are believed to be ordered in a serial hierarchy in terms of the extent to which they are avoided (repressed). Those cues highest on the Avoidance Serial Cue Hierarchy (ASCH) have the highest anxiety loading because they are believed to be the cues previously most closely associated with trauma (primary reinforcement). Furthermore, since these cues are the most completely avoided, their infrequent exposure protects the main source of secondary drive from undergoing extinction (Solomon & Wynne's, 1954, conservation of anxiety hypothesis). The cues low on the ASCH have less of an anxiety loading. They are usually more accessible and identifiable by the patient. They can be deduced usually from a purely descriptive analysis of the patient's behavior.

Symptom-Contingent Cues

The hypothesized cues which are believed to be low on the ASCH are presented first. Many of these cues can be identified as symptom-contingent cues. These are the situational or environmental cues which are highly correlated with the occurrence of the patient's symptom. They can be identified by analyzing the contingencies surrounding the occurrence of the symptom. For example, in the case of a phobic reaction, the symptom-contingent cues might involve the sight of a tall building, the driving of a car, or being confined to a small enclosed space. Whether the symptom involves a compulsive ritual, an obsessive thought, a hysterical fit, or a conversion reaction the strategy is essentially the same, that is, the identification of as much of the stimulus complex as possible surrounding the occurrence of the symptom.

Once the cues associated with the anxiety-evoking situation are deduced, the therapist can attempt to extinguish their anxiety-eliciting properties by verbally describing in detail to the patient the sequence in which the cues occur. At the same time the patient is encouraged to visualize the cues in imagery. Scenes are described to the patient in which he is asked to imagine himself being unable to elaborate his symptom while in the anxiety-eliciting situation. For example, he might be asked to imagine himself climbing the stairs of a feared tall building, being unable to perform his compulsive ritual, or having to visualize the acting out of his feared obsession. In a sense, the therapist forces the patient to be exposed to some of the anxiety-provoking cues that he partially avoids outside of the treatment session by means of his symptom. Therefore, with the avoidance response circumvented, greater exposure to the cues will occur, and subsequently greater extinction will be effected.

Frequently, with his reduction in anxiety, the patient will report a number of other anxiety-eliciting situations in his life which he maintains he previously had forgotten completely. Such information provides further cues. The assumption made is that anxiety which is extinguished to one set of cues will, through the principle of generalization of extinction, make the next set of cues which have higher anxiety-eliciting value more accessible.

Hypothesized Sequential Cues

When the symptom-contingent cues have been extinguished, the hypothesized sequential cues (those hypothesized avoided cues comprising the rest of the total stimulus complex) are introduced. These cues are assumed to be higher on the patient's ASCH and are believed mainly to incorporate the dynamic areas thought relevant to the basic problems of the patient. The cues found most anxiety eliciting usually center about the expression of hostility and aggression directed toward parental figures, retaliation for aggressive acts by the patient with cues depicting various degrees of bodily injury, and those related to experiences of rejection, deprivation, abandonment, helplessness, guilt, shame, and sex. Oedipal, anal, oral, sibling-rivalry, primal scene, and death-wish impulse themes are worked into the hypothesized ASCH, along with the introduction of "acceptance of conscience" cues and other areas somewhat neglected by psychodynamically oriented therapies.

For didactic purposes, the areas which usually incorporate the hypothe-sized sequential cues can be categorized under the following 10 major headings:

Aggression. Scenes presented in this area usually center around the expression of anger, hostility, and aggression by the patient toward parental, sibling, spouse, or other significant figures in his life. Various degrees of bodily injury are described including complete body mutilation and death of the victim.

Punishment. The patient is instructed to visualize himself as the recipient of anger, hostility, and aggression of the various significant indi-viduals in his life. The punishment inflicted in the scene is frequently a result of the patient's engaging in some forbidden act.

Oral material. In this category oral incorporative and destructive scenes involving, for example, eating, biting, spitting, cannibalism, and suck-ing are introduced.

Anal material. Anal retentive and expulsive scenes comprising a variety of excretory and related anal situations are described.

Sexual material. In this area a wide variety of hypothesized cues related to sex are presented. For example, primal and Oedipal scenes and scenes of castration, fellatio, and homosexuality are presented.

Rejection. Scenes where the patient is rejected, deprived, abandoned, shamed, or left helpless are enacted.

Bodily injury. Scenes involving mutilation and death of the patient are introduced where fear of injury appears dominant (e.g., in phobic reac-tions such as falling off a high building, being hit by a car, dying from an infection). This procedure is followed also in cases where suicidal fantasies are present.

Loss of control. Scenes are presented where the patient is encouraged to imagine himself losing impulse control to such an extent that he acts out avoided sexual or aggressive impulses. These scenes usually are followed by scenes where the individual is directed to visualize himself hospitalized for the rest of his life in a back ward of a mental hospital as a result of his loss of impulse control. This area is tapped primarily with patients who express fear of "becoming insane" or concern about being hopeless and incurable.

Acceptance of conscience. Scenes are portrayed in which the patient confesses, admits, and believes he is responsible and guilty for all sins and wrongdoings (as portrayed in scenes from other categories) throughout his life. The surrounding may be described as involving a courtroom scene with all the patient's family and loved ones present. After his confession he is convicted by the court, sentenced to death, and executed. In some cases, after death the patient is instructed to picture himself going before God, and the theme is essentially repeated with God condemning him to eternal suffering. An attempt is then made to fit the patient's "hell" to his "sins."

ANS and CNS reactivity. The sensory consequences of autonomic and central nervous system reactivity may function itself as a cue for anxiety. Scenes are introduced in which the patient is asked to visualize the sensory consequences of his own nervous system (e.g., heart pounding, perspiration increase, increase in muscular tension, involuntary discharge of the bladder or bowels).

In general, most of the above areas are touched upon at one point or another during the patient's treatment. The categories emphasized, and where they fall on the ASCH, will depend upon the patient's history and dynamics. The categories, of course, are not mutually exclusive or all inclusive. From a learning model many of the cues would be expected to occur within the same stimulus complex in which the original conditioning occurred. In practice, many of the scenes presented within a session include cues from more than one of the above categories. These scenes are presented from least to most feared in terms of the hypothesized ASCH. They are repeated until the anxiety reactions elicited by them are markedly reduced or eliminated.

To summarize, the first objective of the implosive procedure is to have the patient imagine and verbalize those important symptom-contingent cues and/or hypothesized sequential cues which, although possessing high-anxiety-eliciting value, are believed to be relatively low on the patient's ASCH. These cues are chosen from the real-life experiences of the patient in which objects or situations are known to have high-anxiety-eliciting value, as in specific traumatic situations, material produced in dreams, or symbolism of a psychoanalytic nature such as snakes, spiders, wolves, or other objects or animals thought to have stimulus-generalization properties (symbolically meaningful to the patient). As each theme is worked through and extinguished, hypothesized cues believed to be higher on the ASCH are introduced. This procedure is continued until all the areas desired to be worked through are extinguished.

VALIDATION

IT was developed by the first author in 1957 (see London, 1964). Since that time, the technique has been applied to a wide variety of psychopathological problems. It appears to be highly effective over a wide range of psychoneurotic disorders including anxiety, phobic, obsessive-compulsive, and depressive reactions and has been applied successfully to psychotic disorders including affective, schizophrenic, and paranoid reactions. It shows promise in the treatment of personality disorders including homosexuality, alcoholism, and speech disturbances. A striking feature of the therapy is the reduced treatment time needed to achieve marked changes in symptomatology (from 1 to 15 one-hour sessions) with total treatment time rarely exceeding 30 implosive hours.

Since "new" therapies frequently appear to be more effective initially, it was thought desirable not to publish the above theoretical approach pending the completion of objective experimental studies. Such confirmation has been reported recently (see Hogan, 1966; Hogan & Kirchner, 1967; Kirchner & Hogan, 1966; Levis & Carrera, 1967). However, further research on the efficacy of the technique, theory, and interaction of the two is still needed before any definite claims can be made.

REFERENCES

Ayllon, T. Intensive treatment of psychotic behavior by stimulus satiation and food reinforcement. *Behavior Research and Therapy,* 1963, 1(1), 53–61.

Bandura, A. Psychotherapy as a learning process. *Psychological Bulletin,* 1961, 58, 143–157.

Black, A. H. The extinction of avoidance responses under curare-like drugs. *Journal of Comparative and Physiological Psychology,* 1958, 51, 519–525.

Brady, J. V., Porter, R. W., Conrad, D. G., & Mason, J. W. Avoidance behavior and the development of gastroduodenal ulcers. *Journal of the Experimental Analysis of Behavior,* 1958, 1, 69–73.

Breger, L., & McGaugh, J. L. Critique and reformulation of "learning-theory" approaches to psychotherapy and neurosis. *Psychological Bulletin,* 1965, 63, 338–358.

Brown, J. S. *The motivation of behavior*. New York: McGraw-Hill, 1961.

Denny, M. R., Koons, P. B., & Mason, J. E. Extinction of avoidance as a function of the escape situation. *Journal of Comparative and Physiological Psychology*, 1959, 52, 212–214.

Dollard, J., & Miller, N. E. *Personality and psychotherapy*. New York: McGraw-Hill, 1950.

Grossberg, J. M. Behavior therapy: A review. *Psychological Bulletin*, 1964, 62, 73–88.

Hogan, R. A. Implosive therapy in the short term treatment of psychotics *Psychotherapy: Theory, Research and Practice*, 1966, 3, 25–32.

Hogan, R. A., & Kirchner, J. H. Preliminary report of the extinction of learned fears via short-term implosive therapy. *Journal of Abnormal Psychology*, 1967, 72, 106–109.

Holland, J. G., & Skinner, B. F. *The analysis of behavior*. New York: McGraw-Hill, 1961.

Hunt, H. F., Jernberg, P., & Brady, J. V. The effect of electroconvulsive shock (ECS) on a conditioned emotional response: The effect of post-ECS extinction on the reappearance of the response. *Journal of Comparative and Physiological Psychology*, 1952, 45, 589–599.

Kimble, G. A., *Hilgard and Marquis' Conditioning and learning*. New York: Appleton-Century-Crofts, 1961.

Kirchner, J. H., & Hogan, R. A. The therapist variable in the implosion of phobias. *Psychotherapy: Theory, Research and Practice*, 1966, 3, 102–104.

Knapp, R. K. Acquisition and extinction of avoidance with similar and different shock and escape situations. *Journal of Comparative and Physiological Psychology*, 1965, 60, 272–273.

Krasner, L. Studies of the conditioning of verbal behavior. *Psychological Bulletin*, 1958, 55, 148–170.

Levis, D. J. Effects of serial CS presentation and other characteristics of the CS on the conditioned avoidance response. *Psychological Reports*, 1966, 18, 755–766.

Levis, D. J., & Carrera, R. N. Effects of ten hours of implosive therapy in the treatment of outpatients. *Journal of Abnormal Psychology*, 1967, 72, 504–508.

Liddell, H. S. The challenge of Pavlovian conditioning and experimental neuroses in animals. In J. Wolpe, A. Salter, & L. J. Reyna (Eds.), *The conditioning therapies*. New York: Holt, Rinehart & Winston, 1965. Pp. 127–148.

Lindsley, O. R. Operant conditioning methods applied to research in chronic schizophrenia. *Psychiatric Research Reports*, 1956, 5, 118–138.

London, P. *The modes and morals of psychotherapy*. New York: Holt, Rinehart & Winston, 1964.

Lowenfeld, J., Rubenfeld, S., & Guthrie, G. M. Verbal inhibition in subception. *Journal of General Psychology*, 1956, 54, 171–176.

Masserman, J. H., & Pechtel, C. Neuroses in monkeys: A preliminary report of experimental observation. *Annals of the New York Academy of Sciences,* 1953, 56(2), 253–265.

Mednick, S. A. A learning theory approach to research in schizophrenia. *Psychological Bulletin,* 1958, 55, 316–327.

Miller, N. E. Learnable drives and rewards. In S. S. Stevens (Ed.), *Handbook of experimental psychology.* New York: Wiley, 1951. Pp. 435–472.

Mowrer, O. H. Motivation and neurosis. In *Current theory and research in motivation—a symposium.* Lincoln: University of Nebraska Press, 1953. Pp. 162–185.

Mowrer, O. H. *Learning theory and behavior.* New York: Wiley, 1960.

Rotter, J. B. *Social learning and clinical psychology.* Englewood Cliffs, N. J.: Prentice-Hall, 1954.

Salter, A. *Conditioned reflex therapy.* New York: Farrar, Straus & Cudahy, 1949.

Shoben, E. J. Psychotherapy as a problem in learning theory. *Psychological Bulletin,* 1949, 46, 366–392.

Skinner, B. F. What is psychotic behavior? In *Theory and treatment of psychosis: Some newer aspects.* St. Louis: Washington University Studies, 1956. Pp. 77–99.

Solomon, R. L., Kamin, L. J., & Wynne, L. C. Traumatic avoidance learning: The outcomes of several extinction procedures with dogs. *Journal of Abnormal and Social Psychology,* 1953, 48, 291–302.

Solomon, R. L., & Wynne, L. C. Traumatic avoidance learning: The principles of anxiety conservation and partial irreversibility. *Psychological Review,* 1954, 61, 353–385.

Stampfl, T. G. Avoidance conditioning reconsidered: An extension of Mowrerian theory. Unpublished manuscript, John Carroll University, 1960.

Wall, H. W., & Guthrie, G. M. Extinction of responses to subceived stimuli. *Journal of General Psychology,* 1959, 60, 205–210.

Weinberger, N. M. Effects of detainment on extinction of avoidance responses. *Journal of Comparative and Physiological Psychology,* 1965, 60, 135–138.

Wolpe, J. *Psychotherapy by reciprocal inhibition.* Stanford: Stanford University Press, 1958.

Yates, A. J. The application of learning theory to the treatment of tics. *Journal of Abnormal and Social Psychology,* 1958, 56, 175–182.

23

THE SYSTEMATIC DESENSITIZATION TREATMENT OF NEUROSES

Joseph Wolpe

Some years ago, studies on the induction and elimination of experimental neuroses in animals (23) showed that these conditions were persistent habits of unadaptive behavior acquired by learning (conditioning); and that their therapy was a matter of unlearning. The central constituent of the neurotic behavior was anxiety, and the most effective way of procuring unlearning was repeatedly to feed the animal while it was responding with a weak degree of anxiety to a "weak" conditioned stimulus. The effect of this was to diminish progressively the strength of the anxiety response to the particular stimulus so that it eventually declined to zero. Increasingly "strong" stimulus situations were successively dealt with in the same way; and finally, the animal showed no anxiety to any of the situations to which anxiety had been conditioned. The basis of the gradual elimination of the anxiety response habit appeared to be an example, at a more complex level, of the phenomenon of *reciprocal inhibition* described originally by Sherrington (17). Each time the animal fed, the anxiety response was to some extent inhibited; and each occasion of inhibition weakened somewhat the strength of the anxiety habit. The experiments suggested the general proposition that *if a response inhibitory to anxiety can be made to occur in the presence of anxiety-evoking stimuli so that it is accompanied by a complete or partial suppression of the anxiety response, the bond between these stimuli and the anxiety response will be weakened.*

I have argued elsewhere (24, 27, 28) that human neuroses are quite parallel to experimental neuroses. On this premise and during the past twelve years, the writer has applied the reciprocal inhibition principle to the treatment of a

Reprinted from *The Journal of Nervous and Mental Disease,* 132, 1963, 189–203, with the permission of The Williams & Wilkins Company (Copyright © 1963, The Williams & Wilkins Company, Baltimore, Md. 21202, U.S.A.) and Dr. Wolpe.

large number of clinical cases of neurosis, employing a variety of other responses to inhibit anxiety or other neurotic responses. In a recent book (27) an analysis has been given of the results in 210 patients, of whom 89 per cent either recovered or were much improved, apparently lastingly, after a mean of about 30 interviews.

In the case of neurotic responses conditioned to situations involving direct interpersonal relations, the essence of reciprocal inhibition therapy has been to instigate in the situations concerned new patterns of behavior of an anxiety-inhibiting kind whose repeated exercise gradually weakens the anxiety response habit (16, 19, 20, 25, 27, 28). Neurotic responses conditioned to stimuli other than those arising from direct interpersonal relations do not lend themselves, as a rule, to behavioral treatment in the life situation of the patient; and consulting-room applications of the reciprocal inhibition principle have been necessary. The most straightforward examples of neurotic responses requiring such measures have been the phobias. Relatively "simple" though they are, they have hitherto constituted a difficult therapeutic problem. For example, Curran and Partridge (2) state, "Phobic symptoms are notoriously resistant to treatment and their complete removal is rarely achieved." A very different picture is in prospect with the use of conditioning methods (1, 4, 10–12, 14, 15), which are no less effective when used for much more subtle neurotic constellations. Examples will be found below.

In the office treatment of neuroses by reciprocal inhibition, any response inhibitory of anxiety may in theory be used. The almost forgotten earliest example of therapy of this kind (7) involved inhibiting the anxiety of phobic children by feeding (just as in the animal experiments mentioned above). Conditioned motor responses have occasionally served the same end (27, p. 173); and Meyer (14) and Freeman and Kendrick (4) have made use of ordinary "pleasant" emotions of daily life (see also 27, p. 198). But the behavioral response that has had the widest application is deep muscle relaxation, whose anxiety-inhibiting effects were first pointed out by Jacobson (5, 6). It has been the basis of the technique known as *systematic desensitization* which, because of its convenience, has been most widely adopted (1, 9, 11, 12).

Though several descriptions of the technique of systematic desensitization have been published (*e.g.,* 26, 27) it is now clear that more details are needed to enable practitioners to apply it without assistance. It is the aim of this paper to present a more adequate account, and also for the first time to give a separate statistical analysis of results obtained with this treatment.

A TECHNIQUE OF SYSTEMATIC DESENSITIZATION

It is necessary to emphasize that the desensitization technique is carried out *only after a careful assessment of the therapeutic requirements of the patient.* A detailed history is taken of every symptom and of every aspect of life in which the patient experiences undue difficulty. A systematic account is then obtained of his life history with special attention to intrafamilial relationships. His attitudes to people in educational institutions and to learning and play are investigated. A history of his work life is taken, noting both his experiences with people and those related to work itself. He is questioned about his sexual experiences from first awareness of sexual feelings up to the present. Careful scrutiny is made of his current major personal relationships. Finally, he is asked to describe all kinds of "nervousness" that may have afflicted him at any time and to narrate any distressing experiences he can remember.

The problems posed by the case are now carefully considered; and if there are neurotic reactions in connection with direct interpersonal relations, appropriate new behavior based on the reciprocal inhibition principle is instigated in the patient's life situation (19, 20, 25, 27, 28). Most commonly, it is assertive behavior that is instigated. When systematic desensitization is also indicated, it is conducted as soon as possible, and may be in parallel with measures aimed at other sources of neurotic anxiety.

Systematic desensitization is used not only for the treatment of classical phobias involving anxiety responses to nonpersonal stimulus constellations (like enclosed spaces or harmless animals), but also for numerous less obvious and often complex sources of neurotic disturbance. These may involve ideas, bodily sensations, or extrinsic situations. Examples of each are to be found in Table 1. The most common extrinsic sources of anxiety relate to people in contexts that make irrelevant the use of direct action, such as assertion, on the part of the patient. As examples, one patient reacts with anxiety to the mere presence of particular persons, another to definable categories of people, a third to being the center of attention, a fourth to people in groups, a fifth to inferred criticism or rejection, and so forth. In all instances, *anxiety has been conditioned to situations in which, objectively, there is no danger.*

In brief, the desensitization method consists of presenting to the imagination of the deeply relaxed patient the feeblest item in a list of anxiety-evoking stimuli—repeatedly, until no more anxiety is evoked. The next item of the list is then presented, and so on, until eventually even the strongest of the anxiety-evoking stimuli fails to evoke any stir of anxiety in the patient. It has consistently been found that at every stage a stimulus that evokes no anxiety when imagined in a state of relaxation will also evoke no anxiety when encountered in reality.

The method involves three separate sets of operations: 1) training in deep muscle relaxation; 2) the construction of anxiety hierarchies; and 3) counterposing relaxation and anxiety-evoking stimuli from the hierarchies.

TRAINING IN RELAXATION

The method of relaxation taught is essentially that of Jacobson (5) but the training takes up only about half of each of about six interviews—far less time than Jacobson devotes. The patient is also asked to practice at home for a half-hour each day.

The first lesson begins with the therapist telling the patient that he is to learn relaxation because of its beneficial emotional effects. He is then directed to grip the arm of his chair with one hand to see whether he can distinguish any qualitative difference between the sensations produced in his forearm and those in his hand. Usually he can, and he is asked to take note of the forearm sensation as being characteristic of muscle tension. He is also enjoined to re-member the location of the flexors and extensors of the forearm. Next, the therapist grips the patient's wrist and asks him to pull, making him aware of the tension in his biceps; and then, instructing him to push in the opposite direction, draws his attention to the extensor muscles of the arm.

The therapist now again grips the patient's wrist and makes him tense the biceps and then relax it as much as possible, letting go gradually as the patient's hand comes down. The patient is then told to "keep trying to go further and further in the negative direction" and to "try to go beyond what seems to you to be the furthest point." He may report sensations like tingling and numbness which often accompany relaxation. When it appears that the patient has understood how to go about relaxing he is made to relax simul-taneously all the muscles of both arms and forearms.

At the second lesson in relaxation, the patient is told that from the emo-tional point of view the most important muscles in the body are situated in and around the head, and that we shall therefore go on to these next. The muscles of the face are the first to be dealt with, beginning with the forehead. This location lends itself to demonstrating to the patient the step-like manner in which tension is decreased; and I do this by contracting the eyebrow-raising and the frowning groups of muscles in my own forehead very intensely simul-taneously, and then relaxing by degrees. The patient is then made aware of his own forehead muscles and given about ten minutes to relax them as far as possible. Patients frequently report spontaneously the occurrence of unusual sensations in their foreheads, such as numbness, tingling, or "a feeling of thickness, as though my skin were made of leather." These sensations are characteristic of the attainment of a degree of relaxation beyond the normal level of muscle tone. At this session attention is drawn also to the muscles in the region of the nose (by asking the patient to wrinkle his nose) and to the muscles around the mouth (by making him purse his lips and then smile). After a few minutes he is asked to bite on his teeth, thus tensing his masseters and temporales. The position of the lips is an important indicator of successful relaxation of the muscles of mastication. When these are relaxed, the lips are parted by a few millimeters. The masseters cannot be relaxed if the mouth is kept resolutely closed.

At the third lesson, attention is drawn to the muscles of the tongue, which may be felt contracting in the floor of the mouth when the patient presses the tip of his tongue firmly against the back of his bottom incisor teeth. Thereafter, with active jaw-opening, infra-hyoid tensions are pointed out. All these muscles are then relaxed. At the same session, the tensions produced in the eye muscles and those of the neck are noted and time given for their relaxation.

The fourth lesson deals with the muscles of the shoulder girdle, the fifth with those of the back, thorax and abdomen, and the sixth with those of the thighs and legs. A procedure that many patients find helpful is to coordinate relaxation of various other muscles with the automatic relaxation of the respiratory muscles that takes place with normal exhalation.

CONSTRUCTION OF ANXIETY HIERARCHIES

This is the most difficult and taxing procedure in the desensitization technique. Investigation of any case of anxiety neurosis reveals that the stimuli to anxiety fall into definable groups or *themes*. The themes may be obvious ones, like fear of heights, or less apparent ones, like fear of rejection.

Hierarchy construction usually begins at about the same time as relaxation training, but alterations or additions can be made at any time. It is important to note that the gathering of data and its subsequent organizing are done in an ordinary conversational way and *not under relaxation,* since the patient's *ordinary* responses to stimuli are under scrutiny.

The raw data from which the hierarchies are constructed have three main sources: 1) the patient's history; 2) responses to the Willoughby Questionnaire (22) ; and 3) special probings about situations in which the patient feels anxiety though there is no objective threat. Abundant material is often obtained by setting the patient the homework task of listing all situations that he finds disturbing, fearful, embarrassing, or in any way distressing.

When all identified sources of neurotic disturbance have been listed, the therapist classifies them into groups if there is more than one theme. The items of each thematic group are then rewritten to make separate lists and the patient is asked to rank the items of each list, placing the item he imagines would be most disturbing at the top and the least disturbing at the bottom of the list.

In many instances, the construction of a hierarchy is a very straightforward matter. This is true of most cases of such fears, as of heights (where the greater the height the greater the fear), or enclosed spaces, or, to take a some-what more complex instance, fears aroused by the sight of illness in others. In such instances as the last, exemplified in Case 1 below, although the items have only a general thematic linkage and do not belong to a stimulus continuum (as do, for example, the items of a height hierarchy), all that has to be done is to obtain a list of situations embodying illnesses in others and then to ask the patient to rank the items according to the amount of anxiety each one arouses.

In other cases, hierarchy construction is more difficult because the sources of anxiety are not immediately revealed by the patient's listing of what he avoids. For example, it may become clear that he reacts to social occasions with anxiety, and that different kinds of social occasions (*e.g.* weddings, parties, and the musical evenings) are associated with decreasing degrees of anxiety. There may then be a temptation to arrange a hierarchy based on these types of social occasions, with weddings at the top of the list and musical evenings at the bottom. Usually, little effective therapy would follow an attempt at desensitiza-tion based on such a hierarchy, and more careful probing would almost certainly reveal some facet of social occasions that is the real source of anxiety. Frequently, fear and avoidance of social occasions turns out to be based on fear of criticism or of rejection; or the fear may be a function of the mere physical presence of people, varying with the number of them to whom the patient is exposed. The writer once had a patient whose fear of social situations was really a conditioned anxiety re-sponse to the smell of food in public places. A good example of the importance of correct identification of relevant sources of anxiety is to be found in a previously reported case (27, p. 152) where a man's importance was found to be due to anxiety related not to aspects of the sexual situation as such, but to the idea of trauma, which in certain contexts, especially defloration, enters into the sexual act.

It is not necessary for the patient actually to have experienced each situa-tion that is to be included in a hierarchy. The question before him is of the order that, "If you were today confronted by such and such a situation, *would you expect* to be anxious?" To answer this question he must *imagine* the situa-tion concerned, and it is usually not much more difficult to imagine a merely possible event than one that has at some time occurred. The temporal setting of an imagined stimulus configuration scarcely affects the responses to it. A man with a phobia for dogs has about as much anxiety to the idea of meeting a bulldog on the way home this evening as to recalling an encounter with this breed of dog a year previously.

A small minority of patients do not experience anxiety when they imagine situations that in reality are disturbing. In some of these, anxiety is evoked when they *describe* (verbalize) the scene they have been asked to imagine. As in other patients, the various scenes can then be ranked according to the degree of anxiety they evoke.

To a therapist inexperienced in the construction of anxiety hierarchies, the most common difficulty to be encountered is to find that even the weakest item in a hierarchy produces more anxiety than can be counteracted by the patient's relaxation. In many cases, it is obvious where weaker items may be sought. For example, in a patient who had an anxiety hierarchy on the theme of loneliness, the weakest item in the original hierarchy—being at home accompanied only by her daughter—was found to evoke more anxiety than was manageable. To obtain a weaker starting point all that was needed was to add items in which she had two or more companions. But it is not always so easy, and the therapist may be hard put to find manipulable dimensions. For example, following an accident three years previously, a patient had developed serious anxiety reactions to the sight of approaching automobiles. At first it seemed that anxiety was just noticeable when an automobile was two blocks away, gradually increasing until a distance of half a block and then much more steeply increasing as the distance grew less. This, of course, promised plain sailing, but at the first desensitization session even at two blocks the imaginary car aroused anxiety much too great to be mastered: and it was revealed that the patient experienced anxiety at the very prospect of even the shortest journey by car, since the whole range of possibilities was already present the moment a journey became imminent. To obtain manageable levels of anxiety, an imaginary enclosed field two blocks square was postulated. The patient's car was "placed" in one corner of the field and the early items of the hierarchy involved a trusted person driving his car up to a stated point towards the patient's car, and bringing this point ever closer as the patient progressed. Another case in whom weak anxiety stimuli were not easily found was a patient with a death phobia, whose items ranged in descending order from human corpses through such scenes as funeral processions to dead dogs. But even the last produced marked anxiety, when they were imagined even at distances of two or three hundred yards. A solution was found in retreating along a temporal instead of a spatial dimension, beginning with the (historically inaccurate) sentence, "William the Conqueror was killed at the Battle of Hastings in 1066."

DESENSITIZATION PROCEDURE

When the hierarchies have been constructed and relaxation training has proceeded to a degree judged sufficient, desensitization can then begin. First "weak" and later progressively "strong" anxiety-arousing stimulus situations will be presented to the imagination of the deeply relaxed patient, as described below.

When relaxation is poor, it may be enhanced by the use of meprobamate, chlorpromazine, or codeine given an hour before the interview. Which drug to use is decided by trial. When pervasive ("free-floating") anxiety impedes relaxation, the use of carbon dioxide-oxygen mixtures by La Verne's (8) single inhalation technique has been found to be of the greatest value (27, p. 166) and with some patients this method comes to be used before every desensitization session. In a few patients who cannot relax but who are not anxious either, attempts at desensitization sometimes succeed, presumably because interview-induced emotional responses inhibit the anxiety aroused by the imagined stimuli (27).

It is the usual practice for sessions to be conducted under hypnosis with the patient sitting on a comfortable armchair. He may or may not have been hypnotized in an exploratory way on one or more occasions during earlier interviews. With patients who cannot be hypnotized, and in those who for any reason object to it, hypnosis is omitted and instructions are given merely to close the eyes and relax according to instructions. (There is a general impression that these patients make slower progress.)

The patient having been hypnotized, the therapist proceeds to bring about as deep as possible a state of calm by verbal suggestions to the patient to give individual attention to relaxing each group of muscles in the way he has learned.

The presentation of scenes at the first session is to some extent exploratory. The first scene presented is always a neutral one—to which a patient is not expected to have any anxiety reaction whatsoever. This is followed by a small number of presentations of the mildest items from one or two of the patient's hierarchies. To illustrate this, we shall make use of a verbatim account of the first session of Case 2, whose hierarchies are given below. After hypnotizing and relaxing the patient, the therapist went on as follows.

"You will now imagine a number of scenes very clearly and calmly. The scenes may not at all disturb your state of relaxation. If by any chance, however, you feel disturbed, you will be able to indicate this to me by raising your left index finger an inch or so. (*Pause of about 10 seconds*) First, I want you to imagine that you are standing at a busy street corner. You notice the traffic passing—cars, trucks, bicycles, and people. You see them all very clearly and you notice the sounds that accompany them. (*Pause of about 15 seconds*). Now, stop imagining that scene and again turn your attention to your muscles. (*Pause of about 20 seconds*). Now, imagine that it is a work day. It is 11 A.M. and you are lying in bed with an attack of influenza and a temperature of 103°. (*Pause of about 10 seconds*). Stop imagining the scene and again relax. (*Pause of 15 seconds*) Now, imagine exactly the same situation again. (*Pause of 10 seconds*) Stop imagining the scene and relax. (*Pause of about 20 seconds*) Now, I want you to imagine that you are at the post office and you have just sent off a manuscript to a journal. (*Pause of 15 seconds*) Stop imagining the scene and only relax. (*Pause of about five seconds*) In a few moments, I will be counting up to five and you will wake up feeling very calm and refreshed. (*Pause of about five seconds*) One, two, three, four, five. (*The patient opened his eyes looking somewhat dazed*).

On being brought out of the trance, the patient is asked how he feels and how he felt during the trance, since it is important to know if a calm basal emotional state was achieved by the relaxation. He is then asked to indicate whether the scenes were clear or not. (It is essential for visualizing to be at least moderately clear.) Finally, the therapist inquires whether or not any of the scenes produced any disturbance in the patient, and if they did, how much. It is not common for a patient to report a reaction to the neutral control scene. It is worth remarking that even though the patient has a signal at his disposal with which to indicate disturbance, the fact that he has not done so during a scene by no means proves that it has not disturbed him at all, for it is a rare patient who makes use of the signal if only mildly disturbed. But the provision of a signal must never be omitted, for the patient will use it if he has a strong emotional reaction, which may not be otherwise manifest. *Exposure, and prolonged exposure in particular, to a very disturbing scene can greatly increase sensitivity.* With less marked disturbance there may be perseveration of anxiety, which makes continuance of the session futile.

At subsequent sessions, the same basic procedure is followed. If at the previous session there was a scene whose repeated presentations evoked anxiety that diminished but was not entirely extinguished, that scene is usually the first to be presented. If at the previous session the final scenes from a hierarchy ceased to arouse any anxiety, the scene next higher is now presented, except in a few patients who despite having had no anxiety at all to a final scene at a previous session, again show a small measure of anxiety to this scene at a subsequent session. It must again be presented several times until all anxiety is eliminated before going on to the next scene.

In order to gauge progress, the following procedure is adopted after two to four presentations of a particular scene. The therapist says, "If you had even the slightest disturbance to the last presentation of this scene, raise your left index finger now. If you had no disturbance, do nothing." If the finger is not raised, the therapist goes on to the next higher scene in the hierarchy. If the finger is raised, the therapist says, "If the amount of anxiety has been decreasing from one presentation to the next, do nothing. If it has not been decreasing, raise your finger again." If the finger is now not raised, this is an indication for further presentations of the scene, since further decrements in anxiety evocation may be confidently expected; but if it is raised, it is clear that the scene is producing more anxiety than the patient's relaxation can overcome, and it is therefore necessary to devise and interpose a scene midway in "strength" between this scene and the last one successfully mastered.

There is great variation in how many themes, how many scenes from each, and how many presentations are given at a session. Generally, up to four hierarchies are drawn upon in an individual session, and not many patients have more than four. Three or four presentations of a scene are usual, but ten or more may be needed. The total number of scenes presented is limited mainly by availability of time and by the endurance of the patient. On the whole, both of these quantities increase as therapy goes on, and eventually almost the whole interview may be devoted to desensitization, so that whereas at an early stage eight or ten presentations are the total given at a session, at an advanced stage the number may rise to 30 or even 50.

The *duration* of a scene is usually of the order of five seconds, but it may be varied according to several circumstances. It is quickly terminated if the patient signals anxiety by spontaneously raising his finger or if he shows any sharp reaction. Whenever the therapist has a special reason to suspect that a scene may evoke a strong reaction he presents it with cautious brevity—for one or two seconds. By and large, early presentations of scenes are briefer, later ones longer. A certain number of patients require fifteen or more seconds to arrive at a clear image of a scene.

The *interval* between scenes is usually between ten and twenty seconds, but if the patient has been more than slightly disturbed by the preceding scene, it may be extended to a minute or more, and during that time the patient may be given repeated suggestions to be calm.

The *number* of desensitizing sessions required varies according to the number and the intensity of the anxiety areas, and the degree of generalization (involvement of related stimuli) in the case of each area. One patient may recover in as few as a half-dozen sessions; another may require a hundred or more. The patient with a death phobia, mentioned above, on whom a temporal dimension had to be used, also had two other phobias and required a total of about a hundred sessions. To remove the death phobia alone, a total of about 2,000 scene presentations were needed.

The *spacing* of sessions does not seem to be of great importance. Two or three sessions a week are characteristic, but the meetings may be separated by many weeks or take place daily. Occasional patients, visiting from afar, have had two sessions in a single day. Whether sessions are massed or widely dispersed, there is almost always a close relation between the extent to which desensitization has been accomplished and the degree of diminution of anxiety responses to real stimuli. Except when therapy is nearly finished, and only a few loose ends of neurotic reactions are left (that may be overcome through emotions arising spontaneously in the ordinary course of living [27]), very little change occurs, as a rule, between sessions. This was strikingly demonstrated by Case 1 (below) in whom the marked improvement of a severe claustrophobia achieved by a first series of sessions remained almost stationary during a three and one-half year interval, after which further sessions overcame the phobia apparently completely.

EXAMPLES OF HIERARCHIES FROM ACTUAL CASES

Single or multiple anxiety hierarchies occur with about equal frequency. Each of the following two cases had multiple hierarchies. (*The most disturbing item, as always, is at the top of each list with the others ranked below it.*)

CASE 1

Mrs. A. was a 50-year-old housewife, whose main complaint was of very disabling fears on the general theme of claustrophobia. The fears had begun about 25 years previously, following a terrifying experience with general anesthesia, and had subsequently spread in a series of steps, each associated with a particular experience, to a wide range of situations. The patient also had other phobias, the most important of which, concerning illness and death, had its origin during childhood. In 46 desensitization sessions between March and July, 1956, all phobias were overcome except the most severe of the claustrophobic possibilities indicated in the first three items of the hierarchy given below, and with item 4 still incompletely conquered therapy was terminated when the writer went overseas for a year. The patient returned to treatment in October, 1959, having maintained her recovery in all areas, but having made very little additional progress. During the next two months, 16 additional sessions were devoted to desensitizing to numerous scenes relevant to the "top" of the claustrophobia hierarchy. She was eventually able to accept, in the session, being confined for two hours in an imagined room four feet square, and reported complete freedom from fear in tunnels and only slight anxiety in "extreme" elevator situations.

Hierarchies

A. *Claustrophobic Series*
   1) Being stuck in an elevator. (The longer the time, the more disturbing.)
   2) Being locked in a room. (The smaller the room and the longer the time, the more disturbing.)
   3) Passing through a tunnel in a railway train. (The longer the tunnel, the more disturbing.)
   4) Traveling in an elevator alone. (The greater the distance, the more disturbing.)
   5) Traveling in an elevator with an operator. (The longer the distance, the more disturbing.)
   6) On a journey by train. (The longer the journey, the more disturbing.)
   7) Stuck in a dress with a stuck zipper.

8) Having a tight ring on her finger.
9) Visiting and unable to leave at will (for example, if engaged in a card game).
10) Being told of somebody in jail.
11) Having polish on her fingernails and no access to remover.
12) Reading of miners trapped underground.

B. *Death Series*

1) Being at a burial.
2) Being at a house of mourning.
3) The word *death*.
4) Seeing a funeral procession. (The nearer, the more disturbing.)
5) The sight of a dead animal, *e.g.,* cat.
6) Driving past a cemetery. (The nearer, the more disturbing.)

C. *Illness Series*

1) Hearing that an acquaintance has cancer.
2) The word *cancer*.
3) Witnessing a convulsive seizure.
4) Discussions of operations. (The more prolonged the discussion, the more disturbing.)
5) Seeing a person receive an injection.
6) Seeing someone faint.
7) The word *operation*.
8) Considerable bleeding from another person.
9) A friend points to a stranger, saying, "This man has tuberculosis."
10) The sight of a blood-stained bandage.
11) The smell of ether.
12) The sight of a friend sick in bed. (The more sick looking, the more disturbing.)
13) The smell of methylated spirits.
14) Driving past a hospital.

CASE 2

Dr. B. was a 41-year-old gynecological resident who had felt anxious and insecure for as long as he could remember. Five years earlier, when anxieties were intensified by divorce proceedings, he had consulted a follower of Harry Stack Sullivan, who had tided him over the immediate situation but left him with attitudes of "acceptance" which had resulted in his becoming more anxious than before. After a few weeks' assertive training, he felt considerably better,

Table 1

BASIC CASE DATA

Patient, Sex, Age	No. of Sessions	Hierarchy Theme	Outcome	Comments
1. F, 50	62	a) Claustrophobia	++++	See case data above.
		b) Illness and hospitals	++++	
		c) Death and its trappings	++++	
		d) Storms	+++	
		e) Quarrels	++++	
2. M, 41	6	a) Guilt	++++	See case data above.
		b) Devaluation	++++	
3. F, 24	17	a) Examinations	++++	
		b) Being scrutinized	++++	
		c) Devaluation	++++	
		d) Discord between others	++++	
4. M, 24	5	a) Snakelike shapes	++++	
5. M, 21	24	a) Being watched	++++	
		b) Suffering of others	++++	
		c) "Jealousy" reaction	++++	
		d) Disapproval	++++	
6. M, 28	5	Crowds	+++	
7. F, 21	5	Criticism	++++	
8. F, 52	21	a) Being center of attention	0	No disturbance during scenes. Was in fact not imagining self in situation.
		b) Superstitions	0	
9. F, 25	9	Suffering and death of others	+++	
10. M, 22	17	Tissue damage in others	++++	
11. M, 37	13	Actual or implied criticism	++++	
12. F, 31	15	Being watched working	+++	
13. F, 40	16	a) "Suffering" and eeriness	++++	This case has been reported in detail (26).
		b) Being devalued	++++	
		c) Failing to come up to expectations	++++	
14. M, 36	10	a) Bright light	++++	
		b) Palpitations	++++	
15. M, 43	9	Wounds and corpses	+++	
16. M, 27	51	a) Being watched, especially at work	+++	No anxiety while being watched at work. Anxious at times while watched playing cards.
		b) Being criticized	++++	
17. M, 33	8	Being watched at golf	+++	
18. M, 13	8	Talking before audience (Stutterer)	0	No imagined scene was ever disturbing.
19. M, 40	7	Authority figures	++++	
20. M, 23	4	Claustrophobia	++++	
21. F, 23	6	a) Agoraphobia	0	Later successfully treated by conditioned motor response method (27).
		b) Fear of falling	0	
22. M, 46	19	a) Being in limelight	+++	
		b) Blood and death	++++	

Table 1—Concluded

Patient, Sex, Age	No. of Sessions	Hierarchy Theme	Outcome	Comments
23. F, 40	20	Social embarrassment	++++	
24. F, 28	9	Agoraphobia	0	
25. F, 48	7	Rejection	+++	
26. M, 28	13	a) Disapproval	+++	
		b) Rejection	++++	
27. M, 11	6	Authority figures	++++	
28. M, 26	217	a) Claustrophobia	++++	
		b) Criticism (numerous aspects)	+++	⎧ Finally overcome completely by use of Malleson's method (13).
		c) Trappings of death	+++	⎩
29. F, 20	5	Agoraphobia	++++	
30. M, 68	23	a) Agoraphobia	++++	
		b) Masturbation	++++	
31. F, 36	5	Being in limelight	++++	
32. M, 26	17	a) Illness and death	+++	
		b) Own symptoms	+++	
33. F, 44	9	a) Being watched	++++	
		b) Elevators	++++	
34. F, 47	17	Intromission into vagina	+++	After 15th session gradual in vivo operation with objects became possible, and subsequently, coitus with husband.
35. M, 37	5	a) Disapproval	++++	
		b) Rejection	++++	
36. F, 32	25	Sexual stimuli	++++	
37. M, 36	21	a) Agoraphobia	++++	
		b) Disapproval	++++	
		c) Being watched	++++	
38. M, 18	6	a) Disapproval	+++	
		b) Sexual stimuli	++++	Instrumental in overcoming impotence.
39. F, 48	20	a) Rejection	++++	Stutter markedly improved
		b) Crudeness of others	++++	as anxiety diminished, partly as result of desensitization, and partly due to assertive behavior in relevant situations.

but was left with the anxious sensitivities ranked in the hierarchies below. After six desensitization sessions he was completely free from anxiety responses to any actual situations similar to those contained in the hierarchies.

Hierarchies

A. *Guilt Series*

1) "Jackson (Dean of the Medical School) wants to see you."
2) Thinks "I only did ten minutes work today."

3) Thinks "I only did an hour's work today."
4) Thinks "I only did six hours' work today."
5) Sitting at the movies.
6) Reading an enjoyable novel.
7) Going on a casual stroll.
8) Staying in bed during the day (even though ill).

B. *Devaluation Series*

1) A woman doesn't respond to his advances.
2) An acquaintance says, "I saw you in Jefferson Street with a woman." (This kind of activity had locally acquired a disreputable flavor.)
3) Having a piece of writing rejected.
4) Awareness that his skill at a particular surgical operation left something to be desired. (Anxiety in terms of "Will I ever be able to do it?")
5) Overhearing adverse remarks about a lecture he delivered that he knows was not good.
6) Overhearing, "Dr. B. fancies himself as a surgeon."
7) Hearing anyone praised, *e.g.*, "Dr. K. is fine surgeon."
8) Having submitted a piece of writing for publication.

RESULTS

Table 1 presents basic details of 39 cases treated by desensitization. These patients, comprising about one-third of the total number so treated up to December, 1959, were randomly selected (by a casual visitor) from the alphabetical files of all patients treated. They are considered to be a representative sample of the total treated patient population. Rather than to summarize results from nearly 150 cases, it was felt desirable to present some details about a more limited series.

Many of the patients had other neurotic response habits as well, that were treated by methods appropriate to them. Interspersed among the 39 cases reported were six others eligible for desensitization who had between two and six sessions, but who are excluded from the series because they terminated treatment for various reasons (even though usually showing some evidence of progress). It is felt proper to exclude these, as in evaluating the therapeutic efficacy of an antibiotic it would be proper to omit cases that had received only one or two doses. Also excluded are two cases that turned out to be schizophrenic. Psychotic patients do not respond to this treatment and of course receive it only if misdiagnosed as neurotic. On the other hand, every presenting neurotic case is accepted for treatment.

Outcome of treatment is judged on the basis of several sources of information. In addition to the patient's report of his reactions to stimuli from the hierarchies during sessions, there frequently is observable evidence of diminished anxious responding, inasmuch as many patients display, when disturbed, characteristic muscle tensions (such as grimaces or finger movements). The greatest importance is attached to the patient's reports of changed responses, in real life, to previously fearful situations. I have not regularly checked these reports by direct observation, but in several cases in whom I have made such checks the patient's account of his improved reaction has invariably been confirmed. In general, there is reason to accept the credibility of patients who report *gradual* improvement. A patient who wished to use an allegation of recovery in order to get out of an unsuccessful course of treatment, would be likely to report recovery rather suddenly, rather than to continue in treatment to substantiate a claim of gradual recovery.

Degree of change is rated on a 5-point scale ranging from 4-plus to zero. A 4-plus rating indicates complete, or almost complete, freedom from phobic reactions to all situations on the theme of the phobia; 3-plus means an im-

Table 2

SUMMARY OF DATA OF TABLE 1

Patients	39	
Number of patients responding to de-sensitization treatment	35	
Number of hierarchies	68	
Hierarchies overcome	45 ⎱	91%
Hierarchies markedly improved	17 ⎰	
Hierarchies unimproved	6	9%
Total number of desensitization sessions	762	
Mean session expenditure per hierarchy	11.2	
Mean session expenditure per success-fully treated hierarchy	12.3	
Median number of sessions per patient	10.0	

provement of response such that the phobia is judged by the patient to retain not more than 20 per cent of its original strength; 2-plus means 30–70 per cent; and 1-plus indicates that more than 70 per cent of the original strength of the phobia is judged retained. A zero rating indicates that there is no discernible change. (It will be noted that only 4-plus, 3-plus and zero ratings have been applicable to the patients in this series.)

Table 2 summarizes the data given in Table 1. There were 68 phobias and neurotic anxiety response habits related to more complex situations among the 39 patients, of whom 19 had multiple hierarchies. The treatment was judged effective in 35 of the patients. Forty-five of the phobic and other anxiety habits were apparently eliminated (4-plus rating) and 17 more were markedly ameliorated (3-plus rating). (It is entirely possible that most of the latter would have reached a 4-plus level if additional sessions could have been given; in cases 16 and 29, progress had become very slow when sessions were discontinued, but this was not so in the other cases.)

Among the failures, cases 8 and 18 were unable to imagine themselves within situations; case 22 could not confine her imagining to the stated scene and therefore had excessive anxiety, but was later treated with complete success by means of another conditioning method (27, p. 174); case 25 had interpersonal anxiety reactions that led to erratic responses and, having experienced no benefit, sought therapy elsewhere.

The 39 patients had a total of 762 desensitization sessions, including in each case the first exploratory session although in many instances scenes from the hierarchies were not presented at that session. The mean number of sessions per hierarchy was 11.2; the median number of sessions given to patients 10.0. It should be noted that a desensitization session usually takes up only part of a three-quarter hour interview period, and in cases that also have neurotic problems requiring direct action in the life situation there may be many interviews in which a session is not included.

At times varying between six months and four years after the end of treatment, follow-up reports were obtained from 20 of the 35 patients who responded to desensitization. There was no reported instance of relapse or the appearance of new phobias or other neurotic symptoms. I have never observed resurgence of neurotic anxiety when desensitization has been complete or virtually so.

DISCUSSION

The general idea of overcoming phobias or other neurotic habits by means of systematic "gradual approaches" is not new. It has long been known that increasing measures of exposure to a feared object may lead to a gradual disappearance of the fear. This knowledge has sometimes (21), but unfortunately not very often, contributed to the armamentarium of psychiatrists in dealing with phobias. What is new in the present contribution is 1) the provision of a theoretical explanation for the success of such gradual approaches and 2) the description of a method in which the therapist has complete control of the degree of approach that the patient makes to the feared object at any particular time. The situations, being imaginary, are constructed and varied at will in the consulting room.

The excellent results obtained by this method of treatment are naturally viewed with skepticism by those who in the psychoanalytic tradition regard phobias and other neurotic anxiety response habits as merely the superficial manifestations of deeper unconscious conflicts. Some attempt to clarify the issue must be made. In the majority of cases a phobia is found to have begun at a particular time and in relation to a particular traumatic event. Before that time, presumably the patient already had his assumed unconscious conflicts, but did not feel any need for treatment. At the very least, then, it must surely be admitted that if through desensitization the patient is restored to the state in which he was before the traumatic event, something important has been gained from the point of view of his suffering. The reply could, of course, be made that unless the unconscious conflicts are brought to light and resolved, the patient will relapse or develop other symptoms; but in keeping with follow-up studies on the results of non-analytic psychotherapy in neurotic cases in general my experience has been that relapse or the appearance of new reactions is rare, unless a major group of stimuli in a desensitized area has been neglected.

At the same time, it is indisputable that only a minority of individuals exposed to a given traumatic event develop a phobia; some predisposing condition or conditions must determine which individuals do. The psychoanalysts are undoubtedly right in insisting on this point. But we are not therefore compelled to accept their version of the nature of the predisposing conditions, especially as the factual foundations of that version are far from satisfactory (30). Objective behavior theory can also point to factors that may predispose an individual to particularly severe conditioning of anxiety. First, some people are apparently endowed with much more active autonomic nervous systems than others (e.g., 18). Second, previous experience with similar stimulus constellations may have induced low degrees of anxiety conditioning which would sensitize a person to the traumatic experience. Third, there may be circumstances in the moment of trauma that may bring about an unusually high degree of focusing upon certain stimulus constellations. The second of these suggested factors is probably the most important, for patients do frequently tell of minor sensitivity having pre-existed the precipitating event. In the course of desensitization, these original sensitivities also come to be removed, along with whatever has been more recently conditioned.

Critics of the conditioned response approach to therapy of the neuroses frequently assert that when the desensitization method leads to recovery, it is not the method as such that is responsible, but the "transference" established between patient and therapist. If these critics were right—if desensitization were incidental to rather than causal of recovery—it would be expected that improvement would affect all areas more or less uniformly, and not be confined to those to which desensitization had been applied. The facts are directly contrary to this expectation, for practically invariably it is found that *unless dif-*

ferent hierarchies have unmistakable common features desensitization to one hierarchy does not in the least diminish the reactivity to another (untreated) hierarchy. For example, a recent patient had both a widespread agoraphobic constellation, and a fear of airplanes, extending to the sight and sound of them. Having constructed hierarchies to both series, the writer proceeded to desensitize the patient to the agoraphobia, but ignored the airplane phobia until the agoraphobia had been almost completely overcome. At this stage, re-assessment of the airplane phobia revealed not the slightest evidence of diminution. This is in accord with observations made in connection with experimental neuroses, in which eliminating anxiety conditioned to visual stimuli does not affect the anxiety-evoking potential of auditory stimuli that were conditioned at the same time as the visual stimuli (23, 27).

From the point of view of the scientific investigator the desensitization method has a number of advantages that are unusual in the field of psychotherapy: 1) the aim of therapy can be clearly stated in every case; 2) sources of neurotic anxiety can be defined and delimited; 3) change of reaction to a scene is determined during sessions (and accordingly could be measured by psychophysiological means); 4) there is no objection to conducting therapy before an unconcealed audience (for this has been done without apparent effect on the course of therapy); and 5) therapists can be interchanged if desired.

SUMMARY

The desensitization method of therapy is a particular application of the reciprocal inhibition principle to the elimination of neurotic habits. The experimental background and some theoretical implications of this principle are discussed.

A detailed account is given of the technique of desensitization and an analysis of its effects when applied to 68 phobias and allied neurotic anxiety response habits in 39 patients. In a mean of 11.2 sessions, 45 of the neurotic habits were overcome and 17 more very markedly improved. Six month to four year follow-up reports from 20 of the 35 successfully treated patients did not reveal an instance of relapse or the emergence of new symptoms.

REFERENCES

1. Bond, I. K. and Hutchison, H. C. Application of reciprocal inhibition therapy to exhibitionism. *Canad. Med. Ass. J.,* 83: 23–25, 1960.

2. Curran, D. and Partridge, M. *Psychological Medicine.* Livingstone, Edinburgh, 1955.

3. Eysenck, H. J. *Behavior Therapy and the Neuroses.* Pergamon Press, New York, 1960.

4. Freeman, H. L. and Kendrick, D. C. A case of cat phobia. *Brit. Med. J.,* 2: 497–502, 1960.

5. Jacobson, E. *Progressive Relaxation.* Univ. of Chicago Press, Chicago, 1938.

6. Jacobson, E. Variation of blood pressure with skeletal muscle tension and relaxation. *Ann. Int. Med.,* 13: 1619–1625, 1940.

7. Jones, M. C. The elimination of children's fears. *J. Exp. Psychol.,* 7: 382–390, 1924.

8. LaVerne, A. A. Rapid coma technique of carbon dioxide inhalation therapy. *Dis. Nerv. Syst.,* 14: 141–144, 1953.

9. Lazarus, A. A. The elimination of children's phobias by deconditioning. *Med. Proc.,* 5: 261, 1959.

10. Lazarus, A. A. *New group techniques in the treatment of phobic conditions.* Ph.D. dissertation. Univ. of the Witwatersrand, 1959.

11. Lazarus, A. A. and Rachman, S. The use of systematic desensitization in psychotherapy. *S. Afr. Med. J.,* 31: 934–937, 1957.

12. Lazovik, A. D. and Lang, P. J. A laboratory demonstration of systematic desensitization psychotherapy. *J. Psychol. Stud.,* 11: 238, 1960.

13. Malleson, N. Panic and phobia. *Lancet.,* 1: 225–227, 1959.

14. Meyer, V. The treatment of two phobic patients on the basis of learning principles. *J. Abnorm. Soc. Psychol.,* 55: 261–266, 1957.

15. Rachman, S. The treatment of anxiety and phobic reactions by systematic desensitization psychotherapy. *J. Abnorm. Soc. Psychol.,* 58: 259–263, 1959.

16. Salter, A. *Conditioned Reflex Therapy.* Creative Age Press, New York, 1950.

17. Sherrington, C. S. *Integrative Action of the Nervous System.* Yale Univ. Press, New Haven, 1906.

18. Shirley, M. *The First Two Years.* Univ. of Minnesota Press, Minneapolis, 1933.

19. Stevenson, I. Direct instigation of behavioral changes in psychotherapy. *A. M. A. Arch. Gen. Psychiat.,* 1: 99–107, 1959.

20. Stevenson, I. and Wolpe, J. Recovery from sexual deviations through overcoming nonsexual neurotic responses. *Amer. J. Psychiat.,* 116: 737–742, 1960.

21. Terhune, W. S. The phobic syndrome. *Arch. Neurol. Psychiat.,* 62: 162–172, 1949.

22. Willoughby, R. R. Some properties of the Thurstone Personality Schedule and a suggested revision. *J. Soc. Psychol.,* 3, 401–424, 1932.

23. Wolpe, J. Experimental neuroses as learned behavior. *Brit. J. Psychol.,* 43: 243–268, 1952.

24. Wolpe, J. Learning versus lesions as the basis of neurotic behavior. *Amer. J. Psychiat.,* 112: 923–927, 1956.

25. Wolpe, J. Objective psychotherapy of the neuroses. *S. Afr. Med. J.,* 26: 825–829, 1952.

26. Wolpe, J. Psychotherapy based on the principles of reciprocal inhibition. In Burton, A., ed. *Case Studies in Counseling and Psychotherapy,* pp. 353–381. Prentice-Hall, Englewood Cliffs, N.J., 1959.

27. Wolpe, J. *Psychotherapy by Reciprocal Inhibition.* Stanford Univ. Press, Stanford, 1958.

28. Wolpe, J. Reciprocal inhibition as the main basis of psychotherapeutic effects. *A. M. A. Arch. Neurol. Psychiat.,* 72: 205–226, 1954.

29. Wolpe, J. Recoveries from neuroses without psychoanalysis: Their prognosis and its implications. *Amer. J. Psychiat.* In press.

30. Wolpe, J. and Rachman, S. Psychoanalytic "evidence": A critique based on Freud's case of Little Hans. *J. Nerv. Ment. Dis.,* 131: 135–148, 1960.

24

ACQUISITION OF IMITATIVE SPEECH BY SCHIZOPHRENIC CHILDREN

O. Ivar Lovaas, John P. Berberich, Bernard F. Perloff and Benson Schaeffer

Abstract. Two mute schizophrenic children were taught imitative speech within an operant conditioning framework. The training procedure consisted of a series of increasingly fine verbal discriminations; the children were rewarded for closer and closer reproductions of the attending adults' speech. We found that reward delivered contingent upon imitation was necessary for development of imitation. Furthermore, the newly established imitation was shown to have acquired rewarding properties for the children.

With the great majority of children, the problem of teaching speech never arises. Speech develops within each child's particular environment without parents and teachers having to know a great deal about how it occurs. Yet, in some children, because of deviations in organic structure or prior experience, speech fails to develop. Children with the diagnosis of childhood schizophrenia, especially autistic children, often show little in the way of speech development (1). The literature on childhood schizophrenia suggests two conclusions regarding speech in such children: first, that the usual treatment setting (psychotherapy) in which these children are placed might not be conducive to speech development (2); and second, that a child failing to develop speech by the

Reprinted from *Science,* Vol. 151, 11 February, 1966, pp. 705–707, with the permission of the American Association for the Advancement of Science (copyright 1966 by the American Association for the Advancement of Science) and the authors.

Study supported by grants from Margaret Sabl of Los Angeles. We express appreciation to James Q. Simmons and the staff at the Children's Unit. Neuropsychiatric Institute, University of California, Los Angeles.

age of 5 years remains withdrawn and does not improve clinically (2). That is, the presence or absence of speech is an important prognostic indicator. It is perhaps obvious that a child who can speak can engage in a much more therapeutic interchange with his environment than the child who has no speech.

The failure of some children to develop speech as a "natural" consequence of growing up poses the need for an increased knowledge of how language is acquired. A procedure for the development of speech in previously mute children would not only be of practical importance but might also illuminate the development of speech in normal children. Although several theoretical attempts have been made to account for language development, the empirical basis for these theoretical formulations is probably inadequate. In fact, there are no published, systematic studies on how to go about developing speech in a person who has never spoken. We now outline a procedure by which speech can be made to occur. Undoubtedly there are or will be other ways by which speech can be acquired. Furthermore, our procedure centers on the acquisition of only one aspect of speech, the acquisition of vocal responses. The development of speech also requires the acquisition of a context for the occurrence of such responses ("meaning").

Casual observation suggests that normal children acquire words by hearing speech; that is, children learn to speak by imitation. The mute schizophrenic children with whom we worked were not imitative. Thus the establishment of imitation in these children appeared to be the most beneficial and practical starting point for building speech. The first step in creating speech, then, was to establish conditions in which imitation of vocal sounds would be learned.

The method that we eventually found most feasible for establishing verbal imitation involved a discrimination training procedure. Early in training the child was rewarded only if he emitted a sound within a certain time after an adult had emitted a sound. Next he was rewarded only if the sound he emitted within the prescribed interval resembled the adult's sound. Toward the end of the training, he was rewarded only if his vocalization very closely matched the adult's vocalization—that is, if it was, in effect, imitative. Thus verbal imitation was taught through the development of a series of increasingly fine discriminations.

The first two children exposed to this program are discussed here. Chuck and Billy were 6-year-old in-patients at the Neuropsychiatric Institute at UCLA. These children were selected for the program because they did not speak. At the onset of the program, vocal behavior in both children was restricted to occasional vowel productions with no discernible communicative intent. These vowel sounds occurred infrequently, except when the children were tantrumous, and did not resemble the pre-speech babbling of infants. In addition, the children evidenced no appropriate play (for example, they would spin toys or mouth them). They engaged in a considerable amount of self-stimulatory behavior such as rocking and twirling. They did not initiate social contacts and became tantrumous when such contact was initiated by others. They evidenced occasional self-destructive behavior (biting self, head-banging, and so forth). Symbolic rewards such as social approval were inoperative, so biological rewards such as food were substituted. It short, they were profoundly schizophrenic.

Training was conducted 6 days a week 7 hours a day, with a 15-minute rest period accompanying each hour of training. During the training sessions the child and the adult sat facing each other, their heads about 30 cm apart. The adult physically prevented the child from leaving the training situation by holding the child's legs between his own legs. Rewards, in the form of single spoonsful of the child's meal, were delivered immediately after correct responses. Punishment (spanking, shouting by the adult) was delivered for inattentive, self-destructive, and tantrumous behavior which interfered with the training, and most of these behaviors were thereby suppressed within 1 week. Incorrect vocal behavior was never punished.

Four distinct steps were required to establish verbal imitation. In step 1, the child was rewarded for all vocalizations. We frequently would fondle the children and we avoided aversive stimulation. This was done in order to increase the frequency of vocal responses. During this stage in training the child was also rewarded for visually fixating on the adult's mouth. When the child reached an achievement level of about one verbal response every 5 seconds and was visually fixating on the adult's mouth more than 50 percent of the time, step 2 of training was introduced.

Step 2 marked our initial attempt to bring the child's verbal behavior under our verbal control in such a manner that our speech would ultimately stimulate speech in the child. Mastery of this second step involved acquisition of a temporal discrimination by the child. The adult emitted a vocal response— for example, "baby"—about once on the average of every 10th second. The child was rewarded only if he vocalized within 6 seconds after the adult's vocalization. However, any vocal response of the child would be rewarded in that time interval. Step 3 was introduced when the frequency of the child's vocal responses within the 6-second interval was three times what it had been initially.

Step 3 was structurally similar to the preceeding step, but it included the additional requirement that the child actually match the adult's vocalization before receiving the reward. In this and in following steps the adult selected the verbalization to be placed in imitative training from a pool of possible verbalizations that had met one or more of the following criteria. First, we selected vocal behaviors that could be prompted, that is, vocal behaviors that could be elicited by a cue prior to any experimental training, such as by manually moving the child through the behavior.

An example of training with the use of a prompt is afforded in teaching the sound "b". The training would proceed in three stages: (i) the adult emitted "b" and simultaneously prompted the child to emit "b" by holding the child's lips closed with his fingers and quickly removing them when the child exhaled; (ii) the prompt would be gradually faded, by the adult's moving his fingers away from the child's mouth, to his cheek, and finally gently touching the child's jaw; (iii) the adult emitted the vocalization "b" only, withholding all prompts. The rate of fading was determined by the child; the sooner the child's verbal behavior came under control of the adult's without the use of the prompt, the better. The second criterion for selection of words or sounds in the early stages of training centered on their concomitant visual components (which we exaggerated when we pronounced them), such as those of the

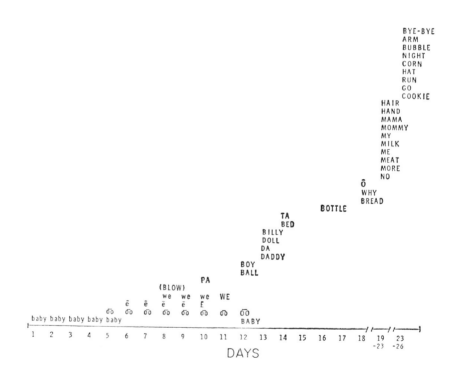

Figure 1

Acquisition of verbal imitation by Billy. The abscissa denotes training days. Words and sounds are printed in lower case letters on the days they were introduced, and in capital letters on the days they were mastered.

labial consonant "m" and of open-mouthed vowels like "a." We selected such sounds after having previously found that the children could discriminate words with visual components more easily than those with only auditory components (the guttural consonants, "k" and "g," proved extremely difficult and, like "l" and "s," were mastered later than other sounds). Third, we selected for training sounds which the child emitted most frequently in step 1.

Step 4 was a recycling of step 3, with the addition of a new sound. We selected a sound that was very different from those presented in step 3, so that the child could discriminate between the new and old sounds more easily. To make certain that the child was in fact imitating, we randomly interspersed the sounds of step 3 with the sound of step 4, in a randomized ratio of about 1 to 3. This random presentation "forced" (or enabled) the child to discriminate the particular sounds involved, in order to be rewarded. There was no requirement placed upon the child in step 3 to discriminate specific aspects such as vowels, consonants, and order of the adult's speech: a child might master step 3 without attending to the specific properties of the adult's speech. Each new introduction of sounds and words required increasingly fine discrimination by the child and hence provided evidence that the child was in fact matching the adult's speech. All steps beyond step 4 consisted of replications of step 3, but new sounds, words, and phrases were used. In each new step the previously mastered words and sounds were rehearsed on a randomized ratio of 1 to 3. The next step was introduced when the child had mastered the previous steps —that is, when he had made ten consecutive correct replications of the adult's utterances.

One hour of each day's training was tape-recorded. Two independent observers scored the child's correct vocal responses from these sessions. A correct response was defined as a recognizable reproduction of the adult's utterance. The observers showed better than 90 percent agreement over sessions. When the child's correct responses are plotted against days of training, and the resulting function is positively accelerated, it can be said that the child has learned to imitate.

The results of the first 26 days of imitation training, starting from introduction of step 3, have been plotted for Billy (Fig. 1). The abscissa denotes training days. The words and sounds are printed in lower case letters on the days they were introduced and in capital letters on the days they were mastered. It can be seen that as training progressed the rate of mastery increased. Billy took several days to learn a single word during the first 2 weeks of the program, but a single day to master several words during the last 2 weeks. Chuck's performance was very similar to Billy's.

After 26 days of training both children had learned to imitate new words with such ease and rapidity that merely adding verbal responses to their imitative repertoire seemed pointless. Hence the children were then introduced to the second part of the language training program, wherein they were taught to use language appropriately.

The imitation training took place in a rather complex environment, with many events happening concurrently. We hypothesized that it was the reward, given for imitative behavior, which was crucial to the learning. To test this hypothesis, the adult uttered the sounds as during the training and the children received the same number of rewards as before. However, the rewards were contingent upon time elapsed since the last reward, regardless of the child's behavior.

The data show a deterioration in imitation behavior whenever rewards are shifted from response-contingent to time-contingent delivery. It is concluded, therefore, that reward immediately following correct, imitative behavior (and withholding of reward following incorrect responding) is a crucial variable in maintaining imitative behavior in these children. The same finding has been reported by Baer and Sherman (3) who worked with imitative behavior in normal children.

Since the child was rewarded whenever he responded like the adult, *similarity* was consistently associated with food. Because of such association, similarity should become symbolic of reward. In other words, imitative behavior, being symbolic of reward, should eventually provide its own reward (Baer and Sherman, 3). To test this hypothesis, both children were exposed to Norwegian words which they were unable to reproduce perfectly when first presented. The adult simply stated the Norwegian word and the child always attempted to repeat it; no extrinsic rewards were delivered. However, occasionally the child was presented with English words which the adult rewarded when correctly imitated. This procedure was necessary to maintain the hypothesized symbolic (learned) reward function of imitation.

The children improved in the imitation of the Norwegian words over time. It is as if they were rewarded for correct behavior. In view of the data pointing to the need for rewards in maintaining imitative behavior, and in the absence of extrinsic rewards, we would argue that the reward was intrinsic and a function of the prior imitation training. There is one implication of this finding which is of particular interest for therapeutic reasons: children may be able to acquire new behaviors on their own. (This finding contrasts with the frequent stereotype of a conditioning product, namely, that of an automaton unable to function independently.)

Currently, three new schizophrenic children are undergoing the same speech training program as Billy and Chuck. After 3 days of training, one of these children achieved a level of imitative behavior similar to that shown by Billy and Chuck after 26 days. It should be pointed out that schizophrenic children are a very heterogeneous group with respect to their speech histories and symptomatology in general, and that Billy and Chuck had failed in development to a profound degree. Insofar as one works with such a diverse population, it is likely that numerous procedures could be helpful in establishing speech.

REFERENCES

1. B. Rimland, *Infantile Autism* (Appleton-Century-Crofts, New York, 1964).
2. J. Brown, *Amer. J. Orthopsychiat.* 30, 382 (1960).
3. D. Baer and J. Sherman, *J. Exp. Child Psychol.* 1, 37 (1964).

25

INTENSIVE TREATMENT OF PSYCHOTIC BEHAVIOUR BY STIMULUS

Teodoro Ayllon

Summary. This investigation demonstrates that extensive and effective behavioural modification is feasible without costly and lengthy psychotherapeutic treatment. In addition, the often heard notion that another undesirable type of behaviour will replace the original problem behaviour is not supported by the findings to date.

INTRODUCTION

Until recently, the effective control of behaviour was limited to the animal laboratory. The extension of this control to human behaviour was made when Lindsley successfully adapted the methodology of operant conditioning to the study of psychotic behaviour (Lindsley, 1956). Following Lindsley's point of departure other investigators have shown that, in its essentials, the behaviour of mental defective individuals (Orlando and Bijou, 1960), stutterers (Flanagan, Goldiamond and Azrin, 1958), mental patients (Hutchinson and Azrin, 1961), autistic (Ferster and DeMyer, 1961), and normal children (Bijou, 1961; Azrin and Lindsley, 1956) is subject to the same controls.

Reprinted from *Behavior Research and Therapy,* 1, 1963, 53–61, with the permission of Pergamon Publishing Company and Dr. Ayllon (Footnotes have been renumbered.)

This report is based, in part, on a two-year research project (1959–1961), conducted by the author at the Saskatchewan Hospital, Weyburn, Saskatchewan, Canada, and supported by a grant from the Commonwealth Fund. Grateful acknowledgment is due to H. Osmond and I. Clancey of the Saskatchewan Hospital. The author also thanks E. Haughton who assisted in the conduct of this investigation, and N. Azrin and W. Holtz for their critical reading of the manuscript.

Despite the obvious implications of this research for applied settings there has been a conspicuous lag between the research findings and their application. The greatest limitation to the direct application of laboratory principles has been the absence of control over the subjects' environment. Recently, however, a series of applications in a regulated psychiatric setting has clearly demonstrated the possibilities of behavioural modification (Ayllon and Michael, 1959; Ayllon and Haughton, 1962). Some of the behaviour studied has included repetitive and highly stereotyped responses such as complaining, pacing, refusal to eat, hoarding and many others.

What follows is a demonstration of behaviour techniques for the intensive individual treatment of psychotic behaviour. Specific pathological behaviour patterns of a single patient were treated by manipulating the patient's environment.

The Experimental Ward and Control over the Reinforcement

This investigation was conducted in a mental hospital ward, the characteristics of which have been described elsewhere (Ayllon and Haughton, 1962). Briefly, this was a female ward to which only authorized personnel were allowed access. The ward staff was made up of psychiatric nurses and untrained aides who carried out the environmental manipulations under the direction of the experimenter. Using a time-sample technique, patients were observed daily every 30 minutes from 7:00 a.m. to 11 p.m.

The dining room was the only place where food was available and entrance to the dining room could be regulated. Water was freely available at a drinking fountain on the ward. None of the patients had ground passes or jobs outside the ward.

Subject

The patient was a 47-year-old female patient diagnosed as a chronic schizophrenic. The patient had been hospitalized for 9 years. Upon studying the patient's behaviour on the ward, it became apparent that the nursing staff[1] spent considerable time caring for her. In particular, there were three aspects of her behaviour which seemed to defy solution. The first was stealing food. The second was the hoarding of the ward's towels in her room. The third undesirable aspect of her behaviour consisted in her wearing excessive clothing, e.g. a half-dozen dresses, several pairs of stockings, sweaters, and so on.

In order to modify the patient's behaviour systematically, each of these

[1]As used in this paper, 'nurse' is a generic term including all those who actually work on the ward (attendants, aides, psychiatric and registered nurses).

three types of behaviour (stealing food, hoarding, and excessive dressing) was treated separately.

EXPERIMENT I

Control of Stealing Food by Food Withdrawal

The patient had weighed over 250 pounds for many years. She ate the usual tray of food served to all patients, but, in addition, she stole food from the food counter and from other patients. Because the medical staff regarded her excessive weight as detrimental to her health, a special diet had been prescribed for her. However, the patient refused to diet and continued stealing food. In an effort to discourage the patient from stealing, the ward nurses had spent considerable time trying to persuade her to stop stealing food. As a last resort, the nurses would force her to return the stolen food.

To determine the extent of food stealing, nurses were instructed to record all behaviour associated with eating in the dining room. This record, taken for nearly a month, showed that the patient stole food during two thirds of all meals.

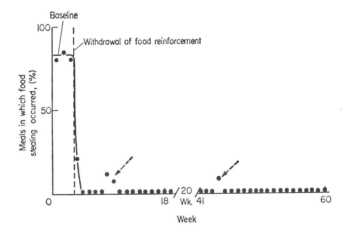

Figure 1

A response, food stealing, is eliminated when it results in the withdrawal of food reinforcement. The dotted arrows indicate the rare occasions when food stealing occurred. For purposes of presentation a segment comprising 20 weeks during which no stealing occurred is not included.

Procedure

The traditional methods previously used to stop the patient from stealing food were discontinued. No longer were persuasion, coaxing, or coercion used.

The patient was assigned to a table in the dining room, and no other patients were allowed to sit with her. Nurses removed the patient from the dining room when she approached a table other than her own, or when she picked up unauthorized food from the dining room counter. In effect, this procedure resulted in the patient missing a meal whenever she attempted to steal food.

Results

Figure 1 shows that when withdrawal of positive reinforcement (i.e. meal) was made dependent upon the patient's 'stealing', this response was

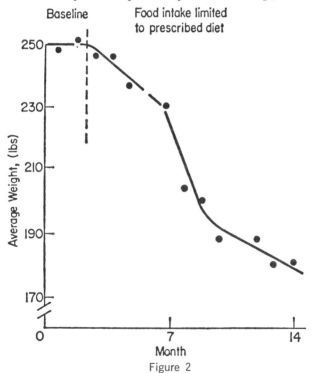

Figure 2

The effective control of food stealing results in a notable reduction in body weight. As the patient's food intake is limited to the prescribed diet her weight decreases gradually.

eliminated in two weeks. Because the patient no longer stole food, she ate only the diet prescribed for her. The effective control of the stealing response is also indicated by the gradual reduction in the patient's body weight. At no time during the patient's 9 years of hospitalization had she weighed less than 230 pounds. Figure 2 shows that at the conclusion of this treatment her weight stabilized at 180 pounds or 17 per cent loss from her original weight. At this time, the patient's physical condition was regarded as excellent.

Discussion

A principle used in the laboratory shows that the strength of a response may be weakened by the removal of positive reinforcement following the response (Ferster, 1958). In this case, the response was food-stealing and the reinforcer was access to meals. When the patient stole food she was removed from the dining room and missed her meal.

After one year of this treatment, two occasions of food stealing occurred. The first occasion, occurring after one year of not stealing food, took the nurses by surprise and, therefore the patient 'got away' with it. The second occasion occurred shortly thereafter. This time, however, the controlling consequences were in force. The patient missed that meal and did not steal again to the conclusion of this investigation.

Because the patient was not informed or warned of the consequences that followed stealing, the nurses regarded the procedure as unlikely to have much effect on the patient's behaviour. The implicit relief that verbal instructions are indispensable for learning is part of present day psychiatric lore. In keeping with this notion, prior to this behaviour treatment, the nurses had tried to persuade the patient to co-operate in dieting. Because there were strong medical reasons for her losing weight, the patient's refusal to follow a prescribed diet was regarded as further evidence of her mental illness.

EXPERIMENT II

Control of One Form of Hoarding Behaviour Through Stimulus Satiation

During the 9 years of hospitalization, the patient collected large numbers of towels and stored them in her room. Although many efforts had been made to discourage hoarding, this behaviour continued unaltered. The only recourse for the nursing staff was to take away the patient's towels about twice a week.

Procedure

The routine removal of the towels from the patient's room was discontinued. Instead, a programme of stimulus satiation was carried out by the nurses. Intermittently, throughout the day, the nurses took a towel to the patient when she was in her room and simply handed it to her without any comment. The first week she was given an average of 7 towels daily, and by the third week this number was increased to 60.

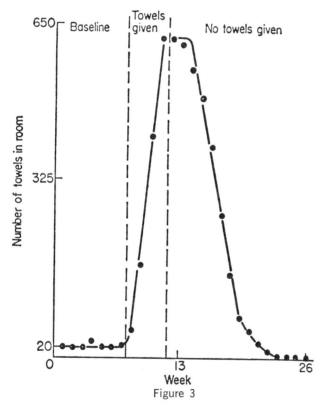

Figure 3

A response, towel hoarding, is eliminated when the patient is given towels in excess. When the number of towels reaches 625 the patient starts to discard them. She continues to do so until the number in her room averages 1.5 compared to the previous 20 towels per week.

Results

The technique of satiation eliminated the towel hoarding. Figure 3 shows the mean number of towels per count found in the patient's room. When the

number of towels kept in her room reached the 625 mark she started taking
a few of them out. Thereafter, no more towels were given to her. During the
next 12 months the mean number of towels found in her room was 1.5
per week.

Discussion

The procedure used to reduce the amount of towel hoarding bears resemblance to satiation of a reinforcer. A reinforcer loses its effect when an
excessive amount of that reinforcer is made available. Accordingly, the response
maintained by that reinforcer is weakened. In this application, the towels
constituted the reinforcing stimuli. When the number of towels in her room
reached 625, continuing to give her towels seemed to make their collection
aversive. The patient then proceeded to rid herself of the towels until she had
virtually none.

During the first few weeks of satiation, the patient was observed patting
her cheeks with a few towels, apparently enjoying them. Later, the patient was
observed spending much of her time folding and stacking the approximately
600 towels in her room. A variety of remarks were made by the patient regarding receipt of towels. All verbal statements made by the patient were recorded
by the nurse. The following represent typical remarks made during this experiment. First week: As the nurse entered the patient's room carrying a towel, the
patient would smile and say, "Oh, you found it for me, thank you." Second
week: When the number of towels given to patient increased rapidly, she told
the nurses, "Don't give me no more towels. I've got enough." Third week:
"Take them towels away. . . . I can't sit here all night and fold towels." Fourth
and fifth weeks: "Get these dirty towels out of here." Sixth week: After she
had started taking the towels out of her room, she remarked to the nurse, "I
can't drag any more of these towels, I just can't do it."

The quality of these remarks suggests that the initial effect of giving
towels to the patient was reinforcing. However as the towels increased they
ceased to be reinforcing, and presumably became aversive.

The ward nurses, who had undergone a three-year training in psychiatric
nursing, found it difficult to reconcile the procedure in this experiment with
their psychiatric orientation. Most nurses subscribed to the popular psychiatric
view which regards hoarding behaviour as a reflections of a deep 'need' for
love and security. Presumably, no 'real' behavioural change was possible without
meeting the patient's 'needs' first. Even after the patient discontinued hoarding
towels in her room, some nurses predicted that the change would not last and
that worse behaviour would replace it. Using a time-sampling technique the
patient was under continuous observation for over a year after the termination

of the satiation programme. Not once during this period did the patient return to hoarding towels. Furthermore, no other behaviour problem replaced hoarding.

EXPERIMENT III

Control of an Additional Form of Hoarding Through Food Reinforcement

Shortly after the patient had been admitted to the hospital she wore an excessive amount of clothing which included several sweaters, shawls, dresses, undergarments and stockings. The clothing also included sheets and towels wrapped around her body, and a turban-like head-dress made up of several towels. In addition, the patient carried two or three cups on one hand while holding a bundle of miscellaneous clothing, and a large purse on the other.

To determine the amount of clothing worn by the patient, she was weighed before each meal over a period of two weeks. By subtracting her actual body weight from that recorded when she was dressed, the weight of her clothing was obtained.

Procedure

The response required for reinforcement was stepping on a scale and meeting a predetermined weight. The requirement for reinforcement consisted of meeting a single weight (i.e. her body weight plus a specified number of pounds of clothing). Initially she was given an allowance of 23 pounds over her current body weight. This allowance represented a 2 pound reduction from her usual clothing weight. When the patient exceeded the weight requirement, the nurse stated in a matter-of-fact manner, "Sorry, you weigh too much, you'll have to weigh less." Failure to meet the required weight resulted in the patient missing the meal at which she was being weighed. Sometimes, in an effort to meet the requirement, the patient discarded more clothing than she was required. When this occurred the requirement was adjusted at the next weighing-time to correspond to the limit set by the patient on the preceding occasion.

Results

When food reinforcement is made dependent upon the removal of super-fluous clothing the response increases in frequency. Figure 4 shows that the

patient gradually shed her clothing to meet the more demanding weight requirement until she dressed normally. At the conclusion of this experiment her
clothes weighed 3 pounds compared to the 25 pounds she wore before this
treatment.

Some verbal shaping was done in order to encourage the patient to leave
the cups and bundles she carried with her. Nurses stopped her at the dining
room and said, "Sorry, no things are allowed in the dining room." No mention
of clothing or specific items was made to avoid focusing undue attention upon
them. Within a week, the patient typically stepped on the scale without her
bundle and assorted objects. When her weight was over the limit, the patient
was informed that she weighed "too much." She then proceeded to take off a
few clothes, stepped on the scale again, and upon meeting the weight requirement, gained access to the dining room.

According to the principle of reinforcement a class of responses is
strengthened when it is followed by reinforcement. A reinforcer is such when
it results in a response increase. In this application the removal of excessive

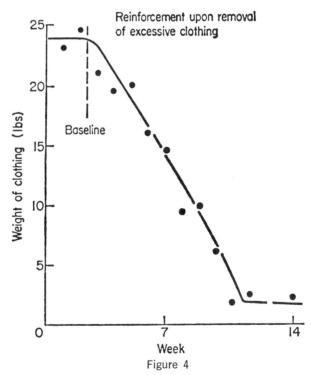

Figure 4

A response, excessive dressing, is eliminated when food reinforcement is made
dependent upon removal of superfluous clothing. Once the weight of the clothing
worn by the patient drops to 3 pounds it remains stable.

clothing constituted the response and the reinforcer was food (i.e. access to meals). When the patient met the weight requirement she was reinforced by being given access to meals.

At the start of this experiment, the patient missed a few meals because she failed to meet the weight requirement, but soon thereafter she gradually discarded her superfluous clothing. First, she left behind odd items she had carried in her arms, such as bundles, cups and handbags. Next she took off the elaborate headgear and assorted "capes" or shawls she had worn over her shoulders. Although she had worn 18 pairs of stockings at one time, she eventually shed these also.

During the initial part of this experiment, the patient showed some emotional behavior, e.g. crying, shouting and throwing chairs around. Because nurses were instructed to "ignore" this emotional behaviour, the patient obtained no sympathy or attention from them. The withholding of social reinforcement for emotional behaviour quickly led to its elimination.

At the conclusion of this behaviour treatment, the patient typically stepped on the scale wearing a dress, undergarments, a pair of stockings and a pair of light shoes. One of the behavioural changes concomitant with the current environmental manipulation was that as the patient began dressing normally she started to participate in small social events in the hospital. This was particularly new to the patient as she had previously remained seclusive spending most of the time in her room.

About this time the patient's parents came to visit her and insisted on taking her home for a visit. This was the first time during the patient's 9 years of hospitalization that her parents had asked to take her out. They remarked that previously they had not been interested in taking her out because the patient's excessive dressing in addition to her weight made her look like a "circus freak".

CONCLUSIONS

The research presented here was conducted under nearly ideal conditions. The variables manipulated (i.e. towels and food) were under full experimental control. Using a time-sample technique the patient was observed daily every 30 minutes from 7:00 a.m. to 11 p.m. Nurses and aides carried out these observations which were later analysed in terms of gross behaviour categories. These observations were in force for over a year during which time these three experiments were conducted. The results of these observations indicate that none of the three pathological behaviour patterns (i.e. food stealing, hoarding and excessive dressing) exhibited by the patient were replaced by any undesirable behaviour.

The patient displayed some emotional behaviour in each experiment, but each time it subsided when social reinforcement (i.e. attention) was not forthcoming. The patient did not become violent or seclusive as a consequence of these experiments. Instead, she became socially more accessible to patients and staff. She did not achieve a great deal of social success but she did begin to participate actively in social functions.

A frequent problem encountered in mental hospitals is overeating. In general this problem is solved by prescribing a reduction diet. Many patients, however, refuse to take a reduction diet and continue overeating. When confronted with this behaviour, psychiatric workers generally resort to two types of explanations.

One explanation of overeating points out that only with the active and sincere cooperation of the patient can weight reduction be accomplished. When the patient refuses to co-operate he is regarded as showing more signs of mental illness and all hopes of eliminating overeating come to an end.

Another type of explanation holds that overeating is not the behaviour to be concerned with. Instead, attention is focused on the psychological 'needs' of the patient. These 'needs' are said to be the cause of the observable behaviour, overeating. Therefore the emphasis is on the removal of the cause and not on the symptom or behaviour itself. Whatever theoretical merit these explanations may have, it is unfortunate that they fail to suggest practical ways of treating the behaviour itself. As a consequence, the patient continues to overeat often to the detriment of his health.

The current psychiatric emphasis on the resolution of the mental conflict is presumably at the basis of the symptoms, is perhaps misplaced. What seems to have been forgotten is that behaviour problems, such as those reported here, prevent the patient from being considered for discharge not only by the hospital personnel but also by the patient's relatives. Indeed, as far as the patient's relatives are concerned, the index of improvement or deterioration is the readily observable behaviour and not a detailed account of the mechanics of the mental apparatus.

Many individuals are admitted to mental hospitals because of one or more specific behaviour difficulties and not always because of a generalized 'mental' disturbance. For example, an individual may go into a mental hospital because he has refused to eat for several days, or because he talks to himself incessantly. If the goal of therapy were behavioural rehabilitation, these problems would be treated and normal eating and normal talking reinstated. However, the current emphasis in psychotherapy is on 'mental-conflict resolution' and little or no attention is given to dealing directly with the behavioural problems which prevent the patient from returning to the community.

REFERENCES

Ayllon, T. and Michael, J. (1959) The psychiatric nurse as a behavioral engineer. *J. exp. anal. Behav.* 2, 323–334.

Ayllon, T. and Haughton, E. (1962) Control of the behavior of schizophrenic patients by food. *J. exp. anal. Behav.* 5, 343–352.

Azrin, N. and Lindsley, O. (1956) The reinforcement of cooperation between children. *J. abnorm. (soc.) Psychol.* 52, 100–102.

Bijou, S. (1961) Discrimination performance as a baseline for individual analysis of young children. *Child Develpm.* 32, 163–170.

Ferster, C. B. (1958) Control of behavior in chimpanzees and pigeons by time out from positive reinforcement. *Psychol. Monogr.* 72, 1–38.

Ferster, C. and Demyer, M. (1961) The development of performances in autistic children in an automatically controlled environment. *J. chron. Dis.* 13, 312–345.

Flanagan, B., Goldiamond, I and Azrin, N. (1958) Operant stuttering: The control of stuttering behavior through response-contingent consequences. *J. exp. anal. Behav.* 56, 49–56.

Hutchinson, R. R. and Azrin, N. H. (1961) Conditioning of mental hospital patients to fixed-ratio schedules of reinforcement. *J. exp. anal. Behav.* 4, 87–95.

Lindsley, O. R. (1956) Operant conditioning methods applied to research in chronic schizophrenia. *Psychiat. Res. Rep.* 5, 118–139.

Orlando, R. and Bijou, S. (1960) Single and multiple schedules of reinforcement in developmentally retarded children. *J. exp. anal. Behav.* 3, 339–348.

26

BEHAVIOR THERAPY AND PSYCHOTHERAPY

Bernard Weitzman

A number of procedures which would, a decade ago, have claimed the status of "psychotherapy" (cf., e.g., Wolpe, 1958) have in the recent past characterized themselves as "behavior therapies." It is intended by its users that this nomenclature shall be pregnant with meaning (cf. Eysenck, 1960). Properly understood, it reflects the long-resisted penetration of clinical practice by that form of "scientism" which, earlier, had a hand in leading academic "psychologists" to their sea change into "behavioral scientists." While attempts to articulate the historical factors which underlie such transformations are always speculative, there seems little doubt that, in the case of clinical practice, the publication of Wolpe's psychotherapeutic manual is one causal nexus. The apparent effectiveness of the techniques devised by Wolpe, in particular the procedure called "systematic desensitization" (cf. Grossberg, 1964), has won him a following, and has invited the use of an argument of virtue by association in a bid to legitimize the host of procedures calling themselves "behavior therapies."

Many psychologists in clinical practice have found quite irresistible the promise of quick and effective results which Wolpe's procedure holds forth, despite a host of objections to it which arise from the various "dynamic" orientations. Others, feeling tempted, have resisted the demons of mechanization and dehumanization, and the danger of "loss of soul" which is understood to be implicit in the Weltanschauung of behaviorism. This resistance is buttressed by theoretical allegiances and made to seem necessary by a variety of therapeutic rubrics, for example, the expectation of symptom substitution, a problem which will be treated in some detail later.

Reprinted from the *Psychological Review*, 74, 1967, 300–317, with the permission of the American Psychological Association and Dr. Weitzman.

The rejection, on grounds of principle, of behavior therapy by the clinical community, and the derogatory treatment of dynamic therapies by behavior therapists, have had the inevitable consequence of generating premature crystallizations of positions in both camps. The lines of battle have been most sharply and articulately drawn in the writings of Eysenck (1960), who asserts:

> . . . behavior therapy is an *alternative* type of treatment to psychotherapy [i.e., it is not ancillary]; . . . it is a *superior* type of treatment, both from the point of view of theoretical background and practical effectiveness; . . . in so far as psychotherapy is at all effective, it is so in virtue of certain principles which can be *derived from learning theory* . . . psychotherapy itself, when shorn of its inessential and irrelevant parts, can usefully be considered as a minor part of behavior therapy. [p. ix]

While the position taken by Eysenck is more extreme than other behavior therapists might prefer, its clarity makes it a useful target for analysis. Some comments on the contents of Eysenck's statement will clear the way for the major substance of this essay, that is, an examination of the grounds upon which clinicians have based their rejection of behavior therapy.

THE THEORETICAL BACKGROUND OF BEHAVIOR THERAPY

The evidence of the practical effectiveness of behavior therapy, while not conclusive, is indeed impressive. However, if one notes (as Eysenck does) that the term "behavior therapy" refers to a large and diverse group of treatment methods, clarity requires that the question of effectiveness must be put to each method. If one extracts from the mass of data the results of systematic desensitization therapy, one is left with an impression which is rather different from that intended by Eysenck. The residue, that is, the evidence of the practical effectiveness of behavior therapies other than systematic desensitization, while interesting, would excite the enthusiasm of few clinicians (cf. Grossberg, 1964). As a first step then, the accuracy of Eysenck's statement might be increased by appropriately reading "systematic desensitization" where he has written "behavior therapy." This sharpening of focus permits a more cogent appraisal of the evidence, and a more lucid analysis of the problems.

An issue of considerable importance is raised by Eysenck's claim of theoretical superiority for behavior therapy. It has been pointed out, from both camps, that analytic theory requires that symptom substitution or recurrence must attend a symptomatic treatment which, by definition, does not affect the dynamic sources of the symptoms. The evidence is rather impressive that neither substitution nor recurrence typically follows treatment by systematic desensitization. When occasional recurrences are reported, they are described as being of low intensity and, apparently, never catastrophic. Wolpe and Eysenck have both explicitly contended that this evidence constitutes a decisive empirical argument against psychoanalysis. A detailed analysis of the theoretical grounds upon which this contention is based will be undertaken later in this discussion. At this point, however, it must be noted that a crucial logical alternative, that is, that systematic desensitization does, as a technique, in some way affect the total psychological matrix, has been given due theoretical consideration by behavior therapists or by psychotherapists. Attempts have been made to demonstrate, *empirically,* the specificity of the effects of systematic desensitization, that is, to demonstrate that desensitization is confined, in the locus of its effects, to the undoing of specific conditioned associations. The evidence, however, is not altogether convincing and certainly not conclusive. As long as the issue is empirically open, the *logical* analysis must be allowed.

When this analysis is undertaken it appears that there are implications of the data for Eysenck's theoretical model which have not been examined, and which seem to indicate that the Eysenckian position is vulnerable to criticisms similar to those leveled at psychoanalysis. Eysenck (1957) views neuroticism as a genetically determined constitutional predisposition. That is, all else being equal, there is a genetic determination of the likelihood that one individual will develop neurotic symptoms more readily than will another individual. Obviously, behavior therapy, in removing symptoms, cannot be expected to alter this genetic base. Thus, the likelihood of developing symptoms, insofar as this is genetically given, will remain constant. It would seem reasonable to assume that, in statistical mass, the number of patients treated as neurotics in any therapeutic setting will contain a disproportionately large number of individuals high in genetically determined neuroticism. If this reasoning is correct, Eysenck's model would seem to predict a high incidence of new symptom formations in patients who have already been treated for neurotic symptoms. Indeed, if one takes seriously the reports of almost total absence of new symptoms in patients treated by systematic desensitization, a problem of some difficulty arises for the Eysenckian model. On the one hand there are difficulties in attempting to solve the problem by entertaining the speculation that a lasting transformation of learning processes has been achieved by this technique if one is determined to deny that there are any nonspecific characterological consequences attending its application. (An analysis of some of the conceptual difficulties for S-R theories in ". . . explaining how *generality* of behavior results from specific learning experiences" has been presented by Breger and McGaugh, 1965, p. 348.) On the other hand, if it is granted that there are such nonspecific consequences, the genetic hypothesis must be formulated in a manner which makes such consequences intelligible. The alternatives for

Eysenck would seem to entail a surrender, both of the current conception of genetically determined neuroticism and of the insistence upon the specificity of the effects of desensitization.

Eysenck's intention, however, is not to burden his own theory with the support of his claim to theoretical superiority for behavior therapy. Rather, the burden falls more broadly on something called "learning theory." An issue which exists for many clinicians seems to pivot about the intrinsic relation which is claimed to exist between behavior therapy and this "learning theory." The clinician is asked to agree that if he accepts the method as therapeutically valid and gives credence to the data which support assertions of its effectiveness, he must "buy" some "S-R" model of man. But what model of man is, in fact, required? A number of comments on this relationship may be helpful.

In the foreword to a volume reporting the outcome of a summer symposium on learning theory (Estes, Koch, MacCorquodale, Meehl, Mueller, Schoenfeld & Verplanck, 1954), the editor writes:

> It might be supposed that there would crystallize out from such a critical and unbiased analysis of theories and the experimental evidence on which they rest, some one basic theory of the learning process which all reasonable persons could accept. If there were any such expectations among the members of the group, they were soon dissipated. Each theory appeared to exist within its own closed system and to defy direct comparison and the pooling of data. Concepts, techniques, apparatus, units of measurement, and definitions of terms were peculiar to a given theory and could not safely be lifted out of their own frame of reference. Each theory, then, had to be examined and analyzed separately for internal consistency and the degree to which it satisfied the logic of science. [p. vii]

In the context of a discussion similar to the present one, Breger and McGaugh (1965, p. 341) conclude that "The claim to scientific respectability by reference back to established laws of learning is . . . illusory." In light of these reports it seems somewhat misleading to speak as if there were a monolithic system properly called "learning theory." Indeed, Eysenck (1960) concedes this point. To the objection that "learning theorists are not always in agreement with each other," he answers:

> . . . those points about which argument rages are usually of academic [theoretical] interest rather than of practical importance. Thus, reinforcement theorists and contiguity theorists have strong differences of view about the necessity of reinforcement during learning and different reinforcement theorists have different theories about the

nature of reinforcement. Yet there would be general agreement in any particular case about the optimum methods of achieving a quick rate of conditioning. . . . [p. 15]

In fact, only an eclectic learning theory which systematically avoids examination of the relations between its own assumptions—that is, a nontheoretical amalgamation of pragmatic principles—can hope to derive the effects of a behavioral setting as complex as the therapeutic interview. Whether or not the methodological consensus which Eysenck assumes really exists (the reader is referred once more to the quotation from Estes *et al.,* 1954), the theoretical limitation which is acknowledged must be as constraining for those procedures called "behavior therapy" as for psychotherapy. That is, if there is no "learning theory" competent to handle the data of behavior therapy, there is no "learning theory" competent to handle the data of psychotherpy. If, then, one accepts the data of behavior therapy, one is faced, not with a set of necessary theoretical conclusions, but with a set of theoretical problems.

THE METHOD OF SYSTEMATIC DESENSITIZATION: AN INQUIRY

Since the most impressive data have been produced by Wolpe's method, it will be worthwhile to turn now to a more detailed consideration of systematic desensitization, and the relation of its practical methodology to Wolpe's conception of it.

Wolpe (1962) has described the genesis of systematic desensitization in discussing his replication of Masserman's (1943) study. Masserman produced "neurotic" behavior in cats by directing blasts of air at the animals as they began to eat. Wolpe, in his replication, demonstrated that the confrontation of appetitive and avoidant drive states is not a necessary condition for eliciting this symptomatology; that is, he obtained apparently the same form of neurotic behavior by shocking cats in the absence of food. (It is worth noting, en passant, that Wolpe has claimed that this demonstration undermines the psychoanalytic theory of the relation of symptom and conflict. While his study does seem to provide evidence concerning necessary conditions, it is not relevant to the premise that drive conflict is a *sufficient* condition for symptom formation.)

Wolpe then "deconditioned" the fear reaction by a procedure in which a gradual, stepwise approach was made to the feared stimuli (the experimental cage and room), each step accompanied by feedings. Feedings, sometimes repeated at a given step, led to extinction of the fear response at that level of approach and permitted feeding to be initiated at the next step. The animals were, finally, free of any signs of neurotic behavior. This result was rationalized by the assumption that the eating response inhibits the occurrence of anxiety and leads to the extinction of the anxiety response to the stimuli which are present at a given step.

Wolpe reasoned that eating is only one of a variety of behaviors which may be used to inhibit anxiety. This thinking led to the application of the procedure to human subjects. Relaxation was substituted for eating as the anxiety-inhibiting response, and the resulting method was called "systematic desensitization."

A description of this method sounds strikingly like the method used by Wolpe to cure his cats: The human subject is trained, by a short form of the Jacobson (1938) method, to develop high-strength relaxation responses. He is then, while in a relaxed condition, presented, one at a time, with preselected stimuli, known to produce anxiety and arranged in a series of intensity or approach steps. When, after one or a number of presentations, a given step elicits no anxiety response, the next stimulus in the intensity hierarchy is presented, until the most intense stimulus produces no anxiety.

In this description, however, is hidden a form of analogy-making which gives comfort to the behavior therapist but which obscures differences of profound significance between the systematic desensitizations of cats and men. The reaction of the clinician, that "they are treating patients the way they treat cats," fails to penetrate the flaws of the analogy. (It is not entirely beside the point to note that this reaction implicitly grants the legitimacy of the behavioristic interpretation of cat behavior. The necessity of that interpretation is, of course, open to question.) It is crucial that the above, stylized description of systematic desensitization be concretized and given a more detailed procedural analysis.

The human subject is trained in voluntary relaxation. The training directs the subject to careful observation of certain internal states, to the discrimination of tensions in the major muscle groups of the body, and to the voluntary cessation of muscular responding. When this highly complex "response" has been acquired, a stimulus is presented. That is to say, the patient is directed by the therapist to *imagine a stimulus* which he has previously described to the therapist and which he has placed, for the use of the therapist, among other anxiety-producing stimuli in a given hierarchical position. The patient is, in fact, required to produce a vivid visualization of a scene. It is this visualization which is the "stimulus" bandied about in discussions of systematic desensitization. As Breger and McGaugh (1965, p. 340) have put it, ". . . the use of the terms stimulus and response are only remotely allegorical to the traditional use of these terms in psychology." The importance of this characterization of the stimulus is underlined by the fact that *inability to produce such visualizations is grounds for rejecting a patient for treatment by this method.* Having "presented a stimulus," the therapist lapses into silence for periods of up to

1 minute. *Any stimulus present in this situation is produced by the patient's internal processes.*

The therapeutic effect of systematic desensitization thus seems to be produced in periods of silence. That is, the therapist describes a scene which, presumably, sets a process in motion. So long as this process continues neither therapist nor patient speaks, and neither acts. There is, thus, for the content of the therapeutic process itself, no response of record. In other words, the question of what transpires during these silences is not, and has not been, asked. In reaction to the formulation of this question, and to frequent spontaneous reports from patients who were concerned that their inability to maintain static visualizations of the scene described by the therapist might hamper therapy, the author undertook regular inquiry into the contents of these silences. Six patients being treated by the method of systematic desensitization were interviewed. An interview was conducted at the end of each session of desensitization, providing a sample of approximately 200 interviews. Without exception, when closely questioned, patients reported a flow of visual imagery. The initiating scene, once visualized, shifted and changed its form. Moreover, these transformations took place continuously and, when the imagining was terminated by the therapist, had produced images which were quite removed in their content from the intended stimulus. These contents, and the transformations they exhibit, compel a characterization as a form of spontaneous and apparently autonomous fantasy familiar to many dynamically oriented therapists and, in fact, a therapeutic focus for those analysts who use Jung's (1959) method of active imagination. (While there is one report in the literature—Weinberg & Zaslove, 1963—of " 'involuntary' manipulations of the imaginal process," during treatment by systematic desensitization, the observed shifts in the intended stimulus are understood by the authors as a form of "resistance" to the treatment.)

What emerges from this inquiry is the information that the initiating scene presented by the therapist undergoes a series of transformations and elaborations which are under the control of the patient's internal, psychological processes. With this information in hand, it is not surprising, to a dynamically oriented therapist, to find that a wealth of dynamically rich and exciting material results from desensitizations obtained with Wolpe's method. For example, in one case, immediately upon conclusion of a desensitization series dealing with the patient's fears about the eventual death of his mother, he spontaneously reported:

> It was as if my feelings about my mother were transformed. Whenever I thought about her dying what I really felt was a fear of my being deserted by her. Now if I think of her dying I feel sorry for *her* [patient's emphasis]. For the first time I feel sorry for her instead of for myself.

Such a reminder of the fact that one is engaging processes of profound depth and complexity is hardly unique in the writer's experience. Opportunities for similar observations will probably present themselves to any behavior therapist who is willing to listen, and might be expected to serve as a caution against the simplistic view that only a stimulus-response connection is being affected by the therapy.

To note that the stimulus of record in this procedure is a self-produced visualization, and then to observe that the period in which the therapeutic effect is produced is characterized by a flow of images and symbolic materials, stretches the analogy to Wolpe's procedure with the cats rather thin. The grounding of behavior therapy in the history of the past decade of experimental psychology, which behavior therapists hope has elevated them above the analytic schools and made a science of therapy, is placed in jeopardy by this finding. I am not aware of the existence, in the literature of experimental psychology generated by learning theories, of anything more than an unpaid promissory note in regard to conceptualizations of this form of cognitive activity.

When one notes, in addition, that in this procedure an internally produced, imagined representation of a stimulus has a reality in terms of its observable and specifiable behavioral consequences, equal to what one might expect of an externally produced stimulus, it is clear that the current conceptual horizons of S-R learning theories have been passed. What in fact seems to be demanded by these data is a conceptualization geared to understanding man as a cognitive being.

In all fairness to behavior therapists it should be noted that Wolpe has offered demonstrations of effectiveness for other procedures, including in vivo presentations of actual stimuli, based on his general principle of reciprocal inhibition, and using responses other than relaxation for the inhibition of anxiety. In addition, other behavior therapies have used therapeutic analogies which are, at least without closer scrutiny, better approximations of laboratory procedures with animals. The present critique, however, is justified by the status of systematic desensitization therapy, and does not require modification if its applicability to behavior therapies is not universal. In other words, the writer is not willing to prejudge the question of whether a single set of processes is responsible for the successes reported by every therapeutic school.

DEFENSE OF PSYCHOTHERAPY

Neither cognitive psychologists nor psychoanalysts have yet seized upon the data of systematic desensitization as providing an opportunity for theoretical growth. Nor have dynamically oriented therapists fulfilled their professional responsibility, which, or so it appears to me, requires the most careful investigation of a method which makes and supports claims to therapeutic efficacy. Here I am in full agreement with Eysenck (1960) when he says:

> . . . I have noted with some surprise that many psychotherapists have refused to use such methods [behavior therapies] . . . on *a priori* grounds, claiming that such mechanical methods simply could not work, and disregarding the large body of evidence available . . . only actual use can show the value of one method of treatment as opposed to another. [p. 14]

An attempt to weaken the claims of behavior therapists of the theoretical superiority of their position by a critical attack may be welcomed by analytically oriented psychologists but is not likely to prove constructive. It is, rather, necessary to turn attention to the attacks made upon psychotherapy and to seek out the legitimate sources of its defense. While this examination is cast in a theoretical context, it should be noted that there is also at issue, waiting off-stage but providing a background of urgency, a question of therapeutic responsibility; that is, what degree of theoretical certainty justifies withholding an available therapeutic method from a client?

The Therapy-Theory Distinction

There are two issues, typically confounded in the literature, which need to be separated before an intelligible analysis can proceed. It is claimed by behavior therapists that the clinical successes of behavior therapy invalidate psychoanalysis. Statistics on rates of "cure" are adduced in support of the claim that behavior therapy is more effective than psychoanalysis. Whatever the persuasiveness of these statistics, final judgment is a complex matter. Definitions of therapeutic practice and diagnostic criteria remain inadequate. The uses of the word "cure" by behavior therapists and psychotherapists are often incommensurable. Regardless, however, of history's verdict on the value of psychoanalytic therapy as it is practiced today, the problem will remain that psychoanalysis as a theory requires evaluation by criteria different from those by which therapy is evaluated.

There appears in many places in the analytic literature the articulation of an awareness of Freud's intention to consider analytic theory and therapy as distinct endeavors. The metapsychology incorporates analytically derived data but goes, with full comprehension of this step, far beyond the data. On the other hand, the metapsychology requires, if it is to be properly implemented in practice, procedures which have not yet been invented. Thus Reich (1949) wrote:

> All problems of techniques converge in the one basic question whether and how an unequivocal technique of analytic therapy can be derived from the theory of the neuroses. . . . Ample experience[s] . . . have shown that we have hardly made a beginning at this task. [p. 3]

A responsible critique of psychoanalysis by behavior therapists would need to make this distinction clear. The adequate response from psychoanalysts would also make this distinction. If behavior therapy is indeed the more effective instrumentality, this fact should instigate a reexamination of the untapped technical resources of analytic theory. One cannot expect progress to follow from defensive denials.

The Problem of Symptom Substitution

On other fronts, genuinely theoretical attacks have been leveled at psychoanalysis. The most potent of these is the claim that, according to analytic theory, symptom substitution or recurrence *must* follow a course of treatment which removes a symptom by treating it directly, that is, without altering the underlying source of the symptom. In fact, analysts have tended to the belief that symptomatic treatment may be worse than no treatment at all, that is, that it may be dangerous. Both Eysenck and Wolpe have stated that psychoanalytic theory is decisively undermined by the failure of this prediction. The expectation of symptom substitution is a clinical prejudice of long standing, but the data seem to require a reevaluation.

Freud (1936) considered the possibility that a symptom may be a behaviorally fixed pattern which has inherited the total cathectic energy of the impulse which existed at its time of origin:

> . . . of the repressed instinctual impulse itself we assumed that it persisted unchanged for an indefinite period in the unconscious. Now our interest shifts to the fate of the repressed, and we begin to feel that this persistence, unchanged and unchanging, is not a matter of course, is perhaps not even the rule. . . . Do there therefore still exist the old desires, of the earlier existence of which analysis in-

forms us? The answer appears obvious and certain. The old repressed desires must still persist in the unconscious, since we find their lineal descendents, the symptoms, still alive. *But this answer is inadequate; it does not make it possible to distinguish between the two possibilities that, on the one hand, the old desire now operates only through its descendents,* the symptoms, *to which it has transformed all its cathectic energy, or on the other hand, that the desire itself persists in addition.* . . . . There is much in the phenomena of both morbid and the normal life of the psyche which seems to demand the raising of such questions. In my study of the breakdown of the Oedipus complex, *I became mindful of the distinction between mere repression and the true disappearance of an old desire or impulse.* [p. 83; italics mine]

Successful symptomatic treatment may be taken as evidence for this second alternative, which might be extended and elaborated in ways entirely compatible with analytic theory.

On another level of analysis, Rapaport (1959) has noted that psychoanalysis is, essentially, a postdictive system. It can rationalize events after their occurrence, but cannot predict these events. This assertion is, in part, based upon Freud's conception of the energetic relations between the systems of the psychic economy. The originally unitary nature of the psychic structure is conceived as remaining, in certain essential characteristics, unalterable. Thus the energetics of those psychic systems which emerge in the course of the development of personality remain highly interactive. This interactivity makes it extraordinarily difficult to predict the consequences of alterations of energy distributions in one psychic system upon the other system. Is it possible, then, to state what follows of theoretical necessity from the removal of a symptom? Such an alteration of experience and behavior is, after all, likely to involve a not inconsiderable redistribution of cathectic processes. From this vantage it would appear that predictions of symptom substitution follow from a clinical rubric, and not with strict necessity from the analytic theory of the neuroses.

These considerations can be carried still further. Another line of analysis arises from the consequences of the thesis that the ego depends, for its development, on the greater efficiency of the secondary, as compared to the primary, process. That is, because the operations of the secondary process lead to increasing mastery of the relation of the psychic structure to object reality, exercise of the secondary process results in the binding of libidinal energies to the service of the emerging ego. Among the services to which energy is bound is that termed "repression." If one now considers the consequences for the ego, in its relations with object reality, of the removal of a symptom, the strands of the analysis come together. The removal of a symptom typically involves an increased mastery of object relations; for example, in the case of the person who is freed to express love, or hostility, or the person who is able, for the first time in a decade, to climb a flight of stairs without trembling. Such increased mastery must lead to an increment in the bound energy available to ego functioning. Even if one must insist that the dynamic source of an original symptom formation remains unaffected by the removal of that symptom, the consideration that an increase in bound energy may well lead to an increase in the effectiveness of repressive cathexes should prohibit any *certain* prediction that symptom substitution must follow.

A final line of analysis of this problem is stimulated by a consideration of Freud's conception of symptoms in their relation to anxiety. It is useful to compare this conception with Wolpe's behavioristic formulation. Wolpe conceives of anxiety as *the neurosis*. As such, it is simply an acquired, that is, learned, maladaptive response. In this formulation anxiety is not given a functional role in the psychic system. Freud, on the other hand, envisions symptoms, that is, maladaptive responses, as means used by the ego to protect itself from danger. Anxiety, in this context, serves as a signal to the ego that a dangerous instinctual demand is growing in strength. In response to this impending danger a symptomatic action is engaged which binds a portion of the energy available to the instinctual demand. This binding reduces the imperiousness of the instinctual demand and permits the ego to avoid engaging it. Thus conceived, the symptom is a behavior substituted for the behavior demanded by the instinctual arousal. It is a maladaptive substitute because the danger to the ego, which may, at the time of symptom formation, have been actual, no longer exists. The ego never discovers that the danger is past because every arousal of the instinct produces a signal of anxiety, which in turn produces a discharge of the instinctual energy through the substitutive action, that is, the symptom. Of immediate relevance to the problem in hand is that in order to bind, successfully, the energy of the instinct, the substitute formation must bear a certain meaningful relation to the original object of the instinct. That is, the symptom formation is governed by the same principles which govern every displacement from an original instinctual object. This is another way of saying that the symptom must contain, in some measure, a symbolically adequate representation of the original object. Thus, for example, an external, phobic stimulus must symbolically represent the meaning of the internal danger.

This analysis leads to another formulation of the belief that symptom substitution must follow symptom removal, but also contains a suggestion of the possible error of this belief. If a symptom is removed, it is argued, the instinctual demand is unaltered, but now the ego has been deprived of its safety valve, that is, of its means of binding the instinctual energy. Without a means of discharge available the urgency of the impulse will increase, anxiety signals will come more and more frequently, and in the end the ego will either be inundated or a new substitute formation, that is, a new symptom, will appear to bind the energy which is pressing forward.

Among the many assumptions, both explicit and implicit, in the above argument, the postulated relations between an instinctual demand and its object underpins both psychoanalytic method and theory. Every displacement of cathexis from an existing object is determined by, and participates in, a system of associative and symbolic meaningfulness. It is this fact which permits the reading of dynamic messages in the overt behaviors of people. It is this premise which permits psychoanalytic theory a solution of the problem of joining an apparently limitless field of variations in human behavior to a limited number of motivational sources. Thus, when a therapist confronts a symptom as a substitute formation he is, by definition, confronting the inner dynamic as well, albeit at a remove. Insight is, after all, conceived as the grasping of this relationship in a particular instance. To speak analytically of treating a symptom is theoretically inexact, unless one envisions the psychic equivalent of a scalpel which can enter a body of tissue, excise a desired portion, and leave lower tissue layers unaffected.

The treatment of a symptom by the method of systematic desensitization has no sensible analogy to such an idealized surgical procedure. On the contrary, the entire ego system is engaged in an eidetic and introspective task. The patient confronts his fear and inhibits his flight reflex. His fear, then, decreases. This fact should not upset the analytic theorist. If, in treating a symptom, we are treating the symbolic carrier of a feared instinctual demand, it satisfies the "logic" of our understanding of unconscious processes to expect far-reaching effects. To the degree to which a substitute formation is an adequate binder of cathectic energy, we may expect that a reduction in the strength of the signal anxiety which sustains this formation will represent an increase in ego tolerance of the instinctual demand. Freedom from fear, theory leads us to expect, is characteristic of increased ego strength, and may signal the possibility of creating more adequate binding behaviors. Why then predict symptom substitution?

It would neither surprise nor distress the author if psychoanalytic theorists should find fault with the above arguments. If a critique leads to a more convincing and elegant penetration of the proper relationship between the data of behavior therapy and analytic theory, the intention of the present analysis will have been realized. What is of importance is that this relationship be examined. The considerations already outlined suggest the futility of the position taken by Wolpe and Eysenck. To maintain that the failure of symptom substitution to occur with any regularity following symptom removal by the interventions of behavioral therapists constitutes a decisive argument against the validity of psychoanalysis, is to seriously underestimate its theoretical resources. Similarly, the unexamined prediction that symptom substitution must occur, as the grounds for a refusal by clinicians to give the use of the technique of systematic desensitization due consideration, must be rejected.

SOME INTERACTIONS OF DESENSITIZATION
WITH PSYCHOTHERAPY

The consequences, for a psychotherapist, of acknowledging the possible utility of systematic desensitization, bear illustration. One may tentatively accept the data which report the effectiveness of this technique and which deny contraindicating consequences. One may use the technique to give relief to one's patients. When the use of this technique is allowed, and when its implications are permitted to interact with an existing analytic, or other, orientation, possibilities occur which, while quite foreign to the behavior therapists, may lead to technical and theoretical growth.

For example, the occurrence of resistance in analytic work lends itself to an analysis which suggests the use of systematic desensitization. Resistance, in general, is assumed to occur when a train of associative production approaches forbidden unconscious material. This approach produces anxiety signals which excite the defenses of the ego and which lead to renewed efforts at repression of the material in question. What would follow if a patient were presented with the associative content which energizes repressive cathexes as a simulus for desensitization?

In order to explore this question, two patients in analytic therapy were given brief training in the relaxation method (Jacobson, 1938) used in preparation for systematic desensitization. (The author is aware of the concern which many therapists will feel in regard to the effects of this procedure upon the transference. While this is a problem of great theoretical importance, an adequate treatment would require at least as much space as is taken by the present article.) When these patients reported dreams for which they were able to produce only sparse associative material, the systematic desensitization procedure was used. Specifically, the patient was asked to relax and was then asked to imagine either the last image of the dream, or another image in the dream which seemed particularly significant or disturbing to him. (The procedure may be described as a marriage of the methods of active imagination as developed by Jung, and systematic desensitization.) When a scene produced no further anxiety reaction, the patient was again asked for associations to the dream. On the 12 occasions (10 with one patient and two with the other) when this procedure was attempted, the outcome was the production of a flood of associative material. Both patients developed spontaneous interpretations of their dreams in the course of this process during six of the sessions in which the method was used. A control for this observation is suggested by a history of unsuccessful efforts by these patients to engage the images in their dreams by the method of active imagination prior to relaxation training. Other explorations suggest themselves, in abundance, upon consideration of the possibilities involved.

A promising area of research which has been opened in the literature is the application of systematic desensitization to the treatment of psychosomatic complaints. Insofar as a conception is entertained in which the breakdown of an organ system is envisioned as a consequence of the repression of impulses to express significant affect, systematic desensitization offers the possibility of direct hypothesis testing. Among the most interesting desensitizations, from a dynamic point of view, are those which free a patient to express his feelings. For example, in two cases which the author has not yet reported in the literature, the desensitization of anxiety produced by impulses to express hostility led to the disappearance of migraine syndromes of extended duration. The time and energy which would be involved in a full-scale, controlled investigation of psychosomatic illness, using the method of systematic desensitization to test the hypothesis of its relation to affect suppression, seems to this writer a small price to pay for the potential gains in understanding and therapeutic power. Applications to general medicine may also be envisioned in areas in which psychosomatic effects are apparent, for example, the postulated relations between preoperative emotional stress and postoperative prognoses. What gains would there be in desensitizing a patient's unrealistic fears about his impending surgery?

An Empirical Critique of Systematic Desensitization and a New Method of Treatment

Dynamic points of view also suggest possible technical innovations in the desensitization procedure itself which are not likely to present themselves to a behavior therapist of a learning theory persuasion. One such suggestion arises from the groundbreaking investigations of Gendlin (1962) undertaken from his Rogerian orientation. Gendlin has described the consequences of attending to internal, felt body-states associated with affective arousal. It is his observation that the decision to remain verbally quiet and passive while directing attention to feelings in the body results in the experience of an increase in the richness and complexity of these feelings and a sequence of transformations of the felt "meaning" of the sensations. There is typically reported a brief, sharp rise in the intensity of the feeling, followed by a decline in the intensity as the associative richness connected with the feeling is directly experienced.

Explorations of Gendlin's procedure, both by this writer and in the reports of patients who were asked to observe themselves in this way, produced descriptions bearing a marked resemblance to the reports of content flow which were obtained from the investigations if imagining during systematic desensitization which were reported earlier in this paper. The possibility presented itself that during systematc desensitization visualizations, time limitations placed on the imagining of a given scene do not permit the patient's feeling to pass the peak of anxiety. It thus appeared possible that the necessity of multiple, hierarchical presentations was an artifact of the technique itself.

Four patients were involved in an investigation of this possibility. Each of two of the patients who were already being treated by systematic desensitization was given a new set of instructions. The patient was told to relax as usual and to imagine the scene presented by the therapist; but as soon as a feeling arose he was to direct his attention to the way his body felt. He was to focus attention on the strongest locus of feeling and to keep watching it no matter what distracting thoughts or images came to mind, and no matter how intense the feeling might become. The patient was presented with scenes from his prepared hierarchies. The first presentation to each patient was made at the beginning of a session in which a new hierarchy was scheduled for treatment, and consisted of the most intensely disturbing scene in that series. A single presentation was limited to 15 minutes. The therapist repeated, every minute, one or another paraphrase of the following: "Attend to the way you feel. Don't talk! Don't think! If thoughts come, let them pass through your mind. Don't attach yourself to them. Keep watching your feelings." Each session consisted of two such presentations followed by half an hour of discussion of the contents which had been experienced. Both of the patients reported intensifications of anxiety, floods of associations, changes in their understanding of what they were feeling, and, finally complete disappearance of any affect they were willing to call anxiety in regard to the contents treated. (The interested reader is referred to Gendlin, since my description of the experienced process would add nothing to what he has already described in detail.) Both patients tell that, *in contrast to their experience with systematic desensitization,* they "made sense to themselves," felt good about themselves and "in touch with themselves" (cf. Gendlin, 1962) after each session. In addition, while the *effects* of desensitization were experienced as "real," the procedure seemed magical and mysterious. By contrast, in this new procedure, the patients felt that *they* had healed themselves.

Four such sessions were conducted with each patient. Each of the "Gendlin-like" sessions was followed by one session devoted to the standard systematic desensitization procedure in order to determine whether desensitization had, in fact, occurred. The first scene presented was, in each case, the same scene which had been created by the "Gendlin-like" procedure in the case of one of the patients, the systematic desensitization presentations of the scenes in *descending* hierarchical order produced no anxiety reactions whatever. In vivo behavior gave strong evidence that desensitization had taken place. In the case of the other patient, two of the four hierarchies followed the above pattern.

The other two hierarchies showed an anxiety residue, although the patient felt that the anxiety was considerably less than he had anticipated when preparing the hierarchies. For each of these hierarchies, a second "Gendlin" session produced apparently complete desensitization.

Two additional patients were treated by the "Gendlin" procedure. In both cases the treatment was begun without prior relaxation training and, consequently, without experience of systematic desensitization. Each of these patients went through a standardized series of diagnostic sessions used in cases intended for treatment by systematic desensitization, which included the preparation of anxiety hierarchies. At the beginning of the first treatment session the patient was instructed to relax as well as he could and to attend to the way his body felt, that is, sensations of his clothing on his body, the chair against his back, the feeling in his "gut," etc. He was then given the instructions which have been described above and was presented with the most intense scene of his lowest hierarchy. One patient was flooded with anxiety and could not bear to continue on this first and two subsequent attempts. The procedure was, therefore, temporarily abandoned. The results with the second patient were identical with those which have been described for patients experienced with systematic desensitization. In this case, however, the "Gendlin sessions" were not alternated with systematic desensitization sessions. The evidence that desensitization occurred is, therefore, confined to self-reports and in vivo behavioral evidence.

The patient with whom the procedure had failed was subsequently trained in relaxation. Treatment by the "Gendlin procedure" was then resumed and, on this attempt, replicated the three cases which have been described. Relaxation training seemed to have had a striking effect. On the occasions of the initial attempts the patient reported poor visualization of the scenes described to him by the therapist. After relaxation training visualizations were vivid and feelings during sessions were sharp and distinct. The patient reported the, to him, fascinating observation that, while the anxiety was as strong during sessions following relaxation training as he remembered it having been before, he felt more in touch with his body and better able to tolerate the feeling. Relaxation training of the Jacobson type may prove to be a means of bringing patients into contact with their internal processes. Rather than fostering repression under the guise of relaxation, as one analyst has expressed his concern (Hillman, 1960), relaxation training may tend to induce an increased receptivity to unconscious contents.

It hardly seems necessary to point out the urgency of attempts to replicate these findings. These results, should they prove replicable, suggest that the use of intensity gradients and other means of controlling anxiety arousal may be unnecessary for desensitization, and call into question a crucial procedural and theoretical emphasis in systematic desensitization. Wolpe came upon this treatment procedure, in part, by analogy to his successful desensitization of conditioned phobic reactions in cats. It does not detract from the impressiveness of the successes this analogy has generated in the treatment of human subjects to suggest a modification and indeed a radical revision of his method. It may be that with human subjects a method which encourages an engagement of the dynamics of the anxiety reaction with a subject's cognitive processes will also produce desensitization.

In spite of the very preliminary nature of the data which has been described, they would seem to offer reason for optimism. Attempts to produce confrontations of the data and method of systematic desensitization with other perspectives and frames of reference may prove to be a source of enrichment of therapeutic practice and theory.

ANALYTIC INTERPRETATIONS OF BEHAVIOR THERAPY

Earlier in this discussion a challenge was made of Eysenck's assertion that the effects of psychotherapy can be understood in terms of principles derived from "learning theory." It remains, for the purposes of this paper, to show that the effects of behavior therapy (systematic desensitization) can be understood in terms of principles derived from analytic theories. In other words, it seems desirable to offer a preliminary demonstration that confrontations of analytic theories with the method of systematic desensitization may be undertaken with some degree of plausibility on theoretical grounds. In what follows an attempt will be made to show that psychotherapists can derive, from their theoretical perspective, means of understanding the effects of the technique of systematic desensitization. That is, some of the resources of analytic theories will be tapped in an effort to frame interpretations of the way in which the specific therapeutic interventions of this form of behavior therapy produce their effects. These interpretations should *not* do violence to dynamic points of view, and *should* lead to a rational expectation that desirable results will follow.

A Psychoanalytic Interpretation of Systematic Desensitization

A number of suggestions have already been made, for example, in the discussion of symptom substitution, which could lead to a rational derivation of the effects of systematic desensitization by psychoanalytic theory. There are, however, in the body of Freud's writings a number of formulations which lend themselves even more precisely to this purpose. For example, Freud (1936) considers that an analysis of anxiety yields three attributes: "(1) a specific unpleasurable quality, (2) efferent or discharge phenomena, and (3) the perception of these [p. 70]." This is true for symptomatic anxiety as well as for signal anxiety which leads to a mobilization of ego defenses and symptom formation. Were it possible to confront the ego with impulses which generate the signals of anxiety, by, for example, asking the patient to imagine himself engaged in the expression of an impulse from which he normally flees, and, were it possible, at the same time, to prevent or inhibit the occurrence of anxiety signals by, for example, inducing deep relaxation and raising the threshold of the discharge phenomena, reality oriented binding of cathexes might be expected to follow. While aware of the oversimplifications in this analysis, the writer fails to see any urgent reason why the suggestions which it makes available should not be explored by the technique of systematic desensitization.

An Interpretation by Complex Psychology of Systematic Desensitization

Within the writings of Jung, as well, is contained abundant conceptual material for analyses similar to that which has been outlined for Freud. Strikingly suggestive parallels may be found in Jung's (1960) monograph on paranoid dementia. The terms of definition of the complex theory as they are presented in that paper lend themselves to our present purpose.

The psyche is conceived as consisting, in part, of an indefinite number of clusters of relatively autonomous associative complexes. Each complex is organized around an emotionally toned content which draws to it materials bearing similarities of meaning and materials which occur as stimulus input during periods of time in which that particular complex is behaviorally dominant. In ordinary circumstances the complex of greatest strength, stability and clarity is called the "ego." The ego depends, for its stability, on the fact that it includes in its associative cluster the range of proprioceptive stimulation produced by normal bodily tone. Most stimuli which occur in the presence of this normal proprioceptive state are drawn into association with the ego complex and share its clarity and stability. When a stimulus, by its associative properties, excites a complex other than the ego, it also excites an alteration in body tone. This altered body tone is part of the ego-alien complex, and induces an alteration of proprioception. It is in such altered states of proprioception that we have emotions. The emotional state is characterized by a weakening of the ego complex, that is, a loss of its usual behavioral dominance, and a change of consciousness best described as a loss of apperceptive clarity. (For an extended theoretical discussion of the far-reaching conclusions as to the nature of consciousness to which Jung was led by these germinal considerations, the reader is referred to Jung, 1954.)

It seems to follow that if a content which ordinarily disturbs the ego complex could be made to occur without producing an alteration in proprioception, that is, without an emotional excitement, the consequence should be an integration of this content to the ego complex. The therapeutic gains would be considerable. If systematic desensitization produces effects which can be understood in this way, many interesting avenues of exploration will be opened to Jungian theorists.

An Interpretation of Systematic Desensitization from the Viewpoint of Interpersonal Psychiatry

From the vantage of interpersonal psychiatry a relatively straightforward interpretation can be formulated. Anxiety, in Sullivanian thinking, has a clearly articulated function in determining personality structure. Anxiety generates and is involved in maintaining a set of defensive processes, primary among which is the "self." Insofar as the habitual responses of the self are designed to avoid anxiety, they tend to have the character of parataxic thinking, that is, thought processes in which association by contiguity rather than connection by rational structure is the guiding principle. An adult who is capable of syntactic or rational thought may, nonetheless, exhibit parataxic habits in the presence of anxiety. Anxiety typically produces this weakening of rational processes. While this set of concepts is already suggestive in the present context, its relationship to systematic desensitization is clarified by a further consideration. Sullivan (1940) supposed that the necessary precondition for emotional states is an increase in skeletal-muscular tension. This increase in tension, when it passes a threshold value, produces that clouding of consciousness which, when we perceive it, we call anxiety. It is this clouding of consciousness which results in the failure of rational thought mentioned above.

It follows that if the adequate stimulus for an increase in skeletal-muscular tension could be presented in such a fashion as to limit, or avoid, the increase in tension which is ordinarily contingent upon it, a clouding of consciousness might be avoided. The stimulus in question should, in these circumstances, come under the scrutiny of the syntactic process and might be expected to undergo rational integration. Systematic desensitization is "tailor-made" for testing this hypothesis, which, should it be validated, provides a possible rationale for the use of this technique by analysts of the interpersonal school.

An Interpretation of Desensitization Therapy by Decision Theory

Psychotherapists who are oriented toward decision-making models of cognitive functioning, and who prefer to avoid dynamic formulations of the analytic variety, should also find little difficulty in rationalizing the use of systematic desensitization. A single example, very loosely based upon the theory of signal detection and focused on the anxiety hysteric, will serve to illustrate this contention. (Another approach, from the point of view of "cognitive" learning theory, is outlined by Breger & McGaugh, 1965.)

Anxiety may be conceived as the adequate stimulus for an avoidance or flight response (signal anxiety in the Freudian sense). Anxiety, thus, reflects an organization of the utilities matrix which controls the decision-making process by which responses to certain stimulus classes are selected. Existing utilities may require that a stimulus class which has the demonstrated power of evoking the anxiety signal be avoided, so that no signal is generated. The situation will now be such that for a given class of stimuli, the threshold of avoidance response has been lowered. In order to insure a high percentage of successes in the avoidance of danger the person is willing to make avoidance responses to a range of contents which include many innocuous stimuli. At the same time, avoidance of the anxiety signal will require that avoidance responses be initiated at the first signs of such proprioceptive alterations as might imply possible anxiety. Given a base level of proprioceptive stimuli which are not perceptually articulate, any given increase (as determined by the utilities) in the intensity of proprioceptive feedback, such as that produced by increased skeletal-muscular tension, may be an anxiety signal. We thus have a person who responds as if there were reason to be anxious to a wide range of stimuli, both external and proprioceptive. We say that such a person has unadaptive anxiety. If, in the therapeutic setting, we alter the a priori possibilities of stimulus input by decreasing the intensity of proprioceptive feedback, we decrease the "false alarm" rate and raise the threshold of avoidance responses to signals of anxiety.

This can be accomplished by inducing a state of skeletal-muscular relaxation. If, at the same time, we decrease the chaos of perceptual inputs by directing a patient to close his eyes and, further, by asking that he produce a vivid visualization of particular stimuli, we once again reduce the a priori possibilities of "false alarms." The experience of specific stimuli which have, in the past, been the occasion for anxiety signals, in the presence of reduced intensity of proprioceptive feedback, might be expected to produce "therapeutic" alternations of utilities matrices. The task of rationalizing the effects of systematic desensitization should not present formidable difficulties for other cognitive theories.

CONCLUSION

This paper has attempted a form of relatively systematic desensitization, in regard to the use of a therapeutic technique, upon the dynamically oriented clinical-academic community. It must, however, be noted that many objections to the use of systematic desensitization which may be raised on analytic grounds have only been lightly touched upon in this paper, or not mentioned at all. The interpretation of the transference relationship, to select only one example, will require a formidable theoretical effort. It would miss the point, quite decisively, to proceed as if no problems remained.

On the other hand, exploratory arguments have been drawn with the intent of persuading psychotherapists of the urgency of examining the grounds of their resistance to the use of systematic desensitization and of reevaluating the theoretical necessity of these grounds. The primary motivation of this attempt is the conviction of the writer (qualified by the obvious need for better controls and further investigation) that systematic desensitization works, that is, that it produces behavioral change, reliably, sometimes dramatically, and thera- peutically. Within the areas to which it has been applied it has demonstrated impressive effectiveness. It remains to determine the best theoretical formula- tion of the processes involved in producing its effects. The limit of its applic- ability and the best form for its application are empirical questions. However, as a source of data and as a source of therapeutic power, it demands exploitation.

The question of the form this exploitation *should* take has led to the theoretical exercises in this paper, and to the empirical investigations described. What shall be the field of investigation, and the theoretical attitude with which this tool will be applied? The stakes seem too high to settle for a battle between behavior therapists and psychoanalysts. That there is danger of this happening has been pointed out by Andrews (1966) in his appeal for more open scientific communication. Everyone, including the patient, is likely to lose in such war- fare. There is room for each persuasion to increase its technical and theoretical sophistication. Preliminary considerations have been presented with the inten- tion of demonstrating that proprietary rights to this technique cannot be estab- lished on theoretical grounds. In other words, there is nothing to fear, in the technique or in the data it generates, for psychoanalytic or cognitive theorists, provided they actively engage the problem. There is no reason to fear that the engagement will force them to "throw the psyche out of psychology." There is reason to think they may emerge from the combat with new strength. Freud (1936) put the alternative succinctly: "When the wayfarer whistles in the dark, he may be disavowing his timidity, but he does not see any the more clearly for doing so [p. 23]." There are theoretical grounds for the use of systematic desensitization, for hypothesis generation, and for experimental tests of its consequences from a variety of points of view.

So long as the relationship of theory to its data is sufficiently loose that logical arguments can take precedence over empirical arguments, and empirical decisions seem out of reach, we can, perhaps, justify uncritical loyalty to our preconceptions. When, however, a means presents itself of bringing our therapeutic concepts to an empirical confrontation we are obligated to do so. None of us can assume that we possess enough foresight to envision the theoretical consequences, the model of man which the data will require. Perhaps it helps to remember the words of the prophet, that the better is always the enemy of the good, and that the good must give way if the better is to be. In any case, whatever the outcome, to collect the data and to construct the model seem to this author to be our professional obligation.

REFERENCES

Andrews, J. D. W. Psychotherapy of phobias. *Psychological Bulletin,* 1966, 66, 455–480.

Breger, L., & McGaugh, J. L. Critique and reformulation of "learning theory" approaches to psychotherapy and neurosis. *Psychological Bulletin,* 1965, 63, 338–358.

Estes, W. K., Koch, S., MacCorquodale, K., Meehl, P. E., Mueller, C. G., Jr., Schoenfeld, W. N., & Verplanck, W. S. *Modern learning theory.* New York: Appleton-Century-Crofts, 1954.

Eysenck, H. J. *The dynamics of anxiety and hysteria.* New York: Praeger, 1957.

Eysenck, H. J. (Ed.), *Behavior therapy and the neurosis.* New York: Pergamon Press, 1960.

Freud, S. *The problem of anxiety.* New York: Norton, 1936.

Gendlin, E. T. *Experiencing and the creation of meaning.* New York: Free Press of Glencoe, 1962.

Grossberg, J. M. Behavior therapy: A review. *Psychological Bulletin,* 1964, 62, 73–88.

Hillman, J. *Emotion.* London: Routledge and Kegan Paul, 1960.

Jacobson, E. *Progressive relaxation.* Chicago: University of Chicago Press, 1938.

Jung, C. G. The spirit of psychology. In J. Campbell (Ed.), *Spirit and nature.* New York: Pantheon, 1954. Pp. 371–444.

Jung, C. G. *The archetypes and the collective unconscious.* New York: Pantheon, 1959.

Jung, C. G. *The psychogenesis of mental disease.* New York: Pantheon, 1960.

Masserman, J. H. *Behavior and neurosis.* Chicago: University of Chicago Press, 1943.

Rapaport, D. The structure of psychoanalytic theory: A systematizing attempt. In S. Koch (Ed.), *Psychology: A study of a science.* Vol. 1. New York: McGraw-Hill, 1959. Pp 55–183.

Reich, W. *Character-analysis.* New York: Noonday, 1949.

Sullivan, H. S. *Conceptions of modern psychiatry.* New York: Norton, 1940.

Weinberg, N. H., & Zaslove, M. "Resistance" to systematic desensitization of phobias. *Journal of Clinical Psychology,* 1963, 19, 179–181.

Wolpe, J. *Psychotherapy by reciprocal inhibition.* Stanford: Stanford University Press, 1958.

Wolpe, J. The experimental foundations of some new psychotherapeutic methods. In A. J. Bachrach (Ed.), *Experimental foundations of clinical psychology.* New York: Basic Books, 1962. Pp. 554–575.

27

SOME IMPLICATIONS OF PSYCHOTHERAPY RESEARCH FOR THERAPEUTIC PRACTICE

Allen E. Bergin

The material to follow is a digest of research findings which have implications for practice and research in psychotherapy. It has been formulated in terms of six conclusions and implications which appear justifiable and defensible. This catalogue of conclusions is based upon a comparative handful of research reports which have been carefully selected from the present empirical chaos for their relative adequacy of conceptualization, design, and outcome. Conclusions have been drawn only in those areas where the results appear to have substance and where they have been replicated; consequently, many areas of study are excluded.

THE DETERIORATION EFFECT

Conclusion 1

Psychotherapy may cause people to become better or worse adjusted than comparable people who do not receive such treatment.

Recently, a curious and provocative finding occurred in the preliminary results of the Wisconsin schizophrenia project conducted by Rogers, Gendlin, and Truax (Rogers, 1961; Truax, 1963; Truax & Carkhuff, 1964). It was that

Reprinted from the *Journal of Abnormal and Social Psychology,* 71, 1966, 235–246, with the permission of the American Psychological Association and Dr. Bergin. (Table 1 has been omitted.)

the patients in psychotherapy tended to become either better or worse in adjustment than their matched control-group counterparts.

At that time three earlier studies were analyzed (Barron & Leary, 1955; Cartwright, 1956; Cartwright & Vogel, 1960) in which similar findings had occurred; but being incidental to other results, they had not been emphasized in proportion to their true import (Bergin, 1963). Since then, four additional studies with similar findings have been discovered (Fairweather, Simon, Gebhard, Weingarten, Holland, Sanders, Stone, & Reahl, 1960; Mink, 1959; Powers & Witmer, 1951; Rogers & Dymond, 1954). In all seven studies, although there tends to be no difference in the average amount of change between experimentals and controls, there does tend to be a significant difference in *variability* of change. The criterion, or change, scores for treatment groups attain a much wider dispersion than do those of control groups, even though the mean change in both groups is quite similar. Typically, control subjects (Ss) improve somewhat, with the varying amounts of change clustering about the mean. On the other hand, experimental Ss are typically dispersed all the way from marked improvement to marked deterioration. Now, frequently documented, this information is alarming to say the least. Psychotherapy can and does make people worse than their control counterparts! Because of the controversial nature of this conclusion, the following material is presented as detailed substantiating evidence in its support.

Table 1 [here omitted] reproduced from Cartwright's (1956) reanalysis of the well-known Barron and Leary study (1955).

Cartwright comments on the data as follows:

> For many scales the variance results suggest that mean differences between the groups are absent because differences of two kinds, opposed in sign, are present. If seems that some therapy patients *deteriorated* to a greater extent than did the waiting-list controls, while some therapy patients *did improve* significantly more than the controls [p. 403–404].

It should be noted that this occurred only for individual and not for group therapy.

It is a fascinating fact that Cartwright's observation has lain unattended in the literature for years, while implicit in his statement is a clear means of resolving much of the controversy over negative results in therapy-outcome studies. It is even more fascinating that Cartwright himself participated in a study (Rogers & Dymond, 1954) in which a similar phenomenon occurred, but just as with the data in the Barron and Leary study it was never emphasized in proportion to its true import. The classic features in this study apparently overshadowed the passing references to a *client-deterioration phenomenon*.

While the study is properly famous for other reasons, it provides supporting bits of evidence for the thesis that negative change in therapy is not an isolated or chance occurrence. A careful reading of the report indicates that of 25 therapy Ss, 6 or 24%, declined in self-ideal correlation between pretherapy and follow-up testing. A quick computation of the mean change in self-ideal correlation indicates that those who increased averaged an increment of .49 in their correlations, whereas those who declined a decrement of −.40, a difference that is striking considering the fact that the mean pretherapy correlations were not different for those two subgroups. While some chance fluctuations in scores are to be expected, these changes in both directions can hardly be attributed to the effects of imperfect test reliability. While Butler and Haigh (1954) do not examine these possibilities in the data, they do allude to them in passing: "It is of interest, though it does not bear directly upon the hypothesis, that there has also been a marked increase in the degree of variation of correlations (self-ideal) over this period [p. 63]."

It may be argued, of course, that decline in self-ideal correlation can be an indication of improved adjustment, particularly when the correlation is extremely high as in the case of some paranoid Ss. However, the pretest correlations of all six Ss who declined in this study were low, ranging from .28 to −.12. The question of whether self-ideal correlations actually measure adjustment at all is still a subject of some debate, so it would seem unwise to draw conclusions about psychotherapy in general from data based on this measure alone. In another section of Rogers and Dymond, an analysis of behavior observations made of the clients independently of therapist progress ratings yielded results similar to those found with the self-ideal measure:

> During the whole period from pre-therapy to follow-up, observers saw a definite increase in the maturity of behavior of those clients whose therapy was rated as successful and a sharp decrease in the maturity of behavior of those clients rated as unsuccessful. The relationship was statistically significant [p. 228].

While there are additional fragmentary evidences of deterioration phenomena in the book, these suffice to illustrate the point.

In a controlled study of counseling with high school students, Mink (1959) observes the same phenomenon: "Counseling affected the expression of social adjustments on the California Test of Personality. The forms of expression indicate both improvement and recession [p. 14]."

The excellent multifactor design executed by Fairweather et al. (1960) yielded similar results:

Generally, significantly different variances occurred on most instruments between treatments and diagnoses. The control group usually had the smallest variance and the three psychotherapy groups the largest [p. 24]. In these three interactions, one or all of the three long-term psychotic groups in psychotherapy demonstrated changes in the maladaptive scale direction [MMPI] while the controls remain[ed] relatively the same or change[d] in the adaptive direction [p. 9].

Cartwright and Vogel (1960) discovered the same type of differential effect in a neurotic sample using different criterion measures:

Thus, as measured by the Q score, adjustment changes, regardless of direction, were significantly greater during a therapy period than during a No-Therapy period [p. 122]. The Post-therapy tests showed those in therapy with experienced therapists to have improved significantly on both tests, whereas those in therapy with inexperienced therapists not to have improved . . . in fact they bordered on a significant decrease in health on the TAT [p. 127].

Turning back several decades to the Cambridge-Somerville youth study (Powers & Witmer, 1951) which was initiated in 1937, the same phenomenon is found with a group of predelinquent boys:

When the Study Services were effectual most of the boys did function better than their C-twins [i.e., members of a matched control group]. This conclusion can be accepted, however, only if its opposite is also accepted: that some of the boys who were not benefited may have been handicapped in social adjustment by the organization's efforts. If this is true, we can conclude that the apparent chance distribution of terminal adjustment ratings . . . was due to the fact that the good effects of the Study were counterbalanced by the poor [p. 455].

Elsewhere the authors indicate that in a significant proportion of cases where the counselor's efforts were judged as poor, the boys "were more socially maladjusted than their control twin [p. 509]." It is unfortunate that this excellently designed and executed study is one leaned upon most heavily by Eysenck (1960, 1965) in his bold denial of the usefulness of psychotherapy, for while the study shows no difference between experimentals and controls, it demonstrates the efficacy of treatment as well as its deteriorative effect.

Finally, to cite the recent Wisconsin project on therapy of schizophrenia which has been published (Truax, 1963) thus far only in tempting bits and pieces:

> High levels of therapist-offered conditions during therapy are related to patient improvement, but . . . low levels . . . are related to patient deterioration, so that if all the therapy combined is indiscriminately compared to control conditions there is little average change. Thus, psychotherapy can be for better or for worse [p. 256].

Since the length of therapy varied in these seven studies from a few months to several years, it seems doubtful that the observed deterioration can be accounted for by the temporary regression that sometimes occurs during treatment. The views of most writers would indicate that the average deterioration due to this effect for a treatment group would be small after brief and lengthy period of therapy but large in between; whereas the findings reported here suggest a consistent, rectangularly distributed, amount of regression, regardless of the length of time transpired prior to obtaining outcome estimates. Unfortunately,

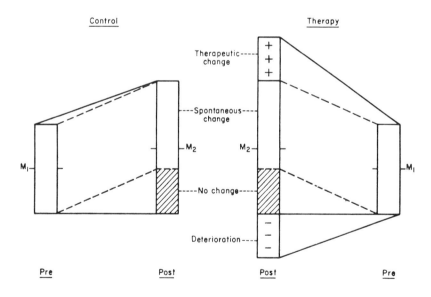

Figure 1

THE DETERIORATION EFFECT

Schematic representation of pre- and post-test distributions of criterion scores in psychotherapy-outcome studies.

so little controlled empirical work has been done with analytic therapies, which are presumably the richest sources of such data, that it is difficult to compare the findings reported here with what might be found if research were done on them.

Fortunately, these various data indicate that psychotherapy can make people considerably better off than control Ss. Therefore, contrary to the notions of some critics, psychotherapy can produce improvement beyond that which may occur due to spontaneous remission alone. Consistently replicated, this is a direct and unambiguous refutation of the oft-cited Eysenckian position (Eysenck, 1960, 1965).

A general paradigm is suggested by the double-edged effect observed in the studies cited which may be schematized as shown in Figure 1. Such a startling phenomenon certainly deserves a name, and *The Deterioration Effect* is suggested here.

It is interesting to note that a phenomenon similar to the great variability in the quality of therapeutic effects noted here has also been observed in relation to the accuracy of diagnostic evaluations (Garfield, 1963). Apparently, even well-known diagnosticians vary greatly in the accuracy of their judgments. When all of these judgments are pooled, average predictions or discriminations often are not different from chance estimates; but some individuals appear to far exceed chance predictions while others actually do worse than chance.

Implication 1

(*a*) The practice of psychotherapy should not be given up as some have advocated. (*b*) Those engaged in this field should be more cautious and critical of their own practices, carefully eliminating any ineffective or harmful therapeutic techniques. They should find out whom they are making worse or better, and how, with all due speed. (*c*) They should find out if some therapists make people better and if some make them worse, or if individual therapists do both. After that, comes the ticklish business of making changes in technique, personality, or personnel as may be necessary to eliminate negative influences and accentuate positive.

NATURAL THERAPEUTIC CONDITIONS

Conclusion 2

(*a*) It has been frequently replicated, and is now a well-established fact, that control Ss who do not receive psychotherapy change positively as a group with the passage of time. This is the so-called spontaneous remission effect (Eysenck, 1952, 1960, 1965). (*b*) Three studies (Frank, 1961; Gurin, Veroff, & Feld, 1960; Powers & Witmer, 1951) indicate that many of these disturbed persons who receive no formal psychotherapy seek and obtain help from various professional and nonprofessional sources such as friends, clergymen, physicians, teachers, and occasionally even psychotherapists (Bergin, 1963).

All this has typically been unknown to the researchers who were depending upon these so-called controls to be a baseline for comparison with their treatment cases. It seems clear that this aid has an ameliorative effect, as the people improve, although it would be impossible to substantiate this fully without further study of the influences upon control *S*s in their "natural" habitat. To the extent that this position is correct, it further undermines the Eysenck-type position, because it shows that control *S*s often change due to the influence of therapy or therapy-like procedures. Thus, "spontaneous remission" is just another name for the effects of informal therapy.

Implication 2

(*a*) Researchers who utilize control groups should carefully ascertain that these groups are indeed controls, or, if necessary, should directly measure the effects of nonexperimental influences which they cannot control. (*b*) The fact that some of these previously uncontrolled influences are much like therapy, but frequently occur outside of a professional setting, implies that nonprofessional help can stimulate positive personality change. This may consist partly of individuals with "therapeutic personalities" who are sought out for counsel and catharsis by many people. It may be also that unrecognized, but powerful, therapeutic agents exist naturally in everyday life. Just as cures for various physical disorders have been discovered by studying health, so it may be possible to discover antidotes for some of the mental disorders that confront us by discovering conditions already existing in "nature" which support or promote personality integration.

INGREDIENTS OF THERAPY

Conclusion 3

Therapeutic progress varies as a function of therapist characteristics such as warmth, empathy, adequacy of adjustment, and experience.

In a recent review, Gardner (1964) cited a smattering of positive results to the effect that the more a therapist has an attitude of *liking and warmth* the more likely he is to obtain positive change in his clients. While some of the studies enumerated are of questionable design or generalizability, they are relatively consistent when compared with many other areas of research.

A recent questionnaire study of patients' retrospective reports regarding their therapeutic experience (Strupp, Wallach, & Wogan, 1964), which was not reported by Gardner, further confirms this general finding. While the study is uncontrolled and appears to be contaminated by artifactually inflated correlations, it is of interest that it strongly emphasizes the importance of therapist warmth and genuineness in relation to patient-perceived outcome ($r = .53$).

Additional data on this point come from the client-centered group in a series of studies with neurotics and psychotics. It should be noted that some of the therapists studied were *not* client-centered. These studies are consistent in discovering a significant relationship between operational measures of Rogers' concept of positive regard and independent indices of therapeutic progress or outcome (Truax & Carkhuff, 1964, 1965a; Barrett-Lennard, 1962). Measures of the therapist's attitudes have included ratings by both the therapist himself and the patient. Three types of analysis have resulted in similar findings and in different studies with different samples of clients and therapists. It has thus become increasingly clear, within the limits of these studies, that a therapist's ability to be warm and positively inclined toward his patients is an effective therapeutic ingredient. The effects of intentional authoritarian demands or other forms of planned therapist aggression which are sometimes advocated have not been studied and thus cannot be compared with these findings.

Acknowledging the past confusion and contradiction involved in studies of *empathy,* it is suggested that the recent data offer promising leads. Analyses of recorded therapist behavior and ratings by clients of their therapists during the process of treatment have yielded consistently positive relationships between empathic understanding and outcome.

The strength of these findings lies in careful design (Rogers, 1961) and in the analysis of therapist behavior *in vivo,* which is unusual in empathy research. A new empathy measure has been operationalized by Truax (1961b) and is defined by Truax and Carkhuff (1964) as accurate "sensitivity to current feelings and the verbal facility to communicate this understanding in a language attuned to the patient's current being [p. 8]." While the scale is still crude and might not be accepted by analysts as measuring their "kind" of empathy, its usefulness has been relatively substantial in these studies.

The third characteristic, *adequacy of adjustment,* has not been studied as thoroughly as the others, but thus far the data are relatively consistent. Those therapists who are more anxious, conflicted, defensive, or "unhealthy" are least likely to promote change in their cases.

Several studies have indicated that supervisor and client ratings of the therapists' competence are negatively related to his degree of anxiety or maladjustment (Arbuckle, 1956; Bandura, 1956; Bergin & Solomon, 1963). Other studies have yielded similar findings when the therapist's actual in-therapy behavior and the patient's response to it was evaluated and used as a criterion of competence. For example, Bandura, Lipsher, and Miller (1960) found that therapists' hostility anxiety was directly associated with avoidance responses to patients' expressions of hostility toward them. The more hostility conflict a therapist had, the more likely he was to avoid his patient's hostility and consequently the patient's self-exploration in this area diminished and his conflicts remained unresolved. A practically identical result was found by Winder, Ahmad, Bandura, and Rau (1962) with regard to dependency anxiety.

In another study (Bergin & Solomon, 1963) it was found that measures of the therapists' degree of personal disturbance correlate negatively with his level of empathy as measured by ratings of tape-recorded psychotherapy interviews. Independent measures of personality strength, on the other hand, correlated positively with degree of "live" empathy. In addition, ratings of therapist anxiety level correlated negatively with independent ratings of therapeutic competence.

Additional data come from the client-centered studies already cited with regard to warmth and empathy, in their examination of therapist congruence. Congruence (Rogers, 1957, 1959) means essentially the healthiness of the therapist in his relationship with his client—his spontaneity, nondefensiveness, openness, or genuineness. Like positive regard and empathy, this variable has also been related to therapeutic progress, and further confirms the general finding of a direct connection between level of therapist adjustment and therapeutic effectiveness.

The three elements of warmth, empathy, and congruence have been found, in the Wisconsin studies, to vary directly with outcome in both negative and positive directions. That is, when these therapist characteristics were at a low level, the patients were getting worse; when they were high, the patients improved (Truax & Carkhuff, 1964). These studies thus provide a partial answer to the question raised earlier as to how negative change occurred in the outcome studies reviewed, although they are limited in that the observed differences were not large, and there is also some question as to whether the division into high and low conditions was done before or after the fact. The other studies cited here in the same realm further clarify the point, although none of the data are precise enough to make practical selection decisions possible.

With regard to the much debated variable of therapist experience, it may be asserted that, in general, more experienced therapists are more effective and successful. This is based on four studies (Barrett-Lennard, 1962; Cartwright & Vogel, 1960; Chance, 1959; Fiedler, 1950a, 1950b, 1951), one of which suggests that highly inexperienced therapists may actually cause patient deterioration (Cartwright & Vogel, 1960).

Implication 3

(*a*) Since psychotherapists are effective partly as a function of personal adjustment, they should be selected for this quality and not solely on the basis of academic and intellectual abilities. Future practice of therapy should therefore be modified by new selection procedures which will bring healthier personalities to bear upon problems of pathology, and by closer self-scrutiny and exposure of one's work among present practitioners.

There is presently no evidence that personal therapy for a disturbed therapist can qualify him for practice and should not be depended upon to perform that function until such evidence is provided. This does not, of course, prove that the experience of being treated cannot be useful to a student therapist whose functioning is within a relatively normal range. There are no studies in which treated neurotics have improved to a level of functioning which is similar to that of control normals even though they do change in level of adjustment; therefore, treatment should not be counted upon to take care of errors in selection. The behavior ratings and personality inventories used in the studies reviewed could provide a beginning in research geared specifically toward the selection problem.

(*b*) Given the necessary personal attributes, therapists should develop their abilities in the realm of warmth and empathic communication, particularly in the case of empathy which is known to be subject to training and experience influences. Further study should be conducted so that clear, measurable standards of performance can be required of aspirants to professional status before they are permitted to practice. As an example, the Truax Empathy Scale (Truax, 1961b) could be used as a beginning to assess one's level of functioning via analysis of recorded interviews.

(*c*) Inexperienced potential therapists should be very carefully introduced to practice with clients, perhaps with much more stringent care than is now commonly exercised. Since all beginners make many mistakes, it may be useful and ethical to have them see more resilient, normal people until they reach a criterion level of interview performance, measured perhaps on dimensions such as warmth and empathy which appear to be accepted by most schools of therapy as vital though not necessarily sufficient for successful treatment.

Conclusion 4

To date, the only school of interview-oriented psychotherapy which has consistently yielded positive outcomes in research studies is the client-centered approach (Rogers & Dymond, 1954; Shlien, Mosak, & Dreikurs, 1962; Truax & Carkhuff, 1964).

The fact that other schools have not subjected their methods to systematic study of this sort is important but it should not deter one from accepting the fact that client-centered treatment has some positive value when properly conducted according to Rogers' (1957) paradigm. The implications for practice seem quite clear, particularly in view of the consistently dismal reports on percentages of improvement in psychoanalytic therapy (Eysenck, 1965; Wolpe, 1964b).

It appears from these reports that the poorest results were obtained with more classical, long-term psychoanalysis, namely a lower percentage of improved cases than the 67% "spontaneous" remission rate. Briefly, analytically oriented eclectic psychotherapy was more promising in that the percentage improvement equaled the spontaneous remission figure. This type of therapy was also used in some of the studies cited in this paper on the deterioration effect; therefore, despite the generally negative evidence, some analytically oriented therapists must be having a positive effect beyond that occurring in control groups.

It should also be noted that the technique of "moderate interpretation" (Speisman, 1959), which derives from the analytic tradition, has potential therapeutic significance. Its definition is very similar to that given for "good" interpretation by various analysts (Fenichel, 1941), and it is related to productive patient self-exploration. It consists of responding to client affect just below the surface and labeling, identifying, or emphasizing it. This does not involve making connections between past and present, being diagnostic or theoretical, nor telling the patient about feelings he "really has" when he's not experiencing them. It is, rather, an instance of good empathy. If one looks carefully at the definitions and operations for identifying accurate empathy and moderate or good interpretation, it is very difficult to distinguish between them. Truax and Carkhuff (1964) refer to this notion in an interesting comment:

> "Accurate empathy" has much in common with the "good psycho-analytic interpretation," in that it makes use of both verbal and non-verbal cues presented by the patient. It differs from some good psycho-analytic interpretations in its insistence that the therapist's empathic response focuses upon feelings and experience of the patient from the patient's own unique viewpoint.

The importance of these observations should not be underestimated, for if they are accurate it appears that effective variables cut across schools of treatment and thus provide the basis for applying techniques on the basis of known effects rather than on doctrines promulgated by warring factions. This also indicates that titles, degrees, or years of training should not define the psycho-therapist, but rather what the individual can do. Thus one might call himself "client-centered" and espouse the teachings of that school while at the same time presenting the low level of therapist empathy found to result in client deterioration. On the other hand, a psychoanalyst might be functioning at a high level according to the client-centered empathy scale.

Conclusion 5

In spite of all so far stated about the possibilities for substantially improving consulting-room effectiveness, some stubborn facts still require confrontation. One is that even when the various sources of slippage and inadequacy are accounted for, interviews still do not generally produce very dramatic changes in people. Another is the now well-known fact that many types of people simply are not helped at all by this procedure.

Studies of the relationship between client qualities and therapeutic outcome indicate consistently and clearly that positive outcome is limited or nil with many personality types. It is common for private practitioners and even clinics either to refuse to treat, or reluctantly to accept for treatment, cases that do not fit their conception of psychotherapy. To a great extent this is realistic because traditional methods do not work with these cases. These "rejects," as compared with "accepted" cases, tend to be less intelligent, less anxious, less educated, less verbal and insightful, more concrete and action-oriented, more severely disturbed, more impulsive in the sociopathic sense, and often find the typical consulting-room procedure rather meaningless (Barron, 1953; Cartwright, 1955; Fulkerson & Barry, 1961; Garfield & Affleck, 1961; Hollingshead & Redlich, 1958; Kirtner & Cartwright, 1958a, 1958b). This general observation has been made fairly frequently by various clinicians and is currently rather well-substantiated by the research literature.

Implication 5

The implication of these data, which only confirm an already widely believed idea, is that novel or modified techniques must be developed for dealing with a vast population whose problems are not amenable to standard methods. The importance of novel approaches is further emphasized by the fact that standard methods are not dramatically effective even in those cases where they are applicable, except in rare instances. The latter unusual cases would be a proper subject of study in themselves and may actually suggest innovations even though they arise in "traditional" therapy.

There are three primary sources of possible innovation that might alleviate this predicament. One is creative work in the clinical setting; another is naturally existing conditions in society; and another is that general area of research which is concerned with personality and behavior change such as studies of learning, attitude change, and personality development.

THE PROMISE OF BEHAVIOR THERAPY

Conclusion 6

Studies of learning have thus far been very fruitful in generating principles and methods for promoting personality change. The work by Wolpe (1958), Lazarus (1963), Lang and Lazovik (1963), Lindsley (1963), and others has been both provocative and fruitful. The cases presented and research studies reported provide more positive evidence of the usefulness of these methods than is the case in any form of traditional interview or dynamic psychotherapy, including client-centered therapy.

They involve clinical adaptation of learning principles, such as counter-conditioning or extinction of anxiety symptoms, positive reinforcement in shaping adaptive responses and developing appropriate discriminations, aversive conditioning of maladaptive approach responses, and modeling. It is the effects of these methods which are important here. Wolpe (1964a) cites over 200 cases of neurosis in 89% of which he has obtained substantial recovery. Lazarus (1963), in England, reports 408 cases with a similar improvement rate. The striking aspect of these results is that they have been achieved with difficult symptom pictures in brief periods of time. Unfortunately, these are clinical reports by individual therapists who rate their own case outcomes. Independent criteria and control Ss are completely lacking, and it is difficult to discern how comparable their cases are with those reported in other studies. Still, it is rare to find such high rates of claimed cure even in the clinical literature.

A number of well-designed studies appear to substantiate the clinical reports of Wolpe and Lazarus. Lang and Lazovik (1963) were able significantly to alter snake phobias with brief desensitization procedures. Effects of testing and training in relaxation were controlled, and no symptom substitution occurred during 6 months of follow-up Lazarus (1961) demonstrated substantial and rapid change of phobic symptoms and impotence by group desensitization methods. A comparison group being treated by traditional interpretive group therapy showed considerably less improvement, only 2 of 17 cases becoming symptom free after 22 sessions. These same cases were subsequently treated by group desensitization and after a mean of 10 sessions each, two thirds were symptom free. Paul (1966) found that desensitization procedures were far more effective in eliminating speech anxieties than brief insight therapy, an attention-placebo condition, and a no-therapy control condition.

In a study of operant conditioning methods, which are different from Wolpe's techniques, King, Armitage, and Tilton (1960) found that substantial changes could be effected even in schizophrenic cases. They were able to produce clinically observable improvement in cases so treated which was greater than the changes occurring in conventional interview therapy, recreational therapy, or no therapy. Ayllon and Michael (1959) effected substantial positive changes in ward behavior of psychotics by programming the reinforcements of their hospital environment according to operant principles. Lovaas, Schaeffer, and Simmons (1966) appear to have induced important changes in the social behavior of difficult cases of childhood autism by systematic use of negative reinforcement. In a review, Lindsley (1963) argues for the general promise of operant techniques, although the evidence thus far pertains primarily to simple motor and verbal behaviors. Conceivably, this approach will prove to be more useful with the more primitive behaviors of psychotics and small children than with the more complex, symbolically involved adult neuroses.

A most interesting development in behavior therapy involves the systematic application of principles of imitative or observational learning. Bandura (1965b) argues persuasively from the vantage point of extensive experimental work (Bandura, 1965a, 1965c) that modeling procedures provide powerful conditions for the acquisition of new responses and the modification of old ones. Though controlled clinical applications have just begun, they already lend considerable substance to Bandura's view (Berberich & Schaeffer, 1965; Frank, 1965; Hoehn-Saric, Frank, Imber, Nash, Stone, & Battle, 1965; Krumboltz & Thoreson, 1964; Krumboltz & Schroeder, 1966; Krumboltz, Varenhorst, & Thoreson, 1965; Nelson & Bijan, 1965; Thoreson & Krumboltz, 1966; Truax & Carkhuff, 1965b). . . .

In spite of the fact that the evidence is favorable, these techniques have been criticized by clinicians as removing symptoms without changing basic pathology and as being limited to very simple neuroses. Neither criticism, however, fits the evidence. Wolpe (1964a) cites data on 88 cases which indicate that a high proportion of complex neuroses can be successfully treated (89%) and in a much briefer time than is typical of traditional methods (Table 2).

The more telling critique of this work is Breger and McGaugh's (1965) point regarding the uncontrolled case reports, which are the basis for the high cure rates, and the rater bias in estimating outcomes encountered in many of the experimental studies. Faulty as a proportion of these reports are, the overall record still represents the best there is in the field of psychotherapy.

In addition to the fact that difficult cases show improvement in a short time, these reports indicate that significant relapses are rare. This is perhaps the most persuasive evidence that behavior therapists are right when they assert that "symptoms" are not symptoms of psychoanalytic-style pathology, but that they are learned behaviors subject to modification via relearning.

Table 2

COMPARISON OF NUMBERS OF SESSIONS IN
COMPLEX AND SIMPLE NEUROSES

Neuroses	N	Median No. Sessions	Mean No. Sessions
Complex	65	29	54.8
Simple	21	11.5	14.9
Total	86	23	45.4

Note.—The total is only 86 because 2 cases that turned out to be schizophrenic are excluded.

Some learning theorists have criticized Wolpe in particular, claiming that his techniques do not derive directly and logically from learning principles and thus do not have the scientific base he claims (Breger & McGaugh, 1965; Mowrer, 1963). While this may be true to some extent, it is irrelevant to the question of the technique's effectiveness and ignores the possibility that these clinical phenomena may eventually become the basis for reformulating learning theories in terms of complex, socially significant human behavior. In this case, one would not expect principles of behavior therapy to conform rigorously to conceptions derived largely from animal research.

Implication 6

The implications of this work seem quite clear. Since these techniques are effective with many types of symptomatology, they should be used. With regard to some of the more complex and difficult problems, behavior therapists argue that it would be better to spend time developing more complex social learning paradigms for treatment than to expend equal energy modifying less promising traditional interview methods. It appears that special effort should be devoted to integrating these methods with others and in some cases substituting them for the other methods. It would seem important to avoid a current tendency to isolate behavior therapies from the mainstream of treatment and thus create another rigid "school" which will gradually become as impervious to new ideas as the traditional schools already are.

CONCLUSION

In conclusion, it is only regrettable that comment upon so many topics of research has had to be excluded. Suffice it to say that the results in many of those not mentioned are not as yet amenable to synthesis. A good example is the material on the patient-therapist relationship. Nearly all of this research actually pertains to therapist qualities and has nothing to do with an analysis of interactional factors. An unusual exception is the work of Barrett-Lennard (1962) which was cited briefly in the discussion of therapist qualities. The few other useful facts in this domain were also included in that section. Another promising line of investigation is that on patient-therapist similarity; but the meaning of the data is still quite ambiguous (Sussman, 1964).

In spite of the fact that much of what is called psychotherapy research is appalling in its inadequacy, to have found a handful of reliable conclusions is gratifying. The groundwork seems well laid by these studies for initial steps at productive innovation in therapeutic treatment.

SUMMARY

A survey of psychotherapy research findings is digested into 6 broad conclusions, and implications for practice and research are drawn from them. They are: (a) Psychotherapy causes clients to become better or worse adjusted than controls, (b) Control Ss improve with time as a result of informal therapeutic encounters, (c) Therapeutic progress varies with therapist warmth, empathy, adjustment, and experience, (d) Client-centered therapy is the only interview-oriented method that has been validated by research, (e) Traditional therapies are seriously limited in effectiveness and are relevant for a small minority of disturbances, and (f) Behavior therapies have considerable promise for enhancing therapeutic effectiveness and should be utilized or experimented with more widely.

REFERENCES

Arbuckle, D. S. Client perception of counselor personality. *Journal of Counseling Psychology,* 1956, 3, 93–96.

Ayllon, T., & Michael, J. The psychiatric nurse as a behavioral engineer. *Journal of the Experimental Analysis of Behavior,* 1959, 2, 323–334.

Bandura, A. Psychotherapist's anxiety level, self-insight, and psychotherapeutic competence. *Journal of Abnormal and Social Psychology,* 1956, 52, 333–337.

Bandura, A. Behavioral modification through modeling procedures. In L. Krasner & L. Ullmann (Eds.), *Research in behavior modification.* New York: Holt, Rinehart & Winston, 1965. Pp. 310–340. (a)

Bandura, A. Psychotherapy conceptualized as a social-learning process. Paper read at the Kentucky Centennial Symposium on Psychotherapy, University of Kentucky, April 1965. (b)

Bandura, A. Vicarious processes: A case of no-trial learning. In L. Berkowitz (Ed.), *Advances in experimental social psychology.* Vol. 2. New York: Academic Press, 1965. Pp. 3–48. (c)

Bandura, A., Lipsher, D. H., & Miller, P. E. Psychotherapists' approach-avoidance reactions to patients' expressions of hostility. *Journal of Consulting Psychology,* 1960, 24, 1–8.

Bandura, A., & Walters, R. H. *Social learning and personality development.* New York: Holt, Rinehart & Winston, 1963.

Barrett-Lennard, G. T. Dimensions of therapist response as causal factors in therapeutic change. *Psychological Monographs,* 1962, 76 (43, Whole No. 562).

Barron, F. Some test correlates of response to psychotherapy. *Journal of Consulting Psychology,* 1953, 17, 235–241.

Barron, F., & Leary, T. Changes in psychoneurotic patients with and without psychotherapy. *Journal of Consulting Psychology,* 1955, 19, 239–245.

Berberich, J., & Schaeffer, B. Establishment of verbal behavior through imitation. Paper read at American Psychological Association, Chicago, September 1965.

Bergin, A. E. The effects of psychotherapy: Negative results revisited. *Journal of Counseling Psychology,* 1963, 10, 244–250.

Bergin, A. E., & Solomon, S. Personality and performance correlates of empathic understanding in psychotherapy. *American Psychologist,* 1963, 18, 393. (Abstract)

Breger, L., & McGaugh, J. L. Critique and reformulation of "learning-theory" approaches to psychotherapy and neurosis. *Psychological Bulletin,* 1965, 63, 338–358.

Butler, J. M., & Haigh, G. Changes in the relation between self-concepts and ideal concepts consequent upon client-centered counseling. In C. R. Rogers & R. F. Dymond (Eds.), *Psychotherapy and personality change.* Chicago: University of Chicago Press, 1954, Pp. 55–75.

Cartwright, D. S. Success in psychotherapy as a function of certain actuarial variables. *Journal of Consulting Psychology,* 1955, 19, 357–363.

Cartwright, D. S. Note on "changes" in psychoneurotic patients with and without psychotherapy. *Journal of Consulting Psychology,* 1956, 20, 403–404.

Cartwright, R. D., & Vogel, J. L. A comparison of changes in psychoneurotic patients during matched periods of therapy and no-therapy. *Journal of Consulting Psychology,* 1960, 24, 121–127.

Chance, E. *Families in treatment.* New York: Basic Books, 1959.

Eysenck, H. J. The effects of psychotherapy: An evaluation. *Journal of Consulting Psychology,* 1952, 16, 319–324.

Eysenck, H. J. The effects of psychotherapy. In H. J. Eysenck (Ed.), *Handbook of abnormal psychology.* New York: Basic Books, 1960. Pp. 697–725.

Eysenck, H. J. The effects of psychotherapy. *International Journal of Psychiatry,* 1965, 1, 97–178.

Eysenck, H. J., & Rachman, S. *The causes and cures of neurosis.* San Diego: Knapp, 1965.

Fairweather, G. W., Simon, R., Gebhard, M. E., Weingarten, E., Holland, J. L., Sanders, R., Stone, G. B., & Reahl, J. E. Relative effectiveness of psychotherapeutic programs: A multicriteria comparison of four programs for three different patient groups. *Psychological Monographs,* 1960, 74 (5, Whole No. 492).

Fenichel, O. *Problems of psychoanalytic techniques.* Albany: Psychoanalytic Quarterly, 1941.

Fiedler, F. E. A comparison of therapeutic relationships in psychoanalytic, nondirective, and Adlerian therapy. *Journal of Consulting Psychology,* 1950, 14, 436–445. (a)

Fiedler, F. E. The concept of the ideal therapeutic relationship. *Journal of Consulting Psychology,* 1950, 14, 239–245. (b)

Fiedler, F. E. Factor analyses of psychoanalytic, nondirective, and Adlerian therapeutic relationships. *Journal of Consulting Psychology,* 1951, 15, 32–38.

Frank, J. D. *Persuasion and healing.* Baltimore: Johns Hopkins Press, 1961.

Frank, J. D. The role of hope in psychotherapy. Paper read at the University of Kentucky Centennial Psychotherapy Symposium, April 1965.

Franks, C. (Ed). *Conditioning techniques in clinical practice and research.* New York: Springer, 1964.

Fulkerson, S. D., & Barry, J. R. Methodology and research on the prognostic use of psychological tests. *Psychological Bulletin,* 1961, 58, 177–204.

Gardner, G. G. The psychotherapeutic relationship. *Psychological Bulletin,* 1964, 61, 426–437.

Garfield, S. L. The clinical method in personality assessment. In J. Wepman and R. Heine (Eds.), *Concepts of personality.* Chicago: Aldine, 1963. Pp. 474–502.

Garfield, S. L., & Affleck, D. C. Therapists' judgments concerning patients considered for psychotherapy. *Journal of Consulting Psychology,* 1961, 25, 505–509.

Grossberg, J. M. Behavior therapy: A review. *Psychological Bulletin,* 1964, 62, 73–88.

Gurin, G., Veroff, J., & Feld, S. *Americans view their mental health.* New York: Basic Books, 1960.

Hoehn-Saric, R., Frank, J. D., Imber, S. D., Nash, E. H., Stone, A. R., & Battle, C. C. Systematic preparation of patients for psychotherapy: I. Effects on therapy behavior and outcome. *Journal of Psychiatric Research,* 1965, 2, 267–281.

Hollingshead, A. B., & Redlich, F. C. *Social class and mental illness.* New York: Wiley, 1958.

King, G. F., Armitage, S. G., & Tilton, J. R. A therapeutic approach to schizophrenics of extreme pathology. *Journal of Abnormal and Social Psychology,* 1960, 61, 276–286.

Kirtner, W. L., & Cartwright, D. S. Success and failure in client-centered therapy as a function of client personality variables. *Journal of Consulting Psychology,* 1958, 22, 259–264. (a)

Kirtner, W. L., & Cartwright, D. S. Success and failure in client-centered therapy as a function of initial in-therapy behavior. *Journal of Consulting Psychology,* 1958, 22, 329–333. (b)

Krasner, L., & Ullman, L. (Eds.) *Research in behavior modification: New developments and implications.* New York: Holt, Rinehard & Winston, 1965.

Krumboltz, J. D., & Schroeder, W. W. The effect of reinforcement counseling and model-reinforcement counseling on information-seeking behavior of high school students. *Personnel and Guidance Journal,* 1966, in press.

Krumboltz, J. D., & Thoreson, C. E. The effect of behavioral counseling in group and individual settings on information-seeking behavior. *Journal of Counseling Psychology,* 1964, 9, 324–333.

Krumboltz, J. D., Varenhorst, B., & Thoreson, C. E. Non-verbal factors in the effectiveness of models in counseling. Paper read at American Personnel and Guidance Association, Minneapolis, April 1965.

Lang, P. J., & Lazovik, A. D. Experimental desensitization of a phobia. *Journal of Abnormal and Social Psychology,* 1963, 6, 519–525.

Lazarus, A. A. Group therapy of phobic disorders by systematic desensitization. *Journal of Abnormal and Social Psychology,* 1961, 63, 504–510.

Lazarus, A. A. An evaluation of behavior therapy. *Behavior Research and Therapy,* 1963, 1, 69–79.

Lindsley, O. R. Free-operant conditioning and psychotherapy. In J. H. Masserman (Ed.), *Current psychiatric therapies.* Vol. 3. New York: Grune & Stratton, 1963, Pp. 47–56.

Lovaas, O. I., Schaeffer, B., & Simmons, J. Q. Building social behavior in autistic children by use of electric shock. In J. O. Palmer & M. J. Goldstein (Eds.), *Perspectives in psychopathology: Readings in abnormal psychology.* New York: Oxford University Press, 1966. Pp. 222–236.

Mink, O. G. A comparison of effectiveness of nondirective therapy and clinical counseling in the junior high school. *School Counselor,* 1959, 6, 12–14.

Mowrer, O. H. Freudianism, behavior therapy, and "self-disclosure." *Behavior Research and Therapy,* 1963, 1.

Nelson, K., & Bijan, G. Teaching social behaviors to schizophrenic children through imitation. Paper read at American Psychological Association, Chicago, September 1965.

Paul, G. L. *Effects of insight, desensitization, and attention placebo treatment of anxiety.* Stanford: Stanford University Press, 1966.

Powers, E., & Witmer, H. *An experiment in the prevention of delinquency.* New York: Columbia University Press, 1951.

Rogers, C. R. The necessary and sufficient conditions of therapeutic personality change. *Journal of Consulting Psychology,* 1957, 21, 95–103.

Rogers, C. R. A theory of therapy, personality, and interpersonal relationships, as developed in the client-centered framework. In S. Koch (Ed.), *Psychology; A study of a science.* Vol. 3. New York: McGraw-Hill, 1959. Pp. 184–256.

Rogers, C. R. A theory of psychotherapy with schizophrenics and a proposal for its empirical investigation. In J. G. Dawson & N. P. Dellis (Eds.), *Psychotherapy with schizophrenics.* Baton Rouge: Louisiana State University Press, 1961. Pp. 3–19.

Rogers, C. R., & Dymond, R. F. *Psychotherapy and personality change.* Chicago: University of Chicago Press, 1954.

Shlien, J. M., Mosak, H. H., & Dreikurs, R. Effect of time limits: A comparison of two psychotherapies. *Journal of Counseling Psychology,* 1962, 9, 31–34.

Speisman, J. C. Depth of interpretation and verbal resistance in psychotherapy. *Journal of Consulting Psychology,* 1959, 23, 93–99.

Strupp, H. H., Wallach, M. S., & Wogan, M. Psychotherapy experience in retrospect: Questionnaire survey of former patients and their therapists. *Psychological Monographs,* 1964, 78 (11, Whole No. 588).

Sussman, A. Patient-therapist similarity as a factor in psychotherapy. Unpublished manuscript, Teachers College, Columbia University, 1964.

Thoreson, C. E., & Krumboltz, J. D. Relationship of counselor reinforcement of selected responses to external behavior. *Journal of Counseling Psychology,* 1966, in press.

Truax, C. B. A scale for the measurement of accurate empathy. *Psychiatric Institute Bulletin,* Wisconsin Psychiatric Institute, University of Wisconsin, 1961, 1, No. 10. (a)

Truax, C. B. The process of group psychotherapy: Relationships between hypothesized therapeutic conditions and intrapersonal exploration. *Psychological Monographs,* 1961, 75 (7, Whole No. 511). (b)

Truax, C. B. Effective ingredients in psychotherapy. *Journal of Counseling Psychology,* 1963, 10, 256–263.

Truax, C. B., & Carkhuff, R. R. For better or for worse: The process of psychotherapeutic change. In *Recent advances in behavioral change.* Montreal: McGill University Press, 1964.

Truax, C. B., & Carkhuff, R. R. Experimental manipulation of therapeutic conditions. *Journal of Consulting Psychology,* 1965, 29, 119–124. (a)

Truax, C. B., & Carkhuff, R. R. Personality change in hospitalized mental patients during group psychotherapy as a function of the use of alternate sessions and vicarious therapy pretraining. *Journal of Clinical Psychology,* 1965, 21, 225–228. (b)

Ullmann, L., & Krasner, L. (Eds.) *Case studies in behavior modification.* New York: Holt, Rinehart & Winston, 1965.

Winder, C. L., Ahmad, F. Z., Bandura, A., & Rau, L. Dependency of patients, psychotherapists' responses, and aspects of psychotherapy. *Journal of Consulting Psychology,* 1962, 26, 129–134.

Wolpe, J. *Psychotherapy by reciprocal inhibition.* Stanford: Stanford University Press, 1958.

Wolpe, J. Behavior therapy in complex neurotic states. *British Journal of Psychiatry,* 1964, 110, 28–34. (a)

Wolpe, J. The comparative clinical status of conditioning therapies and psychoanalysis. In J. Wolpe, A. Salter, & L. J. Reyna (Eds.), *The conditioning therapies.* New York: Holt, Rinehart, & Winston, 1964. Pp. 5–20. (b)

DISCUSSION

As is apparent by now, therapists vary considerably with regard to the level of events upon which they focus. Wolberg has presented a concise summary of classical Freudian theory and technique, with its focus upon underlying personality problems assumed to be the basis of symptomatic behavior. As a consequence of this focus upon inferred personality processes, insight therapists set as their goal the reconstruction of the personality rather than direct elimination of unadaptive behavior. The articles by Stampfl, Wolpe, Lovaas and Ayllon represent a progression toward increasingly behavioristic approaches which view abnormal behavior as resulting from current environmental stimulus conditions, to be modified directly through the application of learning principles.

Stampfl has formulated an interesting method of behavior modification which integrates psychodynamic formulations with an extinction procedure derived from two-factor learning theory. This approach conceptualizes most abnormal behavior as learned responses which enable the person to avoid conditioned anxiety evoking stimuli. Therapy consists of presenting the client with the most powerful anxiety evoking stimuli under conditions in which no actual threat exists, thus extinguishing the conditioned anxiety which motivates maladaptive avoidance responses. Stampfl assumes that the effects of extinction will then automatically generalize to less powerful anxiety arousing stimuli. Wolpe, like Stampfl, utilizes the principles of classical conditioning as the basis of his theory. However, Wolpe relies upon the principle of counterconditioning rather than extinction to reduce conditioned anxiety. The apparent effectiveness of these quite dissimilar techniques for the reduction of conditioned anxiety leads one to wonder whether or not many behavior therapists have not become overly preoccupied with precision of technique and parameters of conditioning stimuli, with consequent neglect of the importance of higher-order, mediational, or cognitive variables as Weitzman suggests.

Implosion and desensitization therapies are applied most extensively to neurotic behaviors. This is undoubtedly related to the fact that both approaches emphasize the elimination of unadaptive behavior and assume that the individual has had a basically sound learning history which will enable him to independently develop more adaptive behaviors once conditioned anxieties are removed. But what of the many individuals whose past experience does not appear to have resulted in a foundation of adaptive interpersonal behaviors? Behavior modification techniques applied to such individuals must include procedures designed to foster adaptive behaviors as well as to eliminate or interfere with unadaptive behavior. The articles by Lovaas and Ayllon are representative of the highly successful applications of the principles of instrumental conditioning to such individuals. This approach represents the endpoint of behavioristic emphasis in that it deals only with observable behavior and consists essentially of providing positive reinforcing stimuli when desired behavior is exhibited and withholding such stimuli when unadaptive behavior occurs. The articles by Lovaas and Ayllon demonstrate effectiveness as well as subtlety in the application of reinforcement principles to the modification of even the most severe patterns of psychotic behavior.

Adherents of each of the approaches discussed above claim that their techniques are effective with most clients. Nevertheless, insight therapists frequently argue that behavior therapists deal only with superficial behaviors and ignore underlying causes, while the behavior therapists point with assurance to research evidence which indicates that their techniques effectively eliminate unadaptive behavior in approximately 85% of their cases and challenge the insight therapists to do likewise. The insight therapists reply that by dealing with the sources of problem behaviors rather than controlling their effects, they undertake a more challenging and ambiguous task which is not always readily specifiable in terms of specific behavior change.

Bergin's article summarizes the conclusions which can be derived from recent research on psychotherapy and indicates some of the complexities of attempting to compare the effectiveness of different therapies. The conclusions that therapy may actually have harmful as well as beneficial effects and that various characteristics of the client-therapist relationship appear to be essential to client improvement no matter what the therapist's approach, have broad implications with regard to both training and research. Weitzman indicates effectively some of the convergences of behavioral and insight approaches and attempts to integrate the findings of each into the method and theory of the other. He outlines the many complexities involved in comparing the effectiveness of insight and behavior therapies, by dealing specifically with the issue of symptom substitution. Within the context of discussing this one issue Weitzman elucidates some of the over-simplifications and misinterpretations of behavioristic attacks upon psychoanalytic theory, as well as the ambiguity and postdictive limitations of psychoanalysis.

GROUP APPLICATIONS OF THE PRINCIPLES OF BEHAVIOR MODIFICATION IN THE MENTAL HOSPITAL

A number of investigators have documented the debilitating aspects of prevailing practices in the modern mental hospital. Regardless of the avowed objective of "curing mental illness," a functional analysis of institutional practices indicates that most mental hospitals are more concerned with the management and social control of patients than with their behavioral rehabilitation. In many ways this inconsistency between avowed purpose and actual practice is a direct result of the inconsistencies inherent in a medical analogy. The medical model encourages patients to adopt the passive, helpless attitude that they have come to be "cured" of something which has happened to them and for which they must be treated in a manner analogous to the treatment of physical illness, i.e., taking medication, bed rest, and passive compliance with the doctor's orders. If one is treating a disease the above approach is most appropriate; however, if the goal is the modification of abnormal behavior and the shaping of functional behavior, then such an approach is in many ways obstructive. Indeed many theorists have attributed the apathy, withdrawal, lack of interpersonal concern, and emotional dullness characteristic of chronic mental hospital patients to the fact that life in a mental hospital results in prolonged withdrawal of the many incentives present in our society which maintain the complex behavioral, cognitive, social and vocational abilities necessary for successful adjustment.

During the past several years, psychologists, working from a behavioral model, have successfully instituted programs which emphasize behavioral development, re-education, resocialization and vocational train- ing, and have established ward structures which parallel the demands of outside society. These programs utilize contingent reinforcements applied on a group basis in order to effect desired changes in behavior.

28

PRELIMINARY REPORT ON THE APPLICATION OF CONTINGENT REINFORCEMENT PROCEDURES (TOKEN ECONOMY) ON A "CHRONIC" PSYCHIATRIC WARD

John M. Atthowe, Jr. and Leonard Krasner

An 86-bed closed ward in a Veterans Administration hospital was used in a 2-yr. study involving the application of a "token economy." For the patients, labeled chronic schizophrenics or brain damaged, every important phase of ward life was incorporated within a systematic contingency program. Patients received tokens for performing specified desirable behaviors involving self-care, attending activities, interacting with others, or demonstrating responsibility. The tokens could be exchanged for the "good things in life" such as passes, movies, and well-located beds. The results at the end of a year indicated a significant increase in the performance of reinforced "desirable" behaviors and a general improvement in patient initiative, responsibility, and social interaction.

Reprinted from the *Journal of Abnormal Psychology,* 73, 1968, 37–43, with the permission of the American Psychological Association and the authors.

Parts of this paper were presented to the annual meeting of the American Psychological Association, Chicago, September 1965. Supported by the Psychology Research Associate Program of the Veterans Administration at the VA Hospital, Palo Alto, California and United States Public Health Service Grants MH 6191 and MH 11938 to Stanford University and The State University of New York at Stony Brook. The authors wish to acknowledge the following staff members and trainees who participated in the program: Dave Panek, Robert Houlihan, Ralph Sibley, Gordon Paul, Lois Brockhoff, Joseph McDonough, Loraine Ceaglske, Martha May, Rose Peter; psychiatric aides Ed Noseworthy, Donald Bradford, Herbert Bowles, Sam Asbury, Kay Key, Harriet Faggitt, Van Cliett, Calvin Johnson, Hope Wood, Wilbert Butler, Doris Hughley, and Alice Bruce; Arlene Stevens, ward secretary; Martha Smiley; W. G. Beckman, ward psychiatrist; J. J. Prusmack, and Thomas W. Kennelly.

Although investigators may disagree as to what specific strategies or tactics to pursue, they would agree that current treatment programs in mental hospitals are in need of vast improvement. Release rates for patients hospitalized 5 or more years have not materially changed in this century (Kramer, Goldstein, Israel, & Johnson, 1956). After 5 years of hospitalization, the likelihood of release is approximately 6% (Kramer et al., 1956; Morgan & Johnson, 1957; Odegard, 1961), and, as patients grow older and their length of hospitalization increases, the possibility of discharge approaches zero. Even for those chronic patients who do leave the hospital, more than two out of every three return within 6 months. (Fairweather, Simon, Gebhard, Weingarten, Holland, Sanders, Stone, & Reahl, 1960). There is certainly need for new programs of demonstrated efficiency in modifying the behavior of long-term hospitalized patients.

In September 1963 a research program in behavior modification was begun which was intimately woven into the hospital's ongoing service and training programs. The objective was to create and maintain a systematic ward program within the ongoing social system of the hospital. The program reported here involves the life of the entire ward, patients, and staff, plus others who come in contact with the patients. The purpose of the program was to change the chronic patients' aberrant behavior, especially that behavior judged to be apathetic, overly dependent, detrimental, or annoying to others. The goal was to foster more responsible, active, and interested individuals who would be able to perform the routine activities associated with self-care, to make responsible decisions, and to delay immediate reinforcement in order to plan for the future.

THE WARD POPULATION

An 86-bed closed ward in the custodial section of the Veterans Administration Hospital in Palo Alto was selected. The median age of the patients was 57 years, and more than one-third were over 65. Their overall length of hospitalization varied from 3 to 48 years with a median length of hospitalization of 22 years. Most of the patients had previously been labeled as chronic schizophrenics; the remainder were classified as having some organic involvement.

The patients fell into three general performance classes. The largest group, approximately 60% of the ward, required constant supervision. Whenever they left the ward, an aide had to accompany them. The second group, about 25%, had ground privileges and were able to leave the ward unescorted. The third group, 15% of the patients, required only minimal supervision and could probably function in a boarding home under proper conditions if the fear of leaving the hospital could be overcome.

In order to insure a stable research sample for the 2 years of the project, 60 patients were selected to remain on the ward for the duration of the study.

The patients selected were older and had, for the most part, obvious and annoying behavioral deficits. This "core" sample served as the experimental population in studying the long-term effectiveness of the research program, the
token economy.

THE TOKEN ECONOMY

Based on the work of Ayllon and his associates (Ayllon, 1963; Ayllon &
Azrin, 1965; Ayllon & Houghton, 1962; Ayllon & Michael, 1959) and the
principle of reinforcement as espoused by Skinner (1938, 1953), we have
tried to incorporate every important phase of ward and hospital life within a
systematic contingency program. The attainment of the "good things in life"
was made contingent upon the patient's performance.

If a patient adequately cared for his personal needs, attended his scheduled
activities, helped on the ward, interacted with other patients, or showed increased responsibility in any way, he was rewarded. The problem was to find
rewards that were valued by everyone. Tokens, which could in turn be exchanged for the things a patient regards as important or necessary, were introduced. As stated in the manual distributed to patients (Atthowe, 1964):

> The token program is an incentive program in which each per-
> son can do as much or as little as he wants as long as he abides by
> the general rules of the hospital, *but,* in order to gain certain ends
> or do certain things, he must have tokens. . . . The more you do
> the more tokens you get (p. 2).

Cigarettes, money, passes, watching television, etc., were some of the more
obvious reinforcers, but some of the most effective reinforcers were idiosyncratic,
such as sitting on the ward or feeding kittens. For some patients, hoarding
tokens became highly valued. This latter practice necessitated changing the
tokens every 30 days. In addition, the tokens a patient still had left at the end
of each month were devaluated 25%, hence the greater incentive for the patient
to spend them quickly. The more tokens a patient earned or spent, the less
likely he would be to remain apathetic.

In general, each patient was reinforced immediately after the completion
of some "therapeutic" activity, but those patients who attended scheduled
activities by themselves were paid their tokens only once a week on a regularly
scheduled pay day. Consequently, the more independent and responsible patient
had to learn "to punch a time card" and to receive his "pay" at a specified
future date. He then had to "budget" his tokens so they covered his wants for
the next 7 days.

In addition, a small group of 12 patients was in a position of receiving what might be considered as the ultimate in reinforcement. They were allowed to become independent of the token system. These patients carried a "carte blanche" which entitled them to all the privileges within the token economy plus a few added privileges and a greater status. For this special status, the patient had to work 25 hours per week in special vocational assignments. In order to become a member of the "elite group," patients had to accumulate 120 tokens which entailed a considerable delay in gratification.

The token economy was developed to cover all phases of a patient's life. This extension of contingencies to all of the patient's routine activities should bring about a greater generality and permanence of the behavior modified. One criticism of conditioning therapies has been that the behavior changed is specific with little evidence of carry-over to other situations. In this project plans were incorporated to program transfer of training as well as behavior change, per se. As a major step in this direction, token reinforcements were associated with social approval.

The attainment of goals which bring about greater independence should also result in strong sustaining reinforcement in and of itself. The aim of this study was to support more effective behavior and to weaken ineffective behavior by withdrawal of approval and attention and, if necessary, by penalties. Penalties comprised "fines" of specified numbers of tokens levied for especially undesirable behavior or for *not* paying the tokens required by the system. The fines can be seen as actually representing a high token payment to do something socially undesirable, for example, three tokens for cursing someone.

METHOD

The research program was initiated in September of 1963 when the senior author joined the ward as the ward psychologist and program administrator. The remainder of 1963 was a period of observation, pilot studies, and planning. Steps were taken to establish a research clinic and to modify the traditional service orientation of the nursing staff. In January 1964, the base-line measures were begun. The base-line or operant period lasted approximately 6 months and was followed by 3 months in which the patients were gradually prepared to participate in the token economy. In October 1964, the token economy was established and, at the time of writing, is still in operation. This report represents results based on the completion of the first year of the program.

The general design of the study was as follows: A 6-month base-line period, a 3-month shaping period, and an 11-month experimental period. During the base-line period, the frequency of particular behaviors was recorded daily, and ratings were carried out periodically. The shaping period was largely devoted to those patients requiring continual supervision. At first, the availability of canteen booklets, which served as money in the hospital canteen, was made contingent upon the amount of scheduled activities a patient attended. It soon became clear that almost one-half of the patients were not interested in money or canteen books. They did not know how to use the booklets, and they never bought things for themselves. Consequently, for 6 weeks patients were taken to the canteen and urged or "cajoled" into buying items which seemed to interest them (e.g., coffee, ice cream, pencils, handkerchiefs, etc.). Then all contingencies were temporarily abandoned, and patients were further encouraged to utilize the canteen books. Next, tokens were introduced but on a noncontingent basis. No one was allowed to purchase items in the ward canteen without first presenting tokens. Patients were instructed to pick up tokens from an office directly across the hall from the ward canteen and exchange them for the items they desired. After 2 weeks the tokens were made contingent upon performance and the experimental phase of the study began.

Within a reinforcement approach, the principles of successive approximation in gradually shaping the desired patient behavior were utilized. Once the tokens were introduced, shaping procedures were reduced. It would be impossible to hold reinforcement and shaping procedures constant throughout the experimental period or to match our ward or our patients with another ward or comparable group of patients. Consequently, a classical statistical design does not suit our paradigm. It is much more feasible, in addition to reducing sampling errors, to use the patients as their own controls. Therefore, we first established a base line over an extended period of time. Any changes in behavior from that defined by the base line must be taken into account. The effects of any type of experimental intervention became immediately obvious. We do not have to rely solely on the inferences teased out of statistical analyses.

Other than an automatic timer for the television set, the only major piece of equipment was the tokens. After a considerable search, a durable and physically safe token was constructed. This token was a $1\frac{3}{4} \times 3\frac{1}{2}$ inch plastic, nonlaminated, file card which came in seven colors varying from a bright red to a light tan. Different exchange values were assigned to the different colors. The token had the appearance of the usual credit card so prevalent in our society.

Whenever possible, the giving of the tokens was accompanied by some expression of social approval such as smiling, "good," "fine job," and a verbal description of the contingencies involved, for example, "Here's a token because of the good job of shaving you did this morning."

RESULTS

There has been a significant increase in those behaviors indicating responsibility and activity. Figure 1 shows the improvement in the frequency of attendance at group activities. During the base-line period, the average hourly rate of attendance per week was 5.85 hours per patient. With the introduction of tokens, this rate increased to 8.4 the first month and averaged 8.5 during the experimental period, except for a period of 3 months when the reinforcing value of the tokens was increased from one to two tokens per hour of attendance. Increasing the reinforcing value of the tokens increased the contingent behavior accordingly. With an increase in the amount of reinforcement, activity increased from 8.4 hours per week in the month before to 9.2 the first month under the new schedule. This gain was maintained throughout the period of greater reinforcement and for 1 month thereafter.

Thirty-two patients of the core sample comprised the group-activity sample. Nine patients were discharged or transferred during the project, and the remaining patients were on individual assignments and did not enter into these

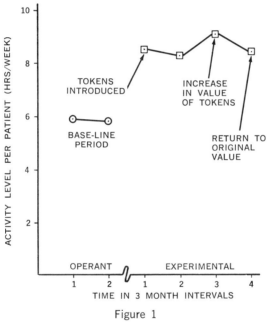

Figure 1

ATTENDANCE AT GROUP ACTIVITIES

computations. Of the 32 patients, 18 increased their weekly attendance by at least 2 hours, while only 4 decreased their attendance by this amount. The probability that this is a significant difference is .004, using a sign test and a two-tailed estimate. Of those patients going to group activities, 18% changed to the more token-producing and more responsible individual assignments within 4 months of the onset of the token economy.

A widening of interest and a lessening of apathy were shown by a marked increase in the number of patients going on passes, drawing weekly cash, and utilizing the ward canteen. Of the core sample of 60 patients, 80% had never been off the hospital grounds on their own for a period of 8 hours since their hospitalization. During the experimental period, 19% went on overnight or longer passes, 17% went on day passes, and 12% went out on accompanied passes for the first time. In other words, approximately one-half of those who had been too apathetic to leave the hospital grounds increased their interest and commitment in the world outside. Furthermore, 13% of the core sample left on one or more trial visits of at least 30 days during the token program, although 6 out of every 10 returned to the hospital.

For the entire ward, the lessening of apathy was dramatic. The number of patients going on passes and drawing weekly cash tripled. Twenty-four patients were discharged and 8 were transferred to more active and discharge-oriented ward programs as compared to 11 discharges and no such transfers in the preceding 11-month period. Of the 24 patients released, 11 returned to the hospital within 9 months.

Independence and greater self-sufficiency were shown by an increase in the number of patients receiving tokens for shaving and appearing neatly dressed. Fewer patients missed their showers, and bed-wetting markedly diminished.

At the beginning of the study, there were 12 bed-wetters, 4 of whom were classified as "frequent" wetters and 2 were classified as "infrequent." All bed-wetters were awakened and taken to the bathroom at 11 PM, 12:30 AM, 2 AM, and 4 AM regularly. As the program progressed, patients who did not wet during the night were paid tokens the following morning. In addition, they were only awakened at 11 PM the next night. After a week of no bed-wetting, patients were taken off the schedule altogether. At the end of the experimental period no one was wetting regularly and, for all practical purposes, there were no bed-wetters on the ward. The aversive schedule of being awakened during the night together with the receiving of tokens for a successful non-bed-wetting night seemed to instigate getting up on one's own and going to the bathroom, even in markedly deteriorated patients.

Another ward problem which had required extra aide coverage in the mornings was the lack of "cooperativeness" in getting out of bed, making one's bed, and leaving the bed area by a specified time. Just before the system of specific contingency tokens was introduced, the number of infractions in each of these areas was recorded for 3 weeks. This 3-week base-line period yielded an average of 75 "infractions" per week for the entire ward, varying from 71 to 77. A token given daily was then made contingent upon not having a recorded infraction in any of the three areas above. This token was given as the patients lined up to go to breakfast each morning. In the week following the establishment of the contingency, the frequency of infractions dropped to 30 and then to 18. The next week the number of infractions rose to 39 but then declined steadily to 5 per week by the end of 9 weeks (see Figure 2). During the last 6 months, the frequency of infractions varied between 6 and 13, averaging 9 per week.

A significant increase was shown in measures of social interaction and communication. A brief version of the Palo Alto Group Psychotherapy scale (Finney, 1954) was used to measure social responsiveness in weekly group meetings. The change in ratings by one group of raters 1 month before the introduction of tokens compared with those of a second group of raters 4 months later was significant at the .001 level. A simple sign test based upon a two-tailed probability estimate was used. Neither set of raters knew which of their patients was included within the core sample. The rater reliability of the scale is .90 (Finney, 1954). Evidence of enhanced social interaction was dramatically shown by the appearance of card games using tokens as money among some of the more "disturbed" patients and an increased frequency in playing pool together.

DISCUSSION AND CONCLUSION

A detailed description of the entire procedures and results is in preparation. However, we wish to point out in this paper the usefulness of a systematic contingency program with chronic patients. The program has been quite successful in combating institutional behavior. Prior to the introduction of tokens most patients rarely left the ward. The ward and its surrounding grounds were dominated by sleeping patients. Little interest was shown in ward activities or parties. Before the tokens were introduced, the ward was cleaned and the clothing room operated by patients from "better" wards. During the experimental period the ward was cleaned and the clothing room operated by the patients of this ward themselves. Now, no one stays on the ward without first earning tokens, and, in comparison to prior standards, the ward could be considered "jumping."

Over 90% of the patients have meaningfully participated in the program. All patients do take tokens, a few only infrequently. However, for about 10%, the tokens seem to be of little utility in effecting marked behavior change. With most patients, the changes in behavior have been quite dramatic; the changes in a few have been gradual and hardly noticeable. These instances of lack of responsiveness to the program seem to be evident in those patients who had previously been "catatonically" withdrawn and isolated. Although most of the patients in this category were favorably responsive to the program, what "failures" there were, did come from this type of patient. Our program has been directed toward all patients; consequently, individual shaping has been limited. We feel that the results would be more dramatic if we could have dealt individually with the specific behavior of every patient. On the other hand, a total ward token program is needed both to maintain any behavioral gains and to bring about greater generality and permanence. Although it was

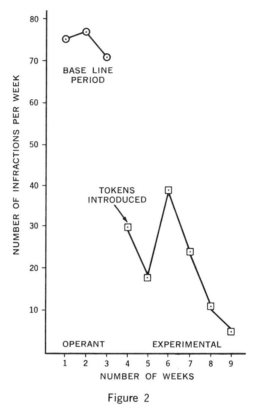

Figure 2

NUMBER OF INFRACTIONS IN CARRYING OUT
MORNING ROUTINES.

not our initial objective to discharge patients, we are pleased that the general lessening of apathy has brought about a greater discharge rate. But, even more important, the greater discharge rate would point to the generalized effects of a total token economy.

The greater demands on the patient necessitated by dealing with future events and delaying immediate gratifications which were built into the program have been of value in lessening patients' isolation and withdrawal. The program's most notable contribution to patient life is the lessening of staff control and putting the burden of responsibility, and thus more self-respect, on the patient himself. In the administration of a ward, the program provides behavioral steps by which the staff can judge the patient's readiness to assume more responsibility and thus to leave on pass or be discharged.

The program thus far has demonstrated that a systematic procedure of applying contingent reinforcement via a token economy appears effective in modifying specific patient behaviors. However, the evidence in the literature based on research in mental hospitals indicates that many programs, different in theoretical orientation and design, appear to be successful for a period of time with hospitalized patients. The question which arises is whether the success in modifying behavior is a function of the specific procedures utilized in a given program or a function of the more general social influence process (Krasner, 1962). If it is the latter, whether it be termed "placebo effect" or "Hawthorne effect," then the specific procedures may be irrelevant. All that would matter is the interest, enthusiasm, attention, and hopeful expectancies of the staff. Advocates of behavior-modification procedures (of which the token economy is illustrative) argue that change in behavior is a function of the specific reinforcement procedures used. The study which most nearly involves the approach described in this paper is that of Ayllon and Azrin (1965) whose procedures were basic to the development of our own program. Their study was designed to demonstrate the relationship between contingency reinforcement and change in patient behavior. To do this they withdrew the tokens on a systematic basis for specific behaviors and, after a period of time, reinstated them. They concluded, based upon six specific experiments within the overall design, that

> the reinforcement procedure was effective in maintaining desired performance. In each experiment, the performance fell to a near-zero level when the established response-reinforcement relation was discontinued. On the other hand, reintroduction of the reinforcement procedure restored performance almost immediately and maintained it at a high level for as long as the reinforcement procedure was in effect [Ayllon & Azrin, 1965, p. 381].

They found that performance of desirable behaviors decreased when the response-reinforcement relation was disrupted by delivering tokens independently of the response while still allowing exchange of tokens for the reinforcers; or by discontinuing the token system by providing continuing access to the reinforcers; or by discontinuing the delivery of tokens for a previously reinforced response while simultaneously providing tokens for a different, alternative response.

In the first year of our program we did not test the specific effects of the tokens by withdrawing them. Rather, we approached this problem in two ways. First, we incorporated within the base-line period of 9 months a 3-month period in which tokens were received on a noncontingent basis. During this period patients received tokens with concomitant attention, interest, and general social reinforcement. This resulted in slight but nonsignificant change in general ward behavior. The results of the experimental period were then compared with the base line which included the nonspecific reinforcement. The results indicate that the more drastic changes in behavior were a function of the specific procedures involved. The other technique we used was to change the token value of certain specific activities. An increase in value (more tokens) was related to an increase in performance; return to the old value meant a decrement to the previous level of performance (see Figure 1).

We should also point out that the situation in the hospital is such that the token economy did not mean that there were more of the "good things in life" available to these patients because they were in a special program. The patients in the program had had access to these items, for example, extra food, beds, cigarettes, chairs, television, recreational activities, passes, before the program began, as had all patients in other wards, free of charge. Thus we cannot attribute change to the fact of more "good things" being available to these patients and not available to other patients.

Thus far, a contingent reinforcement program represented by a token economy has been successful in combating institutionalism, increasing initiative, responsibility, and social interaction, and in putting the control of patient behavior in the hands of the patient. The behavioral changes have generalized to other areas of performance. A token economy can be an important adjunct to any rehabilitation program for chronic or apathetic patients.

REFERENCES

Atthowe, J. M., Jr. Ward 113 Program: Incentives and costs—a manual for patients. Palo Alto, Calif.: Veterans Administration Hospital, 1964.

Ayllon, T. Intensive treatment of psychotic behavior by stimulus satiation and food reinforcement. *Behaviour Research and Therapy,* 1963, 1, 53–61.

Ayllon, T., & Azrin, N. H. The measurement and reinforcement of behavior of psychotics. *Journal of the Experimental Analysis of Behavior,* 1965, 8, 357–384.

Ayllon, T., & Houghton, E. Control of the behavior of schizophrenic patients by food. *Journal of the Experimental Analysis of Behavior,* 1962, 5, 343–352.

Ayllon, T., & Michael, J. The psychiatric nurse as a behavioral engineer. *Journal of the Experimental Analysis of Behavior,* 1959, 2, 323–334.

Fairweather, G. W., Simon, R., Gebhard, M. E., Weingarten, E., Holland, J. L., Sanders, R., Stone, G. B., & Reahl, J. E. Relative effectiveness of psychotherapeutic programs: A multicriteria comparison of four programs for three different patient groups. *Psychological Monographs,* 1960, 74 (5, Whole No. 492).

Finney, B. C. A scale to measure interpersonal relationships in group psychotherapy. *Group Psychotherapy,* 1954, 7, 52–66.

Kramer, M., Goldstein, H., Israel, R. H., & Johnson, N. A. Application of life table methodology to the study of mental hospital populations. *Psychiatric Research Reports,* 1956, 5, 49–76.

Krasner, L. The therapist as a social reinforcement machine. In H. H. Strupp & L. Luborsky (Eds.), *Research in psychotherapy.* Washington, D. C.: American Psychological Association, 1962. Pp. 61–94.

Morgan, N. C., & Johnson, N. A. The chronic hospital patient. *American Journal of Psychiatry,* 1957, 113, 824–830.

Odegard, O. Current studies of incidence and prevalence of hospitalized mental patients in Scandinavia. In P. H. Hoch & J. Zubin (Eds.), *Comparative epidemology of the mental disorders.* New York: Grune & Stratton, 1961. Pp. 45–55.

Skinner, B. F. *The behavior of organisms.* New York: Appleton-Century-Crofts, 1938.

Skinner, B. F. *Science and human behavior.* New York: Macmillan, 1953.

29

EXPERIMENTAL SOCIAL INNOVATION IN MENTAL ILLNESS

David H. Sanders

While recidivism and chronic hospitalization are the foremost problems in mental hospital treatment today, a moment's reflection upon the daily work with mental patients by those of you who work with this marginal group should demonstrate to you that those persons who remain in the hospital can and do establish and maintain a particular role in the treatment setting. However psychotic he may be, each patient becomes defined as a certain person within the hospital. He may act as a clown, an isolate, a leader, or a follower. But, regardless of his role definition, his behavior gives him a known social position which provides him and others with an expected set of behaviors. Once he has established a role, it is extremely difficult for the mental patient to leave the institution and attempt an adjustment in the community. This is true because his well-defined hospital role does not exist in the community. Upon returning to the community he must relinquish the recognized social position that he has so slowly and painstakingly developed in the hospital. And, in addition, he becomes a member of a feared minority group, the former mental patient group. As a former mental patient, he is discriminated against by the people in the community even while attempting to establish a new social role for himself— a task he has failed to perform in the past. Why then should he give up the hospital role in which he has gained a degree of social prestige for a community role where he will be feared and perhaps hated. Under these conditions it is no wonder that when the chronic psychotic patient leaves the hospital, he typically quickly returns. Indeed, it is a wonder that he leaves at all. It seems necessary now to take a new look at how the chronic mental patient can make a transi-

Reprinted from the paper "Behavior Modification and Rehabilitation Facilities: Experimental social innovation in mental illness," with the permission of the Aldine Publishing Company, John Wiley and Sons, and Dr. Sanders.

tion to the community without losing the stabilizing influence of the social position he has had in the hospital.

Today I will be reporting on two longitudinal studies conducted by Dr. George W. Fairweather and his research group, of whom I am one. The first pertains to a hospital treatment program and the second to a community treatment program. The initial research reported is a hospital program in which techniques were developed for organizing patient groups containing mostly chronic psychotics. This research has been pointed towards solving the problem of the high rate of recidivism of previously hospitalized mental patients, particularly chronic institutionalized psychotics.

Despite the fact that a large body of literature maintained that psychotics could not solve problems because of their autism and withdrawn behavior, Fairweather's early studies with small groups of psychotic patients led him to ask two major questions in 1961. They were: 1) Can small problem-solving groups of hospitalized psychotic patients be formed? 2) Can the group members take care of and maintain each other? In other words, could groups, in which the members would become so dependent upon one another as to provide stabilization or support for their members, exceed the support which was unavailable to the individuals themselves? A study to explore answers to these questions established a small-group treatment program and compared it to a traditional treatment program. It clearly showed that problem-solving groups of patients could be formed and that they could take care of each other. Further, these groups of mental patients demonstrated many of the characteristics of small groups in other decision-making situations.

Throughout this research, the meaningful task has involved the current living and future planning for each member of a group. A step level system delineates for the patients, and the staff as well, the task the groups are rewarded for accomplishing. A sample system of rewards and punishments is associated with the performance of the task groups. Each patient is assigned to a task group upon his arrival on the ward, and remains in this group until he leaves. Each group member must go through four steps in order to successfully complete the program, and the group is responsible, as a unit, for each of its individual members. Scrutiny of the step system shows that the rewards increase with the level of responsibility of the task. The first step is that of personal care, punctuality on assignments, and orientation of new members. When in this step, the member receives $10 and a one-day pass per week. Step 2 involves adequate performance in Step 1, as well as qualitatively acceptable work on job assignments. In Step 2, the member receives $15 per week and two one-day passes per week. In Step 3, members are now responsible for Steps 1 and 2 and, in addition, recommend their own money and passes commensurate with individual step level. In Step 3, members are eligible for $20 per week and an overnight pass. In Step 4, the member is responsible for posthospital plans and is entitled to a weekend pass and $25 plus per week. In order to provide forces for cohesion, the task groups are responsible, as units, for the performance of their members, since a meaningful task and rewards alone might not produce the desired cohesiveness where each patient is concerned about every other patient of his group. In view of the fact that it seemed somewhat unrealistic to require that the group be responsible for the behavior of members which it might not be able to control, the determining feature of rewards and punishments is the recommendations of the task groups to the staff. Thus, it is the reality of the task group's recommendations which are rewarded and punished. This permits the staff to make the final decisions by determining the validity of the task group's recommendations. Thus, the staff maintains control of the ward and at the same time allows the patients maximum opportunity for responsible and realistic decision-making behavior.

The task group meets daily by itself four days of the week and on the fifth day meets with the staff to present the evaluation of their group. The group's secretary verbally presents a written account of the week's decisions regarding problems presented to the group by the staff. Daily problems are communicated to the group by the staff by means of a note system. A note is written to a group for each such problem or for relating information to the group, and is signed by the staff member calling it to the attention of the group. The evaluation usually includes recommendations about the progress in step level, money and passes, departure planning, and job performance for each member of the group, as well as an evaluation of the general level of the group's performance. At the completion of the group's formal presentation, the staff retires to a separate room. The staff then reviews the group's solutions to all of its problems during the week as to their reality and appropriateness of the recommended solutions and the responsibility the group is taking for its members. A record of the notes given to the group during the week is kept by the staff and a decision is expected on each note. The staff then discusses the step level recommendations of the group and approves or disapproves them, at which time the staff reports back to the group its evaluation of the group. When a group has not functioned well, demonstrated poor problem solution, overall poor performance, and/or disorganization, the entire group is reduced in step level or the members are frozen in their current step levels, dependent upon the severity of the group's poor performance. During the task group meeting hour, the entire staff is on consultation call and can be summoned to any group to present factual information in order for the group to arrive at a reasonable decision. It is noted that the staff cannot make a decision for the group or any of its members, but can present factual information requested by the group. If a task group member approaches a staff member to solve a problem, he is referred back to his group for solution of the problem and a note is sent to his group informing them of his improper behavior. This deviant behavior is in effect an attempt to take from the group their responsibility, authority, and autonomy.

As previously mentioned, the groups of patients in the small-group program meet daily during the week to transact their assigned business. The meetings are carried on without any member of the hospital staff present and the groups must reach some decision on each of the problems presented to them. These problems range from what to do about a member who never gets to his appointments to helping a group member plan for his release from the hospital. The decisions made by the group on each matter are forwarded to the ward staff as a recommended course of action. The ward staff reserves, at all times, the right to disapprove the group's recommendations and to return the problem to the group for another solution.

This monitoring by the staff is done on all but a few minor areas of the group's responsibilities and culminates in the previously mentioned weekly evaluation of the group by the staff. At this evaluation, the group receives feedback of both information and reward-punishment from the staff for its overall performance during the week.

Staff supervision is necessary because it involves an important aspect of the program. The group must be monitored because its activities are not limited to verbal behavior. It does not simply discuss things, but must actually deal with problems of living as they arise in the behavior of its members and must make decisions on what to do about them. These decisions are expected to be realistic enough to be acted upon, and the group is evaluated by the staff on its ability to show good judgment in dealing with the problems which arise. This means that the group must learn effective methods of dealing with behavior problems, and must accept the responsibility for the behavior of its members— even to the point of planning for release from the hospital. It must learn to punish or reward its members when necessary, to provide help or instruction as needed, and to show acceptable judgment in handling a wide variety of problems. Most elements of the small-group treatment program are concerned with generating and maintaining the exact degree of autonomy control which will elicit such problem-solving behaviors from groups of chronic mental patients in a hospital setting. Let us look at some of the ingredients.

First of all, there is the system of communication. All information passing between the staff and the group takes place through written notes which are placed in designated mailboxes on the ward. The groups receive all their problems by these notes as well as most information, and they send their responses to the ward staff by return mail. Three features of this system are important: 1) Except for emergencies, the ward staff responds to the behavior problem of a group member by writing the group a note and awaiting the group's recommendation. It does not take direct action. 2) The notes to the group are factual and as nonevaluative as possible; it is the group's responsibility to decide if action is warranted and then to recommend such action to the staff. 3) The emphasis is on behavior and not on inferred psychological states. If a group member is absent from his assignment, this is reported to his group; the fact that he also appears confused is irrelevant.

Second, no staff member ever enters a group meeting except when requested to do so by the group, and then is restricted to one of two behaviors: giving information which the group would not be expected to have, or providing support situations which the group cannot handle. The last function is restricted to emergencies and is almost always in response to the group's request. Generally, it is not a good idea for the staff to respond to shouts and heated language from the group meeting rooms because this usually means that a good meeting is in progress, and nothing more.

Third is the weekly evaluation meeting, when the staff meets with each group to review its entire performance for the past week. After the group presents its minutes for the week and each member gives a personal comment, the staff retires to prepare a written evaluation of the group's performance. The group receives a copy of this evaluation and, on the basis of it, the staff rewards or punishes the group, as a whole, for its performance by the amount of weekly cash or pass time which the members may have for that week. Each member is recommended by his group for one of four "step levels" in the program based upon his behavior in the past week. The step levels have different pass and money privileges associated with them and the staff may approve or disapprove such recommendations. The "step level" recommendations are themselves evaluated as an example of the group's judgment.

These are the main components of the experimental program. Integrated into it are the conditions which five studies, over the past few years, have shown to be crucial to the formation of cohesive task groups of chronic patients at Palo Alto. I will list those conditions.

1. The group must be "autonomous" in the sense that they must solve problems and make decisions with no staff present. The presence of a staff member is destructive to the group's cohesiveness since it tends to inhibit discussion and destroy patient leadership. Given the opportunity, the group will gladly defer all decisions to the staff.
2. A communication system must be maintained which allows the staff to present the group with problems without involving the staff in group decisions. This is the purpose of the written notes and evaluations in the program.
3. The task set the groups must be a meaningful one. In this case, it is solving behavioral problems of group members, managing the day-to-day living and working on the ward and planning for discharge.
4. A system of rewards and punishments must be available to the staff

for shaping the group's performance. Without this, the staff cannot change the group's behavior when it is drifting into indolent and maladaptive ways, and groups will not improve in performance without rewards. In a hospital, weekly cash allowance and pass time are obvious and meaningful rewards and these are used in the program.

5. The rewards and punishments must be applied to the group, as a whole, since only in this way can it be preserved as a cohesive unit.

These conditions seem to be minimal for maintaining the kind of task groups I have described in a mental hospital environment.

In describing the small-group program, I have mainly spoken of the mechanics of the system. It is, therefore, appropriate to discuss another important component of the program—the ward staff. One prior study has shown that, with proper training and preparation, staff may be completely replaced without altering the program to any appreciable degree. This points up an important fact: the formal structure of the experimental program is as much for the control of the staff behavior as it is for the shaping of patient performance. A staff that fails to grasp this, that fails to see it (no less than the patients) is bound by the "rules of the game" on the ward and will almost invariably destroy group cohesion and effectiveness.

Perhaps it is especially difficult for a hospital staff to control its behavior in this way. It is hard for some personnel to accept the new role of the "patient" in this sort of program. The medical model of the healer and patient roles is violated by the notion that the "patients" generate their own therapeutic social environment, and that they are responsible for their own behavior and that of their fellows. In this respect, chronic mental hospital patients are generally as well trained as the staff. They are thoroughly conditioned to the "sick" role and will try, in countless and devious ways, to persuade, cajole or trick the staff into resuming responsibility and decision making. If the staff does this, it is fatal to the group's cohesion. An explicit program, with explicit rules of procedure and ward regulations, makes it much easier for the staff to control its own processes and to resist tendencies to violate group autonomy.

However, let me quickly add that these remarks do not mean that the rules of operation are inflexible. Changes are made in the program all the time. The important thing is that such changes are always made in one of two ways. In the first way, the change is made on an experimental basis and controlled observations made of the results on the groups. This allows a meaningful evaluation of its effects. In cases where a problem arises which makes a minor change in ward rules necessary, the staff refrains from simply writing a new regulation. Instead, the problem is presented to the patients' community meeting and it is requested to find a solution and send a recommendation to the staff. Such recommendations are evaluated by the staff and either adopted or the problem returned to the group. In many instances, problems are both raised and solved by the patient group on its own initiative.

The results of this initial longitudinal study showed that the patients in the small-group program demonstrated higher social activity in all situations with increased self-involvement of the most chronic patients. Their expectancies about the future were brighter and they perceived the increased responsibilities required by the program as difficult but rewarding. The small-group patients manifested a pronounced personal involvement in the adjustment of other members of their group; they showed higher morale; and more frequently perceived their fellows as socially desirable. Posthospital adjustment by members of the small-group program was better with regard to employment and social adjustment in the community than that of the members of the traditional program, which was less socially active and more time consuming. Furthermore, many of the most chronic small-group patients were active program participants and some became group leaders. In its unique role as an evaluation team, the staff itself became a cohesive group and its morale and interest were heightened as a result of change in the patient-groups' behavior. All of the above results were obtained while significantly shortening the time patients spent in the hospital.

Despite the success and considerable advantages of the small-group approach, as contrasted with the traditional treatment program, 16.67% of psychotics with over two years' previous hospitalization never left the hospital during the initial year. Moreover, 35.42% of the chronics who left returned to the hospital within six months. Consequently, 52.09% of this population was in the hospital at the termination of the six month follow-up period.

As revealing as the above statistics are, the results pertaining to posthospital employment focus on possibly the paramount problem that must be faced by not only the chronic mental patient, but also by all chronic marginal individuals. Only 24% of the entire research sample was employed full-time during some period of the six month follow-up. While 7% was employed approximately half-time and 16% about quarter-time for some period during the six months, a fantastic 53% was totally unemployed. In the overall sample, the average number of days employed was 53 out of 183 possible days. In other words, only an average of 28% of the possible work time was utilized. This occurred despite the fact that the progressive social system of the small-group program led to a significant difference between the experimental and control groups regarding the number employed.

Further analyses of the data showed that the posthospital adjustment of patients who remain out of the hospital the longest are those who have a socially supportive living situation in the community and are more frequently employed, but specifically in a low status job. These are also the patients who are more communicative with other people. This is probably the most profound and significant result of the study, for it cannot go unnoticed that posthospital adjustment correlates with no significant hospital behavior *but* it is highly related to the posthospital situation to which the patient returns.

The results of this study, published in the book *Social Psychology in Treating Mental Illness: An Experimental Approach,* indicated that a new approach aimed at reestablishing chronic mental patients in the community was in order. The characteristics of such a new program are described in that book in the following manner:

> Such an approach needs to create patient role behaviors within the hospital that are consistent with those of community living. Furthermore, a mechanism to bridge the gap between the protective hospital setting with its minimal demands and the more rigorous demands of community life needs to be found. This is particularly important since, not only must the patient make the transition from a protective living situation but he must also be supported in some measure against the rejecting attitudes of some members of his society who will regard him as a member of a feared minority group— the mentally ill.
>
> A rapprochement between the role requirements of hospital and community membership might conceivably be brought about by establishing reference groups within the hospital who would return as units to the community.

Evidence regarding the patients' community adjustment obtained from the small-group study just mentioned highlighted the fact that the community must be the center of future treatment programs. To be feasible such programs would have to be undertaken with a minimum of professional assistance.

As an outgrowth of the small-group study, the decision was made to examine experimentally the proposition that task groups, trained in decision-making in the hospital, could be moved into the community as units. The belief was that such groups would maintain each person's status and role that had been established in the hospital, thus giving him a stable membership in a social system. The entire social system could then be implanted in the community. To discover whether small groups could be organized and moved as units into the community in order to reduce recidivism and unemployment, Fairweather and his research group applied for a large-scale grant. This provided funds for the planning and execution of the community study that I will now describe.

The goal of this research was to provide a total social subsystem for the rehabilitation of chronic psychotics and to contrast it with an existing hospital small-group treatment program on reduction in the recidivism rate, self-enhancement, and the degree to which hospitalization was reduced.

One program attempted to establish a community lodge which is an extension of a supportive group social system developed within the hospital while the comparative program used the same system in the hospital but afforded traditional types of community assistance following release from the hospital, such as outpatient treatment prescribed by the ward staff, and the like. Both had the same hospital treatment program. Patients participated in three rehabilitation programs or experimental groups, namely: 1) volunteer chronic patients who lived in a community lodge after release from the hospital; 2) volunteer chronic patients who either returned to other community situations or remained in the hospital, this being the volunteer control group; and 3) nonvolunteer chronic patients who either returned to other community situations or remained in the hospital, this being the nonvolunteer control group.

The plan was to organize a task group in the hospital which could then be moved into a community lodge. In the hospital, this group was early presented with problems that they would have to face once they arrived in the community. Such problems as how to organize the lodge and how to purchase and prepare food were discussed and solved by the members of the group. The idea was to train the group in problem-solving behavior while they were in the hospital so that they could behave independently once they arrived in the community. It was hoped that the problem-solving ability acquired by the group during this training period would help them solve the problems they would soon face in the community.

After four weeks of such training, the group moved from the hospital into a motel which had been leased as living quarters. The first evidence that our training program had been a failure occurred at this point. All of the problem-solving ability so assiduously developed in the hospital disappeared. Rather than going about the tasks of preparing food and training members for work that had been developed in the hospital, all of the members gathered around the kitchen. The person who had claimed that he was a cook, couldn't cook. The food that was supposed to have been purchased for the meals had only been partially obtained. And what we, as experimenters, learned at this point was that our earlier work which showed no relationship between hospital and community behaviors had indeed been very accurate. But, of course, this lack of problem-solving behavior was accompanied by a variety of humorous incidents.

During the first day, while most of the people were milling about the kitchen, the leader of the group and his sidekick disappeared. They could not be found anywhere around the lodge site. About two hours later they reappeared. The leader, who wore a baseball hat askew on his head, said, "We have just bought the land next door for a recreation area. We are going to build a bridge over the freeway and put in swimming pools and a playground." When he was asked what they would do for money he said that since we were from a major university he was certain the university could dig up the money for this venture. A carnival atmosphere prevailed. It was unlike anything we had witnessed before. The members acted as if they had been recently freed from a prison and they were bent upon enjoying themselves while the freedom lasted. They began habituating a cocktail bar and became quite well known as "playboys" in the first week of their stay in the community. During that week we learned about medication, too; without our knowledge, one individual quit taking his medication. After about a week, he began setting small fires along a freeway fence. He had to be returned to the hospital. This first behavior problem had a marked sobering impact upon the lodge members for they suddenly became aware of what might happen when their fellow members did not take their medication. And so, the first of a series of rules governing the behavior of lodge members was established. This rule required members to take their medication and if they did not, the business manager, a lodge member himself, would see that their medication was given to them. For the remainder of the four years of our contact with the lodge there were no further difficulties with medication that could not be handled by the lodge members themselves. Another problem that very quickly became defined was that the members did not know how to work by standards that were acceptable in the community. Even though several of them had worked for years in the janitorial service of the hospital, and one had even been a member employee there, their work methods were shoddy and disorganized. Despite this, the group wanted immediately to go to work in the community. So, after some brief training sessions, work began. Advertisements were placed in the local paper and telephone calls were received requesting job estimates from the janitorial service.

The first job the group had to do was for a member of the professional staff of the hospital. Here we discovered again some of the unrealistic behavior that comes from years of divorce from the community. According to the training procedures, the leader of the group was to make the job bid. He walked through the house with the professional person and his wife. They showed him the various areas that needed cleaning. Then they went to the living room and sat down and the leader, with his hat askew and pacing up and down the living room, was asked by the owner of the house how much the job would cost. And, without a flicker of a smile he said, "I think we can let you have it for $1,000." This led to further evidence that training within the hospital had not had the result we had hoped it would. Furthermore, it became clear that a staff member would have to make the job bids if we were to remain in business.

Then we lost our second and third jobs. The first reaction of the group to losing these two jobs was that people in the community would never stop discriminating against former mental patients. But, after several hours of cathartic negativism, a more positive attitude began to emerge and that involved a reassessment of their failures and some concern about "What are we doing wrong for which we are getting fired." With this reassessment and questioning of the value of their work, a training program was put into effect. This training program, unlike the first one, began to show signs of success mainly because the workers were now willing to find out how they might better do their job.

It is important here to review briefly what these first few weeks had accomplished.

1. A social organization was beginning to take shape.
2. In the beginning phases of any new social organization established in the community some social organization has to be imposed by the staff regardless of how much autonomy one wishes to give the members.
3. It became very clear that behavior changed as a direct result of negative feedback from the community. It was only after they had failed in the real life setting that they were eventually willing to take a look at their own behavior and to question its value.

As time passed, a more well-defined social organization began taking shape. Various members were assigned to positions of responsibility. One individual took over responsibility for the kitchen. He purchased all the food, planned and cooked the meals. He eventually became an excellent cook as evidenced by the fact that delivery men who had the lodge on their route frequently arranged their time so that they could spend their lunch hour or leisure time at the lodge. They often stated that the lodge was the friendliest place on their route.

A business manager was appointed and work leaders emerged. And most important, a committee of lodge members was formed to make decisions about the management of the lodge. This committee was designated the executive committee and among other management functions, it had the authority to discipline the members. It played the legislative, judicial, and police roles in this small neophyte society. The work performance of the members began to improve. We found that the members performed best in crews and usually in crews comprised of three people. The person that was responsible for the crew was given the title of crew chief, the next most responsible person was the worker, and the third individual on the crew was a "nebbish." "Nebbish is a word which means "nothing" in Yiddish and this word became adopted in the lodge because one of the supervisors in a fit of disgust once told a worker, "You are a nebbish." He then explained to the group what nebbish meant and this word was then adopted by the lodge members. This working arrangement was quite satisfactory. It was particularly good for the poorer workers who, by this technique, always had a role on a crew.

And, this leads to some statements about the symptoms that these chronic patients had. Throughout their stay at the lodge, they never became completely devoid of symptoms. It was necessary for most people to remain on medication but what happened was that the members became aware of the places in which their behavior was least acceptable. For example, they rarely hallucinated or deluded on work assignments. Let me deviate for a moment to tell you how this worked. One member continuously hallucinated. This was the cause for a great deal of concern by other members when working in a residence or a business where they might be observed. Accordingly, the supervisor of his work crew informed the hallucinating individual that if he hallucinated on the job he would sock him. Henceforth, little hallucinating was done on the job although he did hallucinate in the truck while driving to the job, and, as soon as the job was finished, he began hallucinating in the truck once they left the work area. This is an important point because among their peers, symptoms were readily accepted. Around the lodge, for example, it was quite permissible to exhibit odd behavior because you were accepted as a person regardless of how you behaved. However, when you were in situations other than at the lodge or among your peers, it was important to behave in more normative ways so that you did not bring shame upon the organization. This was a very important aspect of the lodge society. Individuals were not asked to give up totally their symptoms but rather to learn where such behavior was appropriate and where it was inappropriate and to behave accordingly.

As time passed, the organization became well thought of and a pillar of strength in the community. It was initially located at the edge of a Negro ghetto where considerable maladaptive behavior often occurred. We were an integrated group and soon became known as such in the area. We were viewed as responsible people by both the black and white individuals in the neighborhood. Several times people came to our group asking for employment. And, on one occasion, the members saved the life of a service station attendant. The service station, located next door to the lodge, was robbed one evening and the attendant was stabbed in the neck. It was only through quick emergency activity on the part of the lodge members that his life was saved. And you might be interested to know that their behavior was usually approved by individuals with whom they had daily contact. For example, the physician whose office they visited and who treated each member as an outpatient was continuously surprised at these individuals' morale and their interest in the lodge. The physician had had several years experience with chronic mental patients prior to entering private practice and he perceived this group as making the most adequate adjustment possible for such individuals.

But, along with these successes, and particularly the success in work, came additional problems. When the lodge was first organized, the worst possible thing one could do was to return to the hospital. This was an unacceptable form of behavior. Very often individuals would beg members not to return to the hospital by telling them that once they returned they had lost their last chance to again become first class citizens. But as the business became more and more successful, the leaders of the group began concentrating more and more upon the business aspects of the lodge and less and less upon the rehabilitative aspects. Thus, there emerged a new value—the "work-business" value. This value eventually came in conflict with the "rehabilitative" value. As time went on, there was less and less tolerance for the marginal worker. He was often fined for failing to appear for work or working poorly. Eventually, the work norm took preeminence over the rehabilitative norm and when this happened there developed what we called the "revolt of the nebbishes." The marginal workers united and petitioned the executive committee of the lodge for a vote in the decision-making processes of the lodge. The consultant to the lodge by this time had relinquished most of his authority to the group but he still retained the power of veto over decisions made by the executive committee. The executive committee decided to ignore the petition of the marginal workers. The consultant vetoed this decision and further ruled that the marginal workers should now become part of the executive committee so that all matters should be decided in the future by a majority vote of all the members. It is interesting to note here that after this action was taken, the marginal workers soon lost interest in the organization and the executive committee again controlled the organization. It was as if the rebellion was concerned not so much with participating in the decision-making process but rather the right to vote if one wished to do so.

There was another matter which was of deep concern to all of us, and I believe to all of you. . . . That was the negativism with which the members of the lodge viewed professional mental health workers. Shortly after our arrival in the community, the hospital director, knowing that we were hard pressed for employment, offered the group an opportunity to do some contract work for the hospital by keeping up the hospital grounds. This offer was immediately rejected by the group. Their logic was, that if they returned to the hospital grounds, they would be perceived as patients and, hence, put in an inferior social position. They often expressed the feeling that mental health workers are generally unable to view as equals people who have been hospitalized with a mental illness. The accuracy of this perception was demonstrated over and over again as the project progressed. I will select a dramatic example to illustrate this point. One day a crew went to work in a nurse's house. Throughout their 3 to 4 hours of work there, she appeared on the scene several times always with some excuse for returning to the house. The work crew was quite certain that she was there to supervise their work and check on their progress.

To them, this meant that she did not really trust them. By contrast, they worked shortly thereafter for a contractor who had just built a 62-unit apartment building. He handed the keys of the apartments to the crew chief and told him to call the contractor when the work was completed. The contractor did not check on their performance until they had completed the work. This demonstrated to them that he believed they could do the assigned work. It was this form of trust which over and over again was shown by people who were not involved in the mental health field but not by those who were so involved. To illustrate how strongly this affected the lodge members, it is noted here that when they reached a stage where they had done their last job for people from the mental health field, they threw a party to celebrate this occasion. They were now free.

As you may have guessed, the lodge moved successively towards autonomy. The first supervisor of the lodge was a psychologist with many years experience in working with mental patients. As mentioned earlier, he created a rather structural social situation for the first few months of the lodge. A second more autonomous phase was created when a graduate student took over the reins of lodge consultant. He gave more autonomy to the members and gradually the idea began to take shape that lay leaders might be able to do the job even better than professionals. And so we approached the State Bureau of Employment and selected two individuals at random to take over the lodge. One was a man in his early 60's who had been a former salesman for a large department store and a second was a former marble worker who had sustained a back injury and had to leave his trade. To everyone's surprise, morale showed a rapid upswing once the graduate student had gone. Work increased and it was thus found that motivated and interested lay persons can serve as adequate leaders for such community programs.

Eventually, the experiment was ending and it became necessary at this point to discover whether the members could assume full responsibility for themselves. On a prearranged date, the lodge members were informed that gradually over the next several months, the amount of money contributed to their support for food, medication, and so on, from grant funds would be decreased until they were totally on their own. Some of these men had veterans pensions and some did not. By pooling the money from the pensions, plus their income from the business, they were able finally to become completely self-sufficient.

On the day when the lodge was closed, they moved into a middle class neighborhood where they had leased two houses and, of course, the inevitable happened. In the first few days in their new residence, one of the members told the neighbors that they were a group of "nuts from the mental hospital." The children who had been playing in the yard and romping through the house suddenly disappeared and a degree of isolation was established between the neighbors and the group members. Eventually, this isolation disappeared. One of the neighbors had a brother who was then in a mental hospital and she began conversing with the lodge members. Before long, other neighbors again became conversant. Eventually, it was necessary for the members to keep the children out of the house because they were taking too much of the members' time. Today the lodge still exists. These men have been completely on their own for almost two years.

The establishment of this lodge was a very carefully controlled experiment. The lodge members can be contrasted with other patients matched on age, diagnosis, and length of hospitalization. This comparison group participated in the same small-group treatment program on the same ward in the same hospital but instead of moving to the community lodge once they were eligible to leave the hospital they went to the kind of community program that was available to the typical patient who left the hospital either for a visit or by discharge. They participated in such programs as outpatient clinics and home-care situations. At the termination of the study, the sample totaled 333—183 were in the nonvolunteer-nonlodge group; the remainder consisted of 150 matched patients, with 75 in the volunteer-lodge group and 75 in the volunteer-nonlodge group.

I wish now to show you some graphs comparing what happened to the individuals who went to the lodge with those who went into the typical community programs. I would like to show you some rather dramatic information about recidivism, employment, and the comparative costs of these two programs.

Compared to their matched control group of patients, a significantly greater proportion of the individuals in the working-living lodge situation

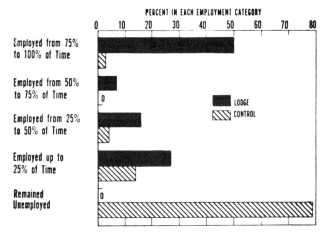

COMPARISON OF THE PERCENTAGE OF TIME EMPLOYED FOR THE LODGE AND CONTROL GROUPS FOR SIX MONTHS OF FOLLOW-UP.

were able to remain out of the hospital and assume employment. Sixty-five percent of the lodge group remained out of the hospital for six months, while 35% of the control group never left the hospital during the first six months and only 24% remained in the community for the full six month period. Fifty percent of the lodge group was employed full time for the entire six month follow-up period, while 79% of the matched controls were unemployed and only 3% worked for the full six months.

COMPARISON OF THE PERCENTAGE OF TIME IN THE COMMUNITY
FOR THE LODGE AND CONTROL GROUPS FOR SIX MONTHS OF FOLLOW-UP

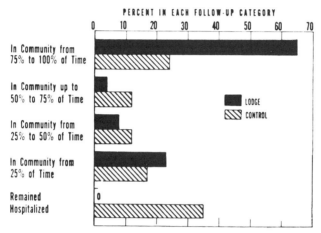

Furthermore, the results obtained for the next two years are shown in this graph.

COMPARISON OF LODGE AND CONTROL GROUPS:
TIME OUT OF HOSPITAL AND FULL-TIME EMPLOYMENT

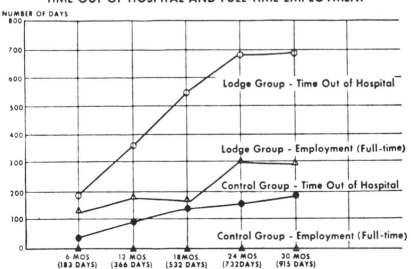

About ⅓ of those who arrived failed. But if a person survived these first few days he usually remained. This may be due to the VA population—none failed in Benton. The average length of time spent at the lodge by failures was less than a month. Seventeen percent of the lodge group left the lodge before the completion of their first six months in the community ostensibly in order to seek other employment. However, most of them remained unemployed after leaving the lodge.

So the community lodge was necessary for the maintenance of continuous employment and other aspects of adjustment. Thus, ⅔ of the members who left the lodge and were followed for as long as two years after leaving the lodge were unemployed during this time. The ⅓ who did obtain employment immediately upon leaving the lodge were employed only an average of 47 days during 18 months of follow-up. On the other hand, the median employment time for the control group was zero days during the entire follow-up period. Thus, the contribution of the lodge to continuous employment is very obvious.

As for other research findings, the lodge maintained but did not grossly affect individual behavioral adjustment. The lodge group revealed themselves to be no less a disabled group when measured in terms of commonly used adjustmental criteria. Their seclusiveness, inarticulateness, eccentric behavior, apathy about goal accomplishment, and passivity in social interaction were no deterrent to their capacity to remain productively occupied in the community

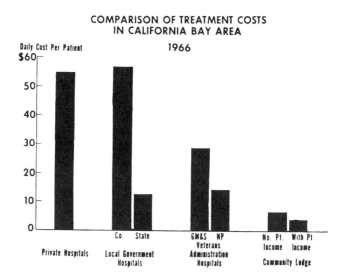

in what was, for them, an appropriately designed social situation. At the same time they could adopt participative social roles within their limited capacities.

The lodge was a much less expensive way of maintaining mental patients in society. This point is clearly illustrated in the graph shown here which compares treatment costs in the San Francisco Bay area. The cost of maintaining individuals in the community lodge ($6.37) was less than half that for hospital care ($14.34 at the Menlo Park Division of the Palo Alto VA Hospital). When the members contributed their earnings toward their own maintenance at the lodge, the cost was further reduced to $3.90 per day per man. In contrast, the costs for treatment at other hospitals in the area were: $55 at the local private hospital; $56.75 at the local county hospital; $12.26 at the local state hospital; and $28.29 at the VA GM&S Hospital.

As far as work is concerned, this group of men had considerably more than 2000 janitorial jobs, some only requiring a day's work, in 2¾ years and they worked almost continuously after the first month that the lodge was in existence. They averaged more than three janitorial or gardening jobs per work day. As a group, they earned more than $52,000 during this period.

In the community lodge a new and meaningful social role was created for these former mental patients and it led to success in both their contribution to the society and their feelings of achievement. It is quite true that the men at the lodge remained out longer because they were placed in the lodge to begin with, and they had jobs because employment was created for them. And, this is precisely the point of the entire community research project: Chronic mental patients are in need of a reference group that they can remain in and which will sustain them. This leads to a more constructive life.

At the lodge, there was continuous social stimulation, employment, companionship, a reason for remaining out of the hospital, the opportunity to do something constructive and to be perceived as a worthwhile human being. These men built for themselves a small society within whose norms they could live. They depended upon one another for survival. They could not do without this social organization. True, this may conceivably have been as far as they could go, and as far as society's usual norms are concerned this may not have been a normal existence. But this was a normal existence for them and it was an existence that was entirely acceptable to the rest of the community around them. As far as the larger community was concerned, these were former mental patients who were continuously moving away from the mental illness stigma because the community viewed the lodge as a residence and a business where fairly responsible men lived and worked at something constructive.

The location of the lodge was highly advantageous with respect both to its functions as a living unit and as a working unit. The lodge was socially compatible with the immediate neighborhood which was of a low social-economic status and persons who lived there had a high tolerance for minority group members. In such an environment a working-living social system of former mental patients had a good chance of being accepted by the neighborhood.

At the same time, the lodge was divided by little more than a freeway from a group of prosperous neighborhoods which provided a strongly expanding market for the janitorial services it offered as a working unit. In the period from 1964 to 1965 when the lodge janitorial business was growing into an established enterprise, the janitorial service industry within this area increased by 11.3%, employed 15.3% more persons, and paid 16.8% more in taxable payrolls. This represented a substantially greater expansion of janitorial services in the lodge trading area than occurred in the surrounding metropolitan area.

Residents and businesses within the vicinity of the lodge were interviewed in reference to their attitudes about having the janitorial service in their neighborhood. In the middle of the interview they were asked if they knew that the men who worked for the janitorial service also lived there and that they were a group of former mental patients. Prior to receiving this information, 81% of this group of interviewees were quite positive toward the lodge in terms of having the business in the neighborhood and using and referring their services. While some people were aware of the primary function of the lodge, it is interesting to note that after the additional information was supplied, 59% of the group remained the same in their attitude toward the lodge, 30% became more positive and only 11% were less positive.

In the course of the interviewing many spontaneous comments were made such as "They are a good bunch of guys" and "I'm not uneasy about a neighborhood with former mental patients because of the experience of living next door to the 49ers".

This group of former patients ranged from the classically characterized alcoholic, psychopath, anxiety and other neurotic reactions, to the schizophrenic of both short and exceedingly long previous hospitalization. It is most important to note that 55% of these men were in the chronically hospitalized category (greater than 2 years previous hospitalization). The mean number of weeks of previous hospitalization for the lodge sample was 292 or 5.6 years. Since the basic mental hospital problem in our society is what to do with the chronic schizophrenic of more than 3 years prior hospitalization, this study is particularly significant. It describes a social system where these people can live in the community and do something constructive. It has been demonstrated that these "long termers" can sustain themselves and that they can work an eight hour day within the framework of a small society. However, just as significant is the adjustment of those who have frequent but short hospitalizations. They, too, present a problem for they might one day become chronically hospitalized. These "repeaters" usually were the leaders of the lodge. They preferred doing things for others more helpless than themselves, and the more disturbed lodge members afforded them this opportunity.

What was the reaction of the hospital to the lodge? To ascertain attitudes toward the lodge program by the professional and nonprofessional staffs of the hospital as well as the patients, questionnaires and structured taped interviews were obtained.

There was no significant difference on the questionnaire among the various professional groups although the psychology and social work groups ranked consistently higher on their attitude toward the lodge than the other professional groups. The most positive attitude of any group on the questionnaires was expressed by the personnel on the small-group experimental ward from which the lodge members came.

The interviews showed both positive and negative reactions in all groups. The negative responses from hospital personnel were stated to be due to a lack of sufficient information about the program so that they could not make any meaningful comment, or, in a few cases, a simple refusal to be interviewed. The positive comments were about the lodge being a very exciting and hopeful program. Many saw it as a very necessary resource for the hospital. Some thought it had influenced their own research and that it had been inspiring and stimulating. One of the psychiatrists said that the favorable comments tended to come from the more progressive physicians and the physicians who are more dynamically oriented; whereas the unfavorable comments came from those who are organically or custodially oriented.

I have presented data concerning the community lodge program. The data have shown that the program was an unqualified success when you consider our initial goal. We have described several aspects of the program, such as the establishment of a work situation and the characteristics of the lodge as a living situation. Now, I shall present a brief description of the lodge janitorial and yard service as a business, and demonstrate to you that former mental patients, living in a group supportive situation, can function at a high level of sophistication and can present to the general public a socially acceptable level of behavior. In doing this I will briefly present you a few of the typical and sometimes complex steps involved in the business of the 49ers Janitorial and Yard Service.

As with any business that offers its services to the public, the 49ers advertised in the usual manner. They had a listing in the yellow pages of the telephone directory, purchased advertising space in the local newspaper, and they printed business cards for distribution in the community. The card is quite complete in presenting basic information such as the kind of services offered, where they could be contacted, and the fact that they were bonded and insured. The card not only presents basic information but also performs the very important function of presenting the services of the business to the public in a socially acceptable form. Thus, their business practices placed these former mental patients on a par with other businesses which provide services to the public.

A potential client, in response to the business card or any other form of advertisement, would contact the 49ers, usually by telephone, and request an estimate for a job. The estimate took place at the client's home or business at a prearranged time and if the estimate was accepted the client's name and the date when the job was to be performed were entered in the 49ers' Job Book. The format of this book also allowed for entries to be recorded for such items as the job number, the cost of the job, and the dates on which the client was billed and paid for the work. On line 9 is the summary statement indicating that the accounts receivable for March 1966 was $1,917.50. This figure represents the dollar value of work completed that month.

They also used a Cash Receipt Book. This bookkeeping instrument allowed for the recording of entries pertaining to the flow of funds into the business. In this regard, entries were made relating to the date money was received in payment for a job, the actual dollar amount of the job, and the client's name. This book was also used for the recording of income from other sources such as the coke, juke box, cigarette and candy machines which the lodge members had installed in the common dining hall. These machines were utilized by both the members and the general public. On line 29 is another summary statement. In this case, the sum of $1,867.34 refers to the total amount of money received, regardless of source, for April 1966.

Now that you have seen how funds flowed into the 49ers Janitorial and Yard Service, let's see how they dispersed some of these funds. I'll describe a page from the payroll ledger of the 49ers. The disbursement of funds to payroll is, of course, a straightforward operation. However, the 49ers had shaped it to fit their particular needs. For example, during this particular payroll period they paid crew chiefs 4.62% of the weekly receipts, deputy crew chiefs 3.61%, and workers 2.61%. Consider the gentleman whose name appears on the first line, Mr. _____, who is being paid by check No. 2309. His wage for the week was $24.61. The sum includes $3.68 for extra work on nights or Saturday and $2.49 as his share of the penalty assessed other workers who, for some reason such as not working, had money deducted from their weekly salary. It was the norm at the lodge to redistribute the amount of money deducted from the salary of the penalized workers among those workers whose work performance was satisfactory or better. Thus, they established an additional reward-punishment system. His withholding tax was $1.60, leaving him with a net pay of $23.01 for the week. Check No. 2309 was drawn on the 49ers' account to pay Mr. _____. It was signed by two people: usually a consultant or lay leader and the 49ers' business manager who was one of the former patients.

Now for a page from the Cash Disbursement Book. In this particular book were recorded such regular expenditures as the amount of the weekly payroll; a sum paid to the Coca-Cola Bottling Company for soda pop purchased by the members for use in their coke machine located on the premises; and another direct financial outlay representing payment for janitorial supplies received from Richco, Inc., a janitorial supply house.

I have presented considerable information to you about a successful community experiment because it is the contention of our research staff that fully 50% of the patients in most mental hospitals could be moved to the community near their hospital in reasonably productive roles if the appropriate situations were established. As I have pointed out earlier, these situations have been arranged in both urban and rural areas. For example, the State Hospital in Benton, Arkansas, a rural hospital, and the Fort Logan Mental Health Center, an urban hospital, have established community lodges and developed work situations for the lodge members. Fort Logan, having established its lodge in the Denver metropolitan area, developed a janitorial and gardening service. However, the Arkansas State Hospital, which established separate community lodges for males and females, employed their men as grounds-keeping crews at the local golf courses and obtained work for their women as nursing assistants in training at the local nursing home. After a one-year period of testing by the employer, the female former patients were hired as full-time employees. Our Arkansas experience leaves no doubt that those who work on hospital wards could adequately handle the community situation. As a bonus, our experience shows that meaningful community roles for both patients and staff enhances the quality of everyone's life.

REFERENCES

1. Fairweather, G. W., Simon, R., Gebhard, M. E., Weingarten, E., Holland, J. L., Sanders, R., Stone, G. B., and Reahl, J. E. Relative effectiveness of psychotherapeutic programs; a multicriteria comparison of four programs for three different patient groups. *Psychological Monographs,* Whole No. 492, 1960, 74, No. 5.
2. Fairweather, G. W. (Ed.) *Social Psychology in Treating Mental Illness: An Experimental Approach.* New York: John Wiley & Sons, 1964.
3. Sanders, D. H. Social psychology in the treatment of mental illness: A model approach for treatment of addiction—the effect of group membership on community adjustment. In *Rehabilitating the Narcotic Addict,* Report of Institute on New Developments in the Rehabilitation of the Narcotic Addict, Fort Worth, Texas, Feb. 16–18, 1966. Vocational Rehabilitation Administration, U. S. Dept. of Health, Education and Welfare.
4. Sanders, D. H. Social innovation in treating mental illness: A community experiment. In *Monograph—An Institute on Interagency Programming for*

Psychiatric Rehabilitation: An appraisal based upon recent legislation and research. Colorado State University Research Foundation, 1967.

5. Fairweather, G. W. *Methods for Experimental Social Innovation.* New York: John Wiley & Sons, 1967.

6. Fairweather, G. W., Sanders, D. H., Maynard, H. M., and Cressler, D. L. *Treating Mental Illness in the Community: An Experiment in Social Innovation.* Book in preparation.

DISCUSSION

The increasing use of group contingent reinforcement procedures is indicative of their effectiveness as a means of counteracting the processes which contribute to progressive institutional dependence and chronicity. The Atthowe and Krasner article clearly demonstrates the effectiveness of a ward incentive program both with regard to inducing more adaptive behavior within the institution, and enhancing the frequency of interpersonal behaviors, social communication, and motivation to return to the community. The increased discharge rate on the token reinforcement program indicates its success in shaping the social and vocational behaviors necessary for life in society.

Despite these encouraging results, previous research indicates that approximately 70% of all chronic mental patients discharged from mental hospitals are readmitted within 18 months. Given the higher discharge rate which results from group reinforcement programs, it seems unlikely that their readmission rate will be significantly different as long as most patients must make the abrupt transition from hospital to the often stressful, nonsupportive conditions existing for mental patients in society. Sanders, Fairweather and their colleagues have developed ingenious methods for facilitating the transition from hospital to self-sufficiency. These methods employ group reinforcement contingencies to foster interpersonal concern, group identification and support, as well as judgmental and vocational competence. This approach facilitates interpersonal concern and group cohesiveness by transferring the responsibility for evaluating and modifying the behavior of individual members to the group. Since follow-up studies indicate that approximately half of those patients hospitalized 2 years or more, when released from the task group system, returned within 6 months, Fairweather, Sanders and colleagues utilized the task group as an agent of transition to the community, and as a source of social support to enhance the probability of successful community adjustment. The results of the community lodge project indicate that the supportive context of the task group greatly enhances the chances for chronic patients to permanently leave the hospital and become self-supporting, productive individuals.

NAME INDEX

477

SUBJECT INDEX